Blind Justice

Miscarriages of Justice in Twentieth-Century Britain?

Blind Justice

Miscarriages of Justice in Twentieth-Century Britain?

John J. Eddleston

ABC-CLIO
Oxford, England
Santa Barbara, California
Denver, Colorado

British Library Cataloguing in Publication Data

Eddleston, John J.
    Blind Justice: Miscarriages of Justice in Twentieth-Century Britain?
    1. Judicial error – Great Britain – History – 20th century
    2. Judicial error – Great Britain – Cases
    I. Title
  345.4'1

ISBNs 1–85109–333–8 (Paperback)
         1–85109–343–5 (Hardback)

ABC-CLIO Ltd,
Old Clarendon Ironworks,
35A Great Clarendon Street,
Oxford OX2 6AT, England.

ABC-CLIO Inc.,
130 Cremona Drive,
Santa Barbara,
CA 93117, USA.

Typeset by ABC-CLIO Ltd., Oxford, England.
Printed and bound in Great Britain by
MPG Books Limited, Bodmin, Cornwall.

I would like to dedicate this book to Yvonne Sandra Berger.
Without her help, patience and understanding,
it would not have been possible.

Contents

Acknowledgements

A book of this size and complexity would not have been possible without the help of my researcher and partner, Yvonne Berger. She has helped me with the research, proof-read every chapter and suggested improvements throughout. Without her efforts this work would have been so much more difficult.

I would also like to take this opportunity to thank the staff of the Public Record Office at Kew, especially those who work in the image library there. I am also very grateful to the staff of the newspaper library at Colindale.

Finally, I would like to thank my publisher and especially Dr Robert Neville, the Editorial and Production Director, who has proved to be most helpful and patient.

Thank you all.

Acknowledgements

Introduction

WHILST I was in the process of writing this book, I mentioned it to a friend of mine. He asked me which famous cases I was including and I mentioned some of the more recent chapters in the volume.

"Yes well, they were all guilty really. They got off on technicalities and it's a pity they didn't hang the lot," he commented. In many cases, that "technicality" was that the people concerned, most of whom had spent years in prison, were innocent.

This narrow-minded, blind and uninformed opinion is, sadly, typical of that of many in British society. The legal system in Britain maintains that a person is, quite rightly, innocent until proven guilty. It is not for the defendant to prove that he, or she, is innocent, the prosecution must prove guilt beyond a reasonable doubt. And here is the crux of the problem. Any person going to serve on a jury, especially in the most serious of cases, that of murder, may well have a feeling, albeit a subconscious one, that innocence has to be proved. After all, the person in the dock has been arrested and charged. There must be something in that. There must be a good chance that they are guilty so the juror asks that innocence be proved.

Even when the evidence is considered carefully, and a juror does ask for guilt to be proved, mistakes can be made. There are many cases in this book where had I been on the jury, listening to the evidence presented at the trial, I would have voted guilty. After all, witnesses can be mistaken, but they do not lie deliberately do they? Policemen do not manufacture evidence, suppress beneficial testimony or beat confessions out of innocent suspects, and scientific or forensic evidence cannot be wrong. Yet the pages of this book show that each of these has occurred and continues to occur.

Many of those accused of murder in these fifty chapters lost their lives at the end of a rope. Others would certainly have done so had we still had capital punishment in force at the time. "Oh no!" you cry, another advocate of the anti-hanging lobby. There can be little doubt that if there were a referendum in this country today, most people would vote to restore hanging. After all, mistakes are extremely rare.

Tell that to Timothy Evans, Derek Bentley or Mahmood Mattan, all of whose stories appear in these pages. All were hanged. All have been pardoned for murders they did not commit. Still, that is only three names. Even if you add those that we still have serious doubts about, such as James Hanratty, there is still only a handful.

Since the dawn of the 20th century there have been almost 800 executions for murder in England, Wales and Scotland. If we graciously allow that four or five may have been innocent, we have less than one per cent of those executed who may not have deserved that fate. Even though the loss of one innocent life is to be regretted, surely it counts for little when so many guilty souls got what they so richly deserved.

Yet when one researches these cases in depth, as I have done, the number starts to rise. This volume is not exhaustive. It contains the names of thirty-eight people who were hanged but I have enough names to fill a second volume, and possibly even a third. In fact, I hold that around ninety of those who were hanged were either innocent, or probably insane, or that there was at least a reasonable doubt. Remember, one does not have to prove innocence. One only has to have a reasonable doubt. So, our five or so cases now become ninety or more, and our one per cent now becomes more than eleven per cent. Suddenly the figures don't look so good.

Very well, the exponents of the rope cry, let's move the goalposts a little. Fair enough, mistakes have been made, so let's just have capital punishment for certain crimes. The usual litany of such crimes includes child murder, mass murder, murder through acts of terrorism, more than one murder committed at different times, and the murder of a policeman.

Unfortunately, that argument too is doomed to failure. This book contains those who were said to be child murderers, such as Louisa Masset, George Alfred Rice and Stefan Kiszko; those accused of mass murder, such as Judith Ward and the Birmingham Six; those said to be terrorist killers, like the Guildford Four; and those claimed to have killed more than one victim at different times, such as Timothy Evans. It even includes one hanged for the murder of a policeman, Frederick Guy Browne.

All right, just convict those who confess and whose confessions are backed up by other evidence. Such was the case with Judith Ward, some of the Birmingham Six and Stefan Kiszko, amongst others.

Murder can never be justified, but then neither can the conviction of the innocent. How can a civilized society claim that killing is wrong and then punish its killers by killing them? And how can a civilized society condone people in its police force who manufacture confessions, manipulate evidence and assault suspects until they will swear to anything? Not one of the policemen in these pages who behaved improperly to secure a conviction has served a single day in prison. Why not have a society which is not afraid or reluctant to prosecute all criminals, including those who wear uniforms and obtain false convictions? Why not have a simple system of punishment whereby any officer shown to have beaten a confession out of someone, or faked evidence or testimony in order to put someone behind bars, is sent to prison themselves to serve a sentence, to the day, the same as that served by the person they had convicted?

British justice leaves a lot to be desired when so many innocent, or possibly innocent, people can be processed through the system and lose their lives at the end of a rope, or serve years of imprisonment, for something they did not do. Until a proper and independent body exists to examine these wrongs and prosecute vigorously and without favour all those who have conspired to maintain them, justice will continue to be blind.

Louisa Josephine Jemima Masset

Hanged at Newgate, Tuesday, January 9th, 1900
For the murder of her son, Manfred Louis Masset, in London

1

AT 6.19 p.m., on Friday, October 27th, 1899, two ladies alighted from a train at Dalston Junction station in north London. Mary Teahan, a governess from Isleworth, and her good friend Margaret Biggs were due to attend a lecture at a school in Tottenham Road, Kingsland, but before they left the station, Miss Teahan needed to use the rest room.

The ladies waiting-room was situated on platform three, and Miss Biggs stayed in there whilst her friend went into the lavatory at the far end of the same room. Inside the lavatory were two water closets and Mary Teahan tried to gain access to the first of these. Unfortunately, something was blocking her way.

The cubicle was very badly lit but in the darkness, Miss Teahan saw something that looked like a child's face. Such a thing, though, was surely not possible, so the shocked woman assumed that what she had seen was in fact another lady, possibly in need of assistance. Miss Teahan returned to the waiting-room, joined Miss Biggs, and together the two ladies walked out on to the platform where they spotted Joseph John Standing, a porter, pushing a barrow. The two ladies told him that they thought there was a woman in distress in the ladies lavatory.

Joseph immediately passed this information on to Mr Cotterell, the foreman porter, and together the two men went to investigate. Sure enough there was someone lying behind the door, but it was not a woman who had fainted. The light was very poor but it appeared to be a small child, covered by a dark-coloured shawl. Joseph Standing wasted no time in going to fetch the station inspector, David Bundy.

By the time Bundy arrived at the cubicle, Standing had collected a lamp to provide adequate light in the dark lavatory. To their horror the men found the body of a boy, naked except for a black shawl covering his midriff. The boy's head lay towards the passage, whilst his feet pointed towards the water closet. There was a good deal of blood on his face and near his head lay a broken clinker brick (a hard brick used as a paving stone). Bundy immediately called for the police and a doctor.

It was 6.55 p.m. by the time Dr James Patrick Fennell made his examination. He confirmed that life was extinct and originally stated that the time of death was at least two hours before. After a subsequent post-mortem examination, he revised his opinion somewhat and said that the boy had died some time between 2.55 p.m. and 5.55 p.m., though he thought that death was most likely to have occurred between two and three hours previously, that is between 3.55 p.m. and 4.55 p.m.

The police investigation moved slowly at first. There had been nothing left on the body to identify it, so details of the crime and a description of the boy were published in the newspapers on the following Monday, October 30th, in the hope that someone would be able to put a name to the poor unfortunate child.

These newspaper reports were seen by Helen Eliza Gentle, a children's nurse who lived with her mother, Mrs Norris, at 210 Clyde Road, Tottenham. She contacted the police and said that she was very much afraid that the description of the dead boy bore a remarkable resemblance to a child she had had in her care until the very Friday that the body was found. Miss Gentle was escorted to the mortuary, and there she positively identified the body as that of Manfred Louis Masset.

According to Miss Gentle, Manfred had been born on April 24th, 1896, meaning that at the time he died, he was three and a half years old. His mother, Louisa Masset, had answered an advertisement that Miss Gentle had placed in a local newspaper soon after the child's birth, and after some discussion she had agreed to leave the child in Miss Gentle's care. The problem was that Miss Masset was not married and, as she had her own living to earn, was not really in a position to look after the boy herself. As a result, in May 1896, Manfred was handed over to Miss Gentle, who was paid thirty-seven shillings per month to bring him up.

This arrangement had continued until very recently. To begin with, Manfred's mother had visited him every fortnight, but once he was older, these visits had increased to once a week. Every Wednesday, Louisa would call at the house and sometimes she would take her son out for a walk. Occasionally, Helen Gentle would accompany her and they often went to the nearby park at Tottenham Green.

On October 16th, a letter, dated two days earlier and addressed to Mrs Norris, was received at Clyde Road. The letter came from Louisa and explained that the boy's father, who lived in France, had asked that his son be sent over to him to be educated. Louisa had agreed to this request and, as a result, she wished to take custody of Manfred on Friday, October 27th.

On Wednesday, October 25th, Louisa had made her usual visit to Clyde Road and final arrangements for the hand-over were completed. Helen Gentle agreed to meet Louisa outside the Birdcage public house on Stamford Hill at 12.45 p.m. on the Friday. She did indeed keep this appointment and the last time she saw Manfred was when he boarded an omnibus with his mother and set off for London Bridge railway station, where they could catch the train for Newhaven and the ferry to France.

29 Bethune Road, Stoke Newington – the home of Louisa Masset (John Eddleston)

The police naturally now wished to interview Louisa, and with this in mind they went to her home at 29 Bethune Road, Stoke Newington. The house was actually owned by Richard Cadisch, who was married to Louisa's sister, Leonie. They confirmed that Louisa had told them the story of a trip to France in order to hand the boy over to his father. She had left the house at 12.30 p.m. on October 27th, and had not returned until 9.00 p.m. on Sunday, October 29th. Since that time there had been no change in Louisa's demeanour, and she had now gone out to attend to some pupils to whom she taught music and French. They had no idea what time she might be expected back. The police decided to wait outside and concealed themselves across the road, waiting for Louisa to return.

In fact, it was during the early hours of Tuesday, October 31st that the police saw a man arrive at 29 Bethune Road. He went inside the house, only to come out shortly afterwards with Mr Cadisch. The officers decided to follow the two men, a journey which took them to Streatham Road, Croydon.

It transpired that Mr Cadisch's visitor had been George Richard Symes, a gentleman married to another of Louisa's sisters, and the two men had returned to Mr Symes' house together. Once the police officers knocked on his front door they found Louisa, in a very distressed state, talking to her two brothers-in-law.

According to George Symes, Louisa had arrived there at around 11.00 p.m. She told him that she had seen a newspaper report stating that the child's body found at

3

Dalston had been identified as that of Manfred Masset and adding that his mother was now sought in connection with his death. Louisa denied any involvement whatsoever in Manfred's death, claiming that someone else had killed him. Now, for the first time, she told her version of what had happened to her son.

Louisa confessed that the story of the trip to France was false. She had spent that weekend in Brighton with her lover, Eudor Lucas, but on the Friday had handed Manfred over to two ladies who said they were starting a private school in Chelsea. She went on to make a full statement outlining her version of events.

Louisa's statement began by referring to an incident that had taken place on Wednesday, October 4th, when she had visited Clyde Road as normal. As was her habit, she had taken Manfred to Tottenham Green where he fell into play with a little girl she knew only as Millie. Nearby, two women sat on a bench and one introduced herself as the mother of Millie. The conversation naturally turned to the children and the women, the older of whom said their name was Browning, said that they were thinking of starting a small private school. Louisa confessed that she was not satisfied with the education Manfred's nurse was providing. In reply, Mrs Browning mentioned that a place might be found for Manfred for a fee of £12 a year for his board and lodgings and ten shillings a month for his education.

The following Wednesday, October 11th, Louisa again took Manfred to the park and again met up with the Brownings. Further discussions on the new school took place, and finally Louisa agreed to place Manfred in their charge. Arrangements were made to meet at London Bridge railway station at 2.00 p.m. on October 27th, when she would hand over Manfred and £12 in cash.

Louisa now had a problem. She had no wish to hurt Helen Gentle's feelings and so she concocted the story of sending Manfred to his father in France. However, since she would have to spend some time away from home in order to support this story, she would take the opportunity to travel down to Brighton and enjoy a short break.

The police listened patiently to this story but still felt that they had enough

The victim, Manfred Masset, whose body was found at Dalston Junction station on October 27th, 1899 (Public Record Office Ref. No. CRIM 1/58/5)

evidence to hold Louisa on a charge of murder. She again vehemently denied playing any part in Manfred's death.

The trial of Louisa Masset opened at the Old Bailey, before Mr Justice Bruce, on December 13th, 1899. The case for the prosecution rested in the hands of Mr Charles Matthews and Mr Richard D. Muir, whilst Lord Coleridge and Mr Arthur Hutton defended. The proceedings lasted until December 18th and, at first glance, the evidence against Louisa seems overwhelming.

To begin with, it could easily be shown that Louisa and Manfred had travelled to London Bridge station, as she had indicated. Helen Gentle had seen her board the horse-drawn omnibus outside the Birdcage. Thomas Bonner had been the conductor on that bus and he told the court that according to his records, his vehicle had left Stamford Hill at 12.48 p.m. He remembered a woman and child sitting together and saw them get off at London Bridge at approximately 1.35 p.m. Bonner had been unable to positively identify Louisa but had been shown a picture of the dead boy and swore that it was the same child.

The next sighting of a mother and child had been made by Georgina Worley, an attendant in the waiting-room on the South London line at London Bridge. She put the time at 1.42 p.m., and said that the couple remained in the waiting-room until around 2.30 p.m. Georgina had spoken to the woman, who explained that she was waiting for someone to arrive at the station. She was unable to state with certainty that the woman was the prisoner, but she believed that to be the case.

There were in fact two ladies waiting-rooms at London Bridge station and the attendant on duty in the other one, the first-class waiting-room, was Ellen Rees. She had only come on duty at 2.30 p.m. on the 27th, and said that shortly afterwards, at about 2.40 p.m., a woman and child had come into her room. Ellen Rees particularly remembered the child because he was crying. She asked the woman what was the matter with him and was told that he was missing his nurse. Ellen then asked how old the boy was and the woman said that he would be four next April. Finally, the woman said that she would go and buy him a cake and the two walked off in the direction of the refreshment room. It was then 3.00 p.m.

So far, little damage had been done to Louisa's story. She agreed that she had travelled to London Bridge and had first gone into Miss Worley's waiting-room, where she had arranged to meet Mrs Browning at 2.00 p.m. When the two ladies had still not appeared by 2.30 p.m., Louisa recalled the other waiting-room and thought that they might have been waiting in the wrong one. She had spoken to the attendant there and had left that room at 3.00 p.m. It was fifty-five minutes later that the ladies finally appeared, apologized for being so late, and took charge of Manfred. Louisa was then just in time to catch the 4.07 p.m. train to Brighton.

The first problem came with the remainder of Ellen Rees' evidence. She went on to say that she had seen Louisa again, at 6.50 p.m., and that this time she was alone. By then, Louisa was in the lavatory and had asked Ellen for a towel so that she could have a wash. Later, she asked her what time the next train to Brighton was and Ellen told her that it was due to leave at 7.20 p.m., advising her that she should hurry if she wished to catch it. In fact, the train was actually due at 7.22 p.m., and left a couple of minutes late. Ellen Rees last saw Louisa at 7.18 p.m., as she left the waiting-room to catch the Brighton train. Since then, she had attended an identification parade and picked out the prisoner from a number of other women.

There were other indications that Louisa had arrived in Brighton long after she had claimed. Alice Rial was a chambermaid at Findlay's Hotel, situated at 36 Queen's Road, Brighton. She testified that it was 9.45 p.m. when Louisa checked in, giving her name as Miss Brooks and reserving a second room for her brother, who was to arrive the following day. Louisa was also seen by the hotel's proprietor, John Findlay, who confirmed that it was quarter to ten when she arrived. The next day 'Mr Brooks', who was of course Eudor Lucas, arrived and occupied the room next door. The two guests paid their respective bills on the Sunday but a couple of days later, whilst cleaning out the rooms, Alice Rial found a pair of toy scales. These were identified by Helen Gentle as a pair she had purchased for Manfred and handed over to Louisa on October 27th.

Further damning evidence had come from Brighton. Eudor Lucas had arrived at Brighton at 3.20 p.m. on Saturday, October 28th. Louisa had met him there at that time. Just ten minutes later, Annie Skeats, an attendant in the ladies waiting-room at Brighton, had found a brown paper parcel. She took the parcel to the cloakroom but when it was not claimed, it was forwarded to London Bridge station where it was opened. The parcel contained a child's jacket and frock and though some of the trimmings had been removed, Helen Gentle was able to identify the items as those Manfred had actually been wearing when she handed him over to his mother. Furthermore, it could be proved that the wrapping used on the parcel had been given to Louisa by Miss Gentle on the 27th, as the brown paper was torn and matched exactly a tear in another piece still at Miss Gentle's home.

When Manfred's body had been found he was naked except for a black shawl thrown over him. Evidence was now called which seemed to link that shawl directly to Louisa.

Maud Clifford was a sales assistant at McIlroy's draper's shop at 161 High Street, Stoke Newington. She testified that on October 24th she had sold a black shawl to a lady fitting the prisoner's description. The shawls had only been in stock for about a week and Maud recalled the customer insisting that the shawl had to be black. Maud had attended an identification parade and picked out Louisa but said that she could not swear absolutely that this was the woman.

Ernest Hopkins Mooney was the manager of that same draper's shop and he said that on October 16th he had purchased fifteen woollen shawls from his supplier. Only three of these had been black and only one of those black shawls had been sold. He produced the two remaining shawls in court and agreed that they matched exactly the one found on Manfred's body.

The prosecution suggested that the motive for Manfred's murder was that he was an encumbrance to the continuing relationship between Louisa and her lover, Eudor Lucas. Eudor told the court that he now lived at 23 Mildmay Grove, Stoke Newington, but he had until recently lived next door to Louisa at 31 Bethune Road. Eudor was French, and since Louisa was half-French it was perhaps natural that they should get on well, despite the fact that she was thirty-six and he had only turned nineteen in November.

Continuing his evidence, Eudor said that he had first met Louisa in September 1898 but they had only been walking out together for the past three or four months. At Whitsuntide, he and two friends had gone with Louisa to Brighton for a weekend break. On that occasion they had also stayed at Findlay's hotel but nothing improper had taken place between them.

The friendship had continued to develop, and about two or three months earlier, Louisa had told him about Manfred. Eudor had thanked her for her candour and told her that it made no difference to their relationship, but he asked her not to mention the child again. He was certainly not distressed by the knowledge that she had given birth to an illegitimate son and they continued to grow closer together. They had not, though, at any stage, discussed marriage.

On either Tuesday, October 24th, or possibly the next day, Eudor and Louisa had met at Liverpool Street station and she had told him that she intended to go down to Brighton on the following Friday. He said that he would like to go with her but would be unable to get down until the Saturday. He went on to tell her that he would catch the 2.00 p.m. train, and she told him that she would be getting one at around 4.00 p.m. on the 27th. They agreed to book in as brother and sister under a false name, and he next saw her at Brighton station on the Saturday afternoon.

Eudor confessed that he and Louisa had first had sex that same evening, and although they had booked separate rooms, they had actually used only one. They travelled back to London on the Sunday, arriving in Bethune Road at a few minutes before 9.00 p.m. Throughout the entire time they were together Louisa was in her usual spirits and gave no indication that there was anything wrong.

Another suggestion made by the prosecution was that Manfred may have been a financial concern and that Louisa may have killed him in order to save Helen Gentle's fees. This motive was largely negated by the evidence of Louisa's sister, Leonie Cadisch.

Mrs Cadisch confirmed that Louisa had lived with her since August 1898. She knew about Manfred of course, and the arrangements made with Miss Gentle for his care and upbringing. In fact, Leonie had issued a guarantee to Miss Gentle that she would pay her the thirty-seven shillings if Louisa should ever default. However, Leonie had never been called upon to make the payments for her sister. Furthermore, Louisa lived at number 29 without any charge, and all the money she earned from her pupils was for her own use. Leonie also believed that Manfred's father supported the boy financially, though Louisa had never actually revealed who he was. In short, Louisa had no monetary concerns.

Turning to the story that Manfred was being sent to France, Louisa had first mentioned this on October 18th but had only filled in the details a week later, on October 25th. Leonie agreed that Louisa had arrived home at 9.00 p.m. on the Sunday and that she had been calm and collected as usual. Leonie also said that she had never seen the black shawl before and though she was not an expert, did not even think it a new one. As for the clinker brick found near Manfred's body, it was true that there were similar bricks in her garden, but there were also such bricks in many other gardens she knew.

Louisa entered the witness box to give evidence on her own behalf. She repeated her story about handing Manfred over to Mrs Browning at London Bridge, and added that her original plan had been to travel with the boy to the school to see him settled in. Once the ladies turned up, Louisa pointed out that she had only minutes until her train left and would not now be able to go to Chelsea. She handed over her son, the parcel of clothing and £12 and asked for a receipt. One of the women said she would go and get some paper and ink from the refreshment room, but they had not returned by the time her train was due to leave. Louisa was not unduly concerned though. They seemed eminently respectable ladies, and she did have their address – 45 Kings Road, Chelsea. Unfortunately, police investigations had since shown that this address was occupied by a respectable dairyman, Henry Willis, who had never heard of either Louisa or the Brownings.

Louisa maintained that she had caught the 4.07 p.m. train to Brighton, arriving there at about 6.55 p.m. Leaving her Gladstone bag at the left luggage office she had gone for a walk down to the sea front. She had thought about taking a walk along the pier but it was rather damp, so instead she went to Mutton's, a restaurant on King's Road where she had something to eat before walking down to the shops in West Brighton. Later, she returned to the station to collect her bag before checking into the hotel. She was certainly not in London as late as 7.18 p.m., when Ellen Rees claimed she had seen her.

Medical testimony was given by Dr Fennell and Dr Thomas Bond. They agreed that the cause of death was suffocation. It appeared that the clinker brick had been used to stun the child before a hand had been placed over his mouth until he stopped breathing. Dr Bond added that in his opinion, the most probable time of death was some two hours before discovery, placing it at around 4.30 p.m.

In the event, the jury took just thirty minutes to decide that Louisa was guilty as charged. Louisa again said that she was innocent, but Mr Justice Bruce then donned the black cap and sentenced her to death.

Let us examine the evidence of the various witnesses more closely. The most damaging witness was undoubtedly Ellen Rees, who claimed that she had seen Louisa as late as 7.18 p.m. on October 27th. Mrs Rees had picked Louisa out at an identification parade and wore glasses to make this identification. She admitted that she had not been wearing those glasses at work on the 27th, but added that she only needed them for reading. Why then did she wear them at the parade? Furthermore, Mrs Rees had seen a photograph of Louisa in her local newspaper even before she came forward to the police. She also said that as many as 200 women passed through her waiting-room on an average day, many of them with children. There was also the possibility that Inspector Forth had assisted Ellen Rees by standing close to Louisa Masset in the parade. He denied any such impropriety, but this does at least reduce the efficacy of Mrs Rees' testimony.

Maud Clifford and Ernest Mooney, the witnesses who had identified the shawl, gave conflicting evidence. At one stage Mr Mooney said that he had never seen such a pattern before, but he then went on to say that such a shawl could be purchased just about anywhere.

Then there is the possibility that Louisa had been telling the truth all along. There is agreement that Louisa was certainly at London Bridge, with Manfred, until around 3.00 p.m. Louisa herself said that this was the case, and this testimony is confirmed by Thomas Bonner, Georgina Worley and Ellen Rees.

It had taken Louisa forty-seven minutes to get to London Bridge – that is, from 12.48 p.m., when the bus left the Birdcage, until 1.35 p.m. We know that she was certainly at the station until around 3.00 p.m. Assuming that she had then travelled straight back to Dalston, catching an omnibus immediately, she could not have arrived there until around 3.47 p.m. This of course fits in with the medical evidence, but we then have to allow for a return to London Bridge station. Louisa could not have arrived back there until around 4.45 p.m. at the very earliest. Therefore, if she caught the 4.07 p.m. train, she was innocent.

It was during the trial that a new witness from Brighton came forward. Henry James Streeter was a waiter at Mutton's restaurant at 81-84 King's Road, Brighton, and he had been working on Friday, October 27th. He particularly remembered the day, as the weather had been very poor. As a result he had only served two customers all day – one a man and one a woman dressed in black. The woman came in at 6.00 p.m. and stayed for forty-five minutes. He and Mr Mutton, the proprietor, both thought they could positively identify the woman if they saw her again. If this were Louisa it meant that she was in Brighton long before 7.18 p.m.

Mr Streeter and Mr Mutton took their concerns to a solicitor, who contacted Louisa's lawyers. They did not see fit to call either man at the trial. Only later, after she had been sentenced to death, were any efforts made to test this possible evidence. Louisa was asked what she had eaten in the restaurant. She made two statements, giving slightly differing versions. In one she said she had had two slices of hot meat with gravy and vegetables, bread and butter, and either ale or beer, costing a total of two shillings and sixpence. In the other she omitted the bread and butter and said that the cost was one shilling and ninepence. Neither agreed with the books at the restaurant, which said that the woman who had dined there had eaten bread and butter and a pot of tea. As a result, the testimony was dismissed as irrelevant and neither witness was allowed to see Louisa.

There were also other witnesses who were never called. David Taylor lived at Holywell Lane, London, but on October 27th, he was on a bus at the corner of Bishopsgate Street and Cornhill at around 3.45 p.m. He saw two women with a child and noted that the child seemed to be very fidgety and petulant. More importantly, John Hughes-Ellis was on a bus which stopped at London Bridge between 3.15 p.m. and 3.30 p.m. on the 27th. He saw two women with a child that seemed unwilling to be with them. The younger woman picked up the child and sat opposite to Mr Hughes-Ellis. The times, of course, do not agree with those given by Louisa herself since she said she did not hand Manfred over until just before 4.00 p.m. However, Mr Taylor admitted that he may have misjudged the time. There was other evidence too, which was never passed on to the defence.

At the end of 1899, a letter addressed to Louisa was delivered to Newgate prison. Dated December 26th, it read "The women of Chelsea must keep out of sight but they are not anxious to hang you. If the porter (a porter) at Dalston junction would speak he could tell who he saw at 4.45 there. Anyhow, put this in your lawyer's hands – it may save you." The letter was never passed on by the authorities.

Of course, all this may be totally valueless. The letter was most likely a hoax but there are only two alternatives – either Louisa was guilty or she was innocent. Which of the two is the most likely scenario?

The only possible motive for the crime was that Manfred was a burden either financially, or to the relationship with Eudor Lucas. There was no evidence that Louisa was in trouble financially, and Eudor swore that they had never spoken of marriage. Louisa, therefore, had no real motive.

Putting this to one side, if Louisa were guilty, she travelled all the way to London Bridge so that she could be seen by witnesses. She then travelled back to Dalston Junction, her local station, killed her son, stripped him naked and threw her shawl over the body even though it might be linked directly to her. She then went back to London Bridge, was seen again, caught a later train than she said and tried to manufacture an alibi by saying she had eaten at Mutton's. This same cool killer, however, then left Manfred's clothing in Brighton station, thus linking herself directly to the crime.

The alternative is that the child was collected at just before 4.00 p.m., taken to Dalston and killed by the Brownings. The clothing was taken from the boy and parcelled up in the brown paper that Louisa had given to them. The following day, one or both of the killers took a trip to Brighton and dumped the parcel in the waiting-room at the station. The killers had been told by Louisa that she intended to travel to Brighton, and children were being murdered for much less than £12 at this time. As for Louisa not recalling what she had eaten at Mutton's, it must be remembered that she was asked two months later, after she had been through the trauma of losing her son and being put on trial for her life. Everyone agreed that Louisa was a loving and dutiful mother. Could that same loving mother kill with no real motive? There was also the fact that she had discussed placing the child elsewhere as early as February 1899.

It has been said that Louisa confessed her guilt before her execution. Even here there is doubt. Some reports state that just before she was hanged she said, "What I am about to suffer is just, and now my conscience is clear". Other sources say that this took place the night before her execution and consisted of just the words, "What I suffer is just". If the words were ever uttered, in any form, they could just as easily have been those of a mother expressing her guilt at handing Manfred over to his real killers. What is not in doubt is that she was hanged at Newgate prison on January 9th, by James Billington and William Warbrick.

It is not necessary to prove that Louisa Masset, or indeed any of the other people in this book, was innocent. The law requires only that there be a reasonable doubt. The fact is that there are equally valid explanations in this case which do not involve Louisa Masset taking the life of the son she loved.

Suggestion for further reading:-

In Suspicious Circumstances (London: Boxtree, c. 1993).

2

Herbert John Bennett

Hanged at Norwich, Thursday, March 21st, 1901
For the murder of his estranged wife,
Mary Jane, on Great Yarmouth beach

JOHN Norton was a conscientious worker, even though he was not yet fifteen years of age. So it was that at 6.10 a.m., on the morning of Sunday, September 23rd, 1900, he was walking towards Hewell's bathing huts on Yarmouth beach, where he worked as an attendant during the season. Before he got there, though, something he saw made him dash back to his employer, Mr Green.

John told Mr Green that there was a woman asleep on some grass that had grown through the sand. John was told to go back and wake her but when he tried to do so, he found that the woman was dead. There were some bruises and scratches on both sides of the woman's face and a piece of mohair bootlace tied so tightly around her neck that it had bitten deep into the flesh. This, plus the fact that the woman's skirt had been pushed up to her knees and her bloomers pulled down to her ankles, left John in no doubt that he was looking at a murder victim. Reporting back to his employer, John was now told to fetch a policeman. He ran off as fast as his legs could carry him.

Constable Edwin Herbert Manship was on duty in The Drive at 6.30 a.m., and was standing close by the jetty when John Norton ran up to him and told the officer what he had discovered on the beach. Constable Manship followed John to a spot opposite New Road, between the barracks and the naval hospital, and there, lying on the slope of a small hill, some twenty yards from the stone pavement, he saw the woman.

She was lying with her head to the south and her hands down by her side, the fingers bent into the palms of her hands. On the right-hand side, near her head, lay a white straw sailor hat with a black band and a black veil with white spots. The woman's bloomers and petticoat had been pulled down, and though he did not disturb the scene, Manship saw that they bore the laundry mark 'No. 599' on the waistband. The bloomers themselves had been unbuttoned at the waist and torn down the crotch for a distance of some eight inches. Looking around, Constable Manship noticed that there appeared to have been a struggle some yards away. It was clear that the woman was dead, so Manship sent John Norton on yet another errand, this time to fetch a cart in order that the body could be taken to the mortuary. As he waited, Constable Manship noted the shoelace around the dead woman's neck. In fact, it was two laces tied together in a reef-knot at the back, and fastened in front with two reef-knots and a granny. Manship knew his knots, having spent many years at sea before he joined the police force.

It was Dr Thomas Lettis, the local police surgeon, who was called to the mortuary to make an initial examination. By then it was 7.45 a.m., and he found that it was absolutely impossible to get even his little finger underneath the shoelace. He too noted the scratches on both sides of the woman's face, under her eyes and on either side of her nose, and the well-marked abrasions under her jaw. Apart from the laundry mark, though, there were no items on the body that might aid identification.

Reports of the find were well-publicized throughout the town, and it was these reports that brought a lady named Eliza Elizabeth Rudrum to the police station that same afternoon. Eliza lived with her husband John, and their daughter Alice at Row 104, number 3, where she sometimes let out rooms. She told the police that just over a week earlier, at 8.50 p.m. on Saturday, September 15th, a Mrs Hood had arrived, with a baby who was some twenty-three months old. She brought no luggage, other than a small brown paper parcel, and asked if she could rent a room.

Mrs Hood stayed in the house for no more than five or ten minutes before going out again, saying that was going to see her brother-in-law off on his train, as he had brought her down. She said she would not be long, but was not back by midnight. When she finally did reappear, Eliza thought that she might be the worse for drink, but she said nothing about the matter to her new guest.

Continuing her narrative, Eliza said that during the rest of the week, Mrs Hood had gone out with the baby each day. Every night she put the baby to bed and then went out by herself. She was always back by 9.00 p.m. however, and Eliza never saw her drunk again.

On Friday, September 21st, Mrs Hood was out again, but on this occasion only came in at around 10.50 p.m., saying that she had lost her way. That same day a letter had arrived for her. It was in a blue envelope and bore the postmark 'Woolwich'. Eliza heard Mrs Hood read out part of the letter, which said "Meet me at the big clock at nine o'clock and put your babe to bed". The following day, the Saturday, Mrs Hood went out alone at some time between 6.30 p.m. and 7.00 p.m. She did not return that night and as soon as Eliza heard about the body being found on the beach, she feared the worst. Eliza was then escorted to the mortuary, where she formally identified the body as that of her guest. At last, a name had been put to the dead woman.

Unfortunately, this did not help the police a great deal. Contacting their colleagues in the Woolwich area, they could find no trace of a Mrs Hood, with a young baby, who had either been officially reported as missing, or who was not at her home address. By the time the inquest opened, the officers investigating the case had come to think that Hood had been an assumed name.

Returning to the Rudrum household, police officers made a careful search of the room occupied by Mrs Hood. Amongst the woman's belongings, the search revealed the return half of a railway ticket from London to Yarmouth, a letter which referred to Bexley Heath, and a photograph of the dead woman and her child which, it was plain, had been taken on Yarmouth beach.

At this time, there were a number of photographers who spent the summer and autumn taking pictures of families on the sands. When the police made enquiries with these gentlemen, they discovered that the photograph had been taken very recently indeed, by James Richard Conyers. He confirmed that he had taken the picture on Thursday, September 20th, some time between 11.00 a.m. and 11.30 a.m. Obviously this was therefore the most recent likeness of the murder victim and as such, it was widely circulated to police forces throughout England, including those at Woolwich and Bexley Heath.

The police were certainly most methodical in their approach to the investigation. The rail ticket showed that Mrs Hood had travelled to Yarmouth from Liverpool Street station. There, a ticket seller confirmed that two tickets had been purchased at the same time. The seller was unable to describe either of the purchasers but this did imply that Mrs Hood had travelled to Yarmouth with someone, possibly her killer.

It was from Bexley Heath that the first breakthrough came. Lilian Langman lived with her parents at Glencaron Villa, Bexley Heath. She had heard of the search for Mrs Hood's home address and reported that in July, a Mrs Hood and her husband had come to look at the house next door, Glencoe Villa. They had liked the house and decided to rent, their furniture arriving about a week later. It seemed, though, that Mr Hood did not actually live with his wife, for he was seldom at the house.

Lilian stated that she had last seen Mrs Hood on September 15th, when she had left the house with the baby and carrying a brown paper parcel under her arm. The following Wednesday, September 19th, Mr Hood called at Glencaron, tapped on the back window and asked if anyone had called at the house. Just over a week later, on Friday, September 28th, Mr Hood was back and was forced to break a window to gain access to Glencoe Villa, as he had no key. He explained to Miss Langman that he wished to collect some clothes to send on to his wife, who was in Yorkshire.

Glencoe Villa had been let through an agent, Messrs Ralph and Sons, of Bexley Heath. When the police checked with that company, they spoke to Walter Edward Hudson, who had arranged the transaction. He was able to provide the officers with two valuable pieces of information. Originally, Mrs Hood had come there from Woolwich Road, London, and secondly, on September 26th, Mr Hood had called at his office to say that he and his wife would no longer require the house. He was told that he would have to take the matter up with the owner of the property. That owner was John Butler, who confirmed that on October 4th, he had received a letter from Mr Hood, asking to break the agreement. Butler had agreed on condition that the rent was paid up to Christmas.

Emma McDonald lived at 30 Woolwich Road, London, and in due course was traced by the police as the previous landlady of Mrs Hood. Mrs McDonald stated that Mrs

Hood and the baby had moved in with her on July 4th, taking a flat on the upper floor. She had also seen Mr Hood, but as far as Emma was concerned, he had only ever stayed at the flat one night. Furthermore, Emma McDonald was able to give the police yet another previous address, 64 Wickham Lane, Plumstead.

The house in Wickham Lane was occupied by a serving policeman, Herbert Elliston, and his wife, Emma. It was Emma Elliston who had dealt with the letting out of two furnished rooms in her home. She reported that on May 12th, the woman in the photograph shown to her had come to stay in the house, with her child and husband, and that their names were not Hood, but Bennett. Finally, the correct name had been put to the dead woman found on Yarmouth beach. She was Mary Jane Bennett, the child was Ruby and the husband was named Herbert John.

Mrs Elliston was able to give the police further valuable information. Mary Jane had been rather deaf and as a result, many of the conversations she had held with her husband had been loud enough to overhear. It was clear that the couple did not live happily and even as they moved in, Bennett had remonstrated with her over her arriving late. To this she had replied "Herbert, the baby was so heavy, also the portmanteau. I could not get here before. You knew the time I was coming. Why didn't you meet me?" Bennett's comment had been "Shut your great mouth. Damn you and Ruby too."

Bennett had some trouble with a sore toe and on one occasion, Mary Jane had brought him some hot water so that he could put a poultice on it. The water, though, was too hot so Mary Jane had to return to the kitchen where she fell into conversation with Emma. Back in her own room, Mary Jane was questioned over what she had said and replied "I told the landlady you had a bad toe". Again Bennett had said "Shut your great mouth", but this time he had added "Don't talk about me".

During the first week that the Bennetts were at Wickham Lane, he appeared to do no work, preferring to spend his time reading *Exchange and Mart*. During the second week he found employment at the Co-operative Store in Woolwich. In all, the family had been there for about six weeks when, after yet another argument, Bennett had told his wife that he wanted them to live separately and suggested that she should get a house for her and the child at Bexley. Emma also heard Bennett say that he had taken a room for himself at Woolwich. Cryptically, Mary Jane had shouted "Herbert, I shall follow you for the sake of the baby and if you are not careful, I shall get you fifteen years". He replied "I wish you were dead and if you are not careful, you soon will be".

The police now had a positive identification of the dead woman, and further investigations led to the whereabouts of her husband, Herbert Bennett. Eventually it was felt that a strong enough case could be brought against Bennett, and he was arrested near his new place of employment, the Woolwich Arsenal, on November 6th. Two days later he was escorted back to Great Yarmouth where, after a number of police court appearances, he was sent for trial at the next Norfolk assizes.

In fact, the case was never to be heard at Norwich. Local press reports had been so vitriolic that it was felt by Bennett's defence team that he would be unable to receive a

16

fair trial in the county where the murder had taken place. On January 18th, 1901, an application was made to have the hearing transferred to the Central Criminal Court. The application was heard by Justices Bruce and Phillimore, who ruled that in the interests of justice, the trial should be transferred.

So it was that Herbert Bennett faced a jury at the Old Bailey on February 25th. The case was before the Lord Chief Justice, Lord Alverstone, and the prosecution case was led by Mr F. C. Gill, assisted by Mr A. H. Poyser and Mr Richard D. Muir. The defence team consisted of the formidable Mr Edward Marshall Hall, who also had two assistants, Mr G. Thorn Drury and Mr Forrest Fulton. The proceedings were to last until March 2nd.

Amongst the earliest witnesses on that first day were John Norton and Constable Manship, who both described what they had found on the beach on September 23rd. They were followed by the first medical witness, Dr Thomas Lettis. In addition to examining the body at the scene, he had also performed the post-mortem, with Dr Charles O'Farrell. There was no fracture of the hyoid bone, though asphyxia from the bootlace had been the cause of death. Dr Lettis had also noticed that there was sand on the woman's right thigh and this, together with some small bruises on the vagina, indicated that the woman had either voluntarily engaged in intercourse, or had been sexually attacked before her death. Under cross-examination, he inclined more towards the view that she had been raped.

Dr Lettis was followed on the stand by Dr Charles O'Farrell. His evidence agreed with that of his colleague, but he added that he believed that the ligature had originally been tied on the woman's chin and then slipped down onto her neck, causing the superficial skin abrasions on her cheeks and chin. Whoever tied the bootlace must have used considerable strength, and after it had been placed around the throat, Mary Jane would not have lived for more than a couple of minutes.

The next witness was William Porter, a labourer who had been on the beach at about 8.00 a.m. on the morning that the body had been found, September 23rd. He had discovered a pair of spectacles some thirty yards from the edge of The Drive and not far from where the body had lain. These had since been identified as those worn by Mary Jane.

The beach photographer, James Conyers, was next to the stand, but his testimony was to be far more important than the mere confirmation of his taking the last picture of the murdered woman. The photograph showed a necklace around Mary Jane's throat, and when the police had searched Bennett's lodgings in Woolwich, a woman's chain had been found. If it could be shown that this was the same chain that appeared in Conyers' photograph, then Bennett would probably be the murderer. Conyers, however, swore that in his professional opinion, the chain around Mary Jane's neck was a rope pattern chain, whilst the one found in Bennett's room, and now produced in court, was a link pattern.

To counter this damaging testimony, the prosecution now called another photographer, Frank Henry Sayers. He also had a studio at Yarmouth, but had taken the mortuary photographs for the police and had since experimented on the beach, trying to recreate the Conyers picture. He testified that the necklace shown in the picture might be either a rope or a link pattern but under cross-examination, he had to say that the one in court did not look the same as the one in the picture.

William Clarke was a butcher of 24 Dock Road, Northfleet, and the father of Mary Jane. He told the court that his daughter had been born on August 28th, 1877, making her just twenty-three when she met her death. From an early age, Mary Jane had been taught the violin and the piano, and seemed to have a natural musical talent. Indeed, eventually she started teaching and it was through this that she first met the prisoner, Herbert John Bennett, when she began to give him lessons.

Bennett and Mary Jane grew close and soon she announced that she was pregnant. Though Bennett's own family opposed the match, they married on July 22nd, 1897. The child Mary Jane carried had died soon after birth but later, in October 1898, Ruby had been born. Giving some details of the family history, Mr Clarke said that by the start of 1900, Bennett ran a grocer's shop at Westgate-on-Sea, but within two months, the shop had burned down. At first the insurance company had refused to honour Bennett's claim, but later had offered a compromise settlement that Bennett had accepted. Soon afterwards, Bennett and Mary Jane told friends and relatives that they were sailing for America, but in fact they went to South Africa. They left England on March 17th, but were back by May 9th, apparently with a good deal of money.

Mr Clarke was also able to say that amongst his daughter's belongings had been a silver watch and a gold chain. He had given the watch to Mary Jane when she was twelve, and though he had only seen the watch a couple of times in the last few years, he was able to produce a receipt for it, showing that it was numbered 132785. In fact, the number stamped on the watch was 132783, but allowing for human error, it was accepted that this watch, which had been found in Bennett's rooms, was the one that Mary Jane habitually wore.

Turning to the gold chain found in Bennett's possession, Mr Clarke said that this had belonged to his mother and had only been passed on to Mary Jane when Mrs Clarke died. Finally, he stated that he had only heard of his daughter's death the day after Bennett had been arrested.

On the second day, Emma Elliston gave her evidence and she was followed by William Clarke, who had been recalled to clear up a point about Bennett's marriage to Mary Jane. He confirmed that the marriage certificate stated that Bennett was twenty-one, but that this had been overstated by a factor of four years. Bennett had been only seventeen when he married, meaning that he was now twenty.

The next witness was Emma McDonald, who told of Mary Jane's stay at her home in Woolwich. She also identified a brooch, produced in court. This rather distinctive item was in the form of a pickaxe, shovel and pail. Next came the house agent, Walter Hudson, who in addition to relating details of the rental of Glencoe Villa also produced a reference that Bennett had forged in order to get the house for Mary Jane.

After Lilian Langman and other neighbours at Bexley Heath had given evidence, the prosecution called two very damaging witnesses, Edward Robert Goodrum and William Alfred Read. Goodrum was the 'boots' at the Crown and Anchor Hotel, Yarmouth, and he told the court that he had been on duty at the hotel on the night of September 22nd. At around 11.45 p.m., he had admitted a man he recognized as the prisoner. He was carrying a small paper parcel, explained that he had missed his last train, and asked for a bed for the night. Before retiring he said he wished to catch the 7.20 a.m. train for London the next day, and he asked to be called by 6.30 a.m. The next morning, Goodrum saw Bennett leave the Crown and Anchor at 6.50 a.m.

This was confirmed by Read, a waiter at the same hotel. Read was also able to state that he had seen Bennett even earlier than September. On August 4th, Bennett had come to the hotel with a young lady, though they had occupied separate rooms. He was also there on September 15th and, of course, on September 22nd.

Comfort Pankhurst lived at 44 Union Street, Woolwich and she told the court that some time around the middle of June, Bennett had taken lodgings at her home. Whilst there he became very friendly with another lodger, John Stevens, and through Stevens he met a young lady named Alice Meadows. Bennett had brought this Miss Meadows to the house a number of times, finally stating that he intended to take her as his wife.

One day, a telegram had arrived for Bennett whilst he was at work. The telegram appeared to come from Bexley Heath and read "Very ill, come at once". Thinking that this might be urgent, Comfort took the telegram to the Co-operative Store and handed it over to Bennett, who told her that it was from his cousin.

On Saturday, September 22nd, Bennett had arrived home from work, which was by then the Arsenal, at some time between 2.30 p.m. and 3.00 p.m. He went out soon afterwards and she did not see him again until the evening of Sunday, September 23rd. He had told her only that he was going to catch a train, and she noted that he wore a grey suit at the time.

Bennett had arrived home at 5.30 p.m., or perhaps 6.00 p.m., on the Sunday, looking rather less smart than he usually did. He changed his clothes and went out soon afterwards. Some days later he left her house and moved to new lodgings at 18 William Street, also in Woolwich.

Miss Pankhurst had referred to a friend of Bennett's named John Stevens. He was the next witness and he said that he had been keeping company with a young lady named Treadwell. She was in service as a cook at a house in Hyde Park Terrace, and one of her fellow workers had been Alice Meadows, a parlour-maid. It had been through this association that Bennett had first met Miss Meadows.

Before moving on to the relationship with Alice Meadows, the prosecution first called Henry Robert Horton, a bookkeeper at the Woolwich Arsenal. Part of Mr Horton's duties included keeping a record of which employees were at work and which were absent. Herbert Bennett had started working there on July 16th, 1900 and had been allocated employee number 5342, though this was later changed to 5069. On September

15th, Bennett was recorded as being off sick, resuming work at 8.00 a.m. on Monday, September 17th. On Friday, September 21st, he worked from 6.00 a.m. until 7.00 p.m., and the next day, September 22nd, he worked from 6.00 a.m. until the normal stopping time for a Saturday, 12.40 p.m.

Bennett had claimed that on the night of September 22nd, whilst his wife was being murdered in Great Yarmouth, he had been out drinking with two friends who he once worked with at the Co-operative. John Cameron said that he had indeed met Bennett, but this had been a week later, on September 29th. He had certainly not seen him on the 22nd and was certain of that date because that was when he bought himself a new suit of clothes. The other drinking companion, William Henry Parritt, confirmed what Cameron had said.

The final witness on this second day was Alice Amelia Meadows of 22 York Road, Stepney. She confirmed how she had first met Bennett, sometime in June, 1900. Bennett had told her that he had a cousin at Bexley Heath and a grandfather, father and stepmother who all lived at Gravesend. At no time did he refer to a wife and child and he always represented himself as a single man.

At about the same time, Alice had expressed the intention of going to Yarmouth for her summer holiday. Miss Treadwell, the same woman who was walking out with John Stevens, had given her two addresses, one of a Mrs Rudrum and the other of a Mrs Newman. Bennett had written to both on her behalf and received two replies, both saying that they were unable to provide rooms for the period in question.

On Saturday, August 4th, she and Bennett had gone to Yarmouth together, staying in separate rooms at the Crown and Anchor. They returned to London on the following Monday and soon afterwards, the subject of marriage had been discussed. Bennett then proposed on August 20th and just over one week later, on August 28th, he gave her a diamond and ruby ring to mark the engagement. Later that same day, the couple travelled to Ireland for a fortnight, again staying in separate rooms. Wherever they went, Bennett seemed to have plenty of money to spare and spent it freely.

Continuing her narrative, Miss Meadows said that on September 14th, Bennett had told her that he was going to Gravesend the next day, Saturday 15th, as his grandfather was rather ill. She next saw him on Sunday 16th, at around 3.30 p.m. On the following Thursday, September 20th, Bennett told her that he was going back to Gravesend and so would not be able to see her on Sunday, the 23rd. However, when September 23rd came, Bennett caught up with her at the Albion Gate entrance of Hyde Park. He explained that there were others in the family looking after his grandfather and he had felt himself to be in the way, so he had come back early to see her. It was then that he gave her a gold brooch with a shovel, a pickaxe and a bucket on it.

It was agreed that she and Bennett would marry at Christmas time. Over the next few days he gave her other gifts, usually saying that he had obtained them from a cousin who was going over to South Africa. All of these items had in fact belonged to Mary Jane.

20

On the Sunday before he was arrested, Bennett had been at Alice's mother's house when the subject of the Yarmouth murder, which had been all over the London newspapers too, had been raised. Alice's sister said that it was curious that nothing had been heard about the killer and compared the mystery to that of Jack the Ripper. Bennett ignored all reference to Great Yarmouth but mentioned that he thought the Ripper had been captured in the United States.

The morning of the third day of the trial was mostly taken up by the cross-examination of Alice Meadows. It was after the defence had finished with her that the Rudrum family were called.

Eliza Rudrum said that on September 22nd, the last time she had seen Mary Jane Bennett, whom she knew as Mrs Hood, alive, she had gone out of the house at some time between 6.30 p.m. and 7.00 p.m. After hearing about the discovery of the body the following morning, she had reported to the police. Later that day, Inspector Lingwood had come to her house and been shown the dead woman's bedroom. The beach photograph, so important in this case, had been found in a drawer.

Turning to the night that Mary Jane had arrived at Yarmouth, Eliza said that when Mary Jane had finally come in that first night, she had gone upstairs with her. Mary Jane had confided that she had had three drops of brandy and a fish supper with her brother-in-law, who had brought her up to Yarmouth. One day during 'Mrs Hood's' stay, the two ladies had gone out together and Mary Jane had pointed out a hotel. Eliza was not sure whether it was the Star or the Cromwell, but she said that this was where her brother-in-law was staying. She went on to say that she had travelled down from York, but added that her brother-in-law was going to get her a house in London so that he could see more of her.

Mary Jane, it seems, was also inventing a past for herself. She told Eliza that she had been married for five years but her husband had died the month before her child was born. Turning again to the subject of her brother-in-law, Mary Jane had intimated that he was in love with her and she would not be surprised if he was following her about. However, in addition to this testimony, Mrs Rudrum had some most curious and interesting information to impart.

She had already told the police of a letter that her guest had received, on Friday September 21st, in a bluish-coloured envelope, which had been postmarked Woolwich. Mrs Rudrum claimed that once she had heard that a man named Bennett had been arrested in connection with the crime, she had suddenly remembered the name. She had searched through her correspondence, which she kept, and found a letter from Bennett, asking if she might put up him and a lady friend. This letter had, of course, been referred to by Alice Meadows, but the significance was that Eliza Rudrum claimed that the handwriting was the same as that on the letter which Mary Jane had received.

John Rudrum was Eliza's husband, and he confirmed that the victim had come to his house at some time between 8.00 p.m. and 9.00 p.m., on the night of September 15th. The following Friday, September 21st, he had seen her at the end of The Row, in the company of a man. It had already been shown that two tickets from London to Yarmouth had been purchased at the same time. Was this man the one who had accompanied Mary Jane to the seaside from the capital? Was he the mysterious brother-in-law?

Alice Rudrum was Eliza and John's daughter and lived with them in The Row. She too recalled the letter in the blue envelope arriving, and she too confirmed that the handwriting was the same as the letter Bennett had written.

On Friday, September 21st, Alice too had seen her with a man at the end of The Row, quite late at night. She was unable to say anything about the man but heard him say, "I am placed in an awkward position just now". If there was a reply, Alice did not hear it, but she did see the couple kiss before the man bade Mary Jane goodnight and walked away.

On Saturday, September 22nd, Alice was out with Miss Briggs, a friend of hers. It was just after 9.00 p.m., and they were near the Town Hall when they saw Mary Jane, alone. Alice spoke to her briefly and Mary Jane said she was waiting for her brother-in-law, who was coming down by train.

The next witness was William Thomas Carver Borking, the manager of the South Quay Distillery public house. He testified that just before closing time on September 22nd, at a few minutes before 10.00 p.m., a lady and a gentleman came into his bar. He swore that the man was Bennett and believed that the woman was Mary Jane. During their stay, the man stood close to the bar, twirling his moustache. The couple left together at about 10.00 p.m. Under cross-examination, however, Mr Borking confirmed that the man he had seen wore a heavy moustache, whilst Bennett's was only slight. This sighting of Bennett at the Distillery was confirmed by Elizabeth Gibson, one of the barmaids there.

Alfred Edward Mason's testimony showed that he might have actually witnessed the murder itself. On the night of September 22nd, he had been out with his young lady, Blanche Smith. Some time before 11.00 p.m., they walked down New Road and on to the beach, where they sat down in a hollow in order to do a little courting. After ten minutes or so they saw a young man and a woman walk on to the beach from New Road. This couple sat down thirty yards away. They were talking loudly, as if quarrelling. They then heard the woman cry out and this was followed by groaning. Neither Alfred nor Blanche took any action.

At about 11.10 p.m., Alfred and Blanche got up to leave and walked towards the spot where the man and woman lay. At one stage they were only five yards away and Alfred could see that the man was lying astride the woman, with his right arm on her chest and his left arm over her right shoulder. Despite the fact that, as they passed, the man lifted his head and looked directly at Alfred, neither he nor Blanche could identify the man or the woman.

Edward Goodrum from the Crown and Anchor was now recalled to show that whilst he claimed with certainty that Bennett was the man he had seen in the hotel, he was unable to describe any of the clothing his customer wore. One further witness, Mr Read, the manager of the same hotel, was then called to confirm that the receipt counterfoils for all the dates mentioned could not be found. There was no hard evidence of any bill paid by Bennett.

The final day of the trial opened with Mr Keates, the landlord of the Crown and Anchor, who again referred to the missing counterfoils. He said that there were a total of thirty sheets missing, including all those on the relevant dates. He could offer no explanation for this.

John Milner Headley was a newsagent based at 18 Howard Street North in Yarmouth, and on September 23rd, he had been at the railway station for the 7.20 a.m. train to London. He saw a man, who he believed to be Bennett, standing at the door of one of the carriages, but the efficacy of his testimony was largely demolished by Mr Marshall Hall, who produced a copy of that day's newspaper detailing all the evidence that he had given. Bennett, it seems, was still being tried by the press, for under cross-examination Mr Headley was unable to confirm that the man he had seen was the prisoner.

Next, evidence was called on the railway timetable. On September 22nd, there was a train from Liverpool Street, London at 5.00 p.m., and this arrived in Yarmouth at 8.28 p.m., showing that Bennett could have been there in plenty of time to commit the murder.

Eliza Rudrum was then recalled. Long after Bennett had been arrested, she had suddenly produced a petticoat which she claimed had belonged to the victim but which had been accidentally put away. This petticoat had been handed over to the police on January 16th, and bore the name Bennet [sic] written in ink. Asked to spell Bennett, Mrs Rudrum claimed that she was unable to do so, but finally she wrote Bennet. She then hesitated before adding the final 't'.

The final prosecution witness was Mr Kaye, a photographic expert from London who testified that on a short exposure, such as that used by Mr Conyers on Yarmouth beach, a chain link necklace might appear to be like a rope chain.

That then was the essence of the case against Bennett. He had lived unhappily with his wife and had expressed a wish that she were dead. He was enamoured of Miss Meadows and therefore Mary Jane was in the way. His alibi that he was out drinking with two friends had collapsed, he could have easily made it to Yarmouth in time to commit the crime, and he had been seen by more than one witness on the Saturday night and Sunday morning. Finally, the brooch he had given to Alice Meadows had belonged to his wife and the silver watch and gold chain found in his lodgings were the same as those taken from the dead woman's body.

The defence opened with a number of expert witnesses on both photography and jewellery. Howard Welby was an expert on gold chains, and he stated that the one in the beach photograph was definitely a rope chain. Thomas Wortley, a manufacturing jeweller, said that the chains were different, as did Thomas File, a photographer. The most important witness, though, was John Sholto Douglas, who lived in Hither Green, near Lewisham in south-east London.

Douglas was a manufacturer of fancy goods and a keen gardener. He remembered September 22nd particularly well, for that was the only Saturday out of four or five at that time when he did not potter about in his garden.

Arriving home at 3.00 p.m., he first had a hot meal and then went out for a walk, leaving his home at 4.00 p.m. He walked to Burnt Ash Hill, on to King John's Palace, where he arrived at 4.45 p.m., and then started for home via Eltham. It was along that journey home that he met a man whom he now identified as Bennett. Bennett stopped Douglas and asked him for a light. The two fell into a conversation, during which Bennett mentioned that he worked at Woolwich and had recently been to Ireland. The town of Bexley was also mentioned.

Douglas wished to get rid of his new companion but was much too polite to say so. Instead, as they reached Lea Green, he offered to buy Bennett a drink. Bennett accepted and the two went into the Tiger public house. Later, as they left, Douglas' companion joked that a namesake of his appeared to live there, and he pointed out a hairdresser's shop. The name over the door was Bennett. The two finally parted at 7.00 p.m. If this were true, then Bennett must have been in London long after he was supposed to have caught the train for Yarmouth. Mr Douglas had seen reports of the police court hearings in the newspapers, recalled his meeting with Bennett, and contacted the defence on November 17th. He had no doubt whatsoever that Bennett was the man he had seen.

Another important witness was Susan Cato of 3 Fairlight Road, Tooting. Once, in September 1899, she had shared a house with the Bennetts in Balham. She swore that Mary Jane was not the conscientious mother that had been portrayed. She neglected the baby, and was seeing another man whom Bennett knew nothing about. One day this man called on Mary Jane and Susan saw that he looked very much like Bennett. She was also able to say that Mary Jane had two watches and two chains. Furthermore, the two watches were very similar to each other.

On the final day, the jury retired at 6.25 p.m, returning at 7.10 p.m. to announce that Bennett was guilty as charged. Asked if he had anything to say before the sentence of death was passed, he replied "I say I am not guilty". Less than three weeks later, on Thursday, March 21st, 1901, Bennett was hanged at Norwich by James and Thomas Billington. As the black flag was hoisted outside the prison, the pole broke and it was some minutes before it could be fixed. Many of the more superstitious onlookers held that this was a sign that an innocent man had been hanged. What is certain is that Bennett made no confession to the crime.

As far as the evidence is concerned, there was a reasonable doubt as to Bennett's guilt. A companion was seen with Mary Jane on Friday, September 21st. Bennett was not absent from work on that day. There is evidence that there were two chains and two watches, and in any case there was no proof that Mary Jane was wearing the watch on the night that she died or that it had been taken from her body. In addition, there was also one witness who swore that he had been with Bennett in London as late as 7.00 p.m. on Saturday, September 22nd, which meant that Bennett could not have been in

Yarmouth in time to kill his wife. There are also at least indications that Mrs Rudrum tried to 'manufacture' evidence. There exist, however, still more facts which increase the feeling of unease about the conviction.

Mr O'Driscoll was a newsagent at Lowestoft. On Wednesday, September 26th, he was serving in his shop when a man came in and asked for a paper with the best account of the Yarmouth murder. The man was given a newspaper, began to read the article, and then groaned and screwed the paper up. O'Driscoll noticed that the man wore boots but only one was laced up. The other had no lace, and the one that remained was mohair. This man was also seen by William J. Overy, an assistant in the shop. Both said that this man was not Bennett.

One final mystery remains. On July 14th, 1912, a young woman's body was found on the beach at Yarmouth. She had been strangled with a bootlace in a manner almost identical to the murder of Mary Jane Bennett. This poor woman was eighteen-year-old Dora Gray, and her murder remains unsolved to this day.

Suggestion for further reading:-

Brian Lane, *The Murder Guide to Great Britain: 100 Extraordinary, Bizarre and Gruesome Murders* (London: Robinson, 1993).

3

John Harrison

Hanged at Walton prison, Tuesday, December 24th, 1901
For the murder of Alice Ann Wright, at Bickerstaffe, Lancashire

O
N February 21st, 1901, a marriage took place at Parr church near St Helens, which was then situated in Lancashire but which nowadays, due to boundary changes, lies in the county of Merseyside.

The couple, who were both in their thirties, were John Harrison and Alice Ann Wright. The marriage was bigamous however, for Alice, who had been born Alice Sutcliffe, had first been married in 1889, in Fleetwood, to a man named James Wright. That particular relationship was not to last, with Alice walking out on James in 1897, after a disagreement about her misconduct. Alice, it appears, was very fond of the company of men and sold her services to them in order to support herself. Indeed, she had served two prison sentences for that very offence.

It soon transpired that this second 'marriage' was based on Alice being the main breadwinner – through using the only skill she appeared to have. George Hill was a police constable at Ormskirk, and in early May two somewhat undesirable people moved into his district. Hill decided that these people, John and Alice, merited close attention and felt it best to keep a watchful eye on them. Though Hill could not actually prove anything, he believed that Alice was plying her trade as a prostitute. On several occasions, he saw the couple walking through the quiet streets of Ormskirk, Harrison following some distance behind his new bride.

On other occasions, Constable Hill saw Alice in the company of different men. On Friday, May 31st, for instance, he saw her at 9.20 p.m. in Dark Lane, Latham, with a man who was certainly not her husband, for Harrison was sitting on a fence some 200 yards away. Ten days before this, on Tuesday, May 21st, Constable Hill had been in Railway Road, Ormskirk, when he saw Harrison walking along the road, whistling brightly to himself. Around fifteen minutes later he was joined by Alice, who greeted him with "Hello Jack". Harrison replied "Well, how have you gone on? You have been a long while." To this, Hill heard Alice say "I've got half a crown", at which point she handed something over to her husband. The last time Constable Hill saw John Harrison and Alice Wright was on Friday, July 26th, again in Ormskirk.

In the meantime, John Harrison had managed to obtain employment for himself. On June 14th, he had started at Rainford Colliery where he stayed until July 19th. One week later, on July 26th, Harrison picked up his last wage packet, which amounted to ten shillings.

Saturday July 27th, 1901, was a bright day. At 8.30 a.m., Richard Gardner was walking to work down Liverpool Road, Skelmersdale, when he noticed two people, walking along on opposite sides of the road. Later, he would identify these two as Harrison and Alice, but now he just saw a man and woman who appeared to be quarrelling. Much of the conversation was indistinct, but at one stage Gardner heard Alice shout, "Bugger you". At this, Harrison walked into the Engine Inn, only to be followed moments later by Alice.

This scene had also been witnessed by George Dawson. He could only say that the time was somewhere between 8.30 a.m. and 9.00 a.m., but he too saw the couple argue, and then walk into the Engine Inn. George, however, also went into the pub, where he saw the couple having a drink, which the woman paid for, taking the money out of a purse. Harrison and Alice left the pub at around 10.20 a.m., and the last Dawson saw of them, they were striding down White Moss Road.

In fact, there was a slight discrepancy about the exact time that Harrison and Alice left the Engine Inn. Though George Dawson claimed that it was 10.20 a.m., it must have actually been somewhat earlier, for by 10.00 a.m., Alice was knocking on the door of Peter Marsh's house at Bickerstaffe. Mr Marsh owned Rose Farm and upon opening the door, he was greeted by Alice who said that she and her husband wished to rent a cottage they had seen on his land.

Mr Marsh walked down to the cottage, called Rose Cottage, where he found Harrison waiting for him. Harrison told Marsh that he was working at Rainford Colliery and had been there for some nine weeks. After some discussion, Marsh agreed to let the cottage to the couple, and he unlocked the door for them. Marsh checked through the place and noted that there was absolutely no furniture on the premises, but that all the windows were unbroken. By the time he left the couple alone together, it was 10.15 a.m.

Rachael Coxhead was just fifteen years old and lived with her father, who farmed land at Ivy Farm, Bickerstaffe, situated some quarter of a mile from the cottage Harrison and Alice had rented. Rachael was on her way to Skelmersdale, and passed Rose Cottage at 1.20 p.m. It was easy for her to pinpoint the time, even though she did not carry a watch, for Rachael had just seen the 1.17 p.m. train from Skelmersdale to Rainford go past.

As she glanced at the cottage, Rachael noticed that the top square of one of the window-panes was broken, and the glass was outside, on the pavement. Obviously, this meant not that someone had broken in, but rather that someone inside had broken the pane, causing the glass to fall outwards. Curious, Rachael tried the front door, which was closed but not locked.

Stepping inside, Rachael saw a white straw hat and some dark-coloured material covering some shape. It was obvious that this shape was a woman for Rachael could also see a human female foot, toes turned upward. Thinking that someone was asleep, and possibly drunk, she closed the door quietly and left.

Forty minutes later, at 2.00 p.m., Ann Kirby, the wife of William, who lived at Coxhead's Cottages, also passed Rose Cottage. She too noticed the broken pane of glass, with the shattered fragments lying outside on the footpath.

Some time before Rachael Coxhead had made her discovery, at 1.10 p.m. to be exact, Richard Evans had been in White Moss Road, Skelmersdale, when he noticed John Harrison walking along towards him. This spot was around three-quarters of a mile from Rose Cottage and as Harrison passed, he hung his head down and tried to whistle.

At 2.00 p.m, Edward Alker was in the outside urinal at the Fox and Goose public house on Wigan Road, Skelmersdale. Whilst occupied in there, Alker noticed a stranger, whom he would later identify as Harrison, walking towards the pub down White Moss Road. The man came into the Fox and Goose, and when Alker returned to the bar, he saw the man served with several pints of beer. Harrison seemed to be somewhat distressed and was almost crying. At one stage he wrung his hands together and muttered "Oh dear my..." Alker watched as Harrison fell into conversation with another drinker, Joseph Pye. The two men were still drinking each other's health when Alker left at 2.45 p.m.

John Harrison was not seen again until 9.00 p.m. that night, when he knocked on Peter Marsh's door. When Marsh admitted Harrison he announced "My wife is dead". Marsh was not sure that he had heard Harrison correctly and replied simply "What?" Harrison then said, "My wife is dead and cold".

Peter Marsh advised Harrison that the best thing he could do would be to report the matter to the police. He then set out with Harrison, walked him part of the way and gave him directions to the local constable's house. During their walk, Harrison remarked "I went towards St Helens and my wife went towards Skelmersdale and when I came back I found her on the floor, dead and cold".

Elizabeth Wragg was the wife of Constable Wragg, the local officer for Bickerstaffe. Harrison arrived at her home at 9.30 p.m. and asked, "Does the policeman live here?" Told that he did, Harrison continued "Will you tell him I want to see him?" Elizabeth informed Harrison that her husband was out, but would probably be back at any moment. She also advised Harrison that if he did not wish to wait he might walk up the road, where he would probably see her husband on duty. She then asked him what this was all about, to which Harrison replied "I have found my wife dead on the ground". He added, "It seems as if someone had been messing about with her throat". He began to cry and sobbed "If I could catch the man that laid a hand on that woman he would never kill any more".

Harrison then left Elizabeth Wragg's house, saying that he would go to find her husband. In fact, he then went on a drinking spree. At 10.00 p.m., he walked into the

Horse Shoe Inn on Liverpool Road, Skelmersdale where the landlord, Peter Arnold, served him with a glass of beer. Harrison drank it down and then asked, "Where can I find a policeman?" Arnold told him that if he went further up the road he would probably find one, and then asked what the matter was. Harrison replied "I had been out of the house for about three hours and when I came back, I found my wife laid on the floor, dead". He then left the pub.

At 10.30 p.m., Harrison was back in the Engine Inn, where he had been with Alice earlier that day. He was served by Sarah Ann Yates, the licensee, and asked her "Do you remember me and my missus being in that room this morning?" Sarah replied that whilst she did not remember him particularly, she did recall serving a man and a woman that morning. To this, Harrison commented "It was my wife and I've found her dead". Sarah, shocked to hear this, ordered Harrison "Sup that beer and get to a policeman". She watched as Harrison then left.

Constable Myles Cundliff was on duty in Sandy Lane, Skelmersdale at 11.00 p.m., when Harrison walked up to him and said, "You are the very man I want. I have found my wife dead in a house on the Moss." He continued "I left home at 2.00 p.m., to go to St Helens and when I came back I found my wife dead". Cundliff asked Harrison if there had been any marks of violence on the body, to which Harrison said "I do not know. I never looked. I came straight away."

Further down Sandy Lane, Constable Cundliff noticed Sergeant Stewart Kidd. The story Harrison had told was repeated to him and all three men then walked to Rose Cottage, which was about a mile away.

The front door to the cottage was closed but not locked, the key being in the lock on the inside. There, in the second room, they found Alice with her head resting on the kitchen step, a straw bonnet over her face. Her long brown jacket and blue bodice were unfastened to the breast. There were marks of violence on her chin and some dry blood nearby. One of the windows had been broken outwards and there was a clear hand mark on the adjacent pane of glass. As Sergeant Kidd examined the scene, Harrison said that he had intended to go to St Helens, adding "I called at Joe Ripley's White Hart Hotel. I walked to St Helens and back. It was near dusk when I got to the Wheatsheaf at Rainford where I had a drink."

Harrison was informed that he would have to accompany the two officers back to the police station. At first he appeared to be reluctant but after a time he calmed down and the three men walked back to Sandy Lane.

It was 1.00 a.m. on the 28th by the time Harrison was interviewed by Inspector Edward Barnes. Harrison informed the inspector that he had arrived home at about 6.00 p.m., and again described finding his wife lying dead on the floor. Leaving Harrison in custody, Inspector Barnes then went to Rose Cottage to see the scene for himself. He noted signs that there had been a struggle in the front room and that Alice had then been dragged to where she lay. One of the windows held four panes of glass. One of the top ones had been broken and there was a clear hand print on the one next to it. Going back to the police station, the inspector examined Harrison and noted a spot of blood on his right ear and another on his right hand. There was a bruise on the second knuckle of his right hand and dried blood around his right-hand thumbnail. Harrison said that he could not account for any of this. He was then searched, whereupon Sergeant Kidd found a purse containing one shilling and threepence, ten pawn tickets, a pocket knife, a small glass spirit level and some photographs. At 7.00 a.m., Harrison was charged with murder, to which he replied "Me kill my wife? I would not hurt a hair on her head, far from that."

John Harrison's trial took place at Liverpool on December 2nd, 1901, before Mr Justice Bucknill. The case for the prosecution was led by Mr Foard, who was assisted by Mr Blackwood Wright. Harrison's defence lay in the hands of Mr F. A. Greer and Mr D. G. Morris.

Harrison's defence was that he had left his wife at around 2.00 p.m., and that someone else must have killed her whilst he was walking to St Helens. He had, of course, not reckoned with Rachael Coxhead finding Alice at 1.20 p.m.

Sergeant Kidd reported the details of a statement Harrison had made, in which he claimed "We came to live at that cottage on the Moss this morning. I left the house at about two o'clock to go to Rainford for my money. When I returned about nine o'clock I found her dead on the floor. She was well and hearty when I left the house." This statement was self-contradictory in parts. Earlier Harrison had said that he arrived home at six, and that he was walking to St Helens.

At another stage, Harrison had claimed that he had had a drink with a man named Harry Dingle in the Prince of Wales pub in St Helens. Henry Dinsdale, who confirmed that he was known as Harry Dingle, said that he had indeed been drinking in the Prince of Wales on July 27th, but he had not seen Harrison on that day.

One of the final witnesses was Dr Joseph Parker Woodhouse, who had been called to Rose Cottage by the police, arriving there at 2.30 a.m. on July 28th. He reported that Alice was about thirty years of age when she died. The post-mortem showed that there were numerous bruises on the neck and throat, and several lacerations that might have been caused by a human fingernail on the right-hand side. Alice's tongue was swollen and pushed forward and her hands were tightly clenched. In his opinion, death had taken place at least twelve hours before his initial examination and the cause was strangulation. He also reported that Alice's body had been very verminous.

It was not surprising that Harrison was adjudged to be guilty and was sentenced to death. At this time there was no appeal court and just under three weeks later, on Christmas Eve, Harrison was hanged at Walton prison, Liverpool by William and John Billington. It was said that he confessed to the crime before he plunged to his death.

There can be little doubt that John Harrison killed Alice Ann Wright, but was he responsible for his actions? At the trial, some evidence had been brought forward to show that he was, at the very least, a strange individual. He was said to be of a sullen disposition and to have eccentric habits. He was often seen muttering to himself as he

31

walked the streets and had acted very strangely since the death of his mother two years before. A local constable, P.C. Wall, had twice seen him enter his home, late at night, and fire a revolver before putting the light on. He was also prone to visit his mother's grave, well after midnight, and sometimes sleep on top of it. There was additional evidence of instability in the family, with an elder brother, James, having hanged himself seven or eight years before.

William Bailey and his wife, of 108 Broad Oak Road, Parr, had known Harrison since childhood. They lived next door to Harrison and had heard the incidents with the revolver. They also reported that he behaved strangely and was highly unsociable.

These antecedents had been examined by Dr Arthur Price, the medical officer at Liverpool prison. He stated that Harrison was a man of good physique and sound health. He was taciturn, bad-tempered and inclined to be suspicious of other people. Turning to the family history, Dr Price said that Harrison's father had died eighteen years before, of stomach cancer. Two years ago, his mother had died of 'grief', and four years ago, his brother James had hanged himself because he had discovered that his wife had been unfaithful. Dr Price claimed that the midnight visiting of his mother's grave had been no more than morbid sentimentality on Harrison's part, and the firing of his revolver in his home had been simply lonesome fear.

There was other evidence that Harrison's personality had changed once his mother had died. He had allowed his hair to grow to a great length and his home had become filthy. This, added to his other behaviour, seemed to indicate that he was certainly not in control of his mental processes during the last few years of his life. He may have taken Alice Wright's life but was his mental state such that this could be described as pre-meditated murder?

Even the authorities at the time must have had doubts about Harrison's death, however the accused's alleged confession seems to have reassured them that Harrison really was both sane and a cold-blooded killer. Indeed, at the inquest after the execution, the coroner remarked, upon hearing the alleged confession, that this was most satisfactory as "....otherwise there was a fear that something had gone wrong".

Arthur Devereux

4

Hanged at Pentonville prison, London, Tuesday, August 15th, 1905
For the murder of his wife and twin sons, at Harlesden, London

ELLEN Gregory was at a loss to understand what was going on. She had not seen her daughter, Beatrice Devereux, or her grandchildren for the best part of three weeks now. In fact, the last time she had seen Beatrice was on Saturday, January 28th, 1905. On that date, Beatrice had called at Ellen's house during the evening. She had been alone and the two ladies went out shopping together. In fact, this would be the last Ellen would see of her daughter for some time, as she was going away to work, but she had written. It was strange that Beatrice had not replied. She was usually a most dutiful daughter.

Ellen returned after only two weeks away, in February, determined that the first thing she would do would be to go around to Beatrice's flat at 60 Milton Avenue, Harlesden, and see what the problem was. She was most shocked to find that not only was Beatrice not in but that she, her husband, and their three children had moved out leaving no forwarding address.

Ellen started knocking on the doors of the neighbours' houses and finally got to speak to Mrs Wells. She had no idea where the family had moved to, but she did recall seeing a furniture van one day. The name of the company was emblazoned on the side, so Mrs Wells was able to tell Ellen that the family had used Bannister's.

Arriving at Bannister's warehouse in Kensal Rise, Ellen Gregory discovered two things. Firstly, the Devereux family had moved on February 7th to a new address in Harrow Road. Two removal men, George Willougby and Harry Allingham, had moved their effects, except for one item. That was Ellen's second piece of information. A large tin trunk, supposedly containing books and chemicals, had been left behind at the warehouse.

The address in Harrow Road was number ninety-two. The owner of that property was a gentleman named John Tabboth, and he told Ellen that he had advertised a bedsitter flat in his home, in early February. On the 6th of that month, Arthur Devereux, Beatrice's husband and Ellen's son-in-law, had called to view it. The rent was five shillings per week but there was apparently one small problem. The flat only had a single bed and Mr Devereux had explained that he would need a double as he also had a five-and-a-half-year-old son. Mr Tabboth agreed to put in a double bed and Devereux said he would move in the following day.

This information intrigued Ellen Gregory, for there were actually five people in the Devereux family. In addition to Arthur there was his twenty-five-year-old wife Beatrice, the five-and-a-half-year-old son, Stanley and two-year-old twin boys, Laurence Rowland Devereux and Evelyn Lancelot Devereux. Stanley was a healthy enough child, but the twins suffered from rickets and could not feed themselves. Both required constant attention from their mother. What had happened to Beatrice and the twins?

Inquiring further of Mr Tabboth, Ellen discovered that Arthur Devereux had mentioned them when he rented the rooms. He had explained that they were away in the country as Beatrice was recovering from an illness. There was one final piece of information. Devereux had moved on again, on February 20th, saying he was going to start a new job in Coventry. The day before this he had asked Mr Tabboth if he could keep Stanley for a short time, until his mother was well enough to fetch him. Mr Tabboth had agreed to this request. In due course, Devereux had sent word that Stanley should be put onto the train for Coventry, at Euston station, on Wednesday, March 25th.

All these investigations had taken Ellen Gregory some time so it was not until April

Mrs Devereux with her eldest son (Public Record Office Ref. No. CRIM 1/97/7)

that she contacted the police and expressed her concerns for her daughter's safety. There had still been no word from Beatrice, and it was now approaching two months since Ellen had seen her.

The police decided that the first thing they should do was to examine the contents of the tin trunk left at Bannister's warehouse. So it was that early on the morning of April 13th, officers attended the warehouse and began their inspection. The trunk was padlocked, strapped and sealed with red wax. The lock was forced and the lid of the trunk lifted. Inside the police found a layer of wooden planks, tightly sealed with glue and Boric acid, making the interior of the trunk totally airtight. Once the barrier of the planks had been breached, the next layer was a quilt and tablecloth. It was only when these were taken out that the final contents were revealed – the bodies of a woman and two small boys. They were formally identified, by Ellen Gregory, as her daughter Beatrice and the twins, Laurence and Evelyn. It appeared that all three had been poisoned with morphine.

It was a simple matter to trace Arthur Devereux. Letters written to John Tabboth, giving instructions for Stanley, had borne the return address of 156 Spon Street, Coventry, the premises of a Mr Bird, a chemist. That same evening, Devereux was visited by officers who told him of the grim discovery in the warehouse, and instructed him that he was being detained on suspicion of causing their deaths. He was then escorted back to London, on the way making the comment "My conscience is perfectly clear as to their deaths but I was wrong in concealing the bodies".

Devereux's trial opened at the Old Bailey on July 26th, before Mister Justice Ridley.

The opened trunk in which the bodies of Beatrice Devereux and her twin sons were found on April 13th, 1905 (Public Record Office Ref. No. CRIM 1/97/7)

The proceedings lasted for three days, during which the prisoner was defended by Mr George Elliott, Mr Arthur Hutton and Mr Cecil Fitch. The prosecution case was led by Mr Charles Mathews, who was assisted by Mr Bodkin.

Ellen Gregory told the court of her own investigations into the disappearance of her daughter and grandsons. She also outlined some of the early history of Devereux and his relationship with Beatrice. They had first met at Hastings in 1895. At that time, Devereux was an assistant in a chemist's shop, and the two had taken an instant liking to each other. They began walking out together and three years later, on November 2nd 1898, they had married, at the Trinity Church, Paddington, in London.

The first marital home had been at Croydon and it was there, on August 24th, 1899, that their first child, Stanley, had been born. Soon afterwards they moved to Stroud in Gloucestershire, and there, on April 5th, 1903, the twins were born. The following year, Devereux had obtained a position as the development manager of a chemist's shop at Kilburn, but on January 2nd, 1905, he had been given notice as the business had not developed as the owner had wished.

Before this, in December 1904, Devereux had taken the top floor at some newly built flats in Milton Avenue. At the time, Devereux had said that he only wanted the flat for six weeks and this, of course, was the last address at which Ellen had known her daughter to live.

William Garforth was the agent for the landlord of the flats at Milton Avenue. He testified that Devereux, using a different surname that sounded like Eggerson, had come

35

to see a flat in December, 1904. He looked at quite a few of the properties and finally, on Christmas Eve, said that he would take number sixty. At the time, Devereux said that he only wanted the place for about six weeks as he intended to share a house with a friend after that. He specifically asked for the top-floor flat and asked if the bottom flat might be left empty so that his family could have some peace and quiet. There were several other flats still empty so Garforth agreed to this request, for the time being.

The family moved in on December 31st, and paid their rent regularly. No notice was given when Devereux moved out and the first Garforth knew of the actual move was seeing a furniture van outside the flat on February 7th. Garforth went to Devereux and asked him if he were moving out and Devereux said that he was, in a day or two. The van was just to take some boxes into storage. That same evening, Garforth saw yet another van outside and again went to Devereux to ask for the rent. Devereux explained that he had decided to move out immediately after all, but would pay the rent from the money he had received for selling some of his furniture. The two men then walked to the Royal Oak together and along the way, Devereux mentioned that his mother-in-law might call round at some time. He went on to say that they did not get on and admitted that he had once threatened to blow her brains out with a revolver if she ever came to his doorstep again.

Mrs Wells lived next door to Devereux and seeing Mr Garforth, she had approached him and pointed out that before he left, Devereux had had a bonfire in the back garden. The next day, February 8th, Garforth went to the garden to check. He also inspected the house, which seemed to be in order except for some screws and some red wax which Garforth found in the back bedroom.

The gentleman who actually collected the rents in Milton Avenue was James Perkins. He testified that Devereux had taken the flat in the name of Egerton. The rent was always paid on time, until February 1st. On that day, Perkins had got no reply to his knocking. He was just about to leave when Devereux came to the door, in his shirtsleeves. He seemed to be perfectly normal in his behaviour. The next time Perkins had called, on February 8th, the premises had been vacated.

The neighbour who had told Garforth about the bonfire and Ellen Gregory about the furniture van was Sarah Wells. She said that the Devereux family had been a very quiet one and she had not had much to do with them. On Wednesday, February 1st, Mrs Wells had heard some strange noises coming from the bedroom next door. It was a sort of metallic sound and went on for some time. Three days later, whilst looking into the yard, she saw Devereux and his son, Stanley, making a bonfire out of some papers. Later that same night, a most curious incident took place.

Stanley was outside in the street and rattled the letter-box to get inside. Someone opened the door but told Stanley that he could not go inside yet. Something was then passed to Stanley through the letter-box.

Between February 1st and February 7th, when Devereux moved out, there was a lot of running up and downstairs in the house next door. There was also the sound of furniture being moved around. On the 7th, Bannister's van called and Devereux and Stanley went away with it. They were both back, though, at some time between 3.00 p.m. and 4.00 p.m. They remained at the flat until another van called in the evening, and Mrs Wells never saw them there again.

Some time around February 17th, Ellen Gregory called, looking for her family. Mr Garforth was around and Mrs Wells called him over and introduced Ellen to him. The three then used Mr Garforth's keys to get into the flat and it was then that they noticed a bottle labelled "Prussic Acid - Poison" on the mantelpiece. There was still some liquid inside the bottle.

There was evidence that Devereux had started to sell off family property soon after his wife and the twins had last been seen. Sarah Flint was a second-hand clothes dealer and she testified that during the first week of February, Devereux sold various items to her. The items were women's clothes and Devereux had explained that they were his sister's and were no good to his wife, who needed the money to pay the rent as he was now out of work. In all, Devereux came in two or three times with women's and baby's clothes, and was paid a total of £2.

Thomas Simms was the yard foreman for Messrs Bannister and Co., of Kensal Rise. He sent Willoughby and Allingham to Devereux's house on February 7th. Two days later, on February 9th, at about noon, Devereux and Stanley came to the yard and asked to speak to him. They were brought across by Allingham, who said "This is the gentleman who owns the trunk that I and Willougby brought back from Milton Avenue on February 7th, to be warehoused". Devereux then asked Simms what the cost of warehousing would be and explained that the trunk contained some chemicals and books. He mentioned that someone might call in a day or so to look at the trunk with a view to purchasing the contents, but went on to say that if his wife's mother came he was not to say anything about it to her.

Harry Allingham had died since the case first came to the magistrate's court but George Willoughby was still alive and was called to give evidence. He described his visit to 60 Milton Avenue and loading up various trunks and other items. The tin trunk was upstairs and was very heavy, Willoughby having to get Allingham to help him slide it downstairs. Seeing this, Devereux had asked them not to tip it, as there were chemicals inside.

Other witnesses reported Devereux's hurried attempts to move from Milton Avenue. Horace Furlong was a bread delivery man, and he called every day at the Devereux house, invariably dealing with Mrs Devereux. On Monday, January 30th, he called as usual but there was no reply. The next day he saw Stanley, who took the bread from him. He called every day without getting any reply until Saturday the 4th, when Furlong knocked again, between noon and 1.00 p.m. This time it was Arthur Devereux who opened the door. Furlong explained that there were three shillings owing and Devereux said he would drop the money off in the shop. He never called and there were never any further replies when Furlong called again.

Henry Brazier delivered milk to the Devereux household. On January 23rd, his five shilling bill was paid by Mrs Devereux. After that date it was always Stanley who took the milk from Brazier, until the 30th when Mr Devereux took it and was told that there were six shillings to pay. Devereux said that his wife would pay but at the moment she was out with the babies. The following day, Devereux cancelled the milk and said that his wife had gone away, taking the babies with her.

Until the end of January, Devereux had worked as a chemist for Frederick George Turner of Kilburn. Mr Turner stated that Devereux had started work on May 28th, 1904, on a salary of two pounds per week. On January 2nd, due to the business not increasing the way he had hoped it would, Turner gave Devereux notice. He finally left the position on January 27th.

The prosecution were claiming that Devereux had murdered his wife and sons because of the financial burden they were proving to be after he had lost his job. Since Beatrice was last seen alive on January 28th, that was the most logical date for the crime to have taken place. So far, witnesses had been called who appeared to show that soon after that date, Devereux was selling off his property, arranging to move house, and covering his tracks. However, perhaps the most damning evidence against Devereux was a letter he had written.

Devereux had known on January 2nd that he was going to lose his job at the chemists in Kilburn. It was crucial then that he find new employment as quickly as possible. On January 13th, Devereux had written to Mr Frederick Bird in Coventry, the gentleman he was eventually to obtain a new position with. In that letter he described himself as a widower with one child. At this time of course, Beatrice and the twins were still very much alive and this letter was held to show that the crime was premeditated.

Medical testimony was given by Doctor Augustus Joseph Pepper and Doctor Robertson, who performed the three post-mortems. When the bodies were found, Beatrice was dressed only in her underwear and there were no marks of violence upon her, apart from a slight bruising on her knees, arms and chin. Death was due to asphyxia. The children were dressed in their nightwear and both had died from asphyxia brought about by the ingestion of morphine.

It was suggested that in order to administer this morphine, Devereux had dissolved it in chloroform and told his wife that this was a cough medicine. Once she was out of the way, the same mixture could then be given to the twins. This was negated by the testimony of Sir Thomas Stevenson, the Home Office analyst, who reported that there was no sign whatsoever of chloroform in any of the bodies.

Arthur Devereux claimed that he had not murdered his wife and children. He claimed that on January 28th, the day Beatrice had last seen her mother, he had returned home and found the house smelling strongly of chloroform. As a chemist he had some of that liquid, and some morphine, in the house, locked away safely in his desk. Beatrice, though, had a key to that desk. He went to check and found that both bottles were now missing.

Going upstairs, Devereux said that he found his wife and the twins, all lying dead in their beds. It was clear to him that Beatrice had killed the children and then taken her own life. In a state of panic, he put Stanley to bed, and then set about putting the bodies into the trunk. As for the letter he had written to Mr Bird, he had written other letters before, in a similar vein, as it was easier to obtain a position in this way.

Though this defence still does not explain the fact that no chloroform was found in any of the bodies, it would, if true, mean that Devereux was not guilty of murder. Was there any evidence that Beatrice was capable of such an act? There was certainly some instability in her family background. In July 1903, her brother Sidney had disappeared. His clothing had been found on Plymouth Hoe and it was presumed that he had drowned himself. Under cross-examination, Ellen Gregory herself had admitted that her daughter suffered from depression and had become very anxious when her husband lost his job at Kilburn. She was also used to seeing her mother every day and was upset that she was now moving away, ostensibly for good. Finally, there was the testimony of Mrs Harries.

Mrs Harries had known Beatrice for many years. She testified that in 1899, Beatrice had called on her, bringing her baby Stanley with her. She was very depressed at the time and intimated that she was considering suicide. Furthermore, Beatrice went on to say that if she did kill herself, she would take Stanley with her rather that leave him to the mercies of the world. Unfortunately for Devereux, the prosecution were able to show that Mrs Harries had herself been confined to mental asylums on several occasions between 1899 and 1905.

In his summing up, the judge made an amazing comment. He stated that he saw no reason for Beatrice to have killed her children and then taken her own life. This was an astonishing thing to say. If Devereux were guilty of murder then his motive must have been the financial concerns after he lost his job. Surely the very same concerns, and therefore at least the same motives, would apply to Beatrice, who also had the burden of two ailing twins and who had, so she believed, lost her daily contact with her mother. If she had no motive to kill, then by the same token, neither did Devereux.

There were other reasons too for stating that Devereux, even if he had claimed those three lives, should not have faced a capital charge, as his own background was far from stable. In 1891, his father had been charged with attempted suicide. A grandfather had already attempted suicide by hanging, in 1862. There was an uncle in an asylum and in 1883, an aunt had thrown herself out of a window. Devereux himself had been sent to a farm in Gloucestershire, in his youth, after he had displayed signs of mental instability.

Devereux had been examined by Doctor H. Maudsley, who reported that although there was no sign of real insanity, the prisoner behaved most erratically. He giggled, grimaced and mumbled when answering questions and made outlandish claims. He said he had helped God create the world, and had written all the books in the world. Dr Maudsley concluded that Devereux was trying to fake insanity and displayed cunning more than instability. This was confirmed by Doctor James Scott, the medical officer of Brixton prison, who also believed that Devereux was feigning madness.

There were, however, other signs that Devereux was not faking his instability. The Reverend J. Kirby had known him for many years and testified that he had always behaved strangely. Once he had posed as an American millionaire. On another occasion he had said he was a famous magician and appeared at an entertainment, managing to clear the hall in under ten minutes.

Then there was the evidence of Doctor Forbes Winslow, who had also examined Devereux. He reported that the prisoner was of very weak intellect. Surely such a man would behave exactly the way Devereux did if he found his wife and two of his children dead when he returned home.

Finally there were also indications that the crime was not premeditated. The tin trunk had been in Devereux's possession for two years, and he did not purchase the wood, glue or Boric acid until February 4th.

In the event, the jury took just ten minutes to decide that Devereux was guilty. On August 15th, Devereux was hanged at Pentonville by Henry Pierrepoint and John Ellis. The doomed man's last words, just before he left the condemned cell, were "I have nothing to add to what I have already said". He may well have been making one last protestation of his innocence.

Richard Clifford Brinkley

5

Hanged at Wandsworth prison, London, Tuesday, August 13th, 1907
For the murder of Richard and Anne Beck, at Croydon

A T the beginning of April, 1907, there were four people living in the house at 32 Churchill Road, Croydon. In addition to the householder, fifty-five-year-old Richard Beck, there was his wife, fifty-seven-year-old Anne Elizabeth, and their two daughters, twenty-one-year-old Daisy Kathleen and Hilda May, who was nineteen. Then, on Friday April 5th, a fifth person came to live there, a lodger named Reginald Clifford Parker, an accountant who was separated from his wife and who took the front downstairs sitting-room and the bedroom immediately above it. For a couple of weeks, they all lived happily enough, but the events of Saturday, April 20th, were to change all that. On that night, the family would be torn apart by tragedy.

Though the future police investigation would lead to disputes over what actually happened on the night of April 20th, some of it can be pieced together from the testimony of independent witnesses. Daisy Beck arrived home from work at 5.00 p.m. The only other person in the house at the time was Daisy's father, Richard Beck, but at some time between 7.00 p.m. and 8.00 p.m., Parker, the lodger, came in with a rather vicious looking bulldog which he tied to the door of the living-room he rented. Soon afterwards, at 8.15 p.m., Daisy went out leaving her father and Parker alone in the kitchen. Whilst she was out of the house, Daisy met up with her mother and sister and at 10.45 p.m., all three women went home together. With them was a male friend of Daisy's, a young gentleman named Alfred Young.

When the four arrived back at 32 Churchill Road, there was no one else there, but fifteen minutes later, just as Alfred was biding them all goodnight, Richard Beck came in by the back door. The entire family then went into the sitting-room which Parker used and there Daisy noticed two ale bottles on the table. There was also a bottle of stout and two glasses, both of which looked as if they had contained some of the beer.

Remembering an errand they had to run, Daisy and Hilda went back out, for perhaps no more than ten minutes. When they returned, Richard and Anne were both by the fire in Parker's sitting-room. Daisy then made herself and Hilda a bite of supper, which they ate in the kitchen. During that time, Parker came back into the house, letting himself in through the front door. He then spent some time in his sitting-room, with Mr Beck, and the two men had some more ale together. In all, Parker stayed for between ten and fifteen minutes before leaving again.

Once the two sisters had finished their supper, Hilda announced that she was going to bed. Daisy, meanwhile, went to join her parents in the sitting-room, as her father began to help himself to some of the stout from the bottle on the table. Richard also poured some into the second glass, for his wife, and offered Daisy a sip of her own.

Anne Beck was not a stout drinker, but had expressed a desire to have at least a taste. She took a mouthful and immediately spat it out into the fire exclaiming that it tasted very bitter and expressing her astonishment that her husband could drink the stuff at all. Richard replied by draining most of his wife's glass, whilst Daisy took a sip from the other.

Within minutes, chaos broke loose inside the Beck home. Anne ran into the kitchen where a loud groan signalled that all was not well. Daisy felt that she was suffocating and collapsed onto the settee. At first, Richard seemed to be unaffected, but as he helped his wife back into the living room he too began to sway and gasp for breath. The shouts from Anne and Daisy brought Hilda rushing back downstairs. Help was sought from a neighbour, who ran for the doctor, but by the early hours of the next morning, both Richard and Anne had lost their lives. Daisy was more fortunate. Though she was very ill, she was rushed to Croydon Hospital where she eventually made a full recovery, finally being discharged on April 24th.

It was 12.35 a.m. on April 21st by the time Doctor William Dempster arrived at 32 Churchill Road. He found Richard and Anne Beck lying on the kitchen floor, unconscious, and could do nothing to save them. Once Daisy had been taken to hospital, Dr Dempster searched around for what might have caused this tragedy and finally his attention turned to the bottles on the table. The two ale bottles appeared to be fine, but when he sniffed at the bottle of stout Dr Dempster detected the pungent aroma of bitter almonds. Someone had placed cyanide inside the bottle, killing two people and placing a third at death's door. The police were now investigating a double murder.

After speaking to Hilda, the only member of the Beck family who had suffered no ill effects, Detective Inspector Fowler learned of the lodger, Parker. Curiously enough, Parker had arranged to sleep somewhere else that night. Though he had been at number thirty-two for two weeks now, this particular night he was staying with a friend of his, Mr Marsh, who lived at 269 Brighton Road. In the early hours of April 21st, officers called at that address, roused Parker from his slumbers and escorted him to the police station. He was there until the early afternoon but the story he told placed police suspicion on the shoulders of another man, fifty-three-year-old Richard Clifford Brinkley.

According to Parker, Brinkley was a carpenter who also dealt in livestock from time to time. These business dealings had brought the two men into contact and as a result,

Parker had known Brinkley now for about three years. Brinkley had asked Parker if he might obtain a guard dog for him, and Parker had arranged to show him a dog which he had obtained from Mr Marsh, who was a dog breeder. That was why he had brought the bulldog home, some time after 8.00 p.m., on April 20th.

According to Parker, he and Mr Beck had been alone in Parker's sitting-room at about 8.20 p.m. that evening, when Parker suggested that they might get some beer in. Beck agreed and offered to go out and buy it. He soon returned with two bottles of Fremlin's Ale, which they began to drink in the kitchen. The two men had not been enjoying their liquid refreshment for very long before they heard a knock at the front door. This was Brinkley, whom Parker had asked to call sometime between 8.00 p.m. and 9.00 p.m.

Parker said that he took his visitor into the sitting-room and was surprised to see Brinkley, a lifelong teetotaller, produce a bottle of Oatmeal Stout. Brinkley explained this by saying that his doctor had advised him to take stout for his health. He then asked if he might have a glass. Parker replied that this was not his place, but added that he would drink up his own ale and then give Brinkley his glass.

Upon receiving the glass, Brinkley poured out some stout and drank it down. He then offered Parker some, who accepted, drinking from the same glass. After he had drained it, Brinkley then said he was thirsty and asked for a glass of water. Parker left the room to get a glass from the kitchen. He was out of the room for no more than three-quarters of a minute, and when he returned, Brinkley drank down the water with relish.

Having finished his drink, Brinkley asked Parker to go for a walk with him, bringing the dog with them. The two men walked for a short time, finally parting close by the Red Deer pub, where Brinkley agreed to buy the dog for £5, if Parker would bring it over to his house the following morning. Parker agreed, saying that he would get Mr Marsh to bring him over in his vehicle.

After saying goodbye to Brinkley, Parker went to Mr Marsh's house and arranged to go over to Brinkley's the next morning. Marsh said that they would have to go very early as he had other business to attend to, and Parker said that would be alright. The two men talked until 10.00 p.m., when they went out for a drink together. Later, Parker called back at number thirty-two to pick up his coat. He had another glass of ale with Mr Beck, but was only in the house for a few minutes. He finally left Churchill Road at 11.35 p.m.

The inference was that the poison must have been placed into the bottle of stout, by Brinkley, in the time that Parker was out of the room fetching him a glass of water. Though no motive for such an action could be suggested yet, the police now decided to investigate further. They soon discovered a witness who claimed to have sold a bottle of Oatmeal Stout to a man fitting Brinkley's description. That was enough to cause Inspector Fowler to decide that he would arrest Brinkley on suspicion.

It was close to midnight on April 21st when Inspector Fowler and Detective Sergeant Walter Easter positioned themselves outside 4 Maxwell Road, Fulham, where Brinkley lived. In due course, Brinkley returned home but was stopped before he could turn his key in the lock. Escorted to the police station he was later charged with the two counts of murder, and with attempting to murder Daisy Beck and Reginald Clifford Parker.

Richard Brinkley appeared at Guildford before Mister Justice Bigham on July 22nd. The trial lasted until July 25th and during those four days, Brinkley was represented by Mr Walter Frampton. Mr Richard D. Muir led for the prosecution, assisted by Mr Heber Hart.

Reginald Parker repeated his story of Brinkley's visit to 32 Churchill Road. By this time, a suitable motive for murder had been determined. Parker, it seems, had acted as a signatory to a will in which Brinkley was the only beneficiary. For some years, Brinkley had been close to the previous occupant of 4 Maxwell Road, an elderly lady named Johanna Maria Louisa Blume. A will had been drawn up on December 17th, 1906 and witnessed by Reginald Parker of 60 Water Lane, Brixton, and Henry Heard of 129 Hollydale Road, Peckham. Parker claimed that he had been tricked into signing the document. According to Parker, Brinkley had said that he was drawing up a list of people who were willing to go on an outing he was arranging, and he asked Parker to sign a piece of paper as confirmation that he would take part. Parker had indeed signed a folded piece of paper and it was obvious now that Brinkley had deceived him into signing the will. That will was now being disputed by Mrs Blume's daughter, and if the case were to reach court, the subterfuge would come out. Brinkley had therefore tried to poison Parker, but the stout had claimed two other lives instead.

Before the case reached court, the body of Mrs Blume was exhumed. After all, the old woman had died just two days after the will was signed, which made it most convenient for Brinkley. No trace of any poison was found in the remains however, and no charges in connection with her death were ever made. Furthermore, although Parker denied ever having signed the will voluntarily, his wife stated that he had told her something about a will and added that Brinkley had promised that there was £100 in it for him once the woman had died. Furthermore, the other witness to the will, Henry Heard, swore that he and Parker had voluntarily signed the will, on December 17th, at Mrs Blume's home. When Heard gave this evidence at the police court, the magistrates made it plain that they did not believe him, and possibly as a result of that, it was decided not to call him to give the same testimony at Brinkley's trial, a bad mistake by the defence.

After Dr Dempster had given his evidence, the prosecution called thirteen-year-old John Holden. John was employed as a Saturday assistant at Mrs Hardstone's off-licence at 149 Brighton Road, Croydon. He said that at 7.30 p.m., on April 20th, a man came into the shop and asked for a bottle of stout. When told by Mrs Hardstone that he would have to pay twopence on the bottle, he stormed out, but he returned at 8.00 p.m. and completed the purchase. At an identity parade, Holden had picked out Richard Brinkley as the man who bought the stout. Mrs Anne Emma Hardstone, however, failed to pick out anyone and expressed great surprise that Holden had managed to.

Augusta Glanville was the granddaughter of Mrs Blume and lived with her at 4 Maxwell Road until Mrs Blume died. Though she could not recall ever having seen

Parker at the house, she did recall Heard coming with Brinkley on Friday, December 14th, 1906. On the night that Mrs Blume died, Brinkley came to the house during the evening whilst the family solicitor, Mr Kent, was searching for a will. Brinkley then produced the will from his inside pocket. Everything was left to him, a sum that in all amounted to over £700. Soon afterwards, Augusta Glanville moved out of the house when Brinkley announced that it was his intention to move in.

Under cross-examination, Miss Glanville admitted that Mrs Blume had always been most fond of Brinkley, and that she had always said that she intended to leave nothing to her daughter or to Augusta herself. Furthermore, towards the last few days of her life, Mrs Blume repeatedly asked for Brinkley to be at her bedside.

The daughter Augusta Glanville had referred to was Caroline Blume, Augusta's aunt. She told the court that she was in the process of contesting her mother's will when, on January 23rd, Brinkley had called at her house in an attempt to get her to drop the case. Furthermore, he also told her that it had been her mother's wish that she and Brinkley should marry, a suggestion that she rejected out of hand.

Caroline Blume had found, soon after her mother's death, that certain articles from the house were being offered for sale at a local furniture shop. Edmund Fowler was now called and confirmed that he was a dealer operating from 584 Kings Road, Fulham. He had indeed bought a number of items but there was nothing sinister in this. He had in fact bought them from Mrs Blume herself, before she died. He had called at the house on two occasions and on the second, Mrs Blume had said that she could not sell any more things as, "I must save a few for Mister Brinkley".

Arthur Vale lived at 76 Limes Road, Croydon, and had known Brinkley for fourteen years. Brinkley did some carpentry work at Vale's house in June 1906, and at that time Brinkley said that he had a dog he wished to poison, and needed some prussic acid. Arthur referred Brinkley to his father, William, who lived in Manor Road, South Norwood, and worked as a consultant on bird diseases.

William Vale confirmed that in June, 1906, he had given Brinkley about a drachm of fluid prussic acid, which is, of course, potassium cyanide. Two or three days later, Brinkley had returned and said that he had spilled the first lot, and had then asked if he might have some more. William gave him another drachm. He was also able to confirm that Brinkley had visited his house since that time, and been left alone in the room where the poison was kept.

This indicated that Brinkley not only had enough prussic acid to kill the Becks, but that he had also been in a position to obtain more once Mrs Blume's will had been contested. It ignores a number of important factors, though. In the first place, what did Brinkley do with the original poison? He obtained this in June 1906, almost a year before the Becks were killed. If he still had that poison, then he had no need to steal more. Secondly, if the original poison had been used, perhaps for some legitimate purpose, and Brinkley had stolen more, then he would have had to work very quickly indeed. The poison bottle was wrapped up and hidden out of sight on a high shelf.

Brinkley was alone only for a minute or so, surely not enough time to steal poison and put the bottle back.

William Vale also raised one other interesting point. He had used prussic acid extensively, and knew its properties well. Once poured out, from one bottle to another, it left a lingering smell of almonds in the air for a few minutes. Vale detected no such odour after Brinkley had been left alone in his office. More importantly, Parker had mentioned no almond odour when he left Brinkley alone with the opened bottle of stout, for less than a minute.

Undoubtedly, Parker was the most damaging witness. He placed Brinkley at the scene of the crime and gave him a motive, but was he a stable man, let alone an honest one? When giving his evidence, Parker had admitted that at one stage he had been in severe financial difficulties, so much so that he was thinking of declaring himself bankrupt. The problem with this was that if he did, his creditors would get most of what he had. For that reason he had come up with a subterfuge. He asked Brinkley to accept an IOU for £30, making him the largest single creditor. Brinkley had agreed but the intended fraud had never actually been carried out, as Parker never went bankrupt. This, though, was a sign of the depth of his trickery.

There was also evidence that Parker was a very unstable character. His wife, Ada Parker, confirmed that he had said something about receiving £100 for witnessing a will. She also told the court of an incident on Saturday April 13th, exactly one week before the murder. Though her husband had moved out of the house at Water Lane, she was still concerned about his health and so went with him to the doctors. The doctor informed her that Parker was suffering from acute depression and might well commit suicide at any time. This was confirmed by the doctor in question, Doctor Etherington.

Scientific evidence was given by a number of eminent gentlemen. Richard Bodmer was the public analyst for the area and he said that whilst the stout bottle gave off a strong odour of prussic acid, there was no detectable smell in either of the two ale bottles or in either of the glasses. Sir Thomas Stevenson was the Home Office analyst and he too said that he could detect no poison in either the ale bottles or the glasses but that he had found traces in the stout bottle.

More damaging evidence was apparently given by Henry Daw, who worked as a railway inspector. He had known Brinkley for a number of years and swore that at 6.00 p.m., on April 20th, he saw the prisoner at Chelsea station. There was a train for Clapham leaving at 6.15 p.m., and assuming that Brinkley caught it, he would arrive at Croydon at around 7.15 p.m. The problem with this evidence was that the railway books showed that on April 20th, no one had purchased a ticket from Chelsea to Croydon.

Only two people had placed Brinkley at Croydon on the night of April 20th. Parker was an unstable character, probably suicidal and certainly a liar on other matters. Holden, the thirteen-year-old shop assistant, was the only person who identified Brinkley when his employer, who was closer and actually served the man, could not make any identification at all. Henry Daw had said he had seen Brinkley at Chelsea station, in time to catch the train for Croydon, but no ticket for Croydon had been purchased there on the day of the murders, suggesting that Daw may well have been mistaken about the date he actually saw Brinkley. Of course, it was also possible that Brinkley travelled without a ticket, but in 1907 guards were positioned at all ticket barriers and it would have been very difficult for Brinkley to pass through the barriers without a valid ticket.

For his part, Brinkley claimed that on the day of the murders he had been nowhere near Croydon. He had spent that afternoon at Mr Snapper's shop in Kings Road, Chelsea, repairing a bicycle for him. He had stayed there until 7.00 p.m., after which he returned home to Maxwell Road, where he stayed for the rest of the night. If this were true, then Brinkley certainly could not have been at Chelsea railway station at 6.00 p.m., and was therefore innocent of the charge. Snapper, however, was not called to prove this alibi. It is true that he did visit Brinkley in prison whilst he was awaiting trial, but the fact that he did not give evidence either at the police court or the trial suggests that he simply could not remember the event. Had he simply denied Brinkley's alibi, he would, of course, have been called as a witness for the prosecution. His non-appearance implies that the bicycle-repairing event did take place, but Snapper could not recall precisely when.

There was little point in calling Brinkley's doctor to testify on the subject of his advising his patient to take stout for his health. This story was put forward by Parker, whom the prosecution admitted was the only other possible suspect in this case. If he was telling the truth and Brinkley had used the phrase to explain the breaking of his teetotal habits, then it would have merely been an excuse to put Parker off his guard and the doctor would have only been able to say that he offered no such advice. If Parker was lying then the phrase was never uttered and once again Brinkley's doctor would only have been able to say that he did not advise his patient to drink stout.

There are other factors that were never properly explained. Parker had claimed that he did not get Brinkley a glass for the stout because this was not his place, yet later he did go to the kitchen and get a fresh glass for the water Brinkley asked for. Furthermore, when Daisy Beck gave her testimony she said that her father had offered her some stout with the words, "There's a drop of stout left in this bottle, would you care to have some?" He then poured the contents into two glasses, each of which was then about half full.

Parker had already testified that Brinkley had poured out almost a full glass. If, as the prosecution claimed, Brinkley had then added poison to the bottle whilst Parker was getting him some water, then no more stout must have been drunk until Mr Beck poured out those two half glasses. This in turn meant that the bottle held just two full glasses, or thereabouts. Unfortunately, no record was made of the size of the bottles or the glasses, however, it may well be that the bottle held more than two glasses. The ale bottles certainly did, for Beck and Parker drank quite a quantity. If this were the case then further stout must have been consumed, most probably by Mr Beck, after any visit by Brinkley. This in turn suggests that the poison was added later than Parker claimed, and may well mean that Brinkley was telling the truth when he said he had never even called at Croydon.

In the event, it took the jury just fifty-five minutes to decide that Brinkley was guilty of murder. In the condemned cell at Wandsworth, Brinkley spoke little of the case, and on the rare occasions he did, it was to restate his innocence. In his last letter, written to his solicitor on Monday, August 12th, Brinkley, referring to Parker, wrote "I don't know how people believe a man like that would put his name to a paper without reading it..." He also referred to Inspector Fowler and Parker having been at school together, and towards the end scribbled "But I have lived a righteous and a sober life, so if it is God's will I am prepared to meet Him at any time, and know I am innocent of these poor people's deaths".

The following morning, Brinkley was hanged by Henry Pierrepoint, who was assisted by John Ellis. He never confessed to the murders of Richard and Anne Beck.

John William Ellwood

| 6 | |

Hanged at Leeds, Thursday, December 3rd, 1908
For the murder of Thomas Wilkinson, at Bradford

THOMAS Wilkinson had been a cashier for Messrs Fieldhouse and Jowett, dyers and sizers of Fieldhead, for more than fourteen of his fifty-eight years. The company had their factory at Legram Street, Listerhills, Bradford but they also maintained a small office in the town at 18 Swaine Street.

The office in Swaine Street was really only ever used on a Friday. It was then that Wilkinson would go into the city centre, carry out any banking operations for the company and cash a cheque to cover the weekly wages. The single room office contained nothing more than a desk, a chair and a high stool, and was reached down a long corridor. Off that corridor there were a number of other offices, belonging to many other businesses, and it was in one of those that Samuel Jowett, who had no connection with Fieldhouse and Jowett, was working on the afternoon of Friday, July 31st, 1908.

It was at 2.30 p.m. when Jowett, a warehouseman for George Armitage Limited, returned from a late lunch and heard a thud coming from the office of Fieldhouse and Jowett, which happened to be next door to his own. At first, Jowett thought nothing of this but when a number of low moans also emanated from next door, he rushed to investigate.

Looking through the small glass window, Jowett saw nothing except for a hat, resting on the desk and a walking stick, hanging upon the wall. Of Mr Wilkinson there was apparently no sign, but when Jowett opened the door and walked into the office, he found Thomas Wilkinson lying face down on the floor, his feet close to the door. Wilkinson was obviously seriously injured. He had a severe head wound and lay in an ever-widening pool of blood. Jowett wasted no time in running for the police.

The first officer on the scene was Constable Laycock. He had been on duty in Forster Square when Jowett ran up to him and told him what had happened. Laycock had not been there for very long when other officers arrived, including a constable who, by coincidence, was also named Wilkinson. Between them, these gentlemen did their best to dress the victim's wounds and it was Laycock who went with him in the ambulance to the Royal Infirmary. In the meantime, an initial search of the office had revealed a poker lying on the floor. This was covered with blood, hair and brain matter and had obviously been used to batter Wilkinson into unconsciousness. Blood was splashed on the office walls to a height of six feet, showing that it had been a frenzied attack.

At the infirmary, Constable Laycock searched Wilkinson's pockets. Here he found a gold watch and chain, nine cheques and less than one pound in coins. There was no sign of the small purse that Wilkinson was habitually known to carry, indicating that robbery was probably the motive for the attack.

The initial police investigation threw up a number of valuable witnesses. Harry Jowett was the manager at Wilkinson's place of work and he told the police that Wilkinson had left the factory at 11.30 a.m., on July 31st. Jowett had given Wilkinson two cheques, to a total of sixty-three pounds, to cover the wages but having checked with their bankers, Jowett was able to confirm that these had not yet been cashed. Other cheques had also been handed over, for Wilkinson to pay into the company account.

These had totalled one hundred and sixteen pounds, ten shillings and fourpence, and of course, since Wilkinson had not gone to the bank, they had not been paid in. This information could indicate that someone who knew Thomas Wilkinson's routine might have gone to the office, believing that the banking had been done, and hoping to steal the wages of sixty-three pounds. The assailant had merely arrived too early, for Wilkinson had not yet had time to go to the bank, and as some sort of compensation, the man had then stolen Wilkinson's purse.

Albert Ashton was an office boy for Fieldhouse and Jowett, and at 11.00 a.m. he had answered the telephone at the factory. The caller did not identify himself, but did ask for Mr Wilkinson. Albert could, of course, only hear half of the conversation that followed. He reported that Mr Wilkinson had explained to the caller exactly what time he would be in the town office. Could it be that his attacker had actually made an appointment to see him? If so, this indicated that the assailant might well be someone whom Thomas Wilkinson knew.

The office boy also supplied another piece of interesting information. At 9.00 a.m., Mr Wilkinson had handed Albert a note and asked him to deliver it to forty-four-year-old John William Ellwood at his home. When Albert arrived at the house, Ellwood was not at home, so the letter was left with his wife. However, it did not escape the attention of the police officers that Ellwood knew Wilkinson and had, until fairly recently, worked for Fieldhouse and Jowett and would therefore know about Wilkinson's Friday routine.

Meanwhile, at the Royal Infirmary, Thomas Wilkinson's condition was not responding to treatment. At 5.00 p.m., his wife was summoned to be at his bedside and at 7.30 p.m., he died. This was now a case of murder and it was news of that crime which brought forward another witness, one whose evidence would give the police the breakthrough they needed.

Isaac Pollard was a cart driver who lived at 6 Back William Street. At some time between 2.00 p.m. and 2.30 p.m., Pollard had been going to his employer's premises in Swaine Street and had passed number eighteen. As he reached that address, Pollard heard a cry of "Oh!", and he stopped to look down the corridor that led to all the offices. A man came out of one of the rooms, carrying in his hand a long thin object, which was wrapped in newspaper. Pollard asked this man what the problem was.

"We are having a bit of bother" replied the man, who looked to be very red-faced. Thinking that whatever was happening had nothing to do with him, Pollard went to his employer's office at 12 Swaine Street, but he only stayed there for a few minutes. As he left, he saw the red-faced man coming out of number eighteen and asked him how he had got on. The man said, "Oh all right" but as he walked off, Pollard could see that the man was rubbing his hands together and they appeared to be covered in blood.

Curious as to what the man had been up to, Pollard now followed him along Swaine Street to Charles Street, across Leeds Road and into Hall Lane. At this point he lost his quarry, so returned to Swaine Street where he spoke to a man he had seen previously, sitting on the steps of number twenty. This man, Henry Mason, was not known to Pollard, but in the brief conversation that followed, Mason said that he too had seen the red-faced man going into number eighteen, and coming out not long afterwards. There was, however, no sign at this stage that anything untoward had taken place and so both Mason and Pollard went about their own business.

At 10.30 p.m. on July 31st, by which time of course, Thomas Wilkinson was dead, Isaac Pollard first heard that there had been a brutal murder at 18 Swaine Street. Pollard immediately went to the police and told them what he had observed that afternoon. He also gave them descriptions of the two men he had seen, Henry Mason and the red-faced man. According to that description, this latter man was "About forty, 5ft 10ins tall. He was very broad set with a very red face and a black, heavy, drooping moustache and a rather prominent nose. He was wearing a brown mixture cloth suit with a green stripe running through it. He also wore a gold albert with a dog-link pattern, which had some sort of shield attached to it. This shield had either a coat of arms or an enamelled figure emblazoned upon it. Finally, the man wore a billycock hat."

It was very late that night when the first of the two men Pollard had described was traced. Henry Mason admitted that he was the man sitting on the steps of 20 Swaine Street. It had been just after 2.00 p.m. when he saw a man enter number eighteen. He had been carrying a long, thin parcel wrapped in newspaper. This was at least eighteen inches long, and may have been as much as two feet long. The man had been inside for two or three minutes when he came out and had a brief conversation with another man, who was, of course, Pollard. This latter man walked away whilst the first man returned to number eighteen. Just minutes later he was back outside again and had another brief talk with Pollard, who had by this time returned.

The description these two men had given fitted the man whose name had already been mentioned by Albert Ashton, the office boy. This was why, at 4.00 a.m. on the morning of August 1st, Detective Sergeant Knowles and Detective Constable Pounds called at the house at 62 Edinburgh Street, where John William Ellwood lived. Told that he was being interviewed about the murder of Thomas Wilkinson, Ellwood replied, "I know nothing about it, but I will go with you". Ellwood was then taken to the Town Hall where, later that day, he was placed into an identification parade. He was picked out by both Isaac Pollard and Henry Mason, and was subsequently charged with murder.

Ellwood's trial for murder opened at Leeds on November 10th before Mister Justice Pickford. The prosecution case was led by Mr C. F. Lowenthal, assisted by Mr Frank Newboult, whilst Ellwood's defence lay in the hands of Mr Charles Mellor, who was assisted by Mr J. J. Wright and Mr Godfrey Ellis.

Albert Ashton repeated his evidence about the telephone call he had taken for Mr Wilkinson. He had heard Wilkinson say, "I can't be there. I am going to my dinner at one. I shall be there between two and two fifteen."

In addition to the details of the cheques he had given to Thomas Wilkinson, Harry Jowett confirmed that he had actually seen Ellwood on the day Wilkinson was attacked. At 4.30 p.m., Jowett had seen Ellwood in Back Edinburgh Street and told him that something had happened at the town office. At the time, reports were unclear and Jowett was not sure whether Wilkinson had suffered an accident or not. He said to Ellwood, "There has been an accident or something at our town office, and Mr Wilkinson has either cut his throat, tumbled off a stool, or there has been foul play". Ellwood made no comment on this and when, seconds later, Jowett's brother had come up to him and said that the medical opinion was that there was no hope for Wilkinson, Ellwood maintained his silence. Harry Jowett was also able to confirm that Ellwood had worked for his company but had been discharged in April 1908 because he had had a disagreement with Walter Jowett, another of the company directors.

Mary Craven was employed by Constantine and Son, umbrella and stick manufacturers of Swaine Street. At around 2.10 p.m., on July 31st, she had seen a tall, well-built man standing in the doorway of number eighteen, and had later seen him talking to Mr Pollard. She too had picked out Ellwood at an identity parade, two days after he had been arrested, so now there were three witnesses who swore that Ellwood had been at the town office at the time of the attack.

Joseph Mason, who was no relation to Henry, worked at the Fountain Brewery, and at some time between 1.30 p.m. and 1.45 p.m., on July 31st, he had seen Ellwood in Manchester Road. He had known Ellwood for sixteen years and they had even served together as soldiers in South Africa. The two men fell into conversation and went for a drink together. At first this evidence might not appear important, but it put Ellwood in Manchester Road, where someone had bought a poker which might well have been the murder weapon.

Samuel Ellis worked at a shop at 89 Manchester Road and sometime between noon and 3.00 p.m., a man came into his shop and purchased a poker for threepence. Ellis had a habit of wrapping purchases in newspaper and this is exactly what he did with the poker. Mr Ellis' evidence, however, was strange to say the least. At the inquest, Ellis had said that he could not positively identify Ellwood, but later, at the police court, he changed his evidence and said that he now certainly could. He also confirmed that he had known Ellwood for many years and had only not given a positive identification before because he wanted to be one hundred percent sure. This ambivalence perhaps damaged the effect of the testimony he had given.

The police of course held that the motive for this crime was robbery. Attempts were now made to show that Ellwood had financial problems. William Richardson was the landlord of the Gardener's Arms, in Melville Street. Ellwood was the secretary of a money club at this establishment and on July 30th, contributions of more than £184 had been given to Ellwood for distribution amongst the club members. Unfortunately for the prosecution, Mr Richardson was able to confirm that every single penny had been properly paid out. Richardson also mentioned that Ellwood had been in his pub at 5.00 p.m. on the day of the murder and had said, "Have you heard the news about Tom Wilkinson? It is a terrible affair. It has been more than a one man job."

Evidence was given that the brown suit with a green stripe had been found in Ellwood's house and had shown evidence of blood staining. Then the time came for the medical evidence. Dr Frederick William Eurich had performed the post-mortem with Dr William Wrangham. He described at least ten violent blows with the poker found at the scene of the crime. The bones forming the back and sides of Wilkinson's skull had been broken into many pieces and the posterior third of the left half of the brain had been excessively lacerated and reduced to a pulp.

The defence called a number of witnesses. Norah Gledhill lived in Cobden Street and she saw Ellwood on the day of the murder. At the time he was wearing a light green cap, not a billycock hat. She remembered it well because it was a windy day and the cap blew off near her gate.

Thomas Gawith was the superintendent of the British Homes Assurance Company and he confirmed that Ellwood had been employed by his company from April 18th at a salary of fifteen shillings a week. He also earned a small amount of commission, which added perhaps another shilling per week to his income. He was therefore in regular employment, with a regular salary and so had no financial concerns.

Ellwood went into the box to give evidence on his own behalf. He explained that before his marriage, he had been in the West Riding Regiment and was discharged in 1894 after serving his country for twelve years. He claimed that he had not been near the office in Swaine Street on the day that Wilkinson had been attacked, but agreed that he did receive a letter from the dead man, on the morning of July 31st. This letter was about a new situation that Wilkinson was helping him to find, and read "Dear Ellwood, I have not seen the gentleman I was telling you about, but will let you know in the course of a few days". Unfortunately, the letter had been destroyed after Ellwood had read it, though he had shown it to his wife first. Furthermore, it was argued that it was unlikely that Wilkinson would send a note to Ellwood if the latter had, as the prosecution claimed, arranged to meet Wilkinson later in town.

The bloodstains on Ellwood's clothing were easily explained. His wife looked after a child during the day and on July 25th the child had fallen in the yard and bled rather badly. He had picked the boy up and would have had blood on his clothing from that accident.

Turning to his movements on the day of the attack, Ellwood said that he had left home at 8.45 a.m., but did not feel well so did not go on his rounds and returned home in the early afternoon. As for the shop where the poker was purchased, he had never been inside it and did not even know where it was.

This was in part confirmed by two witnesses. James Francis Gregory was Ellwood's brother-in-law and lived with him. On July 25th he had heard a cry from the yard and was there as Ellwood rushed out and picked up a small boy who had fallen over, cutting his face rather badly.

Ada Ellwood had been married to the accused man for twenty-two years and they had had four children. Not only did she corroborate the evidence of the child falling and cutting himself, but she added that her husband had been at home between 2.00 p.m. and 2.20 p.m. on July 31st. She also confirmed the contents of the letter John had received from Thomas Wilkinson.

Ellwood's defence team claimed that there was no motive that could be put at their client's door. He had been fond of the dead man and had no reason to kill him. The purse was missing but there was no evidence that it had contained any cash at the time. Ellwood was not in financial difficulties and had one pound, six shillings and tenpence on him when he was arrested. The witnesses who said they had seen him were simply mistaken.

The jury retired at 1.45 p.m. on November 11th and returned at 2.53 p.m. to announce that Ellwood was guilty as charged. Ellwood in response said, "I have nothing to say; not guilty of the charge." He was then sentenced to death.

In truth, there was little real evidence to link Ellwood to the crime. It had been shown that he was fond of the dead man and had no financial problems, thus removing any suggested motive. The bloodstains on his clothing were not consistent with the violent attack that had taken place and had been explained by the aid he had rendered to an injured child. All that remained were the identifications of Isaac Pollard, Henry Mason and Samuel Ellis. The latter had been shown to be highly suspect and whilst the other two had indeed picked out Ellwood at an identification parade, similar such identifications have been shown to be incorrect.

None of this was to save Ellwood's life. In the condemned cell, he apparently slept well and showed no loss of appetite. At 9.00 a.m., on Thursday, December 3rd, 1908, John William Ellwood was hanged at Armley jail by Henry Pierrepoint, who was assisted by his brother, Thomas.

7

Abel Atherton

Hanged at Durham, Wednesday, December 8th, 1909
For the murder of Elizabeth Ann Patrick, at Chopwell

I
N all, there were seven people living in the house at 20 Thames Street, Chopwell, near Newcastle-upon-Tyne, in 1909. The head of the house was Jacob Patrick, a miner, and he shared the home with his wife, Elizabeth Ann, and their four children, Frances, Maggie, Joseph and George Robert. In addition, the family also had a lodger, twenty-nine-year-old Abel Atherton, who was also a miner and worked with Jacob at the Chopwell Colliery.

Abel Atherton was a native of Wigan in Lancashire and had lodged with the Patrick family since 1907 but now, in mid-1909, Abel had grown rather too fond of Frances Patrick, who was by then fifteen years old. Abel went as far as making advances towards Frances and when these were repulsed, he was asked to leave the house, which he did on July 24th, 1909. He moved into new lodgings with Mr and Mrs Forster at Mercy Street, not far away.

Atherton was not happy about leaving Thames Street and began to spread rumours that there was some rather strange behaviour going on in the Patrick household. One of these rumours was that Jacob was sleeping with his own daughter. Yet, despite these comments, he still visited his old lodgings almost every day and was usually made welcome. Things, however, were coming to a head and on Wednesday, August 11th, Abel Atherton embarked on a course of action that would cost him his life.

Early that day, Atherton had said to his landlady, Mrs Forster, that it was a good job that he left the Patricks' house before he did some mischief. He went on to say, "I have carried these about all day" and then produced three shotgun cartridges from his pocket observing, "One was meant for Frances, one for Patrick and one for myself".

At around 6.00 p.m., Atherton was back at Thames Street where he made further allegations against Jacob. Elizabeth said that she was sick of hearing these comments and suggested that he come back when her husband was there and challenge him to his face, if he were man enough. Atherton then returned to his new lodgings and asked Mrs Forster for his gun, saying "I'm going to have a bit of sport". He took the weapon and Mrs Forster saw that he was upset about something, for there were tears in Atherton's eyes. So concerned was Mrs Forster that she tried to get Atherton to leave the gun behind but to this he had shouted, "Stand back or I will shoot you". He then went out of the back door as Mrs Forster ran out of the front door in order to get some help.

It was 6.30 p.m. when Abel Atherton arrived at the back door of 20 Thames Street. Inside the kitchen were Elizabeth Ann Patrick, her daughter, Frances, her son, Joseph, and a neighbour, Mrs Marley. As soon as Atherton walked in the door, Elizabeth saw that he was carrying a gun under one arm and got up from her seat by the fire saying, "You are not going to use that gun". She now ran for Atherton and a brief struggle followed, during which a shot was fired. The pellets passed harmlessly into the street but as the struggle continued between Elizabeth and Atherton, a second shot was heard and Elizabeth Patrick fell to the floor, wounded in her thigh. The shot had severed Elizabeth's femoral artery and she bled to death in minutes.

Seeing that Elizabeth was badly wounded, Atherton now discarded the gun and apparently overcome with remorse, knelt down close to Elizabeth and made as if to kiss her. Then he stood up again, took a knife from his pocket and proceeded to cut his own throat. Atherton then walked outside where he met Constable John Coulson at the top of Blyth Street. Atherton announced, "I am the man you want. She is quite dead. It's a pity I did not manage myself as well. It is a bad job for me." He was then taken into custody and, seeing that Atherton's throat wound was not serious, Coulson escorted the prisoner to his house where he told him he was under arrest for murder. To this Atherton replied, "I think she shot herself, but I have been the instigator of it. I wish I had finished myself at the same time." Later still, Atherton was escorted from Coulson's house to Blaydon Police Station where he was formally charged, and claimed that the shooting was "... a pure accident".

The first Police Court hearing took place on August 12th, at Gateshead. The formal proceedings lasted only a few minutes and only evidence of arrest was given. Atherton, a short, stoutly-built man with a florid complexion, was asked if there was anything he wished to say as to why he should not be remanded in custody. Atherton began, "I never shot the woman. I went to the house..." At this point, the chairman of the magistrates, Mr Robert Middleton, interrupted Atherton and told him that he had better reserve his defence. To this Atherton again stated, "I am not guilty of shooting the woman". He was then remanded for eight days.

The inquest on Elizabeth Ann Patrick's death opened at the Workmen's Institute at Chopwell, before Mr John Graham, on August 13th, 1909. Joseph Patrick, Elizabeth's fourteen-year-old son, was the first witness to describe the events of August 11th and, after hearing his testimony, and that of others, the proceedings were adjourned until August 17th. On that date, Frances Patrick was one of the witnesses and although Atherton himself was not present, he was represented by Mr W. N. Armstrong. Medical evidence was also called as to the injuries Elizabeth had suffered.

Meanwhile, the funeral of Elizabeth Patrick had taken place at Tow Law Cemetery on Saturday, August 14th. The funeral cortege left her home at noon, watched by a large crowd of people. A short service was led by the Reverend T. W. Hanson, the curate of Chopwell, and the choir of St John's Church then sang, "Lead Kindly Light". All of Elizabeth's family, including her mother, Mrs Caygill, were present to pay their last respects.

The final hearing before the magistrates took place on August 27th, when Atherton was committed for trial. He finally appeared before Mister Justice Walton at Durham, on November 10th, 1909, when the case for the prosecution was led by Mr Lowenthal, assisted by Mr A. J. Lawrie, whilst Atherton was defended by Mr Griffiths Jones. The proceedings lasted for two days.

Constable Coulson repeated his earlier evidence and added that when he had searched Atherton at the police station, he had found on him twelve ball cartridges as well as a pocket knife. Atherton had complained at the time that his knife was not sharp enough, presumably referring to his unsuccessful suicide attempt. Coulson went on to describe how on August 12th, Atherton had made a further statement in which he claimed that he had only taken the gun with him to frighten the people in the house.

Jacob Patrick described how he had gone to work at 3.45 p.m. on the day that his wife was killed. As a result of a message he received at work, he rushed home, arriving there at about 7.00 p.m., by which time, of course, Elizabeth was already dead. Jacob went on to describe some of the problems that the family had had with Atherton over his infatuation with Frances, and stated that he had been the one who had told Atherton that he had better find somewhere else to live. The prisoner had visited his house a number of times since but Jacob had never heard him issue any threats, though he had come to hear of the rumours that Atherton was spreading.

Frances Mary Patrick was a most important witness. She described how several times before July 1909, Atherton had put his arms around her and kissed her. She had thought nothing of it at the time but one day her father had taken her to one side and warned her what might happen if she allowed such behaviour to continue. From that time onwards, she was not happy for Atherton to touch her in such an affectionate way.

On Easter Monday, Atherton had been ill in bed at 8.30 p.m. Elizabeth was out of the house at the time and Atherton had asked Frances to bring him some tea. Frances took him up a drink and also some cakes and put them down on a chair by Atherton's bed. She was about to leave the room when he sat up, grabbed her around the waist and pulled her towards him. He kissed her and then made a suggestion that she did not like. Frances had then pushed him away saying, "I will tell if you don't let me go". Atherton had done as she asked and Frances went back downstairs but did not mention what had been said to her parents.

About a month after this incident, Frances' parents had gone out together leaving her alone in the kitchen with Atherton. Once again he grabbed at her and made a suggestion as to what they might do together. Frances shouted for her mother whereupon Atherton immediately let her go and then went out of the house. Again, Frances did not report this to her parents.

Half an hour later, Atherton came back to the house. By now, Elizabeth had returned and Atherton announced that he wanted to leave and was giving a month's notice. Elizabeth asked him what was wrong whereupon Atherton said that he had no fault to find with anyone there. Over the next couple of weeks, Atherton made a few more passes at Frances, all of which were repulsed, and then one day he handed her a note which suggested that she was 'carrying on' with her own father. Frances did not show the letter to anyone but did write back to Atherton, saying that his accusations were untrue. Further notes of a similar nature followed but Frances destroyed them all.

On July 24th, Frances was in the kitchen by the fire when Atherton came in at 11.30 a.m. Yet again he threw his arms around her and kissed her and again made suggestions as to what he would like to do to her. Frances was so upset that she walked out of the house and went to a neighbour's house, where her mother called for her a few minutes later. When her father came home from work that night, Frances finally told her parents what had been going on and said that if Atherton did not leave the house, she would. It was then that Jacob spoke to Atherton and he moved out that same night.

Atherton continued to visit Thames Street and some of those visits ended in some kind of argument. Frances was there when, on August 8th, Atherton had shouted to her, "It was through you I had to leave the house. You have done your worst for me and I will do my worst for you." The following night, Atherton was there again, repeating his allegations of misconduct between Frances and her father and pointing out that if he made an official complaint, the courts would look upon it very seriously.

Coming now to the evening that her mother died, Frances related how Atherton had appeared at the doorway with his gun, and her mother had rushed forward to challenge him. Frances too had run towards Atherton but the neighbour, Mrs Marley, had held her back. From where she was, Frances did not have a clear view of what actually happened so was unable to say if her mother had grabbed the gun barrel or not. However, when giving evidence at the inquest, Frances had said that Elizabeth grabbed the barrel.

Fourteen-year-old Joseph Patrick was also in the kitchen on that fateful day and he now gave evidence that his mother had indeed grabbed the barrel of the gun. After hearing the first shot, Joseph ran from the house to get some help and only heard the second shot some seconds later. Cross-examined by the defence, Joseph agreed that when he first came into the kitchen, Atherton had his right hand in his pocket and carried the gun under his left arm, pointing down at the floor. It was only during the struggle that the weapon was raised up. This suggests that Atherton did not go to the house with the intention of using the weapon, but rather that the shooting had been a terrible accident.

A neighbour, Mary Truden, told the court that she had seen Atherton approach the Patrick house, carrying his gun. He went inside and a couple of minutes later she heard the sound of shooting. Looking at her neighbour's house, Mary saw Elizabeth fall into the street. Seconds later the gun was thrown out and landed close to Elizabeth's body.

Another neighbour, Mary Ann Keogan, also heard the first shot and went outside to see what was going on. After the second shot, she too saw Elizabeth fall out of her house and then saw Atherton standing framed in the doorway. The gun was thrown out and then Atherton knelt down and appeared to kiss Elizabeth.

Inspector Dryden of the Gateshead police told the court of a statement that Atherton had made on August 12th. On the way to the station, the prisoner had stated "There is one thing that consoles me – I didn't shoot, she shot herself. I called at the house to frighten them, but she took the gun from me and shot herself. I would have stopped her but the daughter and Mrs Marley stopped me."

Victor Pape was an expert in firearms and he testified that he had examined the gun and the clothing worn by the dead woman at the time she was shot. By conducting experiments with the gun and trying to reproduce the marks found on the clothes, he was able to determine that the gun must have been fired from a distance of about twenty-seven inches, possibly more. It was, of course, still possible that Elizabeth had grabbed the gun and that in trying to pull it from her, Atherton had accidentally pulled the trigger but Atherton's statement that Elizabeth had shot herself was certainly untenable.

The time came for Atherton to give his own version of events. He explained that after leaving the Patricks' household, he found himself rather short of money and had planned to sell his gun in order to raise some cash. That was why he had taken the weapon from his lodgings and on the way to sell it, he had passed the Patricks' house and decided to call in. Upon seeing the gun, Elizabeth had jumped to the wrong conclusion, rushed across the room and grabbed the gun barrel. He had never pointed the weapon at her, or consciously pulled the trigger and was as surprised as everyone else when the gun went off. It was only when he saw Elizabeth lying on the ground that he realized what had happened and as for his attempted suicide, that was because he felt guilty, not for the shooting itself but because he had not had the sense to take the cartridges out of the gun.

For the defence, Mr Griffiths Jones in his summing-up stated that the dead woman had been like a second mother to Atherton and it was surely unlikely that anyone would want to murder someone who had been so kind to them. It was obvious that the gun had been fired accidentally during the course of a struggle, with Mrs Patrick grabbing the gun barrel and almost certainly causing it to discharge. As such, the killing was also accidental and Atherton was guilty of manslaughter, not murder.

The jury were out for forty-five minutes before returning their guilty verdict. Asked if he had anything to say before sentence was passed, Atherton said "Can I get a fresh trial?" Told that he could not, Mister Justice Walton then passed the sentence of death, whereupon Atherton announced "I am innocent". In due course, an appeal was also lost and the sentence of death confirmed.

Atherton's conduct in the condemned cell was said to be exemplary. He continued to maintain his innocence throughout his time there and managed to convince himself that he would be reprieved. On December 5th, he received notice that there would be no reprieve and after initially being upset, finally resigned himself to his fate.

That same day, Atherton wrote a final letter to his parents, which read "Dear father and mother. I write these few lines to you, hoping to find you all well, as you will very likely know the sad news before you get this letter, that there is no more hope for me in this world. But I will have to put my trust in the Lord. He is the One who we will all have to answer to sooner or later. There is one thing that I will not have to answer for, and that is what I am sentenced to death for, of which I am innocent, and my life is on the hands of those I told you about. You can believe me what I told you; it is the God's truth. It won't do me any good to tell lies. I would not have said anything if I had hold of the gun when she was shot, but I never was in the struggle.

"…You can tell all my friends that I send them my best respects. So I will expect you and Katie, Lizzie and Levi coming on Monday, if you can possibly get. That is all at present. From your innocent son, Abel Atherton."

Atherton rose at 6.00 a.m. on the morning of Wednesday, December 8th, 1909. Dressing in his own clothes for the first time since his trial, he was then seen by the prison chaplain, the Reverend D. Jacob. Later still, Atherton ate sparingly of a breakfast of bread and butter, washed down with tea.

There had been a sharp frost the previous night and probably as a result of that, no one waited outside the prison at 8.00 a.m., when Atherton was placed upon the trapdoor at Durham prison by Henry Pierrepoint and his assistant, William Willis. As the pinioning process was completed, Atherton cried out in a loud voice, "Yer hanging an innocent man". They were the last words he ever uttered.

John Alexander Dickman

8

Hanged at Newcastle-upon-Tyne, Tuesday, August 9th, 1910
For the murder of John Innes Nisbet, on a train near Newcastle-upon-Tyne

THOMAS William Charlton worked as a foreman porter at Alnmouth station in Northumberland. One of Charlton's many duties was to ensure that trains were checked for cleanliness before they made a journey. It was just such a task he was performing on Friday, March 18th, 1910.

The train Charlton was scrutinizing had left Newcastle-upon-Tyne's Central Station at 10.27 a.m. Calling at various small stations along the way it had arrived at Alnmouth at 12.06 p.m., and consisted of an engine and four carriages. The carriage nearest to the engine largely consisted of luggage accommodation but also had three third-class passenger compartments. The second carriage had two third-class compartments with a single first-class compartment in the centre. The final two carriages were all third-class, but the last one also had further room for luggage.

Charlton checked the three carriages furthest away from the engine and found nothing amiss. Then he came to the first carriage and upon opening the door of the compartment furthest from the engine, he immediately saw that there was something terribly wrong.

Three streams of what looked like blood ran across the floor of the compartment, all apparently emanating from underneath the seat that faced the engine. Tentatively Charlton entered the compartment and glanced under the seat. There lay the body of a man, face downwards and close by were a hard felt hat and a broken pair of spectacles. Charlton also saw a return ticket from Newcastle to Widdrington, but he touched nothing and ran to report the matter to his superiors.

The police had no trouble in identifying the dead man. A name band inside the hat revealed that he was forty-four-year-old John Innes Nisbet, a colliery bookkeeper, who lived at 180 Heaton Road, Heaton, in Newcastle. A married man, he had two young daughters, Cicely Gertrude and Lilian.

Further investigations showed that Nisbet worked for Messrs Rayne and Burn, who operated from Beaconsfield Chambers, Sandhill. They owned a number of coalmines, one of which was the Stobswood Colliery which was half a mile from Widdrington, where Nisbet should have got off the train.

The motive for this brutal murder was also readily apparent. One of Nisbet's duties, once a fortnight on a Friday, was to take a cheque drawn on his employer's account at the Collingwood Street branch of Lloyd's Bank in Newcastle, and then deliver the cash to Stobswood for the miners' pay. Thomas Anderson was the manager and cashier for Rayne and Burn and he confirmed that he had handed Nisbet a cheque for three hundred and seventy pounds, nine shillings and sixpence. The police checked with the bank and John Bradshaw Wilson, one of the cashiers, was able to show that Nisbet had been given two hundred and thirty-one sovereigns, two hundred and six half sovereigns, thirty-five pounds and nine shillings in silver and one pound and sixpence in copper. Bradshaw had supplied the gold in three canvas bags, the silver in paper bags and the copper in paper parcels. He had seen Nisbet place all the money into a leather bag, about a foot in length, which he then locked. This bag, and all the cash inside it, was missing. Nisbet had been the victim of a callous robbery that had claimed his life.

It was when the police broke the terrible news to the dead man's wife, Cicely Nisbet, that they received some useful information. The Nisbets were a loving couple and on the days that John had been due to take the wages to Widdrington, it had been his wife's habit to walk down from her home to the railway station at Heaton and wait for her husband's train. They would spend a few seconds in conversation before the train pulled out and continued its journey. Things had been no different on Friday, March 18th.

Cicely confirmed that she had been at the station when the train arrived. She had positioned herself at the end of the platform where the rear of the train would stop, since it was Nisbet's habit to travel in that section of the train. This time, though, Cicely had seen her husband poke his head out of a carriage at the far end, closest to the engine, and she ran down to speak to him.

John Nisbet appeared to be in excellent spirits, no doubt amused by his wife's frantic attempt to get down the platform to where his carriage had stopped. The couple only had a few moments together and she reminded him that her aunt was visiting that evening and told him to be home by 6.00 p.m. Nisbet replied, "No, I will come straight home after I have been to the office".

Already the train was moving and Cicely saw her husband push up the carriage window and take a seat facing the engine. As he did so, Cicely noticed that there was another man in the same carriage. She admitted that she only had a very brief glimpse of him and he had his coat collar up and was in the shadow cast from a bridge. Nevertheless, she was able to supply a basic description. The police now made it their first priority to find this man. After all, if he were not the killer, then he might well have valuable information.

The crime received widespread publicity and this brought forward two more witnesses, Percival Harding Hall and John William Spink. These two men had also travelled on the train, in the same carriage as Nisbet but in the next compartment, closer still to the engine. They, like Nisbet, were cashiers delivering money to a mine for their employer, the Netherton Coal Company.

Hall and Spink explained that they had travelled on the same train as Nisbet, every other Friday, for the past four and a half years. They knew Nisbet as the Widdrington cashier, and sometimes passed the time of day with him. Spink said he had not noticed Nisbet at Newcastle's Central Station, but Hall certainly had. He and Spink were already in the middle of the three third-class compartments in the first carriage, and Hall was looking out of the window when he saw Nisbet walking towards him. Nisbet appeared to be with another man. They were strolling along together and Hall saw them get into the next compartment, the furthest from the engine in this first carriage.

Hall and Spink alighted from the train at Stannington in order to make the short walk to their colliery at Netherton. It was now that Spink saw Nisbet for the first time, sitting in the compartment behind the one they had just vacated. Nisbet was sitting facing the engine and nodded to the two colleagues as they passed. They returned the nod and both Hall and Spink noticed another man in the compartment with Nisbet. This man had a moustache and wore a black felt hat.

The composite description supplied by Mrs Nisbet, Hall and Spink was first published in the newspapers of Saturday, March 19th. It stated that the man was around five feet six inches tall, not very old and had a sallow complexion.

By Monday, March 21st, a medical examination of the dead man had revealed that he had been shot five times. Four bullets had been recovered and these proved to be of two different calibres. Two were nickel-plated and of .250 calibre, whilst the other two were made of lead and were .320 revolver cartridges. This, not unnaturally perhaps, led the police to assume that they were looking for two assailants. Even before this, though, another witness had come forward and his evidence was to change the direction of the investigation completely.

Wilson Hepple was an artist and he too had been at Newcastle's Central Station on the morning of March 18th. He was travelling on the 10.29 a.m. train from platform eight and, finding himself with a few minutes to spare, had strolled up and down outside his chosen carriage. As he did so, two men passed him, some eighteen feet away across the platform, walking to the 10.27 a.m. train. The smaller of these men Hepple did not know, but from the details published in the newspapers, he felt that it must be Nisbet. The two men appeared to be walking together, though Hepple could not swear that they were in conversation. He saw them at the door of a carriage close to the engine, and one had his hand on the door of a compartment whilst the other waited for him to open it.

This testimony seemed to indicate that Nisbet had been in the company of a man who got into the same compartment as he did and was therefore almost certainly the same man seen at Heaton station by the dead man's wife. More importantly, Wilson said he had known this second man for more than twenty years and so was able to put a name to him. Nisbet's apparent companion had been forty-five-year-old John Alexander Dickman.

This information puzzled the police. They had asked for any witnesses to come forward and yet Dickman had not reported to them. This was surely curious behaviour, and it fell to Detective Inspector Andrew Tait to interview Dickman and find out what, if anything, he knew.

It was on the evening of March 21st that Inspector Tait called on Dickman at his home at 1 Lily Avenue, Jesmond. Tait identified himself and told Dickman that a man had reported seeing him with Nisbet, at the station, on the day of the murder. Dickman replied, "I knew Nisbet for many years. I saw him on that morning. I booked at the ticket window after him and went by the same train, but I did not see him after the train left. I would have told the police if I thought it would have done any good."

The house in Lily Avenue where John Alexander Dickman was detained on March 21st, 1910 (Yvonne Berger)

At this stage, Dickman was not even a suspect but he had admitted seeing Nisbet at Newcastle and so Tait asked him if he would accompany him to the police station and make a statement to the officer in charge of the case, Superintendent Weddell. Dickman said that he would and as the two men left the house, Dickman called out to his wife, Annie, that he would soon be home.

It was at the station that Dickman made a long statement, which ran "On Friday morning last I went to the Central Station and took a return ticket for Stannington. Nisbet, the deceased man, whom I knew, was at the ticket office before me and as far as I know, had left the hall by the time I got mine. I went to the bookstall and got a paper, the 'Manchester Sporting Chronicle'. I then went to the refreshment room and had a pie and a glass of ale. I then went to the platform and took my seat in a third-class carriage nearer the hinder end than the front end.

"My recollection is, although I am not quite clear on the point, that people entered and left the train at different stations on the journey. The train passed Stannington station without my noticing it and I got out at Morpeth and handed my ticket, with the excess fare of twopence halfpenny, to the collector.

"I left Morpeth to walk to Stannington by the main road. I took ill of diarrhoea on the way, and I had to return to Morpeth to get the 1.12 p.m. train, but missed it. I had to get the 1.40 p.m. While at Morpeth, after missing the 1.12 p.m. train, I came out of the station on the east side, and turned down towards the town. I met a man named Elliott, and spoke to him. I did not get into the town, but turned and went back to the station, and got the 1.40 p.m. to Newcastle. I got a single ticket for Stannington, but I did not give it up. I gave up the return portion at the Manors. I have been very unwell since I went on this journey to see Mr Hogg of Dovecot, in connection with new sinking operations there."

This was a very curious statement. As it stood it left a good period of time unaccounted for. In addition, Dickman fitted the general description of the man seen in the compartment with Nisbet, he had travelled on the same train by his own admission, and a witness who had known him for many years had actually placed him in Nisbet's company. There was also the fact that Dickman had not come forward when witnesses were appealed for. On the strength of these suspicions, Dickman was cautioned and searched. He was found to be carrying seventeen pounds, nine shillings and fivepence, a not inconsiderable sum, seventeen pounds of which was in gold and wrapped up inside a bag from the Lambton branch of Lloyd's Bank. Bags such as these had been used to wrap the money handed over to Nisbet. Dickman was told that he would be charged with murder, to which he replied "I don't understand the proceedings. It is absurd for me to deny the charge, because it is absurd to make it. I only say I absolutely deny it."

The next day, Tuesday, March 22nd, the funeral of John Innes Nisbet took place at the Jesmond Old Cemetery. On the same day, Dickman made his first appearance before the magistrate's court, where he was remanded until March 30th. Further remands followed and it was not until April 14th that the evidence finally began to be heard. The proceedings lasted for two days, after which Dickman was sent for trial at the next assizes.

It was during the first day of these committal proceedings that an astounding incident took place in the court. Mrs Cicely Nisbet gave her evidence about meeting her husband at Heaton station on the morning that he was killed. It was only after she had completed her testimony, as she left the witness box, that she collapsed in a faint. Once she had been revived she stated that she had caught a side glimpse of the prisoner in the box and he had been in the exact same position as the mysterious passenger in the compartment with her husband. The profile was identical and she was now absolutely certain that the passenger had been none other than Dickman.

Before the trial opened, though, there was yet one further development in the case. On Thursday, June 9th, Peter Spooner, the manager at the Barmoor East Colliery, was making an inspection of a seam at the Isabella pit at Hepscott, situated some three-quarters of a mile south east of Morpeth railway station. As he conducted his review, he noticed something at the bottom of a ventilation shaft. This turned out to be a leather bag and the fact that there were wage slips still inside proved that it had been the one which Nisbet had been carrying when he was shot. The bag had been slit open by means of a sharp blade and most of the contents had been removed. Only a few coppers remained inside, with a few more scattered around the foot of the shaft. Eventually a total of nineteen shillings and fivepence was found. When Spooner took his find to the police he was questioned and confirmed that he and Dickman had once worked together, but he was unable to say with any degree of certainty whether Dickman knew of the ventilation shaft or not, though he thought it highly likely.

The case of the Crown against John Alexander Dickman opened at Newcastle on July 4th, before Lord Justice Coleridge. Dickman was defended by Mr Mitchell Innes, who was assisted by Lord William Percy. The prosecution case was led by Mr E. Tindal Atkinson, assisted by Mr C. F. Lowenthal. The hearing lasted for three days.

The trial opened with details of the timetable of the 10.27 a.m. train. After leaving Newcastle Central, the second stop was Heaton where Nisbet saw his wife. From there it called at Forest Hall, Killingworth, Annitsford, Cramlington, Plessy and Stannington, where it arrived at 11.06 a.m.

The stop after Stannington was Morpeth, where the train arrived at 11.12 a.m and took on water, meaning that it did not leave until 11.16 a.m. From there the train called at Pegswood, Longhirst, Widdrington, which was Nisbet's destination, Shevington, Acklington, Warkworth and finally, Alnmouth where it arrived at 12.06 p.m.

For the prosecution, the important stations were Stannington and Morpeth. It was Stannington where Dickman was supposed to get off and where Hall and Spink did get off, seeing Nisbet alive and well in the process. At Morpeth, Dickman alighted and paid a small excess fare. It was also at Morpeth that a gentleman named John Grant got on to the train. He had actually walked past the third compartment of the carriage nearest to the engine, looked inside and seen that it was apparently empty. Grant finally got into the first compartment, the one nearest the engine, but this testimony meant that Nisbet was almost certainly already dead and his body stuffed underneath the seat, making it look as if his compartment were empty. In short, if Hall, Spink and Grant were all correct, Nisbet must have been shot between Stannington and Morpeth.

Dickman never denied getting off the train at Morpeth, but as if confirmation were needed, the prosecution called John Athey, the ticket collector there. He recalled a man paying him an excess fare of two and a half pence and also handing over a ticket to Stannington. The man had the money ready in his hand so did not have to rummage through his pockets. Athey also said that the man was wearing a greatcoat but he could not see if he carried a parcel or bag of any kind.

There was also confirmation of John Grant's testimony. He said that when he got into the compartment, there was another man already there. This was Andrew Bruce, a carriage inspector for the railway. That morning he travelled all the way to Alnmouth and his own evidence confirmed that of Hall and Spink, for Bruce saw them get out at Stannington and nod to someone as they walked off down the platform. Bruce, however, said he had seen no one get off at Morpeth.

An attempt was now made to show that the man in the compartment with Nisbet was indeed Dickman. Cicely Nisbet repeated her testimony about catching a glimpse of Dickman's profile at the magistrate's court and being convinced that he was the same man. John Spink told his story about seeing Nisbet alive at Stannington and related how he had attended an identification parade at the police station. He had failed to pick Dickman out of the line-up, but confirmed that the man in the carriage looked very much like him.

More damning was the testimony of Percival Hall. He too had attended the identification parade that took place on March 24th. There had been nine men in a row and after walking down the line once, Hall had approached a policeman and asked him what he should do. The officer advised Hall to "...point him out", whereupon he had returned to the line and picked out Dickman. Hall, however, had somewhat qualified this identification by saying "I won't swear that the man I pointed out was the man I saw get in with Mr Nisbet, but if I could be assured that the murderer was there, I would have no hesitation in pointing the prisoner out". This rather ambiguous comment would have repercussions later.

Further damage was done to Dickman's case by Charles Raven. Mr Raven was a commercial traveller from Heaton, and he too had been at Central Station on the fateful day. Raven knew both men in this case, having been acquainted with Nisbet for five or six years, and Dickman for nine. He swore that he had seen Nisbet walking with Dickman. He first saw them together a few minutes before 10.27 a.m., but could not say that they were in conversation together. Raven saw them walk together through the gate that led to platform four. The two men then turned right towards platform five, and vanished from his sight behind the cigar shop. He did not see either man actually get on to the train and so was unable to say whether they travelled together. His testimony, however, did seem to support that of Hepple, Hall and Spink.

In his statement, Dickman had said that he was going to a colliery near Stannington to see Mr Hogg about the sinking of a new shaft. The police had spoken to William Hogg, who said he had known Dickman since the turn of the century when he had been the secretary to a colliery company based at Morpeth. Hogg said that his company was indeed sinking a new shaft at the Dovecot mine, but he had no appointment with Dickman on March 18th and had in fact spent that particular day in Newcastle. Under cross-examination, however, Mr Hogg admitted that there was nothing sinister in Dickman's explanation. He had already visited the site four or five times, each without an appointment, and had made his last visit on March 4th, two weeks before the murder. The prosecution then tried to turn that into something significant again by pointing out that this was also the last occasion that Nisbet had acted as wage cashier. Did Dickman make that trip on March 4th in order to plan the crime he would commit two weeks later?

Attempts were now made to show that Dickman had financial worries. Samuel Cohen was the manager of the Cash Accommodation and Investment Company of Northumberland Street, Newcastle and he told the court that some time around October 15th, 1909, Dickman had come to his office and discussed the possibility of raising a £20 loan. Terms were discussed and a few days later, on October 18th, the loan was accepted. The interest of £1 per month had always been paid but in January, Dickman had renegotiated the loan. The last payment of interest had been made on March 17th, the day before the murder. Some time before then Dickman had introduced another potential client, Mr Christie, who had taken out a loan for £200. Dickman was paid no commission on that loan.

The inference was that Dickman was up to his neck in debt. He had borrowed money and been unable to repay it and had then introduced someone else, possibly in the hope that he would be paid some commission, a hope that was not fulfilled. When questioned by the defence, however, Mr Cohen admitted that since Dickman's arrest, his wife had been in to pay off the loan in full. The Crown never suggested that Annie Dickman had received any proceeds of the robbery, but she was still able to pay off £20. This was hardly a sign of someone in severe debt.

The man Dickman had introduced to Mr Cohen was Frank Christie, and he confirmed that he had borrowed £200 and signed the cheque over to Dickman. This was a perfectly normal transaction, however, since Christie often backed horses through Dickman. Since the loan had first been paid, Christie had had the benefit of about half of the money, the rest being left with Dickman for betting purposes.

Various witnesses were called to testify to the running of various bank accounts in both Dickman's name and that of his wife. Nothing unusual was revealed beyond the fact that all were now slightly overdrawn or had low credit balances. One of the witnesses, Robert Plews Sedcole, gave details of an account Dickman had held at the Lambton branch of Lloyd's. The significance of this was of course that the bank bag Dickman had in his possession when he was arrested may well have come from Nisbet's leather bag, but it could equally have come from Dickman's own banking transactions at that same branch.

The gun or guns used to commit the crime had not been found when Dickman's house was searched. It would strengthen the prosecution case if the ownership of weapons could be traced to Dickman in some way.

Henrietta Hyman ran a stationer's and newsagent's shop at 35 Groat Street, Newcastle. She knew Dickman as Fred Black, and it was in this name that letters were delivered to her shop for him. Most of these letters were to do with betting, but one day in October 1909 a parcel arrived for Mr Black. It was only wrapped in paper and the shape was that of a gun. Dickman made no attempt to pick up this parcel for some considerable time and before he did, a postcard arrived from the company that had supplied the weapon saying that it had been sent in error and asking him to return it. Soon afterwards a second parcel arrived, but this was in a box and Henrietta could not tell what it contained.

It was not until January 1910 that Dickman came into the shop again. He now told her that his correct name was Dickman and that he lived in Lily Avenue. He asked her for a label so that he could send the first parcel back to Glasgow from whence it had come. Since that time, other letters had arrived for Dickman, but he had failed to pick them up and she had now passed them all on to the police.

Another link in the chain seemed to come from Andrew Craig Kirkwood, who worked for W. R. Pape and Co., gunsmiths of Newcastle. His company kept a register of all firearms sold and one entry in his ledger read "John A. Dickinson, Lily Avenue, Jesmond - bought automatic magazine pistol". The name was close enough to Dickman for it to be significant.

Thomas Simpson also worked for Pape's and he gave scientific evidence on the bullets found at the scene of the crime. He agreed that the .250 nickel-plated bullets could have been fired from a gun such as that referred to by his colleague, but the other two, the .320 lead bullets, could not have been fired from the same weapon. In his opinion, two guns had to have been used.

Medical testimony from Dr C. Clark Burman showed that there were five bullet wounds in all. The first was underneath the left eye, and burning around the wound showed that the gun had been no more than two inches away from the skin when it had been fired. This bullet had been recovered and was one of the lead ones.

The second wound was over the left forehead and the bullet had travelled down into the head. Once again the flesh had been charred and this bullet was nickel-

69

plated. The third wound, which was not serious, was behind the right ear. The fourth was behind the left ear and had only grazed the skull, whilst the fifth and last was two inches below the fourth and had again been caused by a lead bullet.

Further scientific evidence was given by Dr Robert A. Bolam, a Professor of Medical Jurisprudence at the College of Medicine in Newcastle. He had examined various items of clothing taken from Dickman and his house. These included a pair of gloves, a pair of trousers and a Burberry coat.

Referring to the gloves, Dr Bolam said that on the palm surface of the left glove, just under the thumb, he had found a small smear of blood, though he was unable to determine if it were mammalian, let alone human.

Turning to the trousers, he had found nine small pinpricks of blood inside the front left pocket. As for the coat, there was a large area of staining on the left front, but the surface was frayed as if it had been rubbed well and it smelled of paraffin. He had found no evidence of bloodstaining but said that the application of paraffin would have negated many of the tests usually performed.

There was only one witness for the defence and that was Dickman himself. He said that on the day in question he had left home at around 10.00 a.m., wearing his suit, a black hat, brown overcoat and brown gloves. He caught the train to Northumberland Street, walked from there to Central Station, and as he queued for his ticket, saw Nisbet immediately in front of him.

Nisbet wished him good morning and left the ticket hall. After buying his own ticket, Dickman said he had gone to the refreshment room and after enjoying a pie and a glass of ale, had taken his seat towards the end of the train.

Reading his newspaper, Dickman had become engrossed in an article about the forthcoming Grand National race at Aintree and had missed his stop. Arriving at Morpeth he thought about simply crossing over the line and catching a train back to Stannington, but thought instead that the walk would do him good. On the way, however, he fell ill and had to lie down in a field for about an hour.

After getting up again he walked back to Morpeth, intending to catch the 1.12 p.m. train back to Newcastle. He missed this, so decided to walk into the town. On the way he met Edwin Elliott and a friend of his, William Sanderson. They had chatted about racing and afterwards Dickman returned to the station, where he caught the 1.40 p.m. train.

Dickman went on to attempt to demolish some of the evidence against him. At the identification parade, Dickman said that Hall had been very reluctant to point him out and it even seemed that one police officer was almost forcing him to make a selection.

The gun sent to him at the newsagents had been returned to Bell Brothers of Waterloo Street, Glasgow and the bank bag that was found on him when he was arrested he had had for perhaps ten years.

Hepple, the artist who said he had seen Dickman with Nisbet, was rather old and deaf, but they were close friends. Surely if Hepple had been sure that it was Dickman he had seen, he would have spoken to him?

The stain on his overcoat had been bicycle oil and in fact he had not even been wearing that coat on the day of the murder. He had no financial concerns and the gold found on him when he was searched at the police station was his method of making a living. He took bets for people, sometimes for large amounts, and this was just cash he held for that purpose. This was also why he was so engrossed in reading about the National.

The jury retired at 12.55 p.m. on July 6th and did not make up their minds until 3.30 p.m. Found guilty, Dickman was asked if he had anything to say. He replied, "I can only repeat that I am entirely innocent of this cruel deed. I have no complicity in this case. I have spoken the truth in my evidence, and in everything I have said." After the death sentence had been pronounced, Dickman half-turned to face the body of the court and exclaimed, "I declare to all men that I am innocent".

Only after the trial did certain information come to light that caused the Home Secretary of the day, Winston Churchill, to refer the matter to the Appeal Court himself, the first time such powers had been used. As a result, Dickman's appeal was heard on July 22nd before the Lord Chief Justice, Lord Alverstone, and Justices Lawrence and Phillimore.

One of the most crucial points to be raised at this appeal was some scandalous behaviour on the part of the police. A letter from the Chief Constable was read out and in this document the police admitted that whilst Hall and Spink had been waiting in a hallway at the police station, they had been invited to look into a room where Dickman was being held. Both men did as was suggested but could only see the top of Dickman's hat. When this strategy failed, the police then arranged for the door of the room to be opened slightly and the two witnesses were again invited to take a look. Hall only saw the back of Dickman and remarked at the time that he thought him more thickset than the man he had seen in the carriage with Nisbet.

Hall was actually called as a witness at the appeal and agreed that this subterfuge had taken place. He claimed, however, that what he had seen had not affected his identification. The judges seemed to accept that and, putting aside the total illegality of the affair, they stated that they thought there was sufficient other evidence to support the conviction. They therefore dismissed the appeal.

The fact remained that no weapon was ever traced to Dickman. None of the money was ever found, two of the witnesses had been largely discredited and even Mrs Nisbet, who made the dramatic identification at the magistrate's court, had to admit that she had known Dickman by sight for eighteen years. As for the stain on the overcoat, Annie Dickman agreed that she had used paraffin to remove an oil stain. She was not called upon to give evidence.

Held at Newcastle prison, Dickman continued to maintain that he was innocent. On the morning of his execution he was advised not to die with a lie on his lips. He made no reply, letting his silence testify to his innocence.

After his death, attempts were made to link Dickman with two other murders. The first was the murder of Caroline Luard in Kent in August 1908, the second was the killing of Hermann Cohen in Sunderland in March 1909. If one examines both cases there is not one iota of evidence linking Dickman to either case. They were merely attempts to further blacken the name of a man who could no longer defend himself.

Suggestion for further reading:

William Beadle, *Wrongly Hanged* (Dagenham: Wat Tyler, c. 1995).

9

Steinie Morrison

Sentenced to death, but subsequently reprieved
For the murder of Leon Beron, on Clapham Common, London

T HERE are some professions where public holidays and celebrations are still nothing more than ordinary working days. One such profession is, of course, the police and it therefore was not unusual for Constable Joseph Mumford to find himself on duty on New Year's Day, Sunday, January 1st, 1911.

The New Year was only eight hours old when Constable Mumford's beat took him on to Clapham Common. Mumford found nothing unusual until he reached the north-west corner of the common, at around 8.10 a.m. There appeared to be something partly hidden in the bushes close to the bandstand and, upon closer inspection, Mumford saw that it was the body of a well-dressed man.

The man was lying on his back. He wore an overcoat trimmed with astrakhan, patent leather boots and a black silk handkerchief had been placed over his face and tucked into his collar beneath his chin. The legs were crossed at the ankles and the arms were by his sides. There were signs that the man had actually been attacked a few yards away and dragged to the spot where he now lay. Mumford did not disturb the scene beyond lifting the man's left hand and checking for a pulse. There was none. Constable Mumford immediately raised the alarm and sent for assistance to Cavendish Road police station.

The body was soon moved to the mortuary at Battersea, where it was carefully undressed before being photographed. It appeared that the man had been battered to death, though there were also three stab wounds to the chest. There had also been some facial mutilations inflicted, for on each cheek were deep S-shaped cuts. However, the officer in charge of the investigation, Detective Inspector Alfred Ward, had no doubts that the motive had to be one of robbery, as the dead man, whose clothing implied wealth, had only a single halfpenny on him.

Though there was nothing on the body that could identify it, Inspector Ward did find a notebook which contained a large number of foreign sounding names, mostly women. This appeared to be a rent book of some kind where regular payments were recorded against the names, suggesting that the dead man might be a local landlord.

In fact, it was an envelope, also found on the body, which was to lead to identification. The envelope bore the name Mr Israel Iglazer and the address 16 Coke Street, an address in Whitechapel.

No one knew Whitechapel and the people who lived there better than Detective Inspector Frederick Porter Wensley, so Inspector Ward asked him to assist, even though that officer was heavily involved in the Houndsditch inquiry into the shooting of three policemen by a group of anarchists. Inspector Wensley soon tracked down Mr Iglazer, who in turn gave them an address at 133 Jubilee Street, also in Whitechapel.

According to Iglazer, the dead man lived in a room at 133 Jubilee Street, with his brother. When the police called at that address, there was no one home so the door was forced. The single room was absolutely filthy but when a search was made, various papers were found including a photograph of the dead man. Mr Iglazer had, it seemed, been correct. The officers waited for the final confirmation from the dead man's brother, once he returned home.

In fact, it was not until the early hours of January 2nd that David Beron returned home. He was somewhat surprised to find two police officers waiting for him, but was even more shocked to be taken to the police station for questioning. He was soon able to prove that he had not seen his brother since Friday, December 30th, but at last the police were able to put a name to the dead man in Battersea mortuary. He was Leon Beron, a forty-eight-year-old Polish Jew.

Leon Beron was something of an enigma. From his native Poland he had first moved to France, finally arriving in England from Paris in 1894. Since that time he had never held down any job or profession and described himself as a dealer in property. It was true that he did own a few slum properties, most of which were rented out to prostitutes, but these brought him in no more than a few shillings each week. Despite this apparent lack of income, Leon Beron was never short of money and dressed in the finest clothes. Those who knew him around the cafes and meeting-houses of the East End believed that he also supplemented his meagre property income by acting as a receiver of stolen goods and financier for burglaries and robberies.

Beron, however, did not have a police record. Indeed, his only official contact with the law had been a couple of years earlier when he reported that two men had tried to steal his gold watch, the chain he wore with it and which bore a £5 piece, and a leather pouch containing twenty sovereigns. On that occasion, the thieves had not been successful but those same items were now missing from Leon Beron's body, reinforcing Inspector Ward's belief that this had been a robbery which ended in murder.

The newspapers of the day were naturally filled with stories of the Houndsditch murders and this new horror led the press to immediately suggest a link between the two crimes. After all, Beron had had the letter S scrawled on his cheeks, and this was believed to be the method by which anarchists branded informers. Perhaps Mr Beron, in addition to acting as a fence and financier for the criminal elements of the East End, had also acted as a police informer. The police, though, were having none of this. They denied any involvement with Beron and persisted in saying that the crime was a simple robbery that had ended in the death of the victim.

As far as Inspector Ward was concerned, the most important thing was to trace Leon Beron's movements on December 31st, 1910. His landlady reported that she had last seen him at noon on that day. Further reports stated that one of Leon's favourite haunts was Snelwar's Warsaw restaurant, situated at 32 Osborn Street, Whitechapel. Customers there stated that Leon had indeed been there for lunch on December 31st, but they had more interesting information than that to impart.

It seemed that of late, Leon Beron had spent a good deal of time at the Warsaw in the company of another man. Indeed, they had been seen together at the Warsaw, later that same day, at around 7.00 p.m. The other man had had a bulky brown paper parcel with him at the time. He had said it was a flute but when the proprietor's ten-year-old daughter, Becky Snelwar, had pulled this parcel from his pocket, it had seemed much too heavy to be a simple flute. Furthermore, the customers were able to put a name to this man. He called himself by various names including Moses Tagger and Morris Stein, but apparently preferred to go by the name of Steinie Morrison.

When a police check was made on Morrison, some most interesting facts were revealed. He had been born in the Ukraine in 1879 and came to England in 1898. He was soon in trouble with the law and was given a one-month prison sentence for theft, in December 1898. Since that time he had rarely been out of prison, his sentences including one of five years for burglary in 1901, and another five-year sentence in 1906. Morrison had only been released on licence on September 17th, 1910. A condition of that licence was that he kept the police informed of his address. The records showed that soon after being released he had taken a job at Pither's bakery at 213 Lavender Hill, close to Clapham Common, and taken lodgings at 26 Grove Street. He had left his job after six weeks and returned to Whitechapel, but he was no longer at Grove Street. That was a violation of the licence and Morrison could be arrested on that charge alone.

In due course, Morrison's new address was traced and shown to be 91 Newark Street. Officers spoke to his landlady, Annie Zimmerman, who confirmed that she had not seen him since the morning of January 1st. Further inquiries revealed that Morrison's behaviour had been rather strange that same morning. First, after leaving his lodgings he had deposited a parcel in the left luggage office at St Mary's station, Whitechapel, using the name Banman. From there he had travelled to Walworth Road where he had called on a jeweller friend, Max Frank, and exchanged £10 of gold sovereigns for banknotes. Since it was believed that a quantity of sovereigns had been stolen from Leon Beron, this only reinforced the police belief that they were searching for the right man. A watch was placed on Morrison's lodgings in Newark Street. All they could do now was wait.

On January 8th, it was Detective Constable Harry Jeffrey and Detective Constable James Bellinger who were detailed to watch Newark Street. At 9.20 a.m., they saw Morrison walk down the street and go into his lodgings. A few minutes later he reappeared, carrying a brown paper parcel and a walking stick. The two detectives then followed him to Cohen's restaurant at 7 Fieldgate Street. A message was sent to the police station and at 10.10 a.m., Inspector Wensley and Detective Sergeant William Brogden joined their colleagues. All four officers then entered the restaurant, to find Morrison seated at a table near the door. The inspector identified himself and told Morrison he was wanted, whereupon Sergeant Brogden seized Morrison and searched through his pockets. Steinie Morrison cried out, "Don't get putting anything in my pockets".

Satisfied that Morrison was not armed, he was then escorted, on foot, to Leman Street police station. During the journey Morrison called out, "This is the biggest blunder you ever made. I suppose it's not the first, but you have made one this time." A large crowd had gathered by now and followed the five men to the police station, shouting abuse as they went. Morrison may well have been relieved when he finally arrived at Leman Street and was placed into a cell.

Later that same day, Sergeant Brogden accompanied Inspector Ward to 116 York Road, an address occupied by Florrie Delton, a prostitute. Morrison had explained that after leaving his lodgings he had stayed with Florrie ever since. A search of those premises was made, and various items of clothing taken away. Later still, Sergeant Brogden took charge of the clothes Morrison was wearing when he was arrested, and an examination showed some blood on the left cuff of his shirt and on his collar and tie.

The time came for Inspector Ward to interview his prisoner. Morrison greeted his visitor with, "I understand that I am detained here on a very serious charge, murder I am told, and I desire to make a voluntary statement". Inspector Ward identified himself and suggested that Morrison tell his story verbally, after which it would be written down and he could sign it. Morrison did so, read through the document and then signed it. He was then taken back to the cells whilst a proper scientific examination of the various items of clothing was made. The next day, January 9th, Morrison was told that he would be charged with the murder of Leon Beron. Later that same day he was placed on an identification parade where no fewer than ten witnesses picked him out.

Steinie Morrison appeared at the Old Bailey, before Mister Justice Darling, on March 6th, 1911. The trial lasted until March 15th, during which time Mr Richard D. Muir led for the prosecution, assisted by Mr William Leycester and Mr Ingleby Oddie. Mr Edward Abinger led for the defence. Originally he was assisted by Mr

Alasdair MacGregor, but when that gentleman fell ill after four days, his place was taken by Mr Roland Oliver.

When the police investigation had first commenced, one of the first questions to be asked was how had Leon Beron and his killer arrived at Clapham Common, and how had the murderer escaped. It seemed a reasonable assumption that a cab might have been used, so various drivers were interviewed and a £1 reward offered for anyone with useful information. This reward suddenly brought three cabmen forward. One of these was Alfred Stevens, who stated that he had picked up two men at the Royal Hotel, Blackfriars, and taken them to Cedars Road, Clapham Common, arriving there at 1.30 a.m. After this, Stevens had returned to the rank at Clapham Cross, where he was approached at 2.30 a.m. by a man who asked to be taken to Kennington.

Stevens took this passenger to the Hanover public house and the last he saw of him, he was walking towards another pub, the Horns. The man seemed to be in a rush and Stevens described him as being five feet ten inches in height, clean-shaven and with a dark complexion. On January 9th, he had seen a picture of Morrison in the newspaper and he was sure that this was the man he had picked up.

Edward Hayman was another cab driver, and he claimed that he had picked up two gentlemen on the corner of Sidney Street and the Mile End Road, at 2.00 a.m. One of these men was Steinie Morrison and Hayman described the other as five feet six inches tall and wearing a dark overcoat and a bowler hat. It was Morrison who engaged the cab and paid at the end of the journey, in Lavender Gardens, Clapham.

The third cabman was Alfred Castling. He had been on the rank at Kennington Church on January 1st when, at 3.30 a.m., two men approached him. Castling was one of the ten people who attended the identification parade at Leman Street police station and he positively identified Morrison as one of his passengers. According to Castling, the two men asked to go to Finsbury Park station and Castling told them there would be a fare of seven shillings. He finally dropped the two in Seven Sisters Road and was given three half-crowns in payment.

What was the value of this testimony? It appeared to show Morrison and Beron taking cabs all over London in the early hours of January 1st. It must be remembered that none of these drivers came forward until the reward had been

Steinie Morrison in the dock, March 1911 (Mary Evans Picture Library)

offered. All admitted that they had either seen pictures of Morrison in the newspapers, or had seen detailed descriptions of him and Beron on posters. Furthermore, at the identification parade, none of the other men were as tall as Morrison, making him stick out like a sore thumb.

Alec Snelwar was the owner of the Warsaw restaurant in Osborne Street and he testified that Leon Beron was a regular customer there. He came in almost every day, and had done so for years. During the last couple of months of 1910, Morrison had also been in most days and over the last two or three weeks of the year, was often in Beron's company.

On December 31st, Snelwar went down into the restaurant at 9.00 p.m., and saw Morrison and Beron together at a table. They left together, at 11.45 p.m., and Snelwar never saw Beron again. The next day, January 1st, Snelwar saw Morrison at some time between 10.00 a.m. and 11.00 a.m. He only came in for about a minute and did not speak to anyone before he left. Snelwar was also able to say that it was common knowledge that Beron carried a good deal of money with him, for he often counted it out in the restaurant. He was also proud of his heavy gold watch and often showed it to people, letting them feel the weight. He had seen Morrison holding the watch on one occasion.

Joe Mintz was a waiter at the Warsaw, having started working there on December 1st, 1910. He had known Beron for about two years and started to see Morrison come into the Warsaw quite often. Morrison got on very well with children and was a favourite of Becky Snelwar, the proprietor's daughter.

On December 31st, Morrison came in between 7.00 p.m. and 8.00 p.m., and handed a parcel over to Mintz, after Becky had playfully taken it out of his pocket, thinking it might be a present for her. The parcel was two feet long and two inches wide, and Morrison told him that it was a flute and he would pick it up later. The 'flute' was very heavy but Mintz did not ask any questions and placed it under the counter. At 11.40 p.m., Morrison asked for a glass of lemonade, then said he wanted his parcel back. Mintz handed it over and five minutes or so afterwards, Morrison left with Beron.

Henry Hermelin was one of the Warsaw's regular customers and actually lived upstairs. He was in the restaurant on December 31st and saw Beron come in some time between 8.30 p.m. and 9.00 p.m. Morrison was already there, and Beron went over to sit next to him. They were talking but Hermelin did not catch any of the conversation, although he too confirmed that Morrison had once held Beron's gold watch and remarked on how heavy it was.

Another of the Warsaw's customers was Sam Rosen, a cabinet maker. He confirmed that Morrison and Beron were together in the restaurant and were still there at 11.30 p.m., when he left. Rosen, however, had seen the two men together early the next morning. According to Rosen's original statement, it was sometime between 12.30 a.m. and 1.30 a.m. on January 1st, and the two men were at the corner of Brick Lane, walking towards Sidney Street.

Whilst it was true that this testimony tied in nicely with that of the cabman, Edward Hayman, who reported picking Morrison and another man up in Sidney Street, Rosen was in fact a most unreliable witness. He had told a slightly different story at the police court and confirmed that one of the dead man's brothers, Solomon Beron, had told him that he must keep to his original statement or he might go to prison. Rosen now maintained that he had seen Morrison and Beron heading towards Sidney Street but he had no idea of the time. He said that he had been threatened by Solomon Beron and by other people, some of whom had said they would shoot him if he did not say that he had seen the two men at about 1.30 a.m.

Jack Taw was only sixteen but he worked part-time at the Warsaw. He was not working on December 31st, but had called into the restaurant at 11.15 p.m. Morrison and Beron were sitting together and left together at 11.45 p.m. At 1.45 a.m., the next morning, Taw was at a coffee stall at the corner of Church Lane when he saw Morrison and Beron together. They were in Whitechapel Road, going towards Mile End. Under cross-examination, however, Taw confirmed that he had not approached the police until January 3rd, and only after he had tried to sell his story to the newspapers.

Another sighting of Morrison and Beron together had been made by Jacob Weissberg, who knew both of them. He had first seen them at the corner of Tucker Street and Commercial Street at 7.30 p.m., on December 31st. The next morning, at 12.45 a.m., he saw them again, this time in Whitechapel Road. Weissberg knew that the time was right because he looked at the church clock.

The confusion over just when Morrison and Beron were supposed to be together was added to by Nellie Deitch, who lived at 401 Commercial Road. She had known Beron for more than twelve years, ever since Leon and his wife had lodged with her father in Brick Lane in the 1890s. On December 31st, Nellie was at a New Year's party at 73 Commercial Street, leaving there at 1.15 a.m. She saw Beron with Morrison, a man whom she had not seen before but at whom she got a good look, between Bedford Street and Philpot Street. The two men were heading for the City. Nellie also attended the identification parade and had no hesitation in picking out Morrison. However, it was shown that in her original statement to the police, made on January 2nd, Nellie had said that this sighting was at 3.00 a.m. Only later did she alter it to 1.15 a.m. She was unable to give a satisfactory explanation for this change of time.

The police certainly seemed to have handled the investigation rather badly. They claimed that no mention had been made of the word murder when Morrison was first arrested, but at the police station he immediately began to talk about a murder charge. Surely this was proof that he knew full well why the police were looking for him and was an implication of his guilt. Under cross-examination, Constable Jeffery first said that he personally did not know that Morrison was wanted for murder, but then admitted that he did. He agreed too that it was customary to tell a man why he was wanted but that in this case, this had not been done. Morrison was simply told that he was wanted and the charge not mentioned.

Inspector Ward told the court that he had visited the scene of the crime before the body was moved to the mortuary. He then confirmed that despite the fact that there were clear footprints around the murder scene, no plaster casts of these were taken, thus losing a potentially valuable clue.

This then was the sum total of the prosecution case. A number of witnesses had come forward to say that they had seen Morrison and Beron together in the early hours of January 1st. Cabmen had described taking Morrison and a companion to Clapham Common and Morrison had known that Beron had money and a valuable watch on his person. What was the defence reply to this?

Annie Zimmerman was Morrison's landlady and she testified that Morrison had come home just after midnight on December 31st. She had locked the door behind him and was sure that she would have heard if he had gone back out because the only other way for him to leave the premises was through his bedroom window, and the frame of that shrieked terribly. This was confirmed by her husband, Morrie Zimmerman. Mrs Grove, a neighbour, told the court that she had seen Morrison coming home and confirmed that it was just after midnight. She then heard the bolt being drawn and locked.

Morrison did give evidence on his own behalf. He claimed that he had been selling some imitation jewellery, at around 8.00 p.m., in the Warsaw restaurant. From there he went to the Shoreditch Empire to see Gertie Gitana, Harry Champion and Harry Lauder. He was there from 8.45 p.m. until 11.10 p.m., in the company of Esther Brodsky and her sister, Jane, who had both been romantically linked with the defendant.

After leaving the two women, Morrison said he returned to the Warsaw to pick up his flute, which he had left there earlier. He did see Beron, but did not speak to him and they certainly did not sit down together. At 11.45 p.m., he left the Warsaw and returned to his lodgings. Morrison admitted that he had passed Beron, on the corner of Sidney Street, but again did not speak to him.

Unfortunately for Morrison, it was soon shown that this alibi was false. Both Esther and Jane Brodsky confirmed the music hall story. This, in itself, did not give Morrison an alibi for the time of the murder, but would at the very least have shown that many of the prosecution witnesses who claimed to have seen him and Beron together in the Warsaw were lying or mistaken. When cross-examined, however, both women said that Morrison had paid the shilling admission for them. It was easily shown that because it was New Year's Eve, the normal admission price had been raised to one shilling and sixpence. Furthermore, Esther was unable to remember a single performer at the show.

Steinie Morrison was the worst possible witness in his own defence. He told lie after lie about his past, claiming that he had been born in Australia when it was easily shown that he was Russian. He admitted having a sudden influx of money soon after Beron's death, but did not say that this had come from a Treasury bill forgery he had perpetrated with others. In order to avoid a fraud charge, he was taking great risks with a murder charge.

One of the last witnesses for the defence was Constable George Graves. The police had consistently denied that anyone had mentioned murder to Morrison before he brought the matter up. Constable Graves, who had been at Leman Street, said that Sergeant Brogden had told the prisoner that he was there on suspicion of murder. It was a small victory for the defence, but by then, the damage had been done.

The jury was out for thirty-five minutes before deciding that Morrison was guilty. He was then sentenced to death. When the judge uttered the words "...and may the Lord have mercy on your soul", Morrison replied "I decline such mercy. I do not believe there is a God in Heaven either." He was then taken to the condemned cell at Wandsworth prison to await the fateful day.

An appeal was heard on March 27th. The defence argued that the evidence given by the three cabmen was unreliable and that all three men had seen a picture of Morrison in the newspapers before they made their identifications. However, the judges ruled that there was enough other evidence to show that the conviction was safe, so the verdict was upheld. Exactly one week before that date, however, the Home Secretary, Winston Churchill, announced that he had commuted the sentence to one of penal servitude for life. Morrison was removed from the condemned cell and escorted to Dartmoor to begin his sentence.

Morrison, however, was not a model prisoner. He continued to maintain his total innocence of the crime and began writing letters of appeal. He went on hunger strikes and began to demand that the death penalty be carried out rather than face life in prison. Slowly, people were converted to his cause and a committee was set up to campaign for his release.

In 1913, a petition was organized, holding 42,000 names supporting Morrison's cause. Pamphlets were published telling the story of the crime and his subsequent imprisonment. It was to no avail, and Morrison continued with violent outbursts, suicide attempts and hunger strikes.

By 1921, these constant tirades against authority had taken their toll on Morrison. At 2.15 p.m., on January 21st, warders went into his cell to discover that he had suffered a heart attack. Though he was given prompt medical attention, Steinie Morrison died at 4.30 p.m. He had, as the State intended, served a life sentence.

It should be remembered that there was never any real evidence against Morrison. The three cabmen had been shown to be unreliable witnesses, there was evidence that the murderer of Beron might have had other motives than mere robbery, Morrison had produced witnesses, such as his landlady, who stated that he was in his room at the time the crime took place, and there was a suggestion that certain police officers had been somewhat circumspect with the truth when it came to the interviews they had conducted with their prisoner. Yet despite all this, a man who was almost certainly innocent spent ten years behind bars.

Suggestion for further reading:

Andrew Rose, *Stinie: Murder on the Common* (Harmondsworth: Penguin, 1989).

George Loake

10

Hanged at Stafford, Thursday, December 28th, 1911
For the murder of his wife, Elizabeth, at Walsall

FOR more than forty years George Loake had worked on the railway, and by the turn of the century, he had been promoted to the prestigious position of driver on express trains. The only thing missing from George's life was the love of a good woman, but as he was a widower with nine children, it might be difficult to find someone who would take on this responsibility. Eventually, though, George found the woman he was looking for in the form of Elizabeth Newith, a divorcee with two children of her own, and in 1903, they married.

At this time, George was already fifty-six years old and his new bride just thirty-eight. Despite this eighteen-year age difference, they seemed to be happy enough together, the entire family moving into a rented house at 110 Portland Street, Walsall. For six years, the Loake family lived in contentment.

In the summer of 1909, George was shunting a train at the Bescot sidings when the engine struck the buffers at some speed, inflicting him with a severe blow to the head. Very badly injured, his workmates ministered to him whilst someone ran to fetch the doctor. Ignoring the fact that there was a massive swelling on George's head, the medical 'expert' deduced that no treatment was necessary and George was simply sent home to recover.

For two long hours, George Loake was in acute pain. So unbearable did the agony become that he rose from his bed, walked down to the canal and threw himself in. He was rescued by his neighbours who then helped Elizabeth to take care of him. Slowly his health recovered, but there was to be more bad news for the Loake family. The railway blamed George for the shunting accident and told him that he would be suspended from his work.

In time, George Loake appeared to regain all of his old health and vigour, but those closest to him noticed that there had been a marked change in his personality. Before he had been a placid, mild man but now he was short-tempered, flying into terrible rages at the slightest provocation. His language became obscene and he took to drinking heavily. Once he was drunk he became even more bad-tempered, and as the days passed, his temper seemed to grow even worse.

In due course George returned to work at the railway, but now he seemed to constantly crave drink. In March 1911, he walked out of the railway yard, leaving his engine unattended, so that he could buy more alcohol for himself. This time his employers felt that he had gone too far and dismissed him. This meant that not only did George lose all his income, but he also lost all the pension rights that he had accumulated over those years of service. George, now sixty-four, did not know where to turn.

With little or no money coming into the house and with so many mouths to feed, it became impossible to make ends meet. The rent on 110 Portland Street fell into arrears and by June, those arrears had reached such a point that the family were evicted from their home. They moved, for a short time, to Navigation Street but one day, when Elizabeth was so desperate for money that she pawned George's boots, he walked out on her. Soon afterwards, Elizabeth took her own two children with her and moved in with George and Jane Dolloway, who lived at 8a The Butts, off Warwick Street.

The Dolloways had once been neighbours of the Loakes in Portland Street but some four years before, George and Jane had rented the cottage at The Butts. They still remained friendly with the Loakes and were pleased to see Elizabeth when she called in early July. Elizabeth was very upset, telling Jane that she had nowhere to go now that her husband had moved out of Navigation Street. She had no food and what little money she did have came from the washing she did for other people. George Dolloway and his wife took pity on their old friend and invited her to stay with them.

Over the next few weeks, George Loake often visited his wife at The Butts. Elizabeth was now slowly putting her life back together and after a few visits, George asked if he might move in with her. Elizabeth was adamant that he could not and even said that if he tried to, she would have him turned out. Some of these conversations were overheard by Jane Dolloway, to whom Elizabeth confided that she would never live with George again.

Monday, August 28th, was a bank holiday. At 10.25 a.m., Jane Dolloway left her house to do some shopping. There were, at that time, only two people left inside the house at The Butts, Elizabeth Loake and Jane's eleven-year-old son, Thomas.

Elizabeth was sitting on a chair by the window, sewing. Thomas stood by the table that was further away from the open front door. Suddenly, George Loake appeared and said something to his wife. Thomas Dolloway could not make out what George had said but he saw Elizabeth get up from her chair and prepare to go outside, presumably to continue the conversation. As Elizabeth reached the porchway, George sprang at her and threw his left arm around her neck. He then lifted his right arm as if to strike Elizabeth. The arm came down and Thomas heard Elizabeth scream out before he ran upstairs, terrified, and locked himself in his bedroom.

Thomas knew that he was safe where he was, at least for the time being, but if he wanted to get out of the house, there was only one way, and that was through the front door, where George Loake might well be waiting for him. The frightened boy thought hard for a few minutes before slowly unlocking his door and venturing downstairs.

There was no sign of either George or Elizabeth, but there was blood on the floor by the front door. Thomas walked outside, and then ran down an entry towards the shops where he knew his mother would be. As he ran, Thomas noticed Elizabeth with a neighbour, Mrs Jones. Though he did not stop to speak to either woman, Thomas could see that Elizabeth was bleeding from a wound in her throat.

Jane Dolloway was in Mrs Cooper's shop in Warwick Street when her son came dashing in and shouted for her to come, as Elizabeth was in the yard. Jane replied that she knew that but Thomas then added, "Come mother, he's cut her throat". By the time Jane and Thomas reached their home, a large crowd had gathered. Jane pushed her way through, only to find Elizabeth lying on the ground with blood on her bodice. A policeman was already there and Jane waited until the doctor arrived before finally going back into her house.

The first police officer on the scene had been Constable Richard Woolley. Constable Woolley was actually off duty at the time and at his home, 24 Upper Forster Street. It was around 10.30 a.m. when William Jones knocked on his front door and told him that there was a woman in Warwick Street with her throat cut. Woolley went quickly to the scene where he found Elizabeth Loake bleeding profusely from a throat wound. Even as Constable Woolley was attending to Elizabeth, George Loake walked down the entry, an open pocket knife in his left hand. The knife was wet with blood, and as Loake raised it to his own throat, Woolley leapt forward striking him on the hand with his truncheon. George dropped the knife and was then asked what he had done. He would only reply "It's all right".

Woolley handcuffed Loake and, leaving him in the custody of some of the men who had gathered around, went back to see how Elizabeth was. By now she had lost consciousness and, seeing that there was no time to lose, Woolley sent another man for the doctor. Dr John George Cooke arrived very soon afterwards. Elizabeth was still alive but minutes later she breathed her last. This was now a case of murder.

The trial of George Loake took place at Stafford on November 20th, 1911, before Mr Justice Pickford. Loake's defence rested in the hands of Mr R. J. Lawrence, whilst the prosecution case was led by Dr Hazell, assisted by Mr Brice. The proceedings were relatively short.

Maud Wilson was Elizabeth Loake's stepdaughter and she told the court what she knew of George and Elizabeth's history. Elizabeth Loake had previously been married to William Newith, by whom she had two children, a boy and a girl. Maud said that until some three months before, the prisoner had worked for the London and North Western Railway Company, and had done since he was twenty-three years old.

The last time Maud had seen Elizabeth was about seven weeks before her death when she had called at Maud's house, 159 Queen Street. She had told Maud that she and

George were not living together anymore, but did not give any reason as to why they had split up.

Maud had last seen George on Friday, August 25th when he too called at her home. She offered him some breakfast, which he accepted, but ate standing up. Through the entire period of his visit, some twenty minutes or so, George had stood by the front door. He did not refer to his wife but said that he was still looking for work. Maud confirmed that George had been acting strangely, especially over the last couple of months. He had started talking to her eighteen-month-old baby about trains, but speaking as if the child were a fully-grown adult. Maud also said that she had lived with the couple until her marriage two years before, and had overheard many quarrels between George and Elizabeth, especially over the fact that Elizabeth used to pawn items of his clothing when she was short of money. Furthermore, the situation was not improved by Elizabeth's own fondness for alcohol. Finally, Maud was also able to tell the court that a week before the attack upon Elizabeth, Loake had said he was going to kill himself.

In addition to saying what she had found when her son took her back home, Jane Dolloway also referred to an incident earlier on August 28th. When she left home to go to the shops, she had passed George Loake at the entrance to the alleyway that led to her home. They had exchanged a pleasant 'Good morning' and George then asked if his wife were at home. Jane confirmed that she was and bade him goodbye. She noticed that he had his hands under his overcoat but George seemed to be perfectly sober and was behaving normally.

Thomas Dolloway was of course a witness to the attack itself, though he said he had not actually seen a knife in George's hand when he struck Elizabeth around the neck. When he ran for his mother, Thomas had seen Elizabeth with Mrs Jones, and Edith Jones now told the court what she knew.

Edith lived at 28 Warwick Street and had only known Elizabeth Loake since she moved in with the Dolloways. She had also seen George occasionally, when he paid visits to his wife. On the day in question, Edith was in the wash-house at the back of her house when she saw George walking up the entry towards the Dolloways'. A few minutes later she heard a scream and a cry of 'Murder'! She ran outside to find Elizabeth staggering down the entry towards her. Edith ran to offer assistance and heard Elizabeth gasp, "He's done it, he's done it". There was no sign of George.

As Edith cradled Elizabeth, the stricken woman cried "Mrs Jones, can't you do something for me?" Edith then ran to the street to look for help. Finding no one there, she returned to Elizabeth and supported her with one arm. At that moment, George Loake appeared, still holding a knife. Edith then dragged Elizabeth down to another alleyway, at which point the policeman arrived.

Constable Woolley told the court what he had seen on August 28th. He added that he had only ever seen George once before, on June 10th, when he had been called out to a house in Navigation Street. Elizabeth Loake had met him outside and said "Come with me, my husband has cut the dog's throat". Inside the house he found a dog with a slight wound in its throat. No further proceedings were taken.

Chief Inspector George Henry Ballance had been at the police station when Loake was brought in. The man appeared to be very sullen and Ballance noticed that he had some slight scratch marks on the front of his throat, and on the right side of his neck. The prisoner gave his name and added that he had worked on the railway until a few months previously. He seemed to be quite rational and muttered "Her should have stuck to me". He was then cautioned, to which he replied "I don't want to say anything about it".

At Chief Inspector Ballance's orders, Loake was taken to hospital where he had his throat bandaged. Whilst that was happening, Ballance went to the scene of the crime where he saw some spots of blood inside the vestibule of the house and other blood marks along the entry way and in a yard at the top. Back at the station, Ballance cautioned Loake again and then charged him with murder. Loake's only comment was the one word 'Yes'.

Constable Thomas Bell had been in charge of Loake in the cells after the Coroner's enquiry. He reported that Loake had said to him "Nobody knows why I done it, only her that's gone. I would not tell anybody, not even my own children. She should not have done what she did. I did not intend to have that done on me." He repeated this several times.

William Henry Alcock was the proprietor of the Coach and Horses in Abelwell Street. For the three weeks prior to the crime, George had lodged with him, normally paying tenpence to a shilling for the weeks rent. On August 26th, William had been in the kitchen after dinner when George handed him 4d saying that he might as well take it, as it would be the last he would get.

John Bartlam worked at the Coach and Horses and he testified that at 5.30 a.m., on August 28th, George had been in the scullery washing and drying some clothing. As he went into the kitchen, John noticed that George had left his soap behind in the scullery and pointed this out to him. George replied that John could keep the soap as he would not be needing it anymore.

Medical evidence was given by Dr Cooke. In addition to attending the scene, he had also performed the post-mortem on the victim. He had noted six wounds on the neck, two on the left forearm and two on the left hand. The cause of death was syncope caused by haemorrhage.

The only defence could be one of insanity. Two of the prisoner's sons, George and Harry, both said that they had heard their father threaten to commit suicide and another doctor, Dr Shore, testified that he had been unable to determine if Loake was sane or insane at the time of the attack. Despite this evidence, the jury had little difficulty in adjudging George Loake to be guilty of murder. An appeal was fought on the grounds that Loake was insane and therefore not responsible for his actions, but because Dr Shore had said that he could not be certain of Loake's mental state at the time of the crime, insanity could not be proved so the appeal was dismissed. Loake was hanged at Stafford on December 28th, by Thomas Pierrepoint and William Willis.

Despite all the evidence of George Loake's terrible accident, the appalling medical treatment he received, his subsequent drastic change of personality and his suicidal tendencies, he had been adjudged to be perfectly sane and therefore responsible for his actions.

Frederick Henry Seddon

11

Hanged at Pentonville prison, London, Thursday, April 18th, 1912
For the murder of Eliza Mary Barrow, at Islington

I T was 8.20 p.m., on the evening of Wednesday, September 20th, 1911 when Frank Ernest Vonderahe called at 63 Tollington Park, Islington. His knock was answered within a minute or so and he saw that the door had been opened by a young girl, who he took to be a domestic servant.

"Could I see Mrs Barrow?" inquired Mr Vonderahe.

"Don't you know she is dead and buried?" replied the girl.

"No..." replied a shocked Mr Vonderahe, who went on to ask when this terrible event had taken place.

"She was buried last Saturday" continued the girl, who then mentioned that if he wished to speak to Mr Seddon, the master of the house, he should call back at nine o'clock.

Frank Vonderahe did indeed return to the house at 9.00 p.m., but this time he had his wife, Julia Hannah Vonderahe, with him. The door was again opened by the young maid but almost immediately, sixteen-year-old Margaret Seddon, the eldest girl, came to the door and apologized for the fact that her father and mother were still not at home. She explained that they had gone to see a show at the Empire and probably would not be back until quite late. Mr and Mrs Vonderahe did not see fit to question such a young girl about such a delicate and distressing matter and so they decided that they would leave their enquiries until the following day.

The person that Frank and Julia Vonderahe had first been asking after was fifty-year-old Eliza Mary Barrow, who was Frank Vonderahe's first cousin. Until July 27th, 1910, Miss Barrow had lived with the Vonderahe family at 31 Eversholt Road, a thoroughfare very close to Tollington Park. After some disagreement over her food, Miss Barrow had expressed a desire to find another place for herself and had finally chosen to occupy four rooms on the top floor of 63 Tollington Park, the home of the Seddon family.

In fact, the family arrangements had been rather more complex than that, for Miss Barrow had not moved out of the Vonderahe home by herself. In addition to Miss Barrow, the Vonderahes had also acted as landlords to Robert Dennis Hook, his wife and ten-year-old Ernest Grant, their nephew. The Hooks had been close to Miss Barrow for some considerable time and Eliza Barrow in turn had become very fond of little Ernest, whom she treated almost as her own child. These four people all moved into number sixty-three, with the Hooks agreeing to look after Miss Barrow in return for their lodgings.

This cosy arrangement had not lasted for very long before Eliza Barrow had had yet another argument, this time with Robert Hook. As a result, at Miss Barrow's request, Mr Seddon had eventually ordered the Hooks to leave his house. They had, rather reluctantly, obeyed that order and, as far as the Vonderahes had been aware, Eliza Barrow had continued to live at number sixty-three, along with little Ernest.

The next day, Frank Vonderahe had to go to work and so was unable to return to the Seddon household. The visit was left to his wife, who took with her Amelia Blanche Vonderahe, her sister-in-law. This time, the two ladies did manage to see the owner of the house, forty-year-old Frederick Henry Seddon, who greeted them in a civil manner.

After some discussion, Seddon explained that Miss Barrow had died on Thursday, September 14th, and had been buried two days later on the 16th. The Vonderahes were fully aware of the fact that Eliza Barrow had been a woman of considerable property and asked about the provisions of her will. Seddon showed them a copy of a will, signed in pencil, leaving all the property to Ernest Grant and his older sister, Hilda, but Seddon went on to explain that in fact there was very little property left to dispose of. He outlined how she had sold the vast majority of her property in order to buy herself an annuity. In effect, she had transferred her property so that she could enjoy a regular income as long as she lived. Now that she was dead, of course, the annuity had died with her.

"Whoever persuaded her to do that was a remarkably clever person", commented Amelia Vonderahe, but Seddon made no reply. Julia Vonderahe then asked why the family had not been informed of the death, whereupon Seddon produced a copy of a letter that he said he had sent to Eversholt Road. That letter, dated September 14th and addressed to Frank Vonderahe, read "Dear Sir, I sincerely regret to have to inform you of the death of your cousin, Miss Eliza Mary Barrow, at 6.00 a.m., this morning from epidemic diarrhoea. The funeral will take place on Saturday at about 1.00 p.m. to 2.00 p.m.

"Please inform Albert Edward and Emma Marion Vonderahe of her demise and let me know if you or they wish to attend the funeral.

"I must also inform you that she made a will on the 11th instant, leaving what she died possessed of to Hilda and Ernest Grant and appointed myself as sole executor under the will."

Far from satisfied with what they had heard, Julia and Amelia Vonderahe left Tollington Park and went home to report what they had been told to their respective husbands. The matter was discussed further over that weekend, and on Monday, September 23rd, Frank Vonderahe called on Seddon again, this time with a family friend, Mr Walker, accompanying him. On this occasion it was Seddon himself who opened the door.

"I have called about my cousin. Could I see the will?" asked Mr Vonderahe. Immediately Seddon went on to the defensive, saying "You are not the eldest of the family and I don't know whether I shall show it to you. Everything is perfectly legal and Miss Barrow did everything by herself."

Trying a different tack, Frank Vonderahe then asked about specific properties that he knew his cousin had owned. One of these had been a public house called the Buck's Head, and when Frank asked who now held the lease, Seddon replied that he did, adding that he also held the lease on the barber's shop next door, and all the rest of her property. Seddon then explained that all this had been signed over to him for an annuity of £3 per week. For the moment at least, that was where matters were left to rest.

The inquest on the dead woman duly opened but the Vonderahe family were far from happy. They thought that the financial dealings that Eliza Barrow had apparently freely entered into during the last year of her life were so irregular that there might be more to this case than a fortuitous death for Mr Seddon and his annuity. Frank Vonderahe decided that the matter should be further investigated and, putting his suspicions on paper, wrote to the Director of Public Prosecutions. That letter was then duly passed on to the police.

After carrying out investigations into the various financial matters, the police felt that it might indeed be worth taking another look at the death of Eliza Barrow. Consequently, on November 15th, her body was exhumed and a post-mortem was performed by Bernard Spilsbury. He removed various internal organs and samples and handed these over to his colleague, Doctor William Henry Willcox, who carried out chemical tests on them. The results of these scientific tests were that Eliza Mary Barrow had been killed by arsenical poisoning. The problem was, who had administered that poison?

There were a number of people in the Seddon household who might well have been responsible for poisoning Miss Barrow. Some of these, including Margaret Seddon, the daughter, and Mary Elizabeth Ellen Chater, the maid, seldom or rarely gave food to Miss Barrow. The more the investigation progressed, the more it seemed likely that the culprit was Frederick Seddon himself. That was why, on December 4th, Detective Chief Inspector Alfred Ward found himself outside 63 Tollington Park, waiting for Seddon to return home.

At 7.00 p.m., Ward saw Seddon approaching and told him that he would be detained on suspicion of murder. Seddon replied, "Absurd. What a terrible charge, wilful murder. It is the first of our family that has ever been accused of such a crime. Are you going to arrest my wife as well? If not, I would like you to give her a message for me."

Though Margaret Ann, Seddon's wife, was not arrested, the investigation showed that most of Miss Barrow's food had been prepared and administered by Mrs Seddon. Eventually it was felt that she could have been at least as responsible as her husband and so, on January 15th, 1912, she too was arrested and charged with murder.

91

The trial of Frederick and Margaret Ann Seddon opened at the Old Bailey on March 4th, before Mr Justice Bucknill. The proceedings lasted until March 14th, during which the Crown's case was given by Mr Richard D. Muir, Mr S. A. T. Rowlatt and Mr Travers Humphreys. The defence was led by Mr Edward Marshall Hall, who was assisted by Mr Wellesley Orr and Mr R. Dunstan. Both prisoners pleaded not guilty to the charge.

It was important to show that the two defendants had a motive to murder their lodger. Frank Vonderahe explained that Miss Barrow had been a spinster and some years before had lived with Ernie Grant's mother, an old friend of hers. When Mrs Grant died, three years ago, Miss Barrow took it upon herself to look after the boy, even though she was no blood relative.

Until July 1910, Miss Barrow had lived with Frank at Eversholt Road, paying thirty shillings a week for the food and lodgings for her and the boy. In due course they had argued over her food, Miss Barrow claiming that it was not properly cooked, and she had moved in with Seddon. Frank and Miss Barrow had remained on good terms and the last time he had seen her alive was in August when he met her by chance in Stroud Green Road.

Turning to Miss Barrow's property, Frank Vonderahe explained that she had owned the lease on the Buck's Head public house and the barber's shop next door. She also owned £1,600 worth of India stock, and amongst her personal possessions was a large chest in which she kept various bags all containing gold coin. He had seen Miss Barrow count this out whilst she was at his house and he saw at least £50 or more. Miss Barrow herself had told him that the chest contained £400 and he had no doubt that she was telling him the truth. Since her death, none of this coin had been found. However, under cross-examination, Mr Vonderahe did have to admit that his cousin had been a very eccentric woman. He also agreed that whilst living at his house, Miss Barrow had expressed concerns about the Buck's Head, as the costs of the lease were increasing and eating into her income. Finally, he confirmed that since Miss Barrow had left his house, he had moved from Eversholt Road to 160 Corbyn Street, but had not notified either Miss Barrow or Mr Seddon about that move.

The financial details were confirmed by Julia Vonderahe, who also agreed that Miss Barrow had been eccentric. She had rather a bad temper and one never knew what she might do next. This was also confirmed by Amelia Vonderahe.

It was now shown that Miss Barrow's property had been obtained by Frederick Seddon. Cecil Vane Dunstan was a senior clerk at the Chief Accountant's Office of the Bank of England. He confirmed a transaction, dated October 14th, 1910, in which £1,600 worth of India Stock was transferred from Eliza Mary Barrow to Frederick Henry Seddon. The transfer document purported to be signed by Miss Barrow, though of course, Mr Dunstan was unable to confirm that the signature was genuine.

William Webb Hale was a member of the Stock Exchange, and acted for Miss Seddon in her financial dealings. Some time before October 14th, 1910, he had received a letter from his client, instructing him to put the transfer of the India Stock in motion. On the

14th, he went with Miss Barrow to the Bank of England. Mr Hale witnessed Miss Barrow's signature on the transfer document and confirmed that it was indeed hers.

The India Stock had not remained in Seddon's hands for very long, however. Arthur Astle was another member of the Stock Exchange, but he had acted for Seddon. Mr Astle told the court that on January 25th, 1911, he sold the stock, on Seddon's instructions. The sale realized one thousand, five hundred and nineteen pounds and sixteen shillings, and a cheque for that amount was handed over to Mr Seddon that same day.

Shortly after the India Stock had been transferred, Miss Barrow's other property was signed over to Seddon. Edwin Russell was a member of Russell and Sons, solicitors of 59 Coleman Street, London. On October 17th, 1910, Seddon called on him with a view to having the Buck's Head and the adjoining shop transferred to him from Miss Barrow. The documents were drawn up and the assignment finally dated for January 11th, 1911. In return for the property, Miss Barrow was to receive an annuity of one pound a week for life. This was in addition to the two pounds a week she had already obtained for the transfer of the India Stock, making her income three pounds per week.

The signature on the transfer of January 11th had been witnessed by Mr Henry William Knight, another solicitor. Mr Keeble, a clerk from Russell and Sons, had previously called on him and asked him to act for Miss Barrow in this matter. On the eleventh, he had attended 63 Tollington Park where he witnessed Miss Barrow's signature. Though she was very deaf, she certainly understood what she was doing and read the material part of the document for herself.

According to the prosecution, in addition to the India Stock and the two properties, Mr and Mrs Seddon also obtained other monies belonging to Miss Barrow. John Charles Pepper was the Chief Clerk at the Finsbury and City branch of the London Savings Bank. He testified that the dead woman had held a deposit account at his bank, which had first been opened on October 17th, 1887. That account continued to be properly run until June 19th, 1911, when it held a credit balance of two hundred and sixteen pounds, nine shillings and sevenpence. A week before that date, Miss Barrow had written to give the required one weeks notice, saying that it was her intention to close the account. On June 19th, Miss Barrow came in with another lady, since identified as Mrs Seddon, and drew out the entire balance. The two hundred and sixteen pounds was handed over in gold and now that money was missing.

An attempt was now made to link Seddon directly to the missing gold. Alfred Hartwell was a director of the London and Manchester Industrial Assurance Company, based in Finsbury Square. He said that Seddon had been employed by the company since 1891. In 1901, he had been made the Superintendent of Canvassers in north London. Up to March 1911, his salary had been five pounds and three shillings per week, but from the 25th of that month, it had been increased to five pounds and six shillings. In addition, Seddon got commission on all the collections. It was standard practice for him to pay all the money into his personal account, deduct his commission and hand over a cheque for the rest, usually on a Thursday. This commission added perhaps thirteen shillings a week to his income.

Harry Carl Taylor was an assistant superintendent for the same company, having Seddon as his immediate boss. It was his routine to go to 63 Tollington Park each Thursday, to assist Seddon in making up the company accounts. Seddon had an office in his basement and they would work there, often until quite late at night, usually with his assistant, John Charles Arthur Smith.

On September 14th, the day that Miss Barrow died, Seddon worked as normal, though he did seem rather tired and said that he had been up all night and an old lady had died that morning. That evening, Taylor saw Seddon put at least two hundred pounds in gold into his safe, when the collection should only have amounted to sixty-three pounds. This was confirmed by John Smith, who said that at one point, Seddon had made to give him the bags and joked that he might as well take his wages now.

The next task was to show that Miss Barrow had not had any severe health problems until the last few weeks of her life. The Seddon family doctor was Dr John Frederick Paul, whose surgery was at 215 Isledon Road, Finsbury Park. He testified that he had first met Miss Barrow on November 15th 1910, when she had called at his surgery. She called again two days later but after that, Dr Paul did not see her again until August 1st 1911, when she was brought in by Mrs Seddon. After examining Miss Barrow, Dr Paul concluded that she was suffering from congestion of the liver and prescribed a rhubarb and magnesia mix. On August 3rd, he repeated this prescription and did so once more on August 17th. One week later, on the 25th, he diagnosed asthma and gave Miss Barrow some chloral hydrate. Dr Paul last saw his patient on August 30th, when he gave her more medicine.

According to statements made by Frederick Seddon and the other members of the household, Miss Barrow had become more seriously ill at the beginning of September. Dr Paul was not available so, on September 2nd, Seddon sent for Dr Henry George Sworn, whose surgery was at 5 Highbury Crescent. Dr Sworn said that when he first saw Miss Barrow she was in her bed and suffering from sickness and diarrhoea. He gave her some bismuth carbonate and morphia.

On September 3rd, Dr Sworn visited number sixty-three again and found Miss Barrow not much improved. On the 4th, he saw her again and noted that she was still sick and that there was an offensive smell in the bedroom, a result of the diarrhoea. Mrs Seddon informed him that Miss Barrow would not take her medicine, so Dr Sworn said that unless she did as he had instructed, she would have to be taken to hospital. Miss Barrow said that she would not go.

Dr Sworn visited 63 Tollington Park every day from September 5th to September 9th. On the last occasion she seemed to be a little better and he told Miss Barrow that he would not visit the next day, unless she suddenly got worse. On the 11th, he called again and found his patient better still. Dr Sworn last saw her on September 13th, between 10.00 a.m. and 11.00 a.m. Miss Barrow was about the same but there was still a most offensive odour in the room. At 7.00 a.m., the next day, he heard that she was dead when Frederick Seddon called at his surgery. Dr Sworn did not bother to visit the house, or see the body, but on what Seddon had told him, made out a death certificate showing that Eliza Barrow had died from epidemic diarrhoea and exhaustion.

Under cross-examination, Dr Sworn said that he did not think that arsenic could be responsible for Miss Barrow's illness. Arsenic acted as an antiseptic and would not have caused the diarrhoea to smell so offensive. The question of poisoning had never entered his head until Chief Inspector Ward had called upon him and questioned him. Dr Sworn added that during his talks with Miss Barrow she had always spoken very highly of the Seddons.

The time came to examine those who had been in the house around the time of Miss Barrow's death. Elizabeth Ellen Chater was the domestic servant and had worked for the Seddons since April 1911. Elizabeth agreed that she had done some of the cooking in the house, but the vast majority of it had been done by Mrs Seddon herself, and Elizabeth had never cooked anything for Miss Barrow. One of the four rooms Miss Barrow rented was a small kitchen and either Mrs Seddon, or Margaret, her daughter, used to prepare Miss Barrow's food, usually in that kitchen.

According to Elizabeth, Miss Barrow had gone on a short holiday to Southend towards the end of August, and had fallen ill when she returned. However, throughout the whole of her stay at number sixty-three, Elizabeth thought Miss Barrow was ill. Elizabeth also told of two visitors coming to the house, Mrs Langley and her child.

Mary Emma Langley lived in Wolverhampton and was Frederick Seddon's sister. She told the court that on September 11th, she and her fourteen-year-old daughter, Frances, had paid a visit to 63 Tollington Park. They had stayed until Friday, September 15th. On the night of September 13th, Mary went to bed quite late and at 1.30 a.m. was woken by what sounded like a thud from the room above hers. That room was Eliza Barrow's bedroom. The next day, her brother told her that Miss Barrow had died early that morning.

Ernest Grant had turned ten years old on May 5th, 1911. Naturally he was rather vague about times and dates, but he confirmed that he and Miss Barrow, whom he called 'Chickey', had been happy at Mr Seddon's house. He recalled a holiday in Southend with Miss Barrow and said that when they returned to London, she fell ill.

Ernest used to sleep in the same bed as Miss Barrow, even though he did have his own room as well. On the night of September 13th, he went to bed with her as usual, but during the early hours he was woken by her moving about in the bed and groaning. She was calling out "What shall I do" and seemed to be in great pain, so he went downstairs to fetch Mrs Seddon, who put a hot flannel on Miss Barrow's stomach. During the next few hours, he went to his bedroom but a number of times, Miss Barrow called out for him and he went to her, only to be sent back to his own bed by either Mrs Seddon or Mr Seddon.

The next morning, two of the Seddon children, Ada and Frederick, took him down to Southend, where they stayed for two weeks. During that time, Margaret came down as well and at one stage, Mr and Mrs Seddon were there and Mr Seddon told him that Miss Barrow had died.

Ernest was also able to confirm the existence of the gold in Miss Barrow's chest. He had seen a number of bags and Miss Barrow had counted it out a number of times in his presence. Each week, Mr Seddon would come up to Miss Barrow's room and give her three more gold coins, which she added to her bags. Those three coins were, of course, the £3 due under the annuity that Seddon had set up.

Margaret Seddon was the eldest daughter of the family, and the second child, her brother Frederick being one year older. Margaret told the court that she used to look after Miss Barrow after the Hooks had left the house. For this task, Miss Barrow paid her one shilling per week. Margaret described how Miss Barrow had occupied four rooms on the top floor. One was her bedroom, one was Ernie Grant's room, one was a kitchen and the other was a spare room.

When Miss Barrow fell ill it had been her and her mother who looked after her. However, Margaret never administered Miss Barrow's medicine. That was always given by her mother. Margaret had not been present at Miss Barrow's death, and had last seen her alive at 10.00 p.m. on September 13th. The next morning she was told of the death and later that same day, Ernie Grant, Frederick, her older brother and Ada, her sister, had gone to Southend. She had followed them down after the funeral.

Margaret also testified that at some time between 3.30 p.m. and 4.00 p.m. on September 14th, she had gone out to post a letter at her father's instructions. Though she did not look at the front of the envelope, her father had said that it was a letter to Mr Frank Vonderahe, announcing Miss Barrow's death. The funeral took place on the Saturday, but only her mother, father and grandfather went.

Margaret's grandfather was William Seddon, and he was the father of the male defendant. He had been a witness to the making of Eliza Barrow's will, on September 11th. William said that his son had called him into Miss Barrow's bedroom to witness the signing. Miss Barrow had signed the document first, followed by himself and then his daughter-in-law, Margaret Ann Seddon. Miss Barrow was certainly fit to sign and fully aware of what she was doing because she asked for her spectacles and read the will through carefully. After signing it, she exclaimed "Thank God, that will do".

Margaret Ann Seddon, the co-defendant, testified that she and her husband had always been on excellent terms with Miss Barrow. Though their guest had complained of minor ailments ever since she arrived at the house, she was never actually laid up in bed until September 1st. Margaret Ann looked after Miss Barrow most of the time, helped occasionally by her daughter. It was to her that Miss Barrow expressed a desire to make a will and she passed this information on to her husband.

Margaret agreed that she had accompanied Miss Barrow to her bank when she closed her account and saw the gold that had been withdrawn, but she had no idea what had happened to it since then. Turning to the food preparation, Margaret said that she prepared most of it herself. By the end of her illness, all Miss Barrow could take was the occasional cup of tea, barley water, milk, soda water or Valentine's meat juice. Finally she confirmed that Eliza Barrow died between 6.00 a.m. and 7.00 a.m. on September 14th.

After the death, some of the family had left London for the coast. Annie Henderson lived at Riveria Drive, Southchurch, Southend-on-Sea and she told of various visits that had been paid to her house. On the Wednesday or Thursday before the August Bank Holiday, two of the children, Ada and Frederick, had come to stay for two weeks. On September 14th they returned, with Ernie Grant. The next day, sixteen-year-old Margaret came down and Annie believed that Mr and Mrs Seddon were also in the area, but staying elsewhere. The children finally left Southend on September 28th.

What had happened to the gold Eliza Barrow had had in the chest in her bedroom? Was there any evidence that Frederick Seddon, or his wife, had misappropriated it? Various witnesses were called to show that Margaret Ann Seddon had changed a number of £5 notes at local shops. Laura Bishop, for instance, was a draper's assistant in Seven Sisters Road and she knew Mrs Seddon as Mrs Scott. She had cashed several banknotes at the shop, writing on the back "Mrs Scott, 18 Eversholt Road, Stroud Green". That address was in fact occupied by Charles Forder and though he did let out rooms, he had never had a guest named Scott, and did not know Mrs Seddon. This evidence was useful only in that it showed Mrs Seddon as someone who had used a false name. There was no link between the missing gold and the banknotes that had been cashed.

More important perhaps was the evidence of Charles James Crisfield, the Assistant Secretary of the National Freehold Land and Building Society at 25 Moorgate Street. Frederick Seddon had taken out a mortgage of £220 on 63 Tollington Park, on November 27th, 1909. On September 19th, 1911, just five days after Miss Barrow's death, Seddon had written to the Society asking how much it would cost to pay back the loan. The letter was answered but no further action on the repayment was taken.

One day earlier, however, on September 18th, Seddon had filled out a form applying for three shares in the Society. These cost £30 each and Seddon paid for them on September 19th, in gold. Later he bought three more shares, and paid for these in banknotes.

There was other evidence that Miss Barrow's property had been stolen after her death. Thomas Wright was a jeweller of 400-402 Holloway Road. On September 15th, Frederick Seddon had called at his shop and bought a diamond ring, which he asked to have enlarged so that it would fit his finger. Later that same day, Seddon, together with his wife, was back with a gold English lever watch. It bore a white dial and Seddon wanted it replacing with a gold or gilt one. He also wanted an inscription removed. That inscription read "E. J. Barrow 1860" and the watch had since been identified as one which belonged to the dead woman.

If Miss Barrow had been poisoned, who had purchased the arsenic which was used? Walter Thorley ran a chemist's shop from 27 Crouch Hill. On Saturday, August 26th, a young girl, who he thought was about fifteen, had come into his shop and purchased a threepence packet of Mather's fly-papers. There were six papers in such a packet. After being spoken to by the police, Thorley had attended an identity parade and picked out young Margaret Seddon.

The prosecution were also alleging that there had been undue haste in seeing that Miss Barrow was interred. William Nodes was an undertaker operating from 78 Stroud Green Road. He had known Seddon since 1901, and had acted for the family before. At 11.30 a.m., on September 14th, Seddon came into the office and said an old lady had died and he wished to make arrangements for her funeral. He added, "It mustn't be expensive" and went on to say that he had only found four pounds and ten shillings in her room and the doctor had to be paid out of that. Nodes agreed to a four pound funeral.

After agreeing a price, Nodes accompanied Seddon back to Tollington Park, to measure up the body. He found that there was a most offensive smell about the place and so suggested that it might be better if the body were moved to his mortuary. Seddon agreed and the arrangements were made. The funeral left Stroud Green Road at 2.15 p.m. on the Saturday. Mr Nodes, however, had one further interesting piece of information to impart. Frederick Seddon left instructions with him that a lock of hair should be cut from Miss Barrow's head. He had done as instructed and given it to Seddon in an envelope.

Seddon had claimed that he had written to Frank Vonderahe to tell him of his cousin's death. That had been partly confirmed by his daughter, Margaret. However, if such a letter had indeed been posted, it had been addressed to 31 Eversholt Road, the only address which Seddon had for Mr Vonderahe. William Dell was now called and said that he had moved into 31 Eversholt Road on September 1st, 1911. Since then, only one letter, a circular, had arrived addressed in the name of Vonderahe. William had written "Not Known" on the envelope and handed it in at the Post Office. However, this evidence was only partly confirmed by William's wife, Eleanor Frances Dell. She did recall the circular but claimed that one or two other letters had also arrived for the Vonderahes. However, nothing had arrived around September 14th.

Medical evidence was given by Bernard Spilsbury. He had performed the post-mortem on November 15th. Upon removing the coffin lid he saw some greenish red staining on the bottom of the coffin and on the pillow upon which Miss Barrow's head rested. A handkerchief had been tied around the head and chin, with a knot on top of the head. The body was that of a well-nourished woman, five feet four inches in height. The entire surface of the body was stained green and Spilsbury found no evidence of disease in the heart, lungs, liver, spleen or kidneys. The condition of the alimentary canal was consistent with death from gastro-enteritis, but the remarkable preservation of the body rendered it more likely that death was due to some irritant poison.

Various internal organs and samples had been examined by Dr William Henry Willcox, who also assisted Spilsbury at the post-mortem. He had found arsenic in all the organs, to various degrees, and estimated that there had been a total of 2.01 grains in the entire body. On November 29th, he had made a further examination of the body and taken samples of hair, skin and nails. These too contained arsenic and in his opinion, a fatal dose had been administered within two or three days of Miss Barrow's death. In addition, Dr Willcox had obtained some of the fly-papers purchased by Margaret Seddon. In one paper he found 4.17 grains of arsenic, in the other 3.8 grains. Finally, Dr Willcox contradicted Dr Sworn, claiming that arsenic would have caused diarrhoea and that the stools would have had an offensive smell.

Frederick Henry Seddon gave testimony on his own behalf. He said that Miss Barrow came to live in his house in July 1910, having obtained the rooms through Gilbert's the Estate Agents. She took four rooms at a rent of twelve shillings per week, arriving with Ernest Grant and Mr and Mrs Hook, Mr Hook being the boy's uncle.

Soon after her arrival, Miss Barrow took exception to something Mr Hook did. He and his wife had taken Ernie out for the day, leaving Miss Barrow to fend for herself. She complained about this and after some argument, asked the Hooks to leave. Seddon, acting upon her instructions, made them vacate the premises.

In October of that year, Miss Barrow had shown him a document relating to the Buck's Head public house in Camden Town. She held a lease on the place, with some sixteen or eighteen years left to run, but she was not satisfied with her investment. She also mentioned that she had some India Stock, which had once brought in £108 a year but which now brought in only £94. She had heard that one of her friends had purchased an annuity and now had no such concerns. She expressed a desire to have something similar but did not want to involve any of her family as they had behaved so badly towards her.

In due course, Seddon granted Miss Barrow an annuity on the Buck's Head and the shop next door. The following January he did the same with the India Stock, and in addition to her £3 a week, Miss Barrow also now lived rent free, thus saving herself another twelve shillings. Referring to his own dealings, Seddon said that after he sold the India Stock he purchased fourteen houses for himself. These would yield him £8 a week in rent.

Seddon then told the court of Miss Barrow's last illness and said that on September 11th, she had asked about making a will. That document was signed and witnessed between 6.00 p.m. and 7.00 p.m., that night. He had visited her every night during her illness and was with her when she died. He had certainly not administered any poison to Miss Barrow and was not responsible for her death. He had no idea what had happened to the gold that she was supposed to have.

On March 14th, the jury retired to consider their verdict. They took one hour to decide that Margaret Ann Seddon was not guilty, but that Frederick Seddon was guilty as charged. Asked if he had anything to say, Seddon referred to the fact that he and the trial judge belonged to the same brethren, Freemasonry, but this did not prevent Mister Justice Bucknill from sentencing Seddon to death.

An appeal was lodged on the grounds that there was no proof that it had been Seddon who administered the poison, but the judges ruled that the evidence was sufficient to show that it must have been Seddon, and so Seddon was hanged at Pentonville on

Thursday, April 18th, by John Ellis and Thomas Pierrepoint. In his last letter to his sister, Seddon maintained that he would die an innocent man.

It seems reasonable to assume that Frederick Henry Seddon stole some of Eliza Barrow's property after her death. However, there are no indications that she was cajoled or manoeuvred into signing over her property for the annuity, as professional men dealing with the transfers reported no signs of duress or uncertainty. It is certain that Eliza was poisoned, but it had been sixteen-year-old Margaret who actually purchased the fly-papers. It is of course possible that if Seddon were the killer, he might have involved his own daughter in the crime, but surely this is unlikely? There is also the fact that this clever man, who it is alleged perpetrated a fraud lasting more than a year in order to obtain all Miss Barrow's property, before murdering her to end the annuity, then put his own neck in the noose by telling the undertaker to save some of Miss Barrow's hair. Why also did he not have the body cremated, if he had something to hide? He must have known that sooner or later, one or more of the Vonderahes would ask some very awkward questions.

So if Frederick Seddon did not poison Eliza Barrow, who did? Both Mrs Seddon and her daughter had the opportunity to kill, but there was one other person who could have administered that fatal dose of arsenic, and that was Miss Barrow herself. The fly-papers were the type that had to be soaked in water and Mrs Seddon had admitted that these papers had been scattered around Miss Barrow's room at her own request. Just before she died, those papers had all been placed in one large bowl, which was located close to where Miss Barrow slept. Could she have drunk this liquid deliberately or accidentally?

It is true to say that the annuity, the missing gold, and Seddon's business dealings created a great deal of suspicion, so much so that he and he alone was held to have a motive for murder. However, there is at least a doubt that Frederick Seddon administered that poison, and for this reason, he should not have been hanged.

Ernest Edwin Kelly

12

Hanged at Manchester, Wednesday, December 17th, 1913
For the murder of Daniel Wright Bardsley, at Oldham

ONE of the duties of night-watchman James Greaves was to check on the booksellers and stationers situated at 43 Yorkshire Street, Oldham. The early morning of Sunday, July 27th, 1913, was no different and at 12.30 a.m., James checked the back of the premises and found the door secure. He then continued on his rounds.

At 3.00 a.m., James Greaves was again at the rear of the booksellers, but this time all was certainly not well. The back door was still closed but when James put his thumb on the latch, the door opened. James pushed the door gently but it would only move for a distance of about six inches. There was something on the floor preventing it from opening any further, and when James forced his head through the narrow gap, he saw two human feet.

Pushing a little harder, James managed to force his way into the shop and found the proprietor, fifty-four-year-old Daniel Wright Bardsley, lying in a pool of blood. To one side of the poor man's head lay an Indian club, and to the other, a dumb-bell. Someone had brutally attacked Mr Bardsley. Touching nothing, James Greaves left the shop and ran to fetch the police.

It was 3.15 a.m. when Greaves arrived at the police station and told Inspector William Johnson what he had found in Yorkshire Street. Both men then went back to the shop and Johnson made a careful examination of the scene.

Daniel Bardsley's feet were now some fourteen inches from the back door. His head was two feet four inches away from some stone steps that led into the shop itself. The man was fully dressed but his hat lay between his head and the steps, indicating that he perhaps had been about to leave the premises for the night when he was attacked.

Bardsley's head was covered in blood. His right arm was drawn up towards his shoulder so that his hand was level with his breast. The left arm lay stretched out by his side, with the hand resting on his abdomen. Under the right shoulder lay one end of the dumb-bell, the rest projecting outwards. Close to the body were a number of letters stamped and ready for posting, again signifying that Bardsley was on his way out when his assailant struck. As for the motive for this terrible crime, that was plain to see, for the cash register drawer was open and empty. Later that morning, when the body was moved, one more significant find was made, for beneath Bardsley's corpse lay a piece of cloth, heavily bloodstained.

Daniel Bardsley had had three employees working for him in the shop; two of these, Annie Leach and Clara Hall, were soon interviewed by the police. Annie said that she had worked for Mr Bardsley for the past eleven years. On the night of Saturday, July 26th, she and Clara had left the shop by the back door at 10.30 p.m. At that time, their employer was alive and well and working upstairs. Half an hour before this, at 10.00 p.m., the iron gates had been placed onto the front of the shop by the third employee, seventeen-year-old Edward Hilton. He had only worked in the shop for three weeks and Mr Bardsley had been far from satisfied with his work.

This testimony was confirmed by Clara Hall, but she was also able to state that during the morning of July 26th, Mr Bardsley had sent her to Mr Hirst's shop nearby, where she picked up six gold rings on approval. These had not been found by the police and so, in all probability, had been taken by the killer. Finally, Clara was able to say that Hilton had left before her, at around 10.10 p.m.

One of the officers involved in investigating the murder was Detective Constable Charles Arthur Jones. He arrived at the shop premises at 10.15 a.m., on July 27th, to find the three employees who had turned up for work as usual. At 10.30 a.m., Jones spoke to Edward Hilton and asked him to accompany him to the police station for further questioning. Hilton readily complied.

As the two men neared the police station, they encountered Detective Inspector Piggott, who asked Hilton what time he had left the shop the previous night. Hilton confirmed that it was at 10.10 p.m, after he had received his wages. He had then caught a tram in front of the shop and gone to meet a friend in the Market Place. Hilton was unable to give the name of this friend, but said that he lived in West End Street.

Whilst Hilton was held at the police station, Constable Jones went to his home at 105 Manchester Street, where he took possession of the clothes which Hilton had been wearing on the night of the attack on Daniel Bardsley. Later, after being questioned about his movements on July 26th, Hilton finally admitted that he had robbed Mr Bardsley but denied having killed him. This Hilton blamed on his partner in crime, twenty-year-old Ernest Edwin Kelly.

Later that same night, Hilton took the police to 119 Ward Street, where Kelly lived, and pointed him out to the police officers. Kelly muttered "Come into the front room and don't let my mother hear". Once inside this room, Kelly continued "I will show you where I put all I got". He then took the officers into the backyard and pointed out a spot near the outside toilet wall. There the police found four of the gold rings, nine shillings and sixpence in silver and one shilling and eightpence in copper. Both men were then escorted back to the police station and charged with murder.

In reply to the charge, Hilton replied "Not guilty. I never touched him with the club. I never touched him with anything. I gave him a drink, that's all." Kelly, though, replied "Guilty for me. I hit him with the club and then threw it down." Kelly then pointed to Hilton before continuing, "He hit him twice with the club and then ran upstairs".

The trial of Ernest Edward Kelly and Edward Wild Hilton took place before Mr Justice Avory, at Manchester, on November 24th, 1913. Mr Gordon Hewart and Mr Henriques appeared for the prosecution, whilst Kelly was defended by Mr Ryecroft.

Detective Inspector Piggott told the court of his initial interview with Hilton. Later, after he had been charged, Hilton said "If you will come with me, I will show you where I have hidden my share of the money". Hilton then took the inspector to Painter Street, where he indicated a dark passageway where there was a hole in the wall. Inside was a handkerchief and when this was unwrapped, Piggott found twenty-five shillings and sixpence in silver, fourpence in copper and the two missing gold rings. Back at the police station, the Indian club was produced and Kelly admitted, "That's mine. I took it to the shop when I went to meet Hilton. I left it in the shop." Ownership of this club was also confirmed by Harry Edwin Kelly, the prisoner's brother, who said it had been lying in their back yard for several years.

Medical evidence was given by Doctor Robert Ashton Jackson, who had performed the post-mortem on July 27th. He said that Bardsley's skull had been extensively fractured, that considerable force had been used and that at least two blows had been struck. As to who struck those fatal blows, the testimony of the two defendants was conflicting to say the least.

Hilton began by saying that he had turned eighteen on August 9th, 1913, less than two weeks after the murder. He had only known Kelly for a few weeks prior to the attack on Mr Bardsley, but admitted that the two of them spent most nights together.

On July 25th, they had agreed to go to Hollingwood Wakes the next day. On the 26th, at around 10.00 p.m., he had seen Kelly in the yard behind the shop and confirmed that he would go to the Wakes with him, when he finished work. Kelly asked him if he had any money and Hilton replied "Not until I get my wages". Kelly went on to ask if Bardsley had any money, and when Hilton confirmed that there was some upstairs in the safe, Kelly suggested attacking him. He then added that he had to go home first, but would be back in a few minutes.

At 10.10 p.m., Hilton saw Kelly in the yard again. They then hid together until they saw Clara Hall and Annie Leach leave. After waiting a couple of minutes to make sure that the girls were not coming back, Hilton went into the shop, unaware that Kelly had followed him.

Inside the back room, Mr Bardsley saw Hilton and asked what he was doing back there. Hilton replied that he had left his apron behind and was told to go into the shop to get it. Whilst in there, Hilton heard a commotion, and going back into the other room he saw Mr Bardsley falling against the steps. Kelly was standing over him, the club in his hand.

Rather than showing concern for his employer, Hilton shouted, "Wait a bit till I get out of the shop or else I'll get catched [sic]". Kelly ignored this and struck Bardsley again, on the left side of his face. He then raised the club for a third time, whereupon Hilton tried to stop him, but Kelly ignored his pleas and delivered a third blow down onto Bardsley's head.

At this point, Kelly dropped the club and Hilton picked it up and placed it on top of a box. Looking down, he saw that his hand was now covered in blood. Kelly, meanwhile, had run upstairs, in order to attack the safe, so Hilton followed him. From upstairs, Hilton could hear Bardsley moaning so he went downstairs, got a tin cup, filled it with water and gave the injured man a drink. He then called up to Kelly "Come down and leave the safe, Mr Bardsley is trying to get up".

After a minute or so, Kelly came downstairs, picked up the club and made to strike Bardsley again. This time, Hilton grabbed his arm and stopped him but Kelly pulled away and hit Bardsley for a fourth time. Then, for some reason, he told Hilton to get a cloth and wipe the blood off Bardsley's face. He did so but then Kelly told him to stuff the cloth into Bardsley's mouth, so that he would not be able to call out for help. It was Kelly who then rifled through Bardsley's pockets, found the rings and money, and handed some to Hilton.

Under cross-examination, however, Hilton admitted that Mr Bardsley had sacked him that night and informed him that he had to leave the following Saturday. He also admitted that he knew about the gold rings, having seen them earlier that day. Finally, Hilton agreed that he had tried to buy a gun three weeks before the murder, but gave the somewhat unlikely explanation that he wanted this so that he could have his picture taken at a studio in Manchester, dressed as a cowboy.

The time came for Kelly to give his version of events. He began by saying that on July 25th, the night before the murder, he and Hilton had gone to the cinema together. As they separated after the show, Hilton asked Kelly to meet him near the shop at 9.50 p.m., the following night. He gave no reason for the request.

At 9.50 p.m., on July 26th, Kelly went to Yorkshire Street and stood waiting opposite the shop. He saw Hilton and asked him if he was going to the Wakes and Hilton replied that he would, once he had his wages. He then added, "I think Bardsley's going to sack me but he has not said anything yet. He will be in by himself tonight, after they have all gone." Puzzled, Kelly asked Hilton why he had said that and Hilton replied that he wanted to rob him, asking Kelly if he had anything they might hit Bardsley with. Kelly told him about the Indian club and Hilton told him to go home and fetch it.

Arriving back at Yorkshire Street, Kelly found the yard door to the shop open and Hilton waiting for him. He asked for the club and Kelly handed it over. They then hid, waiting for the two ladies to leave. Once they had, Hilton suggested that they both take their boots off, so that they would not make a noise. Having done so, they then went into the shop and waited for Bardsley to come downstairs. After some ten minutes, Bardsley came down and locked the back door. The room was quite dark and both

Hilton and Kelly were hiding. This explained how the night-watchman, James Greaves, had found the door locked at 12.30 a.m.

Bardsley, meanwhile, had gone back upstairs and Hilton suggested that they should swap jackets so that his employer would not recognize him on Monday morning. He also handed the club back to Kelly, before going to hide underneath the stairs.

In due course, Bardsley came back downstairs and Hilton shouted, "Hands up!" Rather than comply, Bardsley rushed for the gaslight and turned it up before making a dash for the back door. He had apparently forgotten that it was locked and having failed to open it, ran back into the shop, stumbling as he did so. Kelly swung the club and struck Bardsley on the shoulder, but then immediately threw the club to the ground.

Bardsley's nose was bleeding but he was not seriously injured and was in the act of pulling himself to his feet when Hilton picked up the club and hit him. He dropped the club and went through Bardsley's pockets, before going into the shop, leaving Kelly with the injured man. Kelly heard the cash register ring as Hilton opened it, before both men went upstairs to see if they could open the safe. Whilst Hilton tried to open it, Kelly went back downstairs and gave Bardsley a drink of water. It was also he, Kelly, who mopped Bardsley's face.

Leaving the shop, the two men pulled on their boots and left the yard but as they were walking down the passageway, Hilton announced that he had forgotten something and went back. Kelly saw Hilton go into the shop again and then walked on to Rock Street. Some ten minutes later he saw Hilton by the Market Hotel and they then walked to a public toilet in Newland Street, where they divided the spoils.

If Kelly was telling the truth, then he was not guilty of murder. It was true that he and Hilton had acted together and if Hilton had struck the fatal blow whilst the two were together then Kelly would be equally as guilty of murder. If, however, Bardsley had still been alive when they left the shop, and Hilton had gone back to kill the shopkeeper, then Kelly had played no part in the murder itself.

The key, perhaps, was the piece of cloth that had been used to mop some of the blood from Bardsley's face. According to Hilton, this had been left stuffed in the victim's mouth, whilst Kelly claimed that the last time he saw it, the cloth was lying over Bardsley's face. If Hilton had returned to strike Bardsley again he would not have needed to remove the cloth in order to do so. The fact that the cloth was found beneath the body suggests the possibility that Bardsley was trying to pull himself up again when Hilton re-entered, hit him again, and Bardsley then fell onto the cloth.

The jury retired and returned to announce that they had found both men guilty of murder. Both were then sentenced to death. Hilton, though, managed to escape the noose. Evidence had been called to show that he had been mentally defective since childhood and he had only been seventeen at the time the crime took place. As a result, on December 16th, his sentence was commuted to one of life imprisonment.

The people of Oldham were incensed. They had long considered that if anything, Hilton was the guiltier of the two, and yet he would not now face the gallows. A large crowd gathered outside Oldham Town Hall demanding that Kelly too should be reprieved. The Mayoress wrote a personal plea to the Queen and deputations were made to the Home Secretary. None of this had any effect.

On the morning of the execution, a large crowd walked the seven miles to Strangeways prison, Manchester and although a massive police presence kept them away from the prison gates, they still managed to make their dissatisfaction plain. Meanwhile, inside the prison, Kelly was hanged by John Ellis. In his last letter to his parents, written just hours before he died, Kelly maintained his innocence and claimed again that the fatal blows had been struck by Hilton.

13 Thomas Clinton

Hanged at Manchester, Wednesday, March 21st, 1917
For the murder of Henry Lynch, at Barrow in Furness

O N Saturday, January 13th, 1917, Sergeant Job Barrow was supervisor of the guard at the Cavendish Dock camp of the Royal Welsh Fusiliers at Barrow in Furness. Each guard comprised twelve privates and two non-commissioned officers and at 2.30 p.m., a new guard came on duty. One of the privates in that particular guard was twenty-eight-year-old Thomas Clinton, a native of Manchester.

Almost as soon as the men assembled in the guardroom, Sergeant Barrow heard Clinton complaining to the orderly officer that he had not yet had his dinner. There were no other complaints, and no threats issued. Clinton was merely pointing out that he appeared to have been overlooked at mealtime.

Clinton was due to go on sentry duty at 7.00 p.m. In the time between starting guard duty and sentry duty, all the men were supposed to remain in the guardroom and not leave without express permission from either the sergeant, or one of the officers. If such permission were granted, for any reason, the man had instructions to replace his rifle in the rack on the guardroom wall. He was certainly not allowed to leave with his rifle, unless actually going on sentry duty.

As Sergeant Barrow busied himself with his own duties he did not see a lone figure leave the guardroom, at some time before 3.15 p.m. The first he knew of anything out of the ordinary happening was at some time between 3.15 p.m. and 3.30 p.m., when Barrow heard a single shot ring out. Reacting instantly, Sergeant Barrow turned out the guard as he heard a shrill whistle from one of the sentries, a signal that something was amiss. Within moments, Thomas Clinton was being led back inside the guardroom, under escort. The private had no rifle with him and Sergeant Barrow listened in amazement as details of what had taken place were outlined to him.

It appeared that Private Clinton had simply marched into the company office with his rifle, attracted the attention of Company Sergeant Major Henry Lynch, and then fired one bullet into his throat. Lynch was badly wounded and, despite prompt medical attention, soon succumbed to his wound. Later that same day, Clinton was formally charged with wilful murder.

Thomas Clinton appeared before Mr Justice Shearman at Manchester assizes on February 15th. The prosecution case rested in the hands of Mr A. H. Maxwell, who was assisted by Mr Lindon Riley. Clinton was represented by Mr Gilbert Jordan.

Thomas Francis Albertoni Webb was the captain of 'B' Company of the Fusiliers and he stated that the dead man had been thirty-nine years of age and a serving soldier for the past twenty-one or twenty-two years. At around 3.30 p.m., on January 13th, Captain Webb had been in his quarters which were about twenty yards from the company office. He heard a rifle shot that sounded as if it had come from the orderly room, so he went out to investigate. He saw Sergeant Major Lynch, lying on the parade ground, bleeding from a wound in the upper part of his body. At the time, Lynch was being held upright by Regimental Sergeant Major Williams.

Having been told by other witnesses what had happened, Captain Webb went immediately to the guardroom where he saw Clinton, under guard. Seeing that the man responsible was secure, Webb then went to the orderly room where he found a rifle outside, leaning up against the wall. He took possession of the weapon, later handing it over to Inspector Duckworth when the police arrived. In the presence of the inspector, Webb removed four live cartridges and one spent cartridge from the magazine.

Lance Corporal William John Davies was in the company office between 3.00 p.m. and 3.30 p.m. Sergeant Major Lynch was sitting at a table writing and Davies was facing the door when he saw Clinton walk in, holding his rifle in front of him in the on-guard position. Clinton stopped opposite to where Lynch sat and said "Now then Sergeant Major". Almost immediately a shot rang out, as the muzzle of the gun was some two or three feet from Lynch.

Sergeant Major Lynch turned to his left and threw his hands up to his throat. His head dropped forward on to his chest. Meanwhile, Clinton went back outside and as Davies followed, he saw him drop the rifle and put his hands up to his face. Davies reported the incident to a sentry, who blew his whistle to summon the guard. Two of the guards appeared, took Clinton into custody and marched him towards the guardroom.

Turning around, Davies then saw the Sergeant Major stagger out of the company office and collapse into the arms of Regimental Sergeant Major Williams. Under cross-examination, however, Lance Corporal Davies admitted that Clinton had walked into the company office at a normal pace and his voice had not sounded threatening when he spoke those few words to Lynch. In fact, he sounded much more like he was merely trying to attract Lynch's attention, and Davies thought he might have come in to complain about the rifle.

Another man inside the company office at the time of the shooting was Private William Smithies. He confirmed much of the evidence given by Lance Corporal Davies, whom he had followed out of the office. Lynch was right behind Smithies, walking under his own steam, but collapsed as soon as he reached the parade ground. Smithies caught the Sergeant Major but then the shock of the incident caused him to faint himself. Finally he admitted that although he had heard the rifle go off, he did not actually see Clinton pull the trigger.

Private William Barry was on duty outside the guardroom, which was situated just six or seven yards from the company office. He saw Clinton as he passed by, walking towards the office. Barry testified that as Clinton passed the window of the office before actually reaching the door, he would have been able to see into the office and would know who was inside.

Barry confirmed that as Clinton turned to enter the office, his rifle was in the on-guard position. Three seconds later, Barry heard the report of the weapon and seconds after that, Clinton came out, put his hands to his face and then fell to his knees.

Lance Corporal Davies followed and told him that Sergeant Major Lynch had been shot, so Barry blew his whistle to call out the guard.

As Clinton was taken away, the Sergeant Major staggered out of the office, with his hands held up to his chest or throat. He cried out "I am dead. I am dead." and then fell down, three yards away from where Barry stood. Barry then confirmed that he had never heard Clinton express any ill will towards Lynch.

Sergeant Barrow told the court that every man on guard duty was issued with a rifle and twenty rounds of ammunition in four clips of five bullets. Three of these clips, totalling fifteen rounds, would be placed in the ammunition pouch whilst the last clip of five bullets would be in the rifle magazine. However, no man should have had a cartridge in the chamber of his rifle.

The defence was suggesting that the shooting had been accidental and one way of accounting for the gun being discharged would be if the weapon were dirty. Questioned about this, Barrow said that the rifle Clinton used should not have been dirty as it was the duty of each guard to ensure that the weapons were clean before handing them over to the next man. Barrow admitted, however, that there had been occasions in the past when a man had been issued with a dirty rifle.

Doctor George Alexander had his practice in Barrow in Furness and he was called by the military hospital at about 3.30 p.m. on the day in question. He arrived at the barracks between 3.40 p.m. and 3.45 p.m., to find Lynch lying on the floor of the company office, having been carried back in there by some of the guard. Lynch had a bullet wound in the lower part of his neck, from which blood was oozing. He was still alive but died within a few minutes.

Inspector Charles William Duckworth saw Clinton in the guardroom at 3.50 p.m. on January 13th. He identified himself as a policeman and cautioned Clinton before arresting him on a charge of shooting Lynch with intent to murder. Clinton made no reply. He was then taken to the central police station where he was alleged to have said, "Will you answer me one question? Did the bullet strike him? That's what I want to know. He has been a scamp to everybody in the Company. I am sorry to say he has been a bad 'un." Shortly after this, Inspector Duckworth discovered that Lynch had died from his injuries. He cautioned Clinton for a second time and then charged him with murder. Again Clinton made no reply.

Clinton, though, had made a written statement. In this he said that at 2.30 p.m. on January 13th, he had been warned that he would be needed to mount guard by the Orderly Sergeant. He was informed that he would be required to form part of the TNT guard, whereupon Clinton said that he had a complaint to make.

After the Orderly Officer had inspected the guard, Clinton told the Sergeant to inform the Officer that he wished to speak to him. When Clinton was asked what the problem was, he complained that he had not yet been given any dinner. The Orderly Officer told him to fall in again and then instructed the Sergeant to change him from the TNT guard to the Cavendish Dock guard, as it would be easier for him to get something to eat there.

Clinton marched to the Cavendish Dock guardroom where Sergeant Barrow was in charge. The old guard was dismissed and Clinton and his fellow soldiers were issued with their rifles. The men then went into the guardroom where they took off their water bottles and haversacks and were given twenty rounds of ammunition each. Clinton said that he loaded five rounds into his magazine and then without thinking, walked across to the company office to see Sergeant Major Lynch about his dinner.

Entering the office, Clinton said "Now then Sergeant Major" to attract Lynch's attention. Lynch looked up and gave Clinton a dirty look and before he knew what had happened, the gun went off accidentally. Clinton went on to say that if he had wanted to kill Lynch, he would have easily been able to choose a time when there were no witnesses as the Sergeant Major often passed him whilst he was alone on duty. The statement ended, "All I have left to say now is the people in Barrow won't look upon me as a murderer when they know the truth, they will understand things, and the lads in the camp will also do. I don't think I have one enemy in the whole camp."

Some of this statement was confirmed by other witnesses. Second Lieutenant John Henry Bennett had been the Orderly Officer on January 13th. Bennett would normally have been present at the hut where Clinton should have had his dinner, accompanied by Orderly Sergeant Jones, but he had other duties that day, which left Jones to supervise the meal alone.

At 2.30 p.m., Bennett inspected the guard, after which Clinton stepped forward saying that he had a complaint to make. Sergeant Jones asked for the details and then informed Bennett that Clinton had not been given any dinner. Bennett asked Jones, within Clinton's hearing, if the private had made a complaint at dinnertime and Jones said that he had not.

Bennett told Clinton to fall in whilst he investigated what had happened. He then told Sergeant Jones that Clinton should be placed on the Cavendish Dock guard so he would be closer to Bennett whilst he made enquiries. The guard moved off and Bennett told Jones to try to find out why the soldier had not been fed, and to try to arrange a meal at once.

Bennett then went to the company office, where he saw Captain Webb and mentioned the matter to him. Webb, though, seemed to be more interested in holding a Court of Enquiry on an absentee and a few minutes later, Bennett and Webb left the office together. At this time, Clinton was at the door of the guardroom and Bennett pointed him out to Webb, saying that this was the man who had complained of having no dinner. Webb said he would investigate and Bennett left him to it.

Sergeant William David Jones was the Orderly Sergeant to whom Clinton made his complaint. He began his testimony by stating that he had supervised the feeding of somewhere between eighty and ninety men at 12.45 p.m. He then went off for his own dinner. At 2.10 p.m., the guard fell in at the lower camp and Clinton complained that he had not been fed. After the inspection by Second Lieutenant Bennett, Clinton stepped forward out of the rank and beckoned to Jones, telling him that he wished to speak to the Orderly Officer.

After explaining to the officer that he had not had his dinner, Clinton was told to march to the Cavendish Dock camp whilst Jones was told to go to the lower camp and arrange some food for him. Jones began to obey that order but had only gone forty or fifty yards when Sergeant Major Lynch called him back to give evidence at an enquiry into a deserter. Later he went to the mess to ask about Clinton and discovered that there had been six dinners short that day. These had later been served to six men and Clinton was not one of them. Whilst at the lower camp, Jones heard that there had been a shooting and when he returned to Cavendish Dock, he found Lynch lying on the ground, receiving medical attention. Jones was also able to state that when he made his complaint, Clinton did not appear to be in a bad temper.

For Clinton to be guilty of murder, the prosecution had to show a motive. For that reason they called Sergeant David Edwin Palmer. On November 4th, 1916, Palmer had been stationed at Bebbington and at 2.00 p.m., was in the dining tent, doing some clerical work. Sergeant Major Lynch was also there, as was Clinton. Palmer stated that Clinton had been drunk and had become quarrelsome with the Mess Orderly. Lynch ordered him to be quiet but Clinton ignored him so Lynch had him taken to the guardroom. As he was being escorted away, Clinton struggled and as a result was later brought before the Company Officer, Captain Holden, and charged with being drunk in camp. As a result, Clinton got seven days and a fine of seven shillings and sixpence.

That Clinton held a grudge against Lynch seemed to be confirmed by the evidence of two policemen. Constable Ralph Townson had been on duty at the police station, keeping Clinton under observation, and claimed that he heard the prisoner say, "Did the bullet go near the Sergeant Major? It's a pity it did not kill him. He is a bastard."

Constable James Goad was also at the station when Clinton asked if the bullet had hit Lynch. Goad said he did not know, whereupon Clinton commented "He is a swine. It is a wonder he has not been laid out before. I was as near him as I am to you. I let go at him. He deserved all he got." The problem with both of these alleged statements is that Clinton was apparently asking if the bullet had struck Lynch after he had already been charged with murder! Does this suggest some manufacturing of evidence on the part of the police?

The only motive that the prosecution could suggest was that Clinton had held a grudge against Lynch, for two months, over a trivial offence. It ignored the fact that it would have been impossible to plan the murder, as Clinton was originally not even supposed to be a member of the guard at Cavendish Dock. A much more likely scenario is that Clinton, concerned over the fact that he had missed his dinner, saw Orderly Sergeant Jones marching off to sort the matter out, only for him to be recalled by Lynch. Wanting to know what was going on, he then went to ask Lynch about the delay. Added to this, the testimony of eye witnesses who said that Clinton did not have a menacing tone in his voice, and that he behaved perfectly normally up to the moment of the shooting, indicates that in all probability, Clinton was telling the truth when he claimed that this was an accident. As such, he should probably have been found guilty of manslaughter and sentenced accordingly. This avenue was closed off by the trial judge, Mr Justice Shearman, who astoundingly stated in his summing up that there could be no such verdict, presumably because of a point of law. The jury therefore had no choice but to either find Clinton guilty of murder or acquit him completely. With their hands thus tied, they had little alternative but to return a guilty verdict.

An appeal was lodged on the grounds that the trial judge had misdirected the jury as to the possibility of a manslaughter verdict. However, it was held by the Appeal Court that there had been no such misdirection, and so on Wednesday, March 21st, 1917, Thomas Clinton was hanged at Manchester prison by John Ellis. One cannot help but wonder if the ends of justice had really been served.

William Thomas Hodgson

14

Hanged at Liverpool, Thursday, August 16th, 1917
For the murder of his wife and his daughter,
both named Margaret, in Wallasey, Liverpool

T HERE were four people living in the semi-detached house at 16 Central Park Avenue, Wallasey, in Liverpool, in early 1917. In addition to thirty-four-year-old William Hodgson and his thirty-seven-year-old wife, Margaret, whom he had married in September 1910, there were also the two children – three-year-old Margaret, who had a birthday due on April 27th, and one-year-old Cyril.

By all accounts, the Hodgsons were an ordinary enough couple. Margaret stayed at home to look after the children and William worked as a buyer in the silk department of Robb Brothers, a drapers, in Birkenhead. And yet, on Monday, April 16th, this apparently ordinary family was to make headline news.

At 7.00 a.m, Thomas Robinson, the milkman, delivered a single pint, as he usually did. At this early hour, no one stirred in the Hodgson household and Mr Robinson noticed nothing out of the ordinary.

Next door to the Hodgsons, at number fourteen, lived Eleanor Yates Law and her husband, William. They had known the Hodgsons ever since the family had first moved into number sixteen, in August 1916, and Eleanor saw Margaret most days, though she seldom spoke to Mr Hodgson. There was nothing sinister in this, though. The two families were only on nodding terms even though Eleanor's own daughter often played with little Margaret.

It was around 7.40 a.m. when Eleanor Law rose from her bed and went downstairs. Going through to the kitchen and the pantry beyond, in order to prepare herself a cup of tea, she heard what sounded like a man's footsteps in the yard of number sixteen. She thought nothing of this at the time. William Hodgson habitually rose long before the rest of his family. He would make his own breakfast, then take his wife a cup of tea in bed before making up the fire in the kitchen. Eleanor simply assumed that Mr Hodgson was in his yard fetching some coal from the shed there.

Almost at the same time, Eleanor also heard a little girl's voice, which she assumed to be young Margaret. It seemed to come from either the kitchen or the scullery next door and consisted of the words, "Don't do that". There was no element of distress or anxiety in the child's voice.

At around 8.35 a.m., Eleanor heard a door bang. Again coming from number sixteen, it sounded either like the front door itself, or the inner door of the vestibule that led to the rest of the house. She knew that William Hodgson usually left for work at about 8.30 a.m., and simply presumed that it was him.

Thomas Robinson, the milkman, returned to Central Park Avenue that afternoon in order to collect any empty milk bottles. It was 3.30 p.m. when he arrived at number sixteen, but he could not get a reply to his repeated knocking. He tried the front door, found it open and knocked again on the inner glass door of the vestibule. Still there was no reply. Robinson then closed the front door and walked down the passageway that separated number sixteen from number eighteen. The gate that led into the yard was on the latch and Robinson looked into the yard but again there was no sign of Mrs Hodgson. Finally he closed the gate and left.

Eleanor Law was out for most of that afternoon and when she returned, she could hear baby Cyril crying next door. By 6.00 p.m., when the crying had still not stopped, Mrs Law decided to go next door to see if Mrs Hodgson needed some assistance.

Mrs Law began by knocking on the glass panel in the front door. When she received no reply, and the baby continued crying, she knocked on the inner door of the vestibule before actually opening it, knocking again and calling out for Mrs Hodgson. Still there was no reply.

Tentatively, Eleanor Law walked into the hallway and then on through the door at the far end, into the kitchen. She noticed that the fire was out but it was not until she looked on, into the scullery at the far side of the kitchen, that she saw the feet and part of the lower legs of a woman. Immediately, Eleanor turned on her heels and dashed from the house.

William Thomas Wells was a bricklayer and chimney sweep from Royston Avenue but just after 6.00 p.m., he happened to be walking down Central Park Avenue. He saw an ashen-faced Mrs Law run from number sixteen and stammer something about a body in the scullery. Wells now entered the house to investigate for himself.

Wells did not know the layout of the house so he first walked through the first doorway off the hall. This led into the front parlour and it was there that Wells noted a portmanteau lying on the floor. It was open and some items had been placed inside it, though Wells did not bother to check what they might be.

Leaving the front parlour and going through the next doorway, Wells found himself in the back parlour. There seemed to be nothing out of place there so he then took the third doorway off the hall, and finally entered the kitchen.

Looking around, the observant Wells noted a child's money box lying on the table, next to a woman's purse. Both appeared to be empty. The scullery door was only slightly open so Wells pushed it gently. The sight that met his eyes was to stay with him for the rest of his life.

114

On the floor lay a little girl's body, her head close to the sink in the corner and her feet close to the kitchen door. Close by lay Mrs Hodgson, with her head close to the gas oven and her feet close to her daughter's body. There was a good deal of blood and nearby lay what looked like the murder weapon, a heavily bloodstained axe.

The sound of baby Cyril crying still filled the air and Wells now ran upstairs to see if the boy had been hurt in any way. Fortunately, Cyril had not been injured but he had been alone for some hours. The poor baby was very wet and apparently extremely hungry. Gently Wells carried the boy downstairs and handed him over to another neighbour, seventeen-year-old Hannah Lancaster, who worked as a servant for Mrs Barrow and lived in at number twenty-two. Hannah noticed that baby Cyril was still dressed in his nightclothes and his face was very pale, as if he had been crying for a long time. She took him back to Mrs Barrow's and prepared a bottle of feed, which he drank down with enthusiasm.

The police were soon on the scene and started their detailed investigation. At 6.45 p.m., Dr Thomas William Adam Napier arrived. He noted that both bodies were lying on their backs. Mrs Hodgson had her arms lying across her chest and both bodies were stretched out full with their legs in line with their trunks. In addition to the large quantity of blood, there was also a good deal of brain tissue on the floor and both victims had suffered extensive head injuries. There were many splashes of blood both above and below the draining board, reaching as high as four feet six inches from the ground.

The scullery at 16 Central Park Avenue, where the bodies of Margaret Hodgson and her daughter were found on April 16th, 1917 (Public Record Office Ref. No. ASSI 65/22)

To the right side of Mrs Hodgson lay a hatchet, which later examination would show had been the murder weapon. The assailant had wielded the flat end of the axe in order to inflict the terrible wounds on the woman and her daughter. Dr Napier placed the time of death at eight to ten hours previously, that is, at some time between 8.45 a.m. and 10.45 a.m.

Even as the bodies were being wrapped prior to their removal on a wheeled stretcher, at around 7.30 p.m., Inspector John Bebbington noticed a man standing just inside the kitchen door. Naturally, Inspector Bebbington demanded to know what he wanted, but the man only replied, "What's up here?"

Bebbington assumed that this stranger was most likely the tenant of the house,

115

William Hodgson, and asked for confirmation. The man replied, "I am Mr Hodgson". The inspector gave no information to Hodgson but took him into the back parlour where Hodgson sat down, put his head into his hands and began to cry.

Bebbington and Hodgson were soon joined by Chief Inspector Morris, who told Hodgson not to get excited but confirmed, as if it were necessary, that there was something wrong. Morris then escorted Hodgson to the hallway where he pointed through the doorway into the front parlour where the portmanteau lay on the floor.

Hodgson persisted in wanting to know what was wrong but the Chief Inspector would only say that the Chief Constable knew more, so it would be best if Hodgson went to the police station with Detective Constable Frederick Robinson.

On the way to the police station, Hodgson sat between Constable Robinson and Constable Barnaby. On the journey, Hodgson said "You might tell me what's wrong", but was again told that the Chief Constable knew more. He did not speak again for the rest of the trip.

It was indeed the Chief Constable who told Hodgson that his wife and daughter were dead. He quickly added that the baby was alive and well but upon hearing the news, Hodgson again began to cry. The Chief Constable said that he would need some information and Hodgson then made a brief statement, outlining his movements that day.

According to that statement, Hodgson said he had left home for work at 8.30 a.m. that morning. His wife had just finished dressing their daughter and was about to go upstairs to dress the baby. Hodgson also told the Chief Constable that his wife had spoken about a gardener who had called at the house the previous Saturday, asking if the family wanted any work done. Margaret had informed the man that it was for her husband to make such decisions and told him to call back at some time before 8.30 a.m., or after 7.00 p.m., when William would be there. The police had already noticed that there were signs that the garden had recently been dug over, so this might have been significant.

The Chief Constable made careful notes and after Hodgson had finished making this initial statement, he asked if his wife's family might be informed that she was dead. He also asked that nothing be said about little Margaret's death, as it would upset them too much. Hodgson then asked if he would be allowed to spend that night at his own home. The Chief Constable said that under the circumstances, this would not be permitted.

At this stage, there was no question of arresting Hodgson and he was allowed to leave the station after he had been interviewed. Constable Robinson walked back to Central Park Avenue with Hodgson, noting that as soon as he was outside the station, Hodgson lit up a cigarette. Along the way they met Constable Short, who accompanied them back to Central Park Avenue where Hodgson was taken to Mrs Law's at number fourteen. As they arrived, Robinson asked Hodgson if he had a front door key to number sixteen and when he replied in the affirmative, asked that it be handed over. Hodgson did as he had been asked and then joined Mr and Mrs Law for a bite of supper.

116

Later that same evening, Hodgson was taken back to the police station where he made a detailed written statement. He was then charged with the murders of his wife and daughter.

William Thomas Hodgson was tried at Chester on July 13th, before Mr Justice Avory. He pleaded not guilty, denying vehemently that he had had anything to do with the deaths of his wife and child. All the evidence against him appeared to be purely circumstantial, even though the prosecution had what it believed was one of the oldest motives of all, another woman.

To begin with, the prosecution had to show that Hodgson had the opportunity to commit the murders. Under normal circumstances, a system of clocking on existed at Robb Brothers, where Hodgson worked. Winifred May Jenkins was a clerk at Robb's and she gave evidence that every employee had to register their start times each day. Hodgson had the staff number 'sixty-two', and according to the company records, his entries for the period from January 1st to April 21st, even though he was already in custody by this latter date, showed that the earliest he had arrived was 8.57 a.m., and the latest was 9.23 a.m., which occurred on April 3rd. Throughout that entire period, six days had passed without recorded times and unfortunately, one of those dates was April 16th. There was, therefore, no way to say with certainty what time the prisoner had arrived for work on the day of the murders.

There was also a discrepancy over the time that Hodgson had left home on the fateful morning. He, of course, claimed that he left at his usual time of 8.30 a.m., but this was disputed by the testimony of Eliza Godfrey Ward Westmore, who lived at 15 Central Park Avenue, the house opposite to Hodgson's. She claimed that she was in her front bedroom at 9.00 a.m. on the morning of April 16th when she heard a door bang. Looking through her window she saw Hodgson on his doorstep with a small parcel underneath one arm. As she watched, Hodgson buttoned up his dark overcoat, as the weather was rather bad. He then walked off down the street but stopped after a short distance to flick something off his trousers. He walked a few more steps and then stopped again to repeat the process, before finally continuing his journey.

Next, an attempt was made to show that Hodgson was indeed capable of such a brutal crime. Mary Ellen Smith, the mother of Margaret Hodgson, stated that she had often heard her daughter complain that he would stay out late on Wednesdays, often until 11.00 p.m. When Margaret tried to remonstrate with him about this, he would simply reply that he considered it his night out.

Mrs Smith also explained that Hodgson had a very bad temper. She stayed with them at Central Park Avenue from time to time and on one occasion his daughter had played up when he told her it was time to get out of the bath. Hodgson had slapped the little girl so hard on her bare back that the following day there was a black mark. At the time, Margaret had remarked to her mother "If you had not been here, I should have got that".

Under cross-examination, however, Mrs Smith admitted that Hodgson was unusually affectionate to his children, but she added that nevertheless, they were frightened of him, due to his short temper.

Those Wednesday nights when Hodgson stayed out late proved to be highly significant when Helena Llewellyn gave her testimony. Helena had been a waitress at Evan's cafe on Grange Road, Birkenhead and she explained that whilst working there she had met the prisoner about a year ago. They fell into conversation, one thing led to another and they began seeing each other, usually on Wednesday nights. Hodgson, however, had neglected to mention that he was a married man.

In early 1917, a visit to the doctor had confirmed that Helena was pregnant. A meeting was arranged between Helena, her mother and Hodgson where this information was passed on to him and he promised to stand by her. Repeatedly, Hodgson said that he would sort things out soon after Easter was over. Letters were produced confirming this and here, according to the prosecution, was the motive. Hodgson not only had another woman but she was pregnant by him and pressing him to do the decent thing. If he were to keep his promise, then his wife Margaret had to be removed one way or another.

So far the prosecution had intimated that there was a motive for Hodgson to kill his wife, that he had a bad temper and was therefore capable of such an act, and that he had had the opportunity since there was a dispute over when he left for work, and no proof that he had arrived on time. They now tried to link Hodgson directly with the crime itself.

After his arrest, various items of clothing had been taken from Hodgson and subsequently examined by Bernard Spilsbury, the Home Office pathologist. On Hodgson's trousers, Spilsbury had found two tiny bloodstains on the outer side of the left leg and three spots higher up on the same leg. There was also a single spot on the right leg.

On Hodgson's waistcoat, Spilsbury found six bloodstains, most of which he described as minute. There were four further stains on a blue serge coat and six on an overcoat. Turning to the boots Hodgson had worn on the day of the murder, Spilsbury said that he had found two small stains on the left but nothing on the right. In all, there were twenty-four small stains but Spilsbury also stated that in his opinion, these spots were in the form of clots and that the blood was clotted before it got onto the clothing.

Dr Napier had examined the bodies at the scene of the crime and also performed the post-mortem two days later. He formed the opinion that many violent blows had been struck and that in the case of both victims, most of these blows had been inflicted whilst the victim was lying on the ground. This implied that the killer had struck Margaret and her daughter, rendered them unconscious and then continued raining down blow after blow upon them whilst they lay helpless. Neither victim had eaten anything that day.

It did not take long for the jury to decide that Hodgson was guilty of murder. An appeal against the death sentence was heard on July 31st before the Lord Chief Justice,

Lord Isaacs, Lord Justice Coleridge and Mister Justice Low. The defence submitted that the conviction could not be sustained, but the judges felt that there was more than enough evidence to justify the conviction and the appeal was dismissed. Just sixteen days later, Hodgson was hanged by John Ellis, who was assisted by Edward Taylor.

In reviewing the evidence against Hodgson, one of the most crucial points is when the murders were committed and at what time Hodgson actually left for work. We have already seen that Mrs Law heard a door bang at 8.35 a.m. This agrees with Hodgson's claim that he left at his usual time of about 8.30 a.m. It does not, however, agree with the testimony of Mrs Westmore, who said she saw Hodgson leave at 9.00 a.m. Even if we assume that she was correct and 9.00 a.m. was the right time, it still only gave Hodgson a maximum of fifteen minutes to commit two murders, fake a robbery, clean himself up as best he could, and leave the house – because according to the medical evidence, the earliest time of death was 8.45 a.m.

Next there was the testimony of Hodgson's mother-in-law, which said that he had a temper and his family lived in fear of him. Mrs Law often passed the time of day with Margaret Hodgson, and their children played together. She said she had never seen any marks of violence on Margaret and even Mrs Smith herself admitted that Hodgson was an affectionate father.

If Hodgson were guilty of the murders then he had to have been an accomplished actor too. William Marshall Wilson worked as a warehouseman for Robb Brothers and he testified that he saw Hodgson at work on April 16th. There was nothing unusual in his demeanour throughout that day. In fact, Wilson had called at 16 Central Park Avenue on the Sunday, the day before the murders, to give the family a plant he had grown. The Hodgsons all seemed perfectly happy together.

Turning to April 16th, Wilson said that after work, he and Hodgson had called at the Charing Cross Hotel for a beer, something they frequently did. Still Hodgson's behaviour was perfectly normal and when they parted, at the corner of Wheatland Lane, Hodgson said he had to hurry home as he was baby-sitting whilst his wife and daughter went to the pictures together.

Bernard Spilsbury had found a number of small bloodstains on Hodgson's clothing. It might well be argued that such a murder should have splashed a good deal more blood onto his coat, boots and trousers, but it must also be recalled that Spilsbury described the blood as already clotted when it came into contact with the clothes. Could it not be that these blood spots were formed when Hodgson walked into his house that night?

We now come to Hodgson's motive for the murder, the fact that he had a lover and she was now pregnant. A number of letters which Hodgson had written to Miss Llewellyn were produced in court. The earliest was dated March 24th and the latest, April 14th. Whilst they are indeed penned in affectionate terms, they are full of excuses for him cancelling arranged meetings. If anything, they prove that Hodgson was trying to cool the relationship with Miss Llewellyn. In the final one, written just two days before the murders, he says "My Dear Lena, I was sorry I could not get down last night.

I was really glad to get into bed and I am no better today and if I am no different on Monday I shall not come next week at all, they will have to manage in my dept. I don't suppose the firm will thank me any more for it however I will let you know how I am on Monday if I cannot get down at night. Hope you are keeping better."

The letter was signed "Best love and kisses. Your ever loving boy, Tom." In all his letters, Hodgson had used a false address in Oliver Street, and always signed himself 'Tom'.

The fact remains that in this case, prosecution witnesses gave conflicting testimony as to times, the forensic evidence was inconclusive, Hodgson behaved perfectly normally afterwards and would only have had, at best, fifteen minutes to commit the crime, and there was evidence that his relationship with Helena Llewellyn was cooling. Was this enough to claim a man's life?

Henry Beckett (alias Perry)

15

Hanged at Pentonville prison, London, Thursday, July 10th, 1919
For the murder of four members of the Cornish family,
at Upton Park, London

CHARLES Henry Amey had lived at 11 Stukeley Road, Upton Park, London, for some years. He had known his neighbours at number thirteen, the Cornish family, for at least eight of those years.

It was 6.30 p.m., on Monday, April 28th, 1919, when Charles Amey returned from work. He walked through to the kitchen at the back of the house, in order to make himself a nice refreshing cup of tea to wash away the rigours of the day, but what was to happen in the next few moments would put all thoughts of tea from Amey's mind.

A man's voice called out "Mrs Amey" twice. The sound appeared to come from the garden at the back of the house so Charles opened the door and went out. As he did so, he saw forty-eight-year-old Walter Cornish clambering over the fence from number thirteen, his head covered in blood and an axe clutched in his hand. Cornish cried out "Look at my head!"

Startled, Charles Amey took the axe from Cornish and, looking at the injured man more closely, saw that there was blood oozing from wounds in his head and face. Amey's first thought was to render what practical assistance he could, so he grabbed a handkerchief and tried to staunch the flow of blood from the terrible wounds. Even as he did so, Amey noticed that one of Cornish's fingers had been chopped off so he took Cornish into the scullery where he took a cloth, tore it up and wrapped it around the bleeding man's hand. A blanket was also used to wrap Cornish's head.

It was clear that Walter Cornish was in need of urgent medical attention so Amey supported him as they walked to the nearest tram stop. On the journey to the hospital Amey asked, "Who has done this?" to which Cornish replied, "That soldier".

Charles Amey knew that until fairly recently, the Cornish family had had a guest staying with them, a man who was supposed to be some relative of Mrs Cornish. Persisting in his questioning, Amey asked, "How did it happen?" Cornish replied, "I went indoors and asked him where my wife and children were. He said they had gone to Upton Park station. I went into the scullery, put the frying pan on the gas ring, put a rasher of bacon in the pan and lit the gas. I then felt a blow on my head. I put my hand on my head and received another blow."

Amey did not press his neighbour any further but as they reached the hospital and got down from the tram, Cornish muttered "Mr Amey, when you go back you might go in my house and turn out the gas in case the place catches fire".

Amey handed Walter Cornish over to the tender care of the doctors and nurses at Queen Mary's Hospital, West Hammersmith. There he was treated by Dr William Carey. His patient was still conscious and able to give an account of how he had sustained his injuries, and before Amey left, Cornish also turned to him and sobbed "When you go back to the house I have an idea that he has done my wife and children in".

In due course, Charles Amey did return to Stukeley Road to find the front door to number thirteen closed. He was unsure what he should do but at 7.15 p.m., two police officers, alerted by the hospital, arrived at his house. Amey allowed them through his own home and showed them how they might gain access to number thirteen through the back door. At their request, Amey himself followed them onto his neighbour's property.

Thomas Fitchley was a detective in the Metropolitan Police and after receiving a call from the hospital, he had gone with Sergeant Foster to Stukeley Road. Going into number thirteen with Charles Amey, the three men at first noticed little out of place. The house was tidy enough and there were no signs of a struggle, but going into the hallway they did notice that the floor appeared to have been washed down very recently. Furthermore, at the edge of a door that led to the cellar, there was some blood with human hair adhering to it. The door was locked and there was no sign of a key. On Fitchley's instructions, the door was broken down.

On the cellar steps, the three men found the body of fifteen-year-old Alice Cornish. She was lying on her back with her head thrown back and resting against the wall. The gaping gash in her throat showed that she was beyond all human aid.

At the foot of those same steps there lay another body, that of six-year-old Marie Cornish. She was in a curled position, her hand clutching a quantity of coal dust. She had suffered terrible wounds to her skull and brain, and she too was obviously dead.

When the two officers and Amey had first set foot on Walter Cornish's property, they had glanced inside a shed in the garden, but found nothing untoward. Now, after searching through the rest of the house and finding no sign of Mrs Cornish, they returned to the shed to make a more careful inspection. There was some lumber piled just inside the door and when this was moved, they found forty-three-year-old Alice Cornish. She had a large gash in her throat and the handle of a roasting fork lay embedded in the wound. There was also a large hole in her head, which might have been caused by a weapon such as a pickaxe. One of her fingers had also been cut off, the one that had held her wedding ring.

The police were looking at three brutal murders and one attempted murder and after speaking to Charles Amey, they knew that they were looking for a soldier who had been living at 13 Stukeley Road. Investigations soon showed that he was thirty-six-year-old Henry Beckett, who also used the name Perry, a man who until very recently had served in the Army Veterinary Corp. A check on his criminal record showed that he was well known to the police.

Beckett had first come to the attention of the authorities in 1891. On February 14th of that year he was birched for throwing stones. Four years later, on July 10th, 1895, he was birched again, this time for stealing shoes. His first incarceration came on April 28th, 1897, when he received seven days for stealing food. Almost exactly two years later, on April 8th, 1899, he got four months at Ipswich for breaking into a warehouse.

Beckett was again in trouble in 1900. On May 31st he was sentenced to one month, at Stratford, for stealing clothes. Later that same year, on October 17th, he was in Essex where he got six months for stealing fowl. The following year, on June 1st, Beckett received one month at Havant, for stealing a waistcoat and later that same year, again on October 17th, he received his longest sentence thus far, nine months for stealing tools.

By 1902, Beckett was a free man but on October 30th of that year, he was sentenced in the name of Henry Smith to twenty-one days for stealing wood. A similar offence followed at Saxmundham on January 15th, 1903, for which he got another twenty-one days.

On June 5th, 1903, Beckett received twelve days for horse stealing at Suffolk. His third sentence of 1903, also twelve days for horse stealing, followed at Norwich on July 1st. In 1904, on October 19th, he was sentenced to three years at Essex for stealing a bicycle. Released in 1907, he was given five years on April 11th of that year for shopbreaking at Ipswich. His final sentence, another one of five years, came on April 13th, 1912, when he was found guilty of stealing lead. Significantly, however, none of these many crimes involved any degree of violence.

On Wednesday, April 30th, two days after the attack on the Cornish family, Walter Cornish succumbed to his injuries and died. Beckett, once he was traced, would now face four charges of murder, although there was still no sign of him, despite a full-scale police search.

It was not until May 2nd that Beckett was finally traced. William James Green, who also happened to be a special constable, was serving a woman, Mrs Reynolds, in his shop on Barking Road, East Ham, when he saw a strangely dressed man walk past. The man wore trousers that were much too long for him and when Green took a closer look, he became convinced that it was the man all London was looking for, Henry Beckett. Green began following the man, whilst Mrs Reynolds dashed off to find a policeman.

Constable William Hewson was on duty in High Street North at 11.45 a.m., when Mrs Reynolds came to him and told him that she thought she had seen Beckett. Constable Hewson saw the man approaching and decided to stop him.

"What is your name?" demanded Hewson.

"Jones", replied the man. Hewson continued, "Where are you going?" and the man replied "Home".

"Where do you live?" asked Hewson.

"Forest Gate" came the answer, but Hewson was far from satisfied. Though the man was in civilian clothes he wore a Mons medal ribbon, four chevrons and two wound stripes. Asked to explain himself further, 'Jones' said that he had been demobbed from the army but could not show any papers to prove this. As a result, he was escorted to the police station.

Searched, 'Jones' was found to be carrying two half sovereigns, five one pound notes, eleven shillings in silver, eleven shillings and sixpence in copper, eleven foreign coins and two safety razors. He wore three gold rings but more telling was the notebook that he also carried, for on one page someone had written "Mrs Cornish, 13 Stukeley Road, Forest Gate". He was told he would be detained whilst further enquiries were made.

It was noon by the time Divisional Detective Inspector Francis Hall and Chief Inspector Arthur Neil reached East Ham police station to interview the mysterious Mr Jones. Inspector Hall greeted the man with, "I understand you gave the name of Jones?" but immediately 'Jones' replied "No, my name is Harry Perry. I am also known as Beckett. I am the man you are looking for." He was then cautioned and told he would be charged with murder, to which Beckett replied "Quite right". He then made a statement admitting what he had done at 13 Stukeley Road on April 28th.

Beckett's trial took place at the Old Bailey on May 27th, before Mr Justice Darling. The Crown's case was led by Mr Percival Clarke, assisted by Mr Adrian Clark, whilst Beckett was defended by Mr Fox-Davies.

Charlotte Beatrice Gallagher lived at 75 Upton Park Road, West Ham, and was the sister of Walter Frank Cornish, the dead man. She had identified Walter's body, together with those of his wife, Alice Mary, and his two daughters, Alice Beatrice Dorothy and Marie. However, in addition to this testimony, Charlotte was also able to place Beckett at the scene of the crime. On April 28th, at around 4.05 p.m., Charlotte had called at 13 Stukeley Road. The door had been opened by Beckett and when Charlotte asked if Alice were in, Beckett had replied "She has gone out". Mrs Gallagher then left, but at the top of the street she turned and saw Marie knocking on the door. The door was opened again and little Marie was admitted.

Mrs Gallagher was also able to confirm that Beckett had been staying at number thirteen until April 19th. Whilst he was living there he called at her home on a number of occasions, and Alice Cornish introduced him as her nephew. She stated that during those visits, Beckett had become rather enamoured of her lodger, Mrs Sparks, and marriage had been discussed.

Charles Amey told of his encounter with the battered and bloodstained Walter Cornish, the trip to the hospital, and his later entry into number thirteen. When he first went into the kitchen, Amey saw a soldier's coat and belt on a couch. Later, when the first body was found, Amey became so upset that he had to go outside and stand at the front gate for a few minutes. Returning to the house he saw that the gas ring was on in the scullery. There were the remains of some burnt bacon in the pan.

There were other witnesses who could report on Beckett's escape from the house. Elizabeth Fordree was only thirteen and at 6.30 p.m., she was playing with some friends outside her home at 186 Neville Road, Upton Park. As she played, Elizabeth saw a soldier run into Neville Road from Stukeley Road. At first, she took little notice of him but the man ran into her and pushed her to one side. Now Elizabeth saw that his collar was undone, his hat was on the wrong way round and his face and hands were covered in blood. The man ran off towards West Ham Park. Though Elizabeth did not know the soldier's name, she had seen him before, with Mrs Cornish and the two girls.

Adelaide Williams also lived in Neville Road, at number ninety-six, and on April 28th, she was near her house in the company of her two small children when someone pushed past her, knocking her hat to one side. She saw that the man was dressed in khaki, and his hands were bloodstained. She too identified the man as Beckett.

Doctor John Andrew Garden had been called to the murder house at 9.00 p.m. on April 28th, and after examining the scene he had later performed the post-mortems on the three bodies found there.

Alice Cornish, who was found in the shed, had a wound on the left side of her head some one and a quarter inch by one inch. It was a deep penetrating wound and could have been made by a pickaxe. One inch above this wound was a smaller one. On the right side of the head, towards the back, was another penetrating wound beneath which the skull was fractured. This might have been caused by the heavy knob on the end of a poker found in the house. In the throat was a transverse lacerated wound, three inches long, in which the carving fork had been embedded. The trachea was severed. The ring finger of the left hand had been severed at the joint nearest to the hand and this was possibly the only wound inflicted after death.

The fifteen-year-old daughter, also named Alice, had a lacerated wound on her frontal bone, approximately one inch long. The skull was fractured beneath this and the wound might have been caused by the back end of an axe. There was another wound above the occipital ridge and a large gaping wound in the neck. The arteries and veins on the left side had been severed and the epiglottis removed from the tongue. Alice's head was almost severed from her body and this particular wound might have been caused by the sharp edge of the axe. A hammer had also been recovered from the house and this bore traces of human hair which matched Alice's.

Marie had been found lying with her right hand above her head, grasping some coal dust. Her head, left shoulder and the left side of her face were covered in blood and coal dust. She had a gaping wound in her throat reaching down to the spinal column, and her head too had almost been severed. She also had a lacerated wound over her right frontal bones, which had been shattered to small fragments.

Further medical evidence was given by Dr Carey, the gentleman who had treated Walter Cornish after his admission to hospital. The doctor explained that there was a wound on Walter's head, on the right side, some four to five inches long. Beneath this was a fracture of the skull and the wound might well have been caused by the back of the axe produced in court. In addition, the end of the right forefinger had been cut off. Soon after his admission, Walter fell unconscious. He never awoke and died at 6.10 p.m., on April 30th.

In addition to giving evidence on Beckett's arrest and subsequent interview, Inspector Frank Hall had also attended the murder scene, at 8.30 p.m. on April 28th. After looking at all three bodies he had found the severed portion of Alice Cornish's finger under a bench in the shed. A number of items bore bloodstains including the axe handed to him by Charles Amey, a poker, a hammer and a pickaxe. All of these items had been taken for examination.

Going into the house he saw a soldier's overcoat. Inside the pocket was six shillings in coppers, wrapped in a khaki handkerchief. Nearby was a soldier's belt. In the scullery there was a pail in the sink which had some bloodstained water and a floor cloth in it.

Turning to the interview with Beckett on May 2nd, Hall said that when Beckett was asked to remove a wedding ring he wore, he handed it over saying, "That isn't the one I took from her. I gave that to a woman in Stratford on Monday night." This evidence was confirmed by Chief Inspector Neil, who was present when Beckett made his long written statement. After signing it he commented, "Mrs Cornish received a letter from her sister-in-law at Colchester and it was after that they twitted me and told me to clear out and I was annoyed".

Ettie Emmeline Sparks was a widow who lodged with Charlotte Gallagher at Upton Park Road. She had known Beckett for about a month by the end of April, and he told her that he had been a prisoner of war in the 1914-18 conflict. He also told her that he had been wounded and a scar on his head bore testimony to the truth of that. They had grown close and he had proposed to her. Ettie had accepted and they were due to be married on May 7th.

Beckett's statement was then read out in court. He began by saying that he believed he had been born at Chatham, but his father had died young. Later, his mother remarried. He did not give details of his youth but went on to say that on November 29th, 1916, he had joined the 3rd Suffolk Regiment at Bury St Edmunds and the following year had been sent to Egypt.

After being demobbed, his sister, Mrs Louie Smith, who lived in Ipswich, had told him about his step-aunt, Mrs Cornish. He visited the Cornishs and was made welcome. During his stay there he met Mrs Sparks and soon they were engaged to be married.

In due course, letters arrived detailing his past record and Mrs Cornish asked him to leave her house. He did so, staying at various places until, on April 26th, he went to stay with Mrs Sparks. He stayed with her until Monday, April 28th, when he left the house at 10.00 a.m.

For the rest of that day, Beckett roamed about. He had some beer until, at about 1.30 p.m., he found himself walking past the Cornish family's house. Mrs Cornish saw him and invited him in. She gave him some rough words but then asked him to stay for dinner. For some reason, though, he lost his temper and knocked her down with the kitchen poker.

Beckett went on to explain how he had carried her out to the garden shed where he struck her with a pickaxe. He then returned to the house, found the carving fork, took it back and stuck it in her throat. Then he took a knife and cut off her ring finger, pocketing the wedding ring, before hiding her body under some lumber. By now it was some time between 2.00 p.m. and 3.00 p.m.

After Mrs Gallagher had called, Marie arrived home from school. As soon as she was in the house, Beckett hit her on the head with the hammer. She fell and he picked her up and threw her down the cellar steps. Next, Alice came home and she too was struck with the hammer. Once she had fallen, Beckett said that he hit her across the throat with the axe before carrying her to the cellar too.

Eventually Mr Cornish came home and demanded to know what Beckett was doing there, saying, "What game are you having? I am going to hand you over to the police." The two men had a few words during which Mr Cornish went into the scullery to cook some bacon. He turned his back on Beckett, who hit him on the head with the axe. Beckett then hit him again but Mr Cornish still managed to get away.

After running away, Beckett went to Stratford where he visited a clothes shop and purchased a jacket, waistcoat and cord trousers. He took these items to the docks where he took off his uniform and changed into the new clothes. Over the next day or so he spent a lot of time gambling and sleeping about the docks area before he was finally arrested.

There could be no doubt that Henry Beckett had killed four people and the only possible defence was one of insanity. In Beckett's long statement he had explained how he had been captured by the Turks during the war, and subsequently tortured. In that same campaign he had been wounded in the head by some shrapnel, and blown up by high explosives. Ever since, he had suffered from terrible dreams and had heard voices commanding him to do things.

These claims were supported by medical testimony. Sir Robert Armstrong-Jones, the superintendent of the Claybury Asylum, stated that he believed Beckett to be insane. Dr Stoddart said that he too had examined Beckett and believed the prisoner to be mentally deficient. Another medical witness, Dr Norman, said that Beckett was not capable of judging between right and wrong. To counter this, the prosecution called the medical officer of Brixton prison, who swore that Beckett was quite rational and perfectly sane.

Despite the fact that Beckett, although having a long criminal record, had never committed a violent crime before and had no real motive for the crime, and despite medical evidence and testimony which showed that he might well have severe mental problems, the jury took just ten minutes to adjudge that he was guilty of wilful murder.

On Thursday, July 10th, 1919, Henry Beckett, also known as Perry, was hanged at Pentonville by John Ellis, assisted by William Willis. Whether or not he was truly insane was never really determined.

16

Edwin Sowerby

Hanged at Leeds, Thursday, December 30th, 1920
For the murder of Jane Darwell, at Crofton, near Wakefield

JANE Darwell, a pretty nineteen-year-old girl, worked as a domestic servant at the Royal Oak Inn at Crofton, situated just south east of Wakefield and, in 1920, little more than a village. Jane was not resident at the inn, though, and still lived with her parents, close to the inn, at 16 North's Yard, Crofton. Also in that same street lived twenty-eight-year-old Edwin Sowerby, and he was enamoured of Jane, feelings that were not, apparently, returned. The couple had once, briefly, walked out together but it was clear that Jane believed the relationship had run its course. Indeed, on one occasion, when Sowerby had called at the Darwell house and half-jokingly asked Jane if she loved him, she had simply replied "No". By the latter part of 1920, whatever friendship had existed between the young couple was certainly over.

Monday, October 25th, was an exciting day for the village of Crofton. There was to be a dance at the Crofton Council School, situated at the back of North's Yard. Jane had expressed a desire to go, but first she had to complete her duties at the inn. She would thus go over only for the last hour or so.

It was 10.20 p.m. by the time Jane arrived home from the Royal Oak. She changed quickly and told her father, Charles, that she wanted to be at the dance by 11.00 p.m. Charles Darwell said that he wanted a walk and so was more than happy to escort his daughter to the school hall, leaving her at the front door. He then went home and retired to his bed, confident that Jane would be able to make her own way home once the dance finally ended, in the small hours of October 26th.

At some time after midnight, Charles Darwell was woken by loud screams coming from the Council School. There were various voices raised, people were running from the building, and it was clear that something terrible had happened over there. Charles dressed quickly and ran across to the school, only to find his daughter lying dead, a terrible gash in her throat. The culprit, Edwin Sowerby, had then turned the blade upon himself but his own wound was only superficial. He was taken to Clayton Hospital for treatment but it was clear that there was no danger to his life.

From statements made by the many witnesses at the dance, it was plain that Jane had been murdered by Sowerby. Those who had witnessed the attack said that just as the dancing was coming to an end, Sowerby had walked across the dance floor and slashed Jane's throat, without saying a word to her. Sowerby's dance programme had then fluttered to the floor and upon it he had scribbled "Me and Jane gone for ever, E. Sowerby. With love to all." It was an open and shut case and Sowerby was duly charged with wilful murder, once he had been released from hospital.

Edwin Sowerby appeared at Leeds before Mister Justice Salter on December 9th, 1920. The case for the prosecution was led by Mr H. S. Cautley, who was assisted by Mr Willoughby Jardine. The prisoner was defended by Mr S. Fleming, who sought a verdict of guilty but insane. The proceedings did not last for very long.

There were, of course, a large number of witnesses who had seen the actual attack upon Jane. Perhaps the closest was Richard Sanson, who had been sitting very near to where Jane stood. Sanson saw Sowerby walk up to Jane and put his arm around her neck. Then she exclaimed "Oh!" and a second later blood splashed on to Sanson's face and clothing. He looked up in time to see that Sowerby was just attempting to cut his own throat.

There were, however, quite a few defence witnesses who seemed to confirm that Sowerby had some rather severe mental problems. Doctor Clarke, the family physician, told of a visit he had made to Sowerby's house on October 8th, when he had been called out by Mrs Sowerby. The prisoner was lying in his bed, apparently unconscious, but when Doctor Clarke examined him, he found that he was awake, but had seemingly lost the power of speech. Concerned for his patient, the doctor had called again on October 10th, only to find that Sowerby was out. His mother, however, reported that her son had been complaining of headaches and sleeplessness for the past five weeks. Dr Clarke added that in his opinion, Sowerby had a very weak character.

Mrs Sowerby was also able to tell the court that Edwin had never been the same since he came out of the army in 1918. Ever since that time he had suffered from terrible pains in the head, and his behaviour had changed too.

William Hall was a friend of Sowerby's and he reported a conversation that had taken place on October 21st, just four days before Jane Darwell's death. Sowerby had told Hall that he intended to do away with himself. A similar conversation had taken place that same night between Sowerby and another friend, Sam Bateman. Bateman testified that Sowerby had told him that he intended to put his head on the railway line and end it all.

Of course, Sowerby had taken Jane's life and deserved to be punished for it, but was he sane enough to be aware of what he had done and therefore subject to the ultimate sanction of the law? After a deliberation of twenty minutes, the jury returned to announce that not only was Sowerby guilty, but he was also sane.

It should not be forgotten that when an accused man relies on a defence of insanity, the onus of proof shifts from the prosecution to the defence. A plea of insanity requires that the defence prove that the prisoner is insane and in Sowerby's case, the jury held that they had failed to do this. It may be quite obvious to the reader that Sowerby's behaviour was not that of a man responsible for his actions, but the law was immovable and it seemed of little import that a man's life was at stake.

There was no appeal and when, on December 29th, it was announced that there would be no reprieve, Sowerby's fate was sealed. Precisely three weeks after the trial, on December 30th, he was hanged at Leeds prison by Thomas Pierrepoint, who was assisted by Edward Taylor. The doomed man carried a picture of Jane with him as he walked to the gallows.

It was a very busy time for the hangmen of England for on this same day, Marks Goodmacher was hanged at Pentonville and Samuel Westwood lost his life on the scaffold at Birmingham.

Edith Jessie Thompson

17

Hanged at Holloway prison, London, Tuesday, January 9th, 1923
For the murder of Percy Thompson, her husband, at Ilford

I T had just turned 12.30 a.m., on the morning of Wednesday, October 4th, 1922 when John Webber headed upstairs to his bed at 59 De Vere Gardens, Ilford. Suddenly a scream rang out. It had come from somewhere in the street outside and John knew that it was the cry of a woman in distress. Even as he strained his ears he heard a repeated cry of "Oh Don't! Don't!"

John Webber's house was in a corner position and it sounded to him as if the shouts had come from Belgrave Road. Hurriedly running outside, Mr Webber walked into the middle of Belgrave Road in time to see three people, two women and a man, approaching him from the direction of Courtland Avenue. One of the women was in front of her two companions, as if leading the way, and Webber could see, even in the darkened street, that she was very distressed about something.

The trio passed where John Webber stood and stopped some yards away. One of the three then bent down and struck a match, close to the pavement. Intrigued, Webber walked slowly forward to see what was happening. He was just a few yards from the spot, on the opposite side of the road, when the group turned to look at him and the man remarked "No, that is not him". None of this made any real impression on John Webber however, for his eyes were by now fixed on a fourth figure. Sitting on the cold pavement was another man, his back up against a garden wall.

Webber took another couple of steps forward and politely inquired if the man had fallen. At this, one of the women, the one who had been running in front of the others just a minute or so ago, replied "Yes... No... I don't know." Before Mr Webber could ask any more questions, he noticed that Dr Maudsley was arriving to take charge.

Dr Noel Maudsley lived and worked from 62 Courtland Avenue and had been enjoying a quiet night at home when a Miss Pittard knocked on his door. It was just about 12.30 a.m., and Miss Pittard had breathlessly explained that she and some friends had been walking home from the railway station when a distraught woman had approached them and announced that her husband had been taken ill. As the others had rushed to where the woman said her husband lay, she had gone for the doctor and now accompanied him to the position where the stricken man lay.

Dr Maudsley directed John Webber to tear open the man's clothing so that he might better make his examination. It was all to no avail though. The man was clearly beyond all human help. As the doctor confirmed that the man was dead, the woman who had run for assistance became agitated, distressed and hysterical, shouting that the doctor should have come sooner so that he might have saved her husband.

The doctor now contacted the police station and arranged for the ambulance to be sent so that the body might be taken away. It was Constable Cyril Geal who arrived with that ambulance, and later accompanied the vehicle to the mortuary. There he undressed the body and what he saw led him to make careful notes in his pocket book.

It was 1.05 a.m. by the time Police Sergeant Walter Mew noticed a small crowd of people gathered near an ambulance in Belgrave Road. Noticing Dr Maudsley, Mew asked him what had happened. The doctor replied, "This is a case of sudden death, haemorrhage, from the mouth".

Seeing a distressed woman crying hysterically, Sergeant Mew gently questioned her and determined some basic facts. Her name was Edith Jessie Thompson and the dead man was her husband, Percy. They had spent a pleasant Tuesday evening with a couple of friends at the Criterion Theatre in London. After the show, they had said goodbye to their friends at Piccadilly tube station. From there, Percy and Edith had caught a train to Liverpool Street, where they caught a second train for Ilford. They had then been walking home from the station when Percy had fallen ill and collapsed.

Sergeant Mew now began to escort Edith to her home at 41 Kensington Gardens. On the way, the still sobbing woman asked, "Will he come back?" Sergeant Mew naturally assumed that the poor woman had not yet come to terms with the fact that her husband was dead and so, to placate her, replied 'Yes'. To this, Edith somewhat cryptically answered "They will blame me for this".

At Kensington Gardens, Sergeant Mew handed Edith over to the care of Mrs Lester, who also lived in the house. He then walked around to the house of Richard Halliday Thompson, at 49 Seymour Gardens, Ilford, to inform him that his brother was dead. He also suggested that Mr Thompson might go around to his sister-in-law's house in order to comfort her. Richard agreed that this was a good idea and arrived at Kensington Gardens at 2.00 a.m.

Edith Thompson was still very distressed but Richard still felt that he had a right to know what had happened to his brother. He had not been aware that Percy had any life-threatening illness, though of course he was aware that his brother had been discharged from the army due to a weak heart. Perhaps this had played a factor in his sudden demise?

For the first time, Edith began to explain some of what had happened. She said that Percy had complained of not feeling well as they passed Endsleigh Gardens. A few steps further on he had suddenly fallen forward with a cry and with blood

Edith Thompson and Frederick Bywaters, both hanged for the murder of Percy Thompson (Popperfoto)

issuing from his mouth. He had fallen against Edith and she had tried, in vain, to support him. Percy had staggered on a little way before falling against the wall and sliding down to the pavement. Without delay she had run off to find help and one of the people she found had kindly run for the doctor. Richard ended his questioning by asking Edith if she had seen anyone else. She replied with an emphatic 'No'.

Meanwhile, Sergeant Mew had gone to the mortuary, to find that when the body had been stripped by Constable Geal, a number of stab wounds had been noted. It seemed that this was not a case of sudden illness after all, but that Percy Thompson had been the victim of a vicious attack. Some sort of sharp edged weapon had been used and Sergeant Mew, together with Constable Grimes, now returned to Belgrave Road to search for it. They found nothing but noted a large quantity of blood along the pavement where Percy had lain. In all, the bloodstains stretched for some forty-four yards.

It was obviously important to get to the bottom of this affair so Sergeant Mew now walked back to 41 Kensington Gardens to interview Edith again. He asked if she could account for the cuts he had observed on her husband's neck, but Edith replied "No, we were walking along and my husband said 'Oh!' I said 'Cheer up', thinking he had one of his attacks. He then fell on me and walked a little further. He then fell up against the wall and then on the ground."

Edith was certainly sticking to the illness story, in spite of the evidence to the contrary, so the sergeant now asked her if Percy had had a knife with him, thinking that this might have been a case of suicide and that Edith was seeking to protect Percy's memory. Edith shook her head and said, "No, I did not see a knife or anything". She then allowed the sergeant to examine her handbag. Again, no weapon was discovered.

The police investigation continued and it soon became clear that Edith Thompson might not have been the dutiful wife she had thus far appeared. Stories were circulating about a young man who had once been a lodger at the Thompson household, and who had argued with Percy over the way he treated his wife. That young man was Frederick Edward Francis Bywaters and it transpired that he lived with his mother, Lilian, at 11 Weston Street, Upper Norwood.

It was 11.00 p.m., on October 4th, when Detective Inspector Frank Page of Scotland Yard called at Lilian Bywaters' home. She confirmed that her son was a seaman but that when he was home on leave he usually came to stay either with her, or with the Graydon family, Graydon being Edith Thompson's maiden name. Continuing her story, Lilian said that Frederick had come home on leave on Saturday, September 23rd, and had been at home each night since then.

On the night of October 3rd, Lilian had gone to bed at 10.30 p.m. At the time, Freddie had been out but she heard the bell as he came in later. That morning she had seen him at breakfast at 8.45 a.m. and remarked "You were late last night weren't you? I suppose you went to sleep in the train." He had replied "Yes, I went to Norwood Junction and walked".

Concerned that the inspector should see that her son had nothing to fear from the police, Lilian Bywaters then invited Page to look in Freddie's bedroom. Inspector Page did so. He found no murder weapon but did recover a cache of letters from a suitcase and another small pile from a jacket pocket.

Earlier that day, at 11.00 a.m., Detective Inspector Francis Hall had paid a visit to Edith Thompson's home in Kensington Gardens. He informed her that he was satisfied that her husband had been attacked and stabbed several times and asked her to repeat her story of what had taken place. Edith again said that Percy had been taken ill, and had finally fallen against the wall. She added that they had had no argument or quarrel and had been quite happy together. Finally she confirmed that she had seen no one else. Inspector Hall then asked Edith to accompany him to Ilford police station where she might answer some further questions. She was never to know freedom again.

In the meantime, Frederick Bywaters had been found and also taken to Ilford police station, where he had made a full written statement. Running to three pages it began, "I have known Mr Percy Thompson for about four years, and his wife, Edith, for about seven years".

Frederick went on to confirm that he had lodged with the Thompsons from June 18th until August 1st, 1921 and that he had left the house after an argument with Percy when Percy had threatened Edith with physical violence. The statement went on, "I had always been exceedingly good friends with Mrs Thompson. I was also on visiting terms with the mother of Mrs Thompson, a Mrs Graydon, who resides with her husband and family at 231 Shakespeare Crescent, Manor Park.

"After I left Mrs Thompson I went back to reside with my mother at my present address. On the 7th September 1921 I got a position as writer on board the SS Morea. I sailed on the 9th September and returned to England the end of the following month. Shortly after I came back from the voyage I called on Mr and Mrs Thompson at their address. Mrs Thompson received me quite friendly, Mr Thompson a little coldly but we parted as friends."

Bywaters went on to state that since that time he had met Mrs Thompson from time to time, always by appointment, and detailed meetings they had had in a restaurant in Aldersgate Street. He confirmed that he knew that Edith had an unhappy marriage and that he had written to her on a couple of occasions, addressing her as 'Dear Edie'.

Detailing his movements on the night of the murder, Bywaters said that he knew that Edith and Percy were going to the theatre that evening, but stated that he had visited her parents, leaving the Graydon home at about 11.00 p.m. Catching a train to Victoria he realized that he had missed the last train home so he walked through Kennington, Brixton, Dulwich and Crystal Palace, to Upper Norwood, where he arrived at 3.00 a.m. Bywaters ended by saying that the first he knew of the murder was when he read the details in a newspaper on the morning of October 4th, and added that he was not in the habit of carrying a knife.

The questioning continued and on October 5th, Edith made a two and a half page statement repeating her story of Percy's illness. She also referred to the letters which Inspector Page had discovered in Bywaters' bedroom and shown to her. She continued to deny any involvement in her husband's death.

It was as Edith was being escorted to the canteen that she passed the room where Bywaters was being held. Catching a glimpse of Freddie she became hysterical and cried out "Oh God! Why did he do it? I didn't want him to do it. I must tell the truth." She then asked to make another statement. That statement was very short and read, "When we got near Endsleigh Gardens, a man rushed out from the Gardens and knocked me away from my husband. I was dazed for a moment. When I recovered I saw my husband scuffling with a man. The man who I know as Freddie Bywaters was running away. He was wearing a blue overcoat and a grey hat. I knew it was him although I did not see his face."

Told of Edith's second statement, Frederick Bywaters said he wished to make another of his own. It read, "I wish to make a voluntary statement. Mrs Edith Thompson was not aware of my movements on Tuesday night 3rd October. I left

Manor Park at 11.00 p.m. and proceeded to Ilford. I waited for Mrs Thompson and her husband. When near Endsleigh Gardens I pushed her to one side, also pushing him further up the street.

"I said to him 'You have got to separate from your wife'. He said 'No'. I said 'You will have to'. We struggled. I took my knife from my pocket and we fought and he got the worst of it.

"Mrs Thompson must have been spellbound for I saw nothing of her during the fight. I ran away through Endsleigh Gardens, through Wanstead, Leytonstone, Stratford, got a taxi at Stratford to Aldgate, walked from there to Fenchurch Street, got another taxi to Thornton Heath. Then walked to Upper Norwood, arriving home about 3.00 a.m.

"The reason I fought with Thompson was because he never acted like a man to his wife. He always seemed several degrees lower than a snake. I loved her and I couldn't go on seeing her leading that life. I did not intend to kill him. I only meant to injure him. I gave him an opportunity of standing up to me as a man but he wouldn't. I have had the knife some time; it was a sheath knife. I threw it down a drain when I was running through Endsleigh Gardens."

It is certain that Frederick Bywaters was guilty of murder, but when the charges were made, there were six against Edith. Both Frederick and Edith were charged with murder and conspiracy to murder but, after reading her letters to Freddie, the police also laid four further charges against Edith alone. These were soliciting to murder, inciting to commit a misdemeanour, administering poison with intent to murder, and administering a destructive thing with intent to murder. Though Frederick had wielded the knife, both protagonists would be on trial for their lives.

The trial of Edith Thompson and Frederick Bywaters opened at the Old Bailey on December 6th, 1923, before Mr Justice Shearman. The proceedings lasted until December 11th, during which the case for the Crown was led by Sir Thomas Inskip, who had two assistants, Mr Travers Humphreys and Mr Roland Oliver. Bywaters was defended by Mr Cecil Whiteley, assisted by Mr Huntly Jenkins and Mr Myles Elliott, whilst Edith was represented by Sir Henry Curtis Bennett, assisted by Mr Walter Frampton and Mr Ivan Snell.

One of the early witnesses was Percy Edward Clevely, who lived at 62 Mayfair Avenue, Ilford. He explained to the court that soon after midnight, on the morning of October 4th, he, his wife, Miss Secretan and Miss Pittard had been walking from the railway station towards their home. Between Courtland Avenue and De Vere Gardens, they met a man wearing a blue suit and a fawn-coloured overcoat, which he carried over his arm. The man looked perfectly ordinary and did nothing to arouse their suspicions. The group walked on but just before Endsleigh Gardens, a woman whom he now knew to be Edith Thompson ran up to them and asked for a doctor, saying that her husband had fallen down and was bleeding.

Miss Pittard ran off to fetch the doctor whilst he ran back to where Edith indicated. It had been Clevely who bent down and struck the match so he could get a better view of the stricken man. He agreed that Edith appeared to be very distressed and that she had become totally hysterical when told that her husband was dead.

Much of this testimony was backed up by Dora Finch Pittard. She confirmed that after Edith had rushed up to them, she had gone to fetch the doctor. Miss Pittard heard the doctor ask Edith what had happened, to which Edith replied "I don't know anything at all. I don't remember. Someone flew past and when I went to speak to my husband, blood was pouring out of his mouth."

Detective Inspector Hall told of his investigations and Edith's reaction when she had seen Bywaters at Ilford police station. When, later that day, Bywaters was informed that both he and Edith would be charged with murder, he had said "Why her? Mrs Thompson was not aware of my movements." Told that she would still be charged, Bywaters then insisted on making another statement, his third, in which he denied that she had played any part in his crime. When both parties were formally charged, Edith made no reply but Bywaters shouted, "It is wrong. It is wrong."

Medical evidence detailed the wounds that Percy Thompson had suffered. Dr Percy James Drought, the police surgeon, had performed the post-mortem. He described a number of wounds, mostly superficial, but there was a stab at the back of the neck that was two inches deep. A second wound, some two and a half inches deep, passed from below and upwards towards the lobe of the right ear whilst a third, on the right side of the throat, was again two and a half inches deep. This wound had divided the jugular vein and the carotid artery and penetrated the gullet. It was the direct cause of death.

In his statement, Bywaters had said that he put the murder weapon down a drain. He later made another brief statement enlarging on this and as a result, a police search was made. Detective Sergeant John Hancock now gave evidence that on October 9th, at about noon, he had found a sheath knife in a drain on the north side of Seymour Gardens. It was the last drain in the street, between numbers six and eight. The weapon appeared to be new and was lying under three inches of water.

The case against Bywaters was cast iron, but was Edith Thompson guilty of murder? The prosecution first had to provide a motive for Edith wanting her husband dead and, in effect, she had provided that herself in the letters she had written to her co-defendant.

Inspector Frank Page told the court of the letters he had found at Bywaters' mother's home on October 4th. Another detective inspector, Alfred Scholes, who worked at the port of London, stated that he had gone on board the SS Morea, Bywaters' ship, at Tilbury Docks, at 9.45 a.m. on October 12th. A box belonging to Bywaters was opened and found to contain a number of letters, tied up in bundles. There was also a picture of Edith, but it was the letters that were important and these were now read out in court.

The letters showed that a passionate affair had been taking place between Edith Thompson and Frederick Bywaters. That perhaps gave a motive, but of more import were some of the suggestions made by Edith, for the implication was that she was trying to poison her husband.

In one letter she had written, "I am not going to try any more until you come back. I made up my mind about this last Thursday. He was telling his mother the circumstances of my Sunday morning escapade, and he puts great stress on the fact of the tea tasting bitter, as if something had been put in it, he says. Now I think whatever else I try it in again will taste bitter. He will recognise it and be more suspicious, and if the quantity is still not successful, it will injure any chance I may have of trying when you come back."

In another letter she referred to trying to feed Percy ground glass in his food. She wrote, "I used the light bulb three times, but the third time he found a piece, so I have given up until you come home". Later in the same missive she penned, "I was buoyed up with the hope of the light bulb, and I used a lot – big pieces too, not powdered, but it has no effect. I quite expected to be able to send that cable. But no, nothing has happened from it."

Edith also wrote to Bywaters about fictional characters who managed to rid themselves of unwanted spouses. One such book was called Bella Donna, in which the main character uses digitalin to poison her husband. She wrote to Bywaters, asking him if digitalin were any use.

In one of the final letters, written just days before Bywaters' attack on Percy, Edith had commented that she and her husband had made love that weekend. Witnesses were now called to show that the defendants had met up on both October 2nd and October 3rd. Were they both planning the murder of the man who stood between them?

Charles Higgins worked at Carlton and Priors, the company that had employed Edith. He testified that on October 2nd, she had asked him to take a letter to a gentleman who would be waiting at Aldersgate Street station. Edith described the man to Higgins who duly found him and handed over the letter. Minutes later, Edith handed him a second letter to deliver. On neither occasion did Higgins speak to the man, who was, of course, Bywaters.

Lillian Vallender also worked at Carlton and Priors and she said that on October 2nd, at some time between 4.30 p.m. and 5.00 p.m., Edith had said to her, "Freddie is outside. Would you like to have a cup of coffee with him?" Miss Vallender, who had been on holiday with Edith and knew Bywaters well, went outside, met Bywaters and went to Fuller's restaurant with him. Later Edith came over and Lillian left so that they could be alone together.

Edith Annie Brown worked as a waitress at Fuller's which was situated at 42 Aldersgate Street. She had seen Edith and Bywaters together a number of times in the restaurant. She recalled him coming in with Lillian Vallender on October 2nd and later being joined by Edith. The next day, October 3rd, Bywaters came in alone at around 4.00 p.m. He sat alone until 5.10 p.m., when Edith joined him. He asked her to have coffee with him but she refused and after settling his bill, they left together at 5.15 p.m.

Edith worked in Aldersgate Street, she met Bywaters in that street and evidence was now called to show that the murder weapon had also been purchased in that same street. Henry William Forster was a director of Osborne and Co., tool merchants of 166 Aldersgate Street. He identified the murder weapon as a hunting knife, made by John Watts and Co. of Sheffield, which he had sold for six shillings. The knife was quite distinctive and Forster believed that his shop was the only one in London selling them. Having said that, Forster had to confirm that he had attended an identification parade where he picked out a man who was not Bywaters.

If it could be shown that Edith Thompson had tried to murder her husband by administering poison, then the Crown would have a very strong case that she and Bywaters had worked in tandem to commit the crime which claimed Percy Thompson's life. After the original post-mortem had been carried out, the victim's body had been exhumed so that a second examination could be carried out by Bernard Spilsbury, the Home Office pathologist. That examination was made on November 3rd.

Spilsbury began by referring to the wounds he had observed, concurring with the findings of the earlier examination. However, he also performed a detailed internal examination and reported that he had found no signs of poisoning, nor was there any evidence of glass being administered. There was no scarring of the stomach wall and no scars in either the large or small intestines. Finally, there were no fragments of glass in the appendix.

Spilsbury had taken various organs for chemical analysis and these had been forwarded to John Webster, the senior official analyst for the Home Office. The only substances he discovered were traces of an alkaloid that gave a reaction for morphine, in the liver and kidneys. However, when the dead man's house had been searched, a bottle of medicine called Chlorodine had been found. Such a substance was taken to produce relief for heart patients and of course, Percy Thompson had been discharged from the army for heart problems.

In the event, the jury decided that both defendants were guilty of murder. Immediately Edith screamed out "I am not guilty. Oh my God, I am not guilty." Both were then sentenced to death.

Whilst languishing in the condemned cell, Bywaters wrote out a final confession in which he said that he had been drunk on the night of the murder. He saw the Thompsons walking home together and at one stage, Percy put his arm around Edith. That was the final straw and he leapt out and attacked him. Again he claimed that Edith had known nothing of his intentions and had certainly not persuaded him to act. She was innocent of any crime.

141

On the morning of Tuesday, January 9th, 1923, Frederick Bywaters was hanged at Pentonville prison. He was just twenty-one years of age and walked bravely to the scaffold. The same cannot be said of Edith Jessie Thompson. At the same time, she was taken from the condemned cell at Holloway and had to be half carried to the trap. It has been said that it took as many as five warders to hold her up as John Ellis, Robert Baxter and Thomas Phillips did their work.

There was no real evidence that Edith Thompson knew anything of Bywaters' intentions. Medical and scientific evidence proved that no noxious substance had been administered to Percy, showing that the letters were nothing more than the ramblings of a woman smitten by love. It might well be argued that Edith Thompson was hanged for adultery as much as she was for murder.

John Norman Holmes Thorne

18

Hanged at Wandsworth, Wednesday, April 22nd, 1925
For the murder of Elsie Emily Cameron, at Crowborough, Sussex

DONALD Gilchrist Cameron arrived home from work on the evening of Friday, December 5th, 1924, to find a letter from his daughter, twenty-six-year-old Elsie Emily Cameron, waiting for him on the kitchen table. The brief note informed Donald that Elsie had gone down to Crowborough, in East Sussex, to spend some time with her beau. There was nothing unusual in this. It was something Elsie had done many times over the past couple of years and Mr Cameron saw no cause for concern.

Elsie Cameron had been walking out with John Norman Holmes Thorne, a local man, for some years now. They had first met at chapel and soon started seeing each other on a regular basis. Times were hard, though, and Thorne, who preferred to be called Norman, had been unable to find regular work for himself in London. As a result, he decided to try to set up in business for himself. In 1922 he borrowed £100 from his father and bought himself a small plot of land in Crowborough. In reality this was little more than a field with a couple of sheds on it, but Norman purchased some chickens and started a small poultry farm. At first he would commute between Kensal Rise and Sussex but when this proved to be something of a chore, he moved down to Crowborough permanently, living in one of the huts on his farm. Elsie visited him on a regular basis, staying at one of the other farms nearby, which did bed and breakfast. To all intents and purposes, Norman and Elsie were an ordinary happy couple trying to set up a decent life for themselves and, by late 1924, they were officially engaged.

The Cameron household, at 86 Clifford Gardens, Kensal Rise, London NW10, supported a total of five souls. In addition to Mr and Mrs Cameron and their daughter, the house was also home to Bertha Motture and her husband, Charles William, who had lodged there for some time. Indeed, when Donald Cameron spoke to Mrs Motture, after reading the letter from his daughter, Bertha confirmed that she had last seen Elsie at around noon on that grey December Friday. The girl seemed to be in excellent spirits, showing off a new hairstyle and excited at the prospect of seeing Norman. Though

Bertha had not seen Elsie again that day, she did hear the front door bang at around 2.00 p.m., and presumed that this was Elsie leaving.

The weekend passed and by the time Monday arrived, Elsie Cameron had still not returned home. Usually she only stayed in Sussex for the weekend but perhaps she had decided to stay over for an extra day, as she had done from time to time previously. By this stage, Donald Cameron was perhaps a little concerned, but still not unduly worried.

On Tuesday, December 9th, there was still no sign of Elsie. As if this were not enough, two letters had arrived for Elsie and Mr Cameron saw that the envelopes were in Norman Thorne's hand. Why would Norman be writing to Elsie back in London whilst she was staying down in Sussex? It did not make sense. Determined to find out what was going on, Donald Cameron sent a telegram to Thorne. Dated December 10th, it read "Elsie left Friday. Have heard no news. Has she arrived? Reply."

In due course, a telegram arrived at Clifford Gardens but it did nothing to assuage Donald Cameron's concerns. It simply read "Not here. Open letters. Can't understand. Thorne."

Donald Cameron did indeed open the letters. One, dated December 7th, contained phrases which made it clear that Norman wanted to know why Elsie had not turned up for a prearranged meeting on the previous Saturday. It appeared that she had left London but never arrived in Sussex. Now deeply worried about his

Elsie Cameron and Norman Thorne. Thorne was hanged on April 22nd, 1925, for Elsie's murder (Popperfoto)

144

daughter's safety, Mr Cameron walked to the police station and reported Elsie as a missing person.

The London police passed the report on to their colleagues in Sussex but it was not until Friday, December 12th that Constable Beck paid a routine visit to the poultry farm. Thorne leaned on his gate whilst he spoke to the officer but said he could shed no light on what might have happened to Elsie. He had expected her to come down on Saturday the 6th, but she had not turned up. Constable Beck made a note in his pocket book and went to report to his superiors.

In due course, reports about Elsie's disappearance began to appear in the local newspapers and one of the people who read them was George Adams, a nurseryman of 2 Grovehurst Villas, Blackness, which was close to Crowborough. He and another worker, Albert James Sands, had been walking home, past Thorne's poultry farm, at about 5.15 p.m. on Friday, December 5th. As they strolled down the muddy lane, a young woman carrying a suitcase had passed them, some ten yards from Thorne's gate. Adams and Sands recalled the incident especially because they had stepped aside to allow the woman to pass on a dry part of the track. That woman fitted the published description of Elsie Cameron and so the two men took this information to the police.

Meanwhile, the Sussex police had made no headway in their investigation and so called in the assistance of Scotland Yard. Two detectives, Chief Inspector John Gillan and Sergeant Ambrose Askew, were sent down to Sussex, but the matter was still in the hands of Superintendent Isaac Budgen, who was normally based at Uckfield. As a result of the information given by Adams and Sands, it was Superintendent Budgen who next interviewed Norman Thorne.

It was December 18th when the superintendent visited Thorne at the farm and informed him that two men had reported seeing a woman fitting Elsie's description approaching his farm on December 5th. Thorne replied that he had heard some local gossip to that effect but that the witnesses must be mistaken, as Elsie had certainly never arrived. He then invited the superintendent to have a look around for himself.

Superintendent Budgen did take a look around, accompanied by Inspector George Edwards from the Crowborough force. They found nothing out of the ordinary and left after Norman had made a written statement in which he said that he had last seen Elsie on November 28th. She had not visited on December 5th but he had received a letter from her on that date, saying that she would be down on the Saturday. He had gone to meet her train but there was no sign of her and he had returned to the farm, fully expecting to hear from her in due course. When he did not, he wrote to her at her home address, asking what the matter was. As for the letter from Elsie, unfortunately he had since burned it.

As the investigation progressed, the police officers on the case soon discovered that Norman Thorne might not have been the concerned fiancé that he claimed. In the first place, the recent engagement had only come about because Elsie had announced to her mother that she thought she was pregnant. Mrs Cameron had marched her daughter

145

around to the doctor, who had been unable to confirm that Elsie was with child, but Mr Cameron had then placed pressure on Norman to ensure that he did the decent thing. Secondly, it soon became clear that Norman had another girlfriend, a local woman named Elizabeth Ann Coldicott, who lived with her mother at Springhill, South View Road, Crowborough.

Officers now spoke to Miss Coldicott, who explained that she had first met Thorne at a village dance at Whitsun, 1924. Since then they had seen each other a few times, during which Norman had explained his ties with Elsie. This had not discouraged Miss Coldicott who, from September 1924 onwards, had taken to visiting Thorne at his farm, often staying there until late in the evening. Norman had even told her that he wished to marry her, not Elsie, but added that he would have to be careful how he broke this news to his present fiancée as she was highly-strung and he was not sure how she might take it.

It was December 26th by the time that Thorne was interviewed again. Confronted with knowledge of Miss Coldicott's existence and his fiancée's possible pregnancy, he now admitted that he had had some trouble with Elsie. He described their relationship in detail and admitted that they had engaged in some fairly heavy petting but had stopped short of actual intercourse. He was not sure if she could be pregnant, but if she were in that condition, then he would, of course, marry her. He continued to maintain, however, that he had not seen her on December 5th.

It was now only a matter of time before a proper search of the farm took place. On January 14th, a number of officers arrived with shovels and began digging. Thorne, meanwhile, was taken in for further questioning.

At 8.25 a.m. on January 15th, the first breakthrough came. Constable John Philpott shouted that he had found something in the mud. The soil was scraped away and it was seen that he had found an attaché case. Once the case was opened, the contents were easily identified as belonging to Elsie Cameron.

News of this discovery was transmitted back to the police station and Thorne was informed that the search would continue and that he would be held in custody and probably charged with being responsible for the death of Miss Cameron. Thorne made no reply and the police returned to the muddy field at Crowborough to carry on with their digging.

By 5.00 p.m., nothing new had been found and operations were suspended for the day. Three hours later, however, Thorne announced that he wished to make another statement. This document began "I, John Norman Holmes Thorne, after being cautioned, wish to tell you the truth of what happened on 5th December.

"Between 5.15 p.m. and 5.30 p.m., Miss Cameron entered my hut carrying her suitcase and that was all. I asked her why she had come unexpectedly, and she said she wanted some tea. I asked her where she intended to sleep and she said 'In the hut', and furthermore, that she intended staying until she was married. I asked who would support her and she said 'You will have to'. I said I had to talk it over with mother and

146

The accused man, John Thorne, with a warder at Crowborough station, on the way to Brixton prison during the
Elsie Cameron enquiry (Hulton Getty Picture Collection)

father. She insisted on being married at once. I went to the Cosham's, leaving her in the hut, at 7.30 p.m., to see if I could arrange for her to sleep one night.

"I returned saying she would have to sleep in my bed. I proposed sleeping in a large chair myself. There was an argument between us as to her coming down without making arrangements, and she said it made no difference as we were to be married. I told her I had arranged to meet Mrs and Miss Coldicott at the station to carry their suitcases, and told her to go to bed. I went to the station, and when I returned at 11.30 p.m., the dog came down to meet me. When I opened the door I saw Miss Cameron hanging from a beam by a piece of cord used for a washing line. I laid her across the table and lay by her for about an hour. I was intending to inform the police, but then realising the position I was in, I went to the workshop and chained up the dog.

"I returned to the hut, and took off her clothes, and put her on the table naked. I got my saw and some sacking, tore up her clothes, and burned them in the hut. I laid the sacks on the floor and sawed off her head by the glow of the fire and put it in a sack. I put parts of the body in the sack, intending to carry them away, but my nerve failed me and I put them in the workshop. The next morning, as soon as it got light, I buried them

147

in the chicken run. I then went into the hut and had some coffee and tried to build up evidence to protect myself. I buried her suitcase near the potato patch."

Thorne then told the police precisely where they would find Elsie's remains. The police began digging again and at 11.00 p.m., Elsie Cameron was finally found. Her body had been cut into four pieces. The head had been severed, placed in some sacking and then packed tightly into a biscuit tin. The trunk, with the arms still attached, was also wrapped in sacking and the two legs, hacked off at the upper thighs, were wrapped together in another piece of hessian. Not surprisingly, Thorne was then charged with wilful murder.

Thorne's trial for murder opened at Lewes on March 11th, 1925, before Mr Justice Finlay. The case for the prosecution was led by Sir Henry Curtis Bennett, who was assisted by Mr R. E. Negus. Thorne's defence lay in the hands of Mr James Dale Cassels, who had two assistants, Mr Oakes and Mr C. T. Abbott. The proceedings lasted until March 16th.

There could be no denying that Thorne was guilty of dismembering Elsie Cameron's body and concealing it on his farm. His defence was that he had carried out this terrible act after he had discovered that she had committed suicide. The prosecution, on the other hand, maintained that he had murdered her because she was demanding that he marry her after he had fallen in love with another woman, Elizabeth Coldicott.

The prosecution began by introducing letters that had passed between Norman and Elsie. Two from Norman, one dated November 21st, and the second dated November 25th, showed Norman admitting that he had found someone else and describing himself as being '....between two fires'. Elsie's replies to those letters were read out in court.

The first letter, dated November 24th, read "My Own Darling Norman. Your letter received last night, and I am returning it in this letter, although I don't see why you wanted it back. It was too late to send it on last night. Why should you not go this week as really Norman every day makes a difference to me. You must realise that this worry is dangerous for the baby.

"Why are there one or two things you have not told me, and in what way does it concern me? I don't know I have ever kept a single thing from you, and I don't think it is fair for you to keep things from me. Why did you not tell me everything last Friday?

"What do you mean by between two fires? I want to be married before Christmas and CD [Christmas Day] is only a month tomorrow, and it will also be perfectly obvious to everyone after that: also you must let your people know as soon as you can. I feel ever so worried about things now.

"Please do get married quickly. I can't write any more now. Fondest love and kisses, yours ever."

The second letter contained such phrases as "...You are engaged to me, and I have first claim on you" and "Whatever this girl thinks of me, I have first claim on you... My baby must have a name."

This evidence did perhaps establish a motive, but it was the testimony of one man that would really convict Norman Thorne. The medical testimony would obviously prove to be crucial and the prosecution had obtained the testimony of the eminent pathologist, Sir Bernard Spilsbury.

Spilsbury began by outlining eight separate bruises which he had detected on Elsie's remains, the most telling of which he believed to be one on the right side of the back of the head. The tissues beneath this bruise had been pulped and this was consistent with a crushing blow being delivered. When the police had searched the hut, two heavy Indian clubs had been found and Spilsbury agreed that one of these could have inflicted the injury he had observed. More importantly, Spilsbury stated that he had found no evidence of asphyxia, which would have been the case had Elsie died as Thorne had described. It was true that there were creases in the tissues of the neck, but Spilsbury claimed that these were natural folds and not grooves caused by a washing line cord digging into the neck.

This evidence had to be refuted and so the defence called their own expert medical witnesses, Dr Robert Matthew Bronte and Dr John Smith Gibson. On February 24th, Elsie's body had been exhumed so that these two doctors could carry out a second medical examination, in the presence of Spilsbury. Both doctors agreed that the most probable cause of death was shock due to attempted hanging. The creases in the tissues of the neck were indeed caused by a rope. On the fifth day of the trial, Spilsbury was recalled and even he agreed that if he were wrong about the grooves, then they did indeed show evidence of some injury to the neck consistent with hanging. Furthermore, he was unable to explain how, since Elsie had an abnormally thin skull, a crushing blow such as he had described would not have shattered the head like an eggshell.

Was Elsie Cameron the type of woman to commit suicide? There seems to be a good deal of evidence to suggest that she was. The Cameron family maintained that such a thought would never have entered Elsie's head and yet, on December 16th, well before the discovery of the body, Mrs Cameron had written to Thorne, "...Whatever has happened to her? We get no rest day or night. If it had been a week or two before, I might have thought that she had done something rash."

When Elsie had visited Norman, she was in the habit of staying at one of two farms – 1 Pasture Villas, a house owned by Agnes and Edwin Piper, or 'Corona', the home of Florence and Robert Cosham. Agnes Piper recalled one particular visit when Elsie stayed with her in 1923. The visit was supposed to last for two weeks but Elsie finally stayed for six. At the end of that time she appeared to be very nervous and on the last night, Edwin had to take her to Thorne's farm because she was so bad. Thorne then had to escort her back to London, where she was handed over to her married sister, Margaret Blomfield. Even Margaret admitted that at the time, Elsie seemed to be very distressed.

Alice Mary Hawksworth was a bookkeeper from Willesden and she knew Elsie Cameron well. She recalled a time in September 1924 when Elsie seemed to be very nervous about going to work. She told Alice that she thought everyone was looking at her and laughing at her. One day, Elsie had grabbed Alice's arm and confessed that she thought she was going off her head.

Rose Blythe and Mildred Pearson were shorthand typists who worked in the same office as Elsie. The work all three women had to do was very simple but Elsie apparently could not cope with it. As a result, Elsie only worked with them for six days and at the end of that time had to be taken home in a state of nervous collapse. Rose and Mildred were detailed to escort her and, at the railway station, had to pull her back from the edge of the platform.

Elsie Cameron had made much of her pregnancy in her letters to Thorne, but the post-mortem had shown that she was not, in fact, in that state. Her own doctor, Dr Watson Walker, testified that he had known Elsie as a patient since June 15th, 1921. In November 1924, she had come to see him and explained that she had missed two periods and believed that she was pregnant. He had been unable to confirm this and advised her to return on December 18th, an appointment she was, of course, unable to keep.

Finally there was the evidence of Dr James Woods, a lecturer on mental diseases at St George's Hospital in London. He stated that the descriptions of Elsie's behaviour were consistent with certain mentally neurotic conditions. She appeared to have moods of elation followed very soon afterwards by deep depressions. This was symptomatic of psychosis and such people, in times of stress, might well have suicidal tendencies. Questioned at length about what Elsie's reaction might have been after arriving in Thorne's hut, only to find that he was about to leave to meet her rival, Miss Coldicott, Dr Woods answered that he thought this could cause a sudden suicidal impulse.

In the event, the jury took just thirty minutes to decide that Thorne was guilty as charged and he was sentenced to death. An appeal was heard on April 6th before the Lord Chief Justice, Lord Hewart and Justices Shearman and Salter, on the grounds that the original trial judge had misled the jury on the conflicting medical evidence whilst summing up. However, the Appeal Court held that the judge had summed up in a "... most admirable way", and on April 7th it was announced that the appeal had been lost. Thorne, who was present, seemed to be visibly moved and as he was taken down to the cells, he cried out that he was an innocent man.

On April 22nd, 1925, John Norman Holmes Thorne was hanged by Thomas Pierrepoint and Robert Wilson. It was a significant date, for April 22nd would have been Elsie Cameron's twenty-seventh birthday.

19 Johannes Josephus Cornelius Mommers

Hanged at Pentonville prison, London, Tuesday, July 27th, 1926
For the murder of Augusta Violette Pionbini, at Thundersley, Essex

THE Pionbini family consisted of four members. Ettore, the father, was a waiter at the Cafe Monico in Piccadilly, London and so only spent his weekends at the family home, Sunnyside, which was situated in Kiln Road, Thundersley. During the week, therefore, the head of the house was Ettore's wife, Victoria Maria, and she looked after her two daughters, Olive and Augusta. Together the three women operated Sunnyside as a boarding house, in order to supplement the family income.

During the week Ettore Pionbini lived in lodgings of his own, at 29 Lillie Road, West Brompton, a house owned by his wife. It was there that he became friendly with a man who lived next door at number thirty-one, Johannes Mommers, a painter and decorator who was of Dutch extraction and who preferred to be called Peter. Mommers often did odd jobs for the Pionbini family and it was therefore no surprise that when they decided that Sunnyside could do with a lick of paint, Ettore turned to Mommers and offered him the job. Mommers accepted and moved down to Thundersley, living in at Sunnyside whilst he carried out the work, starting on May 3rd, 1926.

In the days that the work went on, Mommers grew very close to the Pionbini ladies but it was the eldest daughter, twenty-two-year-old Augusta, known as Girlie, with whom he seemed to spend most time. Mommers took Augusta out every now and then but there was never any suggestion that there was anything more than friendship between them. After all, Johannes Mommers was a happily married man and, at forty-three, much too old for Augusta.

On Thursday, May 6th, 1926, Mommers and Augusta spent the day together in Southend. That evening, when they returned, Mommers spoke to Augusta's mother, Victoria, and told her that he needed to go back to London the next day as there was some problem with his bank account. Some money that he had been expecting still had not come through, and he needed to go to the capital to sort things out. Unfortunately, the problem meant that he had no money at the moment and so he asked Victoria if she would lend him the fare. Victoria readily agreed.

The next morning, Friday May 7th, Mommers left Sunnyside at 8.15 a.m. Before he bade Victoria Pionbini farewell he expressed the hope that he might bump into Ettore whilst he was in London as he would, of course, be going home at some stage to see his wife. Late that afternoon, Mommers returned to Sunnyside and said that he had sorted out his finances satisfactorily, but had not seen Ettore.

At 7.30 p.m. that evening, Mommers and Augusta went out for a stroll. It was something they had done many times before and Victoria raised no objections. She and Olive stayed in the house, busying themselves upstairs.

At 9.45 p.m., Victoria Pionbini heard the door which led onto the back garden open. There was a cry and Olive rushed downstairs to see what the problem was. To her horror she found Augusta bleeding from a gash in her throat. Olive ran upstairs for her mother and they both then helped Augusta up to her bedroom. Since the injured woman had gone out with Mommers, and had now returned alone in this state, Victoria asked her if Peter had done this to her. Augusta managed to mumble something but neither Victoria nor Olive could catch what it was.

Victoria Pionbini needed to get some help for her daughter. Going downstairs she dashed to the house next door and called out to her neighbour, Albert Donoghue, "Come at once, Girlie has had her throat cut". Donoghue ran next door and after seeing the extent of Augusta's wounds, went to fetch a doctor and the police. Despite prompt medical attention, however, Augusta Pionbini died from her injury at 10.50 p.m. The police were now urgently seeking Johannes Mommers in connection with a charge of murder.

At the time, the General Strike was still in full swing and many officers found themselves on various duties connected with the strike. One such officer was Inspector Hurrell, who was based at Grays. It was 3.15 a.m. on May 8th when he saw a man near the police station, walking along by the side of the road. It was unusual to see someone at this early hour, so Inspector Hurrell took special notice of him. Just ten minutes later, Hurrell was looking through the day's messages when he came across the report on Augusta's death. The description of the man the police were looking for matched the man Hurrell had just seen, though this was some sixteen miles from Sunnyside. The inspector wasted no time in retracing his steps, taking Constable Sach with him.

The man Hurrell had seen had moved a little further away from the police station but when the inspector reached Grays Hall Hill he saw the man strolling purposefully down the street. When stopped by the policemen, Mommers readily admitted his identity and was then taken back to the station for questioning. Later that same morning, at 11.30 a.m., he was charged with Augusta's murder. He replied "I am saying nothing".

Mommers' trial took place at Chelmsford on June 16th, before Mister Justice Shearman and a jury of eleven men and one woman. The prosecution case rested in the formidable hands of Mr Edward Marshall Hall, who was assisted by Mr G. Rentoul, whilst Mommers was defended by Mr Lucian Fior.

Ettore Pionbini explained how his family had first met Mommers. Up to two years ago all the Pionbinis had lived at 29 Lillie Road. They then bought the house in Thundersley and moved away. The two families had always been friendly and, in all, had known each other for perhaps five years. Mommers had first done some painting at Sunnyside before Christmas 1925, when he had lived there for as long as two months whilst working on the house. He had gone back in May to continue the work.

Olive Ida Miriam Pionbini, Augusta's seventeen-year-old sister, testified that until May 1st, Augusta had been staying at the London flat with her father. She had been there for about three weeks and for ten days of that time, Olive was there too. On May 1st, Augusta returned to Essex and two days later, Mommers came to Sunnyside to start work.

Turning to the night of Augusta's death, Olive said that her sister had been getting ready to go out when Mommers came into their bedroom and said, "Aren't you ready?" Augusta had replied "I won't be a min." and they left together a few minutes later. When Augusta came back to the house, their mother was lying on her bed and Olive was in her own room. The sound of a scream caused her to run downstairs and they helped Augusta up to the bedroom.

Inspector Hurrell said that when he first stopped Mommers he had asked him "Where are you going?" and Mommers had replied "I am walking to London". Hurrell then asked him for his name and Mommers replied correctly. After he had been charged, his clothing was taken for examination because Inspector Hurrell had noticed what appeared to be bloodstains. The inspector also searched the prisoner and found a packet of cigarettes and a box of matches, both of which were bloodstained.

John Webster was an analyst for the Home Office and he had made a scientific examination of the clothes Mommers was wearing when he was arrested. There were a number of recent bloodstains and a handkerchief bore signs of having been recently washed.

Dr J. C. Jameson told the court how he was summoned to Sunnyside to find Augusta lying on the floor in a back bedroom. He helped to lift the girl onto her bed and she died later without ever having spoken in his presence. Death was due to haemorrhage and Dr Jameson was of the opinion that the wound in the throat was not self-inflicted as it was too severe.

George Hobbs was the manager of the White Hart Hotel at Thundersley and he reported that he had seen Mommers and Augusta many times in his establishment. They came in together at 7.30 p.m. on May 7th, and stayed until just after 9.00 p.m.

Though Hobbs could not hear what the couple were talking about, they appeared to be on the friendliest of terms.

This friendliness was confirmed by Edwin Cotter, a commercial traveller who had been another customer at the White Hart that night. He saw Mommers and Augusta together and they left the bar before him. He left at around 9.45 p.m., and was driving home when he saw them again, near Kenneth Road. The girl had her arm on Mommers' shoulder and he had his arm around her waist.

The prosecution case was that Mommers had wilfully murdered Augusta, but no motive could be suggested. Mommers now went into the witness box to give his version of events.

Mommers began by explaining that he was a Dutch subject and had got married, in Belgium, in 1906. In 1914, he had come to England and almost immediately joined the army, serving with the King's Royal Rifles in France. He went on to explain how he had first met the Pionbinis and then turned to the night of Augusta's death.

After leaving the White Hart, Augusta had turned to him and said "Peter, take me away tonight, yes or no?" She had had three whiskies and seemed to be somewhat under the influence so he let her down gently, saying that he could not take her away. At this she started kissing and cuddling him and asked him again if he would take her away. Again he said no and told Augusta that he needed to use the lavatory. His intention was to sneak away and head off to London, but she saw him and ran after him shouting "Peter, Peter, where are you going? Come here, I want you."

Catching up with him she again demanded that he take her away and he refused for the third time. Suddenly there was a flash and she shouted, "If you don't take me away, this is what I will do". Augusta put her hand up to her throat and Mommers saw that she had a black handled razor in her hand. He took it from her and then left to walk to London. He had no idea that Augusta had injured herself. After he had walked for some miles, Mommers took the razor from his pocket and was surprised to see that it was bloodstained. He then threw it away.

At first, this story looked rather implausible but the defence then called Doctor Robert Matthew Bronte, a pathologist, who had also made an examination of Augusta's wound. He disagreed with Dr Jameson because the wound was much deeper on the right side than the left. This indicated that the wound was self-inflicted.

A second expert witness, Doctor Hugh Ernest Griffiths, a Harley Street practitioner, stated that if this were a homicidal wound, it was a very strange one. In fact, it was much more consistent with suicide. He had found a small fingernail mark on the right side of Augusta's face and this may well have been caused by Mommers trying to pull the blade away from the girl's throat. This was confirmed by a third doctor, Charles E. M. Low.

Despite no fewer than three doctors testifying that it was much more likely that Augusta Pionbini had taken her own life, the jury were out considering their verdict for only eight minutes. Mommers was then sentenced to death, but before he was taken down to the cells he muttered "I didn't do it, sir".

An appeal against the verdict was lodged on the grounds that Augusta had committed suicide and so Mommers could not be guilty of murder. However, this was dismissed on July 12th because it was felt that the evidence was strong enough to show that the crime was deliberate and that Mommers must therefore have been the killer. Just over two weeks later, on July 27th, Mommers was hanged at Pentonville by Robert Baxter and William Willis.

20

Bertram Horace Kirby

Hanged at Lincoln, Wednesday, January 4th, 1928
For the murder of his wife, Minnie Eleanor Kirby, at Louth, Lincolnshire

B ERTRAM Kirby's background cannot be said to have been a stable one. In 1915, at the height of the hostilities during the Great War, he had been discharged from the army as insane. Ten years later, in 1925, he underwent an operation on a carbuncle on his neck which, if anything, made him even more prone to mental problems. He had once attempted suicide by taking laudanum, and by 1927, he was suffering from severe financial concerns.

Kirby was a married man, his wife being forty-six-year-old Minnie. The couple had three sons – Ralph, who lived abroad, twenty-one-year-old Harry, who did not get on with his father due to the violence Kirby had shown him, and so lived with Mrs Beatrice Took at 1 St Michael's Terrace, Louth, and eight-year-old Norman, the youngest, who lived with his parents in a bungalow nearby.

On Monday, July 11th, 1927, at 10.00 a.m., Kirby called at Mrs Took's house and asked if she would take Norman in for dinner. He explained that Norman was at school at the moment but said that Minnie had to go down to London about a job, though she might possibly be back that same night. Kirby also added that he had some work at Grimsby which meant that he might not be back, and if that happened he would appreciate it if Mrs Took would let Norman stay the night. Mrs Took agreed and Kirby said he would go down to the school to tell Norman what was happening. A few minutes later, Kirby came back from the direction of the school, carrying a suitcase and a brown paper parcel.

Neither Kirby nor Minnie returned that night, and Norman stayed with his brother at Mrs Took's. The next day, at around 3.40 p.m., Beatrice Took saw Kirby walking towards his bungalow and he asked her if she had seen anything of Minnie. Mrs Took said that she had not, but Kirby added that he had had a letter from his wife, saying that she would be home at about 9.20 p.m. Kirby said that he would call at St Michael's Terrace to collect Norman at 9.30 p.m., and then carried on walking towards the bungalow.

Harry Kirby had last seen his mother on the evening of Sunday, July 10th, when they had gone for a walk together. On the Monday, when he had gone to Mrs Took's

The Kirbys' bungalow in Louth, where Minnie Kirby's body was found on July 12th, 1927 (Public Record Office Ref. No. ASSI 13/57)

for his own dinner, Harry had been surprised to see his brother Norman there too. Mrs Took explained what their father had told her. That same evening, at 4.30 p.m., Harry had called at the bungalow to make sure that everything was all right. There was no answer to his knocking and the entire house was locked up.

On Tuesday, July 12th, Harry went back to the bungalow at some time between 6.00 p.m. and 6.30 p.m., but apparently there was still no one at home. By now, Harry was growing somewhat concerned about his mother's continued absence, so he decided to take his worries to the police. At 8.15 p.m, Harry returned to Kirby's home, this time accompanied by Inspector Davies.

Inspector Harry Davies gained entrance to the bungalow through a broken back window. The rest of the house had been secure and once inside, Davies saw that not only was the back door bolted but also a brush had been wedged against it for extra security. Opening the door to let Harry Kirby in, the two men now began a search of the rooms.

There were three letters on a table in the kitchen. One was addressed 'To whom it may concern' and the others to family members. In that same room, a clothes-horse, fully laden, blocked off part of the room and it was behind that horse that the body of Minnie Kirby lay. She appeared to have been killed with a single blow from a heavy weapon such as the axe, which was usually kept in the workshop, but which was now behind the pantry door.

Bertram Kirby was soon found. At 9.40 p.m., Sergeant Henry Morris and Inspector Davies went to the White Horse Inn, where they saw Kirby playing dominoes with some friends. The two officers called Kirby outside but he calmly finished his pint before obeying their instruction. Once outside the bar Kirby was cautioned, to which he replied "All right now, I want to be fair with you. I am not going to cause any trouble. My God boy, you do not know what things are and I hope you never will. You do not know what I have had to put up with."

On November 1st, Bertram Kirby faced his trial for murder, at Lincoln, before Mr Justice Swift. Kirby's defence lay in the hands of Mr W. Butler, whilst the prosecution case was led by Mr M. Healy.

Harry Kirby explained that his father had been employed as an engineer's timekeeper for the railway until September 1926, when he had tried to set up his own business selling goods on commission. This had failed and ever since, the family had been in dire financial straits.

Next, an attempt was made to determine at what time the attack upon Minnie Kirby had taken place. Thomas James McQuade was an auxiliary postman and he testified that he had delivered letters at the back door of the bungalow at 7.20 a.m., on July 11th. Minnie had certainly been alive and well at that time. The next morning, another delivery was made, again to the back door but this time the blinds were drawn and McQuade put the letters through the box. He could hear someone moving about inside the house, however.

William Henry Grant was a signalman for the London and North Eastern Railway and on July 11th, he was on duty at the Mablethorpe crossing in Slewton Lane. From there he could see the gateway leading to the Kirby bungalow. At 8.30 a.m., he saw Norman leave for school, turn, and wave to someone. Later, Grant saw the prisoner come to the crossing but did not speak to him.

Elizabeth Mary White was in the habit of buying flowers from Kirby, and had last done so on Friday, July 8th. At the time he seemed to be perfectly all right. On the Monday, Kirby called at her house at 10.00 a.m., saying that he wanted to leave a bag and a parcel with her. He called back for them twenty minutes later and seemed to be pale and excited. Elizabeth saw Kirby again, at 3.30 p.m. the next day. He appeared to be shaky and wild.

Sarah Annie Riley ran a second-hand clothes shop and at 10.30 a.m., on July 11th, Kirby came in with a parcel of clothing to sell. Sarah paid him seven shillings and the next day, she paid him a similar sum when he called with a second parcel. Later that same Tuesday, Kirby brought a third parcel, which Sarah bought for four shillings. Kirby had explained that he was going to Mansfield, to a new job, and said that he had also sold the bungalow and lost £200 on the deal.

Ernest Potts was the licensee of the Wheatsheaf Inn at Louth and he reported that Kirby had come into his establishment at 11.10 a.m. on July 11th, carrying an attaché case. He said that he was on his way to Grimsby and left at 11.25 a.m. Ernest saw Kirby again at 5.50 p.m., when he asked for some tea. He then stayed in the bar, playing dominoes, until 9.45 p.m. The attaché case was now missing and when Ernest asked about it, Kirby said he had sent it home. At one stage, Kirby explained that he had sold his bungalow for £450.

George Baker was a gardener who, on July 11th, was working on some land next to Kirby's bungalow. He told the court that at 9.00 a.m., he had seen Kirby come out of the bungalow. He saw him again, at 10.00 a.m., when Kirby went out of his gate and headed off towards the railway crossing.

Inspector Davies stated that when he was arrested and searched, Kirby was found to be carrying an unfinished letter which Minnie had been writing to Ralph, and Kirby said this was the last she had ever written. He was also carrying a bottle of whisky. The other letters, found at the bungalow, were also referred to. In the one addressed 'To whom it may concern' Kirby had outlined that he had fallen on hard times and his wife had realized that the only way out for both of them was death. That was why he had killed her, and all he wanted now was to join her in death. He had also left a letter that arranged for Norman to be cared for, and another one to Ralph, saying that Minnie was dead, and that he was going to join her. There was also a letter in the house, in Minnie's handwriting, arranging to sell the bungalow, which belonged to her.

Dr Henry Stanley Walker had visited the scene of the crime and stated that Minnie was lying on her back with her face towards the window and her feet underneath a table. A pen lay near her right hand. A cushion had been placed underneath her head, and her hair and the cushion smelled of disinfectant. There was blood on the back of Minnie's head and on the cushion, and after examining the head, Dr Walker noticed a V-shaped lacerated wound with a depressed fracture of the skull below it. Dr Walker had also conducted the post-mortem, and said that death was due to shock caused by a hard blunt object coming into violent contact with the back of the skull. There had only been one blow and the back of an axe, found in the pantry, could have inflicted the wound.

Kirby claimed that there had been a suicide pact between him and his wife but the prosecution claimed that the letters had been written after the event in an attempt to throw the police off the scent. Little regard was paid to Kirby's obvious mental problems, the only examination having been carried out at Lincoln prison, where the governor, Mr F. W. Turner, observed that there were no signs of mental aberration in the prisoner.

As stated elsewhere in this book, a defence of insanity carries with it a number of problems, the main one being that the burden of proof shifts to the defence. It was plain that Kirby was mentally unstable but his defence team did not pursue this matter vigorously enough. Under the circumstances, the jury wasted no time in returning a guilty verdict. The original execution date was set for November 23rd, but this was postponed once an appeal was announced. The appeal was fought on the grounds that Kirby had not been responsible for his actions and that therefore the verdict should have been one of manslaughter. However, the Court held that his behaviour before and after the crime showed that he knew full well what he was doing, so in due course the appeal was dismissed and a new execution date arranged.

On January 4th, 1928, forty-seven-year-old Bertram Kirby was hanged at Lincoln by Thomas Pierrepoint and Henry Pollard. However, there can be little doubt that his mental condition, allied to his financial concerns, played a large part in the death of his wife.

Frederick Guy Browne

21

Hanged at Pentonville prison, London, Thursday, May 31st, 1928
For the murder of George William Gutteridge, at Howe Green, Essex

WILLIAM Alec Ward was a postman who drove a route between Romford and Abridge, most of his journey taking him along the B175. Early on the morning of Tuesday, September 27th, 1927, Ward drove through Havering-atte-Bower and Bournebridge before dropping some mail at the little village of Stapleford Abbotts. He then climbed back into his van and continued towards Stapleford Tawney. Having driven over Pinchback Bridge, Ward turned a bend which led into the hamlet of Howe Green. It was then that he saw something at the side of the road. The time was just after 6.00 a.m.

On the grass verge, in a semi-seated position, was the body of a man. His legs extended out into the road and at first, Ward thought that he might have been the victim of a hit-and-run accident. However, on closer inspection, Ward saw that this was no accident. The man was certainly dead, and there were terrible wounds to his head. Furthermore, the uniform the man wore, and other distinguishing features, showed that this victim was someone Ward knew well, thirty-eight-year-old Police Constable George William Gutteridge, who lived in Stapleford Abbotts.

Ward needed to get help and so ran to Rose Cottage in Howe Green itself, and woke the occupant, Alfred Perritt. The two men then went back to where Gutteridge lay and moved the body so that it now lay parallel to the verge. This was done, as Ward would explain later, so that no passing vehicles would run over Gutteridge's legs, which had been stretched out into the road itself.

Perritt looked about and saw that there was a large pool of blood in the centre of the road, and splashes leading back to where the body lay. That, plus the fact that Gutteridge still held a pencil in one hand, suggested that he might have stopped a vehicle and been killed for his trouble.

At that moment, a bus appeared and the two men spoke to the driver, explained that they had found a policeman dead, and asked him to notify the authorities. The driver went on to call the police at Havering but in the meantime, Ward ran to Stapleford Tawney and used a telephone there to alert the Romford police. Soon after, Constable

Albert Blockson was on the scene, taking charge until Detective Inspector John Crockford arrived at 7.45 a.m.

It was Crockford who made the first careful examination of Gutteridge's wounds. The constable had been shot in the head four times, but there were more than four wounds in the body, as some of the bullets had travelled straight through the head, leaving exit wounds as well. Crockford noted two holes on the left side of Gutteridge's face, just in front of his ear. There were two corresponding holes in the right side of the neck, showing that the two bullets had exited at those points. Perhaps the most horrible feature of the case was that the killer, whoever he was, had deliberately fired a bullet into each of Gutteridge's eyes.

The idea that Gutteridge had just stopped some sort of motor vehicle was reinforced by the fact that in addition to the pencil in his right hand, Gutteridge's tunic was partly unfastened and his whistle hung from his pocket by a chain. His notebook lay in the road but his truncheon and torch were still in his pocket. There were no signs of a struggle round about but there were signs, on the opposite side of the road, that a vehicle had recently parked there. Though it was clear that Gutteridge was beyond all aid, Inspector Crockford then went to fetch the doctor.

It was 9.00 a.m. by the time Doctor Robert Arnold Woodhouse arrived at the scene. He examined Gutteridge and announced that his initial findings were that the officer had been dead for between four and five hours, putting the time of death at somewhere between 4.00 a.m. and 5.00 a.m. The body was then finally moved, to the coach-house at the Royal Oak public house.

The investigating officers at the scene later found two spent bullets in the roadway. It was now surmised that Gutteridge had been patrolling his beat in the early hours of September 27th, when he heard a car approaching. For some reason, the constable decided to stop the vehicle and possibly took out his whistle to call the driver to pull over. Gutteridge, presumably after speaking to the driver, then took out his notebook and prepared to write something down. Before he could put pencil to paper, two shots had been fired into his head. He would then have staggered back and fallen against the grassy bank of the road. His assailant then climbed out of the car, walked over to where he lay dying, and shot out both of his eyes. It was plain that the investigation needed the expertise of Scotland Yard, and that same day, Chief Inspector James Berrett and Detective Sergeant John Harris travelled to Essex from London.

The early part of the investigation was aimed at pinpointing the exact time of the attack upon Gutteridge. After speaking to his widow, Rose Annette Gutteridge, the police discovered that Gutteridge had gone out on duty some time after 11.00 p.m., on September 26th. As part of Gutteridge's beat, he was in the habit of meeting a fellow officer, Constable Sydney James Taylor, near Grove House at Howe Green, at around 3.00 a.m. This was the spot where the two officers' beats coincided and the constables would take the opportunity to talk over any cases they might be working on, and exchange information. When Taylor was interviewed, he confirmed that he had met Gutteridge at about 2.40 a.m., and they had spoken for some twenty-five minutes, finally parting at 3.05 a.m.

The spot at Grove House was slightly over a mile from where Gutteridge lived and a mile and three quarters from where Taylor lived. After saying goodnight to Gutteridge, Taylor had walked slowly back to his home, arriving there at 4.20 a.m. He then made himself some cocoa before going to bed. Surprisingly, he had heard no shots fired, though assuming that both officers had walked at their normal speeds, Taylor would certainly have still been within earshot when Gutteridge was attacked, at around 3.35 a.m. There was also no explanation ever given as to why it had taken Taylor so long to complete the short walk home – questioned on these matters, Taylor insisted that he had walked directly home and had heard nothing. Taylor did say, however, that at about 4.20 a.m., almost an hour later, he heard a car being driven past his house.

Other people had also heard things that morning. Lady Decies lived almost exactly opposite the Royal Oak and she told the investigating officers that at some time between 3.00 a.m. and 4.00 a.m., she had been woken by what sounded like revolver shots. Soon afterwards she heard a car drive past. Assuming that this was the killer, and it would seem

The blue Morris Cowley car, which was stolen on the night of PC Gutteridge's murder and used by the killer (Hulton Getty Picture Collection)

likely that his was the only car around at the time, it would mean that he was heading for Romford.

It was then that reports of a car theft came to Chief Inspector Berrett's attention. Doctor Edward Richardson Lovell lived at Shirley, Oak Tree Corner, near Billericay and at 7.30 p.m., on September 26th, he had parked his blue Morris Cowley car, registration TW 6120, in his garage. The following morning he woke to find that the car had been stolen. Local police had found two witnesses who were able to say that they had heard the doctor's car being driven away in the early hours of September 27th.

Thomas George Wilson lived just one hundred yards away from Dr Lovell, and at 2.30 a.m. he had been woken by the sound of a car being started. Seconds later he heard the car being driven off, towards Mountnessing. William Ernest Stevens lived on the Mountnessing road and he was woken by car headlamps flooding his

165

bedroom with light. He was certain that it was Dr Lovell's car as he recognized the rather distinct engine sound.

It now appeared that someone had broken into Dr Lovell's garage near Billericay, at about 2.30 a.m., on September 27th. Stealing the car, he had then driven along the A129 towards Mountnessing. At this point he may have taken one of two routes, either up towards Chipping Ongar and then down through Little End on the A113, into Stapleford Abbotts, a rather tortuous route towards London, or alternatively, down the A12 towards Romford. If he had taken this second route, and the car thief was the man responsible for the murder, then for some reason he must have turned off, up the B175 to Stapleford Abbotts and, after shooting Gutteridge, turned the car around and retraced his route towards Romford. This would have had to be the case because Lady Decies' house was in such a position that in order to pass her house after she heard the shots, the driver would have to have been heading south. That the stolen vehicle was heading towards London was certain, for news now came through that it had been found, in Brixton.

Albert John McDougall lived at 21 Foxley Road, Brixton, and at 7.20 a.m., on September 27th, he had left for work, having to squeeze past a blue Cowley parked by his back door. As he did so, McDougall noticed that the radiator was quite warm. That evening, at 6.00 p.m., McDougall returned home to find that the Cowley had not been moved. He checked with his neighbours to see if it belonged to any of them and after finding that it did not, reported it to Constable Alfred Edmonds. The car was later driven to Brixton police station, where it was examined. An empty cartridge case was found underneath the front passenger seat. It was marked R.L.IV. A check was made on the registration number and the vehicle was traced to Dr Lovell. Chief Inspector Berrett was informed but by then he was already on his way to Basingstoke, for there a man had given himself up and admitted that he was Gutteridge's killer.

It had been 10.25 p.m., on September 27th, when Andrew Baldwing had walked up to Constable Barge in Basingstoke town centre and announced "I wish to give myself up for the murder of the police constable in Essex". Chief Inspector Berrett was informed, and he and Sergeant Harris immediately began the drive to Basingstoke, arriving there at 3.30 a.m., the next morning. Unfortunately, it soon became clear that Baldwing was merely seeking attention and knew nothing of the crime. Berrett then went on to London, to examine Dr Lovell's car.

No fresh leads were forthcoming so on Berrett's orders a list of possible suspects was drawn up. These were men who lived in London, had criminal records, were known to use violence and who had been in possession of firearms. One name on that list was Frederick Guy Browne, whose real name was Leo Browne. He had five convictions for burglary, larceny, forgery and fraud, and had only been discharged from Dartmoor on March 30th, 1927. A married man, he had a daughter and lived with his family in Clapham, running a garage from a yard at 7a Northcote Road in Lavender Hill, Wandsworth. At this stage, however, there was nothing to link him with the crime and so there was no valid reason to obtain a warrant to search his premises.

166

It was not until November that the longed-for breakthrough came. In that month, a van driver in Sheffield was cut up by a car driven erratically. So incensed was he that he took the car's number and reported the matter to the police. A few days later, a keen-eyed constable spotted the car parked in Sheffield and spoke to the driver. He was asked to show his licence and it soon transpired that the car had been stolen some months before.

The car had been sold on by Benjamin Snow of 66 Bayland Street, Sheffield and he was now interviewed about the stolen vehicle. He explained that he had acquired it in good faith, having exchanged for it his Angus Sanderson, registration CW 3291, with a dealer named Guy Browne. It took some time for this line of enquiry to be established but it now meant that the police would be paying a visit to Browne's establishment, the Globe Garage, in Wandsworth.

On January 19th, 1928, Detective Inspector William Barker, Detective Sergeant John Miller, and other officers mounted a watch on the garage. It was growing dark by the time Browne drove up. As soon as he entered the premises, he was told that he was being placed under arrest for the theft of a car, and a search would now be made of his premises. He was asked to turn out his pockets and produced twelve .455 cartridges of the same type used to shoot Constable Gutteridge. Browne commented, "That's done it. Now you've found them it's all up with me."

A number of other items were found in that initial search. Some medical equipment, corresponding with items missing from Dr Lovell's car, was found. Most telling of all was a gun found by Detective Constable Frank Bevis in the Angus Sanderson car, which still stood in the yard. The gun was a Webley and contained cartridges stamped R.L.IV. Browne freely admitted that it belonged to him. Browne's family lodgings at 33a Sisters Avenue were also searched. More medical equipment was found there, along with a nickel-plated revolver and a Smith and Wesson.

Back at the police station, the first mention was made of Gutteridge's murder. Browne denied any involvement, saying that he had purchased the medical equipment at various stages over the past few years. Some of the items he had adapted and used for difficult jobs when he was working on car engines. He made a statement, dated January 22nd, in which he explained that he had purchased the Webley from a sailor at the docks but it had started to go rusty soon afterwards. He claimed that he had never fired it.

A second search of the garage was made, and in due course, a second Webley revolver was found, hidden in a compartment behind the driver's seat in the Angus Sanderson car. Browne made a second statement about this weapon, but refused to give any details about it. On January 23rd, he was charged with car theft.

At this juncture, the matter of the two Webleys needs to be clarified a little, though it will be returned to later. The first Webley, the rusty one found in the initial search, bore the registration number 299431. The second Webley, the shiny one found in the subsequent search, was numbered 351931. Both guns would later be examined by Robert Churchill, the firearms expert, and the one numbered 351931 was shown to be the weapon used to kill George Gutteridge.

It soon came to the attention of the police that until very recently, Browne had employed a man named William Henry Kennedy at the garage. He too had a long police record and had recently served time with Browne, in Dartmoor. Kennedy was traced to lodgings at 2 Hugenot Place, Wandsworth, but his landlady informed the police that on January 21st, a telegram had arrived, calling Kennedy and his new wife to some sort of family crisis.

It was soon shown that Kennedy had in fact sent the telegram himself, as an excuse to leave in a hurry. The missing man was traced to Euston station, where he had boarded a midnight train to Liverpool. He was well known in that city and the police checked on his old haunts. In this way, Kennedy was traced to 119 Copperas Hill. The street was sealed off at 11.00 p.m., on January 25th, and at 11.40 p.m., Kennedy was spotted by Detective Sergeant Mattinson. Kennedy was arrested but not before he had pulled a Savage pistol from his pocket and tried to shoot Mattinson. Luckily for the officer, Kennedy had left the safety catch on. That same evening, Kennedy too was charged with car theft.

On January 26th, Kennedy was escorted back to London. At 7.00 p.m., he was interviewed by Chief Inspector Berrett in connection with the murder of Constable Gutteridge. Kennedy announced, "I may be able to tell you something but let me consider awhile". He then asked to see his wife.

Permission was granted and Kennedy was heard to say to her "Well my dear, you know when I was arrested at Liverpool yesterday, I told you I thought there was something more serious at the back of it? Well, there is. These officers are making enquiries about that policeman murdered in Essex."

Patricia, Kennedy's wife, asked him if he had killed the policeman, to which Kennedy replied "No I didn't, but I was there and know who did. If I am charged with murder and found guilty I shall be hanged and you will be a widow. On the other hand, if I am charged and found guilty of being an accessory after the fact, I shall receive a long sentence of penal servitude and be a long time away from you. Will you wait for me?"

Patricia Kennedy said that she would wait for her husband and advised him to tell the police the truth. He then made a long statement claiming that he and Browne had gone to Essex together to steal a car. On the return journey they were stopped by Gutteridge who, not satisfied with what Browne had told him, had said that he would have to take down some details. At that point, Browne drew out a gun and shot the constable twice. Both men then got out of the car and Browne said he intended to finish him off. Kennedy tried to stop him but Browne fired twice into the stricken officer's eyes.

Later that same day, Kennedy asked to see the two Webley revolvers and correctly pointed out the one used to kill Gutteridge, making a second statement to that effect. Both men were formally charged with murder on February 6th. Kennedy made no reply to the charge but Browne shouted, "It's absurd. I know nothing about it."

The trial of Browne and Kennedy opened at the Old Bailey on April 23rd, 1928, before Mister Justice Avory and a jury of nine men and three women. Throughout the five days of the proceedings, the prosecution was led by Sir Boyd Merriman, assisted by Mr H. D. Roome and Miss Enid Prosser, the first time that a female barrister had appeared in an Old Bailey murder trial. Browne was defended by Mr E. F. Lever, whilst Mr Frank Powell represented Kennedy.

The trial opened with the jury being sent out whilst Mr Lever argued that the two men should have separate trials. Kennedy had admitted his part in the killing and his confession directly implicated Browne. Even though Mr Powell, for Kennedy, supported this submission, the judge ruled against them and stated that they should face their trial together.

One of the early witnesses was Constable Taylor, who again maintained that he had heard no shots. It was shown that Gutteridge had walked just six hundred and thirty-eight yards from the

Constable George Gutteridge, who was brutally murdered in Howe Green, Essex, on September 27th, 1927 (Hulton Getty Picture Collection)

spot where he parted company with Taylor to the location of the shooting. If Taylor had walked at the same pace, he would have been one thousand two hundred and seventy-six yards, or three quarters of a mile, from where Gutteridge died and would almost certainly have heard the shots. Lady Decies was inside her home, at about the same distance from the shooting, but she heard the shots clearly. This mystery was never explained.

No less than four firearms experts agreed that the Webley numbered 351931 was the murder weapon. In addition to Robert Churchill, the guns had also been examined by William Fox, George Perry and George Henry Ibbinson. Furthermore, the ammunition found on Browne was of the same rare type – black powder cartridges issued during the Great War.

Even at this stage, some doubts about Browne's guilt came to the fore. Several police officers agreed that they had not made notes about Browne's various comments during the search until some hours later, and yet every officer agreed word for word with what had been said. Was this evidence of police complicity? The same officers denied asking Kennedy any questions whatsoever, claiming that he made his statement without prompting of any kind, yet his statement was detailed, chronological and answered every single question that the police had.

Kennedy declined to go into the witness box to give his version of events. That would have left him open to cross-examination, so instead his statement was read out. His barrister, Mr Powell, argued that there was no case to answer against him, as he had not even known that Browne had a revolver on the night in question. Unfortunately for Kennedy, Mister Justice Avory ruled against Mr Powell's plea and said it was for the jury to decide on Kennedy's guilt or innocence.

Frederick Browne did go into the witness box, but from the very outset he antagonized the judge and probably the jury by arguing that he could not take the oath to "tell the whole truth" as he did not know the whole truth because he was not even in Essex on the night Gutteridge met his death. After some argument, he finally took the oath.

He began by fixing the date that he moved into Sisters Avenue as Saturday, September 24th, just three days before the shooting. Referring to the medical instruments, Browne again claimed that he had bought these over the years. It then became clear that in Browne's mind, there had been some confusion over the two Webley revolvers.

Browne referred to them as the new one and the old one. It was the old one that he had bought from a sailor and which had gone rusty. The other one, the new one, had never gone rusty and this too belonged to Browne at the time of the search. However, it had not been his gun at the time when Gutteridge was shot.

According to Browne, he had always owned the rusty revolver, the one which bore the serial number 299431. The other Webley, the new or shiny gun which bore the number 351931 and had been identified as the murder weapon, had belonged to Kennedy and Browne admitted that for some time prior to the murder of Gutteridge, he had been trying to persuade Kennedy into swapping it for a Savage automatic. Kennedy had always refused, at least until early October when he showed a sudden interest in exchanging the guns after all. The swap took place on, or about, October 7th, more than a week after Gutteridge's death.

At first glance it looked like this was a case of one defendant trying to blame the other, but there were witnesses who indicated that Browne was telling the truth. Arthur Finch, Browne's brother-in-law, testified that much of the medical equipment had been in Browne's possession for some years and even Dr Lovell, for the prosecution, was unable to positively identify any of it as having been his. Caroline Browne, the prisoner's wife, swore that he had been at home from about 9.00 p.m. or 10.00 p.m. on the night of September 26th, and had not gone out again until some time before 9.00 a.m., the following morning.

This, of course, might have just been a wife protecting her husband but the defence failed to call Mary Eliza Siddals, Browne's landlady at Sisters Avenue. She had told the police that she heard both the Brownes moving about their flat on the night of September 26th. She was sure that Frederick Browne was at home as she recognized his footsteps, and if it was him, then he was home late because she made them both a cup of tea. She did not actually see Browne, however, which was why the defence did not call her.

170

There is also circumstantial evidence that Browne was not involved in the crime. He was certainly a cool individual, having once given a police sergeant a lift in a stolen car he happened to be driving. Would such a man have panicked when stopped by a village constable in a dark country lane, or would he simply have bluffed his way out? After all, Browne habitually carried documentation in false names and would have been easily able to extricate himself from Gutteridge's questioning without resorting to murder.

In the event, the jury decided that both men were guilty as charged. Before sentence was passed, both men made speeches to the courtroom, Browne claiming again that he was innocent. The judge then sentenced them both to death.

The very next day, April 28th, it was discovered that Browne had attempted to kill himself during the night. He had secreted a piece of razor blade and cut his arm and leg in four places. The wounds were not serious. A few days later he made a second attempt, trying to cut his throat with a piece of broken button.

An appeal was heard on May 22nd before the Lord Chief Justice, Lord Hewart and Justices Slater and Branson. Kennedy was present but Browne was felt to be not fit enough to attend. The main grounds were that the refusal to order separate trials had prejudiced the cases of both men. The three judges ruled against the defence and dismissed the appeals. When he heard the news, Browne smashed up his prison cell and went on immediate hunger strike.

There was no reprieve for either man. On the morning of May 31st, 1928, Browne was hanged by Robert Baxter and Henry Pollard at Pentonville prison. At the same time, Kennedy was executed at Wandsworth by Thomas Pierrepoint and Robert Wilson. Browne maintained his innocence to the very end.

Suggestion for further reading:

Christopher Berry-Dee and Robin Odell, *The Long Drop: two were hanged – one was innocent* (London: True Crime Library, c. 1993).

171

22

George Fratson

Sentenced to death at Manchester, but subsequently reprieved
For the murder of George Armstrong, at Rusholme, Manchester

THE good traders of Rusholme had started to feel that there might be something wrong with old Mr Armstrong. It was the middle of the morning on Saturday, May 4th, 1929, a busy shopping day, but George Armstrong's gent's outfitters at 3 Grange Avenue was still firmly locked. Usually, the doors would have been open at 8.00 a.m., and by now, half of the trading day had gone and there was still no sign of the seventy-two-year-old shopkeeper.

Lunchtime came and went, and still the shop did not open. By the afternoon, a number of other shop owners had started to gossip amongst themselves and someone swore that they could see a light on upstairs. The other proprietors around Grange Avenue knew full well that although the shop was a lock-up, Mr Armstrong lived above the premises, despite that being a breach of his tenancy agreement. In fact, that knowledge was a source of much amusement in the area. George Armstrong liked to maintain the charade that he lived elsewhere and would dutifully lock up his shop every night. Then he would walk the streets, often until late at night, waiting for the area to clear. Finally, when he thought no one was watching, he would sneak back into his shop and creep upstairs to the one room he called home. Many people knew about this, but they allowed George to think that he was fooling them all.

When the shop still had not opened by the afternoon, two of the concerned neighbours, Mr Friedland, who ran the chemist's shop next door, and Mr Birch, the owner of the billiard hall, called the police and reported that George Armstrong might well have fallen ill. At 3.20 p.m., Sergeant Walter Humphrey arrived on the scene with one of his constables. The two men tried the front door, the only access to the premises, and found it securely locked. The only thing they could do now would be to smash one of the upstairs windows and gain entry by that method.

Having borrowed a ladder, Sergeant Humphrey climbed to the first floor window and smashed a pane of glass with his truncheon. The blinds were still drawn but Humphrey pushed these to one side and climbed in. The small sitting-room seemed to be orderly but the electric light and the gas fire were still on. The table in the centre of the room showed evidence that there had recently been two men in the room. There were two empty glasses, both of which had contained beer, and a partially empty bottle of beer nearby.

A staircase led from the upstairs room to the shop downstairs. It was when Humphrey walked down that staircase that he found George Armstrong. The body lay on a mat at the foot of the stairs and at first, Humphrey thought that the old man had simply fallen. Taking a closer look, however, it was clear that Mr Armstrong had been the victim of a brutal attack.

Humphrey knew that he would have to send his constable for further assistance so he walked carefully through the shop premises to the front door. On the mat there he found some letters. These had plainly been delivered by the postman that morning, and had not been disturbed. This suggested that the attack upon Mr Armstrong had occurred some time before the post had been delivered. Sergeant Humphrey opened the shop door, told his constable what he had found, and sent him off for the doctor and Inspector Dewar.

It was Detective Inspector Charles Dewar who arrived first, at 3.50 p.m. He began by making an inspection of the premises. The one room upstairs was divided by a partition and there were no signs of any struggle having taken place there. The bottle of beer on the table was a three gill bottle and another similar bottle nearby was totally empty.

Going out on to the landing, Dewar noted that the staircase consisted of eight steps in all, the last step being the landing itself. There Dewar found three empty cardboard boxes, all of which had been smashed. There was some blood underneath one of those boxes. The seventh step had some spots of blood on it and on the fifth, Dewar found a pair of eye glasses. All the other steps, down to where the body lay, also showed signs of blood staining.

Close to the foot of the stairs was a small cash office. On a shelf in that office there were a number of white cardboard collar boxes, some of which had blood on them. There was also a letter on this shelf, and this too was bloodstained. To one side of the cash office, on the wall, were the electric light switches that controlled all the lights throughout the premises. Only one of these switches was bloodstained and when Dewar carefully snapped it on, the area where the body lay was filled with light.

On the floor in the office, Dewar found a lower set of false teeth. The upper set lay beneath the body and would not be found until later. Once Mr Armstrong was moved, the police would also find a pencil, a pair of scissors and a bunch of keys which proved to be those to the shop.

Going into the shop itself, Dewar saw a trail of blood spots from the front door to the body. Near the front door, there lay a bloodstained duster and a piece of brown paper, also stained. To Dewar's experienced eye it appeared that the killer had attacked Mr Armstrong in or near the cash office, and had used the duster and paper to wipe blood from his hands or clothing. It also seemed that he had not had a very successful haul as far as cash was concerned, for the assailant had also taken several men's hats and caps from the counter display.

Dr Thomas Boyd Riddall, of 274 Dickenson Road, arrived at the shop at 4.45 p.m. He noted that the body of George Armstrong lay face downwards between the bottom of the staircase and a small cash desk. The dead man's head was towards the back wall of the shop and his feet pointed towards the shop door, his legs being fully extended. The left arm lay beneath the body whilst the right arm was stretched out at a thirty-five degree angle.

There was a large patch of clotted and fluid blood on the floor to the right side of the head. The body was fully clothed. Turning the body over, Dr Riddall saw that the collar and tie, complete with tie-pin, were both in place. The front of the coat and the waistcoat were both unbuttoned, as were the braces at the front. The top three buttons on the trouser fly were undone, as was the sixth. In fact, since the fifth button was missing, the fly was only closed by one button. The shirt had been pulled up, uncovering the penis, and the pockets of the trousers had been turned inside out. All of the clothing at the front was saturated with blood.

Turning to the injuries Armstrong had received, Dr Riddall saw ten incised wounds on the face and head, ranging in size from one inch to six inches long and in depth from superficial scratches to wounds two inches deep. One cut over the right forehead extended down to the bone. Mr Armstrong had also been badly beaten, as it was plain that his jawbone was fractured.

What looked to be a simple case of murder during a robbery soon developed more complex undertones. A number of witnesses came forward to report that George Armstrong had been rather fond of the company of young men. James Arthur Rogerson, for instance, said that at some time around 11.00 p.m., on Friday May 3rd, he had seen George talking to two men in the doorway of his shop. Both men were aged about twenty-five to thirty, and had a rather military bearing. All three were laughing and joking and seemed to be in excellent spirits. Another neighbour came forward to say that he had seen a young man wearing horn-rimmed spectacles leave the shop soon after 11.00 p.m. He had seen the same young man before, also leaving the shop quite late.

Police investigations into Armstrong's background revealed him to be a widowed father of seven, but he was not apparently close to his children. Leo Armstrong, for instance, one of the dead man's sons, and who now lived at Harrogate, had not seen his father since 1919. The shop had seemingly fallen on hard times, and this was why the dead man had taken to living over the premises. George Armstrong had been carrying out his nightly routine of locking up and then returning to the shop later for over two years.

On May 6th, Dr Riddall performed the post-mortem. This confirmed the fracture of the jawbone and identified four further fractures, all of the skull. In addition to the incised wounds already mentioned, Dr Riddall discovered that the right carotid artery had been completely severed and that most of the stabbing and cutting wounds had been inflicted by a knife four and a half inches long, with a blade one inch wide. Furthermore, his post-mortem revealed that there was no evidence that Armstrong had been a practising homosexual.

It looked as if police efforts were getting nowhere fast so the Armstrong family offered a £50 reward for the apprehension of a man seen by a number of witnesses in the area. A description of this man was circulated and read, "Thirty to thirty-five years old, clean-shaven, brown hair, medium build and wearing a navy blue overcoat, a trilby hat with the brim turned down, black shoes, a soft collar with a blue tie and fancy socks".

This description, together with the not insubstantial reward, led to some interesting side issues in the case. On May 10th, for instance, a hotel guest approached a police constable in Devonshire Square, Blackpool, and informed him that another guest fitted that description. Furthermore, this guest had mentioned that he was glad to have got out of Manchester. The suspicious sounding guest was arrested on the spot and marched off to the police station, where he was able to prove that he had nothing to do with the murder. Indeed, at the beginning of May he had been in South America.

It was also on May 10th, however, that an arrest apparently unconnected to the Armstrong case took place in Preston. George Bowers, also known as George Fratson, had, until very recently, been living in Royton near Oldham, with a family named Jones. George Jones, the householder, worked in a local mill, and it was alleged that on May 2nd, Fratson had gone to the mill and informed Jones that he had been sent by Mrs Jones to collect his wages. Jones handed Fratson a £1 note, saying that it would have to do for now. In fact, Mrs Jones had sent him on no such errand, and a warrant was put out for Fratson on a charge of fraud. It took some time to trace him, but it was that warrant which caused Detective Constable Charles Henry Gregory to travel from Royton to Preston in order to collect his prisoner.

The journey back to Royton was made by train. It was at some point on that journey that Fratson asked, "Have you heard anything about the Manchester murder yet?" Somewhat puzzled, Constable Gregory replied "No, have you?", to which Fratson muttered "No".

The next day, May 11th, at 7.30 p.m., Fratson was being held in the cells at Royton when he called out to the supervising officer, Constable John Waugh, "Is Detective Gregory there? I want to make a confession." Constable Waugh, believing that Fratson wished to admit his guilt in the fraud charge, called for Constable Gregory, who immediately went down to the cells.

Fratson repeated that he had a confession to make and then began, "On the evening of Friday the third of May I was with a man in Manchester and went with him to the shop where the man was murdered". Fratson then went on to make a detailed statement claiming that he had met a man who called himself Jock, outside a billiard hall. Jock asked him for a cigarette and the two fell into conversation. Jock said that he knew where they could get some money but added that they might have to fight for it. Fratson told Jock that he was not afraid, and would go with him. The shop was just a few doors away and Jock went inside. Fratson waited outside for perhaps thirty minutes until he saw a policeman approaching, at which point he ran off. He then gave a detailed description of Jock, which included the fact that he had a gold tooth on one side.

This was most interesting to Detective Constable Gregory, for he knew that there was indeed a billiard hall just a couple of doors away from George Armstrong's shop. If Fratson was telling the truth, then it was clear that this Jock had killed Mr Armstrong whilst robbing his shop. It was now urgent that this information be passed on to Inspector Dewar in Manchester.

If the police thought that the case might now be much simpler to solve, the truth was that if anything it became even more complex. Over the next few days, Fratson made a large number of statements, fifteen in all, none of which bore much resemblance to each other. To begin with, he enlarged upon the mysterious Jock. Next, Fratson admitted that he had actually gone inside the shop with Jock, but had taken no part in the attack upon Armstrong. Eventually, Fratson's statements became complete confessions that it had been he and he alone who had killed George Armstrong. As a result of these statements, Fratson was charged with murder at 9.45 a.m., on May 16th. In reply to the charge he sobbed, "I was drunk. I didn't know what I was doing."

Fratson's trial took place at Manchester assizes on July 8th, before Mr Justice MacNaghten. The prosecution case was led by Mr E. G. Hemmerde, assisted by Mr P. Redmond Barry, whilst Fratson's defence lay in the hands of Mr Harry Allan. Mr Allan would have his work cut out for him, for by now Fratson had retracted his fifteen statements and was claiming that he had been nowhere near the scene of the crime at all.

Many of the prosecution witnesses were serving police officers. Inspector Dewar told the court that he had first interviewed Fratson on May 13th, when the prisoner had made one of his many statements. At 9.15 p.m. the following night, Fratson had said he wished to make yet another statement and after this had been taken down, the prisoner was escorted to the shop. Though the premises were in darkness, Fratson had walked straight to a far corner of the shop, crouched down and picked up the corner of a mat, which was saturated with blood. Fratson then claimed, "I threw the axe under here somewhere. They (Armstrong and Jock) came tumbling down the stairs together and I saw the other fellow strike him across the face with the axe." According to Dewar, Fratson had then gone on to describe wiping some blood from his hands on an old rag before leaving the shop.

On May 15th, Dewar had again interviewed Fratson and had explained that they were having a great deal of difficulty in finding the man with the gold tooth. The next day, Fratson was himself charged with wilful murder.

One of the other officers involved in the investigation had been Detective Sergeant John Blenkhorn. He had first seen Fratson at Royton police station on the morning of May 13th. Fratson had offered to point out for Blenkhorn where the shop was and later that morning, back in Rusholme, had done just that. At this stage, Fratson was still claiming that he had had nothing to do with the murder itself and that after he had fled the scene, he had slept on a bench in Whitworth Park until 3.30 a.m., the next day. Fratson was also escorted to this park, where he pointed out the bench upon which he claimed he had slept.

On May 15th, after having made further statements and claims, Fratson was taken back to Whitworth Park where he pointed out a lake in which he said he had thrown the murder weapon. That lake had been searched carefully, and nothing had been found. Later that same day, Fratson made yet another statement, stating that he alone had killed Armstrong because the old man had "...tried it on with him".

Sergeant Frederick Whitehurst had spoken to Fratson at the police station on May 14th. The shop door had a curious locking system. There was a Yale lock, as might be expected, but the handle used for pulling the door closed at night was in fact a gimlet or awl, punched into the wood. Surely if Fratson knew about that, it would prove that he had been inside the shop? When Whitehurst questioned Fratson about it he replied "With a Yale lock and a gimlet. I pulled the gimlet out and threw it down in the shop when I was leaving." The gimlet had indeed been found to one side of the door.

An attempt was now made to show that Fratson had been in possession of a knife that fitted the description of one of the murder weapons. Before going to lodge with the Jones family in Royton, Fratson had lived with Stanley Banks and his wife at 13 Fifth Avenue, Royton. Mr Banks testified that after Fratson had left, he had noticed that a cobbler's knife was missing.

Fratson had first appeared in Preston on May 6th. James Taylor was the proprietor of a lodging house there at 93 Water Lane and he confirmed that Fratson, calling himself George Bowers, had arrived at his premises at 2.55 p.m. Another one of the lodgers was John Butler and on that same day, May 6th, he saw Fratson in the kitchen. At the time he was wearing a good pair of brown shoes, but their heels had gone soft with all the recent wet weather. Fratson asked another lodger, a man named Collinson, if he had a pair of boots to give him. Collinson obliged, whereupon the prisoner went to the stove and made to throw his old boots into the fire. Butler tried to stop him, but Fratson claimed that they were no use anymore and threw them in.

George Fratson did give evidence on his own behalf. He admitted stealing the £1 from Jones, after which he walked to a hotel in Manchester. On May 3rd, he left Manchester and walked to Atherton, where he looked for work. Failing to find any he walked back to Manchester, arriving there at about 7.30 p.m., when he went on a pub-crawl.

At 10.00 p.m., Fratson left Manchester and began walking to Liverpool. Once there, he threw his cobbler's knife and a hammer into the river Mersey in disgust over not being able to find work. From Liverpool, he walked on to Preston where he arrived on May 6th. Fratson agreed that he had burned his boots, but only because the heels were worn down and they were useless. He should know, because after all he was a cobbler.

Fratson said that his original problems had come about because of a woman he had been seeing in Royton. She had expressed the desire to get married, but he had had to explain to her that he was already married. This depressed him, and by the end of that first week in May he was so down that he decided to kill himself.

On May 7th he had asked James Taylor, the Preston lodging house proprietor, for some paper and an envelope, and had written to his parents in Bury. The letter had been received and was now produced in court. It read in part, "I know you will think me no good for leaving Royton. The young woman I was going out with asked me to get married, so I went away. I thought it was the best plan. I loved her so much that if I had to stop with her much longer, something serious might have happened. Do not be surprised if I come to Bury to finish things off properly, as I am better off dead than living a life of misery."

The decision having been made, Fratson soon found that he had not the courage to carry out his intention. It was then that he heard about the Manchester murder from some of the other lodgers and, after reading accounts of the crime in the newspapers, decided to admit to the crime so he would be hanged.

The jury retired to consider its verdict and returned after almost two and a half hours to announce that Fratson was guilty. The prisoner at the bar paled visibly and announced, "I am not the murderer of Armstrong". He was then sentenced to death.

The only evidence against Fratson was his own statements. There were only two things in those statements that could not have been deduced from the contemporary newspaper reports. The first of these was the existence of the gimlet in the door. The statement relating to that was made on May 14th, the day after Fratson had been escorted to the premises. Besides that, Fratson had admitted knowing the dead man and having been on the premises before, the first time being in 1926. The murder had been a particularly bloody one and yet not one spot of blood had been found on any of Fratson's clothes. The other factor not disclosed in the papers was the finding of a bloodstained rag or duster inside the shop. This could be explained as a rather natural guess on Fratson's part, but it was to prove most damaging to his case.

The original execution was postponed when an appeal was entered. That appeal was heard on July 30th when the defence introduced some new evidence. The prosecution at the trial had been fully aware that a cardboard box had been found in the shop, bearing a bloody thumbprint. In addition, fingerprints had been found on the two beer glasses in the room upstairs. None of those prints were Fratson's and whilst it might be argued that the beer-drinking companion might not be the killer, it was likely that the print on the box belonged to the murderer. Nevertheless, despite this new evidence, the appeal was dismissed and a new execution date set for August 15th.

George Fratson did not hang. On August 9th, less than a week before he was due to die, he received notification that his sentence had been commuted to one of life imprisonment. Fratson, however, continued to maintain that he was totally innocent and asked his defence team to renew efforts to secure his release. As a result, a second appeal was granted, and this was heard on March 24th, 1930.

This second appeal concentrated on the evidence of the bloody thumbprint found at the scene. At the first appeal, the prosecution had claimed that in all probability this print belonged to a rather careless police photographer. It was now shown that this could not have been the case.

In fact, there were two photographers sent to the scene. The first was Sergeant Wilfred Bailey, the official police photographer. He attended the scene, with Inspector Dewar, on May 5th, and took just two pictures, one of the entrance to the shop and one showing the staircase and small office. By this time, the blood would have all clotted so even if, under his Inspector's supervision, Bailey had touched one of the boxes, he would not have had fluid blood on his fingers. The other photographer was Herbert Walter Doughty, the official photographer of the Manchester Guardian newspaper, but his interior shots were only taken on May 16th.

It could be claimed that the evidence did not prove, beyond a reasonable doubt, that Fratson had been responsible for the death of George Armstrong. The only factor in his confessions that could not be explained away was the bloodstained duster, and this was hardly irrefutable evidence. Nevertheless, the appeal court decided that there was enough evidence to uphold the verdict so this second appeal too was dismissed and Fratson was taken back to prison and his life sentence. It might well be argued that he could have been an innocent man.

23	**Henry Daniel Seymour**
	Hanged at Oxford, Thursday, December 10th, 1931
	For the murder of Annie Louisa Kempson, at Oxford

O N the morning of Monday, August 3rd, 1931, George Henry Reynolds, a college servant at Jesus College, Oxford, received a letter at his home, 13 Cambridge Street. The letter, from Mrs Annie Smith, puzzled George. He had been fully aware that his sister, fifty-eight-year-old Annie Louisa Kempson, who lived at The Boundary, St Clements Street, in Oxford, had intended going down to spend a short holiday with Mrs Smith, but according to the letter she simply had not turned up. George decided to check on Annie.

It was around lunchtime when George arrived at The Boundary, but there was no reply to his knocking and the front door was firmly locked. Perhaps Annie had simply been delayed. George sent a telegram to Mrs Smith, asking her if Annie had arrived yet, but at 5.30 p.m., the reply came that there was still no sign of George's sister.

At 5.45 p.m., George, accompanied by his son, Albert Edward Victor Reynolds, returned to the house. Albert had driven the motor cycle with George being seated, rather uncomfortably, in the sidecar. Once again George tried the front door but it was still secure. The two men decided to call again later that night.

By the time George and Albert returned, it was a few minutes before 7.30 p.m. They went around the back of the house and George noticed that there was a bedroom window slightly open. Albert got a ladder, finally managed to gain access to the house and went downstairs immediately to let his father in by the side door.

There were three main rooms downstairs. At the back was a kitchen and small scullery, then there was a middle room, used as a lounge and finally the front room, which looked out onto St Clements Street itself. George and Albert first checked the kitchen, but there was no sign of Annie there. It was only when they went into the middle room that they discovered why Annie had not kept her appointment with Mrs Smith. The body of Annie Kempson lay on the floor, covered over with cushions. Neither of the two men touched anything but left the house immediately to fetch the police.

Outside the house, George spotted a police constable on patrol and told him what he and his son had found. The officer, Constable Samuel Guyte, went into the house with

George whilst Albert rode off on his motor cycle to report the matter at the central police station.

Constable Guyte timed his entry to the house at 7.25 p.m. Guyte noted that there appeared to be no signs of a struggle in the room where Annie lay. There were two cushions placed over the body and Guyte removed these in order to see if he could offer the woman any assistance. It was clear that she was beyond help, so Guyte replaced the cushions carefully, in the same position as they had been before.

Looking around the room, Constable Guyte saw that several drawers in the sideboard had been opened, and their contents scattered around, implying possibly that the motive for this crime had been robbery. Going into the front room, Guyte saw that nothing here had been disturbed. All the windows in the room were secure except for the one furthest from the front door. This was closed, but not fastened shut. On a Chesterfield in that same room, Constable Guyte found a brown paper parcel which, from the shape and feel of it, contained a pair of woman's shoes.

Continuing his check of the premises, Guyte saw a postcard on the mat behind the front door. It was dated August 2nd, as was a Sunday newspaper. There was also an unopened copy of the Daily Mail of August 3rd, presumably delivered that very morning. To Guyte, this showed that the woman had probably met her death before she

The Boundary, St Clements Street, Oxford, where Annie Kempson was found brutally murdered on August 3rd, 1931 (Public Record Office Ref. No. ASSI 84/135)

had had time to open the first of those newspapers, meaning that she had been attacked either on or before Sunday August 2nd.

Going into the kitchen, Guyte saw the remains of a meal on the table. That meal appeared to be a breakfast, which further narrowed down the time of the attack. Now, according to Guyte's thinking, the latest it could have taken place was some time during or after breakfast on August 2nd.

Upstairs, the door of the front bedroom was locked and since there was no key in the lock, Constable Guyte had no choice but to burst the door open. Inside he saw that the room was in total disarray. The drawers were open, papers were scattered about the floor and even the bedclothes and bedding had been pulled back. Another bedroom was also in this same sort of condition.

At 7.50 p.m., Detective Sergeant Goodchild arrived and ten minutes later still, the police surgeon, Doctor Francis Henry Dickson, attended. He began by removing the various items that had been placed on top of Annie Kempson's body. In order, these were a cushion, placed over her head, a small rug which covered her from the head to the lower part of her abdomen, and then two more cushions which had covered Annie's face, shoulders and right arm. It was also noted that Annie's hair was still in curlers.

There were two immediately obvious wounds. The first was a puncture wound in the neck below the lobe of the right ear, whilst the second was a wound on the forehead, extending towards the left eye. Annie had bled from her mouth on to the carpet and there was a dried bloodstain on the carpet underneath Annie's head.

It was obviously important to determine as precisely as possible the time of Annie Kempson's death. In fact, Annie had not lived at the house alone. She had a lodger, a lady named Eleanor Jane Williams, who worked as a waitress at a cafe in Oxford. She too was now on holiday, spending some time with friends at Chipping Norton. When Eleanor was interviewed she reported that she had left for Chipping Norton directly from the cafe, at 3.45 p.m., on Saturday August 1st. The last time she had actually seen Annie alive was at 9.20 a.m. on August 1st, when Eleanor left to go to work.

Various items had been found at the house that might help the police to narrow down the time of Annie's death. For this reason, Eleanor Williams was questioned very carefully on what she and Annie had eaten over the last couple of days they were together.

Turning to Friday, July 31st, Eleanor stated that she arrived home that night at 10.30 p.m., and had a bite of supper and some hot milk. Annie was in the middle room with her at the time and whilst Eleanor drank her milk, Annie enjoyed a snack of tomatoes.

The next morning, Eleanor had gone downstairs at 9.10 a.m. She had eaten breakfast in the kitchen, the meal consisting of bread, butter, marmalade and tea. Annie did not have anything to eat at that time but did have a cup of tea. Asked about what Annie's routine might have been after Eleanor had left for work, she replied that Annie would usually go upstairs first to make the beds. Then she would take the curlers out of her hair, brush it through and then sweep the front path. After this she would wash up the breakfast things. Eleanor also emphasized that Annie never went out in curlers, and was careful not to even let people see her wearing them.

On August 5th, Eleanor Williams was taken back to the house by the police and asked to look over the premises, which had still not been disturbed. She saw that the breakfast things were still on the table in the kitchen, and there were two cups and saucers and a teapot. In the scullery was a pan that had contained boiled milk, just as Eleanor had drunk on the Friday night. Indeed, the cup and saucer she had used were still unwashed on the copper in the scullery.

There was one other indication that Annie had been attacked on the Saturday morning soon after Eleanor had left the house. When she had gone out to work that morning, Eleanor had left a chamber-pot underneath her bed. That chamber-pot had contained a small amount of urine at the time and since it still remained unemptied, it suggested that Annie had been killed on the morning of Saturday, August 1st, as she was a very tidy woman who would not have left either the chamber-pot or the washing up until the following day.

On the same day that Eleanor Williams was taken back to the murder house, Sir Bernard Spilsbury, assisted by Dr Dickson, performed the post-mortem on the dead woman. The two doctors found a total of four wounds. In addition to the two reported at the scene by Dr Dickson, they also discovered a lacerated wound at the back of the head and abrasions over the spine between the shoulders.

There was food in the small intestine, which consisted largely of partly digested tomato skins. There was also bread and butter in the stomach itself. The medical opinion was that Annie had been lying on the floor when the neck wound was inflicted. The head wounds had been caused by a heavy blunt instrument, having a flat and circular surface about one and a quarter inches in diameter. This was, in all probability, a hammer. It was surmised that the blow to the back of the head had been inflicted whilst Annie was standing, and all the other wounds had been inflicted whilst she was unconscious on the floor. The incised wound in the neck had been inflicted by something with a sharp edge, possible a chisel. Finally, the time of death was consistent with the morning of Saturday, August 1st, most likely between 10.00 a.m. and noon, although this was not definite.

It was also on August 5th that Sergeant Goodchild conducted his own careful search of the murder house. That search was to yield a most valuable clue for, in the scullery, Goodchild found a visiting card. It was obviously a card left by a traveller, a representative of Tellus Limited, a company that manufactured vacuum cleaners. The card also bore a name, Henry Daniel Seymour.

A check of police records led to some very interesting discoveries about Seymour. To begin with, he had a long criminal record. His first jail sentence had been one of six months, handed down in Johannesburg, South Africa, on December 29th, 1906. Three more prison sentences had followed, all in South Africa, and totalling eleven years, the last one being on April 20th, 1914, when Seymour got an extra twelve months for

184

attempting to escape. After the Great War, Seymour had come to England and had since served two sentences there. The first, of twenty months, was awarded at the Old Bailey on April 13th, 1920, for shopbreaking. The last sentence, of five years, had been handed down at Maidstone on February 16th, 1923, for larceny in a dwelling house. Seymour had finally been released, on licence, on November 12th, 1926, but this was not his last run in with the law. At Plymouth on July 31st, 1930, he had pleaded guilty to malicious wounding and had been bound over for two years. The original charge had been one of attempted murder. Furthermore, he was now a wanted man once again, a warrant having been issued by the Metropolitan Police for fraudulent conversion (theft by fraud). All in all, it seemed that a talk with Henry Seymour might well lead to further information in this case.

Seymour was a married man, but was now separated from his wife who lived at 6 Carlton Vale, Maida Vale. She had recently moved from 3 Bassett Road, North Kensington, so mail to both addresses was now opened in an attempt to trace Seymour.

In fact, it was not until August 15th that Seymour was traced to lodgings at 17 Loder Road, Preston Park, Brighton, where he had taken rooms in the name of Harvey. On that day, Detective Sergeant Percy George Scales and two fellow officers of the Brighton force positioned themselves outside number seventeen, and waited for Seymour to appear. At 1.05 p.m., a man fitting Seymour's description walked down the street and up the steps which led to number seventeen. Sergeant Scales stopped the man and announced "We are police officers. You are wanted by the Metropolitan police. Your name is Seymour." The man replied "You have made a mistake". Scales now removed the man's hat, and continued "I am satisfied you are Seymour and use the name of Harvey. You will have to come to the police station." He was then taken into custody.

The next day, August 16th, Seymour was interviewed by Chief Inspector John Howell of the Metropolitan Police. Howell had first been called in to assist in the Oxford murder on August 4th and now, at 3.30 p.m. on the 16th, he cautioned the man he had been looking for since the discovery of the traveller's card in Oxford.

Seymour greeted the caution with "Go on, lay your cards on the table and tell me what you want me for and tell me your names". Chief Inspector Howell identified himself and all the other officers in the room, to which Seymour commented "Yes, now carry on Mr Howell. Is it about the murder at Oxford?" Howell replied that it was and told Seymour that his visiting card had been found at the scene, as had a vacuum sweeper made by the company he represented. Furthermore, a man fitting Seymour's description had been seen at the house before 10.00 a.m. on the Saturday, and since then the police had discovered where Seymour had stayed, determined that he had no money, and that he had had a new hammer and chisel with him at the time. Finally, Howell said that on the strength of what they had discovered so far, Seymour would be returned to Oxford and there charged with murder.

"Right" replied Seymour, "Now I know the state of affairs, I suppose it is my turn to explain my side of the situation". He then made a statement which was taken down in writing. Afterwards, Seymour was escorted back to Oxford and charged, at 10.00 p.m. that same night, with wilful murder.

Henry Daniel Seymour appeared at Oxford before Mister Justice Swift on October 20th. The proceedings lasted until October 25th and during that time, the prisoner was defended by Mr W. G. Earengey and Mr E. R. Guest. The case for the prosecution was led by Mr St John G. Micklethwait, assisted by Mr Wilfred Price.

It was important to determine Seymour's movements as accurately as possible around the time of the murder. He had claimed that he could account for his movements throughout the entire weekend, apart from a brief time on the Saturday morning, August 1st.

Charles William Parkinson was the licensee of the Greyhound Hotel, Market Square, Aylesbury. On July 22nd, Seymour had called at the hotel, booked a room and signed the register. He remained there from July 22nd and had bed and breakfast each day. On the 28th, Parkinson presented Seymour with a bill for two pounds, six shillings and fourpence, which he paid.

On July 31st, Seymour left the hotel immediately after he had eaten his breakfast, but when he had not returned to his room by 11.30 p.m., Mr Parkinson determined that he would contact the police. After all, his guest had received a second bill, for fifteen shillings, which had not yet been paid.

On August 1st, Mr Parkinson went into the police station to make his complaint against his missing guest. However, on his return to the hotel, at around 1.00 p.m., he found that Seymour had returned. "You had better come with me to the police station" said Parkinson, "I have only just come away after reporting you as missing". Seymour asked if he might go upstairs first and get his razor but Parkinson insisted that he must go to the police first. Seymour now changed tack and said that he was hungry, walked out of the hotel, and never returned. A couple of hours later, Sergeant Leonard Giles attended the hotel in response to the complaint, only to be told that he had missed Seymour. For the time being the matter was allowed to rest there.

Sergeant Giles confirmed this testimony and also stated that once he had heard that Seymour was a wanted man, he had returned to the Greyhound, on August 4th, and examined two suitcases which Seymour had left behind. Later still, Sergeant Reginald Read collected those suitcases, which contained, amongst other things, a bathing costume, a towel, a brace and bit and a hammer. There was no sign of either a screwdriver or a chisel.

So, the only night that Seymour had not spent at the Greyhound, was the night before the murder, July 31st. Alice Mary Andrews was an old customer of Seymour's and had bought one of the Tellus cleaners some years before. Alice, a widow, lived with her son at 1 Gipsy Lane, Oxford, but at 2.30 p.m. on July 31st, she was on Headington Hill, walking towards the city, when she saw Seymour walking towards her.

The two exchanged pleasantries and Seymour said it was his intention to call on her. This was something he did with all his customers, in order to check that the goods he had sold to them were still in first-class working order. As they spoke, Seymour mentioned that he had thought of going to Eynsham, where he could have had a swim, but it had looked a little thundery and so he had thought better of it.

At 8.00 p.m. that same evening, Seymour called at Alice's house and said he had been to Eynsham after all. He added that whilst he had been in the water, two boys had been at his clothes and he had had to chase them off. Only then did he discover that they had taken thirty shillings out of his pocket, leaving him all but penniless. He asked Alice if she might lend him some money so he could get back home that night.

Alice gave Seymour four shillings and sixpence. He said he intended to catch the 9.15 p.m. bus to Thame and left the house soon afterwards. At 10.30 p.m., Alice was in bed when she heard a knock at the front door. Her son answered it, then came upstairs and told her that someone wanted to see her. Going downstairs, Alice saw that it was Seymour again. He had missed his bus and needed a bed for the night. Alice kindly agreed and offered him some supper, but Seymour said he only wanted some cocoa.

It was some time between 10.45 p.m. and 11.00 p.m. when Seymour finally retired for the night. The next morning, August 1st, he was up at 8.15 a.m. After going to a local barber's shop for a shave and then returning for something to eat, he left the house at 9.30 a.m.

Mrs Andrews had one more important piece of information to give to the court. On the night of July 31st, Seymour had left his coat in the hallway. The next morning, as she was cleaning the hall, she noticed a hammer and chisel, wrapped in brown paper, in his pocket.

Some of this was confirmed by Alice's son, Percival Stuart Sandon Andrews. He too heard the story of the two boys stealing Seymour's wallet, and saw the two brown paper parcels, which were partly torn, showing clearly that they contained a hammer and a chisel. At no time did Seymour try to conceal these tools.

The last two witnesses had shown that Seymour was at Gipsy Lane until 9.30 a.m., apart from a short period when he went out for a shave. Lovell Charles Archibald Pearce was a hairdresser at 4 Grays Road, Headington and he confirmed that at some time between 8.00 a.m. and 9.00 a.m., on August 1st, a man called at his shop for a shave. The man said he was a commercial traveller and had come to Oxford from Aylesbury but had missed his last bus home the previous night. He also told Pearce that he was staying with Mrs Andrews.

There were two witnesses who seemed to confirm Seymour's acquisition of a hammer around this time. Albert Edward Fulkes was an assistant at his brother's ironmonger's shop in London Road, Headington. At 8.00 p.m., on July 31st, a man had come into the shop and purchased a hammer for one shilling and sixpence. This was confirmed by Alfred Welham, the manager, who also stated that it was shop policy to wrap purchases in brown paper.

What had Seymour done after leaving Alice Andrews' house at 9.30 a.m., on August 1st? Florence Hilda Collins was another of his ex-customers, having bought a cleaner some four years before. On August 1st, she was in London Road between 11.00 a.m. and 11.30 a.m., when she saw Seymour standing at a bus stop. They said "Good morning" to each other and he told her that he was going to go down to Brighton for a short holiday. As they talked, Florence saw a bus arrive and Seymour was going to get on it when she pointed out that it was not the one he wanted. They talked for perhaps five minutes in all before she left him at the stop.

If Seymour were the killer of Annie Kempson then the murder had to have taken place between 9.30 a.m. and 11.30 a.m., the latest time that Seymour was seen at the bus stop by Florence Collins. In fact, this time could be narrowed down even further. Sergeant Goodchild had walked from 1 Gipsy Lane to Annie Kempson's house and timed it at twelve minutes. This meant that for Seymour to be the killer, the earliest time of the attack would have to be 9.42 a.m. Furthermore, the bus stop in London Road was twenty-two minutes walk from the house in St Clements Street, and a check of the timetable showed that the bus left at 11.03 a.m. This in turn meant that Mrs Collins had seen him at the earlier of her estimated times and also that for Seymour to be the killer, the latest possible time of the murder had to be around 10.41 a.m.

Annie Kempson had been seen alive at 9.20 a.m., on August 1st, by her lodger, Eleanor Williams. Witnesses were now called to try to prove that no one had seen her after this time.

Ruth Steele was an old friend of Annie's and on July 31st, the two ladies had gone into Oxford shopping. During the day, Annie bought herself some new shoes but as she was not going directly home, she asked Ruth if she would take them with her and bring them around the next day. Ruth agreed and the two friends parted at 7.00 p.m.

The next morning, at 11.00 a.m., Ruth went to Annie's house and rang the bell. Annie was rather deaf and might not have heard so Ruth knocked hard on the front door three times. Still there was no reply. Looking around at the front of the house, Ruth saw that the window furthest from the front door was open at the bottom. Ruth pulled the window up a little further and threw the shoes inside the front room, seeing them land on the Chesterfield. She then pulled the window all the way down, and left. Ruth ended her testimony by saying she had not noticed if the window was also open at the top.

Julia Anne Life was another friend of Annie's and had seen her in Oxford at 6.30 p.m., on July 31st. On August 1st, Julia called at Annie's house at 9.30 a.m., but there was no reply to her knocking. At 10.00 a.m., she called again and noticed that the window at the front was open a few inches at the top, though the bottom portion was closed. Annie called for a third time at 8.00 p.m., and saw that the window was still open at the top, so she closed it.

The testimony of these two witnesses was most interesting. Julia Life had called at 9.30 a.m., and found the top of the front window open but the bottom part closed. If Seymour were the killer then Annie still had to be alive at this time because Seymour was only just leaving Mrs Andrews' house. Furthermore, the window was not open at the bottom at 10.00 a.m., when Julia called again, but it was at 11.00 a.m., when Ruth

Steele arrived. Someone, either Annie Kempson herself, or her killer, had to have opened that window between 10.00 a.m., and 11.00 a.m.

Charles James ran a general shop that was situated almost directly opposite to Annie Kempson's house. She was a regular customer there and as such, Charles knew the woman very well. In fact, he had tended her garden for her for the past ten years.

Mr James stated that on Saturday afternoons, Mrs Kempson was in the habit of visiting her husband's grave in the local churchyard. On most of the return journeys she would call in at his shop and so he had expected her to call in on the afternoon of August 1st. She never appeared, and when he went to the churchyard himself on August 3rd, he noticed that Mr Kempson's grave had not been attended to.

There were witnesses who reported seeing someone else call at Mrs Kempson's house on August 1st. Violet Reeves was a daily help at the Duke of York public house in St Clements Street and from the front door step she could see Mrs Kempson's house. Between 9.40 a.m. and 9.45 a.m., Violet saw a man call at the house and knock twice. He did not get a reply and went away. Violet described the man as wearing muddy brown trousers, a blue coat, a cap and carrying a mackintosh over his left shoulder. This was almost certainly not Seymour because Alice Andrews had said that when he left her house in Gipsy Lane he was wearing a dark suit and a trilby hat, though he did have a mackintosh.

A more interesting sighting was made by James Horne, who lived in George Street. James had an allotment and left his home to go there on the morning of August 1st. Walking up George Street to St Clements Street, James saw the front door of Annie Kempson's house. It was 9.56 a.m., and there was a man knocking on the door. After a few seconds the door was opened and the man made a bit of a bow and then stepped inside. The man was wearing dark trousers, a dark coat that was rather long and carried a light coat over his left shoulder.

This testimony raises interesting questions. If the time of death had been accurately determined, this man was almost certainly the killer. Medical and other evidence indicated that Annie had been killed between 9.42 a.m. and 10.41 a.m., on August 1st. This man called at the right time but was it Seymour? Witnesses had said that Seymour was wearing a dark suit but the man seen by Horne was wearing a long dark jacket. There was also a major problem for the prosecution in that a large number of people had now reported seeing Annie Kempson alive and well after 10.41 a.m.

William Law said he had seen Annie in Pembroke Street, Oxford, at 11.20 a.m. on August 1st. Sarah King, who knew Annie very well, said she had seen her go into a baker's shop in London Place at 11.30 a.m. This was confirmed by Evelyn Barrett, an assistant in that shop, who said that she served Annie at about that time.

Another shop assistant, John Woodward, who worked in a grocer's shop on the opposite side of the road to where Annie lived, said that he served her at some time between noon and 1.00 p.m. Frederick Taylor, a painter who had known Annie for twenty years, said that he had seen her at about 12.30 p.m., and Kate Barron, who had known Annie all her life, said that she saw her near her house at just before 3.00 p.m. If any of these six witnesses were correct, then Seymour had to be innocent.

There is one other curious factor in the case. Eleanor Jane Williams, the lodger, told the police that there had been a number of rather petty robberies over the months immediately before Annie Kempson had been killed. Things in the house had been moved, and small items had been stolen. The matter was reported to the police for it appeared that someone was calling regularly at the house, gaining access somehow, and stealing things, but there was never any sign of a forced entry.

Despite these factors, the jury took just thirty-eight minutes to decide that Seymour was guilty. An appeal was entered and heard over two days, November 23rd and 24th, before the Lord Chief Justice, Lord Hewart, and Justices Avory and Hawke. Here, it was held that all six witnesses had been mistaken about which day they had seen Alice. Furthermore, little store was placed on the fact that Sir Bernard Spilsbury had examined the hammer found in Seymour's possession and confirmed that it did not fit the wounds on Annie's head, and that no blood had been found on Seymour's clothing. The appeal was therefore dismissed.

Just over two weeks after the appeal was lost, on December 10th, 1931, Henry Daniel Seymour was hanged at Oxford prison.

24

Peter Queen

Sentenced to death at Glasgow, but subsequently reprieved
For the murder of Christina Gall, at Glasgow

PETER Queen had not had the easiest of lives. Born in 1900, the son of a Glasgow bookmaker, Peter married when he was just eighteen years old. Unfortunately, his new bride turned out to suffer from chronic alcoholism and by the time Peter was twenty, she had been sent to an institution. A saddened Peter moved back in with his parents, and tried to put the past behind him.

Peter was the eldest child in the Queen family and it soon became clear that Mrs Queen would need some assistance with the younger members of her brood. So it was that in 1924, a young woman was employed as a nursemaid to these children. She was twenty-one-year-old Christina Gall, known to her friends as Chrissy.

Chrissy Gall was one of six children and had left school at the age of fourteen in order to go into domestic service, one of the few career choices open to a young girl at that time. Her new position meant that she would have to live in and it was not long before she and Peter found themselves attracted to each other. The attraction became something deeper and before long, the two were lovers.

At first glance, it would seem that there should have been few problems for Peter and Chrissy. The attraction was mutual, neither was involved with anyone else, and they had every opportunity to consummate their passions for each other. There was, however, one problem, and that was guilt.

Christina Gall had been brought up in a good Christian background and felt from the very outset that what she was doing was wrong. True, Peter was married in name only, to a wife who lived in an institution, but he was, nevertheless, a married man. All her religious beliefs told Chrissy that she should not be involved with this man, but the frisson between them was such that she could not help herself. This dichotomy tore away at Chrissy, who found herself having to lie to her parents about the situation.

Some respite was obtained when Chrissy found herself a new job, in a factory, and soon afterwards, returned to the family home to look after her mother, who was very ill. The relationship with Peter continued, though, the two of them meeting

191

secretly as often as they could. The circumstances continued to gnaw away at Chrissy, however, and she began to drink rather heavily. Peter had seen all this before, with his wife, and tried his best to persuade Chrissy to stop drinking. This in turn added yet more pressure and Chrissy became depressed, resulting in further prolonged drinking bouts. Thus, the vicious circle of drink, depression and guilt began to take its toll.

Mrs Gall soon succumbed to her illness and passed away. For three months, Chrissy stayed with her father, John Gall, in order to look after him, but soon he announced that he wished to move in with another of his daughters. Chrissy would have to find new lodgings for herself. She turned to Peter for assistance and he helped her to find a place in a house owned by James Burns, a close friend of his, who lived at 1 Hayburn Street. For a time, Chrissy lived there alone, but in December 1930, just before Christmas, Peter moved in with her.

To all intents and purposes, Peter and Chrissy were an ordinary married couple. They told the neighbours as much, but even this basic deception preyed upon Chrissy's mind. She hated being greeted as Mrs Queen and began drinking even more, causing arguments and friction between her and Peter. He tried his very best to help, as did James Burns and his wife, Fay. On one occasion, Fay Burns went round the flat, finding all the hidden bottles of drink and pouring them away. It was never enough, for Chrissy always had yet another bottle hidden somewhere else.

As the drink led to further depression, Chrissy began to talk about killing herself. Once, when sitting alone with Fay, she remarked that she was going to "...make a hole in the Clyde". She even started for the door in order to carry her threat out but Fay managed to stop her, undress her and put her to bed.

The deception over her relationship with Peter continued and some of the subterfuge Chrissy used was rather complex. She took to visiting her sister only on Wednesday afternoons, because she had told her family that she had a job in service and this was her only time off. There were further discussions about suicide and once, Chrissy went to bed leaving all the gas taps on in the flat. Luckily, it was Fay Burns who came to the rescue again. She smelled the gas, turned off the taps and mentioned it to Peter when he came home from work.

Peter felt that a new start might do them good, so in the summer of 1931, he and Chrissy moved to fresh lodgings, at 539 Dumbarton Road. For a short time, things did get better but soon Chrissy was back on the drink and feeling as depressed as ever. This was underlined on Thursday, November 12th, when James and Fay were invited to number 539 for tea. James tried to hang his coat up on a peg behind the door, only to find that the peg had been snapped off. He made a joke about Peter breaking up the happy home but a straight-faced Peter retorted that the peg had been broken the night before, when Chrissy had tried to hang herself. It had failed to support her weight and he had found her lying on the floor behind the door. When asked about this, Chrissy would only say that she had been a damned fool and promised to make a fresh effort to curtail her drinking.

Two days after this, on Saturday, November 14th, Leonard Johnston, who was Fay Burns' brother-in-law, called at the Queen household. He found Chrissy alone, as depressed as ever. He, rather naively, advised her to stop drinking as it was damaging her health. Chrissy shouted back "Don't I know that! But do you understand the problem? Do you understand the pretension of it all? I am fed up with life. I have to tell lies wherever I go. Some day Peter will find me behind the door..." The sentence was never finished, but the inference was clear.

Something had to be done to sort things out. After much discussion, Peter suggested to Chrissy that she might take a break, or a brief holiday, away from Glasgow. At first she said that she would not go, but eventually Peter persuaded her to have a few days away. It was finally agreed that Chrissy would take her young niece, Nessie, who had recently been ill, off to Aberdeen on November 23rd.

Before Chrissy could take her trip, though, there were other incidents that added to her concerns. On Thursday, November 19th, Chrissy went to see her father at his place of work, to tell him of her forthcoming holiday plans. He was too busy to see her, but arranged to see her the next night, at her sister's house in Shettleston Road. Next, Chrissy went to visit her sister, arriving there at about 2.45 p.m. There, she met up with Robert Simpson Gall, her brother, who preferred to be called Bert, and the two of them had a drink together. Chrissy stressed, however, that she was expected back by Peter at 5.15 p.m.

In fact, Chrissy did not get home at 5.15 p.m. She and Bert left her sister's house together and went to visit a pub. They both drank whisky and beer and before they left, Chrissy bought herself a gill bottle of whisky. By the time she did get back to Dumbarton Road, it was 9.00 p.m., and Peter was waiting on the landing.

Naturally Peter said that he had been very worried about her, but Bert Gall reassured him and Peter was content to remove Chrissy's shoes, which were soaking wet from the bad weather. Peter then sat her down in front of the fire, but immediately Chrissy asked him for a pencil and a piece of paper and scribbled a quick note. The note was to ask Peter not to let Bert know that this was where they lived together. Peter, even though he was probably sick of lying to protect Chrissy's family, told Bert that this was his aunt's house and added that they would have to make a move soon as Chrissy had a long way to go before she got home. This rather crude machination seemed to work and after having a nip of whisky for the road, Bert allowed Peter to walk him to the tram stop.

The next day, Friday, November 20th, Leonard Johnston's wife, Helen, called on Chrissy at 2.30 p.m. Once again, Chrissy was extremely drunk and talking about committing suicide. Ten minutes later, Peter arrived home and Helen suggested that he should call the doctor out, as she feared for Chrissy's safety. Peter agreed that it was a good idea. At 4.00 p.m., Helen was back, this time with Leonard, to see how

Chrissy was feeling and what the doctor had said. Peter informed them that the doctor was too busy to call but had agreed to pop in the following morning. Chrissy, meanwhile, was in bed and sleeping peacefully.

The Johnstons stayed until 11.00 p.m. that night, and enjoyed a pleasant evening with Peter. At one stage, Chrissy woke up and even ate a light snack. She announced that she felt much better now and the Johnstons were much encouraged by what they saw.

It was 3.00 a.m., on Saturday, November 21st, when Peter Queen walked into his local police station, put his house keys on the counter, and told the two officers there, Lieutenant Walter Doherty and Constable Alexander McLeod, that his wife was dead. What words he actually used would later be the subject of much argument but the police held Peter in the station whilst officers went around to 539 Dumbarton Road.

There was no sign of any struggle in any of the rooms. Going into the bedroom, they found Chrissy lying in bed with the bedclothes pulled up to her chest. Her right arm lay under the covers, beside her body, but her left arm was stretched out along the pillow. Her tongue protruded slightly from her lips and a thin rope lay knotted around her neck, tied at the front in a simple half-knot.

One of the officers loosened the knot, which was still quite tight, and upon examining the rope, found that it had been recently cut from a pulley washing-line in the kitchen. Though a full medical report would be needed, it seemed clear that Chrissy Gall had been strangled and since the only other person present in that room had been Peter Queen, he was the obvious culprit. At 5.30 a.m. that same day, Peter was charged with murder. He replied "I have nothing to say".

The murder trial took place at Glasgow on January 5th, 1932, before Lord Alness, the Lord Justices-Clerk. The case ran until January 11th, during which time Queen was defended by Mr R. MacGregor Mitchell and Mr Robert MacInnes. Mr John Cameron prosecuted for the Crown, assisted by Mr J. B. M. Young.

Many of the earlier witnesses were police officers who were so evasive in their answers that the judge himself had to take a hand in the questioning. The crucial evidence related to what Peter had said when he first entered the police station. He claimed that he had said, "Go to 539 Dumbarton Road. I think you will find my wife dead. Don't think I have killed her." According to the two police officers, though, that last sentence had actually been "I think I have killed her". However, under cross-examination, both Doherty and McLeod admitted that neither of them had made a note of what Peter had said.

Friends and neighbours, including James and Fay Burns, told the court of the loving devotion and patience Peter had always shown to Chrissy. They told of her drinking, her depression and the repeated threats to kill herself. The only difference of opinion came when the Johnstons gave their evidence. Leonard Johnston said that Chrissy had certainly not been sober, but had not been so drunk that she could not walk unaided. His wife, Helen, disagreed and claimed that Chrissy had been in a helpless condition when they left. This was a crucial point, for the defence were claiming that Chrissy had committed suicide, and in order for that to be the case, she would have had to cut the rope herself.

The medical evidence would be of the utmost importance. The two pathologists who had carried out the post-mortem, Professor Andrew Allinson and Doctor John Anderson, had testified at the magistrate's court that this could not be a case of suicide. It had to be murder and therefore Peter Queen was guilty. To explain this, two expert witnesses were called at the trial.

Professor John Glaister said that several facts excluded the possibility of suicide, including the attitude of the body and especially the positions of the arms. If one allowed for Chrissy having put the noose around her own throat, she would then have been unable to tuck one arm under the covers whilst waiting patiently for death. Professor Andrew Allinson agreed with these comments and claimed that the fracturing of the cricoid cartilage would have involved a good deal of pressure. The defence, however, called two most eminent witnesses of their own.

Sir Bernard Spilsbury argued that the fibres in the rope were such that as it was pulled tight, the fibres would act as a sort of brake and prevent the rope from slipping. He argued that there were three factors which led him to believe that this was a case of suicide. Firstly, the room in which Chrissy's body had been found was undisturbed. Her nightcap was still on her head and her dentures were still in her mouth. Secondly, there was no bruising to the deeper parts of the neck or the thyroid, showing that relatively little force had been used to pull the cord tight. Finally, the cord had been positioned low down on the neck with the knot to the right of centre. This was inconsistent with homicidal strangulation, where the cord is usually positioned far higher. In fact, Spilsbury announced that he would still believe that this was a case of suicide even if Queen had admitted to being the killer.

Professor Sydney Smith stated that the facts could suggest either murder or suicide, but he leaned towards thinking that it was suicide. He confirmed much of what Spilsbury had said and agreed with those general conclusions.

In his summing up, the judge agreed that "...Evidence is scanty and unconvincing in so far as it supports the theory of homicide by the accused". Despite all these doubts, the jury took just two hours to decide, by a majority verdict, that Peter Queen was guilty as charged, having murdered Chrissy because he could no longer face her constant drinking and the problems that caused. The jury did, however, add a strong recommendation to mercy.

The execution was originally set for January 30th, but this was postponed when an appeal was entered. This was heard over two days, the 26th and 27th of January, the judges finally concluding that there was enough evidence to uphold the conviction.

195

A new execution date was set, February 13th, but the jury's recommendation eventually carried the day and a reprieve was announced. Peter was removed from the condemned cell and began his life sentence. Eventually he was released and spent the rest of his days in obscurity. He died in May, 1958.

George Alfred Rice

25

Hanged at Manchester, Wednesday, February 3rd, 1932
For the murder of Constance Inman, at Manchester

A T 6.30 p.m., on the evening of Tuesday, September 22nd, 1931, pretty eleven-year-old Olga Roberts was playing in the street outside her home at 73 Victoria Road, Manchester when she spied her close friend, Constance Inman, running from the area behind her own house at number fifty-six.

Though Constance was only eight years old, she and Olga quite often played together and so Olga called out for her to come and join her in some game or other. Constance appeared not to hear this request for she failed to answer, so Olga called out again. This time, Constance did hear and shouted back that she was going to play with some other children. Under normal circumstances, Olga would have dropped what she was doing and gone with her friend, but she was under express orders from her mother not to stray from the front of the house. Lately there had been some reports of a man accosting children in the area and Olga had been told not to move out of sight from her home.

There had actually been two reported incidents involving this man. In the first, a young girl had been attacked in Raincliffe Avenue and had only described what had happened to her when she arrived at school. She told her teacher that the man had said he would show her some cigarette cards, but when she walked off with him, he had assaulted her.

The second attack had actually taken place in Victoria Road itself. The man had tried to entice a little boy away, but fortunately the child's mother had seen the conversation taking place and had come out of her house to chase the man away. The only description of this man was that he was smartly dressed, middle-aged and rode an old and rather battered bicycle.

Even as Olga Roberts watched her friend disappear down the street, the child's mother called her in for her evening meal. Olga thought nothing more about the incident with Constance until around 7.00 p.m., when Christopher Inman, Constance's father, knocked on the front door of number seventy-three to ask if Olga had seen anything of his daughter as she had not come home for her own meal. Olga told Mr

197

Inman what she had seen but it was little help and Christopher Inman continued along the street, knocking on doors and asking if anyone had seen anything of little Constance.

By 8.55 p.m., Mr Inman had been joined by his wife, Lilian, and some of his friends and neighbours. It was not like Constance to stay out like this and the Inmans had begun to fear for their daughter's safety. When, finally, they heard that Constance had mentioned to her sisters that she had arranged to meet a man who was going to show her some cigarette cards, thoughts of the attack on the girl in Raincliffe Avenue came flooding back. It was time to bring in the police.

In fact, it was not the police who discovered what had happened to Constance Inman. Jane Birkett worked as a domestic servant for Mrs Warne, who lived at 42 Park Range, Victoria Park. At 8.20 a.m on September 23rd, Miss Birkett opened the study window of the house in order to let in some fresh air. This particular window overlooked some of the back gardens of Dickenson Road, and in one of those gardens, Miss Birkett spotted what looked like a large doll. Looking more closely, though, Jane Birkett saw that the doll was in fact a little girl who seemed to be lying perfectly still in the long grass of the rather unkempt garden.

Jane Birkett's first thought was that the girl might be playing some game, but when she still had not moved a few minutes later, it became clear that the child might be ill and in need of some assistance. Miss Birkett walked out into the garden and shouted "Little girl, are you hurt?", but there was no reply.

Going back into the house, Jane Birkett reported what she had seen to her employer, Mrs Warne. At first, Mrs Warne told her maid not to be so silly but once she had seen that Jane was very distressed, she told her that it might be best if she investigated further, if only to put her mind at rest. Jane Birkett then returned to the garden, this time with a set of ladders, and carefully climbed over the fence into the long grass. Gingerly she touched the girl's hand. It was ice-cold and Jane Birkett realized immediately that the poor child was dead.

It was not long before Superintendent Townsend, Superintendent Fisher, and other less senior police officers were on the scene. They noted that the body was that of a young girl, around ten years old at most. She lay on her back with her knees raised a little and her head inclined slightly towards the left. Her dress had been pushed up but her underclothing had not been touched, and there were none of the more obvious signs of a sexual assault. Some of the clothing bore signs of what might have been blood and there was froth near her mouth, indicating possible strangulation. Finally, a string of blue and white beads, which the girl wore around her neck, had been broken.

Dr Arnold Renshaw, the pathologist, arrived on the scene at 9.45 a.m. His initial examination noted some irregular marks on the girl's flesh – nineteen on her right arm and a further six on her left. He concluded that these were almost certainly insect bites, caused after death, and had played no part in her death. There were two abrasions, one on the left knee and another on the left side of her head, but these appeared to have been caused by the child falling. Of much greater significance were three small red marks on the girl's throat and a fourth on her larynx. These might have been caused by someone's fingernails, or possibly by the string of beads being pulled tightly around the little girl's neck. Either way, it appeared that she had died through some external violence and therefore this looked to be a case of murder, though a detailed post-mortem would reveal more.

Of course, only one child had been reported missing in the area and since the clothing matched that described by Christopher Inman, it seemed reasonable to assume that Constance had been found. Later that same morning, Mr Inman reported to the mortuary and there positively identified the body as that of his daughter.

The police officers investigating the case now began calling on all the houses in Dickenson Road, where Constance's body had been found. That afternoon they called at number ninety-seven and what they heard there appeared to be most illuminating.

Number 97 Dickenson Road was a large house, split into a number of separate lodgings or flats. On the ground floor lived Annie Francis Broadhurst and her husband, John Joseph Broadhurst, who acted as caretakers for the property. In the same lodging lived their maid, Rose Powell. On the same floor, Eva Radford occupied two rooms. The rest of the house was empty except for the attic, where a thirty-two-year-old unemployed labourer, George Alfred Rice, who actually used the surname Price, lived alone.

When the police spoke to Annie Broadhurst she stated that at around 11.15 p.m., on September 22nd, she and Rose Powell had been alone in the kitchen when they heard a strange noise that seemed to come from the foot of the stairs. It sounded as if someone had stumbled and this was followed almost immediately by a light thud and the noise of someone dragging something across the landing floor, towards the back door.

Annie and Rose were sure that they were being burgled and so Mrs Broadhurst ran to the front bedroom. If there were someone trying to escape from the house then he would have to leave by either the back door or the front. If he ran out of the front door, Annie Broadhurst would see him. If, however, he escaped out of the back door, then he would have to get out into the street down a passageway at the side of the house. Either way, he would eventually pass her field of vision and she would be able to see who it was.

To Annie's surprise, no one appeared and after ten minutes of waiting, she and Rose heard the unmistakable sound of the back door being bolted. There then came the sound of footsteps across the hallway and someone climbing the stairs. There was only one explanation. The noises had to have been made by the man who lived in the attic, George Alfred Rice.

There was even more information from Rose, Annie and her husband, John. On September 23rd, at around 12.45 p.m, they had all been at John's mother's house at 73 Dickenson Road. By now, Constance had been found and her death was the main topic of conversation. Rice came into the house and Rose asked him if he had heard the terrible news about poor Constance. Rice said he had, and added that he had bought himself a newspaper that gave him all the details. This was extremely curious for Rice could neither read nor write. Later, Annie heard Rice remark rather cryptically, "You will see, they will take me because I am out of work".

When the police spoke to Eva Radford, the other occupant of the ground floor, they found that Rice was behaving somewhat strangely on the morning of September 23rd. It was 6.30 a.m., and he was already up and about, which was totally out of character. He was, after all, unemployed and therefore had no need to rise early. Usually he was seldom seen much before noon. Furthermore, when Eva went to the front door to collect her mail at 7.30 a.m, Rice was busily sweeping the stairs. This was a job he did every week, but always on a Saturday, never on a Wednesday.

It was 4.00 p.m. by the time Detective Sergeant John Blenkhorn called on Rice in his attic flat. Asked to account for his movements the previous evening, Rice stated that he had left the house at 6.25 p.m., on September 22nd. He had walked to the corner of Wilmslow Road, where he stood around until about 7.00 p.m. before popping into a shop on Walmsley Road for some cigarettes. From there he returned home and, seeing Eva Radford, asked her to make sure that the back door was left open for him that night as he was going to see a film at the Ardwick Empire and might be back a little late.

Continuing his narrative, Rice said that he then went back out and caught a tram to Brunswick Street. From there he went to the Empire to see the film. Afterwards he walked back along Brunswick Street, passing a jeweller's shop where there was a large clock, before arriving at Upper Brook Street from where he caught the tram home.

Having listened to this story, Sergeant Blenkhorn said that he was not completely satisfied and insisted that Rice accompany him to the police station, pending some further inquiries. At this, Rice handed over two tram tickets, together with the torn portion of a picture house ticket, to prove that he was telling the truth.

George Rice was taken to the station and kept in the cells overnight. He woke at 4.30 a.m., and greeted Sergeant Blenkhorn with "Give me another cup of tea and I'll tell you all that happened". He then made a detailed statement, which was read back to him, before making his mark, in the presence of other officers, to signify that it was a correct version of what he had said. At 1.00 p.m., he was charged with murder.

Rice's statement began with his reference to purchasing cigarettes at a shop in Walmsley Road. It continued, "I met a little girl in Dickenson Road, Rusholme, about 7.15 on Tuesday night. I done it. I met her near home. I had never seen her before. I took her down by the side of the house where I lived and took her behind the garage. I was cuddling her, but I did nothing wrong to her.

"I must have hit her on the head or something. I do not know what happened. She collapsed at my feet. I spoke to her and could get no answer and so left her." The statement went on to describe his movements afterwards, and his encounter with Mrs Radford in the hallway. He continued, "I then left and went to the second house [the second showing of the film] at the pictures. I then returned on a tramcar to Dickenson Road. I went behind the garage, where I had left the girl. When I touched her I found she was going cold and appeared to be dead.

"I picked her up in my arms and carried her to the bottom of the garden and laid her gently on the grass at the bottom of the garden. I then went into the house and went to bed. This is the truth. I can't tell you anything more. When I first took the girl behind the garage my nerve seemed to go and I went dull."

Rice's trial opened at Manchester on December 14th, before Mr Justice Finlay. The case for the Crown was led by Mr J. C. Jackson MP, who was assisted by Mr P. Redmond Barry. Rice was defended by Mr E. G. Hemmerde and Mr T. H. Hinchcliffe. The case lasted for two days.

There could be no doubt that Rice had been present when Constance Inman breathed her last, but was he guilty of murder? The prosecution suggested that Rice had enticed the girl to the garage near his home and had killed her whilst either raping her or attempting to rape her. In such a case, the medical evidence would prove crucial.

Dr Renshaw, who had examined Constance's body at the scene and later performed the post-mortem, had discovered that both of the dead girl's lungs were congested and appeared to be collapsed. She had bitten her tongue in three places and during the police court hearings, Dr Renshaw had testified that this was evidence of asphyxia. That asphyxiation could have been caused either by direct pressure on the neck, or by someone holding the child's clothing so tightly that the beads around her neck had choked her. On October 1st, under oath, he had stated that there was no definite evidence of rape and that the marks on Constance's throat were too close together to have been caused by fingernails. They were almost certainly caused by the beads of her necklace. In short, Constance had not been sexually abused and had not been manually strangled.

At the trial itself, however, Dr Renshaw gave a different version of events. Now he determined that Constance had been raped and that her assailant had grabbed her so tightly that all the air had been squeezed out of her body. In effect, she had been crushed to death.

When the time came for Rice to step into the witness box, he denied that he had ever held Constance so tightly as to crush her. He had simply cuddled her and she had collapsed at his feet. As for his confession, that was nothing of the kind. He had been woken by Sergeant Blenkhorn and told to make his mark on a piece of paper, which he did. The sergeant, of course, denied that this evidence had been manufactured, but it should be remembered that Rice could neither read nor write and was of low intellect. Despite this, he had apparently made a grammatically correct statement apart from the one clumsy phrase, "I done it".

In his summing up, Mr Justice Finlay told the jury that if they came to think that the child had died as a result of violence whilst being raped then this was a case of murder. If, however, they felt that he had only indecently assaulted her, then they could return a verdict of manslaughter. In the event, the jury returned a verdict of guilty of murder and Rice cried bitterly as the sentence of death was passed.

An appeal was heard on January 18th, 1932, before Justices Avory, Talbot and MacNaghten. Once again, the defence referred to the entire matter of whether

Constance Inman had been raped or not. There was no evidence of a struggle, no signs of bruising and none of the child's clothing had been torn or removed. The worst that could be suggested was that Rice had indecently assaulted her, and if that were the case, then the correct verdict was one of manslaughter.

The verdict was given by Mr Justice Talbot, who remarked that there was ample evidence that extreme violence had been used against the child, though of course there was absolutely no proof of this whatsoever. As a result, the appeal was lost. Just over two weeks later, on February 3rd, Rice was hanged at Strangeways prison by Thomas Pierrepoint. It was reported that the condemned man had to be half-carried to the scaffold.

Was Rice guilty of murder? What other explanation could there possibly be? It is, of course, possible that Constance died during an attempted or actual rape, despite the lack of any conclusive medical evidence. It is, however, equally possible that she died from vagal inhibition. This is a phenomenon where sudden pressure on the neck, even quite light pressure, can cause death. Rice's statements consistently referred to Constance falling down at his feet and this, together with the small bead marks on her neck, suggests that it is possible that he was simply cuddling her when the necklace tightened around her throat and killed her. If such were the case, then Rice was guilty of manslaughter and not murder.

One thing is certain and that is that Rice was not the man who had attacked the girl in Raincliffe Avenue, or tried to abduct the boy from Victoria Road. Both attacks had been committed by a man with an old bicycle. Rice did not own such a vehicle and did not fit the description of the man who did.

William Burtoft

26

Hanged at Manchester, Tuesday, December 19th, 1933
For the murder of Frances Levin at Manchester

THROUGHOUT England, the summer of 1933 was a record breaker. For days upon end, an unrelenting sun beat down upon baking cities, towns and villages. Even normally rain-soaked Manchester basked in the heatwave, and one of the most spectacularly hot days was Wednesday, July 19th.

At the northern end of Cheetham Hill Road stood the imposing structure of Claremont. Situated at number 453, it was home to six people. The head of the house was a sixty-one-year-old widow, Frances Levin. She shared the house with her two brothers, two of her daughters and the family maid, seventeen-year-old Freda Phillips, who had lived in since February of that year.

By all accounts, the Levin family was a close one and as such, it was customary for its members to take lunch together whenever they could. On July 19th, however, the family was not complete. Only Frances, one of her brothers, Louis Henry Davis, and her two daughters enjoyed a light snack in the stiflingly hot front room of the house.

Once the meal was complete, Frances expressed a desire to check how much money she had in her purse. Clara, one of her daughters, duly brought her mother's handbag and then watched as she counted out the few coins that were inside her purse. Frances, it transpired, had just nine shillings. Satisfied, she closed her purse, shut it inside her handbag and placed it down onto the floor.

Clara and her sister left the house to return to work at 1.45 p.m., leaving their uncle, Louis, with their mother, who by now had taken up a comfortable position on the couch which stood in the bay window of the front room. Brother and sister chatted about various family matters for perhaps another half an hour, after which Louis went up to his bedroom. He was only in there for a few minutes and when he went back downstairs, he saw that the maid, Freda, was attending to his sister. Bidding Frances a fond farewell he then left the house by the front door, making sure that it was securely locked behind him.

By now it was almost 2.30 p.m. Louis, an antiques dealer by trade, would normally have returned to his shop but this day was to be different. For some reason, he decided to take particular advantage of the glorious weather and walked on to Cheetham Park instead. He remained there for more than two hours, only finally returning home at 4.40 p.m.

Back in Claremont, Frances Levin had asked Freda to bring her something to read. Freda duly obliged, bringing some books and magazines. Seeing that her employer was settled down, Freda then went through to the kitchen at the back of the house, where she used her electric sewing-machine to repair some clothes. Freda positioned herself close to the back door, which had been open all day in order to let at least some air into the room.

Freda Phillips worked at her machine for an hour and at 3.30 p.m., decided to finish off the last of her work by hand, in her bedroom, on the second floor of the house. The back door remained open, however.

Upstairs, Freda positioned herself near her window, from where she could see across to the house next door, a surgery occupied by Dr Lees and his family. As she looked out, Freda noticed that Samuel Norman Woodcock, Dr Lees' chauffeur, was working on the doctor's car, in the driveway. Samuel had started that work at 3.15 p.m., and, as Freda took her seat by the window, he looked up and saw her. The two exchanged polite waves.

At 4.00 p.m., Samuel Woodcock found that in order to complete his task, he needed a new part for the engine. He climbed onto his bicycle and peddled off to Brocklehurst's Garage, further up Cheetham Hill Road. He was away for no more than fifteen minutes and at some time during that period, Freda Phillips looked down from her bedroom window in time to see a man walking down the path at the side of the house. He passed from the back of the house, through a wicker gate at the side, and headed for the front gate.

The sight of this stranger did not, apparently, unduly upset Freda. Just a couple of days earlier, a man had called to see the family with a view to purchasing some chickens they kept at the back of the house. At the time, he had intimated that he might call again and since this man did look something like that visitor, Freda simply assumed that he had been true to his word and visited Claremont again.

Freda only caught the briefest glimpse of this visitor and, of course, was looking down on him from above. She noticed only that he was perhaps five feet nine inches tall, was dressed in working clothes and wore a brown coat, dark brown trousers, a pinkish-brown shirt and a light trilby hat. He was of medium build and around forty-five years of age.

By 4.15 p.m., Samuel Woodcock had returned on his bicycle and gone back to work on Dr Lees' car. From time to time he glanced up and saw Freda, still at her window on the second floor of the house next door. Then, at about 4.30 p.m., Freda caught his attention and signalled that she was going back downstairs. Samuel nodded his understanding and watched Freda depart.

It was perhaps just two minutes later when Samuel heard Freda calling him from the kitchen steps of number 453. There was an element of panic or distress in her voice and so Samuel dropped what he was doing and dashed next door. He passed through the lattice wicker gate at the side of number 453 and noticed that it was closed but not latched. He was grateful for that since he knew that this particular gate was very difficult to open.

Going to the back of Claremont he found Freda waiting for him. She beckoned Samuel into the kitchen and pointed out what looked like a poker, lying on the floor. Samuel bent down to pick the poker up, but at the last moment, he noticed that the square end of it was covered with what looked like blood. Even as he drew back his hand, Freda pointed out to him a shirt which had seemingly been taken down from a clothes rack nearby and then thrown onto the kitchen table. That shirt was also heavily stained with blood.

Samuel now asked Freda who else was in the house. The nervous maid explained that she was alone except for Mrs Levin, who was resting in the front room. The two then walked down the hallway to the lounge door, which was closed.

Samuel Woodcock knocked on the door but there was no reply from inside the room. He knocked again, this time calling out Mrs Levin's name, but again there was only silence. Turning the handle slowly, Samuel pushed the door open and stepped into the front room, leaving Freda waiting in the hallway.

Frances Levin was still on the settee positioned in the bay window but she was not resting peacefully. Her head was a mass of blood and there were splashes of the crimson liquid on the walls, curtains, pictures and floor. The cushion on which Frances' head lay was also heavily stained with blood, although curiously, there was no blood on the front of the settee.

Slowly Samuel walked towards the dreadful scene and as he did, Mrs Levin's eyes flickered open. She seemed unable to speak and rapidly slipped back into merciful unconsciousness. Closing the door behind him, Samuel went back out into the hallway and, without telling her what he had found, escorted Freda out of the house through the front door.

One might have thought that Samuel Woodcock's first action would have been to dash next door to his employer's house. After all, it was clear that Mrs Levin was still alive and in urgent need of medical attention. Samuel's employer was a doctor and surely such a course of action would have been sensible but instead, Samuel ran further up Cheetham Hill Road to a telephone box, from where he called the police ambulance.

As soon as he had finished his call, Samuel noticed a police officer standing on the corner of the street. This was Constable James Turner and he listened as Samuel blurted out his story. The two men then dashed back to Mrs Levin's house, where they found Freda Phillips waiting for them at the front gate.

Constable Turner went into the front room by himself. He noticed that Frances was lying on her back with her head slightly inclined towards the right and thus looking away from the bay window. Her knees were drawn up a little and her left arm rested on the settee. Her right arm hung off the side of the settee and almost touched the floor. As the officer tried to render basic first aid to the stricken woman, she again opened her eyes but made no attempt to reply when Constable Turner spoke to her.

Satisfied that he had done all that he was able to, at least until the ambulance arrived, Constable Turner now made an inspection of the room itself. There were no obvious signs of disorder. No ornaments or other items had been broken or scattered about and there were no indications of any struggle having taken place. On the settee itself lay two magazines, a newspaper and a book and there were other magazines on the floor immediately in front of the settee. The centre portion of the bay window was open to a distance of about six inches, no doubt to allow some air into the room.

Constable Turner was also able to determine that the motive for this crime might well have been robbery. On the lid of the piano was a woman's purse, which looked as if it had been thrown there. It was half-open and contained no cash.

In due course, the police ambulance arrived, driven by Constable Cecil Hartman. He and Turner lifted the still form of Frances Levin onto a stretcher and carried her into the ambulance so she could be rushed to the Jewish Memorial Hospital. As the ambulance sped away, Detective Inspector William Malcolm Page arrived to take charge of the investigation.

The hospital timed Mrs Levin's arrival at 4.45 p.m. She was attended to by Dr Isaac Goldberg, who noted that his patient was deeply unconscious and required immediate treatment for extensive scalp wounds and a fractured skull.

The front room of 453 Cheetham Hill Road, Manchester, where the murder of Frances Levin took place (Public Record Office Ref. No. ASSI 52/424)

206

Dr Goldberg noted too that both of Frances Levin's hands were bruised and that the bones in her left hand were broken. This injury had almost certainly been sustained as she tried to ward off a blow. Mrs Levin received the best medical care available but despite Dr Goldberg's efforts, she died at 8.53 p.m., without ever regaining consciousness.

It seemed reasonable to assume that the killer had been the man whom Freda Phillips had seen leaving the back of the house as she looked down from her bedroom window. Her description of that man was extremely basic but it was felt that he might well be one of the many homeless and unemployed people who were roaming the streets of Manchester at this time. As a matter of routine, the description, and the suggestion that the man might be a vagrant, were circulated to all police forces. Railway and bus stations were checked, taxi-drivers spoken to and lodging houses visited. None reported seeing any bloodstained man on the day of the attack.

Two days after the crime, on July 21st, the police officers working on the case announced that they had now examined the murder weapon, which was not, after all, a poker but a heavy iron tool kept in the kitchen and used to lift the grate. There were no fingerprints at all on this weapon but this was not unexpected. The police surmised that the killer had taken it from the fireplace, used it to batter Mrs Levin as she lay in her front room and had later returned it to the kitchen, where he wiped it on the shirt. There was, however, one development. A single foreign print had been found on Mrs Levin's handbag, and since all the cash inside had been taken, the motive for the crime was confirmed as robbery. This rogue print would later prove to be significant.

It seemed as though the investigation was running out of steam. The days passed and no arrest was made. From time to time, the police would release some titbit of information to the press, but the sought-for arrest would not come.

On July 25th, for example, a definite line of inquiry was announced. A bloodstained man had been seen and officers had managed to track his movements. A few days before the murder, he had been in Ormskirk. On July 19th, he had been seen in Manchester and since then had been traced to Redcar and Darlington. The public were asked to look out for a man whose clothing would be bloodstained. Later, this too would become significant.

The breakthrough, when it came, occurred not in Manchester but in Hyde, Cheshire. At 10.30 p.m., on July 26th, a man was arrested for vagrancy. The local police noticed that the man fitted the very general description that had been circulated by the Manchester force and a preliminary talk with the man revealed that he had been in the city on the day Mrs Levin was attacked. For that reason, news of the arrest was flashed through to Manchester and at 1.30 a.m., on July 27th, Inspector Page and Inspector Arthur Willis travelled to Hyde where they took the man into their custody and escorted him back to Manchester. Their captive was forty-seven-year-old William Burtoft.

What happened in the interview room at Manchester will be detailed later, but it ended with Burtoft being charged with the murder of Mrs Frances Levin. Later that same day, Burtoft made his first appearance before the magistrates and the press reports of the day carried descriptions of this somewhat significant individual. He was said to be a short, stocky man who only had one eye and whose face was somewhat red and weather-beaten from the amount of time he had spent living rough.

Burtoft's trial for murder finally opened at Manchester assizes on November 13th, before Mr Justice Atkinson, a gentleman who had only been appointed to the bench on May 15th. The case for the prosecution was led by Sir Walter Greaves-Lord MP, who was assisted by Mr E. Shackleton-Bailey. Burtoft's defence rested in the hands of Mr B. S. Wingate Saul, and the proceedings lasted for two days.

Freda Phillips was an important witness as she was the only person who had seen the killer, walking past her window from the back of the house. She told the court what she had seen and also referred to an identification parade that she had attended on July 28th. The police had arranged that she should, as far as possible, be in the same position as she had been when she saw the man on July 19th, so she was positioned in a high window, looking down upon a courtyard. A number of men had walked past her but she had failed to pick anyone out. A second parade had taken place a few minutes later, but again she had been unable to identify anyone as the intruder.

Samuel Woodcock told what he had found when he first went into the front room of 453 Cheetham Hill Road. No reference was made to the fact that the simplest course of action for him would have been to run to his employer, Dr Lees. That action had been brought out in the magistrate's court hearings however, and Samuel had stated that the reason he had gone to telephone the police instead was that he believed his employer might be asleep.

The evidence of these two witnesses did serve one purpose, and that was to narrow down the time of the attack upon Mrs Levin. Samuel Woodcock had been away from his employer's house from just before 4.00 p.m until around 4.15 p.m. Working back from the time that Freda saw the man walking down the path, the time of the attack must have been close to 4.00 p.m. If Burtoft were the killer, then it was important now to show that he could have been in Cheetham Hill Road at this time.

Amy Wale lived in Stockton Street, Moss Side, but at 2.45 p.m. on the day of the murder, she was at 13a Elizabeth Street, a lodging house run by Bertha Edwards, one of her closest friends. These two ladies both testified that Burtoft called at the house at this time and was given some tea and sandwiches by Bertha. Burtoft stayed there until 3.15 p.m, during which time he mentioned that he had no money but might have some later. He mentioned that he was going to knock on doors and try to sell some cards he had, in order to earn a few pence. Finally, Bertha stated that the lodging house was some fifteen minutes walk from Cheetham Hill Road, meaning that Burtoft could have been there at any time from 3.30 p.m. onwards.

The next definite sighting of Burtoft had been made by an old friend of his, James Hughes, at 4.20 p.m. James ran a newsagent's shop at 9 Angel Street, but at that time he was in Kane's lodging house at Angel Meadow, when Burtoft entered with his hands thrust deep into his pockets. James greeted his old friend but Burtoft appeared not to recognize him. He simply walked through to the kitchen and began washing his hands.

Three days later, on July 22nd, James Hughes saw Burtoft again, this time in the George and Dragon public house. Once again Burtoft did not recognize his friend, but after James had spoken to him and reminded him who he was, Burtoft joined him in a drink. Later, they left the public house together and as they did, Burtoft asked Hughes if the police were visiting all the lodging houses in connection with the Cheetham murder. Hughes replied that they were, to which Burtoft commented "I'll beat it..." He then walked off alone.

Returning to the events of July 19th, the next witness, Dorothy Roberts, said that she ran a cafe at 33 Swan Street. At some time between 4.45 p.m. and 5.00 p.m. on that date, Burtoft had come into her establishment and purchased a cup of tea and a meat pie, for five pence. Dorothy was absolutely certain that Burtoft was the man, as her customer only had one eye, and was the only customer at the time. She went on to say that he was wearing a light-coloured but rather dirty trilby hat, a brown coat and a pair of dark trousers.

It was when the time came for the police officers involved in the case to give evidence that the legal arguments began. As soon as Inspector Page stepped into the witness box, Mr Wingate Saul objected to the admissibility of his testimony. The jury were asked to leave the court and Burtoft went into the box to give his version of his interrogation. The judge considered the arguments and finally ruled that the police evidence could be heard.

Once the jury had been recalled, Inspector Page began his testimony. He first spoke of what he had seen when he attended 453 Cheetham Hill Road, and then began his evidence on Burtoft's interview.

Inspector Page stated that this interview had taken place with Detective Inspector Willis and Detective Sergeant Blenkhorn present. Burtoft had been asked to account for his movements over the past few days and seemed happy to detail where he had been and what he had done on July 18th, 20th, 21st and 22nd. He had spoken for perhaps half an hour without interruption, and when he had finished, Inspector Page pointed out that he had made no reference to the day of the murder. Burtoft had hesitated for a few moments and then said, "Go on, I want to tell you everything, write it down". He had then made a statement admitting that he was the killer. The inspector ended his evidence by denying that any threats or inducements had been made to Burtoft, and by insisting that Burtoft's statement had been totally voluntary.

The statement Burtoft signed deserves to be quoted in full. It began, "Go on, I want to tell you everything, write it down. I admit being the murderer of Mrs Levin owing to drinking methylated spirits and also to the maid being where she was, the old lady lost her life. I was cool, calm and collected, of course. When I got in the front room there, the old lady got up and asked who was this and I went back and got the poker off the fire range and struck her repeatedly.

"When I left the house she was not dead but owing to the state of my nerves, I thought everyone was looking at me. I went down Angel Meadow into Kane's lodging house, washed my hands and threw the handkerchief down the lavatory and pulled the chain. Then I walked calmly into Swan Street and had a bit of tea and jumped on a tram for Oldham. I wasn't three minutes in the house. I was selling discharged soldiers' cards. Big Bertha will tell you I left her to sell some.

"I had no intention to do it but, well, I did it. I was sorry when I thought about it after. After I did it I took the poker back into the kitchen and wiped it on a shirt to remove my finger prints."

Inspector Willis also referred to the identification parade that Freda Phillips had attended. In the gap between the two parades, Burtoft had asked for a cigarette. Detective Sergeant Samuel Yarwood had handed one over at which point Burtoft had remarked, "Why all this messing? You know I sold some of the cards in the side streets and called at the doctor's house next door."

It might seem at first glance that Burtoft was determined to put his head inside the noose, but let us examine his apparent statements with more care. Taking his comments to Sergeant Yarwood first, Burtoft claimed that he had first called at Doctor Lee's home.

Henry Rourke Willcock was in Dr Lees' surgery at 2.50 p.m., and as he waited to be seen, he glanced out of the window in time to see a man walk down the path and knock at the front door. The man was of medium height, stocky and wore a trilby hat. Willcock's statement appears to confirm that this was Burtoft, however, there are three difficulties with this assumption. Firstly, the sighting took place seventy minutes before Mrs Levin was attacked, so what did Burtoft do in the meantime, secondly, Willcock made no mention of Burtoft's most distinguishing feature – the fact that he only had one eye, and thirdly, he was at Elizabeth Street until 3.15 p.m.

We can now turn to Burtoft's written statement to the police. In it he claims that after attacking Mrs Levin, stealing her money and then having a bite to eat, he caught a tram to Oldham. However, three days later, Burtoft was seen in Manchester by James Hughes. Are we to assume that having escaped from the city, Burtoft returned after three days and then left again, this time for Cheshire? Or, were the statements being made to fit the facts?

Another point arises from the description of the murder itself, in that same statement. Burtoft claimed that he entered the room, Mrs Levin got up and demanded to know who he was, and he then returned to the kitchen for the murder weapon. However, Mrs Levin was found lying in the same position she had been in when Freda Phillips last saw her. The only possible explanation for this, if Burtoft were the killer, would be that after he went to the kitchen to pick up the poker, Mrs Levin calmly lay down again to await his return!

For his part, Burtoft claimed that he had been forced into signing that confession. He had been questioned intensely and offered a tumbler of whisky, which as an alcoholic he had found impossible to resist. He also said that things got so bad that at one stage he had written on a piece of paper, "This is to certify that I have been subjected to the third degree, which I cannot stand any longer". This, of course, was denied by the police.

Before one decides whether Burtoft was telling the truth or not, it should also be remembered that the single fingerprint found on Mrs Levin's handbag was never referred to as evidence, thus indicating that it did not belong to Burtoft. Furthermore, Burtoft's clothing had been examined and no trace of blood whatsoever had been detected. This was despite the fact that the murder scene had splashes of blood all over the place and the assailant must certainly have been stained in some way.

The jury retired to consider their verdict but returned after an hour to ask for clarification on one part of the evidence. The judge said he was unable to recall the police surgeon who had examined the premises but confirmed that according to his testimony, no blood had been found on the front of the settee. The inference was that the jury were considering the point of no blood having been found on Burtoft, and that this might satisfy them that he could possibly have committed the crime without being splashed. However, such a position would have to ignore the fact that there was blood found on the floor in front of the settee, indicating that blood must have spurted forwards and towards the assailant.

After a further hour's deliberation, the jury returned to announce that Burtoft was guilty and he was sentenced to death. An appeal was heard on December 4th, before the Lord Chief Justice, Lord Hewart and Justices Avory and Lawrence. The main grounds were that the confession was inadmissible, but the judges ruled that it was for the defence to prove that it had been obtained under duress. This had not been done and so the appeal inevitably failed.

Five months to the day after the attack upon Mrs Levin, on Tuesday, December 19th, 1933, William Burtoft was hanged at Manchester. The fact remains that there was no hard evidence to link Burtoft to the crime except for his own confession, which he claimed the police had forced him into signing.

David Maskill Blake

27

Hanged at Leeds, Thursday, February 7th, 1935
For the murder of Emily Yeomans at Middleton Woods, near Leeds

GEORGE Newton was an elderly man but he was still in good health and looked forward to his daily walk through Middleton Woods. A man used to rising early, by 8.00 a.m., on Wednesday, October 17th, 1934, George was already pacing through the deep leaf litter surrounding the bare trees, enjoying the crisp morning air.

By 8.30 a.m., George was turning off the main track and heading up a narrow pathway. As he strolled, something caught his eye. Bending down he saw that it was a woman's glove. Thinking that some lady might simply have dropped it, George picked it up. Walking a little further he saw a young woman, lying on the ground.

At first, George thought the woman was asleep, though this was an unusual place to take a nap. Then he felt that she might have fallen ill, so he gently shook her shoulder to see if he could rouse her. Only then did George see that there was a pink chiffon scarf knotted tightly around her throat and that blood had issued from her mouth.

George immediately dashed off to alert the authorities. Officers were soon on the scene and, searching the area, found the dead woman's handbag in the undergrowth. Inside were articles that bore a name and address. The body was apparently that of twenty-three-year-old Emily Yeomans, who had lived at 69 Garnet Place, off Dewsbury Road, in Leeds.

Police investigations revealed that Emily had been a waitress who worked at the Lyon's Cafe in County Arcade. A native of Barrow-in-Furness, she lived with her uncle, Joseph Adams. It seemed that Emily had been a happy enough young woman whose only real love was dancing. She had been a shy girl and her uncle knew of no regular boyfriend.

According to Mr Adams, Emily had arrived home from work at around 4.20 p.m., on the evening of Tuesday, October 16th. Joseph had not actually come in himself until a few minutes later, and Emily had announced that she was going out that night. He assumed that, as usual, she was going dancing in the city centre. Uncle and niece then sat down to a snack of tea and currant bread, chatting to each other about what they had been doing during the day. Later still, Emily wrote a letter to her mother, who still lived in Emily's home town of Barrow.

Joseph went on to say that he and Emily had left the house together at 7.50 p.m. As Emily walked eastwards down Oakley Grove, Joseph turned the other way and headed west. As they walked away from each other, Joseph turned at one stage and waved to Emily as she, apparently, met up with a male friend on the corner of Dewsbury Road and Trentham Street. As Joseph watched, they walked off together, the man on the inside, close to the buildings and Emily on the outside, nearest to the road, the couple soon vanishing out of sight behind the buildings in Dewsbury Road.

That night, Joseph Adams had arrived home at some time between 10.00 p.m. and 10.15 p.m. There was no sign of Emily but there was nothing unusual in that. Indeed, only a few nights before, Emily had not come in until 2.30 a.m. Joseph went to bed and slept soundly but when he rose the following morning and saw that Emily's room was still empty, he grew rather concerned and considered whether or not he should contact the police. In the event, officers brought him the terrible news of her death before he could report her missing.

Further inquiries led to three potentially important witnesses coming forward. During his statement, Joseph Adams had mentioned that when he and Emily had parted, there had been three youths sitting on a window-sill at Verity's butcher's shop on the corner of Dewsbury Road and Oakley Grove. Perhaps they had also seen the man whom Emily met. The three boys were soon traced. Albert Deighton Bethall, Lawrence Trilk and Jeffrey Charles Sutton were all fourteen years of age and they confirmed that at 7.50 p.m., on October 16th, they had seen Emily Yeomans walk past them.

All three boys knew Emily, and indeed her uncle, quite well and after she had passed the group, Emily briefly vanished out of sight behind a bend in the line of houses before the boys saw her again. This time she was with a man, near Dr Swanton's gate, in Dewsbury Road. The boys had not actually seen Emily meet him, but they could certainly give a description of him. They agreed that he was somewhat taller than Emily, who was 5ft 2ins. Though the boys had only caught a glimpse of the man's face, the police at last had some idea about the man they were looking for.

Detective Chief Inspector James Craig, who was in charge of the case, released this description to the press on October 18th. It read, "About 24 years of age, 5ft 6ins to 5ft 8ins in height; medium build, clean shaven, hair brushed well back and appeared to be greased. Wearing blue suit, no head-dress, no overcoat; of smart appearance." Later, the police were informed that a man fitting this description had been seen coming out of the woods, by a tram driver, on the morning that Emily's body was discovered.

It was not until two days later, on Saturday, October 20th, the same day that Emily's body was buried, that the first breakthrough came. The police announced that a man had been detained, pending a forensic examination of his clothing. This man would prove to play a crucial role in the case but at the time, he was not named by those involved in the investigation. Since he was the first suspect, he would always be referred to as 'Man Number One'. About all the police would admit was that Man Number One had been out with Emily on at least one occasion. He was placed in an identification parade and picked out by two witnesses but finally, after being held for almost sixty hours, he was released without charge.

In an attempt to break the case, the police offered two separate rewards for information. The chief constable offered £50 for information leading to the man's conviction and £20 for information which led to the identity of the man seen with Emily in Dewsbury Road on the night she was last seen alive.

On October 24th, the police received some interesting news. Norah Menzies was the wife of the licensee of the Mulberry Tree Inn, Folly Lane, Leeds and one of her regular customers had been saying that he knew the identity of the man who had been seen with Emily in Dewsbury Road. This information was passed on to the police and after interviewing Mrs Menzies and her customer, Albert Schofield, Chief Inspector Craig, along with Detective Inspector Murgatroyd and Detective Sergeant Binns, called at 33 Lady Pit Lane and there took into custody twenty-nine-year-old David Maskill Blake.

When he was first questioned, Blake denied even knowing Emily Yeomans. This would later prove to be a very costly mistake since it was only when faced with cast-iron evidence that he had been out with her that Blake said he had known her after all, though he still denied seeing her on the night she died. In due course, Blake made a written statement, which read "I am making this statement of my own free will. I have been cautioned by Chief Detective Inspector Craig, that anything I say now may be given in evidence.

"You will wonder why I never admitted that I knew Emily Yeomans at the time I was arrested on suspect [sic] of murder. The reason why was I am not sure of this date, Thursday or Friday, that I met Emily Yeomans coming from a dance at the hour of two a.m., of which I knew she had gone. I walked up the street with her, that is in Dewsbury Road, and we stood round the corner talking and messing about for a matter of an hour and a quarter.

"I knew that she was living with her uncle, but I thought they called her Adams. We were messing about for an hour and a quarter and a policeman came down the road, stood about thirty or forty yards away, and we packed up and said goodnight as she told her uncle she would not be long. I promised to meet her the following Thursday at nine o'clock at night. I was there at nine p.m. She did not come and then I connected her with this murder. I am not the man who met her on Tuesday night, the night of the murder, and that is the truth, Inspector.

"I have met her on several occasions and had drinks with her. I mean she had drinks with me. The reason I did not like saying anything was because of my previous convictions and reading about scientific microscopical inspections on her clothing knowing full well they were practically bound to be on mine. I think this is all I can say, Inspector.

"Also, I am not the man that emerged from the woods on the Wednesday morning of the finding of the body.

"This statement had been read over by me; it has been made voluntarily and it is true."

215

The police now had two suspects but although there was forensic evidence and identification evidence linking Man Number One to the crime, various other witnesses seemed to prove that it was Blake who had met Emily on the night she was killed. So it was that Blake, and not Man Number One, was charged with murder.

During the various police court appearances, evidence was given that the digestion of the raisin skins that Emily had eaten put the time of her death at between two and four hours after she had consumed them. Since Joseph Adams had said that they had had the currant bread at just before 5.00 p.m., this put the time of Emily's death somewhere before 9.00 p.m. on October 16th. This would prove to be crucial when Blake faced his trial. That trial opened on December 12th, 1934, before Mr Justice Goddard and a jury of ten men and two women. Blake's defence lay in the hands of Mr C. Paley Scott and Mr H. B. Hylton-Foster, whilst the prosecution case was led by Mr J. Willoughby Jardine and Mr G. H. B. Streatfeild. The hearing lasted until December 15th.

Joseph Adams told the court of the events of October 16th and also spoke of another encounter, which had taken place on the previous Friday night. Emily had been on a late shift and so only got home from work at 7.00 p.m. By 7.50 p.m., she had gone out again, saying that she was going to a dance. Joseph went out himself, returned home and then went to meet Emily near the Dewsbury Road police station. He saw her there at 1.45 a.m., on October 13th and saw that she was with a man, and another couple. Seeing that Emily was not alone, Joseph told her to 'hurry up' and then went home to wait. Emily had come in some forty-five minutes later. This testimony, of course, agreed with Blake's own statement to the police since he had referred to meeting Emily on a Thursday or a Friday night.

George Newton explained how he had found the body and pointed out that Emily was lying not far from the tramlines that led to Leeds city centre. In fact, the tramlines could be seen from where the body lay and this made the evidence of two more witnesses quite significant.

Bert Foulds was a tram driver, working on the Leeds to Middleton route. At about 7.15 a.m., on the morning of October 17th, he saw a man who looked rather like the suspect being sought by the police. This man was standing in the woods, very close to where Emily's body was found just over an hour later. Another tram driver had also passed close by at 7.00 a.m., and from his tram, he saw a man emerge from the woods at a distance he estimated as just a few yards from where Emily's body lay. These two sightings were, of course, well after the time of death, but the police felt that the killer might well have returned to the scene of his crime. Neither of these witnesses had picked out Blake at his identity parade however, yet Bert Foulds had picked out Man Number One at an earlier parade.

Albert Bethall, Lawrence Trilk and Jeffrey Sutton, the three youths on the butcher's window-sill, had also attended those two identification parades. Two of the boys were unable to identify anyone, but after asking the men to turn around, Lawrence Trilk did point to the man that he thought most resembled the one he had seen. Once again, this

216

was Man Number One. Thus, two men had picked out Man Number One and no one had picked out Blake.

The next witness was Albert Schofield, a boot repairer of 6 Buckton Street, Leeds. Schofield had only become acquainted with Blake on August 25th, but the two men had soon become friends and had started going out together to various dance halls and clubs. Schofield was a member of the 43 Club situated in Rialto Yard, Briggate and this was where Schofield's narrative of his and Blake's movements began.

According to Schofield, he and Blake had met in the 43 Club at around 3.20 p.m., on October 11th. They had stayed there, drinking, until some time between 7.00 p.m. and 7.30 p.m., when they had moved on to the Imperial at Beeston. They only finally split up at closing time, 10.00 p.m. Blake, though, had apparently met someone else afterwards for when Schofield saw him again, on Saturday, October 13th, Blake explained that he had met a girl in Dewsbury Road. Blake went on to say that this girl worked in the Lyon's Cafe in town and her name was Yeomans, and that he had arranged to meet her again on the coming Tuesday.

On October 16th, the day Emily Yeomans met her death, Blake and Schofield met each other again, by arrangement, at the corner of Boar Lane and Briggate, at 3.20 p.m. From there they went to the 43 Club again, leaving at around 7.20 p.m. The two men walked on to Dewsbury Road, where Blake told his friend that he had arranged to meet a woman near the traffic lights, close to the Hunslet Road police station. However, when they reached these lights, Blake said "No, further on", and they walked on to the bottom of Trentham Street, where Blake said he had agreed to wait. Schofield now walked on alone, up Trentham Street.

By now it was around 7.50 p.m., and Schofield watched with interest as a girl appeared from Oakley Grove and crossed to where Blake was waiting. The couple then strolled off down Dewsbury Road, with Blake on the inside. Though he could not positively identify the girl, Schofield was telling the court that he had actually witnessed the meeting between Emily Yeomans and David Maskill Blake.

Blake was actually engaged to be married at this time, and Schofield had arranged to be his best man. According to Schofield, he next saw Blake outside the registry office on Wednesday, October 17th, whereupon Blake produced a copy of the Evening Post, and pointed out a headline that referred to the murder of Emily Yeomans. Blake had then said, "Didn't I tell you I had met a girl named Yeomans who worked at Lyons?" Schofield had agreed that he had, and Blake then continued "Look at that" and handed over the paper for Schofield to read.

On October 19th, Schofield and Blake met in the Mulberry Inn. By now the description of the wanted man had been published, and Schofield remarked that it fitted Blake very well. The following Monday, October 22nd, they were back in the Mulberry and Blake, speaking about the reward offered for information, had said to Schofield, "Now's your chance to get twenty quid. We will see if you are a pal or not." Schofield had replied "I will have nothing to do with it", and said that he held no idea that his friend might be the killer.

This statement appears not to have been the truth however, for Schofield had been talking of his suspicions in the pubs he frequented, and this had come to the attention, first of Norah Menzies at the Mulberry and then finally, of the police. They had come for Schofield on Wednesday, October 24th, and only then had he told them of the things he had seen and Blake's possible involvement in the crime.

The prosecution now called Arthur Jubb, who lived in Duncombe Street, off Park Lane. At some time between 11.00 p.m. and 11.30 p.m., on October 18th, Jubb was walking down Bond Street when he saw Blake and asked him if he could change a two shillings and sixpence piece. Blake said that he could not but the two men fell into conversation and went for a walk. Eventually, Jubb invited Blake back to his house and it was there that Blake picked up the evening newspaper and began reading about the murder.

Jubb told Blake to make himself comfortable and take off his coat but as he did so, something rattled inside his pocket. Blake then took out a tube of cream and a compact containing face powder, asking Jubb if he wanted them for his wife. Jubb replied that she did not use such things but Blake put them on the mantelpiece anyway and told Jubb he could do what he wanted with them.

At one stage, Jubb saw that Blake's trousers were ripped on one leg and Blake told him that he had torn them on some barbed wire on the previous Tuesday. It was not until 8.15 a.m., on October 19th, that Blake left, taking with him an envelope bearing Jubb's address which Jubb had handed over in case Blake ever wanted to call again. That envelope was found on Blake when he was arrested and when the police spoke to Jubb, he handed over the cream and powder, which he said had remained untouched on the mantelpiece.

It was the compact that was to prove significant. The paper lid had a small tear in it and no fewer than five women who worked with Emily Yeomans, at the cafe, said that her compact had had just such a tear. Eva Ogier, one of those witnesses, had known Emily for eleven months, and had even been out dancing with her. Eva was also able to tell the court of a man she had seen out with Emily and stated positively that this was not David Blake.

Irene Walker and Mary Halton were two more waitresses and both reported the same tear. However, both of these witnesses also admitted under cross-examination that they believed Emily's box to be somewhat more dirty and battered than the one shown to them in court. Irene Walker further admitted that she had never heard Emily refer to a man named Blake, but she had spoken to her about Man Number One. Indeed, it had been Irene who first introduced this man to Emily, not being aware at the time that he was a married man. Finally, Margaret Longe and Alice Watts also agreed that Emily's compact had been torn just like the one they now saw.

The time had come to call the medical and forensic evidence. Dr Cyril Robert Manley, the city analyst, had examined the contents of the powder compact. One of Emily's fellow waitresses had once given Emily some of her own powder when she complained that the brand she was using was too light. Dr Manley had tested the contents of the box given to Jubb, hoping to show that it was a mixture of two types. Curiously, he found only thirty grains of face powder. The remaining one hundred and seventy grains of 'powder' turned out to be pure boracic acid. It was never explained how this had got into the compact, or who might have put it there.

Dr Hoyland Smith, the police surgeon, had examined Emily's body *in situ* and later performed the post-mortem with Dr Cyril John Polson. He testified that Emily's skirt had been pushed up at the back and opened up the front. There was bloodstaining in the genital region and though her underclothing was in place, there was evidence of sexual penetration. The pink scarf had been wound four times around Emily's throat and the cause of death was asphyxia due to strangulation.

Dr Gerald Roche Lynch was the senior analyst to the Home Office and he had been given the dead woman's clothes to examine. Later, he was also given several items of male clothing including a coat, a waistcoat and a pair of trousers belonging to Blake. Dr Lynch said that he had found blood on the man's trousers, on the lining behind the fly. There were also smears of blood in the pocket lining, consistent with a bloodstained hand being put into that pocket. Finally, Dr Lynch found evidence of semen staining on the trousers, close to the fly buttons.

Of even more interest was the evidence given by Professor Frederick Tryhorn, of University College, Hull. On October 19th, Professor Tryhorn received Emily's coat, her brown skirt and other items of clothing. On the coat was a short hair, two inches in length, which was a human pubic hair. There was also a single fibre that turned out to be from some navy blue worsted material.

The professor testified that the hair could have come from Blake and that the fibres matched his navy blue suit, which had a small triangular tear on the trousers. This tear, incidentally, could well have been caused by barbed wire and there was some of this wire close to where Emily had been found. However, Professor Tryhorn had also examined clothes taken from Man Number One. His suit was brown, so the navy blue fibre could not have come from that garment, but samples of his hair had also been taken and the hair found on Emily's coat could also have come from him.

Professor Tryhorn continued by saying that in addition to the hair, he had also found some red wool fibres on Emily's skirt and some small fragments of feather on her jersey. At the time of the attack upon her, Emily was wearing a red jumper. Those fibres could then have come from her own jumper, but Man Number One also had a red jumper and they could have come from that. Finally, on Man Number One's trousers, Professor Tryhorn found small pieces of feather, which matched those found on Emily. There was, therefore, forensic evidence linking both suspects to the dead woman.

219

Blood had been found on Blake's clothing and this had to be accounted for by the defence. In order to do so, some of the history of Blake's new wife had to be considered.

Before her marriage, Jean Blake's surname had been Whitehead. Jean Whitehead had a baby who was now seven months old and Blake had never denied that he was the father. Jean's family, though, had not approved of the match and a good deal of animosity existed between Blake and the Whiteheads.

Thomas Whitehead, Jane's brother, testified that on August 25th, Blake had been involved in an argument at their home. A fight had broken out which ended with Blake having to be admitted to hospital for treatment to a head wound after Thomas had struck him with a poker. Confirmation of this hospital treatment was given by Eleanor Thomas, the nurse who treated Blake. Before Blake was seen, he was asked to remove his clothing and as Eleanor treated him, she noticed that the bundle of clothing he carried was navy blue. This explained the presence of blood on Blake's blue suit.

Right up to the moment of his arrest, Blake had lived with his married sister, Florence and her husband, Albert Norman Bousfield, at 33 Lady Pit Lane. Space there was at a premium, so even after Blake and Jean had married, she continued to live with her family at Buckton Place and Blake resided at the Bousfield home.

Albert Bousfield said that he had returned home from work at 6.00 p.m. on October 16th, the day of the murder. He had something to eat and then settled down to sleep on the settee in the living room whilst his wife busied herself upstairs with the household chores. At the time, Blake was certainly not in the house. It was then no later than 7.00 p.m.

At about 8.00 p.m., Florence Bousfield, who was still upstairs, heard Blake calling her from downstairs. He was asking if she knew where he might find a razor blade. Florence confirmed that she did not actually see her brother, but she knew his voice and swore that he was home at that time.

When Albert woke from his nap, at 9.00 p.m., Blake was not there, but some twenty-five minutes later, Jean came in and within three minutes, Blake followed her into the house. The next day, October 17th, Florence noticed that Jean had left behind her powder compact and a tube of face cream. She pointed these out to her brother and he picked them up and put them into his coat pocket. This testimony not only removed the importance of the powder compact, but gave Blake an alibi until around 8.00 p.m. By this time of course, Emily Yeomans had already met the man on Dewsbury Road.

The Bousfields were also able to give other information that helped Blake's defence. They confirmed that on the night he had been involved in the fight with Thomas Whitehead, he had been wearing his blue suit. They were also able to state that on October 14th, Blake had been on a friend's motorcycle when he had been involved in an accident. As a result of that, Blake had injured one of his hands and had also torn his trousers. This was confirmed by the friend in question.

The time came for David Blake to step into the witness box and give evidence on his own behalf. He admitted that he had first met Emily Yeomans about three weeks before

220

she died and had been out with her three or four times since then. He had last seen her on Friday, October 12th, when she had told him that she was going to a dance. He did not like dancing, but arranged to meet her afterwards. They finally met at about 1.20 a.m., and were together for about an hour.

Blake agreed that he had arranged to meet Emily again, but this was not on the Tuesday she died, but on the Thursday, October 18th. He said he had never told Schofield that he was seeing a girl named Yeomans. He had mentioned a girl and had said that her name was Emily, but he had thought that she had the same surname as her uncle, Adams.

On the day of the murder Blake said he had met Schofield and they had been to the 43 Club together. Whilst there he told his friend that he had arranged to meet Jean in Vicar Lane at 9.00 p.m., so he could not stay for too long. They left the club at 7.30 p.m., and far from walking down Dewsbury Road to meet Emily, he had climbed onto a tram at Hunslet Hall Road.

It was just after 8.00 p.m. when he arrived at Lady Pit Lane, a time confirmed by his sister, and he saw his brother-in-law asleep on the sofa. Blake shouted upstairs to where Florence was, and asked her for a razor blade. He shaved and washed and then went to meet his wife. Unfortunately, he missed his wife and so walked back home, arriving just a minute or so after she had.

Blake went on to deny that he had been obsessed with the murder and though he had purchased a copy of a newspaper carrying a report of the crime, he had bought this for the racing. Only later did he see the crime headline and this so surprised him that he pointed it out to Schofield outside the registry office.

Having heard all the testimony, the jury took seventy-five minutes to decide that Blake was guilty and he was sentenced to death. Only now could it be revealed that Blake had something of a history of crime against the person.

He had two previous convictions. One of these had taken place at Christmas, 1929. A young girl, visiting her sister in Castleford, missed her last bus and set off to walk home. En route she met two girls who had a man with them and he offered to escort her home. On the way, the man battered and almost choked her, taking from her a gold necklace. That man was Blake, and for that offence he received a sentence of three years.

Even before this, whilst serving in the Army in India, Blake had been involved in several offences which culminated in the rape and assault of an old native woman. Blake was charged, along with others, and was given a prison sentence, but this was subsequently quashed on a technicality.

Blake's appeal was heard on January 21st, 1935 before the Lord Chief Justice and Justices Avory and Swift. Here, the difficulties with the prosecution case were pointed out again.

The defence stated that according to the medical evidence, Emily had been killed at some time between 8.00 p.m. and 9.00 p.m., at a distance of some 2,000 yards from where Blake lived, and there was testimony that he was at home soon after 8.00 p.m.

Furthermore, two of Emily's workmates had failed to identify the compact as the one that she had owned. In addition, one of the tramcar drivers and one of the young boys who had seen Emily meet a man had made positive identifications of Man Number One, and forensic evidence linked that man to the crime.

Finally, there was doubt over the evidence given by Schofield. He had claimed that he had seen Blake and a woman walk off together, yet if his story were true and he had been there, he would have been unable to see down Dewsbury Road from the far end of Trentham Street. In short, there was sufficient evidence to suggest that the prosecution had failed to prove their case beyond a reasonable doubt. It was not necessary to prove Blake innocent, only to show that the case against him had not been proved.

In giving their judgement, the judges stated that there were a number of suspicious elements to Blake's behaviour, including the fact that when first interviewed he had denied even knowing Emily. In addition, if the jury accepted Schofield's evidence, then there was no doubt that Blake was the man who met Emily on the night she died and this, together with other evidence that linked him to the crime, was more than enough to demonstrate his guilt.

On Thursday, February 7th, 1935, despite a petition carrying over 10,000 signatures pleading for a reprieve, David Maskill Blake was hanged at Leeds by Thomas Pierrepoint and Alfred Allen. It was the day before Blake's thirtieth birthday.

Man Number One vanished back into the pages of history and was never named at the time. Prior to Blake's arrest he had been the chief suspect and would almost certainly have been questioned again had Blake's name not entered into the frame. Man Number One was a major suspect in a murder case and whilst there is no proof that he was guilty, his very existence certainly weakened the case against Blake. However, as in the case of James Hanratty, which is also featured in this book, the police appear to have simply stopped looking once they became convinced that they had got their man.

During his cross-examination of Chief Inspector Craig at Blake's trial, Mr Paley Scott handed him a piece of paper on which he had written a name and asked Mr Craig to confirm that this was the identity of Man Number One. That confirmation was given and the piece of paper, Exhibit 23, was entered into evidence. That exhibit shows that Man Number One was a gentleman named Joseph Talbot.

Charlotte Bryant

28

T HE early 1920s were a time of trouble throughout Ireland and the British Army were present in force. Occasionally, local girls were known to fraternize with these soldiers and some of these relationships even led to marriage. One such liaison took place in Londonderry between Frederick Bryant and Charlotte McHugh. Charlotte decided that she would have a much better life living in England and the couple became engaged, eventually marrying in Wells, Somerset, on October 5th, 1922. At the time, Frederick was twenty-four and Charlotte just nineteen.

Unfortunately for Charlotte, life in England was not much easier than it had been in Ireland. Once he left the army, Frederick took a job as a farmhand. The pay was poor but luckily this new position did carry with it a tied cottage near Yeovil. As for the family income, well Charlotte knew a good way to supplement that. Whilst Frederick was working, she would take men back to the cottage and entertain them for a few shillings. The local populace was scandalized but Frederick, who knew all about it, merely commented, "I don't care what she does. Four quid a week is better than thirty bob." Over the next seven or eight years, four children were born to the union, possibly not all of them Frederick's, but the couple remained together and seemed to be happy enough with their curious living arrangements. All this was to change, though, in 1933, when, just before Christmas, Charlotte met a gypsy named Leonard Edward Parsons, who also called himself Bill Moss.

Parsons had only recently split from his common-law wife, Priscilla Loveridge, the mother of his children, but he instantly fell for Charlotte. The two became very friendly and she invited Parsons to spend Christmas with her family at the cottage. Not only did Frederick not object, but he took an instant liking to the gypsy and they became firm friends too. It was Frederick who confirmed that Parsons could stay as long as he liked and who offered him the spare room. Once more the surrounding area was filled with gossip, for no sooner had Frederick left for work in the mornings than Parsons would climb into bed with Charlotte. It seemed that everyone knew what was going on. It was only a matter of time before Frederick's employer found out too and when he did, he dismissed Frederick on the spot for letting such things take place under his roof.

It was perhaps this dismissal which finally spurred Frederick into action. He ordered Parsons to pack his bags and go. Parsons did so but Charlotte collected her own belongings and announced that she was leaving too. Frederick raised no objections and in due course, Parsons, Charlotte and two of her children moved out. Two days later, though, Charlotte was back home with her husband.

There were always jobs around for farm labourers and it was not long before Frederick found alternative employment at Coombe. There was another cottage with the job and so Frederick, Charlotte and their children moved in and tried to rebuild their lives together. They had not been there for very long when a telegram arrived for Charlotte. It had been sent by Parsons, who seemed to have forgotten that Charlotte could neither read nor write. The message, asking her to meet Parsons at Bradford Hollow, was read out by Frederick, who told Charlotte that she should meet Parsons as arranged but that he would go too and give Parsons a piece of his mind.

It was perhaps a sign of Parsons' rather smooth talk that when the meeting took place not only did he manage to placate Frederick, but the two became friends again and Parsons was invited to move into the new cottage. It seemed that nothing had changed.

In 1935, Charlotte found herself pregnant with her fifth child and the chances were that it was Parsons who was responsible. At about the same time, Frederick Bryant began suffering from stomach pains and Dr Edgar McCarthy had to be called out. He diagnosed gastro-enteritis and prescribed some medicine, which seemed to do the trick, for Frederick made a full and rapid recovery.

A few months later, Parsons announced that he was thinking of finding fresh lodgings for himself. At about the same time, Frederick suffered another bout of stomach pains and this time was seen by Dr McIntosh, as Dr McCarthy was on holiday. He too thought that the patient was suffering from gastro-enteritis, and again the problem soon responded to treatment. Soon afterwards, Parsons moved out and Charlotte became friendly with a neighbour, Lucy Ostler, a widow with seven children of her own. So close were the two women that Charlotte even asked Frederick if Lucy and her children could move in with them. For once, Frederick put his foot down and said no.

On Saturday, December 21st, 1935, Frederick Bryant had another attack of stomach pains. Charlotte ran for help to Lucy Ostler, saying that Frederick had eaten too much sausages and bacon. The two women went back to the cottage to find Frederick writhing on the floor in agony, groaning "I'm dying".

Fortunately, Lucy was a trained nurse. She attended to Frederick before sending for Dr McCarthy. When he arrived he asked what Frederick had eaten and Charlotte replied, "Bread and cheese. He gorges himself on bread and cheese."

Dr McCarthy thought that it would be best if Frederick were taken to hospital, but the patient refused to leave the cottage. A brief argument followed between the two men, but Frederick would not budge. Finally, Dr McCarthy wrote out a prescription and said he would call back the next day. Frederick, however, refused to take the medicine when Charlotte collected it for him. Meanwhile, Charlotte had other things on her mind for whilst Lucy looked after Frederick, she paid a visit to Weston-Super-Mare where Parsons was now living on a gypsy encampment. Unfortunately for Charlotte, Parsons was not at home but his ex-lover, Priscilla Loveridge, was. She made it quite plain to Charlotte that she had no chance of getting Parsons back.

The next day, Sunday, December 22nd, Frederick was far worse and Dr McCarthy said that there would be no argument this time, he had to be admitted to hospital. It was 1.30 p.m. by the time Frederick arrived at Sherbourne hospital, and upon arrival he was immediately given fresh medication. By 2.10 p.m., his condition had not improved and the nurse looking after him felt that the ward sister should be informed. After they had conferred, they called for Dr McCarthy, who was elsewhere in the hospital, and he arrived at Frederick's bedside at 2.40 p.m. Minutes later, Frederick Bryant died. A telegram was sent to Charlotte to inform her, and later that same day, she and Lucy Ostler arrived at the hospital.

This was perhaps the first sign Charlotte received that the authorities were far from satisfied with the way Frederick had died. Going to the reception she explained who she was and added, "I've been to the undertaker. He told me I have to come here and collect the death certificate." She was informed that the doctor had not signed the certificate, and that there would have to be a post-mortem and an inquest. Dr McCarthy, meanwhile, had contacted the coroner and told him that he could not sign a certificate, and the coroner, in turn, had passed this information on to Superintendent Cherrett.

It was Christmas Eve when two policemen arrived at the cottage to take away seven bottles of medicine. Charlotte, Lucy Ostler and all the children were there at the time. At one stage, when Charlotte was out of the room, one of the policemen asked Lucy what Frederick had eaten for breakfast on the day he fell ill. Lucy informed him that Charlotte had told her that it was sausages and bacon.

It was after Christmas by the time Dr Gerald Roche Lynch, the pathologist, had finished his examination of Frederick's remains. Dr Lynch found 4.09 grains of arsenic in Frederick's internal organs. The cause of death had been arsenical poisoning, but who had administered that poison? The most likely candidate was Charlotte, but she could not be arrested without evidence. A police search of every chemist in the county was made. None reported a transaction in the name of Bryant in their poisons register.

On January 4th, 1936, the police were back at the cottage to escort Charlotte and her children to the Stourminster workhouse. This was done so that a thorough search of the farm could be made. The land was dug up, a brook was drained, the lane leading to the cottage was excavated and even four family pets, a dog, a cat and two pigeons, were put down so that they could be examined for traces of arsenic. The only piece of evidence these efforts revealed was a battered empty green tin, which had once contained Eureka weed-killer. Even if this had contained the arsenic, there was still no way of proving that Charlotte had purchased it.

225

As part of the investigation, the police spoke to everyone who had ever known the Bryants. It was this approach that led Detective Sergeant John Tapsell to speak to Gladys Kent, the manageress of a shop in Sherbourne, who recalled writing a rather passionate letter for Charlotte, to a man named Leonard Parsons. She recalled that the address was somewhere in Swanage, but this had been two years before.

From Swanage, the police traced Parsons to the Rothwell Green area, near Wellington in Somerset. Finally, they tracked him down and he was taken to Sherbourne, where he was interviewed by Detective Chief Inspector Bell. Parsons spoke freely of his affair with Charlotte and said that she had told him several times that it would not be long before she was a widow. Over the next few days, Bell also spoke to Lucy Ostler, who, under pressure to say what she knew, began to say things about Charlotte.

It was undoubtedly Lucy Ostler who did the most damage to Charlotte. She told Bell that Charlotte had told her eldest son to get rid of a tin and that on December 26th, when she had wanted to use the wash house, she could not light the boiler as it was choked up with rubbish and partially burned clothing. Checking through the ashes, Lucy had found a burnt green tin, which was labelled weed-killer. Still Lucy had not finished talking though. She mentioned the visit to the hospital to pick up the death certificate and Charlotte asking her what an inquest was. When Lucy told her, Charlotte had remarked "If they can't find anything, they can't put a rope around my neck". There was also the uncertainty over what Frederick had eaten for breakfast. Charlotte had told her that it was sausages and bacon, but she had told the doctor that it was bread and cheese. Finally, on the night of December 21st, when Charlotte got back from Weston, they had all gone to bed in the cottage. During the night, Lucy heard Charlotte giving Frederick some meat extract, and a few minutes later, Frederick was vomiting violently.

Though there was no hard evidence against Charlotte, the police now had proof of the affair with Parsons, his comments on things Charlotte had said about wanting Frederick dead and Lucy Ostler's damning testimony. It was felt that this was more than enough to proceed. On February 10th, Charlotte was arrested and charged with the murder of her husband.

The trial opened at Dorchester on May 27th, before Mister Justice MacKinnon. The proceedings lasted until May 30th, during which time Charlotte was defended by Mr J. D. Casswell and Mr L. R. Dunne. Sir Terence O'Connell appeared for the Crown, assisted by Mr Cyril Asquith and Mr John Maude.

The prosecution began by confirming that the most exhaustive enquiries had failed to produce any evidence that Charlotte Bryant had purchased arsenic in any form. Indeed, the only chemist who had an entry in his register for arsenic was based in Yeovil. He had sold a tin of weed-killer to a woman on December 21st and attended an identification parade on January 15th. He had failed to pick out Charlotte.

After Parsons and Lucy Ostler had given their damning testimony, Mrs Priddle, the wife of Aubrey Robert Priddle, who had been Frederick's employer at Coombe, was called. She told the court that some time in 1935 she had purchased a gallon tin of weed-killer for use on her garden. Once the tin was empty she used it to put some paraffin in when Charlotte needed some. From time to time, Charlotte continued to use the tin to collect more paraffin. The defence had therefore explained the empty poison tin found on Charlotte's land.

Lily Elizabeth Bryant, Charlotte's ten-year-old daughter, said that Lucy Ostler was present when the boiler was raked out after Frederick had died, but that there was no burnt tin amongst the ashes. Furthermore, Lily had seen Parsons with a dark blue bottle when he lived at the house.

Ernest Samuel Bryant, Charlotte's twelve-year-old son, said that on the day after his father had died, he was at home with his mother and Lucy Ostler. There was some conversation about a chemist's shop, but it had been Lucy who did all the talking, implying perhaps that Lucy Ostler had been trying to lead Charlotte into incriminating herself.

Charlotte gave evidence on her own behalf. She denied ever saying that she wanted to get rid of her husband, and insisted that she had not spoken about his death to Lucy Ostler or to Parsons, and had never administered poison to Frederick. She had been a happy woman until Parsons came into her life and it had been he who had done all the running. He was the one who wanted her to leave her husband.

About the only signs of arsenic found in the cottage had been some amongst the dust of the pockets of an old coat, and some amongst the ashes taken from the boiler. Charlotte said that she knew nothing about the coat and even tried it on in court to show that it did not fit her. The boiler ashes were more damning, though. Doctor Lynch said that he had found 149.5 parts of arsenic per million, when the normal portion in household ash should have been 48 parts per million.

The judge told the jury that they had two questions to consider. The first was, did Frederick Bryant die of arsenic poisoning and the second was, if so, was it administered by his wife. In the event, the jury took one hour to decide that Frederick had been poisoned, and the joint testimony of Parsons, Ostler and Dr Lynch on the arsenic found in the boiler ashes convinced them that it was Charlotte who had given it to him. She collapsed in the dock as the guilty verdict was announced.

The evidence, however, was far from complete. A few days after the verdict had been given, Professor William Bone of the Imperial College of Science read a report of the judge's summing up and realized that Dr Lynch had made a terrible mistake. Professor Bone then wrote to Mr Casswell, Charlotte's barrister, and pointed out that the normal amount of arsenic in household ash was not 48 parts per million but at least 148 parts per million and usually closer to 1,000 parts per million. There had been no extra arsenic in the boiler ashes, proving that no container which had held arsenic had been burned there.

On the strength of that new evidence, an appeal was entered. This was heard on June 29th before the Lord Chief Justice, Lord Hewart, and two of his colleagues. They refused to even hear the new evidence, Lord Hewart explaining this by saying "It would be intolerable if this court, at the conclusion of a capital charge, or any other case, were to listen to the afterthoughts of a scientific gentleman who brought his mind controversially to bear on evidence that has been given.

"We adumbrated that possibility and we set our minds like a flint against it. It is clear that there was no mistake in the court below." Such was the value of a human life to the Lord Chief Justice of England.

On July 14th, Charlotte, who had learned basic reading and writing skills whilst in prison, sent a telegram to the King. It read "Mighty King, have pity on your lowly, afflicted subject. Don't let them kill me on Wednesday. Ask them to give Mrs Van der Elst an opportunity of saying what will prove my innocence. From the brink of the cold, dark grave I, a poor helpless woman, ask you not to let them kill me. I am innocent." The lady Charlotte was referring to was a famous campaigner against the death penalty, and the evidence that Charlotte wished to make public was that Frederick was in the habit of taking the occasional sip of sheep dip, which contained arsenic, as a tonic. The telegram never even reached the King. It was diverted to the Home Secretary.

On July 7th, an application to the Attorney General for a fiat for the case to be sent to the House of Lords was rejected and Charlotte's fate was sealed. Just before she was hanged she used what writing skills she had to scribble a note reading "It's all —— fault I am here. I listened to the tales I was told. But I have not long now and I will be out of all my troubles. God bless the children." The prison authorities released the letter but blanked out the name of the person Charlotte had accused.

British justice submitted Charlotte to one final agony. Fearful of public demonstrations the authorities brought her execution forward by one hour, thus snatching the last sixty minutes of her life from her. She was hanged at Exeter by Thomas Pierrepoint, who was assisted by his nephew, Albert.

Robert William Hoolhouse

29

Hanged at Durham, Thursday, May 26th, 1938
For the murder of Margaret Jane Dobson,
at Wolviston, County Durham

A T 11.00 a.m., on Tuesday, January 18th, 1938, Henry Dobson left his farm, High Grange Farm, at Wolviston, and travelled to the auction mart at Sedgefield. Whilst there, a number of pigs attracted his eye and he purchased them, making arrangements for them to be delivered later that day, once the market had closed for business. He then made his way home, arriving at High Grange at about 2.30 p.m.

One hour later, at 3.30 p.m., Henry and his wife, sixty-seven-year-old Margaret Jane Dobson, sat down to a snack of bread and boiled beef. Minutes later, Henry went back to work, carrying out the many duties that a busy farmer has to do.

It was around 4.30 p.m. when Margaret walked into the yard where her husband was working and announced, "I am going out to Wolviston and may go to Dyke House". That address was where Mrs Thompson, Margaret's cousin, lived, so Henry knew that she would probably be gone for some time. For the rest of that afternoon, Henry Dobson supervised the milking until, at 5.30 p.m., the cattle wagon arrived with the pigs he had purchased that morning.

There were three men in that cattle delivery wagon, Percy Swales, Thomas Nelson and John Henry Burns. As they unloaded the pigs, Swales mentioned something about a farm hand in the field next to the long lane that led from the main road to the farmhouse. It seemed to be just the conversation of working men and Henry Dobson took little interest in what was said. Some fifteen minutes later, the unloading was complete and the cattle van was making its way back down the track to the road.

Some time later, Henry Dobson shut the poultry up in the shed, went inside the farmhouse and sat near his roaring fire. By now it was 6.30 p.m. He picked up his newspaper and settled down to read. By the time he had finished it was 8.30 p.m., and there was still no sign of his wife. Becoming a little uneasy, Henry took up a lamp and walked down to the gate at the main road.

Dyke House was near Hartlepool and Henry waited at the gate whilst two of the buses from West Hartlepool passed. Neither of them carried Margaret and Henry

229

decided that in all probability his wife had gone on to see their daughter, who lived in Newcastle-upon-Tyne. It was something that she had done before and, if that were the case, she might not return until the following day.

Going back to the farmhouse, Henry sat down by his fire again, watching the clock until it was 11.00 p.m. Then he picked up the lamp once more and walked back to the main road where he watched the last bus pass. Now it was certain that Margaret would be away for the night. Henry went back to his warm living room. It was now 11.35 p.m.

The next morning, January 19th, Henry Dobson was up and working by 5.00 a.m. He made sure that his men were busy milking the cows before going back into the house at 6.40 a.m., to make himself some breakfast. Henry then went outside to get the milk ready for shipment before going back into the farmhouse to make another breakfast, this time for one of his men, Bob Irvin.

Henry's duties kept him busy until 10.00 a.m., when the farm hands took their morning break. By this time there was still no sign of Margaret, and Henry, growing anxious again, decided to walk into Wolviston village from where he would be able to telephone his daughter in Newcastle in order to confirm that Margaret was there. So, wrapping up against the cold, Henry set off towards the main road.

The track was curved so Henry decided to take a short cut through a field of clover. It was whilst he was walking that he noticed something in the field. It was a dark object and impossible to make out from a distance. Retracing his steps, Henry went to investigate.

Only when he stepped down from the raised trackway did Henry Dobson see what the dark object was. It was the body of his wife, Margaret, and she was clearly beyond all help. Henry climbed back onto the trackway and went to fetch the police. On the way, he met William Tomlinson and told him that he thought Margaret had been murdered.

Constable John Robert Chapman was on duty in the High Street, Wolviston when, at 10.40 a.m., he saw Henry Dobson beckoning him. Going up to the farmer, Chapman heard him say, "Oh my wife has been murdered. She is lying on the ploughed field in a terrible state."

At that precise moment, Chapman noticed Dr Craven passing in his car so he flagged him down, told him what Mr Dobson had said, and asked the doctor if he would take him and Dobson back to the farm. Dr Craven did as he had been requested and then walked with the officer and Henry Dobson to the point where the body lay.

Margaret Dobson lay on her back, her head pointing to the east. There was blood on her face and she lay in the classic rape position with her legs apart and her knees drawn up. After confirming that the poor woman was dead, Dr Craven drove into Billingham where he reported the matter to Inspector Proud. On the inspector's instructions, Dr Craven then drove back to the scene, taking Sergeant Farthing with him. The sergeant then took charge of the scene until other senior officers arrived.

230

After speaking at length to Mr Dobson, the police decided that their first move would be to interview the three men who had delivered the pigs to High Grange Farm, on the Tuesday afternoon. The driver of that vehicle had been Percy Swales. He confirmed that he had driven his van to Sedgefield market at 4.30 p.m. Eight pigs had been loaded for Mr Dobson and he and his men had left Sedgefield at 5.00 p.m. They drove directly to the farm and turned the van into the long track that led to the farmhouse. Some fifty yards down the lane he noticed a man standing in the ploughed field to the right side of the track. As the van lights caught him, the man held up his arms as if he was going to fall forward and indeed, he then dropped down as if trying to hide.

Swales had turned to his two companions and commented "Hello, what's on here?" Even as he spoke these words he noticed a pedal bicycle lying on the grass at the left hand side of the verge and had to swerve the van to avoid running over it. Stopping, Swales stuck his head out of the window and called out "Eh, what's the game here?"

The man in the field shouted back, "I have had one over the nine, don't stop". Swales, assuming that the man was drunk, simply went on his way and delivered the pigs. By then, it was approximately 5.30 p.m. Whilst the van was being unloaded, Swales mentioned to one of the farm hands that one of his mates seemed to be the worse for wear in the top field, but the hand replied that no one was missing from the farm. When Swales and his men drove off fifteen minutes later, there was no sign of the man and the bicycle had gone.

Thomas Nelson had been sitting in the passenger seat of the delivery van and he confirmed all that Swales had said. Between them, these two men were able to say that the man in the field had been around five feet nine inches or five feet ten inches tall, aged about thirty and wearing a cap, a short brown smock, breeches and leggings, and that the bicycle was a racing model with black handlebars.

The third man in the van was twenty-year-old John Henry Burns, who said that it was around 5.10 p.m. when Mr Swales turned the van into the farm track. Burns was sitting in the back of the van and so did not see the man in the field, but he did hear Mr Swales call out to him. From his vantage point, Burns could see the bicycle though, and he confirmed that it was a racing bike.

When these three men were taken back to High Grange Farm to point out where they had seen the man, they indicated a spot which corresponded exactly with a large vehicle track in the mud, just where Swales said he had swerved. By now, Margaret Dobson's body had been moved but the location was precisely where she had been found. It was obvious that the man, whoever he was, must have seen Margaret's body and the likelihood was that he was the killer. This, in turn, placed the time of the murder at around 5.10 p.m. on January 18th, a time later confirmed by the post-mortem.

The police investigation was still in full swing when, at 9.00 p.m., on January 19th, Herbert Collins walked into the police station at Stockton-on-Tees and asked to see Detective Sergeant Edward Foster. Collins was an ex-policeman who now worked for Bert Smith, a gentleman who operated a threshing machine that he hired out to the farms around the area of Wolviston. Collins, it appeared, had some most interesting news to impart.

Earlier that same day, at a few minutes to 6.00 p.m., he had been with Smith at the newsagent's shop near the Wellington Hotel in Haverton Hill. There were notice boards outside the shop referring to the murder, and there they saw a young man they both knew, looking at the headlines. This man was twenty-year-old Robert William Hoolhouse.

Collins and Smith both thought that Hoolhouse looked a little agitated, rather pale and somewhat nervous. There were also some scratches on his face, which looked quite fresh. The two men asked Hoolhouse what had happened and he replied that he had had an accident and fallen from his bike. At this point, Smith asked Hoolhouse why he had not been to work as he usually followed the threshing machine, but had not on this particular day. Hoolhouse retorted, "I was up at Wolviston last night to find out where the machine was, and I have also been to Wolviston today".

Smith then said, "You are looking pretty white. You look as if you have had a shock", to which Hoolhouse said "Yes, I haven't got over it yet". Smith, continuing, then asked Hoolhouse what time he had been up at Wolviston, to which the reply was "I went by bus. I left Wolviston between seven and eight o'clock and I went to see some people named Lax at Husband's House, Wolviston." Smith then went into the newsagent's, leaving Hoolhouse talking to Collins.

It seems that Collins now took over the interrogation of Hoolhouse, saying "You used to work for Dobson didn't you?" Hoolhouse admitted that he had and Collins pointed out that because of that, it was likely that the police would want to interview him at some stage. To this, Hoolhouse said, "I bloody well hope not. I met a girl and went to the pictures at Billingham and came out between ten and eleven p.m."

Putting aside the rather stilted manner in which Hoolhouse is supposed to have spoken, Collins, Smith and another man, James Fulcher, who had been nearby, all thought that this behaviour of Hoolhouse's was very suspicious. He and his father had once worked for Dobson and had left under something of a cloud. Hoolhouse had admitted that he was at Wolviston and his face bore fresh scratches. Surely it was Collins' public duty to report this to the police.

Sergeant Foster listened to Collins' story and then went to interview Bertram Smith, before reporting the matter to his superiors. As a result, the decision was taken to interview Hoolhouse and, at 12.20 a.m. on January 20th, a number of officers gathered at Haverton Hill police station. By the time they arrived at 6 Pickering Street, where Hoolhouse lived with his mother and father, it was 1.15 a.m.

There were three officers in all, Constable Joseph Hodgson, Sergeant Vickers and Inspector Joseph Proud. It was Hoolhouse's father who came to the door. Inspector Proud identified himself and asked if Robert were there. Even as the inspector asked if he might see Robert, he came downstairs partly dressed saying, "I have done nothing wrong. What do you want me for?" He was asked to come to the police station for interview and he dressed immediately, without protest, and went to the station with Constable Hodgson.

Meanwhile, Inspector Proud made a search of Hoolhouse's bedroom, with Mr Hoolhouse's permission. There, on a bolster on the bed, were a number of stains that looked as if they might be blood. The inspector asked if he might take the bolster. Mr Hoolhouse handed the item over with the comment, "They are from boils my son had recently".

Back at the police station, Hoolhouse was cautioned and was then asked to give an account of his movements from noon on January 18th to 6.00 p.m. on January 19th. He co-operated and began by saying that he was at Haverton Hill until 12.30 p.m., on the 18th. Leaving home he then cycled to Wolviston, where he remained until 3.30 p.m., staying at William Husband's house where he saw a young lady he was friendly with, Dolly Lax. He then rode home, arriving back at Pickering Street at about 4.00 p.m. On that return journey he fell off his bicycle and sustained the scratches to his face.

Continuing his statement, Hoolhouse said that he was at home until 6.30 p.m., when he caught the bus for Wolviston, the one which went through Billingham. Once again he went to William Husband's house, arriving there just after 7.00 p.m. Some fifteen minutes later, he and Dolly Lax caught the bus back to Billingham and, after she had called at a friend's house with a parcel, they went to the pictures together, not leaving until 11.00 p.m. From there he saw her safely to her own bus stop before catching his bus back to Haverton Hill, getting home at 11.30 p.m. After having some supper he then went straight up to bed.

If this statement were true, then Hoolhouse could not possibly have been involved in the death of Margaret Dobson. She had been killed some time after 5.00 p.m., and according to Hoolhouse's narrative, he was at home between 4.00 p.m. and 6.30 p.m.

However, when the police interviewed Dorothy Elizabeth Lax, she said that it had been 3.45 p.m. when Hoolhouse arrived at her house on January 18th, only leaving one hour later at 4.45 p.m. This would have given him plenty of time to cycle to High Grange Farm and attack Mrs Dobson.

Meanwhile, the police had obtained a change of clothing for Hoolhouse. He had then handed the items he had been wearing over for examination and a number of red stains had been noted on his shirt cuffs, his jacket, his cap and on his handkerchief. Hoolhouse explained that most of this could be accounted for by the fact that he had cut himself shaving on the Tuesday night.

It was 6.45 a.m. on January 20th by the time Hoolhouse was informed that the times on his statement had been checked and found to be inaccurate. He replied, "I must have made a mistake. I got to Wolviston about three o'clock on Tuesday." He later claimed that everything in his statement was true except for some of the times. He had arrived at William Husband's house at 3.45 p.m. on the 18th, stayed for about an hour and then cycled home, arriving there at about 5.00 p.m.

The police were sure that they had enough evidence to prefer a charge against Hoolhouse. At 7.15 a.m., he was told that he would be detained on suspicion of causing the death of Mrs Dobson. He replied, "I have nothing to say to it. I have given my statement, and I have nothing to add to it."

Robert William Hoolhouse appeared before Mister Justice Wrottesley, at Leeds, on March 28th, 1938. During the three-day trial he was represented by Mr Arthur Morely and Mr W. A. Macfarlane. The case for the Crown was led by Mr C. Paley Scott, who was assisted by Mr A. P. Peaker.

The early witnesses, Henry Dobson, Percy Swales, Thomas Nelson, Constable Chapman and Dr Craven, spoke about the finding of the body, and the man seen in the field at the spot where Margaret Dobson lay. Mr Dobson, however, added the fact that Hoolhouse and his father had once worked at High Grange Farm, but that a few years before, there had been an argument and the family had been sacked and asked to leave their cottage.

These witnesses were followed by Walter Nelson, who lived at Cowpen Bewley. He told the court that at 1.15 p.m., on January 18th, he had entered the Blue Bells Inn at Newton Bewley. There were two men at the bar. One was a commercial traveller but the other was Robert Hoolhouse. The traveller seemed to be in a very generous mood for he ordered that everyone's glass be filled up at his expense, and Nelson heard Hoolhouse ask for a King's Ale. It was 3.00 p.m. by the time Nelson left the pub, Hoolhouse leaving at the same time. Nelson then saw Hoolhouse mount his bicycle and ride off in the direction of Wolviston. He was wearing a trilby hat and a brown coat and, at the time, there were no scratches on his face.

Ronald Walter Baldry was a patrol officer for the Automobile Association and at 3.00 p.m., on the day of the murder, he was cycling along the West Hartlepool to Stockton road, heading towards Wolviston. As he reached a point about one hundred yards on the Wolviston side of Newton Bewley, he noticed Hoolhouse standing in a grassy field, urinating against a fence. Baldry shouted a greeting and Hoolhouse called back "Hello, wait a bit, I am coming up". Baldry then rode on slowly until Hoolhouse caught him up on his own bicycle.

As the two men spoke, Hoolhouse stated that he had been drinking at the Blue Bells. They rode on, as far as Radburn's shop in the High Street, Wolviston where Baldry got off. Hoolhouse rode on, saying that he was going to see his girl. By then it was 3.25 p.m. Baldry was also able to confirm that Hoolhouse had been wearing a dark brown trilby, a Burberry-style raincoat, a blue navy suit, and brown brogue shoes. The position of the two cycles meant that Baldry only saw the left side of Hoolhouse's face, and that was certainly not scratched.

The girl Hoolhouse had referred to was nineteen-year-old Dorothy Elizabeth Lax, who lived with her uncle, William Husband, at the Red Lion Inn, which was no longer used as a public house, in High Street, Wolviston. She stated that Hoolhouse had arrived at her home at 3.45 p.m. According to her, Hoolhouse was wearing a light cap, blue overalls, a light raincoat and brown shoes. He stayed for an hour and left by the back door.

At 7.40 p.m. that evening he was back. At the time she was standing at the front door with her aunt, Beatrice Husband, and Hoolhouse did not come into the house. Hoolhouse and Dorothy caught the bus into Billingham, arriving there at 7.50 p.m. After calling at Mrs Watson's house in Station Road, they went to the cinema together and saw a film entitled 'Under Two Flags'. This finished at about 10.40 p.m., after which Hoolhouse saw her to her bus stop. The bus came at 10.50 p.m. Dorothy confirmed that she did not recall seeing any scratches on Hoolhouse, however she added that she had not taken particular notice of his face.

Beatrice Husband was able to confirm some of this testimony. She was at home when Hoolhouse first called at 3.45 p.m., and agreed that he was wearing blue overalls, a light raincoat and a light cap. He was there for about an hour and during that time she saw no marks on his face. That evening, she was talking to Dorothy Lax at her front door when Hoolhouse came to take her to the pictures. Again, she did not notice any marks on his face.

Arthur Nicholson was the postman at Billingham. He knew the prisoner quite well as Hoolhouse had once acted as a temporary postman. On January 19th, Nicholson had actually called at High Grange Farm to deliver a registered packet to Mr Dobson. It was then some time before 10.30 a.m., and there was no reply at the farmhouse. Walking away, Nicholson found Mr Dobson near the gate at the main road, and got him to sign for the packet there. Curiously, Henry Dobson said nothing about finding the body of his wife.

At 5.50 p.m. that same day, Nicholson was collecting mail at Haverton Hill when he saw Hoolhouse close to the Clarence Street postbox. By now, news of the murder had spread like wildfire and Nicholson asked Hoolhouse what he thought about it. Hoolhouse replied, "I am just going to get the paper to read about it".

The next three witnesses, Bertram Atkinson Smith, Herbert Edward Collins and James Fulcher, told the court of their suspicious encounter with Hoolhouse at the newsagent's shop. It was, of course, this meeting which caused Collins to go to the police and Hoolhouse to be named as a suspect. Smith, though, had one further damaging piece of testimony to give. He claimed that at one stage he had said to Hoolhouse, "Isn't that a terrible murder, you will know about it of course?" Hoolhouse said that he did, whereupon Smith continued "How do you know?" and Hoolhouse replied that the postman had told him. The court had already heard from Arthur Nicholson, whose testimony implied that Hoolhouse had already known about the murder when he saw him near the postbox.

There then followed a series of seven police witnesses, the first of whom was Sergeant Harry Gordon Farthing. When Dr Craven had returned to Wolviston to get further assistance, Sergeant Farthing had gone back with him to High Grange Farm. Once other officers had arrived, Farthing made a search of the immediate area but found nothing of interest. Later, at 3.40 p.m., Sergeant Farthing had supervised the removal of the body to the mortuary.

Constable Joseph Hodgson was the local officer at Haverton Hill and had accompanied Inspector Proud and Sergeant Vickers to Hoolhouse's home at Pickering Street at 1.15 a.m., on January 20th. He confirmed Hoolhouse's denial that he had done anything wrong, and his subsequent detention at the police station. The following day, Hodgson had returned to Pickering Street at 4.30 p.m., again with Inspector Proud, and a search was made of the premises. Constable Hodgson was present when the inspector took a waistcoat from the door that led from the kitchen to the scullery. In the pocket of that coat was a knife and Mr Hoolhouse confirmed that it belonged to his son.

After Inspector Proud had given his testimony about finding the bloodstained bolster at Hoolhouse's home, the prosecution called Detective Sergeant Ralph Walton Lee. He had arrived at the murder scene at 11.15 a.m. on January 19th. Lee made a careful inspection of the scene and noted that two small patches of blood on the soil indicated that Mrs Dobson had attempted to get back on her feet after being attacked and in doing so had moved some three feet six inches to the east. Furthermore, there was blood on the left hip of Mrs Dobson's knickers, and the position of these stains showed that they had been pulled down by the assailant's hand, meaning that he had blood on his hand when he did so.

Detective Sergeant Edward Foster had been at the murder scene since 11.00 a.m., and had measured the various distances involved in this case. The body lay at a point 173 feet from the main road, and 1570 feet from the farmhouse. More importantly, Sergeant Foster, and indeed the scene-of-crime photographs, indicated that when she was found, Mrs Dobson had still been wearing her brown woollen gloves.

Sergeant Foster noticed a number of indistinct footprints around the body. Later, plaster casts of those footprints were taken by Sergeant Lee. One was shown to be that of Mr Dobson, who admitted that he had stepped down into the field to take a look at his wife's body. This print was actually superimposed on another, which, by implication, belonged to the murderer. That print did not match any of Hoolhouse's shoes or boots.

The time came for the medical and forensic evidence. Dr Henry Anstey Cookson was the pathologist at the Sunderland Royal Infirmary, and he had carried out the post-mortem on Mrs Dobson. He reported a number of wounds, including a stab wound above the left breast and another on the left side of the neck. Both had penetrated to a depth of one and a half inches and were half an inch wide. There were also a number of bruises and scratches on the body, but the cause of death was haemorrhage, shock, and heart failure.

Dr Cookson had determined that Mrs Dobson's blood was group two. The knife found in Hoolhouse's waistcoat had been examined and shown to have minute amounts of blood in the thumbnail groove. However, there was too little to even prove that it was human blood. A number of articles of Hoolhouse's clothing had also been examined and blood had been found on a handkerchief, a shirt, and a brown tweed cap. Some of this could be typed and the blood on the shirt cuffs and the handkerchief was, indeed, group two.

236

It was this point which led to a major blunder by the defence. Mr Morley, Hoolhouse's barrister, in addition to advising his client not to give evidence on his own behalf, had also refused to allow his client to be blood tested. Dr Cookson had already stated that group two was one of the more common groups, held by about thirty-eight per cent of the population. It had been shown that Mrs Dobson was group two, but the refusal to allow Hoolhouse to be tested allowed the blood evidence to apparently link him directly to the crime. Yet it can be shown that Hoolhouse was almost certainly group two. The handkerchief taken from Hoolhouse bore blood that was group two. It also bore stains which turned out to be pus. Hoolhouse's father had volunteered that this blood had come from some boils that Robert had, which had burst. The presence of pus seems to prove the truth of this, therefore it is as likely that the blood was Hoolhouse's own.

Returning to Dr Cookson's testimony, he was also able to confirm that Mrs Dobson had been raped, and there was extensive semen staining on her body. No semen stains had been found on any of Hoolhouse's clothing.

The prosecution case, in essence, was that Hoolhouse bore a grudge against the Dobson family because he and his father had once been dismissed. On the day in question, having had some alcohol, Hoolhouse cycled to High Grange Farm, saw Mrs Dobson, attacked, raped and stabbed her, sustaining scratches on his face and blood on his clothing, before returning home as if nothing had happened. When he was spoken to by the police, he deliberately lied to hide the time he was actually in Wolviston.

The jury retired at 1.35 p.m. on March 30th. At 3.55 p.m., they asked to see Hoolhouse's two statements and his bicycle, which was indeed a racing bike with black handlebars, but which was undamaged. At 5.55 p.m., they finally returned to announce that he was guilty as charged. The execution was originally fixed for April 21st, but cancelled when an appeal was submitted. That appeal was dismissed on May 9th, on the grounds that the evidence was more than enough to support the conviction, and despite a petition containing over 14,000 signatures asking for clemency, Hoolhouse, who had by now turned twenty-one, was hanged at Durham prison on May 26th, by Thomas Pierrepoint.

Was there any chance that Hoolhouse was guilty of the crime that claimed his life? The blood evidence has already been considered, and largely shown to be inconclusive. The witnesses who saw Hoolhouse before 5.00 p.m., on Tuesday, January 18th, all said that he was wearing blue clothing. Ronald Baldry said it was a blue navy suit, and both Dorothy Lax and Beatrice Husband said he wore blue overalls. All three of these witnesses, in addition to Walter Nelson, also reported a brown coat over the blue clothing, and yet the man seen in the field by Percy Swales and Thomas Nelson when they delivered the pigs to High Grange Farm was apparently wearing a brown smock, breeches and leggings. Furthermore, he was said to be aged around thirty, while Hoolhouse was only twenty.

It was true that Hoolhouse bore scratches on his face. These consisted of three marks, one longer than the others. The two shorter ones met the third at a point, to produce a sort of arrowhead shape, and the inference was that Margaret Dobson had inflicted these as Hoolhouse attacked her. The trouble with this is that Mrs Dobson had still been wearing her woollen gloves when she was found. The prosecution suggested that she still might have caused the wounds, even though the gloves remained in place. To demonstrate this, a secretary with quite long fingernails donned the gloves in court and tried to scratch the face of a police volunteer. The officer's face was not marked in any way.

Perhaps the testimony of people who were interviewed by the police but who, through the incompetence of the defence, were not called to give evidence at the trial, should also be considered. Bert Husband, who was no relation to Beatrice, was a bricklayer at the Salt Union, Haverton Hill. On January 18th, at 4.05 p.m., he was riding his bicycle up Hope Street, Haverton Hill, in the company of Jack Steel. These two men both saw Hoolhouse walking towards his house in Pickering Street.

Doris Teale lived next door to the Hoolhouses, at 4 Pickering Street, and at some time between 4.30 p.m. and 5.00 p.m. on the 18th, she was cleaning one of her bedrooms. She looked out into the yard of number six and saw Robert come out of the coal cellar and go in through his own back door. Finally, Frederick Robert Hoolhouse, the accused's father, confirmed that he was home between 4.40 p.m. and 4.45 p.m., and that his son was certainly in by 5.00 p.m.

Perhaps the most damning part of the Establishment's killing of Robert Hoolhouse came in a letter, dated March 31st, from the Director of Public Prosecutions, sending the documents to the Home Office. In part the letter read, "...I think it right to add that the evidence against Hoolhouse was, in my opinion, never strong. On the other hand, the jury may well have been influenced by his refusal to submit to a blood test and by his failure to give evidence on his own behalf." It seems that even servants of the State felt uneasy about this case.

30

Joseph Myatt
Sentenced to death, but subsequently reprieved
For the murder of Frances Stevens, at Breadsall, Derbyshire

A T 2.00 p.m., on Saturday, November 11th, 1939, Richard William Jarvis Bridgett, a farmer, drove a horse and cart up to a field on Mill Farm at Breadsall, intending to collect some hay for his animals. In fact, there were a couple of other jobs which required attention in this field, and Richard Bridgett spent some time repairing fences before he climbed back into his cart in order to load up the remaining hay. It was now 2.45 p.m.

As Bridgett stood on the back of the cart so that he could climb up on to the stack itself, he noticed a shoe sticking out of a pile of hay that lay on the ground. Intrigued, Mr Bridgett jumped down from the cart and gave the shoe a gentle poke with his hayfork. The way the shoe moved showed plainly that there was a body hidden in the hayrick. Richard Bridgett touched nothing and ran to fetch the police.

Constable James Hardie Scott was on duty at Little Eaton when Bridgett dashed up to him and told him what he had found in one of his fields. Constable Scott passed a message about the discovery to his divisional headquarters before going back to Lime Lane and the field where the body lay. He noted that the hayrick was in the furthest corner of the field, some one hundred and twenty yards from the road. After careful examination of the hayrick, Constable Scott discovered that the body, that of a woman, was lying close to the foot of the stack, almost in the centre of the side that was furthest from the road. The entire body, apart from the feet, was covered by hay and Scott remained on guard at the scene until his colleagues arrived.

Detective Constable James Richardson arrived at the scene at 3.40 p.m. He began by checking the area around the haystack to make sure that there was no evidence that might be disturbed when the straw was removed from the body. Finding nothing, Richardson then moved the hay from the opposite end of the stack from where the shoe lay. This revealed the face and neck of a woman who had sustained obvious facial injuries and who had a scarf tied tightly around her neck. A piece of the same material that made up the scarf lay on the ground eight inches from the woman's head.

239

Slowly and carefully the officers removed all the hay from the body. Once this had been done, a crumpled, bloodstained petticoat was found, lying between the woman's left arm and her body. Later, although it was plain that the woman was dead, Dr Frederick William Schofield attended and confirmed that she had perished some days before. The body was then removed to the mortuary so that a post-mortem could be carried out.

One of the first tasks that the police had to concern themselves with was identifying the body. Extensive inquiries were made in Breadsall, Chaddesden, Morley and Smalley. This painstaking approach led, on November 13th, to the confirmation that the woman was forty-one-year-old Frances Stevens from Ockbrook, who was known to her friends as Fanny. She had been living in the Derby area for the past six weeks and prior to that, had been staying in Uttoxeter.

This identification was made by Mrs Isabella Roache, who lived at 29 Suffolk Avenue, Chaddesden. She had known Fanny well and the dead woman had actually been living at her home for the past month or so. On Sunday, November 5th, Isabella's husband, Peter Roache, had been in hospital and she and Fanny had gone to visit him at around 1.40 p.m. As the two women approached the infirmary gates, Fanny saw a soldier whom she said she knew, and went over to speak to him. Isabella went into the infirmary alone and did not see Fanny again until she identified her body at the mortuary. Isabella was also able to tell the police that during the time Fanny had been living with her, she had received visits from five different soldiers.

Since the last sighting of Fanny Stevens had been made on the afternoon of November 5th, the police now issued a newspaper appeal for any witnesses who might have seen her after this time. In the Derby Evening Telegraph of November 13th, 1939, an article on the front page gave details of the identification and gave a detailed description of the dead woman. In part it read, "When the body was found the woman wore a coat of rough, fawn tweed, with a brown and orange fleck, and a half-belt at the back. She had a sandy fawn skirt of hopsack tweed and under this a frock of dark brown flowered print, which appeared as a blouse above the skirt. She had a small grey felt hat, brown artificial silk stockings and dirty brown shoes, size five, with a single strap."

The police appeal for help soon brought forward other witnesses who reported that Fanny Stevens had been seen a number of times in the company of a thirty-six-year-old farm labourer named Joseph Myatt, who lived in a lodging house at 10 St Alkmund's Churchyard, Derby. As a result, at 6.00 p.m., on November 14th, Detective Chief Inspector Gray and Sergeant Oliver Fairbrother went to the lodging house, where they first saw Myatt. He readily admitted that he had known the dead woman and agreed to accompany the officers to the police station to make a written statement, describing his movements on November 5th.

This first statement, made from 6.15 p.m. until 8.05 p.m., was a most curious document. Myatt began by saying that at 11.15 a.m., on November 5th, a fellow guest had approached him and said that there was a woman outside asking for him by name and requesting that he take her for a walk around Darley Park. At first, Myatt had refused and had asked the message carrier to tell her to go away. Eventually, however, he did go out to her and though he had never set eyes on this woman before, he agreed to go for a walk with her. The statement went on to say that they stayed in Darley Park until 3.15 p.m., during which time Fanny stated that she was meeting a man with a car, at Bransford. As a result, Myatt walked with her to the bus station and saw her get on the Ashbourne bus, after which he returned to his lodging house.

There were, of course, two problems with this statement. In the first place, Myatt was claiming that a perfect stranger had asked for him by name at his lodgings and he had gone for a walk with her, and secondly, the timetable he outlined did not agree with the last sighting of Fanny Stevens, by Isabella Roache. Consequently, Myatt was held in custody whilst further inquiries were made.

At 9.10 p.m., Sergeant Fairbrother went back to Myatt and asked him if he wished to change anything in his statement. Myatt, who had, of course, had time to think things over, replied, "Yes, I want to tell you the truth. I haven't slept for a week for thinking about Sunday and that woman." He then made a second statement, which was completed at 10.20 p.m.

In this second document, Myatt admitted that he had known Fanny Stevens for a couple of weeks before November 5th and had been out with her twice. He still maintained that she had called for him at his lodgings on that Sunday, but now put the time at 2.15 p.m. Together they walked down to St Mary's Bridge and there boarded a bus for Little Eaton, getting off at the Breadsall turning. The statement continued, "We went up Breadsall Road till we came to the signpost which says to Breadsall Moor. When we got to the church, we went into the field opposite the church. As we got so far down the fields we came to a huge stack. She said to me 'What are you going to do?' I said 'Nothing'. I simply got my temper and by getting temper I kicked her in the face as she lay down by the stack. She shouted. I put the paid [sic] to her by finishing her off with the heel of my shoe. Her scarf was round her neck and I tied it, and the end of the scarf came off in my hand. I covered her over with some hay and came away.

"My scarf had some bloodstains on and so had the shoes. On the following Saturday night I was in a public house when I heard some people talking about the murder. I started to cry, I used my scarf to wipe my eyes. I noticed bloodstains on the bottom of the scarf, so when I got back to the kip [sic] I put the scarf behind the kitchen door, and as far as I am concerned it is still there. When I was going to bed I noticed bloodstains on the left boot toe, so I put them under my bed and the next day I asked a man who had two pairs of boots if he would give me a pair, and he gave me the boots I am wearing now. On the Monday morning I put the bloodstained boots at the bottom of the garden and covered them over with some rubbish."

Acting on this information, Sergeant Fairbrother and Chief Inspector Gray went back to the lodging house, at 11.00 a.m. on November 15th, but could find no trace of the scarf or the boots Myatt had referred to in his statement. At one stage, Myatt was even taken, under escort, to St Alkmund's Churchyard, and he pointed out the pile of rubbish where he claimed the boots were hidden. This was taken apart but again no trace of the missing boots could be found. Nevertheless, at 4.50 p.m. that same day, Myatt was charged with murder. In reply to the charge he remarked, "I did her in, but I didn't mean to do it".

Even though he was due to appear before the magistrates the next morning, Myatt was still not finished with his confessions to the police. At 10.30 p.m., Myatt asked to see Sergeant Fairbrother, to whom he explained that the first two statements were not correct and that he wished to make a third. Sergeant Fairbrother advised the prisoner to sleep on this and make his decision in the morning, when he was fresh. The next morning, at 10.00 a.m, Myatt said he had not changed his mind and his third statement was then taken down.

The statement began by again outlining how he and Fanny had come to the field where her body would subsequently be found. Myatt said that there were two rows of barbed wire around the haystack but they had climbed under these, gone to the stack and had intercourse. As soon as Myatt had finished, Fanny said that she wanted some money from him but he claimed that he did not have any. At this, she had grabbed him around the waist, shaken him and said that she could hear money rattling. He persisted in saying that there was no cash, to which she replied that she would get it off him one way or another.

Myatt continued, "I did no more but I caught her in the mouth with my fist and she fell to the ground. Whilst she was on the ground I hit her again with my fist on the side of her face. She was moaning and I catched [sic] her with my boot in the face. She had a scarf round her neck, tied once. I tied another knot and I pulled it tight. The bottom of the fringe came off in my hand and I threw it down. She had light coloured stockings on tied with string above the knee. She had no knickers on while I was with her that day. She had two frocks on; one was a white one and one was a fawn one. I pulled her to the stack and covered her with hay and left her. I walked away across the fields and saw a man coming towards me so I went in the opposite direction and that brought me on to the same road I had come along with the woman. I got through a gap in the hedge on to the road and I turned to the left and at the end of the road I turned to the left again and went past the Windmill Inn and on to Derby.

"When I left the woman it was just getting dusk so it was about seven o'clock when I got to the kip in St Alkmund's Churchyard and I stayed at the kip all night. I never went out again. I am very sorry I have come to this. I never intended to do anything like that."

Joseph Myatt appeared at Derby on Monday, February 19th, 1940, before Mr Justice Oliver and a jury of nine men and three women. The Crown's case was led by Mr Richard O'Sullivan, who was assisted by Mr Arthur Ward, and Myatt's defence rested in the hands of Mr T. Norman Winning and Mr Geoffrey Smallwood.

The first witness was Detective Inspector James Brailsford, who said that he had taken various photographs of the place where the body was found. When questioned by Mr Winning for the defence, however, Inspector Brailsford admitted that there were no signs of any struggle having taken place at the haystack. Furthermore, in his statements, Myatt had referred to the field being opposite a church, but Inspector Brailsford confirmed that there was no church within half a mile of the location.

Doctor Schofield was then called to describe the injuries Fanny Stevens had suffered. He stated that when he had made his first examination, at the murder scene, he had noted a number of footmarks near the body and underneath it after the body had been moved. These were of a larger shoe size than the woman's and could have been caused by someone carrying the body to the spot. However, Dr Schofield also said that in his opinion, since the body lay in a natural attitude, it had not been placed there and it was more likely that the attack had taken place close to the haystack. Cross-examined by Mr Winning, Dr Schofield confirmed that his initial belief had been that the woman had been knocked down by a motor car and then carried to the haystack, though he had since concluded that death was due to strangulation. He also agreed that there must have been a most violent struggle for the injuries he noted to have been inflicted.

The post-mortem had been carried out by Dr Schofield and Dr Gladstone Rule Osborn, a pathologist from the Derbyshire Royal Infirmary. Cataloguing the bruises and injuries he found, Dr Osborn said that there was a bruise on one side of the face, close to the left eye, and others at the angle of the jaw. Fanny's upper lip was bruised and torn and there were other marks on the left side of her forehead and on the left cheek. There were six separate bruises on the outside right forearm and others on the left hand and right elbow. A front tooth had been knocked out and two others were loose.

Turning to the scarf found around Fanny's neck, Dr Osborn said that it had been wound round three times and tied in the front with a single knot, the pressure fracturing the hyoid bone. Death had taken place two to three hours after Fanny's last meal, which had consisted in part of potatoes. Dr Osborn was also able to say that the dead woman had had sex prior to death, and that had the scarf not been tied around her throat, she would have undoubtedly recovered from her other injuries. Cross-examined by Mr Winning, Dr Osborn also stated that all the injuries were consistent with a violent struggle and that he would have expected to find signs of that struggle at the scene, along with some bloodstaining. In addition, Fanny's attacker might well be scratched or have received injuries to his fist from Fanny's teeth.

Noel Beeston, the deputy lodging-housekeeper at 10 St Alkmund's Churchyard, was then called. He reported how he had told the police, after Myatt had first been questioned, that he had seen the prisoner wearing different boots. He could not recall when Myatt had stopped wearing the old ones but thought it might have been as long ago as two weeks before his arrest. Beeston was also able to say that he had always found Myatt to be quiet and inoffensive and had never noticed any scratches or injuries to his face or hands.

James Frederick Powell was a fellow lodger at the house where Myatt lived and he stated that he had given Myatt a pair of boots in November. Powell could not remember precisely when this was, but it was either the Thursday or the Friday before Myatt was first interviewed. The boots were a little too small for Myatt and Powell had no idea what he did with his old pair. However, Powell also stated that the boots he had given to Myatt were not the pair he was wearing when the police picked him up.

Sergeant Fairbrother was called to describe his interviews with Myatt. Fairbrother freely admitted that after speaking to Myatt for an hour or so he had come to the conclusion that he was far from normal mentally. The defence had produced documentation showing that Myatt had the mind of a child of twelve, and Sergeant Fairbrother said that this did not surprise him.

Another police witness was Detective Superintendent Alan Evans, who had first interviewed Myatt on November 14th. He told the court that Myatt had said that he was a native of Congleton and had three sisters and two brothers. He had left the town three years before and had since done odd farm jobs in Derbyshire, including some for a Mr Shaw at Breadsall. The story Myatt told in this interview was rambling and often contradictory. He had no idea who the man was who told him that there was a woman outside asking for him and then detailed the walk they had taken, saying that Fanny had said she was meeting a man at the wholesale market. He went there with her and gave her tenpence, with which she bought a cup of tea and a couple of ham sandwiches, in a cafe opposite. This statement was in direct contradiction to the known facts, Fanny's last meal being a meat and potato pie that she had eaten with Isabella Roache. There was also the not insignificant fact that the cafe Myatt referred to was closed on a Sunday.

Myatt then said that he had walked Fanny to the bus station and had seen her get onto a bus. He went on to say that she had paid threepence for her ticket, and when asked how he knew this, since he had remained behind in Derby, he had no answer. After relating all this, even Superintendent Evans admitted that he thought there was something wrong with Myatt, adding, "I formed the opinion that he was a man capable of talking rubbish". He also agreed that there was no evidence against Myatt apart from his own statements, and that other men had been suspected of the crime.

One man in particular had been a prime suspect. On November 5th, a blue car had been seen parked outside the field where Fanny's body was later found. The driver of this car was located and interviewed. The man had a criminal record but his story that he had been looking for rabbits was believed and he was allowed to go. Finally, Superintendent Evans said that the soldier seen with Fanny Stevens was certainly not Myatt and had never been traced.

The defence called no witnesses apart from Dr C. M. Dickinson, the medical officer of Leicester prison, where Myatt had been held. Dr Dickinson outlined Myatt's family history, saying that a maternal aunt and uncle were at present in an asylum, as were some of Myatt's cousins. Myatt could only read and write very simple words and was unable to perform the calculation twenty-seven shillings minus one shilling and sixpence. In Dr

Dickinson's opinion, all of Myatt's statements were unreliable and he often contradicted himself in an obvious fashion. There was also the fact that when asked what he thought the punishment for this crime might be, Myatt had replied that it might be a fine of five shillings.

In many ways, the summing up was as important as the trial itself. For the prosecution, Mr O'Sullivan said that the defence had implied that Myatt had heard about the case from the newspapers and had concocted his confession from those reports. However, there were several points in Myatt's statements which could not have been gleaned from the papers, including the fact that Fanny had had sex before she died, or that she was not wearing knickers.

For the defence, Mr Winning said that there was not a shred of evidence against Myatt apart from his own statements to the police. No one had seen Myatt close to the spot where the body was found and his description of the area was in error. There were no signs of a struggle at the spot and yet Myatt had described a violent assault upon Miss Stevens. The fact remained that the only real evidence against Myatt was his own, inaccurate, confession.

The jury took seventy minutes to decide that Myatt was guilty, though they did add a recommendation to mercy because of the prisoner's mental condition. An appeal was entered and heard on March 18th before Justices Hawke, Charles and MacNaghten. Here, the defence again referred to the fact that only Myatt's own statements had convicted him. Had he stayed silent he would probably never have been charged, and the statements themselves were contradictory. Allied to this, Myatt was undoubtedly of well below normal mental ability. However, the three judges again pointed out the various facts which Myatt had mentioned and which only the killer could have known. The conviction was safe and the appeal was dismissed.

In the event, Myatt's mental condition and the jury's recommendation did save his life. On March 25th, exactly one week after the appeal had been lost, the Home Secretary announced that he had advised His Majesty to commute the sentence to one of life imprisonment.

31

David Miller Jennings

Hanged at Dorchester, Thursday, July 24th, 1941
For the murder of Albert Edward Farley, at Dorchester

D AVID Miller Jennings was a native of Warrington who, perhaps seeing that war with Germany was imminent, and wishing to serve his country, joined the army in December, 1938. His first, and only, taste of action was as a member of the British Expeditionary Force, when he was one of the thousands of men evacuated from Dunkirk.

After arriving back in England, Jennings was sent to various camps before arriving at Marabout barracks, in Dorchester, in November 1940. There, he shared a billet with five other privates, Analy, Kay, Hood, Hall and Bowker. Soon after arriving at Dorchester, Jennings received a letter from home. This did not, though, contain the usual good news from his family, but a note from his girlfriend saying that their engagement was off.

Sunday, January 26th, 1941, seemed to be a normal enough day. At 9.15 a.m., Jennings, along with the other soldiers, went on church parade. Two hours later, at 11.15 a.m., he was at the NAAFI in Princes Street. Jennings did not stay there for long, returning to his barracks at noon so that he could have something to eat.

After his meal, Jennings got himself ready for a session on the rifle range. He was there from 1.00 p.m. until 6.00 p.m. Half an hour later he had his evening meal and then changed into a suit so that he could go out on the town.

It was 6.50 p.m. when Jennings and Private James Torkington left the camp together. Their first port of call was the George public house, where Jennings had five beers with whisky chasers. The two friends played some darts before joining two other soldiers, Private Joseph Gerald Riley and Corporal Frank Leith. Leith noticed that Jennings was spending quite freely, especially after he had had to borrow five shillings from Leith the previous day. He spoke to Jennings about it and Jennings admitted that he had borrowed another fifteen shillings, from another soldier. The men carried on drinking, though, and another half pint had been consumed before the four men went on to another pub, the Antelope.

Jennings, Torkington, Riley and Leith were in the Antelope from 8.25 p.m. until 9.45 p.m. More drink was consumed and the four enjoyed another game of darts, whilst Jennings continued to spend freely. Then another pub, the Ship, was visited. When this closed, the four went to a milk bar for some tea and a pie. They finally returned to the camp at 10.35 p.m.

Back in his own billet, Jennings saw that at least two of his comrades, Hall and Bowker, were in bed and apparently fast asleep. He then changed his shoes, and when he saw that Hall and Bowker had woken, Jennings told them that he was going to the toilet. When he returned, Jennings picked up the rifle that he had left underneath a window after finishing on the rifle range that afternoon. He then loaded five rounds of ammunition into the weapon, and picked up another clip of five rounds. Hall asked him what he was doing and Jennings replied that he was going to do a break-in. Hall tried to dissuade Jennings but he would not listen to reason. He left the camp and walked back to Princes Street and the office that was opposite the NAAFI building.

Jesse Bryan Broughton was a garage proprietor and lived opposite the NAAFI building. At some time just before midnight, he was in bed and half-asleep when he heard four quite loud thuds sound out. It was easy to place the time because moments later, the clock struck twelve. By 12.15 a.m., Jesse was wide awake. It was then that he heard the unmistakable sound of five shots being fired, one after the other. There was then a pause, before a sixth shot rang out. Some thirty seconds after this final shot, Jesse heard the sound of footsteps running away.

Approximately half an hour after Jesse Broughton had heard those sounds, David Jennings arrived back at his hut. In order to get to his billet he had to walk through one occupied by Riley and Leith. Jennings looked rather flustered, as if he had been running, and went into his own room without a word, closing the door behind him. Concerned about his friend, Leith followed Jennings into his room, Riley going in a few moments later.

Corporal Leith asked Jennings where he had been and Jennings replied, "I've broken into the NAAFI and shot a civvy bloke". Leith immediately went to report the matter to a superior officer. Meanwhile, Riley noticed that Jennings had a cut over his right eye, which was bleeding, so he took his friend into the toilet and helped him to wash out the wound. A short time later, Sergeant Walter March arrived to question Jennings.

March asked Jennings what had happened and was told "I've shot a man". Jennings was asked where this had happened and replied "In the NAAFI". He was then asked if he had been drinking and, surprisingly, answered no. He went on to explain that he had suffered the cut over his eye when he had tried to shoot open a safe, and a piece of metal had flown up into his face. March then asked Jennings if he had hit anyone, and Jennings replied that he did not know. Finally, when asked why he had done this, Jennings said "To tell you the truth sergeant, I am broke. I am short of money."

After interviewing Jennings, Sergeant March and Corporal Leith walked to the NAAFI in Princes Street. There they found the body of sixty-five-year-old Albert Farley, a man who worked in the coffee bar there, and who was also acting as temporary caretaker, and had therefore been sleeping on the premises. The two soldiers then returned to camp and called the civil authorities, who took Jennings into custody.

David Jennings faced his trial at Dorchester, and one of the early witnesses was Dorothy Warren. Dorothy was the manageress of the NAAFI and she explained that since January 26th, Farley had had to sleep on the premises on a bed at the end of the canteen. On this particular night, the cash box had been left unlocked on the lowest shelf of the display counter. It held the usual £2 float, in silver and copper. Dorothy had left the canteen at 11.10 p.m., making sure that the door was locked and bolted. Farley was then alone on the premises.

Jennings had broken into the recruiting office opposite the NAAFI, making an attempt to blow open the safe there, which was where he sustained the injury to his eye. Daisy Howe was the caretaker of that office and she told the court that she had locked the building up at 2.45 p.m., on Saturday, January 25th. At that time, there was no damage to the safe, nor were there any spent cartridge cases on the floor.

Private Torkington told of the pub-crawl on January 26th. When they arrived back at the barracks with the food they had purchased from the milk bar, they all went into Jennings' room to eat their chips. After that, Torkington had gone to bed, and the next thing he knew was being woken by Leith, at 3.00 a.m.

Private Wilfred Bowker was one of the men Jennings shared a billet with. He stated that the four drinking companions had arrived back at the camp at about 10.30 p.m. Jennings was laughing and said that he had had a good time. The men ate their food and after ten minutes or so, the others all left. Jennings sat on the edge of his bed, took off his boots and pulled on a pair of running shoes. He then went out.

It was about an hour later when Jennings returned. He burst into the room, carrying a rifle and with blood pouring from a wound over his right eye. He was breathing heavily. As Jennings sat down again, Leith came in and asked Jennings where he had been. According to Bowker, Jennings told Leith that he had done a break-in at the NAAFI, and added that he thought he had shot a man but was not sure whether he had hit him or not. Jennings explained that he had been firing shots all around the NAAFI when an old man came out of the front door and ran at him. Jennings fired a warning shot but did not know if it hit the man or not.

Corporal Leith testified that he too had also seen Jennings leave the hut on the night of January 26th, and had asked him where he was going. Jennings had replied that he was going to the lavatory. Leith went back to sleep but at some time between 11.30 p.m. and midnight he was woken by Private Hall, who said that Jennings had told him he was going on a break-in and had still not returned. Leith went to look for Jennings but could not find any sign of him.

When Jennings did return, Leith followed him into his billet and asked him what had happened. Jennings replied, "I tried to do a bust. I've killed a man." Jennings then immediately said that he was not sure if he had killed him or not. Later, Leith went with Sergeant March to the NAAFI. There they found the left-hand door slightly open. There was a light on inside and the dead man was lying behind the right-hand door. He was on his left side, his head and shoulders up against the right-hand wall and his feet against the door. Upon examining the man, Leith saw that he had a wound below his left breast.

It had been police Sergeant Harry Lill who attended the camp after being called out by Sergeant March. After examining the scene of the crime, Lill went to arrest Jennings and cautioned him on a charge of murder. Jennings covered his face with his hands and said "Oh my God!" As the caution continued, Jennings interrupted and the sergeant had to begin again.

At 5.40 a.m., at the police station, Jennings said that he wished to make a statement. In this, he outlined his drinking session with his friends. Then, once he had changed his footwear and picked up his rifle, he went into town. Jennings first went to the office opposite the NAAFI, broke a pane of glass in the door and then unlocked it. Going inside, he struck a match and found the safe in a corner. He tried to shoot the lock off but succeeded only in injuring himself above the eye.

Leaving the office, Jennings then went to the NAAFI itself. He fired three rounds through a side door, and then heard a voice shout from inside. He tried to run away but when he turned around, he saw someone opening the doors from the inside. Jennings turned and fired, just to scare the man off, before running back to his camp.

The prosecution argued that Jennings had gone to the NAAFI, run off after hearing Farley's voice, turned and shot him deliberately. The defence argued that Jennings had hit Farley accidentally whilst shooting in the direction of the door, making this a case of manslaughter. Unfortunately, their case was severely weakened by the fact that Jennings would then have had to almost step over the body in order to rifle the cash box and take most of the £2 float. However, it could also be argued that Jennings was so drunk at the time that this might not have even registered with him.

The most likely scenario is that Jennings, heavily under the influence of alcohol, fired indiscriminately either in Farley's general direction or at the door, in order to scare Farley off. If that were the case, then Jennings hit Farley accidentally, making this a case of manslaughter, not murder. It should also be remembered that Jennings made no attempt to conceal what he had done once he returned to his billet.

In the event, though, the jury felt that the prosecution case was strong enough and Jennings was found guilty of murder. An appeal was lodged on the grounds that the shooting had been an accident and that the verdict should therefore have been one of manslaughter. However, the court felt that there was enough evidence to confirm the murder verdict so the appeal failed, as did representations from the army to the Home Office for mercy. Even though there was a strong argument that the killing had been an accident, and that Jennings was therefore only guilty of manslaughter, he was hanged at Dorchester on Thursday, July 24th, 1941. He was the last man ever to be executed at that prison.

32

Howard Joseph Grossley
Hanged at Cardiff, Wednesday, September 5th, 1945
For the murder of Lily Griffiths, at Porthcawl

THERE could be no doubt that thirty-seven-year-old Howard Joseph Grossley, a Canadian soldier, shot and killed his lover, twenty-nine-year-old Lily Griffiths, but even the victim agreed that this was not a case of murder!

Grossley was a married man, but his wife had remained in Canada when he came over to Britain with the Army, in 1940. He met Lily, a single woman, soon afterwards and they started living together as man and wife. A son was born to the union in 1943. By all accounts, Lily and Grossley were very happy together and stayed with each other throughout the war years.

In due course, the Allied troops invaded Europe and the Axis forces were pushed back deep into Germany. The war was coming to a close and Grossley was fully aware of the fact that one day soon he would be sent back to Canada, leaving Lily and his son behind, possibly for ever. This began to prey on his mind and he became very concerned about his position.

On March 3rd, 1945, Grossley and Lily went to live with Jennie Blodwen Atkinson at 227 New Road, Porthcawl, which is situated just a few miles west of Bridgend. The couple had previously stayed at the house, just for a week, in the summer of 1944, but they now wished to take up a more permanent residency there. Three days later, on March 6th, Lily brought her son, who was by now two years old, to the house and Jennie too noticed that they all seemed to be very happy together.

Lily Griffiths left 227 New Road at 12.15 p.m., on March 12th, to attend a job interview at the Bridgend arsenal. When she returned, Lily told Grossley that she had been successful but had been told that she could only start work there the following week, as she had a rather bad cold at the time. Some time later, Lily announced that she was taking the boy to Aberdare, and the ever-dutiful Grossley walked her to the bus-stop.

At 6.00 p.m, the Atkinson family, along with Grossley, were listening to the radio when a news item said that a number of German prisoners had escaped from a camp near Bridgend. This led Jennie Atkinson's young son to comment that if he had possession of Grossley's gun, he would go out and look for them. Hearing this, Jennie's

251

husband, Ernest Atkinson, asked his house guest if it were true that he had a gun in the house. Grossley admitted that it was and when Ernest's son asked if he might see it, Grossley told him that it was upstairs in a green bag in his bedroom. The boy dashed upstairs and returned with the weapon moments later.

Ernest now asked Grossley if the revolver was loaded, and was surprised to hear him say that it was. Ernest naturally asked him to unload it, which he did before showing the entire family exactly how it worked. Once the gun had been examined by everyone, Grossley took it back from Ernest's son and reloaded it before placing it in the inside pocket of the battledress that he was wearing. Ernest Atkinson then asked Grossley if he intended taking the gun out with him when he went to meet Lily later on and Grossley replied that as a soldier, he always carried it and added that he might well meet some of the escaped German prisoners.

At 6.30 p.m, Grossley left the house in New Road. Soon after this, Jennie Atkinson went to the pictures, not returning home until 10.00 p.m. At that time, Lily Griffiths was back and was sitting in the kitchen, knitting a pair of socks for her son. Minutes later, Grossley came in and Lily asked him where he had been. Grossley simply replied 'Out', but he then produced a ring from his mackintosh pocket and said it had been given to him. He appeared to have been drinking, though Jennie would not have said that he was drunk, and he walked to the door of the room, beckoning with his head for Lily to follow him. The two lovers were then heard going upstairs, and though that was the last either Jennie Atkinson or her husband saw of them that night, they did hear the front door open and close, at 11.00 p.m, as if someone were leaving.

John Carter Clare lived at 175 New Road, and he and his wife had retired for the night at 11.00 p.m., on March 12th. Less than an hour later, at 11.55 p.m, Clare heard a scream, which sounded as if it had come from a woman, and which was followed almost immediately by a loud report. Clare looked out of his window, and though he could not see too clearly in the darkness, there was someone standing in the shadows in an alleyway that was about four houses away from his own.

That scream, and the report that followed it, had also been heard by other occupants of New Road. Lilian Elizabeth Harvey, a single woman, lived at number 181, and had gone to bed at 11.30 p.m. She too heard the scream and what sounded like a shot, as did four men who were all at number 183, the house next door.

Arthur James Speck, George Isaac Lewis, Frank Jones and Fred Aston were all busily repairing a radio inside 183 New Road when, at around 11.55 p.m, they heard a shot ring out. All four men left the house via the back door to investigate, and two of them, Speck and Aston, looked over the wall that divided the house from the narrow lane which ran alongside it. Neither man saw anything but then, as Lewis and Speck waited by the gate, the other two went down the lane, towards New Road itself. As they fumbled along in the darkness, they suddenly saw someone flashing a torch and as they walked towards the beam, a soldier stepped forward and said "Fetch a doctor, I have shot my dear wife".

252

All four men had heard this comment and they now all ran to the soldier to offer what assistance they could. The soldier, Grossley, was in a very distressed state and now asked if one of them would go to his landlord, Mr Atkinson, and tell him what had happened. It was Arthur Speck who, walking past the soldier, was the first to come upon the form of Lily Griffiths. She was lying on the ground and, as Speck examined her, Grossley came forward, fell to his knees nearby and cried "My darling, what have I done?" Lily, who was still conscious, replied "Don't worry dear. You couldn't help it."

At this point, Speck believed that someone else must have attacked both Lily and Grossley, and so he asked the injured woman who the man was. Lily said that she did not know, whilst Grossley pointed towards some allotments nearby and said that two men had run off in that direction. George Lewis also heard Grossley add that the assailants had been escaped German prisoners who had stopped them and demanded her handbag and his clothes. Grossley claimed that he had tried to wrestle with one of the prisoners, had pulled out his revolver and had managed to get between the German and Lily. During the struggle, his revolver had unexpectedly gone off and Lily had been hit by accident. Lewis then ran to the nearest telephone box and rang for the police and an ambulance.

In fact, there was no need to contact the police. Constable Thomas Lewis had been on duty, with War Reserve Sergeant Thomas Nicholas, at the junction of John Street, South Road and New Road, when he heard the shot coming from somewhere down New Road. He arrived on the scene within minutes and, in the lane that ran between numbers 181 and 183, he found Frank Jones, who told him what had happened. Grossley was still in a very distressed state and greeted Lewis with "Oh dear, oh dear, I have shot my wife. Two men attacked us. I missed them and shot my wife."

Lily Griffiths was obviously in some distress for she asked Constable Lewis for something to kill the pain she felt. Having told the injured woman that medical help was on its way, Lewis turned to the task of investigating the incident and asked Grossley where the revolver was now. Grossley, saying "I have an automatic here", took the weapon from his coat pocket and handed it over to the officer without protest. Lewis then informed Grossley, quite properly, that once his wife had been taken to the hospital, he would have to come along to the police station to answer further questions.

A few minutes later, Constable Lewis began escorting Grossley to the police station at Porthcawl, and on that journey, he administered a caution after Grossley had asked if he thought Lily might die. Grossley did not speak until he arrived at the station, at 12.15 a.m., on March 13th, when he was handed over to Inspector William Matthews.

Inspector Matthews listened as Constable Lewis said, "This man has shot a woman believed to be his wife, near New Road schools. She is in a bad condition. Here is the gun he used." The weapon was then given to the inspector, who broke it open and found one spent cartridge and six live rounds. By now, Grossley was sobbing hysterically and repeatedly intoning, "I have shot my wife". Inspector Matthews asked Grossley if he wished to state exactly what had happened and inquired if he wished to make a written statement. Grossley said that he did, whereupon he was cautioned again. After finishing the document, Grossley was told that he would be detained pending further inquiries.

It had been midnight when Dr Robert Hodgkinson arrived at New Road to attend to the injured woman. Lily complained again that she was in terrible pain, and after a quick examination at the scene, Dr Hodgkinson administered an injection of morphine before ordering that Lily, who was in shock, be taken in the ambulance to Bridgend hospital. In the lane, the doctor had observed what looked like recent bruises on Lily's face and legs and later, at the hospital, once the patient had been undressed, he saw more bruises on her body and arms. In Dr Hodgkinson's opinion, considerable force would have been needed to cause some of these marks and some might even have come as the result of a kick. This cast new light on the 'happy' relationship that had supposedly existed between Grossley and Lily Griffiths and, since Lily needed an operation which might prove dangerous, she was told by Dr Hodgkinson that she should make her own statement, saying what had happened to her. Lily agreed, made her statement and was then, at 4.00 a.m, taken down to the operating theatre.

Lily's condition did not improve. On March 14th, Dr Hodgkinson aspirated two pints of blood from the left side of her chest. At 4.00 p.m. that same day, Lily, who was three to four months pregnant, was aborted, but none of this made her condition any better. She was informed that it was likely she would die and so, later that day, she made a dying deposition.

On March 15th, Grossley was charged with attempted murder and appeared before the magistrates at Bridgend. Detective Inspector Lancelot Bailey explained that there were still more inquiries to be made and asked for a remand of fourteen days. In the event, a seven-day remand was ordered and Grossley was told that he would be brought back to court on March 22nd.

In fact, matters moved more rapidly and, on March 16th, Lily Griffiths died. As a result, when Grossley made his next court appearance, it was a very brief one and he was remanded again. On March 29th, the charge against him was changed to one of wilful murder, and after a final hearing, on April 24th and 25th, he was sent for trial on that charge.

Howard Grossley faced Mr Justice Singleton at Swansea on July 11th, 1945. The case lasted for two days, during which time the prisoner was represented by Mr H. Glyn-Jones, who maintained throughout that his client should be facing no more serious a charge than one of manslaughter. The case for the prosecution rested in the hands of Mr Ralph Sutton.

Evidence of identification was given by Catherine Davies, Lily's married sister. Catherine stated that although she knew all about the relationship between Grossley and Lily, she had only recently discovered that Grossley had a wife back in Canada. Catherine added that after the shooting she had visited Lily in hospital every day until the evening of March 15th, and had identified the body the following day.

254

Dr Hodgkinson had observed many bruises on Lily's body and Shirley Jones, of 227 New Road, was now called to say that when she had seen Lily, at 8.00 p.m., on March 12th, there had been no bruises visible on her face or arms. Shirley was Jennie Atkinson's niece and was staying in the Atkinson house.

William Rees Thomas, a taxi-driver of 16 Nicholls Avenue, stated that at 8.00 p.m., on March 12th, he had driven his cab to the Esplanade Hotel. Grossley was there, drinking, and the two men fell into conversation, having a pint of beer together. From there, he, the prisoner and two other men went to the Victoria Hotel, where Grossley had a further four pints. When Thomas left, at 10.00 p.m., Grossley was still there.

Lilian Harvey, of 181 New Road, in addition to saying that she had heard the scream and the shot, said that the following morning, March 13th, she had gone into one of the rooms downstairs with her landlady, Mrs Lilian Newlyn. They had found a spent bullet on the settee that lay on the opposite side from the window. This was confirmed by Lilian Violet Newlyn, who reported that on March 12th, the window in that room had been perfectly fine but on March 13th, she had found some glass on the floor and noticed a hole in one of the window panes.

In addition to Dr Hodgkinson, medical testimony was also given by Dr Jethro Gough and nurse Beryl Edwards. Nurse Edwards said she had been on duty in Lily's ward on the morning of March 15th and had heard Lily exclaim, "I am going to die". The nurse was present when Lily's dying deposition was taken and, after the document had been finished, heard her say, "This is the God's honest truth".

Dr Gough had performed the post-mortem, assisted and observed by Dr Hodgkinson. Dr Gough observed that the whole of Lily's left eye was bruised, and there were other marks on her chin, left upper arm and on the lower part of her abdomen. All of these had been inflicted within a few days, with the possible exception of one on the arm which might have been as much as a week old. The single bullet had entered the body on the left side of the chest, passed through the left breast, the stomach, liver and left lung before coming out close to the last rib on the left side. This wound had caused the left lung to collapse and death was due to a septic infection in the chest cavity.

The prosecution scenario was that Grossley had deliberately killed his wife and then tried to say that they had been attacked by two escaped German prisoners, in an attempt to avoid detection. The one problem with this was that even the so-called murder victim agreed that the entire affair had been a tragic accident. Lily's original statement, taken when she was first admitted to hospital, said that after going up to their room, Grossley had asked her to go for a walk with him. She had agreed and they had left the house together at around 11.00 p.m. There had already been much discussion between them over Grossley's impending return to Canada and he had suggested beforehand that it would be best for everyone if he took his own life.

At the end of the lane, Grossley had taken out his revolver and said, "I will finish myself now". They had struggled and she had tried to take the gun away from him, but he pushed her back and almost immediately she heard a loud report and felt a searing pain in her chest. Grossley flew into a panic and cried out that he had not meant to do it, but Lily's statement added that there were elements of self-preservation involved. Before he had gone to look for help, Grossley had asked her to say that two Germans had attacked them if anyone asked. Lily's statement ended with the confession that Grossley had sometimes beaten her, but only when he had a few drinks and the next morning he would have no memory of what he had done.

Lily's second statement, her dying deposition, was then read out. She began by again saying that they had gone out together for a walk but then stopped her testimony and cried, "I can't stand this". Lily then asked for her earlier statement to be read out to her, and after this was done said that all she wished to add was, "Howard would never hurt me. He has always been good to me." She was then cross-examined on what she had said and stated that Grossley had always been kind but that four years ago he had been in an accident which had caused his back to be badly burnt. He had never been quite the same since and seemed to suffer from head pains a lot. Before they went out on March 12th, he had said to her that he was going to do away with himself to make things easier for her. She ended by repeating yet again that the gun had gone off accidentally, during a struggle.

George Edward Lewis Carter, a chemist from the Forensic Science Laboratory at Cardiff, had made a careful examination of Lily's clothing. He had found no scorch marks around the bullet entry hole and from this, and his knowledge of the wound itself, he concluded that the gun had been held at a distance of sixteen to twenty inches from Lily when it was fired. This reduced the strength of Grossley's argument that the gun had gone off during a struggle, although Lily could, of course, have been pulling away from him at the time the gun was fired. The gun itself, a Colt 38, had been examined by Francis Edward Morton of Birmingham, an expert with thirty-four years of experience. He had fired it a number of times and found no mechanical fault. The pull was six pounds, which was quite normal for a weapon of this type, and he found that he could not make the gun go off accidentally without having his finger on the trigger.

One of the final witnesses was Detective Inspector Lancelot Douglas Bailey. He said that during the early days of the investigation, Grossley had stuck to his story of the two German prisoners attacking him. After much questioning, the prisoner admitted that this was a lie and claimed that the gun had gone off accidentally when he had struggled with Lily. He had wanted to shoot himself but she tried to stop him and was hit accidentally. When Lily had given her dying deposition, Grossley had been present with his solicitor. As he entered the room, Lily gasped "Howard, do you know I am dying?" but he had not answered and she then gave her statement.

Grossley did not give evidence on his own behalf and it was left to the jury to decide whether they believed this was all a tragic accident or not. In the event, they decided that Grossley was guilty as charged and he remained silent as the death sentence was intoned, although he did turn very pale. An appeal was heard on August 21st before Justices

256

Wrottesley, Croom-Johnson and Stable, but they felt that there was no reason to interfere with the verdict.

There can be little doubt that the shooting of Lily Griffiths was a tragic accident. Grossley had taken the gun out either to shoot himself or, as is more likely, to pretend that he was going to do so in order to exact sympathy from Lily. She had taken his threat seriously, struggled with him, the gun had gone off, and she had been fatally wounded. In other cases, dying depositions have been enough to condemn a prisoner. In this case, the same weight should have been given to Lily's deposition, in which instance Grossley would have been found guilty of manslaughter not murder.

None of this succeeded in saving Grossley's life and, just over two weeks after his appeal had been lost, on Wednesday, September 5th, 1945, Howard Joseph Grossley was hanged at Cardiff prison.

33

Martin Patrick Coffey
Hanged at Manchester, Wednesday, April 24th, 1946
For the murder of Henry Dutton at Manchester

HARRY Dixon, a lorry driver, and his mate, Frank Laverty, were driving down Great Jackson Street in Manchester at 2.35 p.m., on Monday, November 26th, 1945, when they saw an elderly man stagger out of a dilapidated building and collapse on the pavement. Rushing to his aid, Dixon and Laverty saw that the old man had been shot. They wasted no time in calling for medical and police aid.

The wounded man, seventy-two-year-old Henry Dutton, was still conscious and managed to tell the first officer on the scene, Constable Frederick William Magerkorth, that just five minutes before he had been found, a young man had walked into his shop at number fifty-seven and demanded all the money on the premises. When Dutton had moved towards the man, two shots had been fired, both of which had hit home, one in the stomach and one in the thigh.

After Constable Magerkorth had accompanied Mr Dutton to the Manchester Royal Infirmary, he returned to the scene of the shooting and made a search of the premises. Inside the shop he found two empty cartridge cases, which he handed over to Inspector Stainton, along with a bullet he had found on the stretcher used to take Henry Dutton into the infirmary. Meanwhile, Mr Dutton's condition was said to be critical and he was visited at the infirmary by his wife and son.

At around 5.00 p.m., the following day, November 27th, three men were walking down Market Street when they were approached by a fourth, who identified himself as a plain-clothes police officer. One of the three, twenty-four-year-old Martin Patrick Coffey, was wanted in connection with a minor matter and was asked to accompany the officer to the police station. Coffey offered no resistance and his two companions, John Irvine and William Phelan, watched as he was escorted away.

At the station, as he was waiting to be interviewed, Coffey was seen by Detective Inspector Frank Stainton, who noticed that the young man fitted the description given by Henry Dutton. As a matter of routine, Coffey was told that a shooting was being investigated and was asked to give an account of his movements on the 26th. Coffey replied, "That's easy. I wasn't in Great Jackson Street and I haven't shot anybody. I stayed at the Salvation Army at Francis Street on Sunday night and occupied bed 290. I left the Salvation Army on Monday morning at half past eleven. I went to London Road station and hung about there until one o'clock. I then went to the amusement arcade in Deansgate and from there to the Salvation Army for dinner where I stayed until half past two. From there I went up Cheetham Hill Road."

At this point, there was nothing to connect Coffey to the shooting of Henry Dutton, beyond the fact that he fitted the description of the assailant. Indeed, the police seemed to be convinced that the man they were looking for was still at large, for whilst Coffey was in custody, another armed robbery took place at a sub-post office in Chorlton-on-Medlock. A young man had pointed a gun at the two assistants and demanded the money in the till. On this occasion, though, he had fled empty-handed, without causing any injuries.

On Friday, November 30th, four days after he had been shot, Henry Dutton's condition worsened and late that afternoon, he died. This was now a case of murder and it was that knowledge which brought John Irvine, one of the two men who had been with Coffey when he was arrested, to the police station where he asked to see Detective Chief Inspector Stainton.

At that interview, Irvine told the chief inspector a most curious story about an event which he said had occurred at around 4.00 p.m. on the day after the shooting. He had been at the Salvation Army hostel in Francis Street with Phelan, Coffey's other friend, when Coffey came over to them. Irvine said that he was reading out details of the shooting, from a newspaper. As he finished the article, he noticed that Coffey was laughing, and asked him what he found so amusing. Coffey replied, "I am laughing up my sleeve at the description in the paper".

Puzzled by this behaviour, Irvine said he had pressed his friend and asked him what he meant, whereupon Coffey said, "It was me that done the job". Coffey added that he had gone into the shop at 2.00 p.m., and said "I went into the shop and asked the old man in the shop if I could have a look at an overcoat that was hanging up. The old man took the overcoat down and put it on the counter for me to examine. I then pulled out a gun as the old man made to go round the back of the counter. I told him to hand over all the money that was under the counter. He put two or three thousand pounds on the counter. As he was fumbling to pull out some more money there appeared in his hand a gun. I shot the gun from his hand and wounded him on the wrist. He then pulled a whistle out of his pocket and blew it two or three times. I then fired two or three rounds into his stomach. The old man staggered after me as I made to go out of the shop."

According to Irvine, he had found this story very difficult to believe but had decided to humour Coffey. For that reason, he asked him where the gun was now. At first, Coffey avoided the question, only saying that he had climbed onto a bus after the shooting, and confirming that he was alone and not with a partner as the newspaper report suggested. William Phelan, who had been present throughout, had said he did not believe the story either and went to have a wash, leaving Irvine and Coffey alone.

Continuing his narrative, Irvine said that some ten minutes after this conversation had taken place, he and Coffey had left the hostel together. As they were walking, Coffey had suddenly left him standing in the street whilst he dashed into a bombed-out house nearby, reappearing moments later carrying a piece of rag. Unwrapping this small parcel, Coffey revealed a gun, which he showed to Irvine, who suggested "You had better give it to me in case you get into any more trouble". Coffey duly handed the pistol over, warning Irvine to be careful as the magazine was full.

Irvine ended his story with details of Coffey's arrest as the three friends were walking down Market Street at 5.00 p.m. that same day. As Coffey was taken away, Irvine had turned to Phelan and told him for the first time about the gun Coffey had given him. He and Phelan had then gone to Irvine's lodgings at 3 George Street, where they examined the gun together and unloaded the magazine. The weapon was now placed on top of a cupboard, for safekeeping.

After listening to this story, Chief Inspector Stainton went back to George Street with Irvine and collected the gun. He then returned to the police station and confronted Coffey with the weapon and Irvine's statement.

At this second interview, the chief inspector was accompanied by Detective Sergeant Crowe and Detective Sergeant Arthur Ormston. After Coffey had been cautioned, the chief inspector said, "Since I saw you on Tuesday last, the pawnbroker from Jackson Street has died. I have made further inquiries and I have traced an automatic pistol, which I believe had belonged to you. I am now definitely of the opinion that you are the person who shot the pawnbroker with this pistol."

Coffey paused for a few seconds and then replied, "You are right. That's my pistol. I did it. I would have told you before but I was frightened that the old man would die. Now it doesn't matter. I will tell you the truth." He went on to make a full statement, admitting his responsibility for the death of Henry Dutton.

Coffey's trial took place on March 12th, 1946, before Mr Justice Morris. Coffey was defended by Mr Kenneth Burke, whilst the prosecution case rested in the hands of Mr F. E. Pritchard.

The two most important witnesses for the prosecution were undoubtedly Irvine and Phelan. Irvine told his story again and much of his testimony was backed up by Phelan. There were, however, discrepancies in their individual stories. For instance, Irvine insisted that Coffey had told him that the shopkeeper had a gun, but Phelan claimed he had said nothing of the kind.

Another important witness was Albert Louis Allen, an Associate of the Royal Institute of Chemistry, who worked at the Home Office Forensic Science Laboratory at Preston. He had visited the scene of the shooting and traced the path of the bullets fired. He was able to determine that they had been fired from a position by the entrance door, just inside the shop. He had also examined the pistol, a self-loading 7.55 mm calibre weapon which had to be manually cocked before the first shot could be fired. The bullets recovered from the shop had been fired from that gun but of course Allen's expert testimony showed that Coffey's supposed confession was inaccurate, since Coffey had claimed that he fired the gun whilst at the counter.

In his summing up, Mr Burke for the defence said that his client liked to romance and that the only real evidence against him was his statements to his friends at the hostel and his statements to the police, and there were obvious discrepancies between these. It was only their evidence that had ever placed the murder weapon in Coffey's possession. It was also obvious that Coffey had deliberately embellished his so-called confession, the details of which did not fit the scientifically proven facts. He had exaggerated the amount of money likely to be found on the premises, and had told a story that simply did not fit the facts – he had spoken of a few thousand pounds being stolen when no such figure was ever kept on the premises, and there was also no evidence that the shopkeeper had ever owned a gun, as Coffey had claimed.

The jury took just forty-five minutes to decide that Coffey was guilty and he was duly sentenced to death. An appeal was entered and this was heard on April 9th. The judges decided that there was sufficient evidence to convict Coffey even without his confession, and the appeal was therefore dismissed.

On Wednesday, April 24th, Martin Patrick Coffey was hanged at Strangeways prison, Manchester. It was true that the murder weapon had been found, but there was only Irvine's word that it was handed to him by Coffey, and only Coffey's confession to link him to the crime. That confession was full of errors and inaccuracies and Coffey was known to be an unsophisticated young man who liked to invent stories in order to boost his own ego. Even if his hand had been the one which held the gun on that fateful day, surely his behaviour afterwards shows that there was a good deal of mental instability in Coffey's emotional make-up, and that too should have been reason enough to save him from the gallows.

Either Coffey was totally innocent of the crime that claimed his life, or he was not totally responsible for his actions and still should not have faced the ultimate sanction of the law.

Walter Graham Rowland

34

Hanged at Manchester, Thursday, February 27th, 1947
For the murder of Olive Balchin, in Manchester

ALTER Graham Rowland was a very worried man. His concerns had all started with a rather minor offence when Rowland, who lived at 2 Cheetham Hill, Mellor, in Derbyshire, had taken a taxi ride to Blackpool and then neglected to pay the £3 fare. As a result, a complaint had been made to the police and he had finally received a summons telling him to appear in court at Stockport. The first hearing had been adjourned and now, on Friday, March 2nd, 1934, he was due to make his second appearance.

The matter, though, had been preying on Rowland's mind and he had even tried to borrow the money from his employer, Mr Renshaw, in order to pay off the debt to the taxi company in the hope that this would put an end to the matter. This attempt had not, however, succeeded. The owner of the taxi firm had explained that much as he would like to help, the matter was now out of his hands and would have to be dealt with by the police and the courts.

As the days had passed, and the date of this second court appearance had grown ever closer, Rowland had even intimated to his wife, Annie May, that they should leave the area and start afresh somewhere else. When Annie pointed out that they did not have the money to do such a thing, Rowland had suggested breaking open the electricity meter and using the cash it held to escape from Mellor. Annie May told him not to be so stupid but nothing, it seemed, could stop her husband worrying.

On the date of the adjourned hearing, Annie May woke at 9.15 a.m. Rowland was already up and about and brought her a cup of tea in bed. Once again, Rowland spoke of his worries and confided in Annie May that he did not think he could face going to court, even though it would certainly mean a warrant being issued for his arrest. Nevertheless, at around 11.00 a.m., Rowland went out, leaving Annie May to take care of their two-year-old daughter, Mavis Agnes.

Annie May Rowland busied herself with the household chores and, by 3.00 p.m., she was upstairs, cleaning out the bedrooms. Some thirty minutes later, Annie noticed her husband's working trousers hanging over a chair near the window and as she straightened them, she noticed that there was something hanging out of one of the pockets. To Annie's surprise, this turned out to be a woman's stocking but even as she gazed at it, Annie May heard her husband coming home. Knowing that he hated her looking through his pockets, she hurriedly pushed the stocking back where she had found it.

For the next couple of hours, Rowland seemed to be on tenterhooks. More than once he went to the front door, opened it, looked out and then rushed back inside and locked the door behind him. Annie May asked Rowland what the trouble was and he explained that he had not gone to court after all, and was afraid that the police would come for him at any time. He was still in this state at 5.20 p.m., when Annie left the house to visit some friends at New Mills. At the time, little Mavis was playing on the living room carpet and Annie told Rowland not to put her to bed before eight or even half past, as otherwise she might not sleep through the night.

It was 7.45 p.m. by the time Annie May returned home, to find the house in darkness. The front door was closed but not locked, and as Annie entered the cold house she snapped on the light to see a towel and the evening paper lying on the table. Annie called out for her husband, but there was no reply to her shouting so she went upstairs to see where he was, and to check on Mavis.

Going into the front bedroom first, Annie found no trace of Rowland. In the back bedroom, nothing had apparently been disturbed but upon looking into the child's cot, Annie saw that Mavis was very pale and that her tongue was protruding from between her lips. Pulling the bedclothes down a little, Annie saw to her horror that there was a woman's stocking tied tightly around the little girl's throat. Annie wasted no time in frantically untying four knots and as the pressure around Mavis' throat was released, a sickening hissing sound escaped from the child. Annie Rowland picked up her daughter and ran next door for help.

Olive May Brough lived with her husband, John, at 1 Cheetham Hill. It was almost 8.00 p.m. by the time Annie Rowland, carrying the baby in her arms, dashed in through the back door and explained what she had found. Annie left Mavis with Mrs Brough as she ran to fetch the doctor. Whilst Annie was gone, Olive Brough walked about the room nursing the still bundle, though she could not help but notice that Mavis' face was very white and her lips were blue. Olive also saw that the stocking was still loosely tied around the child's throat. There was yet another knot to unfasten before it could finally be removed.

At 8.15 p.m., Annie May Rowland returned to Olive Brough's house with Dr David Dougall Hepburn Craig and Police Sergeant Wilfred Coates. By now, Mavis had been placed into a pram and it was there that Dr Craig examined her and confirmed that she was dead. He noted a purplish groove around the child's neck, some quarter to a half inch in width, and estimated that death had taken place within the last two hours, and in his opinion, the latest time of death would have been one hour before. This put Mavis' death at some time between 6.15 p.m. and 7.15 p.m. Sergeant Coates,

264

meanwhile, had checked Rowland's house and found that the electricity meter had been broken into. He then contacted his station and had details of Walter Rowland circulated to forces in the immediate area.

It was not long before a number of witnesses were found who had seen something of Rowland on that evening of March 2nd. Percy Jackson was thirteen years old and a member of the local boy scouts group. Percy lived at 6 Green Doors on Cheetham Hill and knew the Rowland family quite well. The scouts met every Friday night and at some time between 6.00 p.m. and 6.30 p.m., Percy had been on the way to the scout hut when Walter Rowland stopped him and asked if he had seen the paperman. Percy said that he had not, whereupon Rowland picked up Mavis, who had been playing on the pavement in front of the cottages, and took her inside.

The paperman, or newsagent, that Rowland had been referring to was James Horsfield, and he told the police that he had delivered papers to the cottages at Cheetham Hill at 6.30 p.m. on Friday evening. For a few minutes, Horsfield had spoken to Mr Burdekin, who lived at number three. Horsfield explained that he had had to talk rather loudly, as old Mr Burdekin was rather deaf. His voice had probably carried quite a distance as a result and as they talked, Rowland came to Mr Burdekin's front door and asked Horsfield if he might buy a newspaper. Horsfield handed over a copy of the Evening Chronicle and saw Rowland return to his own house. A few minutes later, as Horsfield passed down the hill, he heard the door being bolted at number two and saw that the blinds had been pulled down.

There was one other man who had seen something of Walter Rowland that night. James Hambleton lived at a house named Heatherick on Moor End, Mellor and at 6.50 p.m., he was near the Devonshire Arms Inn. As Hambleton watched, the bus from New Mills came down Cheetham Hill and stopped at the inn. Hambleton was well acquainted with Rowland, and he was certain that Rowland was the man who got off the bus and ran across the road to catch another bus a few yards further down the road. This bus went to Stockport and pulled out a minute or so after Rowland had climbed on. The search for Rowland now moved to Stockport.

Samuel Henderson lived at 28 Hayfield Street, Portwood, Stockport and at 8.30 p.m., on March 2nd, he had walked into the Touchstone Inn where he noticed a man drinking alone. Henderson fell into conversation with the stranger and they both bought rounds of drinks. Henderson's new friend seemed to be somewhat nervous and at one stage asked which was nearer, New Brighton or Blackpool. Told that it was New Brighton, the stranger said that he was thinking of going there on business, if he could get a woman to go with him. When, a few minutes later, an attractive woman came in alone, the man persuaded Henderson to go over and ask her if she wanted a drink.

Eliza Ann Burke lived at 12 Reddish Road, Stockport and although she was a married woman, she quite often went out drinking alone. It was nearly 8.50 p.m. when she entered the Touchstone and almost immediately, Samuel Henderson came over and said that his friend wanted to buy her a drink. The three sat together for a time, the stranger introducing himself as Walter Rowland. Soon, Henderson realized that he was playing gooseberry and went off to drink by himself at the opposite end of the bar. He was still in the Touchstone when Rowland and Eliza Burke left together.

When Rowland had first explained to Eliza that he was going to New Brighton and that he would like her to go with him, she had refused. Eventually, though, she gave into his charm and agreed to accompany him. Rowland asked where they might get a taxi and at 9.20 p.m., he and Eliza walked down to Shepphard's Garage in Wellington Road, where they asked the proprietor to telephone for a cab for them. The first taxi arrived within five minutes, but the driver did not relish the thought of a trip to New Brighton and said that he would return to base and send out one of his colleagues. As a result, it was almost 10.00 p.m. before a second driver, William Grimshaw, pulled up in Wellington Road.

It was not until just after midnight that the taxi arrived in New Brighton, since the male passenger had asked Grimshaw to stop once on the journey. Once they were in the town, Grimshaw was told to find a Mrs Hudson's house in Lyme Grove. He had no idea where that address was and none of the people he asked for directions had any idea either. Even an attendant at a garage had never heard of Lyme Grove, and so Grimshaw parked in Birch Grove and made no objection when his male passenger said he would go off and make enquiries whilst Grimshaw and Mrs Burke waited in the cab.

When his passenger had still not returned after twenty minutes, Grimshaw went in search of his man and found him close to the police station. A brief argument ensued during which Grimshaw demanded payment for his fare. The passenger now produced an envelope upon which he said was his name and home address. He explained that he did not have any money on him and had thought that the woman was going to pay the fare. It was all a simple misunderstanding and if Grimshaw would call at the address he would receive his money without further delay.

William Grimshaw gazed at the envelope and noted the name 'Rowland' and an address at Mellor. Even as he read the words, Grimshaw recalled a case he had seen in his newspapers only that afternoon in which a man named Rowland had been accused of 'bilking', or avoiding a taxi fare. Concerned that he was about to become the second victim of the same man, Grimshaw determined to bring this matter to the attention of the police.

In fact, Rowland had only just walked out of the police station situated just a few yards away. It had been 12.45 a.m. on March 3rd when Rowland went to the station desk and spoke to Constable William Allan Wesley. He explained that he had just come from Stockport in a car with three of his workmates, but that they had separated during the night and as a result, he had now been left behind with nowhere to stay for the night. Constable Wesley said that a colleague of his, on duty outside, might be able to assist Rowland in finding somewhere to stay. It was while Rowland was looking for this second policeman that Grimshaw spotted him. Rowland walked up to Constable Joseph Ryan, who was on duty at the corner of Rowson Street and Victoria Road, and said that his

Walter Graham Rowland under police escort. Rowland was hanged on February 27th, 1947, for the murder of Olive Balchin (Popperfoto)

267

sergeant (mistaking Constable Wesley's rank) had sent him to ask after lodgings for the night. Even as this conversation was taking place, an irate Grimshaw interrupted and shouted, "Wait a minute officer. I want this man's name and address as I have driven himself and a woman to here from Stockport and now he says he's got no money."

In order to sort this matter out, Constable Ryan suggested that they all go back inside the police station. Once again Rowland produced his envelope and was then taken into a back office by Constable Wesley, who asked about the fare that had apparently been avoided. Rowland replied with, "Ring up the police at Mellor. They will tell you something more serious than that." Rowland then asked to use the lavatory, a request that was granted.

Telephone calls were made to Derbyshire and at 8.00 a.m., on March 3rd, Sergeant Coates and Constable Percy Radford Merrey arrived at Wallasey, the station to which Rowland had now been transferred. There, Rowland was told that he would be detained for the murder of his daughter. Upon hearing this Rowland turned pale very rapidly, swooned and had to be supported. He was formally charged with murder at 11.45 a.m., and one hour later, made a full written statement, claiming that he had left his daughter alive and well after reading in the local newspaper that a warrant had indeed been issued for his arrest after his non-appearance in court.

The trial of Walter Rowland opened on Monday, May 7th, 1934. Rowland was represented by Mr H. Rhodes whilst the Crown's case was led by Mr R. K. Chappell, who was assisted by Mr F. Atkinson. The proceedings lasted for two days.

For the prosecution, Mr Chappell began by explaining some of the geography of the case. He stated that Mellor was only just inside Derbyshire and was situated about five miles west of New Mills. Also to the west, about 730 yards from Rowland's cottage, was the crossroads where the Devonshire Arms was situated, and all these locations would play a part in the evidence he would call. Mr Chappell went on to say that Rowland had been a casual labourer but was not at work on March 2nd, since he was due in court at Stockport to answer a charge. Had he attended court, Rowland might well have successfully defended the charge but if he failed to turn up at all, as indeed he did, then it was certain that a warrant for his arrest would be issued.

The first witness called by the prosecution was Annie May Rowland, the prisoner's wife, who was heavily pregnant with her second child, due at the end of the month. She began by saying that she had married the prisoner on September 5th, 1931 and that Mavis had been born on February 21st, 1932. She went on to tell the court of the worries her husband had had over his court appearance and of his suggestions that they run away together, at one stage suggesting that they go to Ireland. She went on to tell of the discovery of the stocking in Rowland's pocket, her visit to relatives at New Mills later that day, and what she had discovered when she finally returned to the cottage that evening.

Annie May confirmed that Rowland had always expressed love for his daughter and had seemed to be devoted to her. After he had been arrested, she had visited him in prison and they had spoken of the crime. When Rowland had said that he was innocent, she had asked him who could have done it then, and he had replied "My dear, I think you must have had a brainstorm and done it yourself". Mrs Rowland also confirmed that some weeks before this incident, she had suffered a nervous breakdown and had gone away for ten days to recover.

The suggestion that Annie May was responsible for her daughter's death was largely dismissed by the evidence of Dr Craig. In addition to attending the scene of the crime, he had also performed a post-mortem on Mavis and this had shown a bloody froth in the child's windpipe and lungs, confirming that the cause of death was strangulation. He repeated under oath that the child must have been dead at least an hour before he made his initial examination, showing that the very latest time that Mavis could have died was 7.15 p.m., and even this was highly unlikely, death almost certainly taking place well before this time. Annie May was then in New Mills and there was no way therefore that she could be responsible for Mavis' death.

Annie May had referred to finding a stocking in Rowland's trouser pocket. Sergeant Coates now testified that after carefully searching Rowland's home, he had found the trousers referred to but there had been no stocking there. However, when Rowland was searched at Wallasey, a woman's stocking was found on him and tests had revealed that this was the twin to the one found around Mavis' throat. Referring then to the electricity meter, Sergeant Coates said that this had been forced at the hinge and when he inspected it, only one shilling remained in the cash drawer. That drawer had since been removed and sent to the fingerprint office at Scotland Yard for examination.

Constable Wesley testified that he had asked Rowland to come into the back room at the New Brighton police station because the light was better there and he could get a better look at the man. Rowland unfastened his coat and Constable Wesley saw a newspaper there. Rowland handed it over and said that there was an article in it showing that he was wanted at Stockport, but that there was something more serious at Mellor. Later, Constable Ryan had escorted Rowland to Wallasey and some time later still, Ryan had telephoned the police at New Brighton and told them that Rowland had admitted leaving something behind when he used the station toilet. Constable Wesley checked the cubicle and on top of the cistern found a chisel. Tests had since shown that this might well have been used to force the meter at his house.

Rowland always claimed that the 'something more serious' he was referring to was his forcing of the electricity meter at his home and the theft of its contents. The prosecution now called Eliza Burke, the woman who had accompanied Rowland on his trip to New Brighton. She told the court how she and Mr Grimshaw had waited in his cab and how Grimshaw had left to find his missing passenger. Mrs Burke had seen the two men involved in an animated discussion with a policeman and had followed them all into the police station. She heard Rowland say, "You might as well ring up Mellor police station" and saw him point to an article in the newspaper he held, saying that he was wanted for something. The policeman asked him what for and Eliza Burke heard Rowland reply, "Murder".

Rowland gave evidence on his own behalf. He denied Mrs Burke's suggestion that he had ever mentioned that he was wanted for murder. When he had been in the police station at New Brighton he had no idea that his daughter was dead and it came as a total shock to him when he was charged. He was guilty only of breaking into his electricity meter and had no involvement in the death of Mavis.

The jury retired at 5.15 p.m., and the verdict, when it came, was that Rowland was guilty of murder, though a recommendation to mercy was added. Almost immediately an appeal was entered, and this was heard on June 6th, before the Lord Chief Justice, Lord Hewart, and Justices Humphreys and MacNaghten. The grounds of the appeal were that all the evidence produced had been circumstantial and that Rowland maintained that he was innocent of the charge. The only thing to connect Rowland to the crime was the silk stocking found in his pocket and he could have picked this up in the house at any time. Giving the court's judgement, Lord Hewart stated that it was clear that Rowland had been in charge of the child at the time of the murder. He went on to say that the jury had, for some reason which was not clear to him, recommended Rowland to mercy, but that this was not a matter for the court. The appeal was dismissed.

Rowland's execution date was set for Thursday, June 21st, at Manchester but just two days prior to this, on June 19th, the Home Secretary announced that he had recommended that the King should commute the sentence to one of life imprisonment. Rowland was taken out of the condemned cell and sent to Parkhurst prison on the Isle of Wight, to serve his life sentence.

Under normal circumstances, that might well have been the last that history heard of Walter Graham Rowland, but for the Second World War. At that time, Britain needed all the fighting men she could find and a system was introduced whereby long-term prisoners could be released if they went into the armed forces. Rowland took advantage of that scheme in 1945, but hostilities ended soon afterwards and he was demobbed, a free man once again. Just a year later, his name would once again be linked to a brutal murder.

On the morning of Sunday, October 20th, 1946, a woman's body was discovered on a blitzed site close to the junction of Deansgate and Cumberland Street, Manchester. The woman had been battered to death and the bloodstained hammer used to inflict the injuries upon her lay close by, as did a piece of brown wrapping paper which bore the impression of the hammer, implying that it might have been purchased only recently. The police had no trouble in identifying the dead woman, for an ID card, found in her pocket, confirmed that she was a forty-year-old prostitute named Olive Balchin, a native of Birmingham.

Investigations showed that Olive, who actually used four names and carried two different identity cards, had only come to Manchester eleven days before her death, and was registered as a resident of the Ashton House women's hostel in Corporation Street.

The hammer found near the body was of the type used by leather-beaters, and the police now began a systematic investigation of all such workers, and men who worked with soft metals, in an attempt to trace the ownership of that particular hammer. Their efforts soon produced three valuable witnesses.

Norman Mercer, the landlord of the Dog and Partridge, a pub on Deansgate, said that he had been walking his dog at around midnight on October 20th, when he saw a man and a woman arguing, close to the spot where Olive's body was subsequently discovered. Mr Mercer gave the police a detailed description of the man, "Aged thirty to thirty-five, five feet seven inches tall, proportionately built, clean-shaven, round faced, dark hair and wearing a blue suit".

The next witness was Edward McDonald, a salesman, who told the officers investigating the case that he had sold a hammer, which might have been the murder weapon, on October 19th. The description he gave of his customer was in some ways similar to that supplied by Norman Mercer. Furthermore, Mr McDonald said it was his habit to wrap all purchases and the type of paper he used was of the same type as that found at the murder scene.

Finally, the police interviewed Elizabeth Copley, a Lyon's waitress, who said that on the afternoon of the murder, she had served two women, who were with a man, in her cafe in Market Street. Elizabeth positively identified the younger of the two women as Olive Balchin, and said that the man with her was carrying a parcel that might well have been the hammer, wrapped in paper.

On October 22nd, Dr J. B. Firth, the director of the Home Office forensic science laboratory at Preston, visited the bomb-site, accompanied by a number of police officers including Superintendent W. Ashcroft, Detective Sergeant W. Trippier and Detective Constable Hesketh. Samples of soil, cement, brick dust and other debris were taken. Before returning to Preston, Dr Firth also spoke to the heads of the newly established murder squad, the first in the city of Manchester. Detective Superintendent William Malcolm Page and Detective Chief Inspector Frank Stainton gave Dr Firth all the details of the case.

On October 24th, a photograph was published of a model wearing Olive's clothes. Although the picture was in black and white, details were given of the blue coat with its distinctive white buttons, the brown beret, and the black shoes. Olive had been wearing these items at 8.00 p.m., on Friday, October 18th, in Littlewood's cafe in Piccadilly. A friend of hers had seen her with a man and had asked Olive to come away with her. Olive had replied, "No, I am going with him". Olive had also worn the same outfit the following day, October 19th, when she had been seen in the Lyon's cafe, by Elizabeth Copley, at 5.00 p.m.

On October 26th, the police announced that they had found a paper money bag amongst Olive's possessions. This bag, from the Midland Bank, had been stamped 'Birchfield Road Depot', together with a date in October. It also bore the initial 'SG', but no sooner had this clue been announced than the police traced the man who had given the bag to Olive. He was able to prove that he had no connection with the crime. That same day though, the police finally made the breakthrough they needed.

Information had been given to the police about a resident of a Service's transit dormitory, in Millgate, who seemed reluctant to venture out of his room during the day. Since this man also fitted the general description of the man wanted in connection with the death of Olive Balchin, two police officers, Detective Sergeant Blakemore and Detective Constable Nimmo, visited the dormitory where they interviewed the man. The officers later claimed that they were greeted with, "You don't want me for the murder of that woman do you?"

The man went on to admit that he did know Olive, but had not been with her on the night she died, adding, "I am admitting nothing because it is only a fool's game to do that. I can account for where I was. I was home at New Mills when she was murdered." Nevertheless, the man was taken in for further questioning. His name was Walter Graham Rowland.

At the police station, Rowland said that he had known Olive for about eight weeks and that during this time, he had been intimate with her and now suspected that he may have caught a sexually transmitted disease from her. That comment seemed to indicate that Rowland might well have a motive for murder, and this was reinforced when at one stage during the questioning, Rowland remarked that if Olive had given him a disease, then she had deserved all she got. When, on October 27th, Rowland was placed in an identification parade where he was picked out by Edward McDonald, the man who had sold the hammer, the last piece of evidence seemed to fall into place and Rowland was charged with the murder of Olive Balchin.

Walter Graham Rowland faced his second trial for murder, at Manchester, on December 12th, 1946, before Mr Justice Sellers. The jury of three women and nine men heard the evidence detailed by Mr Basil Neild and Mr B. S. Wingate Saul, whilst Rowland's defence was put by Mr Kenneth Burke and Mr H. Openshaw. The hearing lasted until December 16th.

Much had been made in the police court about the fact that the man described by the various witnesses had been dark haired, whilst Rowland was blond. An attempt was made to show that under certain circumstances, Rowland's hair might appear much darker, especially if he used grease to keep it in place. The prosecution called Captain Reid, the manager of the Salvation Army Hostel at Chorlton-on-Medlock, in an attempt to prove this point. Rowland had stayed at that establishment for four nights, starting on October 21st, and Captain Reid stated that when the prisoner first arrived, his hair appeared to be dark and greased.

To counter this, Rowland's mother was called. She confirmed that her son had never used grease on his hair. She had actually bought him some in 1945, when he was on leave from the Army, but he had refused to use it, saying that his friends would think he had gone soft, and handed it on to his brother. The most she had ever known Walter to do was to use water to keep his hair in place.

Edward McDonald, the man who had sold a hammer which might have been the murder weapon, testified that he had now positively identified it as one he had sold to Rowland for three shillings and sixpence, at 5.40 p.m., on October 19th. He also confirmed that he had attended an identification parade at the police station and had picked out Rowland from a line of men. However, under cross-examination, Mr McDonald admitted that his original statement to the police had stated that his customer had been dark-haired whilst Rowland was blond. He had also said that the man he served was thin-faced. Rowland was quite chubby.

Norman Mercer, the pub landlord, had also attended that identification parade and picked out Rowland, as had Elizabeth Copley, the cafe waitress. It should be remembered, though, that Mercer saw two people arguing on a dark bomb-site at around midnight. He could not possibly have obtained a good view of either the man or the woman involved. Furthermore, Elizabeth Copley had said that she saw Rowland at around 5.00 p.m. There is a good deal of evidence that Rowland was not even in the city centre at this time. In his statements to the police he had said that he was in a pub named the Wellington, in Stockport, at that time. He also had two extremely good witnesses whose testimony indicated that he was telling the truth.

Rowland claimed that he had stayed in the Wellington until it was quite late and at one stage two policemen in uniform entered one of the bars, walked through the pub and left through the other bar. Sergeant Jones was then called to testify that he and a constable had done precisely that at 10.30 p.m.

Continuing his testimony, Rowland said that after leaving the Wellington he had caught another bus, this time to Ardwick, and after purchasing fish and chips, had gone to a lodging house at 81 Brunswick Street, where he signed the register at about 11.00 p.m. This register was produced in court and it did indeed show that Rowland had been in Ardwick, miles away from where Olive Balchin was murdered.

There was, however, some very damaging testimony from Dr J. B. Firth, who had taken samples from the murder scene. He had examined Rowland's clothing and had found, in his trouser turn-ups, brick dust, cement, charcoal, clinker and weathered leaf tissue, all of which matched samples from the bomb-site. In itself, though, this was curious. Even if Rowland had committed the crime and been involved in a frenzied attack upon Olive, would he necessarily have accumulated so much debris in his turn-ups? Or could that evidence have been contaminated in some way?

On December 16th, Mr Justice Sellers took one hour and fifty minutes to sum up the evidence for the jury. The jury retired, and in due course returned to court to announce that Rowland was guilty. He was sentenced to death, for the second time, and the very next day, the defence team announced that their client would almost certainly appeal.

That appeal was due to be heard on January 27th, 1947, but three days prior to that, the case took a startling turn when David John Ware, a young man serving a sentence for larceny at Walton jail in Liverpool, admitted that he was the man who had killed Olive Balchin. Consequently, when January 27th came, the three appeal court judges,

Lord Goddard, the Lord Chief Justice, and Justices Humphreys and Lewis, decided to adjourn the case for two weeks whilst the matter could be investigated.

David Ware had made a very detailed statement to the police, claiming that he had been to a picture house in Belle Vue with Olive, whom he had met for the first time on the night he killed her. As for the time of the murder, Ware said it was at 10.00 p.m., on October 19th, and not at midnight as had been stated at Rowland's trial.

Rowland's appeal was reconvened on February 10th, and the defence were allowed to call two new witnesses. Henry Somerville testified that he had been in the Wellington Hotel, in Stockport, some time after 10.15 p.m., on the night of October 19th. A man he now identified as Rowland had sold him some cigarettes. The other witness was Walter Haydn Elwood, who was manager of the Plaza Cinema, which was just up the road from the Wellington. Rowland had claimed that when he finally left the pub, there were crowds of people coming out of a cinema. Mr Elwood said that on October 19th, the film finished at around 10.12 p.m., and there would have been crowds around the Plaza after that time. Mr Elwood was also able to state that to get from the area of the Wellington to Deansgate would take at least twenty-five minutes by bus.

For the Crown, Mr Neild admitted that all this evidence negated the testimony of Elizabeth Copley, but there remained the evidence of two others who had picked Rowland out as the man seen arguing with Olive and buying a hammer. The Lord Chief Justice announced that the appeal would be dismissed and the reasons would be put in writing.

Rowland, who was present in the court, did not accept this judgement lightly. Grasping the rail of the dock he shouted, "I am an innocent man. This is the greatest injustice that has ever been offered in an English court." Four warders tried to remove Rowland but he continued to call out, "Why did you not have the man here who has made the confession? I am not allowed justice because of my past." The warders finally managed to prise Rowland's fingers away from the dock but as he was taken down to the cells, he screamed, "It would have knocked the bottom out of British law if you had acquitted me and had proved me innocent. I say I am an innocent man before God."

The written judgement of the appeal court was given on February 17th, when it was read out by Mr Justice Humphreys. According to that document, the reason why Ware had not been heard was that the appeal court was not the proper place. The judge said, "It is no light matter to reverse the finding of a jury which has convicted a person of murder", possibly implying that it was a light matter to allow a man to hang for a crime he may not have committed. The judgement continued, "If we had allowed Ware to give evidence and he had persisted in his confession, the court would have been compelled to form some conclusion of his guilt or innocence and express that opinion in open court. The court would have been engaged in trying not only Rowland, but also Ware."

An inquiry into Ware's confession was announced by the Home Office and this was put into the hands of Mr John Catterall Jolly, a noted barrister. That report was sent to the Home Secretary on February 25th, and its conclusions made public on the following day. It was an astounding document.

Mr Jolly said that Ware had now admitted that his statement to the police had been false. On February 22nd, Ware had written, "I have never seen the woman Balchin, who was murdered in Manchester, in my life. I did not murder her and had nothing whatsoever to do with the murder.

"I made the statements out of swank more than anything, but I had a feeling all along that I wouldn't get very far with them. My health has not been too good since the outbreak of war, and I really do feel I want some treatment.

"I also thought I was putting myself in the position of a hero... I wanted to get myself in the headlines. In the past I wanted to be hung. It was worth while being hung to be a hero, seeing that life was not really worth living."

Mr Jolly had come to the conclusion that Ware had gleaned the details of the crime from press reports and other such sources. There were no points in his 'confession' that could not have been obtained from the newspapers and Ware had even referred to his victim as Olive Balshaw, an error made in early newspaper reports. Furthermore, he had been forced to alter the actual time of the attack from the correct time of midnight on October 19th to 10.00 p.m., since a lodging house register had been produced showing that Ware was asleep in bed at midnight. Ware had even gone so far as to prick his fingers and put spots of blood on his coat sleeves so that forensic evidence would be found to back up his fake story.

Rowland's defence team pointed out many of the inaccuracies in Mr Jolly's report. They found thirteen separate items in Ware's original confession that could not have been obtained from any press articles. For instance, Ware had said the woman wore a double-breasted coat and this was not revealed by any newspaper. Furthermore, Mr Jolly had said that a lodging house register proved that Ware could not have been with Olive at midnight and yet exactly the same type of evidence had been produced for Rowland but it had been concluded that this was a forgery!

Rowland's last chance was a recommendation for a reprieve from the Home Secretary, Mr Chuter Ede. This never came and at 9.00 a.m., on Thursday, February 27th, 1947, Walter Graham Rowland was hanged at Strangeways, by Albert Pierrepoint, as a crowd of one hundred people gathered outside the prison gates.

Some days after Rowland had been placed into his unmarked prison grave, the text of his last letter to his parents was published. This read, "Dear Mother and Dad, I understand just how you must have been feeling today when you came to see me for the last time in this world.

"I ask you to forgive me for trying to cheer you up in the way I did. I just had to keep you up, for I would have broken down myself. I am sure you will understand, Mother and Dad. You know I have told you the truth all along, and you have promised never to doubt or cease from seeking the truth of my total innocence. The truth will out in God's own time, so just go on with this firm belief in your hearts. Please do not mourn my passing.

"I am going into God's hands and into His keeping. I shall walk beside you until we meet again. I am just going on before, away from the injustices and the strain of all the past long days.

"When you receive this letter I shall be at my rest, so do not grieve my passing. Hold up your heads, for I die innocently. I die for another's crime... Before my Maker, I swear that I am completely innocent of the death of that poor woman. May God bless you and comfort you until we meet again... Goodbye in this world. Your innocent and grateful son, Walter."

In time, the disquiet expressed in some circles over the execution of Walter Rowland disappeared, until, that is, another trial, at Bristol, on November 22nd, 1951. It was on that date that David Ware was found guilty but insane of trying to kill a woman named Phyllis Fuidge by hitting her repeatedly, on the head, with a hammer. Ware had surrendered himself to the police on July 13th and, whilst being interviewed by the police, had once again admitted that he had been responsible for the death of Olive Balchin in Manchester in 1946.

At the time of writing, Rowland's conviction has not been declared unsafe, he has received no pardon and as such, he may hold the 'distinction' of being the only man reprieved for a murder he did commit and hanged for one he possibly did not.

Suggestion for further reading:

William Beadle, *Wrongly Hanged* (Dagenham: Wat Tyler, c. 1995).

Sydney Archibald Frederick Chamberlain

35

Hanged at Winchester, Thursday, July 28th, 1949
For the murder of Doreen Primrose Messenger,
at Haldon Moor, Devon

LFRED Speer worked as a roadman for the County Council and lived at Council Cottages, Ideford, in Devon. Saturday, February 19th, 1949, was an ordinary work day for Alfred, until he reached the main Newton Abbott to Exeter road, close to Beggar's Bush, for it was there that he found the naked body of a young girl. Alfred called out the police, who were on the scene within minutes.

Superintendent Stone, based at Newton Abbott, took charge of the investigation, and was assisted by Detective Superintendent Harvey and Detective Inspector Longman. Together the three officers made a check of any girls who had been reported as missing and this led to the rapid identification of the body. The victim turned out to be fifteen-year-old Doreen Primrose Messenger, who lived with her parents in Meadow Way, Heavitree, Exeter and who had been reported missing at 3.00 a.m. that morning.

The formal identification was made by Doreen's mother, Blanche Edith Messenger, who informed the police that her daughter had left school the year before, when she was fourteen, and had gone to work for the bookbinding department of James Townsend and Sons. Blanche also said that she had last seen Doreen on Friday the 18th, before she left for work. She had never returned home that evening but Blanche had her suspicions where Doreen had gone afterwards, for she also told the police that her daughter had been involved with a thirty-one-year-old married man, Sydney Chamberlain, who lived at 7 Ellis Place, also in Heavitree.

Chamberlain was interviewed at his home later that same day and not only admitted his involvement with Doreen, but also that he was responsible for her death. He was then taken to the police station where he made a lengthy statement before being charged with murder.

Sydney Chamberlain's trial took place at Exeter before Mister Justice Jones, on June 16th. During the two-day trial, Chamberlain was represented by Mr Henry Elam and Mr R. Ormrod. The prosecution case was led by Mr J. D. Casswell and Mr A. S. Trapnell. The defence was one of insanity.

The most important part of the prosecution evidence was Chamberlain's own voluntary statement. This began, "Last Friday I seen [sic] Doreen in the dinner time. She told me she wanted to see me in the evening." It went on to describe how Chamberlain had agreed to meet her after she had finished work. He was a little late for the meeting, and by the time he finally arrived, Doreen was waiting for him on the corner.

In the next part of the document, Chamberlain described how he and Doreen had first driven to Teignmouth, intending to go to the pictures, but Doreen had then changed her mind. They had a walk together and then Doreen asked Chamberlain to take her up to their special place, Haldon Moor. He continued, "We pulled into our little place there, and got in the back of the car. We was talking and that, and as we was kissing each other she said to me that she had been getting into trouble at home through going out with me. Her father had told her that if he caught her going out with me he would put her into a home, but she was not going to leave me. Then she said a bit of a funny thing. She said rather than leave me she would rather be dead."

The statement then described how, once they had finished kissing each other, they both got back into the front of the car and Chamberlain started the engine, intending to take Doreen home. She began to cry and when he asked her what the matter was, she told him that she did not like leaving him. He switched the engine off again and they stayed, cuddling, until it began to go dark and the stars began to come out. Seeing how late it was Doreen remarked, "I am bound to get a hiding when I get home". After asking Doreen if she really wanted to go home, and hearing her reply that she did not, Chamberlain went on to say what had happened next.

"I knew I could not find a place to take her because she was under age and the police would be bound to look for her. I put my hands on her neck and pressed on them. She never moved or anything. She just looked at me. I felt her start to shake, so I took my hands off her throat and said, 'Are you all right?'. But all she done was just kissed me. So then I put my hand on her neck and finished what I had done, or started to do. Then she went limp, but she was still breathing, so I took my belt off and put that round her neck and twisted it."

Chamberlain went on to say that after Doreen lost consciousness, he lifted her out of the car and placed her on the ground outside. Having taken all of Doreen's clothes off, except for her stockings, Chamberlain then lay down next to her until he started to feel cold. He then took the belt off Doreen's neck and covered her over with her dress and coat. He then kissed her goodbye and returned home.

This statement did not, however, refer to the fact that Doreen had had sexual intercourse. George Alexander Carey Lynch, the pathologist who performed the post-mortem, stated that the cause of death was asphyxiation and that Doreen had either engaged in sex just before she died, or someone had had intercourse with her soon after death.

When Superintendent Harvey gave evidence he first spoke of the interview he had conducted with Chamberlain, but then turned to Chamberlain's background.

Chamberlain was known to the police, and his record included a sentence of two years, in November 1940, for being armed with an offensive weapon, a hammer, and assaulting with intent to rob. The superintendent admitted that he had personally known Chamberlain for some years and considered him to be of below average intelligence. He had also twice threatened to commit suicide.

Further evidence of his unstable background came from his sister, Florence Annie Oxenham, who told the court that when she was about eight years old, the family had lived in Wales. At the time, Chamberlain was twelve, and one day, for no apparent reason, he stabbed her underneath the left eye with a pair of scissors, as a result of which she lost her sight in that eye. She also said that her brother suffered from fits and quite often an ambulance had to be called to attend to him.

Florence went on to describe two separate incidents where Chamberlain had attacked people for no reason, not remembering afterwards what he had done. This might well have been an hereditary trait, for her father too suffered from these fits. He would often fall unconscious, sometimes for as long as half an hour.

Another witness for the defence was Doctor Paul H. Sandifer, a neurologist at the Mount Vernon Hospital in London. He believed that Chamberlain was suffering from petit mal and defective reason. He was certainly a psychopath with a mental age of eleven. He had been smiling as he described to the doctor how he had sex with Doreen's body, almost congratulating himself on having achieved something so difficult.

The jury, however, had no trouble in deciding not only that Chamberlain was guilty, but that he was also sane, despite the medical evidence that he obviously had severe mental problems.

An appeal was entered, on the grounds that Chamberlain was not responsible for his actions due to his mental state. It was held, however, that his confession was so detailed that he could not have been suffering from any mental aberration at the time of Doreen's death. The appeal having failed, Chamberlain was hanged at Winchester prison on July 28th, the executioner being Albert Pierrepoint, who was assisted by Harry Allen. At the time, there were just four police officers outside the prison, positioned there in case there was a public demonstration.

Timothy John Evans

36

Hanged at Pentonville prison, London, Thursday, March 9th, 1950
For the murder of his daughter, Geraldine Evans,
at Notting Hill, London

D ETECTIVE Constable Gwynfryn Howell Evans was on duty in Merthyr
Tydfil's police station, at 3.10 p.m., on Wednesday, November 30th, 1949,
when a young, rather frightened looking man came in and asked if he might
speak to either an inspector or a sergeant.

Constable Evans told him that there was not another officer available, to which the
man asked if he might talk to Evans alone. Constable Evans hesitated, wondering what
could be so important, but the stranger continued "I want to give myself up. I have
disposed of my wife."

Immediately the young man was cautioned but he persisted, "I put her down the
drain". Asked if he knew the implications of what he was saying he went on, "Yes, I know
what I am saying. I cannot sleep and I want to get it off my chest." He then agreed to
make a formal statement but asked that it be written for him, as he could neither read
nor write himself. He was then taken into the CID office where he was handed over to
Detective Sergeant Gough, who carefully took down the statement before reading it
back and having it signed and witnessed.

The man who had walked into the station and spoken to Constable Evans was in fact
a namesake of his, twenty-five-year-old Timothy John Evans, a local man who had, until
very recently, been living in London with his wife, nineteen-year-old Beryl Susanna, and
their fourteen-month-old daughter, Geraldine. As he sat down with Constable Evans
and Sergeant Gough, his story slowly unfolded.

Timothy Evans' first statement, for he was to make others later, began by outlining
that around the beginning of the previous month, October, his wife had informed him
that she was expecting another baby, and was approximately three months gone. Evans
had expressed the opinion that one more would not make any difference but Beryl had
said that she wanted to get rid of it. Despite his protestations that she would make
herself ill, Beryl went ahead and bought a syringe with which she began trying to abort
herself. This, of course, failed to work but Beryl was determined and told her husband
that she had bought some tablets that might do the trick.

On Sunday, November 6th, Beryl had told Evans that the tablets were not working and that if she could not find a way to get rid of the baby, she would do away with herself and Geraldine. Once again Evans had told his wife not to be so silly but when he got up for work the next day, Monday the 7th, she said that she was going to see a woman who would help her.

Evans went to work as normal but at around 9.00 a.m. that same day he pulled up his van at a transport cafe somewhere between Ipswich and Colchester. He ordered his cup of tea and breakfast and soon fell into conversation with a man sitting opposite to him. They talked of various things until the stranger commented that Evans seemed to be worried about something. Evans then confided in the man about Beryl's pregnancy and the fact that she wanted to abort the child. The man then told him to wait for a minute, went outside and came back with a small bottle wrapped up in brown paper, saying "Tell your wife to take it first thing in the morning before she has any tea, and then to lay down on the bed for a couple of hours and that should do the job".

Evans took the bottle and that night, when he arrived home, he hung his coat up in the kitchen. Beryl asked him for a cigarette and when she went through his pockets to find one, she discovered the bottle. He then explained to her about the man in the cafe, what they had spoken about, and what he had said she must do.

On the morning of the 8th, Evans went to work again, having warned Beryl not to take the stuff in the bottle. That night, though, when he returned home, he found that there was no light in his flat. Going into the bedroom he saw baby Geraldine in her cot but Beryl was lying on the bed and, to his horror, he found that she was dead.

Not knowing what to do, Evans fed the baby and then sat up all night, thinking. Between 1.00 a.m. and 2.00 a.m., he got up, carried his wife's body downstairs and opened a drain outside the house. He then pushed her body head first into the drain before going back inside.

The next morning, Evans still went into work. He got someone to look after Geraldine then went into work and said he wished to leave his job because he had found a better one elsewhere. Later he sold his furniture, for which he got £40, the items being collected on the Monday morning, November 14th. That same day, once the furniture had been collected, Evans caught the 12.55 p.m. train from Paddington to Merthyr, where he had been ever since.

Faced with this statement, the Merthyr police felt that the first thing to do was to check out the details. The Metropolitan police were contacted and they in turn sent a telegram to the Notting Hill police, asking them to check out the drain outside Evans' London address, 10 Rillington Place. That afternoon, officers went to Rillington Place and found the drain exactly where Evans had said it was. However, it took three burly officers to lift the grating, a task which Evans claimed to have accomplished all by himself. Once opened, the drain was found to contain nothing out of the ordinary and a message to that effect was sent back to Merthyr.

It was 9.00 p.m. by the time the Welsh police faced Evans with the news that no body had been found down the drain and that it would have been impossible for him to lift it alone. He was asked if he wished to make another statement and said that he would.

This second statement took almost three hours to dictate, write, read through and finally sign. It began by saying that the story of meeting the man in the cafe and the disposal of his wife's body had not been true. Evans went on to blame another resident of 10 Rillington Place for his wife's death, Mr John Reginald Halliday Christie.

Before examining this second statement in detail, it is necessary to discuss the living arrangements at 10 Rillington Place, Notting Hill, London. The house, the last in a terrace of dismal run down properties, had three floors, each of which had been divided into flats. The ground floor flat was occupied by Reginald Christie and his wife, Ethel. The first or middle floor had just one occupant, Mr Kitchener, whilst the Evans family lived on the top floor. The entire property had just one outside toilet, accessible through the back yard. At the time of these incidents, though, Mr Kitchener was in hospital so his flat was empty.

Evans' second statement said that about a week before his wife died, which would be sometime around November 1st, he had been approached by Mr Christie, who had

The infamous house at 10 Rillington Place, Notting Hill, London, home to both Timothy Evans and Reginald Christie (Hulton Getty Picture Collection)

283

pointed out that he knew about the tablets Beryl was taking, and why she was taking them. He continued, "If you or your wife had come to me in the first place, I could have done it for you without any risk".

According to Evans he then asked what medical qualifications Christie had and Christie replied that he had trained as a doctor before the war, showing Evans some medical textbooks as proof. Evans, of course, could not read, so much of this was lost on him but Christie went on to say that the 'stuff' he used would kill one person in every ten that took it. Evans said he was not interested and went up to his own flat.

Once inside the top floor flat, Beryl began talking about the same topic, having evidently already either been approached by Christie directly, or having confided in him herself. Evans told her that she was not to have anything to do with such things but Beryl said it was her business, not his, and she would do as she pleased.

On Monday, November 7th, when he came home from work, Beryl told Evans that the arrangements had been made and that Mr Christie was going to carry out the job the following morning. Evans took no notice of it, and did not argue with his wife. The next morning, November 8th, he went off to work as usual, but before he left the flat, Beryl had said, "On your way down tell Mr Christie that everything is alright. If you don't tell him I'll go down and tell him myself." Evans had done as his wife asked.

That evening, when he arrived home, Christie was waiting for Evans and said, "Go on upstairs, I'll come behind you". Evans went into his kitchen and lit the gas, whereupon Christie continued, "It's bad news. It didn't work". Beryl's body lay on the bed, covered with an eiderdown. When Evans pulled this back he saw that she had been bleeding from the mouth and nose and from the 'bottom part', meaning the vagina.

Christie then lit the fire in the kitchen before leaving, saying that he would return after Evans had fed the baby. Later, Christie said that Beryl had died at about 3.00 p.m., the cause being her stomach, which was 'septic poisoned'. Christie then left again, only to return fifteen minutes later to say that he had forced the door of Mr Kitchener's flat so that they could put the body in there temporarily. When Evans asked Christie what he intended to do with Beryl, he replied that he would put her down one of the drains.

There followed some discussion about how they would both get into trouble if the police were called and eventually Evans agreed to let Christie organize both the disposal of the body and someone to take care of Geraldine. The next morning he told Evans that he knew a couple in East Acton who would look after the baby.

On Wednesday, November 9th, Evans got home from work at 5.55 p.m. Christie again met him and said that the couple from East Acton would be over the next day. That night, Evans fed his daughter as usual and the following morning he packed some clothes for her, again on Christie's instructions. The next evening, Christie told Evans that the couple had been and that Geraldine was being well looked after. Asked about Beryl's body, Christie confirmed that he had put it down the drain.

Later that same night, Evans went to his mother's house at 11 St Mark's Road and told her that Beryl and the baby had gone away to Brighton for a holiday. As Beryl originally came from that seaside town, and her family still lived there, this was a most plausible excuse. On the Friday, November 11th, Evans sold his furniture to a shop in Portobello Road but was told that it would not be picked up until the following Monday. That Sunday, Evans also arranged to sell his wife's clothing as rags.

Monday, November 14th arrived and Evans started the day by ripping up his wife's clothes and the eiderdown and blankets. A man called at 9.00 a.m., and took these away in two sacks. At 3.00 p.m., the furniture van arrived, cleared all the items and paid him £40. The few items that were left, including vases, a clock, some dishes, the baby's clothes and the pram, were given to Christie.

There was now nothing to keep Evans in London so he packed his suitcase and headed for Paddington, where he deposited the case in the left luggage. He then went to the pictures and a pub before picking up the case just after midnight and catching the 12.55 a.m. train to Cardiff. Finally, after arriving at Merthyr, he went to his aunt's house at 93 Mount Pleasant, where he had been ever since.

Almost as soon as this statement was complete, Evans began telling the police fresh stories, which cast doubt over the validity of some of his previous testimony. He admitted that Christie had not moved Beryl's body by himself, saying that he had heard him 'puffing and blowing' on the stairs and gone to help him. It was clear that Timothy Evans was a stranger to the truth but before progress could be made, Beryl's body had to be found. The London police were contacted again and officers, including Detective Inspector James Neil Black and Chief Inspector George Jennings, went back to 10 Rillington Place.

In fact, there had been a major oversight in the search of the dark house at Rillington Place. Outside, in the yard at the back, was a wash-house. Chief Inspector Jennings asked if this had been searched and was informed that it had been. What actually transpired is that some of the officers thought it belonged to the property next door and others genuinely believed that it had already been examined. As a result, the wash-house lay untouched as the police searched the rest of the property.

On December 1st, Evans was questioned again. Now he gave more information, which further diluted what he had said in his second statement. Evans admitted that he had returned to London from Wales, going down to the capital on November 21st and returning to Merthyr on the 23rd.

It was on Friday, December 2nd, that the breakthrough came. Early that morning, the police took statements from Ethel Christie. Soon afterwards, Inspector Black and Detective Sergeant Corfield travelled up to Wales to escort Evans back

The wrapped body of Beryl Evans on a mortuary slab (Public Record Office Ref. No. CRIM 1/2035)

285

to London. Later still, at 11.50 a.m., Detective Chief Superintendent Barratt and Chief Inspector Jennings returned to Rillington Place and finally investigated the wash-house.

The two officers found a large package, wrapped up in a green table cover and a blanket and tied very tightly with a sash-cord. The parcel had been hidden behind some timber, underneath the sink. Chief Inspector Jennings removed the timber and pulled out the package which, when it was cut open, was shown to contain the doubled-over body of a woman with her head shoved down between her feet. Behind the door, which opened inwards, hidden behind some more timber, lay the body of a baby girl. She was clothed in a pink woollen coat, a flannelette frock, vest and white plastic knickers. Beryl and Geraldine Evans had been found.

It was 9.35 p.m. by the time Evans and the escorting police officers arrived at Paddington. From there, Evans was taken to Notting Hill police station where in one of the offices, Evans was shown the rope, wrappings and clothing which had been removed from the two bodies. The prisoner was then cautioned again and made a brief statement, which was taken down in writing. This statement began, "She was incurring one debt after another and I could not stand it any longer, so I strangled her with a piece of rope and took her down to the flat below the same night, whilst the old man was in hospital.

"I waited till the Christies downstairs had gone to bed, then took her to the wash-house after midnight. This was on the Tuesday, 8th November. On Thursday evening after I came home from work I strangled my baby in our bedroom with my tie and later that night I took her down into the wash house after the Christies had gone to bed."

At this point, Evans began to cry and after he had signed this third statement sobbed, "It is a great relief to get it off my chest. I feel better already. I can tell you the cause that led up to it." Chief Inspector Jennings asked Evans if he wished to make a further statement explaining exactly what had taken place and Evans agreed. This fourth statement was the longest yet, not being completed until 11.15 p.m.

In this final statement, Evans began by outlining his work history and then referring to Beryl getting into debt. Eventually, the rent fell into arrears and Evans told his wife that if she did not improve, he would leave her. She countered this with "You can leave any time you like". A number of arguments followed during the early part of November. These culminated in one on November 8th, when she started yet another row when he came in at night. Evans admitted hitting Beryl across the face but she then hit him back, so in a fit of temper he grabbed a piece of rope from a chair and strangled her with it.

That night, before 10.00 p.m., Evans carried Beryl downstairs to the kitchen of Mr Kitchener's flat before returning to his own flat and making the baby some food. After putting Geraldine to bed, Evans waited for the rest of the house, meaning of course the Christies, to go to bed. He then went down to Mr Kitchener's flat, wrapped Beryl's body in a blanket and table cloth before going downstairs and opening the back door. Beryl was then carried to the wash-house and dumped underneath the sink.

The next day, after seeing that Geraldine was fed, Evans went to work as normal, as he did on Thursday, the 10th. He left his job on that day and at night, when he got home, he strangled Geraldine with a necktie before putting her body in the wash house too.

After making this statement, Evans was taken down to the cells for the night. The next morning, December 3rd, he was charged with the murder of his wife. Eventually, on December 15th, he was also charged with the murder of baby Geraldine.

No matter how many murders a prisoner is accused of, in most British trials it is customary for the accused to answer to just one charge. When Timothy Evans appeared at the Old Bailey on January 11th, 1950, before Mr Justice Lewis, he was charged only with the murder of his daughter. During the three-day trial, the case for the prosecution was led by Mr Christmas Humphreys, who was assisted by Mr Henry Elam. Evans' defence lay in the hands of Mr Malcolm Morris.

The early witnesses were all police officers, the first being Chief Inspector Jennings. They were followed by Professor Donald Teare, the pathologist who had performed the post-mortems on both bodies.

Referring first to Beryl Evans, Professor Teare said that death was due to asphyxia caused by strangulation by means of a ligature. There were a series of abrasions on the right side of the throat and another group on the left of the back of the neck. Deep bruising had occurred in the muscles on the right side of the voice box and small haemorrhages were detected on the chin and in the lungs.

At the time of her death, Beryl was four months pregnant but there was no evidence of any interference with that pregnancy. Turning to the rest of the body, Professor Teare reported a bruise on the inner left thigh, four inches above the knee, and another on the inner side of the left calf, just below the knee. These, along with some bruising in the lower part of the back wall of the vagina, were consistent with forced sexual intercourse.

Geraldine Evans still had a tie fastened extremely tightly around her neck when she was found, and Evans had previously identified this tie as belonging to him. There were no other signs of injury and the cause of death was again asphyxia caused by strangulation.

The next two witnesses were even more damaging to Evans' defence. They were Mr and Mrs Christie. Reginald Christie began by outlining the living arrangements at 10 Rillington Place and by confirming that Mr Kitchener had gone into hospital in early November 1949.

Christie recalled that the last time he saw Beryl Evans was at about lunch-time on November 8th. She was going out with the baby at the time. Later that same day, Christie, a noted hypochondriac, went to the doctor's and by the time he returned home, it was about 7.00 p.m. At midnight, after he and his wife had retired for the night, he was startled by a loud bang. This was followed by the sound of something heavy being moved. He looked out through the window to see if there was anyone outside but there was no one there.

287

The next evening, Christie saw Evans at some time between 10.30 p.m. and 11.00 p.m. Christie was at his bedroom door as Evans came in. Ethel called out that she would put the hall light on so that he could see better but Evans shouted back that he could manage. Ethel then asked about his wife and baby to which Evans replied, "I am by myself. They have gone away to Bristol."

On Thursday, November 10th, Christie saw Evans at 7.00 p.m. Evans knocked at his door and said, "I've packed my job up. I had a row with the guvnor. I've been down to Brighton and brought three customers' orders back and he played hell with me. I told him that if he could find anyone better for the job to give me my cards." He then announced that he would be going to Bristol in a few days as he had the chance of a job there.

On Friday the 11th, Evans told Christie that he had arranged to sell his furniture. Three days later, on Monday the 14th, Christie saw a van arrive and take the furniture away. Later, Evans showed him a roll of banknotes and fifteen minutes later still, he left Rillington Place with a large suitcase. This was the last that Christie saw of Evans until Wednesday, November 23rd, when Evans called again at between 5.30 p.m. and 5.45 p.m. Christie greeted him with, "What on earth are you doing here? I thought you were in Bristol." Evans replied, "I went to Bristol and I've been to Cardiff, Birmingham and Coventry and back to Cardiff and I couldn't find a job". He then said that Beryl had walked out on him, taking Geraldine with her.

Ethel Christie confirmed much of what her husband had said. She referred to the loud bang that woke her up early on November 9th. She was also able to confirm most of the other conversations Reginald had had with Evans. Talking of the wash-house she pointed out that the boiler there was broken and as such, she had not used it in some time. In fact, the tenants only ever used it for the water tap in there.

Violet Gwendoline Lynch lived at 93 Mount Pleasant, Merthyr Tydfil, and was Evans' aunt. She testified that he came to her house on November 15th, saying that his wife and child had gone to Brighton for a holiday. He stayed at her home until November 21st, when he returned to London. On the 23rd, he was back and said that he had seen Beryl but she had walked out of their flat and had left the baby in bed, so he had given Geraldine to some people from Newport to look after.

A day or so later, Violet wrote to Evans' mother in London and the reply, received on November 30th, stated that there had been no sign of Beryl or Geraldine for the past month. Evans claimed that his mother was telling lies but he then refused to eat his breakfast and went into Merthyr, where he walked into the police station and gave himself up.

The next witness was Constable Evans, who had been the officer the prisoner first spoke to in Merthyr police station. He was followed by Detective Inspector James Neil Black, who had charge of Evans as he was escorted from the police station at Notting Hill to the West London Magistrate's Court on December 3rd. Evans had said, "There is something I meant to tell you Mr Black". Evans was reminded that he was under

Timothy Evans arriving back in London under police escort. Evans was hanged in March 1950 for the murder of his daughter, Geraldine (Popperfoto)

caution but continued, "After I killed my wife, I took her wedding ring from her finger and sold it to Samuel's at Merthyr for five shillings". Though Evans did not know it at the time, officers in Merthyr had already recovered that ring from Samuel's Ltd of 119 High Street.

The jury retired on January 13th and had little trouble in deciding that Evans was guilty of murder. An appeal against the death sentence was dismissed on February 20th and just over two weeks later, on Thursday, March 9th, 1950, Evans was hanged at Pentonville by Albert Pierrepoint and Syd Dernley.

There the case would have rested but for the arrest and conviction of John Reginald Halliday Christie, for murder, in 1953, and his execution, also at Pentonville, on July 13th of that year. It is true that Christie was a mass murderer, a strangler by means of a ligature and that he confessed to the murder of Beryl Evans. A campaign for a pardon for Evans started in earnest, gaining momentum through the efforts of Ludovic Kennedy and his book, *10 Rillington Place* (London: Victor Gollancz Ltd, 1961). A subsequent enquiry decided that Evans was innocent of the charge that had cost him his life and a Royal pardon was granted on October 18th, 1966. Conversely, though, there is a strong possibility that Timothy Evans did indeed kill his wife and his daughter.

Those who argue for Evans' innocence propose that Christie, who had already murdered at least two women by this time, and who would go on to claim many more victims, did indeed offer to abort Beryl and, using his infamous gassing technique, killed her and raped her. This scenario would therefore suggest that in his many statements to the police, Evans was telling more of the truth in his second Merthyr Tydfil statement.

The trouble with this is that in that document Evans said, amongst other things, that Beryl had bled from 'the bottom part' and that Christie had moved Beryl's body, though later Evans amended this latter comment by admitting that he had assisted Christie. The post-mortem showed no attempt at abortion and no bleeding from the vagina. Furthermore, when a second post-mortem was carried out, once Christie's infamy was assured, no traces of carbon monoxide poisoning were found. Allied to this, there are two statements which show, quite clearly, that Evans was apparently dragging something around at midnight on November 8th. True, one of those statements came from Christie himself but the other was from Ethel Christie and it is unlikely that she would have been prepared to lie for her husband. Ethel treated Christie with disdain and contempt and would never have allowed him to tell her what to say. There is also the fact that the post-mortem photographs, preserved in the Public Record Office in London, show that Beryl had been subject to some violence before she died. Violence was certainly not Christie's hallmark.

There are, however, other problems even if we assume that Evans did indeed kill his wife and child. If this were the truth, then the fourth statement, the second one made at Notting Hill, would be nearer the mark. In this he actually refers to moving his wife's body on November 8th, which would fit in with Mr and Mrs Christie being disturbed by a loud thud. Evans then goes on to say that he placed the body in the wash-house that same night. This is highly unlikely since there were workmen in the house from October 31st and they used that same wash-house to store their tools. They might well have missed the parcelled up body of Beryl Evans but it is more likely that the body was not placed there until after they finished work, which was on November 11th, the Friday. Beryl's body may have remained in Mr Kitchener's flat all that time.

No one will ever know the truth of what went on in 10 Rillington Place. If Timothy Evans did not kill his daughter, then he deserved to be pardoned. If, however, he did kill Beryl, and Geraldine, then there is still an argument that he should not have hanged. Medical examinations showed that he had an I.Q. of just sixty-five and doctors believed him to be an inadequate psychopath with schizoid traits. He may well have been a brutal killer but on medical grounds alone, Evans did not deserve to face death at the end of a rope.

Suggestions for further reading:

John Eddowes, *The Two Killers of Rillington Place* (London: Warner Books, 1995).

Ludovic Kennedy, *10 Rillington Place* (London: Victor Gollancz, 1961).

37

Patrick Turnage

Hanged at Durham, Tuesday, November 14th, 1950
For the murder of Julia Beesley, at Stockton-on-Tees

O N Friday, July 28th, 1950, a ship, the SS Absalom, docked at Billingham Reach on the river Tees. One of the men on board that vessel was a thirty-one-year-old merchant seaman named Patrick Turnage, whose home was South Africa, but who had actually been born in India. Though Turnage could not have known it at the time, he had just reached his last ever port of call.

The following day, July 29th, in the nearby town of Stockton, seventy-three-year-old Julia Beesley was putting on her make-up, so that she could go out. Her son, Robert Arthur Beesley, watched as she did. He knew that his mother liked to hit one or two of the local pubs on a Saturday evening, and in all probability would come home late. Still, as long as she enjoyed herself, what did it matter?

Robert was also out that evening but by 8.30 p.m., he was back home, at 18 Northbourne Road. His mother was not home yet, but there was nothing unusual in that. No doubt she'd get back once the pubs were shut. Robert noticed that the newspaper had been taken out of the letterbox and, since it was usually delivered at some time between 5.00 p.m. and 5.30 p.m., it was safe to assume that Julia had only gone out after it had been delivered.

After a while, Robert went out again, finally returning to Northbourne Road at 10.40 p.m. Still there was no sign of Julia but Robert, as yet unconcerned, took himself off to bed. The following morning, though, Julia Beesley had still not come home. She had never stayed out all night before and Robert began to worry. When she still had not put in an appearance by 11.00 a.m. on that Sunday, July 30th, Robert took his concerns to the police.

In fact, it was not the police who found Julia Beesley. John Thomas Walker was a charge-hand and he was cycling along a track at 1.40 p.m. that same Sunday when he saw what looked like a leg, sticking out of some grass. Walker dismounted from his bicycle and went to take a closer look. What he had seen was indeed a human leg and from the stocking, Walker could see that it was a woman. Without disturbing the scene, Walker climbed back onto his bicycle and peddled off to fetch the police.

Detective Constable James William Dawson arrived on the scene at 3.00 p.m. As part of his investigation, Dawson interviewed a number of sailors who were on board ships tied up at the jetty. At 5.20 p.m., Dawson boarded the Absalom, and one of the first people he saw there was Patrick Turnage.

Turnage approached Dawson and asked if he were a policeman. Dawson said that he was whereupon Turnage remarked, "I may be able to help you about that woman last night. I had a woman here at the boat last night, but she left and I looked for her for a long time, but I couldn't find her. I have her handbag here. It has about seventeen shillings in. She threw it on the deck from the jetty."

Upon hearing this, Dawson accompanied Turnage to his cabin and collected the brown plastic handbag, which Turnage took out of a drawer. Items inside confirmed that it had belonged to the dead woman and as a result, Turnage was taken to the police station at Billingham, where he was interviewed by Detective Chief Inspector John George Rowell.

It was 6.45 p.m. when Rowell saw Turnage. The latter made a brief statement outlining that the dead woman had accompanied him to the docks, but had then been unable to get on to the ship and so had stormed off in disgust. He had gone to look for her but failed to find any trace of her. Later, though, at 8.55 p.m., Turnage suddenly said, "I have been thinking about what actually happened along the road, but I was too scared. Don't think I didn't want to tell you."

Chief Inspector Rowell cautioned Turnage and asked him if he wished to make a formal written statement. Turnage agreed and then told a new version of what had happened the previous night.

Turnage's statement began by outlining the fact that his father now lived in Calcutta, but that he had emigrated to Durban in South Africa three years before. The ship on which he worked, the Absalom, had left London on July 24th, sailed to Middlesborough to take on lumber and had then arrived at Billingham on July 28th.

The next day, July 29th, Turnage was shopping in Middlesborough from 3.00 p.m. until 5.00 p.m. He then returned to his ship but went out again at 8.00 p.m., first for two or three pints in the Station Hotel at Billingham, before catching the bus into Stockton. Once there, Turnage visited another pub, the Blue Post, where he consumed four more pints of beer. From there he went on to another pub, whose name he could not recall, before returning to the Blue Post where he talked to the girl pianist and arranged to meet her after she had finished work. By the end of the night, Turnage had drunk eight or nine pints.

Once the Blue Post had closed, Turnage waited outside for the lady pianist but after half an hour, she had not shown so he knocked on the door. A man opened it and told him that the girl had left fifteen minutes before.

Deciding that he'd better go back to his ship, Turnage was making his way to Billingham when he saw a woman and asked her where he might catch a bus. This woman was Julia Beesley and she told him that all the buses had stopped by this time, but they fell into conversation and at one point he said that he was from a ship and Julia asked if he would show her over it. Turnage replied that he would need his captain's permission and even if he got it, there were no lights on board so she would not be able to see much. Julia, though, was not to be put off and continued asking until finally, Turnage gave in.

Since there were no buses, it made sense to hail a taxi. This took them to the wharf where Turnage paid the fare. He and Julia then walked to the gangway of the ship, which was nothing more than a ladder. Turnage had no trouble in boarding but Julia could not get across more than a couple of the rungs. She grew frightened and went back to the shore.

The ship's donkeyman was on deck and he offered to give Julia a hand but she was annoyed by now and threw her handbag at him. The bag fell onto the deck as Julia shouted to Turnage that she was going home. Turnage replied that he needed to go to the toilet first, but once he had been, he would walk her back to the main road. Three or four minutes later, Turnage was back on deck, but there was no sign of Julia so he walked up to the road to see if he could find her.

It was at this point that Turnage's story changed from his original statement, in which he had claimed that he had never seen Julia again. He now admitted that he had caught up with her, at a building just past the railway line. They had walked together, towards the road and he noticed that she was carrying something. Turnage asked what it was and Julia replied that it was her drawers and that she wanted him to have sex with her and pay her £1.

Turnage said no, and pointed out to Julia that she was old enough to be his mother. At this, she started to pull at his tie and the front of his trousers so he pushed her away and told her to go home. He turned to go back to his ship but Julia followed him and started calling him names. Once again he pushed her away but this time she fell back into a ditch. He tried to help her up but she was limp and still.

At first, Turnage thought that Julia had fainted. He looked around for some water, and then went to the watchman's hut for help. There was no one around so he returned to the ditch and tried to lift Julia. She was still not moving so he returned to his ship, too scared to tell anyone what had happened. After considering this statement, Chief Inspector Rowell charged Turnage with murder. He replied, "I did not murder her sir".

The police knew that this would be a very difficult case in which to get a conviction for wilful murder. For that reason, they gathered as much evidence as they could, in order to make such a charge stick.

One of the pubs that Turnage had referred to in his statement was the Station Hotel, Billingham. Thomas Francis Davies was the relief manager at that hostelry. He had seen Turnage in the buffet bar several times between 8.00 p.m. and 9.30 p.m. on the night of July 29th, Turnage asking for cigarettes at one point. Davies had also seen a woman who fitted the description of Julia Beesley, that same night. He had first noticed her at 8.30 p.m., and again at 9.30 p.m, and thought that she might have been slightly drunk.

At no stage did he see Turnage talk to Julia, but he did remember seeing one of his barmaids remonstrating with Julia for accosting men at the bar. Julia then went and sat quietly in the corner of the bar and Davies did not remember seeing her again.

Emily MacDonald was one of the barmaids in the Station Hotel. She did not recall Turnage, but she had seen Julia, not long before closing time. Julia had taken a bottle of beer away with her, leaving minutes before 10.30 p.m. Emily said that Julia did not appear to have had too much to drink.

William Duffy was also at the Station Hotel on July 29th. He was part of a wedding party and arrived at 8.00 p.m. About an hour later, Duffy noticed Turnage who asked him if he should wait to be served by a waitress or just go up to the bar for a drink. A few minutes later, Turnage returned and asked Duffy if this were the Station Hotel. Duffy confirmed that it was and Turnage then mentioned that he had heard that a man might 'get a woman' there. Duffy said that he was in the wrong pub and Turnage then mentioned the Blue Post, which Duffy said was in Stockton.

Turnage's statement had also mentioned the woman pianist at the Blue Post. This was Evelyn Levaine Thorpe, a married woman. She stated that Turnage had come into the pub at about 9.55 p.m., and had sat down next to her. He said that he liked her playing and offered to buy her a drink, which she accepted. Turnage then asked if anyone were taking her home, to which she replied no, adding that she usually stayed after closing time to help wash the glasses.

According to Evelyn, Turnage was the last customer to leave that night. Some time later there was a loud banging on the door. The landlord answered it and said something to someone outside. Evelyn left the pub by another door, at 11.00 p.m.

The evidence thus far showed that finding a woman had been high on Turnage's list of priorities that night. This was confirmed by Henry Biwer, a conductor on the 64 bus, which left Middlesborough at 7.34 p.m. Turnage was on that bus, and asked to be put off at Billingham Reach Wharf. He fell into conversation with Biwer and told him that he was South African. Then he asked Biwer if he knew where he might find a woman and Biwer suggested going to a pub. Later on that same bus journey, Turnage approached a woman who was carrying a bunch of flowers and asked her if he could buy one. She said that she would give him one for free.

Charles Ernest Bainbridge was the taxi driver who had taken Julia and Turnage from Stockton back to the wharf at Billingham. It was some time after 11.10 p.m. when Bainbridge saw Turnage at the rank in High Street, in the company of a short old lady who smelled of drink. As they climbed into the taxi, a couple of men approached and asked Bainbridge if he could take them to South Shields. At this, the woman, Julia, became excited and demanded to know where they were going.

Turnage calmed Julia down but Bainbridge by now had had second thoughts and tried to get Julia out of his cab. He opened the door for her, but she refused to move so eventually he drove them towards the wharf. As the vehicle turned into Church Road, Bainbridge heard Turnage mutter, "You keep quiet. We are going down to the ship."

The fare came to ten shillings, which Turnage paid, even though he complained at the price. Bainbridge pointed out that it was, after all, almost midnight, and Turnage looked at his watch and confirmed that it was 11.50 p.m. The two passengers left the cab and Bainbridge asked them to move out of the way so he could turn around. Julia suddenly demanded to know where the cab was going and Bainbridge replied, "Back to Stockton". "What about me?", muttered Julia and Bainbridge asked Turnage if he should come back later to pick the lady up. Turnage said yes, and mentioned a time of 2.00 a.m., but Julia said that that was too late and eventually a time of 1.30 a.m. was agreed upon. However, as Julia walked away, Turnage put his head into the taxi and said, "Forget about it. She's not going back. She's staying all night."

The watchman on the Absalom had been Charles Bellamy and he told the police that at some time between midnight and 12.30 a.m., he had seen Turnage coming down the gangway. There was a woman on the quay, at the end of the gangway, and she was shouting that she was not going to be drowned. Bellamy pointed out to Turnage that women were not allowed on board but Turnage replied, "You know me watchman".

Soon, the woman started to walk away as Turnage went to his room. Minutes later, Turnage was back on deck and then Bellamy saw him go down on to the quay. He next saw Turnage at about 1.30 a.m., in the mess room. He asked Turnage if he had seen the lady but Turnage said that he had not and then asked Bellamy to make him a cup of tea. After drinking that, Turnage retired to his cabin but not before asking Bellamy to call him at 6.30 a.m., as he wanted to see a morning paper.

Medical evidence would prove crucial in this case, and the post-mortem had been carried out by Dr David Ernest Price, a Consultant Pathologist. An external examination showed that Julia was wearing no knickers, a pair of pale blue ones having been found near her body. There was an earring in her right ear, but none in her left. She wore the remains of a broken necklace.

There were a number of small bruises on the body, including one on the right ear, one on the right side of the jaw, one on the point of the chin and one on the scalp at the back of the head. There were small haemorrhages in the deeper layers of the scalp, and signs of asphyxia including some bruising to the muscles on the right side of the voice box. Death was due to asphyxia, caused by pressure on the neck, but the wounds seen there could have been caused by the necklace. Dr Price confirmed that the pressure necessary to cause death could have come from the tightening and twisting of Julia's clothing around her neck. Some force would have been required and death would have occurred in a minute or two.

The case of the Crown against Turnage was due to be heard on October 28th. It was looking extremely unlikely that a murder charge could be won and most of those involved in the case felt sure that Turnage would escape with manslaughter and a consequent term of imprisonment. Then, on October 25th, just three days before the set date, Turnage asked to see Chief Inspector Rowell.

The meeting took place at Durham prison and Turnage said that it was his intention to plead guilty to the charge. Turnage was advised to see his legal representative but once he had, he again asked to see Rowell and added that he wished to make another statement.

In this new statement, Turnage claimed that on July 30th [sic] he had determined that he was going to do some woman in that night. He had thought of killing a woman for several months and would have done it in London but a favourable opportunity never presented itself. The reason for his hatred of women and his desire for revenge was that he had contracted venereal disease.

Turning to his encounter with Julia he claimed that once they were alone near the wharf he had grabbed her by the throat and squeezed her until she went limp and fell. He waited for a minute but it was clear that she was not dead so he pulled her into a sitting position and squeezed her windpipe with all his strength for three minutes or more. Then he pushed her into the ditch and covered her over with grass. He had hoped that the body would not be found until his ship had sailed. He ended by saying that his previous statement was "...a lot of rubbish and all lies".

The trial did take place on October 28th before Mr Justice Hallett, and despite the best efforts of his barrister, Mr Herbert Shepherd, Turnage insisted on pleading guilty. The judge informed Turnage that he would still call Chief Inspector Rowell to outline what had taken place over the last few days, but after that officer had given evidence, the plea was accepted and Turnage was sentenced to death. The entire proceedings lasted for just seven minutes.

Patrick Turnage had deliberately chosen to die. Whilst in the condemned cell he told prison officers that he simply could not face up to fifteen years in jail and had pleaded guilty in order to avoid that fate. In reality, it is almost certain that the death of Julia Beesley was not a deliberate act and that no murder had been committed.

No appeal was entered and on the morning of Tuesday, November 14th, 1950, Steve Wade and Syd Dernley entered the condemned cell at Durham prison to perform their dread task. There was the briefest flicker of fear on Turnage's face. Then he smiled and stood to face the two men who would end his time in jail.

Dennis Albert Reginald Moore

38

Hanged at Norwich, Thursday, July 19th, 1951
For the murder of Eileen Emily Rose Cullen, at Norwich

DENNIS Moore had first met twenty-year-old Eileen Cullen in June, 1950. There seemed to be an instant attraction between them and before long, this had developed into a love affair.

Eileen, her two sisters, and her parents lived with her grandmother at 16 Buxton Road, Norwich, and it was there, on November 20th, that a party was thrown to celebrate Eileen's twenty-first birthday. At that same party, the young lovers announced that they were going to get engaged. It was this rather sudden declaration that caused Eileen's father, Ronald Charles Cullen, to take Dennis to one side and ask him if Eileen might possibly be pregnant.

Dennis was apologetic but admitted that Eileen had mentioned something along those lines to him already. Ronald reassured the young man by saying that he had no objections to the match but suggested that it might be a good idea to get confirmation. So it was that on December 8th, Eileen and Dennis called at the surgery of Dr Frederick Blake Champion, her family doctor. Here, Eileen announced that she had not had a period since September 28th, and asked for a pregnancy test. The test was done and when Eileen made her second visit to Dr Champion, on December 30th, her suspicions were confirmed. Wedding plans were now made and after some family consultation, the date was set for February 17th, 1951.

Dennis visited Eileen at her home most days, usually around 7.30 a.m., or perhaps a little later, as he was on his way to work. He would call again after work and certainly did so on Saturday, February 3rd, because Dennis, Eileen and her sister, Evelyn, all went out shopping together, not getting back to Buxton Road until around 5.20 p.m. After enjoying a bite to eat together, Dennis and Eileen went back out, at 6.30 p.m., to visit the doctor's again.

It was some time between 7.00 p.m. and 7.30 p.m. by the time the couple arrived at Dr Champion's surgery. They were only there for ten minutes or so, and discussed Eileen's forthcoming confinement, and the arrangements they should make. The lovers then walked off together, to a meadow in Oak Lane, where there was a brick-built cowshed in a field.

Joan Evelyn Harrison and her husband, Bert, were the licensees of the Park House pub and that night, at 8.00 p.m., Joan was busy behind the bar when she saw Dennis Moore come in alone. He seemed to be untidy or dishevelled and wore no overcoat. Walking up to the bar he did not ask for a drink but did buy ten cigarettes. This transaction was witnessed by one of the customers, Charles William Betts. Soon after making his purchase, Moore turned on his heel and left the pub.

Sergeant Thomas Royland was on duty in the police station at 9.50 p.m., when the telephone rang. Answering it and identifying himself, Royland heard a man who identified himself as Dennis Moore. The voice continued, "I have murdered Irene Colman [sic]. I am standing on the island at Catton Grove Road by Woodcock Road. I will stay there until you arrive but please don't tell my people." The line was not very clear and it may well have been that Sergeant Royland misheard the woman's name but after making a careful note of the conversation, Royland asked the caller for his name and address and heard the confirmation "Dennis Moore, 70 Woodcock Road". Royland told Moore to stay where he was and then passed the information on to Detective Constable McClennan and Constable Lines.

When the two officers arrived at the traffic island referred to in the telephone call, they found a young man waiting patiently. Constable John McClennan asked the man if he were Dennis Moore, to which the man replied "Yes. I have strangled my girl Eileen Cullen. I'll show you where she is." Moore then climbed into the police car and directed McClennan along Oak Lane to the meadow that was halfway down the road. Once in the meadow, Moore pointed out the brick hut, which was set back some fifty yards from the road.

"She's in there", said Moore and immediately he began to cry, and ran towards the building. The officers caught up with Moore and stopped him at the door to the hut. A torch was then shone into the hut and the light fell upon the body of a woman. Moore then pushed forward and fell down across the body, repeatedly crying, "I love you..."

Once Moore had been restrained, Constable McClennan made a careful examination of the body. Eileen had a woollen scarf wrapped around her head and covering her face. When this was unwrapped, McClennan saw a tightly knotted silk scarf bound around the neck. Quickly, he untied the knot in case Eileen were still alive. Meanwhile, Constable Lines went for help.

Moore and McClennan were left alone at the hut and the detective constable now cautioned the tearful man and informed him that he would be arrested. Moore replied, "I strangled her with my hands until the blood came out of her mouth and I knotted the scarf around her neck, wrapped my scarf around her face, covered her with my coat. I went to the pub and got some cigarettes and then I rang the police. I knew it was no good running away."

At 10.20 p.m., Dr William Lincoln Horn arrived at the scene and certified that life was extinct. He placed the time of death at sometime between one and two hours previously, indicating that Eileen had died between 8.20 p.m. and 9.20 p.m.

Back at the Thorpe Road police station, Moore made a long written statement in which he began by confirming that he had first met Eileen on June 4th of the previous year, when he and some friends had cycled down to Yarmouth where she and her sisters had also ridden. They had all got on famously, and had cycled home together.

The statement also referred to the first time the couple had had sexual intercourse, Moore claiming that this had taken place in September, once again in October and a couple of times in November. There had been another lovemaking session in January, and that night, Moore had wanted sex again.

Turning to the events of that night, Moore wrote, "After we left the doctor's we went for a walk into a meadow at Old Catton. On the way we were quarrelling because I had suspected her father of having had intercourse with her. She denied this, but would not swear to it on the Bible. She had previously told me that her father had had intercourse with her when she was very young.

"I got very angry with her as we walked along, over this same matter. We went to a brick cattle shed in a meadow and standing up we commenced kissing and cuddling, during which time I asked her again and she said 'No'. I felt I wanted to have intercourse with her very badly. I put my arms around her and squeezed her to me very tightly. The next thing I realised she had fallen to the floor and her mouth was all bleeding. I then realised I had hold of her throat and I just couldn't leave go. After that I took her scarf, put two knots in it and tied it around her neck very tight. I then took my own scarf off and wrapped it around her mouth."

The statement then described how Moore had put his mackintosh over Eileen's body before walking to the pub for his cigarettes and then telephoning the police. Towards the end, though, he again turned to the events inside the hut saying, "When I realised what I had done, I sat in the porchway of the shed and took her lipstick out of her handbag and I wrote with her lipstick 'I love her - goodbye'. I felt like running away but I thought twice and came for the police, because I thought it would be better for me. I never carry a knife about with me, but the knife lying on the table looks like my mother's bread knife. I don't remember taking it to the shed. We had got over our tiff when this happened.

"I can't remember putting my hands around her throat. All I know is I had them tightly around her throat when she fell to the floor. I couldn't leave go. I loved her too much. I wouldn't have hurt her, not for anything in the world." This statement, admission of guilt though it was, made no reference to the fact that Eileen's throat had also been cut and the bread knife mentioned had been found at the scene of the crime.

Dennis Moore appeared at Norwich, before Mr Justice Parker, on May 31st, 1951. Throughout the two-day trial, the Crown's case was led by Mr John Flowers, who was assisted by Mr Edward Clarke. Moore was defended by Mr F. T. Alpe and Mr Michael Havers.

Despite Moore's admission that he was the person who had killed Eileen, his defence was that he was not responsible for his actions. Crucial to this would be the obtaining of the bread knife used to cut Eileen's throat. If Moore had deliberately taken the knife out with him, then the crime would obviously have been premeditated and he would be guilty of murder. If, however, it could be shown that he had returned home, collected the knife and returned to the hut to inflict further injuries, then the crime might not be premeditated and a defence of insanity would stand more chance of success.

Victor William Sewell was Moore's brother-in-law and he ran a stall on Norwich market. On February 3rd, Sewell was running the stall as usual when, at about 4.10 p.m., Moore, along with Eileen and Evelyn Cullen, came up to return ten shillings he had borrowed from Sewell's father-in-law. The bread knife found in the hut had been on the stall that afternoon and Gerald Moore, the prisoner's brother, who worked on the stall, had been told to put everything away, whilst Moore was there. The knife had been used to clean some celery and Sewell said that he certainly had not taken it with him that night.

Victor was living with the Moore family at 70 Woodcock Road and was at home that night at 8.00 p.m., when Dennis Moore came in alone. He asked his mother for a pencil but she said that she did not have one so he left again. During his brief stay, Mrs Moore had asked her son where Eileen was and Moore had replied, "She's outside".

Gerald Maurice Martin Moore was the prisoner's brother and, on February 3rd, he had been working on Sewell's stall on the market. When he tidied up, Gerald put the bread knife underneath the stall in a box. Dennis was standing close to the box when he was at the stall but Gerald did not see him take the knife. That night, the box was taken back to the family home.

Bessie Moore, the prisoner's mother, seemed to settle the subject of the knife when she told the court that it had certainly been in her house on the evening of February 3rd. She had used it to prepare some food and had put it away again at 7.30 p.m. This seemed to prove that Dennis, returning home at 8.00 p.m., had indeed taken the knife out and then returned to the hut to cut Eileen's throat.

Dr David Hamilton Fulton was the pathologist who conducted the post-mortem on Eileen. He reported extensive bruising around Eileen's right eye and many petechial haemorrhages in both eyes, eyelids and across the forehead. There were a number of superficial cuts in the skin of the neck and a number of abrasions that could have been caused by the bread knife. The cause of death was due to asphyxia, caused by a ligature, and there was no sign of recent sexual intercourse.

Evelyn Rosemary Cullen was one of the dead woman's sisters and had been out shopping with her and Moore on the fateful day. Besides the notepaper that Moore had scrawled his message on, in lipstick, there was also an envelope near the body and this had originally been addressed to Eileen in what looked like a child's hand, and claimed to be from someone named Brian. Evelyn testified that her sister had had an admirer, a twelve-year-old schoolboy who lived opposite, and he sometimes sent affectionate notes to Eileen. This must have been one such missive and as such, might have been in Eileen's handbag at the time of her death.

The defence were suggesting that Moore had not taken the bread knife out with him when he and Eileen had visited the doctor's surgery on February 3rd. Moore claimed that he had acted under some sort of blackout. Was this consistent with his history?

Irene Grace Rambling was one of Moore's ex-girlfriends, who now lived in London, and she testified that after she and Moore had once argued, he had tried to strangle her. The attempt had not been a serious one but Moore had had no memory of it after it was over.

Robert William Rickers had done his National Service with Moore and he told the court of an occasion when they had been stationed at Colchester. Moore had been play-fighting with another soldier, named Baxter. After some high-spirited fun, Moore had become very excited and suddenly grabbed hold of Baxter's throat. Had other men not pulled Moore off he might well have killed him, and yet they had been friendly just moments before.

Moore had been examined in prison by Dr John V. Morris, who said that there appeared to be an unreasoned jealousy of his prospective father-in-law, Ronald Cullen. This had probably been brought on by the constant rejection of Moore's sexual advances towards Eileen, who, according to Moore, had indicated that she found the sexual act repellent. This sexual rejection and frustration could easily lead Moore to periods of uncontrollable anger.

Despite this evidence, which showed that the crime was almost certainly not premeditated and that Moore had a history of violence accompanied by memory blackouts, the jury found that he was indeed guilty of murder and he was sentenced to death.

An appeal was heard on July 2nd, before the Lord Chief Justice, Lord Goddard, and Justices Hilbery and Ormerod. The grounds for the appeal were that Moore was not guilty of murder due to his mental state. However, as the defence had not proved insanity during the original trial, the grounds for the appeal were in effect superfluous, so the case was dismissed within five minutes. On Thursday, July 19th, 1951, Moore, who was still only twenty-two, was hanged at Norwich prison.

<table>
<tr><td>

39

</td><td>

Mahmood Hussein Mattan

Hanged at Cardiff, Wednesday, September 3rd, 1952
For the murder of Lily Volpert, at Cardiff

</td></tr>
</table>

T HE general outfitter's shop at 203/204 Bute Street was well-known in Cardiff. Run by forty-one-year-old Lily Volpert, the premises officially opened for business each day at 9.00 a.m., and closed at 8.00 p.m. Lily, though, would often stay open longer, for she also sold cigarettes and acted as a pawnbroker.

On the night of Thursday, March 6th, 1952, there were actually four people in the living room at the back of Lily Volpert's shop. In addition to Lily herself, there was her sister, Doris Miara, Doris' ten-year-old daughter, and Lily's mother, Fanny Volpert. It was eight o'clock but, as usual, the shop door still had not been locked for the night. It therefore came as no surprise when the shop bell rang and Lily got up to see to her customer. As Lily left the living room, Doris glanced after her sister and, looking through the connecting door, saw a tall coloured man waiting to be served, inside the shop.

William James Archbold lived a little further up Bute Street, at number 199. He walked past Lily's shop at 8.20 p.m., and was surprised to see that the lights were still on and that the premises were apparently still open. Even for Lily, this was rather late but nevertheless opportune since William found that he needed some cigarettes.

Going inside the shop, William stood for a couple of minutes, waiting for someone to come through from the back to serve him. When no one appeared, he tapped on the counter but still no one came to attend to him. Frustrated, William turned to leave. It was only then, as he glanced to the right, that he saw why he had been ignored. Lily Volpert lay on the shop floor, her throat slit from ear to ear. Without waiting another moment, William Archbold ran to fetch the police.

The nearest police station was on the corner of Bute Street and Maria Street, so William did not have to run far. His arrival at the station was logged at 8.28 p.m. by Sergeant Cecil Walsh, who listened to William's story before going to the shop, accompanied by Constable John Davies.

The two police officers noted that the front door to the shop was open a couple of inches. Going inside they saw Lily's body and a trail of blood running from where she now lay, towards a recess near the stock room. A second blood trail led to the shop door

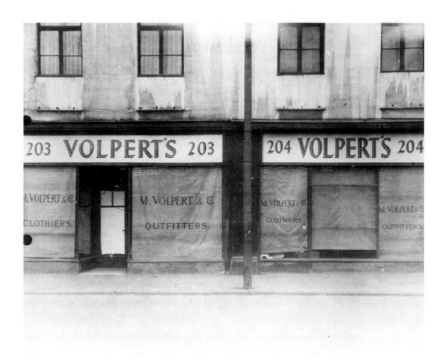

The shop in Bute Street, Cardiff, where Lily Volpert was murdered on March 6th, 1952 (Public Record Office Ref. No. ASSI 84/135)

itself. Only now did Sergeant Walsh and Constable Davies go into the living quarters at the back of the shop, where they found the rest of the Volpert family completely unaware of what had happened to Lily. None of them had heard any argument or struggle, but in due course, Doris Miara was able to show that the motive for this terrible crime had been robbery. An amount between £100 and £120 was missing from the shop till.

Other police officers were soon on the scene and by 9.30 p.m., Dr Andrew Henry Mitchell had arrived. He made an initial examination of Lily's body and noted a deep cut in the throat which ran from below the centre of the chin right around to the back of the neck on the right side. There were three other cuts, each only about an inch long, and about half an inch apart. The blood trails suggested to Dr Mitchell that Lily had been attacked towards the rear of the shop and had somehow managed to drag herself to where she now lay.

Doris Miara reported her sighting of the coloured man who had come into the shop just after 8.00 p.m. It now became imperative to find this man and therefore, early inquiries concentrated on the numerous lodging houses in and around Bute Street. Many of these had large numbers of foreign clients and quite a few were coloured. So it was that as part of the initial investigation, Detective Sergeant David Morris and

306

Detective Constable Lavery called at one such lodging house, situated at 42 Davis Street, at 10.25 p.m., that same night.

The proprietor of the house in Davis Street was Ernest Leonard Harrison, who informed Morris and Lavery that he had three tenants who might possibly fit the description of the wanted man. These were Lloyd Williams, a Jamaican, Mahmood Hussein Mattan, a Somali, and a gentleman named James Monday. Sergeant Morris said he wished to speak to all three men and was told which rooms they occupied.

The first door that Morris knocked upon was that of the middle room on the ground floor, the room that Mattan occupied. From within a voice called out "Who is there?" and Morris identified himself as a police officer. Immediately, the door was opened and Mattan invited the two officers into his room.

The questioning was routine and Mattan was asked to account for his movements earlier that night. He explained that he had been to see a film about the Korean War, which had been followed by a second feature, a cowboy film. The room was then searched but nothing of significance was found. There was no cache of money and no weapon that might have inflicted Lily Volpert's wounds. During this search, however, Mattan became rather excitable and shouted, "What are you looking for? Why do you come to my room? Have you a warrant?"

The other two lodgers were spoken to later and since Indian hemp had been found in Lloyd Williams' room, he was arrested for that offence. As the police escorted Williams from the house, Mattan stood next to James Monday and remarked, "That's the man they are looking for".

The day after the murder, Friday, March 7th, Ernest Harrison told Mattan that he would have to vacate his room. Mattan appeared to ignore this request and started talking instead about the murder of Lily Volpert, saying again that it must have been Lloyd Williams who had committed the crime. This fascination with the murder was reported back to the police and led to Sergeant Morris returning to Davis Street in order to speak to Mattan for a second time.

When he was spoken to, Mattan denied saying anything to Mr Harrison about the crime but was, nevertheless, asked to go to the police station to make a written statement. Mattan said that he would be happy to oblige.

That statement was timed at 10.45 a.m., on March 7th. The entire document took just ten minutes to dictate. It began, "I am at present unemployed and reside at 42 Davis Street, Cardiff.

"On the evening of Thursday the 6th March 1952 I went to the Central cinema at about half past four and came out at half past seven. After coming out of the cinema I went straight to my lodgings at 42 Davis Street, and I went in the front room to talk to Mr Harrison. I later went to bed.

"When I left the cinema I went along Bridge Street, past the public baths, to Adam Street. I have not been down Bute Street since last Sunday [March 2nd]. I did not go down there last night.

307

"I was in the cinema on my own. I did not speak to anyone on the way home. I was wearing a black hat, fawn mackintosh and carrying an umbrella when I went to the cinema last evening."

This statement would, of course, be easy to check. The police first spoke to Ernest Harrison. If he confirmed that Mattan was back at Davis Street, talking to him, soon after 7.30 p.m., then Mattan could not possibly be involved in the murder of Lily Volpert. Unfortunately, Mr Harrison put the time of Mattan's appearance at closer to 9.00 p.m. He had come into the house and walked into the front room, where Mr Harrison was lying ill in bed. James Monday had also been there and when he was interviewed, he too said that it was well after 7.30 p.m. when Mattan came in, though he put the time at somewhere between 8.30 p.m. and 8.45 p.m. Furthermore, both men thought that Mattan was unusually quiet and not his usual self.

The police decided to investigate Mattan's movements more closely. In his statement he had mentioned walking down Adam Street on his way home from the cinema. Margaret Barry ran a general store at 4 Adam Street and when she was interviewed she said that she knew Mattan well as a regular customer. He called into her shop most days to buy his cigarettes and she recalled that he had been in on March 6th. It was about 7.30 p.m., and Margaret was just getting ready to visit a friend of hers who lived in Hodges Row. Mattan asked her for a packet of Players but she told him that she did not have any left in stock and he left empty-handed.

Thus far, all the evidence against Mattan was circumstantial. He was tall and coloured and lived near the shop. He had been seen not too far away, in Adam Street, at 7.30 p.m., asking for cigarettes. Might he then have walked on to Lily Volpert's shop to buy some from her and then taken the opportunity to rob and kill her? It was then that a vital witness came forward to put Mattan at the scene of the crime.

When Harold Cover first spoke to the police he said that he had been outside Lily Volpert's shop at around the time that the crime must have been committed. Mr Cover reported that he had seen two coloured men standing outside the shop. One had a gold tooth and a scarred face whilst the other was over six feet tall. This was not significant because neither description fitted Mattan. Later, however, Mr Cover amended his story and said that he had seen a group of coloured people, who might have been Maltese, standing near the shop. As he walked on, Mr Cover said that he saw yet another coloured man walk from the doorway of the shop, pass the group of Maltese and speak to him. That man was Mahmood Hussein Mattan.

Mattan had claimed that he had not walked down Bute Street on the night of the murder but Harold Cover's evidence put him there at the time of the attack. The police, though, still did not have enough evidence to charge him but such concerns were taken out of their hands on March 11th when Mattan stole a raincoat from a company called J. J. Woodford Limited. He was arrested on that charge and appeared before the magistrates on March 15th.

308

Meanwhile, other witnesses had been traced and spoken to. Two employees of the Central cinema had been interviewed. The commissioner, Charles Alfred Reginald Jones, said that he had come on duty at 3.30 p.m., on March 6th. It was some fifteen minutes later that Mattan, a regular customer, came into the cinema. Jones, however, had not seen Mattan leave, though he admitted that there had been a large crowd that night and he might easily have missed him.

Kenneth Gerrard Powell was the assistant manager of the cinema and he confirmed that there were two features on the night of the murder. The first was called "Steel Helmet" and was about the Korean War. The other was a western, "Outlaws of the Rio Grande".

More important testimony came from Abdul Monaf, who lodged at 34 Angelina Street. He and others often played cards with Mattan and he told the police that on the night of March 8th, Mattan had played poker and lost £7.

There were other signs too that Mattan had suddenly come into money. Hector Macdonald Cooper was the chief security officer at the Somerton Park greyhound track. There had been complaints made about Mattan trying to borrow money from other punters and Cooper had warned him that if he persisted, he would be asked to leave. On March 7th, the night after the murder, Mattan was back at the track and apparently flush with cash.

May Gray was another witness who claimed to have seen Mattan with a wad of banknotes. Mrs Gray ran a second-hand clothing shop from 37 Bridge Street and

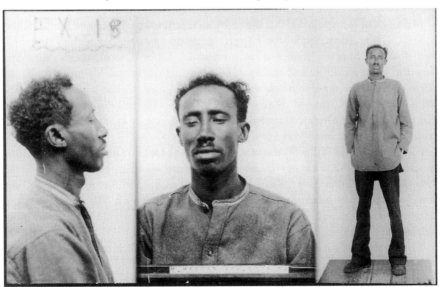

Police photograph of the man accused of Lily Volpert's murder, Mahmood Hussein Mattan (Public Record Office Ref. No. ASSI 84/135)

Mattan had often purchased items from her. He had last called at her shop between 8.30 p.m. and 9.00 p.m. on the night of the murder, but she told him to call back the next day as he did not have any money. In reply Mattan had said, "Yes, I have got money", and showed her a brown wallet stuffed with notes.

As a result of all this testimony, Mattan was charged with murder at 5.00 p.m. on March 16th. His trial opened at Swansea on July 22nd, before Mr Justice Ormerod. The prosecution case was led by Mr H. Edmund Davies, who had two assistants, Mr Alun T. Davies and Mr Bryan Rees. Mattan was defended by Mr T. E. R. Rhys-Roberts and Mr Peter Morgan. The proceedings lasted until July 24th, when Mattan was found guilty and sentenced to death. An appeal was entered and heard on August 19th before Justices Oliver, Devlin and Gorman, who ruled that the verdict was safe. As a result, Mattan was hanged at Cardiff, on September 3rd, as rain drizzled outside.

However, an examination of the evidence of the most damaging witnesses leads to the conclusion that the conviction of Mahmood Hussein Mattan was unsafe.

May Gray said that she had seen Mattan, with a wallet full of money, at some time between 8.30 p.m. and 9.00 p.m. Mattan claimed that he was back in his lodgings by this time and even his landlord and James Monday confirmed that he was certainly there by 9.00 p.m., at the very latest. Under cross-examination, Mrs Gray admitted that she had first heard of the murder the morning after it had taken place, and in her own mind had already connected Mattan to the crime. She did not come forward, though, for five days and much was made of the fact that in those intervening days, the Volpert family had offered a reward for information.

Mrs Gray, of course, denied that she had been motivated by that reward but Mr Rhys-Roberts for the defence produced a sworn statement from another witness, Elizabeth Ann Williams, Mattan's mother-in-law, who stated that at the magistrate's court, Mrs Gray had approached her and said that she was going to say that Mattan had a wallet full of cash and asked her to do the same. Mrs Gray denied this and countered with the claim that Mrs Williams had threatened her. So serious did this dispute become at the trial that Mr Justice Ormerod ordered that the two women be kept apart. Surely all this made Mrs Gray's testimony suspect to say the least?

Returning to Mrs Williams, she was the mother of Laura Mattan, who had married the prisoner in 1947. That union had produced three sons but the couple had parted some eighteen months before. Laura had then gone to live with her mother at 8 Davis Street whilst her estranged husband took lodgings at number 42. The couple remained on good terms, though, attributing their split to the pressures on them from other people who could not accept a mixed-race marriage.

Turning to the night of the crime, Elizabeth Williams testified that Mattan had called at the house at a couple of minutes past 8.00 p.m. He had asked her if she wanted any cigarettes but she had told him that she did not have any money so he went away. Since this was about a mile from the scene of the murder, it meant that if Mrs Williams was telling the truth, and if Mattan was back in his lodgings when James Monday said he was, then Mattan could not have been the killer of Lily Volpert, nor could he have been in May Gray's shop.

The most damaging testimony had come from Harold Cover, since it was he who put Mattan in Bute Street on March 6th and the jury placed a great deal of faith in his evidence. He had, of course, told different stories at different stages. Furthermore, seventeen years after Mattan had been executed, Cover himself was sent to prison for the attempted murder of his eighteen-year-old daughter, Elaina, whose throat he had cut from ear to ear.

There were also witnesses who were never called. One such witness was Esther Williams, who had passed Lily Volpert's shop just after 8.00 p.m. She had seen a tall, coloured man outside the shop and attended an identification parade. She failed to pick out Mattan.

Even more significant was the experience of twelve-year-old Joyce O'Sullivan. She had been sent on an errand to Lily's shop and as she ran there, she saw a coloured man standing in a doorway close by. After the murder, Joyce took her story to the police, who then organized a totally illegal identification parade. This consisted of Joyce sitting in a corridor and one man, Mattan, being brought out for her to look at. Even so, Joyce stated positively that Mattan was not the man she had seen. Details of this parade were not even passed on to the defence.

All of these questions were resolved in 1998 when the case of Mahmood Mattan was passed back to the Appeal Court on the grounds that Harold Cover's evidence had been discredited. Cover's description also matched that of another man, Tehar Gass, another Somali, even down to the fact that Gass had a gold tooth. Gass was charged with a separate murder, that of Granville Jenkins, in 1954. Found guilty but insane, he was subsequently deported to Somalia. The jury at the original trial was also not informed that Gass had been interviewed in connection with the murder and had admitted to being in Lily Volpert's shop on the day that she was killed.

Mahmood Mattan's conviction was quashed on February 4th, 1998. It had taken British justice forty-six years to realize that Mattan was innocent all along. In giving the judgement of the Court of Appeal, the Vice President could only conclude that "capital punishment was not perhaps a prudent culmination for a criminal justice system which is human and therefore fallible".

Derek William Bentley

Hanged at Wandsworth prison, London,
Wednesday, January 28th, 1953
For the murder of Sydney Miles, at Croydon

40

AT 9.15 p.m., on Sunday, November 2nd, 1952, Edith Alice Ware was just tucking her daughter, also named Edith, into bed in the front bedroom of their home at 74 Tamworth Road, Croydon, when she glanced out of the window towards the warehouse that was almost exactly opposite.

As Edith watched, two young men walked from the side passage entrance of Barlow and Parkers' warehouse and stopped at the kerb at the end of the pavement. Suddenly, the shorter of the two climbed over the metal gates at the side. The other one stayed on the pavement for a few moments, looking up and down, before he too climbed over the gates.

Edith called for her husband, John Ware, and told him what she had seen. It seemed reasonable to assume that the two men were intent on breaking into the warehouse so John ran to a nearby telephone box and rang the police.

What precisely happened next has been the subject of much debate over the years. What is certain is that one of the first police officers on the scene was Detective Constable Frederick Fairfax, who arrived at 9.25 p.m., with Constable Norman Harrison and other uniformed officers, in a police van. Fairfax was certainly the first officer to climb over the metal gates at the side of the warehouse. There were signs that someone had recently climbed up a drainpipe in order to gain access to the roof, so Fairfax decided to use the same route.

Once he was on top of the roof, Fairfax saw two young men, some fifteen yards in front of him and to his right. They stood between the roof lights and a lift shaft. As Fairfax approached the two, they backed behind the lift shaft itself but the detective got closer until he was only some six feet away from them. He then announced, "I am a police officer, come out from behind that stack". One of the men replied, "If you want us, fucking well come and get us". Fairfax said "All right", darted behind the stack and grabbed hold of the taller of the two men, pulling him to the opposite side of the lift stack.

The man whom Fairfax had grabbed was nineteen-year-old Derek William Bentley. The smaller man, still free on the roof, was sixteen-year-old Christopher Craig, who was armed with a pistol. For the next half-hour or so, as reinforcements continued to arrive, Craig held off the police, shooting many times in their direction. One of those shots struck forty-two-year-old Police Constable Sydney Miles and killed him. Finally, when Craig ran out of ammunition, he dived off the roof into a greenhouse in a nearby garden, injuring himself, but eventually he was also arrested and both he and Bentley were then charged with murder.

The trial of Bentley and Craig opened at the Old Bailey on December 9th, before the Lord Chief Justice, Lord Goddard. The proceedings lasted three days, during which the prosecution was led by Mr Christmas Humphreys, assisted by Mr John Stuart Bass. Bentley was defended by Mr Frank Cassells whilst Mr Parris represented Craig. The vast majority of the witnesses were serving police officers.

The first witness was Chief Inspector Percy Law, who had taken various photographs of the scene on November 3rd, the morning after Sydney Miles had been killed. These were put in as evidence to assist the jury in visualizing the scene as the other witnesses gave their testimony. To further assist, Constable Bernard Charles Beard produced scale plans of the rooftop and the surrounding streets.

After Edith Ware had told the court what she had seen as she looked out of her daughter's bedroom window, the prosecution called their first major witness, Detective Constable Fairfax. He testified that after he had apprehended Bentley, Craig had darted to the opposite side of the lift stack. Fairfax had then moved around the stack with a view to arresting Craig as well, at which point Bentley broke away from him and shouted, "Let him have it Chris". Immediately there was a loud report, a flash and something struck Fairfax in the right shoulder. The force caused him to spin around and fall to the floor but he was soon up and saw the two men moving away from him, one to the right and one to the left.

Rushing at one man, Fairfax struck him with his fist and knocked him to the ground. A second shot rang out as Fairfax saw that it was Bentley he had hit. He then dragged Bentley in front of him, as cover, before pulling him behind one of the roof lights. Fairfax then rubbed his hands over Bentley's clothing, believing that he too might have a gun. Though there was no revolver, Fairfax did find a knuckleduster in Bentley's right hand coat pocket, took it and put it on. In Bentley's right-hand breast pocket, Fairfax also found a knife at which point Bentley commented, "That's all I've got guvnor. I have not got a gun."

Fairfax informed Bentley that it was his intention to work him around the roof to the doorway in the lift stack. Bentley commented "He'll shoot you", but Fairfax pushed Bentley in front of him to the doorway and then behind the wall so that they would be out of Craig's line of fire.

From somewhere in the darkness behind him Fairfax heard Constable McDonald's voice call out, "I have tried to climb the drainpipe, but can't make it. Can you help me up the last bit?" Fairfax then went to the edge of the roof and assisted McDonald over the last few feet of his climb, pulling him on to the flat roof. The two officers then returned to the lift stack where they both held Bentley.

314

Barlow and Parker Limited, Tamworth Road, Croydon. It was on the roof of these premises that PC Sydney Miles was shot dead on November 2nd, 1952 (PA/News)

According to Fairfax, McDonald then asked him what sort of gun Craig had. Before he could reply, Bentley said "He's got a Colt .45 and plenty of bloody ammunition for it too". It was then that the door in the lift stack burst open outwards and, from inside the stairwell, other officers called out to Fairfax who told them that he was around to their right and the man with the gun was to their left.

As soon as this information had been passed on, Fairfax saw Constable Miles jump from the doorway. Another shot rang out and Miles fell to the floor. Fairfax dashed out to assist him as yet another shot was fired. Fairfax fell to one knee and grabbed hold of Miles' shoulder as Constable McDonald grabbed the stricken man's legs. They then dragged Miles behind the lift stack wall but upon examining him, found that he was already dead.

It was then that Constable Harrison jumped out of the stairwell and ran around the wall to where Fairfax and McDonald still held Bentley. The decision was made to move Bentley downstairs and Fairfax went first, the other officers pushing Bentley after him. As he reached the stairwell, Bentley called out "They're taking me down Chris".

At the bottom of the stairs, Fairfax handed Bentley over to Inspector Bodley before collecting a police gun and going back onto the roof. At the top of the stairs, Fairfax called out "Drop your gun. I also have a gun." To this, Craig replied "Come on then copper, let's have it out".

Fairfax leapt from the doorway onto the roof, and Craig fired again. Running in a semi-circular direction, Fairfax ran towards Craig, firing twice as he did so. It was then that Craig vanished over the side of the roof and when Fairfax looked over the edge he saw that Craig had crashed down into a greenhouse. Other officers arrested Craig as Fairfax was taken to Croydon Hospital so that his wound could be treated.

Fairfax was treated by Doctor Nicholas Jaswon, who reported that the officer came in at 10.30 p.m., on November 2nd. He had a searing wound over the skin of his right shoulder but there was no fracture of the collar-bone. The bullet had passed across his skin but had not penetrated it, and was actually found at the back of his trousers, caught in the top of his braces.

The next witness was Dr David Haler, who had performed the post-mortem on Sydney Miles. He said that Miles had been a well-built, muscular man in perfect health. There were two wounds in his head. One, at the inner side of his right eyebrow, was a wound of entry of a large calibre bullet. The other was an exit wound, slightly to the right and at the back of the head. Death had been virtually instantaneous.

Lewis Charles Nickolls was the Director of the Metropolitan Police Laboratory at New Scotland Yard and he had examined the .45 Colt revolver that Craig had used on the rooftop. The barrel of the gun had been sawn-off but was still in good working order. It had a normal trigger pull but would have been rendered inaccurate by the removal of the barrel. There had been two bullets in the gun which, though struck by the firing pin, had failed to go off.

Doctor Douglas Freebody was a consultant at Croydon General Hospital and he had examined Craig when he was brought in by the police. Craig had sustained a fracture of the dorsal spine at the level of the seventh dorsal vertebrae. There was also a fracture dislocation of the breastbone and a fracture of the lower left forearm.

Constable Fairfax had told the court that the first officer to join him on the roof had been Constable McDonald. The prosecution now called Constable James Christie McDonald to confirm some of what Fairfax had said.

McDonald said that he had arrived at the warehouse at 9.25 p.m. He had travelled in a police car driven by Constable Miles, and they saw a police van arrive at the same time. Constable Fairfax was one of the men in that van and, after climbing over the side gates, McDonald pointed out to Fairfax some wet footprints on a window ledge at the side of one of the drainpipes, indicating that someone had recently climbed up that pipe. Fairfax climbed up that same pipe and pulled himself onto the roof, but when McDonald tried to follow, he found that he could not make the last six feet or so.

Thinking that there might be another way to get on to the roof, McDonald began to climb back down. It was as he did so that he heard someone he now knew to be Bentley shout out, "Let him have it Chris". Two or three shots rang out so he shouted up to Fairfax for help over the last part of the climb, and went back up the pipe. Fairfax did help him over the last few feet and once he was on the roof, McDonald saw his fellow officer with Derek Bentley by the staircase head.

Craig shouted "Come and get it", and another shot was fired. Quickly McDonald dashed behind the staircase wall and grabbed hold of Bentley. Fairfax informed him that he had been shot in the shoulder to which Bentley remarked, "I told the silly bugger not to use it".

Looking around the wall, McDonald saw Craig on the westerly corner of the roof. There was a police officer, Constable Harrison, on a sloping roof near a chimney-stack, and Craig fired twice towards him. McDonald confirmed that Bentley had told them that Craig had a .45 and plenty of ammunition, and soon afterwards, Constable Miles was shot as he ran out of the stairwell.

According to McDonald, they were then joined by Constable Jaggs, who had also climbed up the drainpipe. These three officers then manhandled Bentley downstairs and as they pushed him through the doorway, Bentley shouted "Look out Chris, they're taking me down".

Constable Robert Jaggs testified that as he was climbing up the drainpipe, he heard two shots ring out. Once he reached the roof he saw Craig on the westerly corner of the roof.

The flat rooftop of Barlow and Parker Limited, Tamworth Road, Croydon. It was here that Christopher Craig shot and killed PC Sydney Miles. (Public Record Office Ref. No. CRIM 1/2282)

Behind the staircase head were Constables Fairfax and McDonald, the prisoner Bentley and the body of Constable Miles. Another shot was fired and Craig shouted, "Come on you brave coppers. Think of your wives." Jaggs then heard Bentley say, "You want to look out, he will blow your heads off". Soon afterwards, Jaggs helped to push Bentley towards the stairwell but he then stayed at the top of the stairs whilst Fairfax took Bentley down. A few minutes later, Fairfax returned with a gun. Craig fired again and as Fairfax ran out, firing, Jaggs heard a click as if Craig's gun was empty. Craig then backed to the edge of the roof and shouted "Give my love to...", followed by a name which Jaggs missed. He then jumped off the roof and crashed into the greenhouse in the garden below.

Constable Norman Harrison had been one of the officers travelling in the police van with Fairfax, and so was one of the first officers on the scene. Whilst Fairfax was climbing over the gates, Harrison went around into Upper Drayton Place where he climbed over a fence and eventually got on to the roof of a factory at 25 Tamworth Road. From there he climbed down into the garden of number twenty-six, before eventually gaining access to the sloping roof of the warehouse.

Harrison could see Fairfax on the flat roof and saw him take hold of Bentley, who pulled away and shouted "Let him have it Chris". Two shots were fired in quick succession and as Fairfax struggled with his prisoner, Harrison moved along the roof until he saw Craig move towards him and fire at him. A bullet hit the roof somewhere behind him and as Harrison edged back, another shot was fired, this time hitting a chimney-stack. Harrison dropped his torch, which rolled down into the gutter, but fortunately he escaped injury.

Trying a different approach, Harrison then went into the warehouse and up the staircase that led to the roof. Constable Miles was immediately in front of him and Harrison saw him kick the door open and rush out. Another shot was fired and Miles fell. Soon after this, Harrison ran out onto the roof himself, and threw his truncheon at Craig. He also threw a bottle of milk and a piece of wood as Craig shouted, "I am Craig. You have just given my brother twelve years. Come on you coppers, I'm only sixteen." Harrison then dodged behind the stairhead wall to join Fairfax and the others and helped to push Bentley down the stairs. Constable Harrison reported that as Bentley called out that they were taking him down, Craig shouted back "Are they hurting you Derek?"

Constable Stuart Stanley Lowe arrived at the warehouse at 9.45 p.m. He heard some shots fired and climbed up to the roof by means of the drainpipe. He saw Constable Miles lying dead and then climbed down again. From there, Lowe went into the garden where the greenhouse stood. Looking up he saw Craig on the edge of the roof and heard him shout, "Yes, it's a Colt .45. Are you hiding behind a shield? Is it bullet proof? Are we going to have a shooting match? It's just what I like." He then paused before shouting, "Have they hurt you Derek?"

As Lowe watched, Craig pulled the trigger four times but Lowe only heard four clicks. At first he thought that the weapon must be empty but then Craig pointed it upwards, pulled the trigger again, and a shot was fired. Only then did Craig shout "See, it's empty". He then stood right on the edge of the roof, called out "Well here we go..." and leapt off, crashing into the greenhouse. Lowe ran forward to grab Craig, who struggled and muttered "I wish I were fucking dead", before adding "I hope I have killed the fucking lot".

Sergeant Edward Roberts was in the street outside the warehouse when Inspector Bodley handed Bentley over to him. Roberts cautioned his prisoner, saying "I am taking you to Croydon Police Station where you will be detained in connection with the shooting of Police Constable Miles". To this Bentley replied, "I didn't have the gun. Chris shot him." Bentley was then taken to the police station and on the way said, "I knew he had a gun but I didn't think he would use it. He has done one of your blokes in." This statement was confirmed by Constable Henry Thomas George Stephens, who was also in the car.

Constable James Ross arrived at the warehouse at 9.55 p.m., in time to see Craig dive head first off the roof. The following morning, at 2.30 a.m., Ross was observing Craig in a private ward at the hospital and Craig commented, "Did I really hit a policeman?" Ross did not reply but later Craig also said, "I got the gun from a house in Purley. There are plenty more where that came from."

There was a great deal of disagreement over the words that Craig used when he leapt from the warehouse roof. Constable James Cobban Gordon was inside the stairwell as Craig jumped, and he testified that the words used were something like "Cheerio, I'm going".

Detective Sergeant Stanley Shepherd went to the hospital to see Craig at 11.00 p.m. on the night of the shooting. He asked Craig how he felt and Craig replied, "It's my back, it hurts". Later that same night, Craig said, "I had six in the gun. I fired at a policeman. I had six Tommy gun bullets." Shepherd cautioned him but Craig continued, "Is the copper dead? How about the others? We ought to have shot them all." Soon afterwards, Detective Chief Inspector Smith arrived and informed Craig that he would be charged with murder, to which Craig said, "He's dead is he? What about the others?"

On November 3rd, at 1.15 a.m., Shepherd went to Craig's home at 9 Norbury Court Road and carried out a search of the premises. He found a .45 bullet in Craig's bed, and the sawn-off piece of the barrel underneath the floorboards in the attic. There was also a good deal of ammunition in a tin box.

At 4.00 a.m., that same morning, Shepherd interviewed Bentley at Croydon police station. Bentley said, "I didn't kill him guv. Craig did it." Bentley was cautioned and said he wished to make a statement. The statement began by giving Bentley's address as 1 Fairview Road, London Road, Norbury. It continued, "I have known Christopher Craig since I went to school. We were stopped by our parents going out together, but we still continued going out with each other. I mean, we have not gone out together until tonight.

"I was watching television tonight (2nd November 1952) and between 8 p.m. and 9 p.m., Craig called for me. My mother answered the door and I hear [sic] her say that I was out. I had been out earlier, to the pictures, and got home just after 7 p.m.

"A little later, Norman Parsley and Frank Fazey called. I did not answer the door or speak to them. My mother told me that they had called and I then ran out after them. I walked up the road with them, to the paper shop where I saw Craig standing. We all talked together and then Norman Parsley and Frank Fazey left. Chris Craig and I then caught a bus to Croydon. We got off at West Croydon and then we walked down the road where the toilets are – I think it is Tamworth Road.

"When we came to the place where you found us, Chris looked in the window. There was a little iron gate at the side. Chris jumped over and I followed. Chris then climbed up the drainpipe to the roof and I followed. Up to then Chris had not said anything. We both got out on to the flat roof at the top. Then someone in a garden on the opposite side shone a torch up towards us. Chris said 'It's a copper, hide behind here'. We hid behind a shelter arrangement on the roof. We were there waiting for about ten minutes. I did not know he was going to use the gun.

"A plain clothes man climbed up the drainpipe and on to the roof. The man said 'I am a police officer – the place is surrounded'. He caught hold of me and as we walked away, Chris fired. There was nobody else there at the time. The policeman and I then went around a corner by a door.

"A little later the door opened and a policeman in uniform came out. Chris fired again then and this policeman fell down. I could see that he was hurt as a lot of blood came from his forehead just above his nose. The policeman dragged him round the corner behind the brickwork entrance to the door. I remember I shouted something but I forgot what it was. I could not see Chris when I shouted to him – he was behind a wall.

"I heard some more policemen behind the door and the policeman with me said, 'I don't think he had many more bullets left'. Chris shouted 'Oh yes I have', and he fired again. I think I heard him fire three times altogether. The policeman then pushed me down the stairs and I did not see any more.

"I knew we were going to break into the place. I did not know what we were going to get – just anything that was going. I did not have a gun and I did not know Chris had one until he shot. I now know that the policeman in uniform that was shot is dead.

"I should have mentioned that after the plain clothes policeman got up the drainpipe and arrested me, another policeman in uniform followed and I heard someone call him Mac. He was with me when the other policeman was killed."

Continuing his evidence, Shepherd said that after the last sentence, Bentley had written "Tis as be", which was his attempt at putting "This has been..." Bentley could not finish the wording and so it was written for him. He then signed it. In fact, he signed it twice, the first time misspelling his own name and writing "Derk".

At 5.30 a.m., Detective Chief Inspector John Leslie Smith informed Bentley that he would be charged with murder. He replied, "Chris shot him. I hadn't got a gun. He was with me on the roof and shot him between the eyes."

DCI Smith confirmed what Shepherd had said about Bentley making his statement. Smith later made a search of the warehouse roof and found a number of spent cartridge cases. He also examined the gun that Craig had used. It was a six-chambered revolver with unspent bullets in the first and fourth chambers. The other chambers all held spent cases.

It seemed that Craig was more than willing to talk about what he had done. Constable Vincent Denham was on observation duty in the hospital at 6.30 a.m., on November 3rd, and he reported that Craig had said, "Is he dead?" Denham asked what he meant and Craig replied, "That copper. I shot him in the head and he went down like a ton of bricks."

Constable Ernest Brown was another officer on hospital duty and he told the court that on November 6th, Craig had said to him, "If I hadn't cut a bit off the barrel of my gun I would probably have killed a lot more policemen. That night I was out to kill because I had so much hate inside me for what they done to my brother. I shot the policeman in the head with my .45. If it had been the .22 he might not have died."

Thomas Sheppard was yet another officer set to guard Craig in his hospital bed. On November 5th, Craig was extremely chatty to him. At 2.10 p.m., he asked, "Is the policeman I shot in the shoulder still in hospital? I know the one I shot in the head is dead." At 3.35 p.m., Craig said, "What do you get for carrying a knuckle-duster? Bentley had mine." Finally, at 3.45 p.m., he asked, "Did you see the gun I had? It was all on the wobble so I took it to work and sawed two inches off the barrel."

The final police witness was Constable John Smith, who said that between 5.00 p.m. and 6.00 p.m., on November 3rd, he had heard Craig say, "You are coppers. Ha! The other one is dead, with a hole in his head. I'm all right. All you bastards ought to be dead."

After Craig's father, Niven Matthews Craig, had confirmed that his son was born on May 19th, 1936, Dr J. C. M. Matheson, the Medical Officer of Brixton prison, stated that he had made a number of examinations of Bentley. He was the third of a family of five and in September 1948 had been sent to the Kingswood Training School at Bristol. He had been there until July 28th, 1950, and tests showed that he had an IQ of sixty-six and a reading age of just four and a half years. An electrocardiogram (ECG) examination at the Burden Neurological Institute suggested that Bentley suffered from petit mal. He was illiterate and had a mental age of eleven or twelve.

The jury took seventy-five minutes to decide that both Bentley and Craig were guilty as charged, though they did recommend Bentley to mercy. Craig, being under the age of eighteen, was ordered to be detained during Her Majesty's pleasure, but Bentley, being nineteen, was sentenced to death.

Over the next few weeks, strenuous efforts were made to secure a reprieve, but it was all to no avail. The grounds for Bentley's appeal were twofold. First, the defence maintained that there had been misdirection by Lord Goddard in that he summed up Bentley's defence in one sentence but summed up the prosecution case in four or five pages. Secondly, the defence argued that the "joint venture" with Craig had ended with Bentley's arrest and not with the shooting of PC Miles. However, on January 13th, the appeal court judges ruled that there had been no misdirection and that the joint venture had continued after Bentley's arrest. His appeal dismissed, Bentley was hanged at Wandsworth on the morning of January 28th, 1953, by Albert Pierrepoint and Harry Allen.

There are a number of reasons why Derek Bentley should never have suffered the ultimate sanction of the law. First, and most obvious, was his medical and personal history.

One of a set of twins, his brother had died within two hours of his birth and Derek himself was not expected to survive. Survive he did, but at the age of four he fell from a lorry he was playing on. Landing on his head, Derek had to be rushed to hospital where it was said that the fall had brought on an epileptic seizure. His parents were told that he would never be the same again.

At the age of seven, during the Second World War, a bomb fell on the air-raid shelter that Derek and his family were occupying. Derek had to be dug free, only to suffer a similar fate when he was eleven and a flying bomb fell on the family house in Blackfriars.

In March 1948, Derek was charged with attempted shop-breaking and theft. Bound over for two years he was later in trouble again for taking tools left on a bomb-site. For that offence he was sent to the approved school in Bristol, from where he was released in 1950. These factors alone indicate that Derek Bentley should not have hanged, but there were other reasons too.

During the trial, Lord Goddard interrupted constantly. His interventions were almost always to underline a point for the prosecution and during his summing up, he continued to show this bias, putting on the knuckle-duster found on Bentley, describing it as a fearsome weapon and smashing it into the woodwork of the bench. He failed to point out that Bentley had said that Craig gave him this even though he did not want it, and that it had been found in Derek's right-hand pocket. Derek Bentley was left-handed.

A muscular-looking Derek Bentley. Bentley was hanged on January 28th, 1953, for the murder of PC Sydney Miles (Popperfoto)

There are also the curious words which three police officers said that Bentley shouted, "Let him have it Chris". The inference was that Bentley had called out for Craig to shoot Fairfax and indeed, the first shot was fired immediately after this. Bentley claimed that he had never uttered those words. Surely if he had, he would have claimed that he meant "Hand the weapon over", but he persisted in saying that he had not said the words. On July 11th, 1940, two men named Ostler and Appleby were also hanged for the murder of a policeman. These two had broken into a warehouse and when they were interrupted by a policeman, Appleby said "Let him have it, he is all alone". Although Ostler did the shooting, Appleby was also hanged as he had been said to have incited Ostler to fire. The case bears striking similarity to that of Craig and Bentley.

There is still one final point. There was another officer on the roof that night, one whose name was never mentioned by any of the other officers there. Constable Claude Pain claimed that he travelled in the police van with Fairfax, and as Fairfax climbed the drainpipe, he obtained a ladder from one of the neighbours and reached the roof at the same time as DC Fairfax, before the first shot was fired. Pain stated that Bentley never said "Let him have it Chris", and in fact spent most of the time on the roof crying, once Fairfax had been shot.

This evidence was never given at the trial because Constable Pain's testimony did not agree with that of his colleagues and his statements would have implied that they were lying in order to incriminate Bentley. The defence, therefore, were never made aware of his participation in the night's events. The other officers, on the other hand, were recognized as heroes. Fairfax received the George Cross, whilst Harrison and McDonald got the George Medal and Jaggs was awarded the British Empire Medal. Constable Pain was not mentioned at all.

The State dragged its feet, as it always does when there is a possible miscarriage of justice. Eventually, in the early 1990s, it was acknowledged that Bentley should not have hanged due to his mental subnormality. It was not until 1998, however, that a full pardon was finally granted. For Derek William Bentley, unlawfully killed by the State, it came just forty-five years too late.

Suggestion for Further Reading:

M. J. Trow, *'Let Him Have It Chris': the Murder of Derek Bentley* (London: Grafton, 1992).

Desmond Donald Hooper

41

Hanged at Shrewsbury, Tuesday, January 26th, 1954
For the murder of Betty Selina Smith,
near the Shropshire Union Canal, Shrewsbury

DOROTHY Smith was a worried mother. Her twelve-year-old daughter, Betty, was very late coming home. It was not like her to stay out this long. Concerned, Dorothy pulled on her coat and went to a neighbour's house. It was now the early hours of Wednesday, July 22nd, 1953.

The previous evening, Betty had enjoyed herself at the school social and by 8.30 p.m. had been heading home to 14 Deer Park, 3 Site, Atcham Camp, a hutted area which had been used as an American air base during the Second World War, and which was now occupied by a large number of families. Betty, though, had not stayed at home. She had only been there a few minutes when she told her mother that she was going to visit Mr and Mrs Hooper who lived at 15 Brown Ditch, also on the Atcham Camp. They were a couple she had offered to babysit for occasionally.

The Hoopers had a seven-year-old son, Keith, and Betty spent an hour or so playing dominoes with him. When the time came for Keith to go to bed, Betty prepared to leave for home. Keith's father, twenty-seven-year-old Desmond Donald Hooper, bade Betty goodnight. It was then around 10.40 p.m.

Back at Betty's home, her mother had fallen asleep in front of the wireless. When she finally woke, it was late and Betty still had not returned home. Dorothy Smith climbed onto her bicycle and rode to the Hooper home, which was just a few hundred yards from Deer Park. By now it was some time between midnight and 12.30 a.m., and the house was in darkness.

Mrs Margaret Daisy Hooper opened the door and explained that she was alone with her two children. Her husband had left a note saying that he was popping out, and he had not yet returned. Dorothy Smith asked about her daughter but Margaret knew nothing about the matter and advised Dorothy to wait until Desmond came home.

The two women talked and waited but in fact it was not until 1.45 a.m. that Desmond came back, and immediately, Dorothy thought that his appearance was rather strange. He was wearing no tie, his trousers were wet and muddy and he was sweating quite heavily. Told that Betty had not arrived home, Hooper said that he would telephone for the police but then curiously asked that they should not say what time he had actually come in.

A widespread search for Betty was launched on July 22nd. The officer in charge was Detective Superintendent Evans. He was extremely concerned that Betty had been the victim of foul play. She had never wandered off like this before, wore no coat when she vanished and had no money with her. Ponds on the estate were dragged and emptied, the undergrowth around the woods was searched, but nothing was found. The police appealed for help from anyone who might have seen Betty and a description of her was issued. According to this, she was between four feet seven and four feet eight inches tall, of good build with brown hair and blue eyes. When last seen she had been wearing a pink, lemon and black check dress with short sleeves and edged with white.

The search continued until 10.00 p.m. on July 22nd, but nothing was found. The following day also proved to be fruitless. It was not until July 24th that a jacket was found near the top of an old air shaft on a disused stretch of the Shropshire Union Canal, some two miles from Betty's home. Though the jacket was a man's, the shaft was checked as a matter of routine and there, some forty feet down and lying in a few feet of water, Betty's body was discovered. A man's tie was knotted around the girl's throat, with a double knot. The knot also had some strands of oats intertwined with it and since such oats grew in the field where the shaft lay, it seemed likely that Betty had met her death in that field before her body was thrown down the shaft.

The jacket found at the top of the shaft was double breasted, blue and had a chalk stripe in it. It was now urgent to determine to whom that jacket belonged.

Returning to Mrs Smith, the police now heard her relate something more of her visit to Desmond Hooper's house in the early hours of July 22nd. Moments before Hooper had come in, she and Mrs Hooper had apparently heard a man's voice outside, as if he were engaged in conversation with someone. When Hooper came in, his wife asked him where he had been and he replied that he had been up to Harris' farm to get some pigeons. She then asked him who he had been talking to outside and he said that he had spoken to no one. Mrs Hooper called him a liar and then asked where his two jackets were. Desmond said that they were hanging up behind the bathroom door but when she said they were not there, he commented that they must be around the house somewhere.

It seemed significant that there had been some conversation about missing jackets a full two days before the man's jacket had been found at the top of the shaft where Betty's body lay. Inquiries were made and two witnesses, Bernard Hooper, Desmond's brother and a tailor, George Herbert Lee, identified the jacket as one belonging to Desmond. Lee had had cause to repair the jacket some time before, and recognized his own stitching. Furthermore, there was no one to confirm Hooper's story that he had gone to a farm to collect some pigeons. The farmer, Richard Edward Harris, knew nothing about it and certainly had not seen Hooper on July 22nd. That was enough for Superintendent Evans. Hooper was arrested and charged with murder.

The trial opened at Shrewsbury on November 23rd and lasted until November 27th. The judge was Mister Justice Cassels and during the five-day hearing, Hooper was defended by Mr G. G. Baker and Mr Peter Northcote. Mr E. Ryder Richardson led for the Crown, assisted by Mr Paul Wrightson.

Dorothy Mary Smith, who since her daughter's death had remarried and was now Mrs Webb, told of Betty's return home from the social at 8.30 p.m. on July 21st. She had stayed at home for just fifteen minutes before going out again, to the Hoopers' home. After she had spoken about her visit to the Hoopers' house in the early hours of July 22nd, Mrs Smith turned to Desmond Hooper's arrival home. He was wearing a greenish-blue jacket, which was quite dark. After talking to him about Betty's disappearance she, Desmond and Mrs Hooper had gone back to her house to see if Betty had arrived home in the intervening period. After this, Hooper telephoned the police but she also spoke to the officer at the other end so that she could describe the clothes that Betty had been wearing.

That telephone call had been taken by Constable William John Patrick, who timed it at a few minutes before 3.00 a.m. It was taken on the emergency line and, after Hooper had told him that a young girl was missing, a woman had come on the line to give details of the girl's clothing.

Superintendent Evans spoke of the search for the missing girl and the eventual discovery of a jacket at the edge of the air shaft. In fact, the jacket was hanging over the edge as if an attempt had been made to throw it down the shaft. In the pockets were a single cigarette paper and a sevenpence bus ticket, dated May 27th. In due course, Superintendent Evans had shown the jacket to Hooper, who said "Well that's not mine. I never had one like it in my life. Where did you find it?" Mrs Hooper was present at the time and she interjected with, "You did have a blue one".

Witnesses were then called to link Hooper with the jacket found at the murder scene. Gerald Thomas Vaughan Reynolds was a local gamekeeper who knew Hooper quite well. He testified that he had seen the prisoner wearing a blue striped jacket like the one now produced in court. Edward Coup, who lived at 17 Deer Park and so was a close neighbour of the Smiths, said that he too had seen Hooper wearing the blue striped jacket. However, Mr Coup also stated that when he had seen Hooper at 9.00 p.m. on July 21st, Hooper had not been wearing the jacket then and in fact, he had not seen him wearing it for the past two months.

Bernard George Hooper, the prisoner's brother, said that he had received a blue striped suit from his father in 1950. After some months of use he had had a motor cycle accident whilst wearing the suit and it had been damaged. His other brother, Herbert Hooper, took the suit in for repairs and soon afterwards, the jacket was sold to the prisoner for seven shillings and sixpence. This had been in 1951. The story was confirmed by Herbert Hooper.

The jacket would prove to be a crucial piece of evidence but there was proof that someone else had worn it, at least on one occasion. The bus ticket found in the pocket showed that someone wearing it had made a trip on May 27th, and that person was not Hooper.

Daisy Annie Lloyd lived at 19 Deer Park and she testified that some time in early summer, she had taken some clothing to a cleaners in Shrewsbury. This clothing had been from both her family and the Hoopers. Her son, seventeen-year-old Clive, was with her on that trip. However, according to Mrs Lloyd, he was not wearing a blue striped jacket at the time.

First, the date of that trip to the cleaners had to be established. Irene Roberts was a supervisor at the Salop Steam Laundry in Shrewsbury, and upon checking her records she found that on May 27th, a two piece ladies suit had been received in the name of Hooper, as had a green jacket. There was also a brown and yellow tweed skirt in the name of Lloyd. That the visit was on May 27th was confirmed by Joan Parley, a bus conductress who stated that the sevenpence ticket was one that she issued at Wrekin View on May 27th. The bus left between 1.30 p.m. and 1.35 p.m.

Mrs Lloyd had denied that her son, Clive, had worn the blue striped jacket on his trip into Shrewsbury on May 27th. Clive Albert Lloyd, though, told a different story. He had certainly worn a blue jacket similar to the one found and had borrowed it from Hooper. He had, though, returned the jacket the same day.

This was a very important point. The bus ticket found in the pocket of the jacket was later shown to be from the journey that Lloyd and his mother made on May 27th. There could be no doubt, then, that Lloyd had worn the jacket found at the murder scene, at some time. It was crucial, therefore, for the prosecution to show that the jacket had always belonged to Hooper and that it had been returned to him well before the murder. It was Clive Lloyd's testimony which established this.

That Lloyd was economical with the truth was obvious from a curious incident that had taken place after Hooper had been arrested. One night soon afterwards, at 11.00 p.m., according to Margaret Hooper, the prisoner's wife, Lloyd had called at her house suggesting that they should have sex and had then produced a condom to underline his request. At first, Lloyd denied that any such incident had taken place but under cross-examination he admitted that a complaint had been made against him, and that the police had then called at his house and warned him to stay away from Mrs Hooper. Finally, he admitted that the incident with the condom had taken place after all.

Continuing his testimony, Clive Lloyd admitted that he had been out with Hooper a number of times and on one occasion they had been to the shaft where Betty's body was found. Lloyd denied vehemently, however, that he had told Hooper that he had a grudge against Betty Smith, that he intended to do something to her, and that the shaft was a good place to hide a body. He did admit, however, that Betty had hit his younger sister Maureen a number of times, though he added that this did not mean that he bore Betty any animosity.

328

There were other links between the Hoopers and the Lloyds. Albert Lloyd testified that he had spent the evening of July 21st with Mrs Hooper. He had called for her and they had gone to a pub together at 8.30 p.m., remaining there until closing time. From there they had returned to Hooper's house, arriving there at 10.55 p.m. Desmond Hooper was not at home but he had left a note on the table. Mrs Hooper read this but did not divulge the contents. Lloyd stayed at the house for an hour, leaving at 11.55 p.m., by which time, Hooper had still not returned home.

Constable Eric Charles Ellis recalled a visit he paid to Hooper's house on July 22nd. Hooper confirmed that Betty Smith had been at his house on the evening of the 21st. Before she left, at 10.40 p.m., he had given her some women's magazines and then stood watching by the gate as she ran off towards her home. Later he had scribbled a note for his wife and gone up to Mr Harris' to see if he could find some of his homing pigeons, which he believed had gone up there.

The prosecution were suggesting that Betty Smith may have been seen with the person who killed her. Walter Derek Colley had been visiting a friend on the estate and was heading home at 11.25 p.m., on July 21st. On Berwick Wharf Road he switched on his headlights and, within 300 yards of the Upton Magna turning, saw a man and a girl walking towards Uffington.

The man was wearing a dark suit or a dark sports jacket and trousers, was of normal build and about five feet ten inches tall. The girl was wearing a dark cardigan or blazer, with a light-coloured frock underneath. It should be recalled that Betty's frock was predominantly a dark check so there is a possibility that this was not in fact Betty, though the couple were walking towards the spot where the body was subsequently found.

There was one witness for the prosecution who, had he been telling the truth, might have fatally damaged Hooper's case. Frank Baker was a fellow prisoner at Shrewsbury and he claimed that on one occasion he had had a brief conversation with Hooper who, after discussing what they were both in for, had admitted "I did it. The police have only got circumstantial evidence against me, and it is up to them to prove it. I was having an affair with the girl and I had to get shut of her."

Under cross-examination, Baker admitted that he had not been aware that any prisoner held on a capital charge is not allowed out of his cell without a warder being present. Baker had apparently had a conversation with Hooper without a guard present and was expecting the court to believe that Hooper had confessed to him less than two minutes after first speaking to him. Though Baker was called at the final magistrate's court hearing, his testimony was ruled to be inadmissible and he was not called at the trial.

Further evidence to discredit Baker, if such were needed, came when Professor John Mathieson Webster, who had performed the post-mortem, gave his testimony. He swore that there was no sign of any sexual interference and that Betty was still a virgin when she died. So much for the affair which she was supposedly having with Hooper.

Professor Webster went on to say that the injuries were consistent with Betty having been stifled first, strangled whilst laying on the ground, close to the air shaft, kicked violently in the stomach and then thrown down the shaft whilst still alive. She had actually died from asphyxia, consistent with drowning.

For the defence, three members of the Hooper family were called. Margaret, the accused's wife, said that the note left for her on the table had read "Gone for pigeons. You know where." She had burned the note soon afterwards. She denied asking her husband about his missing jackets whilst Mrs Smith was in the house but had referred to a smock coat which he said was still at work. He had not come home white-faced, sweating or trembling and she had not heard a conversation outside moments before Desmond came in. What she heard was him humming to himself. He had never owned a blue jacket with a chalk stripe and the tie found around Betty's throat was not his.

Marion Hughes was Hooper's sister-in-law and said that she had stayed with the Hoopers on a number of occasions. She had never seen a jacket like the one produced. More valuable evidence was given by seven-year-old Keith Hooper, who said that very soon after he had gone to bed he heard Betty shout "Ta ta" and run off down the road. He then heard his father come back inside and make himself a cup of tea before going back out. If this were true then Hooper stayed inside for at least ten minutes after Betty had left, leaving plenty of time for her to have arrived home. Desmond Hooper then gave evidence on his own behalf. He had never owned the jacket and did not lend it to Lloyd. He had no reason to dislike Betty Smith, or to murder her, and was not guilty of this crime.

In the event the jury, after deliberating for one hour and twenty-five minutes, disagreed and Hooper was judged to be guilty as charged. On January 11th, 1954, an appeal was fought before Lord Goddard, the Lord Chief Justice, and Justices Byrne and Parker, on the grounds that the jury at the original trial had not been properly directed on certain matters of evidence. However, the judges ruled that there was abundant evidence that the defendant had committed the crime, so the appeal was dismissed. Hooper was hanged at Shrewsbury on January 26th, by Albert Pierrepoint and Robert Leslie Stewart.

Whether Hooper killed Betty Smith or not, whoever did kill her showed signs that there was a good deal of anger or possibly even hate behind the crime. Betty was taken to the field where the air shaft lay, attacked and strangled. She then lay on the ground, unconscious but apparently dead, and her assailant had probably believed that she was dead. Despite this he then kicked her in the stomach, injuring her liver. Perhaps this kick pushed her body down the shaft or perhaps the killer then threw her down.

Hooper had no reason to hate Betty. For him to be the killer the motive would have had to have been a sexual one. If Hooper were guilty then the most likely scenario is that he took Betty to the field to seduce her, she rejected him and this then angered him and caused him to attack her. However, he would have known that he would be the first person that the police spoke to about her disappearance and this still does not explain how he had time to wave her goodbye at 10.40 p.m., enjoy a cup of tea and then catch up with her in order to try out his seduction. Why had he not simply tried to rape her whilst they were alone in his home?

The person who did kill Betty Smith killed her in anger. There is, at the very least, a reasonable doubt that Hooper was not the one who demonstrated that anger on the night of July 21st.

42

Frank Stokes

Hanged at Durham, Wednesday, September 3rd, 1958
For the murder of Linda Violet Ash, at Gosforth, Newcastle-upon-Tyne

I N March 1957, the British Parliament passed the Homicide Act, which limited capital punishment for murder to five possible categories. From that time on, a killer could only be executed for murder in the course or furtherance of theft, murder by shooting or causing an explosion, murder whilst resisting arrest or during an escape, murder of a policeman or prison officer or lastly, two murders committed on different occasions. This somewhat ludicrous state of affairs meant that a burglar who killed whilst stealing from a shop, for instance, would face the death penalty, whilst someone who poisoned all the members of his family at the same time would face a life sentence. It was this idiosyncrasy in the law that was, in 1958, to cost a man his life for the sake of a cheap purse.

Linda Violet Ash was a seventy-five-year-old widow who lived in a house in Marlborough Avenue, Gosforth, Newcastle-upon-Tyne. She lived on the ground floor, whilst the first floor was let out to Mrs Sybil Mary Tate and her husband. Mrs Ash did not let out rooms for financial reasons, but rather because she was afraid to be alone in the house, especially at night. Although she was getting on in years, Mrs Ash was still sprightly enough to lead a full and active life, although the upkeep of the garden of the property was largely beyond her. This was why she placed an advertisement in a nearby newsagent's window, offering payment to anyone interested in helping out.

On the morning of Monday, April 14th, 1958, Sybil Tate was downstairs talking to Linda Ash when someone knocked on the front door. It was a man whom neither lady had seen before and he announced that he had seen the advertisement for a jobbing gardener, and was interested in discussing terms. As Mrs Tate left, Violet and the stranger were still talking on her front doorstep.

It was late afternoon, at around 5.30 p.m., by the time Sybil Tate called again on her downstairs neighbour, after her return from work, but now she received no reply to her knocking. It was unusual for Violet to be out at this time and so, thinking that her neighbour might be at the back of the house, Mrs Tate walked to the kitchen door at the rear. The door was unlocked but when Sybil Tate pushed it open, she saw immediately why Linda Ash had not answered her call. Mrs Ash lay on the kitchen floor, her head a mass of blood. Someone had battered her until she was close to the point of death.

Linda Ash, however, was still alive. Rushed to the Royal Victoria Infirmary, she died from her injuries the following day without ever regaining consciousness, making this a case of murder. Detectives interviewed Sybil Tate and other neighbours, who reported a man who had knocked on their doors and asked for directions to Mrs Ash's home. A description was pieced together and, on the day that Mrs Ash died, the police announced that they were satisfied that the man who had called about the gardening job was almost certainly the same man who had battered her to death. He was described as being forty to fifty years old, five feet ten inches tall, with fair hair and light-coloured eyes. He was also described as being thin featured, clean-shaven and having a pallid complexion and a somewhat arrogant manner.

It was also on April 15th that the officers in charge of the case stated that they believed that robbery was not the motive in this case. Mrs Ash's daughter, Joyce Marion Pantridge, who lived at Broadway West, also in Gosforth, had been over the house at the request of the police and said that not only had nothing apparently been taken, but that nothing even seemed to have been disturbed. The police were also able to say that the attack appeared to have been a sudden one. A household hammer had been used to inflict the injuries and since there was no evidence of bruising to Linda Ash's arms or hands, it was unlikely that she had had time to defend herself.

By April 16th, a medical examination of the body had revealed that Linda Ash had been struck from behind and had received four separate blows. The particular blow that had proved fatal had hit Violet behind the ear and towards the back of her head and it appeared that this, and indeed the other blows, had been inflicted by a right-handed man. Two hammers had been found in the house and the larger of these showed evidence of bloodstaining and fitted the wounds on Violet's skull. That same evening, the officer in charge of the case, Detective Superintendent John Patterson, the head of the Northumberland CID, stated that a request for assistance had been made to Scotland Yard and that night, he briefed two detectives who had travelled up from London – Superintendent Leslie Davies and Sergeant Sydney Gentle.

The investigation was certainly widespread and thorough. Late on the evening of April 16th, police in north Cumberland picked up a man who fitted closely the description pieced together by Sybil Tate and the other neighbours. This man had been spotted in a cafe at Brampton and after he left, the police were called and the man was picked up at Warwick Bridge. He identified himself as forty-three-year-old William Sharpe, a man who was a keen gardener and known to travel throughout the north of England doing odd gardening jobs to earn his living. He was questioned for five-and-a-half hours before the police were satisfied that he had nothing to do with the murder of Mrs Ash, and released him.

On April 17th, the case took a new turn when it was revealed that after a second inspection of the murder scene, it had become apparent that cash may have been taken and that robbery may have been the motive after all. If this could be proved, of course, the case would become a capital one and the miscreant, once he was found, would face a sentence of death by hanging.

Still there were no fresh developments in the case. By April 24th, the police had drawn up a list of fifty or more jobbing gardeners and said that every one of them would be traced and checked out. When the breakthrough came, however, it was not in the north of England, but in London.

At 1.00 a.m. on April 25th, forty-four-year-old Frank Stokes walked into Cannon Row police station in the capital and told the officer on the desk that he wished to give himself up for the murder of a woman. Stokes then went on to say that he was the man the police were looking for in connection with the murder of Mrs Linda Ash, in Newcastle. At 4.00 a.m. that same day, Superintendent Davies and Sergeant Gentle returned to London and questioned Stokes closely. Again he admitted that he had killed Linda Ash.

According to Stokes' story, he had seen the advertisement in the newsagent's window and, after asking for directions, had knocked on Mrs Ash's front door. After discussing what the job involved, Stokes had said that he wanted four shillings an hour for his labour. Mrs Ash had said that this was too high a figure so he left the house but stopped on the corner and thought things over. In due course, Stokes returned to the house and told Mrs Ash that he would accept her offer, which had been sixpence less, at three shillings and sixpence per hour.

Mrs Ash now went into the kitchen and began to remove some tools from underneath her sink. Throughout this time she was muttering something about people not being able to make up their minds. She passed a hammer to Stokes and as she continued complaining, Stokes said "You agreed three shillings and sixpence an hour, why bring it up again? Why keep going on about it?" Linda Ash, though, persisted in mumbling about people swapping and changing until finally, in a temper, he lashed out with the hammer and struck her on the back of the head. Stokes went on to say that he had removed nothing from the house, except for the front door key, which he had used to lock the door after he left. He then handed this key over to Superintendent Davies.

There was, however, a problem for Frank Stokes. When he had first walked into Cannon Row and admitted his guilt, Stokes had, as a matter of course, been searched. Amongst the property found on him was a woman's purse. It was a cheap, common purse as might be purchased in many stores throughout the country but it resembled one that Joyce Pantridge had said belonged to her mother. If Stokes had taken that single item from Linda Ash's house, then he had killed her during a theft and would be charged with the capital offence.

After Stokes had been interrogated, he and the two Scotland Yard detectives, Davies and Gentle, returned to Newcastle and it was there, on April 27th, that Frank Stokes was charged with murder during the furtherance of theft. His trial opened at Leeds on July 21st, 1958, before Mister Justice Edmund Davies. The Crown case was led by Mr Bernard Gillis, assisted by Mr Rawdon Smith, whilst Stokes' defence lay in the hands of Mr G. S. Waller, assisted by Mr W. Steer. The jury were all male and the proceedings lasted for three days.

There was, of course, no doubt that Frank Stokes had killed Mrs Linda Ash. When asked to plead to the charge, Stokes had replied "Not guilty to capital murder but guilty to murder". The prosecution now had to show that the cheap purse found on Stokes had come from Mrs Ash's home, in order to obtain the maximum penalty under the law.

Joyce Pantridge wept in court as she reported how she had seen her mother lying in a pool of blood on her kitchen floor on the evening of April 14th. The day after this she had returned to the property with two policemen and made a careful inventory of the things she found there. All her mother's jewellery was safe in a box on the dressing table but the only money in the house was a sixpence and a one shilling piece in a purse on the dressing table. Her mother had been in the habit of keeping money in the house and there was usually at least a few pounds in notes in a wallet, and on a second examination a day or two later, she had noticed that this purse was missing. Her husband had seen the purse a day or two before the attack and there had certainly been banknotes in it then. Joyce believed that there might have been £10 or even £15 inside the purse when it was taken.

Mrs Pantridge was not absolutely sure what colour her mother's wallet was. It may have been navy blue, or it may have been black, but it was very similar in design to the black one found on Frank Stokes when he was charged. Under cross-examination from Mr Waller, Joyce Pantridge admitted freely that the wallet found on Stokes was of a very common type and that the most she could say was that it was similar to her mother's. She could not positively identify it as hers.

Frank Stokes stepped into the witness box to give evidence on his own behalf. He explained that although he was a hotel porter by trade, he had done work as a gardener on previous occasions. Seeing the advertisement in the newsagents he had gone to apply for the position. At this point, Mr Waller asked Stokes, "What was in your mind when you went to that house?" To this, Stokes had replied, "Merely to seek a job".

Stokes repeated the evidence that he had given in his statement to the police about the original disagreement over the fee per hour and added that when he returned to the house a few minutes later he had said that being an old lady she might not be able to afford four shillings and so he would knock it down to three shillings and sixpence. Mrs Ash agreed to this figure and then outlined what duties she expected of him. One of the jobs was the mending of a fence at the back of the

336

property and it was for this reason that she handed him some tools, amongst which was a hammer.

Coming now to the actual attack itself, Stokes said, "I struck her once. Then she fell on the ground and I struck her again after." Believing that Mrs Ash was dead, Stokes had turned off the radio so that the neighbours might think she was out, and left immediately after locking the front door. He did not take any property from the house, apart from the front door key, which he said he had found actually in the lock.

After leaving Marlborough Avenue, Stokes had gone to Newcastle Central station and bought himself a ticket to London. That ticket cost him some four pounds and eight shillings and that was money which he had had on him when he first went to Mrs Ash's house. In fact, he had had about eleven pounds on him when he called at Marlborough Avenue. As for the wallet that was found on him, he had stolen that on April 15th from a house in Whitehall Court in Ewell, Surrey. Once again he had answered an advertisement for a gardener and the black wallet had come from that location. Unfortunately for Stokes, however, this could not be proved.

In the event, the jury, having heard all the evidence decided that not only was Stokes guilty of murder, but that the wallet had come from Linda Ash's home and that Stokes was therefore guilty of murder during the furtherance of theft. There was only one sentence for that offence and Stokes listened apparently unmoved as Mister Justice Davies sentenced him to death.

The appeal was heard on August 20th before the Lord Chief Justice, Lord Goddard, and Justices Cassels and Ashworth. In fact, this would be the last murder appeal heard by Lord Goddard before he retired on September 30th.

For the defence, Mr Waller claimed that the trial judges had not impressed upon the jury that before they could return a verdict of capital murder, they had to be satisfied that Stokes had the intention to steal at the time that the assault took place. Furthermore, Mr Waller suggested that the judge prejudiced Stokes by admitting the part of his voluntary statement in which Stokes admitted that he had stolen a wallet from a house in Surrey. This would surely predispose the jury to believe that a man who admitted one theft could just as well be guilty of another. The final point of the appeal was that the judge had represented to the jury that Stokes was a bogus gardener when there was evidence that he had done previous work of this kind.

In reply, Lord Goddard stated that on the first point, if the jury were satisfied that Stokes had gone to the house in order to steal, then that was enough in the eyes of the law. When it came to the statement which the defence claimed had incriminated Stokes, Lord Goddard said, "If a man chooses to say something that incriminates himself, why should it not be used as evidence? What a man says has always been admissible as evidence. In this case he was giving an explanation about a wallet found in his possession, and a wallet was missing from Mrs Ash's house." As for the third comment, that Stokes was a bogus gardener, Lord Goddard stated, "He might have been the most skilful gardener that ever existed, but he did not go to the house to get a gardening job. On his own confession, he went there to steal." That last sentence was, of course, completely at odds with what Frank Stokes had said. He had never admitted to anything of the kind, but nevertheless, the appeal was dismissed.

On Monday, September 1st, it was announced that the Home Secretary could find no grounds for recommending Her Majesty to intervene and as such there would be no reprieve. At 9.00 a.m., on the morning of Wednesday, September 3rd, 1958, Frank Stokes was hanged at Durham jail. There were just sixteen people outside the prison at the time – fifteen women and one man, who was a friend of the murdered woman's family.

43

James Hanratty

Hanged at Bedford, Wednesday, April 4th, 1962
For the murder of Michael John Gregsten, at Clophill, Bedfordshire

THE morning of Wednesday, August 23rd, 1961, seemed just like any other to farm worker Sidney Charles Burton. He was up at his usual early time and as he walked towards his place of work, it was still only 6.35 a.m.

Strolling towards the rather eerily named Deadman's Hill, just outside Clophill, he suddenly heard a strange noise. Listening carefully, Burton thought that he heard a woman groaning. Perhaps someone had had an accident. It was when he went to investigate that he found something much more terrible. A young woman lay close to a man in the lay-by. Both had been shot and whilst it was clear that the man was beyond all human aid, the woman was still alive and conscious. Burton reassured the injured woman and ran off to find help.

Running down the road, Burton soon found John Kerr, an undergraduate student at Magdalen College, Oxford. Kerr, as part of his studies, was conducting a traffic survey and at 6.00 a.m., he had positioned himself in an RAC (Royal Automobile Club) box on the A6 road, so that he could record all the vehicles passing in either direction. Burton rapidly described what he had found in the lay-by and the two men then dashed back to see what they could do.

Arriving at the lay-by, Kerr noted that the woman was lying on her back. Her face, hair and the top half of her clothing were spattered with blood and her skirt was pulled up to her waist. Kerr took off his leather jacket and, after pulling the woman's skirt down, covered her to keep her warm. The man was lying beside her and Kerr saw for himself that he was clearly dead. He also felt that there was a chance that the woman too might succumb to her injuries. Aware of how vital it was that he carefully record anything she might say, he turned over one of his traffic census forms, took out a pen and gently began to question the stricken woman.

The woman explained to Kerr that she and her friend had been held up by a man with a gun. It was a .38, she recalled, and the assailant had shot them both. She went on to say that the ordeal had started at around 9.30 p.m., the previous night, near Slough. Kerr then asked the woman to describe the man and wrote down that he was a little over five feet three inches tall, had large staring eyes, and light, fairish hair. The car that she and her friend had been in, and which had been taken by the gunman, was a grey Morris Minor, registration number 847 BHN. Finally, the woman gave her name as Valerie Storie and her address as 15 Anthony Way, Slough. The dead man, her companion, had been thirty-four-year-old Michael Gregsten.

Whilst John Kerr was taking these details and doing his best to comfort Valerie Storie, Sidney Burton dashed off to call the police and an ambulance. Medical assistance and police officers were soon on the scene but at 8.00 a.m., the first of a number of curious events which were to feature in this case occurred. John Kerr was approached by a man in uniform, who wore a flat peaked cap. He naturally assumed that this man was a senior police officer and explained to him about the description of the assailant that he had scribbled down on his traffic form. The officer suggested that it might be best if the paper were handed over to him for safe keeping and Kerr readily complied with the request. That piece of paper, a vitally important piece of evidence, was never seen again.

It was not long before Valerie Storie was being interviewed in hospital by Detective Superintendent Terence Acott, the officer in charge of the case. She explained that she had first met Michael Gregsten when they both worked for the Langley Road Research Laboratory. They had been lovers for the past four years, despite the fact that Gregsten was a married man. Indeed, Valerie said that Janet Gregsten, the dead man's wife, knew all about the relationship.

Turning to the evening of Tuesday, August 22nd, Valerie said that she and Gregsten had gone to have a drink at one of their favourite public houses, the Old Station Inn at Taplow. From there, they drove a couple of miles down the road, turned into a quiet lane and finally into a deserted cornfield, another favourite spot of theirs. They were both fond of motor rallying and were discussing the next meeting that they were going to attend when, after some thirty to forty-five minutes, someone tapped on the driver's window.

Both Gregsten and Valerie looked out at the man who was standing there but by now it was getting quite dark and they could only see him from his shoulders to his waist, so they had no idea who he was, or what he looked like. At this stage, all they could tell was that he was wearing a dark suit and a white shirt and tie.

Gregsten started to wind down the window to find out what the man wanted but even before the window was all the way down, a gun was poked into the car and the man spoke for the first time. "This is a hold up, and I am a desperate man. I have been on the run for four months. If you do as I tell you, you will be all right." He then asked Gregsten for the car's ignition key. Valerie had tried to stop Gregsten from handing it over but he had pointed out that the man had a gun and so he had to do as he had been told.

Once the man had the key he ordered Gregsten to open the rear door so that he could get into the vehicle. Gregsten leaned backwards, pulled the handle that opened the door and the man climbed in. He was wearing a handkerchief or piece of cloth tied over his face, so Valerie and Gregsten still could not tell what he looked like.

For a time, the man spoke rather pointlessly. He referred to the gun and said that it was loaded, tapping one of his jacket pockets and saying that it too was full of bullets. He said that he felt like a cowboy and the gun was a cowboy's gun. Finally, he said that he was hungry and had not eaten for two full days. From time to time, either Valerie or Gregsten tried to turn around in order to be able to see what he looked like and so be able to give a better description later, but the intruder always told them to keep looking to the front.

After a few minutes of conversation, the man handed the ignition key back to Gregsten and told him to drive further into the field. Up to this point, the car had only been just inside the field, and would have been easily seen by any passing vehicle. Once Gregsten had done as the man asked, he demanded that they both hand over their watches and any money that they might have. Gregsten handed over his watch and all his cash but Valerie, showing a rather high degree of presence of mind under the circumstances, managed to take the banknotes out of her wallet and stuff them down her brassiere. She then handed over her watch and the empty wallet.

Although Valerie Storie could not see the man's face clearly at this stage, she had noticed his speech patterns. He appeared to have a cockney accent and, typical of that accent, he pronounced 'th' as 'f'. So, thinking became 'finking' and things became 'fings'. He was quite softly spoken, though, did not have a very deep voice and appeared to be around twenty years of age.

After an hour in the field, the intruder decided that it was time to move on. Gregsten turned the car around and approached the gate which led out onto the quiet road. He was told to turn right, towards Maidenhead. It was then that Valerie remembered that the man had said he had not eaten for two days and she said that she knew a place in Slough where he could buy some milk and chocolate from vending machines. The man agreed that this was a good idea but when they did finally stop at a machine, it was discovered that no one had a sixpence piece. Gregsten suggested that they might ask a passer-by for change but the assailant then pointed the gun directly at Gregsten's head and said that he had a better idea. He knew of a cafe near Northolt where he could get something to eat.

During the next part of the drive, Valerie and Gregsten spoke to the man a good deal, trying to find out as much as they could about him. He responded by saying that his name was Jim. He claimed that he had never had a chance in life. Even as a child he had been locked up in a cellar for days on end by his parents and only given bread and water. He had been in remand homes or Borstal ever since the age of eight and had recently done five years for housebreaking.

In due course, the car reached London Airport and Jim asked how much petrol there was in the tank. Although there were actually a couple of gallons, Gregsten lied and said that it would probably only take them another twenty miles or so. Jim then ordered that he pull into a garage and ask the attendant there for two gallons of fuel. Thinking that Gregsten might seize the opportunity to escape, Jim pointed out "I have got the gun pointing at you and if you try and say anything else or give the man a note or make any inclination [sic] that anything is wrong, I will shoot".

The attendant at the garage was a gentleman named Hirons and he did indeed put two gallons into the car's tank. Gregsten handed over a one pound note that had been returned to him by Jim, and got a ten shilling note and a threepence piece in change. Getting back into the car, Gregsten offered the money to Jim who took the note but handed Valerie the threepence, saying that she could have it as a wedding present.

From the garage, Gregsten drove through Hayes, where he was told to go straight on so that he reached the A4010. Various other directions were given until the car pointed towards Harrow and then on towards Stanmore. It was close to Kingsbury that Jim told Gregsten to be careful as there were some roadworks around the corner.

At Stanmore, Jim allowed Gregsten to stop the car again and buy some cigarettes. Again, he warned him first that he should not try anything silly. Back in the car, Gregsten handed the cigarettes to Valerie who lit two. One she handed to Gregsten, the other to Jim and as he took it, she saw for the first time that he was wearing black gloves.

The car continued northwards, passing through Radlett and St Albans, then along the A6 through Luton, Barton and Silsoe. Finally, Jim said that he was tired and wanted a 'kip'. At his instructions they pulled into a couple of country lanes but each time, rather surprisingly perhaps, Valerie pointed out that they might be seen from the main road. Jim apparently took her advice and finally settled for the lay-by on Deadman's Hill. Gregsten was ordered to turn the car around, so that it faced in the direction they had just come, and then turn off the engine and the lights. By now it was almost 2.00 a.m. on August 23rd.

Jim repeated that he needed a kip, but said that he would first have to tie them both up, otherwise they might escape and raise the alarm. There was a small rug in the front of the car and Jim's first suggestion was that they cut this up so that he could use the strips as rope. Gregsten replied that they did not have anything to cut it with so Jim said, "Let me look in the boot of the car to see if you have any rope". He and Gregsten both then got out of the car and looked in the boot. Jim found a small piece of rope and when they both returned to the car, he told Gregsten to take his tie off as well.

Jim then ordered Valerie to turn around, face him, and put her hands out with the wrists together so that he could tie her up. She did as he asked but held her hands apart a little so that the bond would be quite loose. Jim then tied her wrists together with Gregsten's tie before using the rope to fasten her wrists to the car door handle.

This left the problem of what to do with Gregsten. "I have to find something to tie you up with", said Jim, and Valerie suggested tying them together so that he could escape without them following him. Throughout this ordeal there had been a duffel bag in the front of the car. This contained some washing but Jim now noticed it and told Gregsten to hand it over.

Gregsten picked up the bag with both hands and turned towards the centre of the car to hand it over. The bag was halfway across the seats when Jim fired his gun twice, in

342

quick succession. Gregsten fell forward over the steering wheel, two bullets in his head, and Valerie began to scream.

"Stop screaming" ordered Jim. Valerie did so but cried out, "You shot him you bastard. Why did you do that?" "He frightened me. He moved too quick. I got frightened", replied Jim. Valerie begged Jim to let her drive Gregsten to a doctor but all the killer would say was "Be quiet, I'm finking".

Valerie and Jim talked and argued for perhaps another twenty minutes, Jim repeatedly telling her to be quiet as he was still 'finking'. Finally he reached into the duffel bag, took something out, and threw it over Gregsten's head. He then turned towards Valerie and ordered her to kiss him. She refused but it was at that point that a car, passing on the main road with its headlights on, lit up the interior of the car and Jim's face. Though the light was only on his face for a few seconds, Valerie saw him clearly. She saw that he had very large pale blue staring eyes, and brown hair combed back with no parting.

Once again Jim told Valerie to kiss him, brandishing the gun as he did so. This time she obeyed but during the kiss, she leaned across and tried to grab the gun. Jim was too strong and too quick and managed to hold on to it. "That was a silly thing to do", he said, adding, "I thought you were sensible. I cannot trust you now."

Jim ordered Valerie to get out of the car and join him in the back, threatening to shoot her if she did not obey. Slowly she climbed out, but when he opened the rear door and told her to get in with him, she refused. Jim then climbed out himself, forced her into the back seat, and followed her in.

Again he tried to kiss her, during which time she managed to take the cash out of her brassiere, £7 in total, and hide it in the pocket of the mackintosh that she was still wearing. Jim did not see any of this and now ordered Valerie to take her knickers off. At first she refused but after some argument, she did as he had asked. Then Jim calmly put the gun on the back window shelf of the car, unzipped his trouser fly and raped her. He then took the gun back and allowed Valerie to put her knickers back on.

By now it was almost daybreak and Valerie begged Jim to take the car and go. After some thought, Jim agreed that he would leave her there with Gregsten and drive off alone. Together they then pulled Gregsten's body from the driver's seat, after which Jim asked her to explain to him how the car worked, especially the gears. Valerie showed him and, leaving the car engine running, went to sit down next to Gregsten.

Valerie promised that she would not go for help. During this time, Jim was standing quietly behind her. Then the car engine cut out and Valerie was told to start it up again. Jim then asked her to show him the gears for a second time, after which Valerie returned to where Gregsten lay. Jim was still behind her and she heard him say "I think I had better hit you on the head or something to knock you out, or else you will go for help".

"No I won't. I won't move. Just go", replied Valerie. She then took a £1 note out of her pocket and handed it to him. Jim took it and began to walk away. Suddenly he stopped. Valerie heard him turn and immediately he began to fire. She felt a bullet strike her, and then a second hit home. Valerie fell to the ground but Jim kept on firing. Then there was a pause and a clicking sound. He was reloading and soon another three shots rang out, though these seemed to strike the concrete somewhere above Valerie Storie's head. She knew that he intended to kill her so she lay perfectly still. She felt him touch her, checking whether she were alive or not and then, finally, he slammed the car door, turned on the headlights and drove off towards Luton.

It was not very long before Superintendent Acott had his first breakthrough. The stolen Morris car had been found abandoned in Avondale Crescent, Ilford, close to Redbridge Station. Unfortunately, Jim, whoever he was, had left no fingerprints or other clues, but an appeal for witnesses who might have seen the vehicle soon brought results.

John Skillett had been driving to work at 7.00 a.m., on August 23rd. With him in the passenger seat was his friend, Edward Blackhall. As Skillett drove down Eastern Avenue, Ilford, he noticed a grey Morris Minor, the driver of which appeared to be in some sort of hurry, for his driving was somewhat erratic. The Morris pulled across from the nearside lane to the outer lane, cutting up Skillett and almost hitting the car in front. Soon, the driver stopped at the traffic lights and Skillett pulled up close behind him. As the lights changed, the Morris shot off at speed and pulled back into the nearside lane. Appalled at this terrible driving, Skillett determined to give the driver a piece of his mind and accelerated so that he could overtake him. He finally caught up with the Morris at the roundabout near Gant's Hill Station, and asked Blackhall to wind down his window so that he could shout across. Skillett told the man he should not be on the road but the driver merely looked towards him, smiled, and then drove off. Both Skillett and Blackhall were interviewed and asked to give a description of the driver.

James Richard Trower was in Redbridge Lane, Ilford, at approximately 7.05 a.m. He had just parked his car and walked up to the front door of Paddy Hogan, a workmate, to offer him a lift. As he waited for Hogan to answer the door, Trower heard a car changing gear quickly. The noise attracted his attention and he turned in time to see a Grey Morris Minor drive past and turn into Avondale Crescent. Both Trower and Hogan were interviewed and they too were asked to give a description. It was the efforts of these gentlemen that caused Superintendent Acott to issue not one, but two identikit pictures of the wanted man. One had been drawn up by Valerie Storie and the other, largely, by Trower and Skillett.

It was important to give as much publicity as possible to the investigation and Superintendent Acott announced at a press conference that in his opinion, the motive for this crime had been sexual. The killer had, from the very outset, wished to possess Miss Storie, and Gregsten had been killed for that purpose. In Acott's opinion, the killer was a sex maniac and it was likely that someone else knew about the crime, as Jim would need to change his clothing, or have it cleaned, in order to get rid of the blood that would have spilled on to him when Gregsten was shot.

The very next day, August 24th, the murder weapon was found. A cleaner named Cooke was working on a number of buses and when he came to work on one of the number 36A buses, he found something hidden underneath the back seat. Unwrapping the handkerchief that was wrapped around the object, Cooke found that he had discovered a .38 revolver with five boxes of cartridges. Forensic tests soon showed that it was the weapon used to kill Michael Gregsten.

Superintendent Acott believed that the killer had to be lying low somewhere. True, he might have his own home in which to do so, but it was also possible that he lived in rented rooms, or even a hotel or guest-house. As a result, the police made an appeal to all landlords and landladies to report any guest or tenant who might have been behaving suspiciously since the night of the murder. It was this appeal which brought the next break in the case.

A woman staying at the Alexandra Court Hotel in Seven Sisters Road, Finsbury Park, complained to the manager that the guest in the room next to hers was keeping her awake. He paced about in his room and talked to himself all through the night. The manager checked his register and found that his guest, Peter Macdougall, had booked in on August 23rd. Since that time, little had been seen of him. The police were notified and went to speak to Mr Macdougall. He confirmed that his real name was Peter Louis Alphon and stated that on the previous night, the 22nd, he had stayed at the Vienna Hotel at 158-162 Sutherland Avenue, in Maida Vale. He had booked in there after visiting his mother in Streatham. Satisfied that Mr Macdougall, alias Mr Alphon, had an alibi, the officers made a note of what had been said and returned to the police station.

On September 7th, Mrs Dalal of East Sheen answered a knock on her front door. She had advertised a room to let and the man standing before her now said that he wished to take a look at it. Mrs Dalal showed him up to the room but as soon as they were there, the man leapt upon her, hit her on the head and tied her hands behind her back. He then threw her onto the bed and announced that he was the A6 killer. He then began to lift her skirt, at which point Mrs Dalal managed to scream loudly, forcing her attacker to flee. The police took the connection seriously. After all, it was clear that Mrs Dalal's assailant had had some form of sexual assault on his mind, and Valerie Storie had been raped. It might well be the same man.

The reports on Louis Alphon were processed and, as a matter of routine, the manager of the Vienna Hotel in Maida Vale was interviewed. He was William Nudds, a known criminal, who had previously used at least eight aliases and had a long record of offending. His last conviction, though, had been in November 1950 when he received nine years for stealing cars and obtaining money by false pretences, being finally released from jail on July 14th, 1958. He now insisted that he was going straight, though he worked at the Vienna under a new name, that of Glickberg. He was running the hotel with Florence Snell, who lived with him as his wife.

Nudds was more than happy to make a statement to the police. He did recall Peter Alphon, who had stayed at his hotel under the name of Frederick Durrant, giving a home address of 7 Hurst Avenue, Horsham. According to Nudds' statement, Alphon had not spent the night of August 22nd in his room. He had first occupied room twenty-four but had not seemed to be happy with this so Nudds said that he would try to move him, if he could. During the day, room six became available and Nudds reserved it for Alphon, moving his luggage for him from room twenty-four.

By late that night, Alphon had not returned so Nudds scribbled a note saying that room six was now his and left the key. The next morning, every one of the guests attended breakfast, except for Alphon, so Nudds went to his room and knocked on the door. Alphon was just pulling his trousers on and said that he did not want any breakfast. Nudds asked him what time he had arrived back the previous night and Alphon replied that it was some time around 11.00 p.m. Nudds knew that this could not be true as he and Mrs Snell had not gone up to bed until after midnight.

It was that same Vienna Hotel which was to play the next part in the murder case. On September 11th, a routine inspection of the hotel was made by Mr Crocker, who managed four London hotels. He was shown around by Mrs Galves, the housekeeper, and in due course, they came to room twenty-four. At one stage, Mr Crocker noticed that the fabric of an old chair in an alcove was torn. He moved the chair and something fell out on to the floor. To his surprise, Mr Crocker saw that it was a spent cartridge case. He then made a careful examination of the chair and found a second case. Both these cases were handed over to the police who, after examining them in the laboratory, were able to show that they had certainly been fired from the .38 revolver that had killed Gregsten.

Here then was a quandary. The murder had taken place on the morning of August 23rd. Peter Alphon had occupied room twenty-four on the night of the 22nd, and had apparently not been in his room until very late. The previous night, the same room had been occupied by someone giving the name J. Ryan and the address 72 Wood Lane, Kingsbury. It was possible that either man was the killer. For now, though, the police concentrated their efforts on Peter Alphon, especially when his mother was interviewed and denied that her son had been to see her on the 22nd.

A description of Alphon was published. In that description he was described as being five feet nine inches tall, of slim build with a pale complexion and dark brown hair brushed back. He had hazel eyes and a small straight nose with thin lips and a rounded chin. He was known to speak like a Londoner and had a quiet voice.

In fact, it was not until around midnight on September 22nd that Alphon gave himself up to the police. He was placed in an identification parade and picked out by Mrs Dalal as the man who had attacked her. Alphon, though, had an alibi for that particular night and so, on October 3rd, he was freed by the magistrates. Soon afterwards, Superintendent Acott was asked about the elimination of this particular suspect and gave a number of reasons why he did not believe Alphon to be connected with the A6 murder.

The first of those reasons was that he was not called Jim or James. It seemed to escape Acott that the killer might well have given a false name in order to throw the investigating officers off the scent. Secondly, Alphon was twenty-nine whereas Valerie Storie had described her assailant as being in his early to mid-twenties. He was, at five feet nine inches, too tall and he had hazel eyes, not the distinctive blue described by Valerie. He pronounced his 'th' correctly and was generally well spoken whilst the killer had what appeared to be a Cockney accent. There was no proof that Alphon ever used the word 'kip' and he was generally not hesitant in his speech as Jim had been. Finally, Alphon had not been picked out of a line-up by Miss Storie, though she had picked out another man, an innocent member of the public, who bore a resemblance to Alphon. The police search now turned to Mr J. Ryan, the man who had stayed in the room where the cartridges were found on August 21st. Furthermore, it was soon shown that J. Ryan was an alias used by someone already known to the police. Superintendent Acott was now looking for the man who used that alias, James Hanratty.

On October 6th, at 12.15 p.m., Acott was on duty in his office at New Scotland Yard when the telephone rang. The caller identified himself as Jimmy Ryan and said that he was speaking from a telephone box, though he would not say where. He had discovered that he was wanted in connection with the A6 murder and wanted to say that he had nothing to do with it. He also told Acott that he was worried and asked if he could ring back later. Acott agreed that he would be available between 10.00 p.m. and midnight.

A few minutes after 11.00 p.m., the telephone rang again. It was Ryan again, saying that he had already called the Daily Mirror for advice, but they had said that they could not help him. He again denied any involvement in the murder and said that on the night of August 22nd, when Gregsten and Valerie had first been abducted, he had been in Liverpool. He had gone up there to sell some stolen jewellery to three men he knew and, for obvious reasons, was not prepared to name them. Finally, at Acott's request, he gave the police the address of Louise Alderson in Sussex Gardens, London. Alderson was a woman he knew and with whom he had left some of his clothes. After Hanratty had hung up, the call was traced to a public phone box in Slough.

The next day, October 7th, at 5.26 p.m., Hanratty rang Acott for the third time. He said that he was now in Liverpool. He had been to see the three men that he had spoken about but they had told him that they did not want to get involved and so were unable to supply him with an alibi. Hanratty then gave a few more details about his movements around the dates in question. He had booked into the Vienna on August 21st. Next morning, after breakfast, he had gone to Paddington station, thinking that the trains for Liverpool left from there. Realizing his mistake, he went on to Euston and caught a train for Lime Street. He then stayed in Liverpool until Friday, August 25th, when he returned to London. That call too was traced. Hanratty was indeed in Liverpool.

James Hanratty was to remain free for another four days. On October 11th, two observant uniformed police officers spotted him in a cafe in Blackpool. He was immediately arrested on a holding charge of housebreaking and word was sent down to London and Superintendent Acott that his man was now in custody. By the following day, October 12th, Acott was in Blackpool, interviewing Hanratty.

Hanratty, it seems, was confident that the murder charge would not be pinned on him. He greeted Acott by asking if he had picked up his clothing from Sussex Gardens.

347

Told that the various items had been collected, Hanratty continued "I want to tell you about the suits you found there. I read in the papers that you'd sent my clothes to the laboratory for tests. Let me tell you there's blood on the green suit but it's my own blood from a cut on broken glass. The blue suit's all right. You won't find any blood on that. That's the suit I wore all that week at the Vienna Hotel and in Liverpool. It was a suit I bought just before the murder."

In fact, no blood had been found on any of Hanratty's suits, but it was the blue suit which Hanratty admitted wearing on the night of the murder that most interested Acott. The police had found the trousers and waistcoat of that suit, but the jacket was missing. Had Hanratty dumped it because it alone was bloodstained? Hanratty denied this. He said that he had disposed of it, in Stanmore, but not because it was bloodstained but because it was torn. On October 1st, well after the murder, Hanratty had broken into two houses, next door to each other, in Stanmore. Gaining access to one he had torn his jacket and, finding a black jacket inside the house, had stolen it and thrown the damaged one away. Acott said he would check up on this story and left Hanratty in the cells.

Contacting the police at Stanmore, Acott found that there was no report of a double break-in at adjacent houses on or around October 1st. It was clear to the superintendent that Hanratty was lying. It was now time to see if any of the witnesses in this case would pick him out of an identification parade.

Hanratty was escorted to Bedford and placed into a line-up on October 13th. There he was picked out by John Skillett, the driver of the car that had been cut up by the grey Morris, and James Trower, who had called for his friend Paddy Hogan. Edward Blackhall, the passenger in Skillett's car, picked out another man. The next day, another parade was organized at Stoke Mandeville hospital where Valerie Storie was now being treated. This time she asked that all the men in the line-up be made to say "Be quiet will you, I'm thinking". After hearing all the voices, she identified Hanratty as her assailant. It was enough for Acott and Hanratty was charged with murder.

James Hanratty's trial opened at Bedford on January 22nd, 1962, before Mister Justice Gorman. The case, which was to prove to be the longest murder trial in British history up to this point,

James Hanratty, executed on April 4th, 1962, for the murder of Michael Gregsten (PA/News)

lasted until February 17th. During that time the Crown's case was led by Mr Graham Swanwick whilst Hanratty was defended by Mr Michael Sherrard.

One of the first and most important witnesses was, of course, Valerie Storie. She described her terrible ordeal and was then cross-examined at length on the two identification parades that she had attended. At the first she had picked out a man who bore a resemblance to Alphon, but had not picked out Alphon himself. Furthermore, she could not now describe the man she had selected, even though she had got a very good look at him. Now she was claiming that she could identify Hanratty, with certainty, after only catching a very brief glimpse of him in the headlights of a passing car. Furthermore, whilst she denied that she had ever described the killer as having anything other than staring blue eyes, there was also the testimony of John Kerr, who swore that when he first spoke to Miss Storie she had said that the man had large staring eyes and light, fairish hair. At the time of the attack, Hanratty's hair was jet black, having only recently been dyed. Of course, John Kerr's traffic census form, with his on-the-spot notes of what Valerie had said, had mysteriously disappeared.

Next there was the testimony of John Skillett, who described his encounter with the bad driver. At the roundabout, after Edward Blackhall had wound down the passenger window, Skillett had called out "Are you fucking mad or something? You ought to get off the fucking road." Though Mr Skillett had continued to drive his vehicle he claimed that he had had a good view of the driver's face and swore that it was Hanratty. However, his passenger, Mr Blackhall, who would have had a much better and closer view, did not identify Hanratty. Yet this same witness was careful enough to note that the Morris had three red stripes on its back bumper and a torn green label. Furthermore, under cross-examination, John Skillett admitted that the one reason he had picked out Hanratty at the parade was because the driver had dark hair and Hanratty was the only one on the parade with dark hair.

More curious still was the evidence of James Trower, who had called for his friend, Paddy Hogan, in Redbridge Lane, Ilford. Trower said that he called each day to give Hogan a lift into work. On the 23rd, he parked as usual and then heard the Morris coming from the direction of Eastern Avenue. Trower estimated that he had had three full seconds to see the driver and had no hesitation in picking out Hanratty at the identification parade. It was curious then that the prosecution did not call Mr Hogan to back this testimony up. It was left to the defence to call Paddy Hogan, who said that on August 23rd, Trower was late in calling. So much so that far from waiting inside his house for him, Hogan was outside. It was as he stood there, and well before Trower arrived, that he saw the grey Morris pass and turn into Avondale Crescent, where it was later found by the police. In fact, Trower did not arrive until fifteen minutes later and so could not possibly have seen the driver.

William Nudds, the by now ex-manager of the Vienna Hotel, had made three statements to the police, each contradicting the other. In the first statement he said that it had been Alphon who behaved suspiciously and was not back in his room until well after midnight on the day in question. Then he changed his mind and said that Alphon had been back before 11.00 p.m. after all. Nudds admitted that he would have said anything to help the police out. He was a compulsive liar who, soon after this trial was over, would face further criminal charges and end up back in prison.

On November 30th, Roy Langdale, a prisoner at Brixton, made a statement to the police. In this he claimed that he had befriended Hanratty, also held at Brixton, and that they had spoken often. According to Langdale, Hanratty had admitted his guilt and had asked him if he knew how one might get a pawn ticket backdated. Langdale also claimed that Hanratty had told him that his suit had been sent to the cleaners after the murder, as he was sure that Gregsten's blood must have been on it. However, it was a simple matter for Mr Sherrard to prove that the suit had been cleaned long before the murder and, at a time when Langdale claimed that Hanratty was hiding up north somewhere, he had actually still been in London.

Superintendent Acott was not given an easy time by the defence. When he had first spoken to his prisoner, Hanratty had volunteered the information that he had worn a dark blue suit on the night of the murder, not the green one, yet it was the green one that Hanratty said might have his blood on it. Furthermore, he had voluntarily given the address where all that clothing could be found, hardly the actions of a guilty man.

Hanratty had claimed that he threw away the blue suit's jacket after the murder, as late as October 1st, because it was torn. The black jacket he had replaced it with had supposedly been taken from a house that Hanratty had burgled and Acott had found no trace of such a burglary. Now it transpired that two houses in Dennis Lane, Stanmore, were broken into on the same night, and from one of them, the thief had taken a black jacket. There was other evidence too that Hanratty had committed those break-ins for he described how in one of the houses the owner had cut off the electricity whilst he was away on holiday and Hanratty had taken a coloured candle from one of the rooms, to light his way. When the reports were checked, one of the householders had said that he had found the remains of a coloured candle in a sink.

Superintendent Acott also had to admit that at the time of the murder, Hanratty's hair was black. Carol France, the daughter of a friend of his, had dyed it for him three weeks before the murder, and Hanratty continued to wear it black until October. The killer had been said to have brownish hair. There were other points too that Acott admitted did not fit Hanratty. Jim had needed to be shown how to use the car's gears but Hanratty was an accomplished driver. The killer had said that he had been in institutions since he was eight but Hanratty had first been in trouble when he was sixteen. The killer had told how his parents had locked him in a cellar but Hanratty had never lived in a house with a cellar. The killer had not eaten for two days but Hanratty had breakfast at the Vienna on the morning of August 22nd. The killer had been sleeping rough and had been in a remand home, neither of which fitted Hanratty. Of course, the killer might have been lying about his background yet Acott had partly eliminated Alphon on what the killer had said. The police, it seemed, wanted things both ways.

There was also the problem of the spent cartridge cases found in the Vienna Hotel. If Hanratty were the killer then he would have had to have left them behind when he vacated his room on August 22nd. The police seriously claimed that it was their opinion that Hanratty had used the chair for target practice, loosing off two rounds before he checked out, without apparently disturbing any of his fellow guests.

Charles France had been a friend of Hanratty's and it had been his daughter, Carol, who dyed Hanratty's hair for him. Now, though, France was acting as a prosecution witness. He testified that Hanratty had once said to him that a good place to hide something was underneath the seat on a bus, as it would not be found until the bus was cleaned. France, however, was clearly not a reliable witness. Three days before the trial started he had attempted to kill himself and in March, he would try again, this time succeeding.

There were, in fact, five reasons for considering Hanratty to be the killer. Of these, most, if not all, had been discounted. First there was the identification. Valerie Storie had, possibly, given different descriptions and only saw the killer very briefly. Skillett must have had a poor view of the Morris driver and Trower might not have seen him at all.

Next there were the factors which Jim had applied to himself and which apparently fitted Hanratty, however, there were in fact more differences than similarities. Thirdly, there was the supposed confession to Langdale, largely discredited under cross-examination. Fourthly, there were the cartridge cases found in Hanratty's room at the Vienna and which had, apparently, lain undisturbed for many days. Finally, there was the finding of the murder weapon in a location about which it was said Hanratty had spoken. France was unstable and may well have had a score to settle, Hanratty having admitted to some heavy petting with France's young daughter.

The case was certainly going well for Hanratty when he stepped into the witness box to give his own version of events. He began by admitting that he did have a criminal record, largely for housebreaking. There were no crimes of violence or of a sexual nature recorded against his name.

Hanratty described how he had first gone to stay with Charles 'Dixie' France in July 1960. It was there, some time in late July 1961, that Carol France had dyed his hair black. Turning to France's evidence about the hiding place, Hanratty admitted that he had once mentioned to his friend that if he stole a large amount of jewellery he would sort it out on the top deck of a bus, keeping the good stuff and putting the rubbish under a seat, but he had never said that this was a good hiding place.

In July 1961, Hanratty had met Louise Alderson, who ran an antique shop in Greek Street, Soho. They did some business together, and it was at her address that he met one of his girlfriends, Mary Meaden, at whose address he left some of his clothes.

Hanratty said that on August 21st, he had slept in room twenty-four of the Vienna Hotel, arriving there at about midnight. The next day he went by train to Liverpool and left his suitcase at Lime Street's left luggage office. He noticed that one of the attendants there had something wrong with one of his hands. The defence had since found a man named Usher who worked there and who had two fingers missing from one hand.

In Liverpool, Hanratty needed to find an address that was either Carlton or Tarleton Place or Street. He looked around without finding it and finally walked into a sweetshop on Scotland Road to ask for directions. There was a woman behind the counter, and a little girl. The woman told him that he had come too far and had to go back into the city centre. He eventually found the address, but did not manage to contact his friends.

That night, the same night that Gregsten and Valerie Storie were taken prisoner, Hanratty went to a Lyon's cafe in Lime Street and then went on to a billiard hall nearby. He saw a man on the stairs and asked him if he wanted to buy a gold watch. The man seemed to take umbrage at this, said he was the manager and ordered Hanratty to leave, as he did not want anyone trying to sell things on his premises.

If it could be proved that Hanratty stayed in Liverpool on the night of August 22nd, then he was in the clear. The defence had already traced Mr Kempt, the manager of the Reynolds Billiards Hall in Lime Street, and he recalled an encounter with someone who tried to sell him a watch. He knew that it was some time towards the end of August but could not confirm the precise date.

More promising was the testimony of Mrs Olive Dinwoodie. She confirmed that she was in a sweetshop on Scotland Road on both August 21st and August 22nd. On one of those days a man did come in and ask for directions to Tarleton Road. She only knew of a Tarleton Street and directed him accordingly. Though at first Mrs Dinwoodie could not accurately fix the date, she finally decided that it must have been the 21st. However, Hanratty had mentioned a little girl being present in the shop, and as Mrs Dinwoodie's granddaughter had not been present in the shop until after 4.45 p.m. on the 22nd, it seemed quite possible that Hanratty was telling the truth. Furthermore, Mrs Dinwoodie also confirmed that Hanratty resembled the man she had seen.

The prosecution now tried to contend that Mrs Dinwoodie was mistaken about the date and that Hanratty had gone up to Liverpool on the 21st in order to produce an alibi for himself. After all, Mr Kempt could not say what date he had seen the man on the stairs and Mrs Dinwoodie had originally felt that she had seen her customer on the 21st. Nevertheless, the fact remained that there must have been a good deal of doubt in the jury's collective minds when Hanratty dropped a bombshell. He wished to change his alibi.

Hanratty had always claimed that he had gone to Liverpool to find three men who he expected to buy some stolen jewellery from him. His barrister had told him that in order to prove this alibi he would have to name those men. Hanratty refused to do so and now said that there was another way he could prove that he was not in Bedfordshire when the murder took place. He had lied when he said that he had stayed in Liverpool until the 25th. Yes, he had gone to that city and his stories about the left luggage, the sweetshop and the billiard hall were true, but he had then gone on to Rhyl that same night.

Hanratty returned to the witness box and was now questioned on this amendment to his alibi. He now said that he had gone to Rhyl and stayed there until the 24th, when he returned to Liverpool in order to catch the train back to London. Asked to describe what had happened, Hanratty said that when he arrived in Rhyl he found it hard to find a room. Eventually he came upon a small private house with a Bed and Breakfast sign in the window. A woman who wore glasses answered the door. She had greyish hair. Inside the hallway there was a coat-rack, a mirror and a large plant in a bowl. There was a green bath in the attic and he had paid twenty-five shillings for the two nights. He could not say precisely where the house was but he could hear trains from his bedroom, though he could not actually see the tracks.

Hasty attempts were made to find the house and soon the defence had traced Mrs Grace Jones, who lived at Ingledene, 19 Kinmel Street, Rhyl. Her house matched Hanratty's description and she agreed that Hanratty had stayed there sometime between August 19th and August 26th. There was a visitor's book at the hotel but signing it was not compulsory and many guests did not bother to do so. Hanratty, if he was a guest, was one of those who had not signed.

Continuing his narrative, Hanratty said that he had returned to Liverpool on August 24th, from where he sent a telegram to Charles France reading "Having a nice time. Be home early Friday morning for business. Yours sincerely Jim". The night train from Lime Street arrived at Euston at 6.00 a.m. on Friday the 25th. Later that morning he went around to France's house where he had some breakfast. The following day he visited Louise Alderson and a few days after that, on September 4th, he went to Ireland. Before going, though, Carol France had tinted his hair again as the roots were just beginning to show through.

After five days in Ireland, Hanratty returned to London and was back to his old trade of breaking into houses. On the last night of September, into the early hours of October 1st, he broke into the two houses in Stanmore, stealing the black jacket and throwing away his blue one. Finally, after discovering that he was wanted in connection with the A6 murder, Hanratty began telephoning the police and telling them that he was innocent of the crime.

The jury retired to consider their verdict and after six-and-a-half hours deliberation returned to ask the judge for clarification on the definition of reasonable doubt. Mister Justice Gorman told them that they had to be certain and sure of Hanratty's guilt in order to convict him. They then retired again and spent three more hours in conference. Finally they returned to announce that Hanratty was guilty.

An appeal was entered and heard on March 13th before the Lord Chief Justice, Lord Parker and Justices Ashworth and Atkinson. They saw no reason to interfere with the verdict. Just over two weeks later, on Wednesday, April 4th, James Hanratty, still only twenty-five, was hanged at Bedford jail by Harry Allen. In his last letters to his parents and brother he again repeated that he was innocent and was to die for another man's crime.

The Hanratty case did not end there. In 1963, Peter Alphon confessed to Jean Justice that he was the killer of Michael Gregsten and had decided to frame Hanratty by planting the cartridges in the Vienna. This led to a debate in the House of Commons but the Home Secretary refused to order that the case be reopened. Over the next few years, Alphon alternated between confessing to the crime and then withdrawing that confession, at one stage claiming instead that the framing of Hanratty had been carried out by Charles France, who was paid to put the bullets in the hotel room and the murder weapon on top of a bus.

In 1967, Alphon called a press conference in Paris and stated that a wealthy London businessman had paid him to end the relationship between Gregsten and Valerie Storie. Later he withdrew this story too and confirmed that he was in fact innocent of the crime. However, in the same year the new Home Secretary, Roy Jenkins, announced an investigation into Hanratty's Rhyl alibi. This was carried out by Chief Superintendent Douglas Nimmo, who reported that the alibi could not be substantiated.

Nevertheless, the case remains full of curiosities. Two days after Hanratty's trial had ended, the Daily Sketch carried a story which, if true, is one of the most astounding coincidences in the annals of true crime.

According to this story, on August 31st, Janet Gregsten, the dead man's widow, had been helping her brother-in-law, William Ewer, in his antique shop in Swiss Cottage. The shop was situated in an arcade and as Janet put something in the window she saw a man enter the dry cleaners opposite. Janet pointed and declared, "That's the man the police are looking for. That's the man. He fits the description."

Ewer tried to calm his sister-in-law but when Janet persisted, he went into the dry cleaners and asked about the customer who, by then, had left. He had given the name of J. Ryan and an address in St John's Wood. The coincidence did not end there, though. The very next day, September 1st, Ewer was in a cafe in Finchley Road when he saw the same man. He followed him out of the cafe to a florist's shop. Ewer immediately telephoned Scotland Yard but by the time the police arrived, the man had gone. The police checked inside the florists and found that the man had paid to have some roses sent to his mother. The name and address was that of Mrs Hanratty, 12 Sycamore Grove, Kingsbury.

When this story broke, both William Ewer and Janet Gregsten dismissed it as a fantasy from the press, but a number of reporters working for other newspapers reported overhearing Ewer as he gave the story to a couple of reporters in a bar during the last week of the trial. Whatever the truth, it is certainly an astounding story.

In the final analysis, was Hanratty guilty of murder? The evidence against him was very weak, but it can be settled for all time. The killer of Michael Gregsten left behind crucial evidence that could prove his identity. He had raped Miss Storie and from the semen he left behind, the police were able to determine that the killer was blood group 'O'. Incidentally, both Hanratty and Alphon were group 'O', as are thirty-six per cent of the entire population.

In the 1960s that was all that could be determined but now we have DNA testing. Such testing has already been carried out on the semen staining and on cell samples taken from Hanratty's brother. Even now, the results are the subject of obfuscation. Some reports claim that they confirm Hanratty's guilt, others that they are inconclusive and that the results can only ever be finalized when Hanratty is exhumed and samples are taken from his body.

However, there is one final twist. Further samples were taken from James Hanratty's mother. At the time of writing, the results of tests on those samples have not been made public but on March 29th, 1999, it was announced that the case is to be sent back to the Court of Appeal. Surely if those samples prove that Hanratty was the killer after all, there would be no grounds for sending the case to appeal. Possibly, thirty-seven years after his death, the courts will finally decide that James Hanratty was hanged for a crime he did not commit.

Suggestion for further reading:

E. F. L. Russell, *Deadman's Hill. Was Hanratty Guilty?* (London: Secker & Warburg, 1965).

44
Colin Lattimore, Ronald Leighton and Ahmet Salih

Sentenced for the murder of Maxwell Confait, at Catford, London

A T around 1.20 a.m., on the morning of Saturday, April 22nd, 1972, firemen were summoned to a blaze at 27 Doggett Road, Catford, London. They found the basement and ground floor of the house well ablaze but still managed to bring the fire under control within ten minutes. Only then did the officers on the scene discover the body of a young man in the back bedroom upstairs, but he had not been a victim of the flames for a mark around his neck showed that he had been strangled.

The police arrived at 1.45 a.m., and were followed by the police surgeon, Dr Angus Bain, some fifteen minutes later. Dr Bain confirmed that the young man was dead, and that the cause of death was asphyxia. An initial estimate of the time of death, based on the onset of rigor mortis, lay between 8.00 p.m. and 10.00 p.m. on April 21st. This was slightly extended by Dr James Cameron, the pathologist, who arrived at Doggett Road at 3.45 a.m. Dr Cameron believed that the man had died between 7.45 p.m. and 11.45 p.m.

A police search of the premises showed that the blaze had been started deliberately. The officer in charge of the investigation, Detective Chief Superintendent Alan Jones, soon discovered that the dead man was a twenty-six-year-old transvestite homosexual prostitute named Maxwell Confait, who preferred to be known as Michelle.

The fire had originally been reported by a neighbour, but had first been discovered by Confait's landlord, a West Indian named Winston Goode. Mr Goode told the police that he had first met Confait a couple of years before, at about the same time as Goode's marriage had broken up. Goode's wife and family still lived in the same house, but they now led separate lives.

Continuing his story, Goode said that in February 1972, Confait had moved into the house at Doggett Road, and they had become close friends, though Goode denied that any homosexual relationship had existed between them. The arrangement was that Confait paid rent of £2.50 per week and cooked meals for Goode whilst he was out at work.

Turning to the night of the fire, Goode said that he had been asleep in his room, which was in the basement, when he was woken by the sound of the flames. He ran upstairs to call his wife and children out and then shouted up to Confait, but received no reply. However, when Mrs Goode was interviewed she reported that her estranged husband had appeared to be behaving somewhat strangely when he woke her and the children. His eyes were wide and he did not seem to know what he was doing. Indeed, so concerned was she that she sent a neighbour after Winston when he went off to telephone the Fire Brigade. The neighbour had found him still fumbling with the dial and had had to complete the call for him.

Further interviews with Winston Goode showed that Confait was about to leave Doggett Road. In addition, Goode admitted to feeling jealous when Confait had informed him that he was going to move in with one of his lovers. Was this a motive for murder? The police certainly thought so and at this early stage were concentrating their efforts on Winston Goode, when circumstances took them off on a different track.

On April 24th, two days after the fire had been discovered in Doggett Road, three more fires broke out close by. One was on a railway embankment behind Doggett Road, another was in a hut in Ladywell Fields and the third was in a derelict house in Nelgarde Road. Perhaps these fires, also started maliciously, had a connection with the death of Maxwell Confait.

At 5.20 p.m., that same day, Constable Roy Cumming stopped a young man who was loitering in Nelgarde Road, close to where the fire had been. The man gave his name as Colin Lattimore and when asked about the fire which had been set earlier that day, he admitted that he was responsible. Constable Cumming, aware of the possible links with the Confait case, asked Lattimore if he knew anything about the fire in Doggett Road and Lattimore replied, "I was with Ronnie. We lit it, but put it out. It was smoking when we left."

The Ronnie to whom Lattimore had been referring was fifteen-year-old Ronald Leighton, who lived in Doggett Road itself. Lattimore was taken to Leighton's house by the police, who found Leighton with another friend of his, fourteen-year-old Ahmet Salih. All three were then taken to Lewisham Police Station, where interviews were conducted by Superintendent Jones, Detective Inspector Graham Stockwell and Detective Constable Peter Woledge.

Despite the fact that two of the suspects were under sixteen, and Lattimore, although eighteen, was educationally subnormal with a mental age of eight, those interviews were not conducted in the presence of either a solicitor, or any of the boys' parents. Later, both Lattimore and Salih claimed that Woledge assaulted them during their interviews and Leighton said that he was pushed about. Whatever the truth of these allegations, both Lattimore and Leighton admitted to killing Confait and starting the fires at Doggett Road and the other three locations. Salih admitted to helping to start the fires but denied any involvement in Confait's death. All three were then charged with murder.

On May 26th, the murder charge against Salih was dropped and he was then allowed bail on the arson charges. His two co-defendants remained in custody.

The final magistrate's hearing took place just a few days later, on June 2nd, at Woolwich. The police scenario was that Leighton had done the actual killing, Lattimore had placed a piece of flex around Confait's throat and Salih had later assisted in starting the fire. Both Dr Bain and Dr Cameron appeared to give evidence and both said that they had now narrowed the time of death to between 6.30 p.m. and 10.30 p.m. Though all three defendants had alibis for these times, they had nevertheless confessed to being involved, and so they were sent for trial.

At this stage, the boys' defence team was confident that they would secure an acquittal. On April 21st, Lattimore had been at a remedial day centre until he went home for his evening meal. Afterwards he went with his brother, Gary, to the Salvation Army Youth Club, where they were both seen by various witnesses. Everyone agreed that Lattimore was there until around 10.30 p.m.

Salih and Leighton had spent the day together at Leighton's house. There were two witnesses to this, Salih's sister, Periuan and a friend of hers, Deborah Ricketts. The two boys walked the girls to the bus stop outside the cinema at 9.15 p.m. After this they went to a shoe shop they had noticed, in Sangley Road, and decided to break in to see what they could steal. They returned to Leighton's house to get a screwdriver, went back to the shop and broke in, stealing a few pounds from the till. Later, for some reason, they decided to break in again but were arrested by the police as they left. The time of this arrest was 1.30 a.m. on April 22nd.

The trial opened at the Old Bailey, before Mister Justice Chapman, on November 1st, 1972. The proceedings lasted until November 24th, during which Mr Richard Du Cann led for the prosecution. Lattimore was defended by Mr John Marriage, Leighton by Mr Cyril Solomon and Salih by Mr Brian Watling.

What should have been an easy case to win for the defence turned into something else when it became time for Dr Bain and Dr Cameron to give their evidence. Now they had changed their minds. Taking into account various factors such as the heat in the bedroom affecting the onset of rigor mortis, they now believed that Confait could have died as late as 1.00 a.m., on April 22nd. None of the three had an alibi for that time. Lattimore said that he was at home at that hour and the other two claimed to be breaking into a shop for the second time. None had any reliable confirmation of where they were for the times between 10.30 p.m. on the 21st until some time before 1.30 a.m. on the 22nd, when Salih and Leighton were arrested by the police.

The confessions now carried much more weight and, as a result, it took the jury only three-and-a-half hours to return their verdicts. Lattimore was found guilty of manslaughter and arson and ordered to be detained under the Mental Health Act without limit of time. Leighton was found guilty of murder, arson and burglary and was sentenced to be detained During Her Majesty's Pleasure. Salih was adjudged to be guilty of arson and burglary and was given four years.

An appeal was fought on July 26th, 1973, on the grounds that the original time of death had been correct and that the three defendants therefore had alibis. However, the

Appeal Court ruled that the times given in the trial itself were reliable and that therefore the three had no alibis. This ruling combined with the various confessions made by the three boys was enough to lose them the appeal. The case would then have sunk into obscurity but for the efforts of Colin Lattimore's father, George, who began writing letters and highlighting problems with the case. Two of those letters in particular bore fruit. One, to the local Member of Parliament, Mr Carol Johnson, caused him to take the case up and write to the Home Office, who informed him that in order to reopen the case, fresh evidence would be needed. The other letter was to the National Council for Civil Liberties, who decided to put the medical evidence on the case into the hands of the famous pathologist, Professor Donald Teare.

In April, 1974, Professor Teare stated that in his opinion, the fire would have had no effect on rigor mortis. Both Dr Bain and Dr Cameron had been right first time. Maxwell Confait had died between 6.30 p.m. and 10.30 p.m., on April 21st. Once again, the alibis were viable.

On May 22nd, 1974, Winston Goode, the first suspect in the murder of Maxwell Confait, committed suicide by taking cyanide. A police enquiry was then set up into his death, and was asked to pay particular attention to any possible involvement in the murder of Confait. As part of that enquiry, a secret report was commissioned from another noted pathologist, Professor Keith Simpson. His report agreed with the findings of Professor Teare. Confait had died well before the time quoted at the trial.

On June 18th, 1975, Roy Jenkins, the Home Secretary, announced that the case had been sent back to the Court of Appeal. That appeal was heard on October 6th, before Lord Justice Scarman, Lord Justice Ormond and Mister Justice Swanwick. They listened to the new evidence and then reserved their judgement for a week. It was not until October 17th that they ruled that all three appellants must be exonerated from any involvement in Confait's death, and that they must be released from prison immediately. This, of course, implied that the confessions they had made were false and, since they contained facts that the defendants could not have known, must have been prompted by one or more police officers. An inquiry was held but no blame was attached to any particular officer, so no charges were ever laid against the police.

Mistaken medical testimony and improper police behaviour had deprived three innocent young men of more than three years of their freedom.

Judith Minna Theresa Ward

45

Jailed for life for the murder of twelve people near Gomersal, Yorkshire

THE coach was very crowded, and by the time it left the Hartshead Moor service station on the M62, there were even people sitting on suitcases in the aisle. Most of those occupying seats and crowding into the spare spaces between them were servicemen, but some had their families, wives, and children with them. Many were dozing, others were singing. The driver, Roland Handley, a director of the company who had supplied the coach, glanced at his watch. They were into the first ten minutes or so of Monday, February 4th, 1974.

The black-and-white liveried coach had started its journey from Manchester bus station at 11.00 p.m., on Sunday, February 3rd. Chartered to take soldiers and airmen back to Catterick and RAF Leeming, it had also stopped at Oldham, at 11.20 p.m., and then at Queensgate in Huddersfield, at 11.55 p.m., to take on extra passengers. Now Roland Handley was driving through the thick freezing fog of this dismal February morning, his next stops the camps themselves. It was a trip he had made many times before, for the run was a regular weekly one.

At 12.20 a.m., the coach had reached a spot near Gomersal, between Chain Bar and Gilderstone, when a large explosion ripped through the back, strewing wreckage, debris and bodies along the motorway. Somehow, Roland Handley managed to wrestle with the controls and pull the vehicle over onto the hard shoulder, even though he had been injured by flying glass when the windscreen had shattered. Now all that could be heard was the shouting and screaming of those who had been injured.

A total of eleven people lost their lives in the initial blast. Four of those came from one family – Corporal Clifford Houghton, his twenty-four-year-old wife Linda, and their two sons, Lee aged five and two-year-old Robert, had been sitting on the back seat, and all died instantly. All the other seven were servicemen – Signalmen Michael Eugene Waugh, Paul Anthony Reid and Leslie David Walsh, Lance Corporal James John McShane, Fusilier Jack Thomas Hynes and two Gunners, Leonard James Godden and Terence Griffin. Another fourteen people were injured and one of those, Fusilier Stephen Walley, would die later from his wounds, bringing the death toll up to twelve. This

The devastated coach, blown-up on the M62 motorway near Gomersal, Yorkshire, in the early hours of February 4th, 1974 (Reproduced by courtesy of the Yorkshire Evening Post)

carnage had to be the work of a terrorist organization, and the first suspects were the Irish Republican Army (IRA).

The officer placed in charge of the inquiry was Detective Chief Superintendent George Oldfield, who would, three years later, achieve fame as the head of the squad hunting the Yorkshire Ripper, Peter Sutcliffe. For now, though, he concentrated on trying to determine who had planted a bomb on a coach and taken the lives of so many people.

Chief Superintendent Oldfield had been able to determine that the device had contained some fifty pounds of explosive, and by interviewing survivors, discovered that there had been a smell of marzipan after the blast, indicating that the explosive had been based on nitro-glycerine. Where, though, had that bomb been placed on the coach?

Before leaving Manchester, the coach had been left unattended in a car park adjoining Princes Street, in the city centre. Roland Handley recalled checking the vehicle out before he drove it to the bus station, and said that it did not appear to have been tampered with. Once at the Chorlton Street station, he simply left the boot open so that the squaddies could throw their luggage inside. The same thing happened at Oldham but there had definitely been no cases put into the boot at Huddersfield. Forensic tests had shown that the timer might have been set an hour or more before the blast, so it was possible that the bomb had been placed on the coach in Manchester, Oldham, or even when the driver stopped at the service station.

An appeal for witnesses who might have seen anyone loitering near the rear of the coach was made and this led to a search for seven people seen near the Princes Street car park on Sunday, just before the coach was moved. These included three West Indian men and three white women, but early efforts concentrated on the seventh, a man described as having prominent sideburns, an attractive face, and carrying a black executive-type briefcase. Meanwhile, a group of Conservative MPs, sensing the mood of the general public, demanded the return of capital punishment for such acts of terrorism that resulted in the deaths of victims.

In fact, it was not until the early hours of Thursday, February 14th, that an arrest was made. Constable Ron Barnes and a colleague were patrolling the streets of Liverpool. Strolling down Church Street they saw a young woman in a shop doorway. She appeared to be nervous and was looking up and down the street and trying, unsuccessfully, to light a cigarette. Church Street was close to the Pier Head and boats left from there for Ireland. As a matter of routine, the two officers decided to stop the woman and question her.

The woman gave her name as Judith Theresa Ward and produced a driving licence in that name showing an address in Edward Street, Newry, in Northern Ireland. She said that she was on her way back to Newry but had no money and no ticket on her. A quick check showed that the woman, whose real name was Judith Minna Ward, Theresa being merely a confirmation name, had had previous encounters with the police and had known IRA sympathies. She was taken into the police station whilst further inquiries were made.

Judith Ward was questioned for twenty-four hours. During that time she was searched and scrapings were taken from beneath her fingernails. When those scrapings were subjected to forensic tests at RARDE, the Royal Armament Research and Development Establishment at Woolwich, they tested positive for nitro-glycerine, indicating that Judith had handled that explosive recently. Finally, under further interrogation, she admitted her part not just in the M62 blast but also in two other explosions, one at Euston station in London and the other at the National Defence College at Latimer in Buckinghamshire. She was then charged with twelve counts of murder and various other offences.

Having made a total of seventeen appearances before the magistrates, Judith Ward was finally sent for trial. Those proceedings opened on October 3rd, 1974, at Wakefield, before Mister Justice Waller and a jury of nine men and three women. The trial lasted until November 5th, during which Judith was defended by Mr Andrew Rankin and Mr Logan Petch. The case for the prosecution was led by Mr John Cobb, who had two assistants, Mr Peter Taylor and Mr Brian Walsh.

Some of the history of Judith Ward came out during the early days of the hearing. In February 1971, she had joined the Women's Royal Army Corps (WRAC) and after basic training at Guildford, had been posted to Catterick, in the March of that same year. Ward had asked to be posted to Northern Ireland but this was refused and she was posted instead to Aldershot. When the Army refused to allow her to buy herself out, Ward went absent without leave in October. In May 1972 she was picked up by the authorities and, after being fined £20, was discharged in June.

After leaving the forces, Judith went to Stockport for a short time, living in Stanbury Place, Otterton, Stockport, but then, in July, she went to Ireland where she stayed until September. She was not heard of again until 8.45 a.m., on August 26th, 1973, when she was found sleeping on the concourse of Euston Station by Sergeant McGrath. He conducted a search of Ward's rucksack and found papers and a scrapbook which showed sympathy for the IRA cause. As a result, Special Branch were called and an officer was sent to interview her. She was released without charge later that day.

On September 10th, at 1.15 p.m., a bomb exploded at Euston station. Soon afterwards, Judith Ward and another woman, Elaine Gateley, were seen at one of the barriers, shouting abuse. At one stage Ward had apparently called out "If the IRA had done it, it would have been a bigger and better fucking bang. They would have done it properly." That night, after this had been passed on to the authorities, Ward was picked up and found to have papers on her referring to the IRA and Sinn Fein. She also had a list of telephone numbers.

During that interview, Ward volunteered that she was working as a chambermaid at the London Park Hotel, situated at the Elephant and Castle. She stayed there until November 9th, 1973, and the following day was stopped at Holyhead as she was about to board a boat for Dublin. Once again IRA literature was found but Ward was not detained.

By November 23rd, she was back in Stockport but in the following year she replied to an advertisement in *Horse and Groom* magazine for a position taking care of horses in Chipperfield's circus. She was interviewed on January 24th, and got the job, starting straight away and moving into one of the caravans that the travellers used. The circus then carried on with its tour of the country, leaving Belle Vue, Manchester on February 2nd, and travelling down to Oxfordshire. Witnesses were now called to back up the prosecution's case. For security reasons, many of those witnesses were never named.

WRAC Private Margaret Mary Blake was called to confirm Ward's army service. Margaret had joined the WRAC in December 1970, a few months before Ward, and had met her at Catterick. The two women had little to do with each other and soon afterwards, Margaret was posted to Aldershot, Ward following her later. One day, the two women travelled down to London together and Margaret noticed that Ward seemed to have a lot of luggage with her. She explained this by saying that she was taking some clothes home to Manchester but actually failed to return from that leave. Some months later she was returned to barracks under close arrest and when Margaret spoke to her, Ward said she had been "...helping people out in Northern Ireland". She then qualified this by saying that she had been helping them to blow pubs up. Margaret noticed that Ward had the initials IRA scratched into one arm and claimed that she was now a Lieutenant in that organization.

In early September 1972, Ward was certainly in Ulster because she was picked up by the Royal Ulster Constabulary (RUC), in Londonderry, on September 3rd. Interviewed by Detective Constable Patrick McNulty, Ward again claimed to be involved with the IRA, saying that she used the name Theresa O'Connell and carried messages concealed in her clothing into Long Kesh prison. She also referred to two men, Paddy McNally and Seamus Quigley, who had asked her for a map of the Aldershot camp where she had been posted.

Later there was an explosion there and Ward then realized why they had wanted her drawing. McNulty telephoned this information through to London but was told that Ward had already been seen and that no further action was necessary.

Elaine Gateley, who shared a room with Ward at the London hotel where they both worked, testified that Ward used to sell the IRA publication *Struggling for Freedom* outside the hotel. She also sold Gaelic newspapers in Kilburn. This further underlined Ward's Republican sympathies.

A woman named only as Wendy said that she had worked for Chipperfield's circus and shared a caravan with Ward. One day, Ward was arguing with a man named Michael Austin, about the violence in Northern Ireland. During that conversation, Ward said that she was from Newry and spoke about how bombs were made. Wendy thought that Ward was implying that she was involved in their manufacture, but she also believed that Ward was only joking.

Another witness was a soldier who had survived the bomb blast. He said that he was a regular traveller on that route. For a few Sunday nights before the explosion he had seen a car parked near Portland Street, in Manchester. It was an old Austin, with running boards, and the man in the driving seat always seemed to be watching the coach. The car was there again on the night of February 3rd.

On March 20th, Ward had been interviewed at Risley remand centre by Detective Inspector Walter Boreham. She spoke of two IRA members, Keiron McMorrow and Marlene Coyle, saying she had met them in Manchester when they were living in the Longsight area of the city. She added, "You won't get them anyway, they are gone". Ward then said that on February 2nd she had gone to Derby to collect the explosives with McMorrow and had spent the night with him in the car, with the bomb in a holdall in the back. There was a code in the holdall itself. If it were green, Marlene Coyle would plant the bomb, if it were khaki, then McMorrow would. The holdall they collected from Derby was brownish in colour so it would be McMorrow who planted the bomb on the coach. Ward then claimed to have waited in the car whilst McMorrow went to plant the bomb.

Another officer involved in those interviews at Risley had been Detective Chief Superintendent Brian Waite. Ward had confessed to him too that she had carried the M62 bomb, but she regretted the loss of life it caused, especially the deaths of the children. She had been told that the bomb would be timed to go off in the bus station.

Chief Inspector Edwin Sanderson had interviewed Ward at Dewsbury in April. She had told him that her boyfriend had been Michael McVerry, who had been shot by British soldiers soon after she had married him. However, there was no record of such a marriage taking place, which showed that Ward was romancing.

Though Ward had confessed to her involvement in three bombing incidents, including the M62 bomb, it could easily be shown that she was prone to invent stories about herself. There was no evidence, apart from her own statements, that she had ever been an active member of the IRA; her supposed marriage to McVerry was easily demonstrated to be an invention; and, most importantly of all, doubt was also cast over the validity of Ward's statement about her whereabouts on the day the bomb was planted. This doubt was raised when another unnamed witness, the elephant groom at the circus, was called to give evidence. He told the court that on the night of February 3rd, he and Ward and a number of other employees had been in the Blue Boar pub in Chipping Norton, Oxfordshire. They went there at 8.00 p.m., and stayed until 10.45 p.m. Ward had a lot to drink and had to be helped back to her caravan.

This testimony plainly showed that Ward's "confession" was nonsense, however the prosecution next attempted to demonstrate the existence of hard evidence which connected Ward to the bombs themselves. This evidence was provided by three scientific experts, and was enough to convince the jury of Ward's guilt.

Walter Norman Elliott was an explosives expert of twenty years standing. He had tested for nitro-glycerine in Ward's caravan at the circus. He had taken a large number of swabs but only two proved positive, and he had to admit under cross-examination that other test articles known not to have been in contact with the explosive had tested positive as well. Swabs taken from Ward's hands after the Euston explosion had tested positive too. However, swabs taken from two other people had also tested positive, but it was thought that this might have come about from them touching some of the debris, so no charges were placed at that time. These inconsistencies should have immediately invalidated the tests used, but they did not.

Douglas Geoffrey Higgs was a Principal Scientific Officer at Woolwich and he had examined the debris from the M62 coach. He found what appeared to be parts of an alarm clock and some wiring. Swabs he took were negative for nitro-glycerine, so he was unable to say what type of explosive was used, as there were no traces of it left.

Doctor Frank Skuse had been a Home Office analyst since 1963 and he took swabs from Ward's hands after her arrest on February 14th. The tests he conducted showed traces of a commercial explosive. Furthermore, whilst tests made on some of Ward's clothing, which had been found in a holdall, showed the presence of nitro-glycerine, other tests on other items proved negative, showing that the explosives could not have contaminated her clothes whilst in the holdall.

The time came for Judith Ward to step into the witness box and give her own testimony, which she began to do on October 21st. She began by saying that she had left school at sixteen and started work as a trainee groom at a riding school in Wiltshire. In 1966, she took a similar job at a school near Newry in Northern Ireland, leaving this in October 1970. She had no connections with any political organization.

In October 1970 she returned to her parent's home in Stockport, worked in a bakery for a time, and then applied to join the WRAC. She had wanted to be a driver but they told her that she was too small and suggested instead that she train as a communications centre operator. After training at Guildford she spent some time at Catterick, where she put Northern Ireland as her first choice for her next posting. She did this for no particular political reasons.

366

After she had left the Army, she went back to Stockport and one day a man called and asked her to help the IRA by passing messages for them. She refused at first but eventually agreed. Continuing her narrative, Ward claimed that she had married McVerry on August 15th, 1973, just three months before he was shot dead in a gun battle with British soldiers. Before this she had refused to spy for the IRA even though her husband was a serving member of the Provisionals.

After McVerry was shot, on November 15th, 1973, Ward said she was asked to 'suss out' Manchester airport. Some time later she was also asked to do the same at Euston station. After the bomb had gone off there she left her address in London because she was concerned that she might be linked with the IRA.

Ward admitted that she had spoken about Molotov cocktails whilst working with the circus at Belle Vue. She left the circus on February 4th and moved into a flat owned by a man named Jim Mooney, in Kilburn. A few days later, Joe Coyle arrived and left behind a piece of paper with things on it about explosives and the name of a man who could supply them. She got frightened, left the flat and spent a few days living rough in a railway carriage at Euston.

Judith Ward cried in the witness box as she was asked why she had made up stories to the police admitting her involvement. She replied that she was afraid of a man that she knew as Hardy and who came from Manchester (Ward later identified 'Hardy' as McMorrow, upon being shown a photograph during the trial). Later, the men she knew claimed responsibility for the M62 bomb and the one at the Latimer College, but Ward insisted that she was not associated with either of them, as she did not agree with the violence.

One of the offences that Judith Ward had been charged with was the bombing of the Latimer College, which took place after the M62 explosion. The defence now called Ernest Mayall, who was brought to the court from prison where he was serving a two-year sentence for theft and deception.

Mayall said that a few days before the Latimer incident he had met Ward in London, and spent the weekend with her. On the day of the Latimer attack, he and Ward and another girl were in a block of flats near Euston station. At 6.00 p.m. that evening, he and Ward caught a coach to Cardiff where they booked into a hotel in his name. She did not leave him until 3.00 p.m. the following day, meaning that she could not have been involved in the Latimer bombing, as she had claimed in one of her statements to the police.

In his closing speech for the defence, Mr Rankin asked if Judith Ward were guilty, why did she not flee the country as soon as the M62 coach had exploded. Instead, she went to London and made no attempt to conceal her identity. She had applied for a job with horses in Cambridgeshire, hardly the actions of an IRA fanatic, and had no specialist knowledge of the coach from Manchester to Catterick. Thousands of people knew about that route and professional terrorists would not need advice and help from someone like Ward on where to plant the bomb. As for the confessions, Ward had been shown to be a romancer and the jury had to decide whether she made her statements in order to achieve notoriety and a place in Irish folklore.

The jury found Judith Ward guilty on all counts. For the Euston bombing, she received five years. For the M62 coach blast she was given twenty years to run concurrently and for the Latimer College bombing, another ten years, consecutively. For the twelve murders on the M62, Ward was given life sentences with no recommendation as to the minimum term she should serve.

In effect, Judith Ward was found guilty for three principle reasons. Firstly, she had admitted her part in all three outrages. Secondly, she had been physically at or near all three locations, though doubt had been cast on her presence at Latimer. Thirdly, scientific evidence had linked her with explosives. However, if we accept that she invented dozens of stories about herself and subsequently retracted her confessions, then that removes the first two of those reasons, as it had only been her statements that put her in two of the locations. Now, only the scientific evidence remained.

Judith Ward languished in jail until June 4th, 1992. It was on that date that the case was heard again by the Court of Appeal, with Justices Steyn, Glidewell and Nolan revealing that it had come to their attention that the scientific evidence, the one remaining tenet of the case, had been manufactured.

Three government scientists had withheld material evidence and misled both the prosecution and the defence at Judith Ward's trial. This was done to promote the cause that Ward had been in contact with nitro-glycerine. In addition, the West Yorkshire police force had sent only 225 statements to the Director of Public Prosecutions, yet they had taken over 1,700. Many of the remaining statements showed her tendency to fantasize and would have greatly assisted the defence. In short, the police had been selective in what evidence they used against her, and the scientific evidence had been falsified.

On June 5th, the first day of freedom for Judith Ward in almost eighteen years, the Deputy Chief Constable, Paul Whitehouse, expressed his regret at her prison ordeal and the time she had spent in prison because of an "...unsafe and unsatisfactory conviction".

Once again, language had been carefully selected, describing the conviction as unsafe. It would have been more accurate to clearly state that Judith Ward was, and always had been, innocent of all the charges against her. It should also be remembered that had those vociferous Conservative MPs in February 1974 had their way, Judith Ward would have been hanged for something that she did not do.

	The Guildford Four
46	*Patrick Armstrong, Gerard Conlon,*
	Paul Michael Hill and Carole Richardson
	Jailed for the murder of five people at Guildford, Surrey

T HE night of October 5th, 1974, was a typical Saturday night in Guildford. Like in so many other towns across the country, the pubs were filled with people anxious to cast away at least some of the cares of the working week. The only difference as far as Guildford was concerned was that it was an Army town, and many of the drinkers there were serving in the forces.

The Horse and Groom in North Street was quite full. Groups of friends sat around tables, talking and laughing. Others stood at the bar, ordering drinks and putting the world to rights. Then, at 8.50 p.m., their world was shattered when a bomb exploded. More than fifty people were hurt, many of them seriously, but five people, Women's Royal Army Corps (WRAC) Private Caroline Jean Slater, WRAC Private Ann Hamilton, Guardsman William McKenzie Forsyth, Guardsman John Crawford Hunter and a civilian, Paul Cray, were killed.

Most of those who were injured needed help to get out of the rubble that had only moments before been a packed and lively pub. One man, though, Jim Tydeman, staggered out of the wreckage and, suffering from concussion, managed to walk down North Street and then turn into Swan Lane. There he found another pub, the Seven Stars, went inside and ordered himself a fresh pint of beer.

It was not long before the manager of the Seven Stars, Owen O'Brien, heard about the blast at the Horse and Groom and walked down North Street to see for himself what had happened. He then returned to his own pub and, concerned for the safety of his customers, ordered that the place be cleared. Jim Tydeman was one of the drinkers ushered out into the night air. Meanwhile, Owen and his staff began a search of the bars, to see if any suspicious looking packages had been left there.

Just as the last customers were leaving the Seven Stars, at around 9.25 p.m., a second bomb exploded there. Thanks to Owen O'Brien's prompt action, there were no fatalities. Eight people were injured, amongst them six members of the bar staff, but no more lives were lost. Nevertheless, the police were still looking at five cold-blooded murders.

By the following morning, more than one hundred extra detectives had been drafted into Surrey. The investigation was headed by Mr Christopher Rowe, the Assistant Chief Constable of Surrey, who was assisted by Detective Chief Superintendent Walter Simmons. The initial line of inquiry was threefold – to gather intelligence about who might have planted the bomb, to sift the wreckage for forensic evidence, and finally, to locate every single customer who had been in either of the two pubs that Saturday night. In all, this was close to four hundred people, and somewhere amongst those people were the ones who had planted the two devices.

A timetable was drawn up, and the night of the explosions sectioned off into five-minute intervals. In this way, if one of the customers gave the times when he was in one of the pubs, and detailed where he was sitting or standing, the customers he observed could then be traced and fitted in with the evidence gathered thus far. This meant that each witness's testimony was reinforced and clarified. By the end of the exercise, anyone unaccounted for would then fall under deep suspicion and all efforts would be made to trace them.

Almost immediately, the inquiry began to run into trouble. Descriptions of three people whom the police wished to trace were released. One of these was a tall dark man who had been seen in the Seven Stars at 8.40 p.m., carrying a brown paper bag. He was thirty to thirty-five years old, five feet six inches to five feet eight inches in height, and of slim build and with a thin face. The other two were both women seen in the Horse and Groom. Both were young, one blonde and one brunette. They had been seen talking to soldiers just ten minutes before the first bomb exploded. Only later was it shown that these two women were Ann Hamilton, who had died in the blast, and Isabella Price, a victim who had been badly injured.

It was always going to be difficult to trace customers in the Seven Stars, as that pub had a disco on the night of October 5th and many people came and went. With the Horse and Groom, the police had more luck and eventually released details of one man who had been seen by other customers but not yet traced. Known as the 'man in black', he was said to have been wearing a three-quarter length black coat, have been unshaven and possibly carrying a plastic holdall.

By October 25th, Chief Superintendent Simmons was announcing that in fact, only two people from the Horse and Groom remained to be traced. This couple had been seen sitting in the very alcove where the bomb had been planted. One was the 'man in black', but his description was more detailed now. He was aged between twenty and thirty and was between five feet ten inches and six feet tall. He had dark brown hair that reached his collar but was thinning on top. The man had sunken cheeks and a rather prominent nose. He was clean-shaven, but had a five o'clock shadow. His companion was a woman in her early twenties. She was between five feet two inches and five feet four inches tall, slim and with dirty blonde or possibly light brown shoulder-length hair, which was parted in the middle. Together they were referred to as the 'courting couple'.

It soon became clear that the couple might still be active in their terror campaign. On November 7th, at 10.17 p.m., a bomb was thrown through the window of the King's Arms pub in Woolwich. This time, twenty-six people were injured and two, a barman named Alan Horsley and a soldier, Gunner Richard Copeland Sloane Dunne, were killed. A car had been seen driving away at speed and witnesses said that it had contained two women and a man. One witness, William Fairs, described the getaway car as a Mark II Cortina, either dark red or maroon, being driven away without any lights. Such a car had been reported stolen from Ifield Road, Fulham, on October 7th.

On November 20th, identikit pictures of the courting couple seen in the Horse and Groom were published. Just three days later, on November 23rd, three more bombs exploded in London post boxes. Fortunately there were no deaths but twenty people were injured. Two days before this, on November 21st, two bombs had exploded in Birmingham pubs, and that outrage is the subject of another chapter in this book.

On November 30th, two more explosive devices were thrown at the Talbot Arms in Little Chester Street, Belgravia. One failed to detonate but the other injured five people. The unexploded bomb yielded valuable information and two sets of fingerprints. However, before this, on November 28th, the first arrest had been made.

There were conflicting stories about just how Paul Michael Hill had fallen into the police net. Some said that when the pictures of the two suspects were circulated in Northern Ireland, a sergeant in Army Intelligence had recognized one as Hill. Other stories involved a police informer who was paid £350 for naming Hill. The official story was that the intelligence officer had said that the woman in the sketch was in fact a man named Hill.

Whatever the truth of this, Hill was arrested on November 28th, at 29 Aldermoor Avenue, Southampton, where his girlfriend lodged. The arrest was made by Detective Sergeant Anthony Jermey and Detective Chief Inspector Richardson. Hill was first taken to Shirley police station before being escorted to Guildford.

After days of questioning, Hill made a statement admitting that he had come over to England with a friend named Gerry Conlon and that they, along with another man, Patrick Armstrong, had planted the bombs. This led, on November 30th, to a massive round up of suspects including Hill's aunt and uncle, Anne and Frank Keenan. Hugh and Kathleen Maguire, who lived in Paddington, were also picked up, as was Gerry Conlon, who was arrested in Belfast. Another of those who was picked up was Carole Richardson, and she told the officers where Patrick Armstrong, who had been her boyfriend, was living in a squat.

Having heard of his son's trouble, and the fact that he had been taken to England for interview, Gerry Conlon's father, Guiseppe Conlon, travelled from Belfast to London on December 2nd. He stayed with relatives at 43 Third Avenue, Harlesden, but that house was raided the following day. The householders, Anne and Patrick (Paddy) Maguire, their children, and Guiseppe Conlon, were all taken into custody. That same day, Patrick Armstrong was also picked up, along with another suspect who had been named, Paul Colman.

Over the next few days, various suspects made statements incriminating themselves and others. Armstrong admitted his part in the bombings and implicated Gerry Conlon and Carole Richardson. Carole herself admitted to a doctor that she had taken part in the Guildford bombings but said that they had both been 'throw-bombs', like the bombs at Woolwich. In fact, both of the Guildford devices had clearly been time bombs.

On December 7th, six people were charged with the murder of one of the pub victims, Caroline Slater. These six were Patrick Armstrong, Anne Maguire, Brian Anderson, Paul Colman, John McGuinness and Carole Richardson. Paul Hill and Gerard Conlon had already been charged some days before.

In addition to the eight who were charged with murder, Patrick O'Neill, Guiseppe Conlon, Sean Smyth and Patrick Maguire were charged with possession of explosives, Sean Mullin was charged with conspiracy to cause explosions and two of the Maguire children, Patrick and Vincent, were charged with handling explosives.

The police argument was that Anne Maguire and others had manufactured the bombs at her home, 43 Third Avenue, and the others had taken them to the Guildford pubs. Whilst the confession evidence was, of course, important, the only hard forensic evidence against any of the defendants was that tests had shown that Anne and Patrick Maguire, their two sons, Patrick O'Neill, Sean Smyth and Guiseppe Conlon had all handled explosives.

In the event, four of those charged were soon to be released, the police believing that they did not have a strong enough case against them. John McGuinness, Sean Mullin, Brian Anderson and Paul Colman were all now freed. This left just five charged with murder. Meanwhile, the first cracks were beginning to appear in the confession statements. Those who had admitted their parts now claimed that they had been subjected to a torrent of police brutality and that the confessions had been beaten out of them. Carole Richardson's confession was even further weakened by the evidence of Frank Johnson.

Frank was a close friend of Carole and he recalled that on the night of the bombings he, Carole and Lisa Astin had all attended a concert at the South Bank Polytechnic in London. Frank went to the police and told them his story. He was immediately told that since Carole had admitted her part, she must be guilty and if he was now saying that she was with him then the implication was that he was involved in the bombings too. Frank finally left the police station relieved that he had not been charged along with the others.

If the authorities thought that with the arrest of this so-called terror group, Britain would now return to peaceful times, they were soon shown to be wrong. On December 19th, a bomb exploded outside the Selfridges store in Oxford Street and three days later, another bomb was thrown at Edward Heath's flat in Belgravia, though Mr Heath was not home at the time.

The New Year dawned and still the bombings continued. On January 23rd, 1975, a device exploded at the Woodford Waterworks in London. Four days later, seven time bombs were planted at locations around the capital.

On February 24th, the murder charge against Anne Maguire was dropped, though she was still charged with possessing explosives. The committal proceedings were opened on March 17th and to their credit, both Frank Johnson and Lisa Astin gave evidence about Carole Richardson's attendance at the concert at the London Polytechnic. A month after this, on April 15th, Paul Hill was charged with another murder, that of an ex-soldier, Brian Shaw, in Belfast. This was yet another crime to which Hill had apparently confessed.

For that single murder, Hill was tried in Belfast on June 17th. The proceedings, before Mister Justice Kelly, lasted seven days after which Hill was found guilty and sentenced to life imprisonment.

The main trial of the four remaining murder suspects opened at the Old Bailey before Mister Justice Donaldson on September 16th, 1975, and lasted until October 22nd. Hill refused to enter any plea, shouting "I refuse to take part in this. I refuse to defend myself. Your justice stinks."

The prosecution was led by Sir Michael Havers, with Lord Wigoder acting for Conlon. Hill was defended by Mr Arthur Mildon whilst Mr John Leonard acted for Armstrong. Carole Richardson was defended by Mr Eric Myers.

There were fifty-nine prosecution witnesses, the vast majority of these being serving police officers who had been involved in the various arrests and interviews. Since the defence rested on alibi, that the four were elsewhere when the bombs were planted, and on the claim that the confessions were false and had been extracted under duress, there was a long procession of police officers denying that any impropriety had taken place.

Detective Sergeant John Donaldson denied that any violence had been used, as did Detective Sergeant Anthony Jermey. Detective Inspector Timothy Blake said he had never even interviewed Conlon, but could not then explain how Conlon knew he was a Roman Catholic and had a tattoo of a dagger on his arm.

Detective Chief Inspector Lionel Grundy and Detective Constable Peter Lewis denied knowing of any violence being inflicted on Conlon. Detective Chief Inspector Brian Richardson said that he had never shown a gun to Hill or pointed one at him. Detective Chief Superintendent Simmons denied threatening to kill Conlon or saying that he would have rumours spread to Belfast that he had informed on the IRA. Detective Chief Inspector Alan Longhurst denied that he had not even informed Carole Richardson that she had been arrested for five full days. Woman Police Constable Anita Mills said that there had been no assault upon Carole and finally, Assistant Chief Constable Rowe had not assaulted either Hill or Armstrong. Who were the jury to believe, the four people standing in the dock or a large number of police officers, many of them holding senior rank?

All four claimed to have alibis for the time of the bombings, though some of these were stronger than others. Conlon's alibi was certainly the weakest. He claimed that he had spent all day in London but could produce no witnesses to confirm it. He had spent most of the time with a friend, Patrick Carey, but Carey was not called to give evidence.

He was now back in Northern Ireland and said he could not recall the night with any degree of certainty.

Armstrong claimed that he had spent the night of October 5th, 1974, at a squat in Linstead Street in Kilburn with Thomas and Jacqueline Walker. They confirmed this story but their testimony was weakened by Thomas recalling an argument with Armstrong, which Jacqueline said did not take place. Another squatter, Thomas Lewiston, agreed that Armstrong had spent his nights at Linstead Street but could not recall this particular date.

Hill claimed to have been with his girlfriend, Gina Clarke, at her home in Southampton. This was confirmed by Gina and her landlady, Kathleen Crosbie, but in one of his statements to the police, Hill had admitted telling Gina to give him an alibi. Hill now claimed that this statement, like his confession, had also been beaten out of him by the police.

It was Carole Richardson who had the strongest alibi. Her claim to have been at the concert in London has already been referred to. The defence now called Simon Moodie, who was the accommodation officer at the South Bank Polytechnic. There was a concert by a group named Jack the Lad on October 5th and Moodie saw Carole arrive at some time between 7.45 p.m. and 8.00 p.m. Frank Johnson also confirmed this and said that Carole was with him for some time before this, but he was shown to have two convictions for possessing LSD, implying that he might have been under the influence of the drug on that night. The same was true of Lisa Astin, who admitted that she habitually took LSD, barbiturates and amphetamines. Furthermore, to show that Carole could have attended the concert and still been involved in the bombings, the police had timed the journey by car from Guildford. Two journeys were made, one taking sixty-four minutes and the other just fifty-two.

The jury duly returned guilty verdicts on all of the charges. All four were given life sentences. For Carole Richardson, there was no recommendation as to the length of time she should eventually serve. For Conlon, the judge recommended that he serve not less than thirty years. Armstrong was given not less than thirty-five years and as far as Hill was concerned, life was to mean just that.

The second trial in connection with the bombings, that of the so-called Maguire Seven, opened on January 27th, 1976, again at the Old Bailey and again before Mister Justice Donaldson. This trial was to last until March 4th, with much of the scientific evidence relying on the TLC or Thin Layer Chromatography test. This apparently showed that the hands of some of the defendants and a pair of gloves found at Third Avenue had tested positive for nitro-glycerine. Douglas Geoffrey Higgs, the Principal Scientific Officer at RARDE, the Royal Armament Research and Development Establishment, described this test as absolutely infallible. As a result, all seven were found guilty of various possession and handling offences.

Anne Maguire was given fourteen years, as was her husband Patrick. Guiseppe Conlon, Patrick O'Neill and Sean Smyth were all given twelve-year sentences and the two children received youth custody sentences, Vincent Maguire for five years and his brother Patrick for four.

The case would then have been quietly forgotten, but unknown to the general public, the authorities were already aware that these prosecutions were not as secure as they had at first seemed.

On December 12th, 1975, four terrorists were arrested in Balcombe Street, London, after holding a family hostage for a week. These four were named Joseph O'Connell, Harry Duggan, Hugh Doherty and Eddie Butler, and when Butler was interviewed, he freely admitted that his first 'job' had been the Woolwich pub bombing, a crime which had been included in the litany of charges against Hill and Armstrong. Butler claimed that neither of those men were at the scene and added that he had never even heard of them.

This information came to the attention of Mr Alastair Logan in May, 1976. Mr Logan was one of the defence solicitors for the Guildford Four and he now arranged to meet Butler at Wandsworth prison. That meeting took place in June, but Butler refused to say any more until Brendan Dowd, another terrorist already jailed for offences in the north of England, had given his permission. Some time later, Mr Logan met up with Dowd, and Dowd described the devices used in both the Guildford and Woolwich explosions in accurate detail.

Logan now asked Dowd to give him some information about the Guildford incidents that only the genuine pub bomber could know. Dowd replied that he recalled "...two old guys with shopping bags". These two men, Leslie Hutton and Arthur Jones, had indeed been in the Horse and Groom pub, after spending the day shopping together in Guildford. They had left the pub at around 7.00 p.m., and this information had never been made public.

This fact was highly significant for it showed that Dowd had been in the Horse and Groom on the day of the bombing. This in turn meant that Patrick Armstrong or either of the other two male prisoners could not have been there, for the police had made great store of the fact that they had traced every customer except for the courting couple. The male part of that couple now had to be Dowd. This in turn threw doubt on all of the confessions and meant that the Guildford Four were innocent.

The trial of O'Connell, Duggan, Doherty and Butler opened on January 24th, 1977, again at the Old Bailey. Three of the defendants refused to enter pleas because the indictments against them did not include the Guildford or Woolwich bombings. Nevertheless, all four were convicted of other offences.

On October 10th, 1977, the appeal of the Guildford Four opened. It should be remembered that by this stage, all the other trials were over. Dowd and the others were in prison and had admitted more than once that they were responsible for the Guildford and Woolwich bombs. However, the judges refused to allow the jury to consider this new evidence, so the appeal ended on October 28th in dismissal. After all, the Guildford Four had confessed, hadn't they?

On January 23rd, 1980, Guiseppe Conlon died in prison. That August his case was debated in Parliament, but still the guilt of the Guildford Four and the Maguire Seven was accepted. The other ten prisoners remained behind bars continuing their sentences.

Anne Maguire was the last of the Seven to be released, on February 22nd, 1985. The Guildford Four were to remain in prison for another four years, despite growing public disquiet over their convictions. Their freedom, when it did come, proved that there had indeed been police corruption and impropriety on a massive scale.

On October 17th, 1989, three judges, The Lord Chief Justice, Lord Lane and Justices Glidewell and Farquharson announced that the prisoners would be released after the formality of a hearing at the Appeal Court in two days time. At that hearing the senior prosecutor announced, "It is my onerous duty to have to inform the court... that evidence of great significance has come to light. That evidence throws such doubt upon the honesty and integrity of a number of Surrey officers investigating these cases in 1974 that the Crown now feels unable to say that the conviction of any appellant was safe or satisfactory."

The evidence referred to was that the draft notes of three interviews with Armstrong over three different days had been typewritten with many alterations. This in itself was not significant. What was significant, however, was that in their final altered version, the notes matched word for word another set of interview notes which were supposed to

Gerry Conlon waves to well-wishers moments after his release from jail on October 19th, 1989 (Mike Fisher/Reuters/Popperfoto)

have been transcribed during another, later interview with the prisoner. The draft notes must have been made before that transcript, which was used at the trial, and since this transcript could not now have been a verbatim report of what took place, it followed that the interview and statement must have been manufactured.

The Guildford Four were released on October 19th, 1989, though Hill was re-arrested afterwards and flown to Belfast to hear his appeal against the remaining murder charge, that of Brian Shaw. That 'confession' too was now, of course, totally unreliable.

The Four had spent almost fifteen years in prison for crimes they had not committed. On the same day that British justice admitted its mistake, October 19th, the Home Secretary, Douglas Hurd, announced that the convictions of the Birmingham Six were sound.

Suggestion for further reading:

Grant McKee and Ros Franey, *Time Bomb – The Guildford Four* (London: Bloomsbury, 1988).

47

The Birmingham Six

Paddy Hill, Hughie Callaghan, Richard McIlkenny,
Gerry Hunter, Billy Power and Johnny Walker
Jailed for life for the murder of twenty-one people in Birmingham

THE call to the offices of the *Birmingham Post and Evening Mail* was timed at 8.11 p.m., on the evening of Thursday, November 21st, 1974. The voice, with a calm and measured Irish accent, said "There is a bomb planted in the Rotunda and there is a bomb in New Street, at the tax office". The caller also gave a recognized Irish Republican Army (IRA) code word.

There had already been a number of bombs planted in and around Birmingham and other cities in the Midlands over the previous few months, so the call was taken very seriously indeed. News of the warning was passed on to the police, who in turn notified officers patrolling in the area of the city centre. Constable Brian Yates received news of the threat over his radio at 8.15 p.m. He was actually in New Street at the time and made straight for the Rotunda. Once there, he met up with Constable Derek Bradbury and Woman Police Constable Margaret Adams, who had also been notified by radio. Inside the Rotunda there were also two sergeants, already in the process of organizing a search of the building. The three constables were told to search the even-numbered floors of the building and climbed into a lift in order to begin their duties. As the lift doors closed, it was 8.17 p.m., just six minutes after the warning, but already it was too late.

At the foot of the Rotunda was a pub named the Mulberry Bush. It was packed with drinkers when the device that had been planted there exploded. The police officers on the scene now had other duties, moving the injured out into St Martin's Circus, and waiting for the fleet of ambulances to arrive.

Some 300 yards further up New Street was a second crowded bar, The Tavern in the Town, built into the cellar and first floor of the building which also housed the tax office. One of the barmen, John Boyle, heard the blast at the Rotunda and decided that it would be a good idea to check the front of the Tavern for any suspicious packages. He found nothing and was just returning to his duties inside the bar when the second bomb exploded.

A total of nineteen people were killed immediately. Two more died in the days and weeks to follow, bringing the death toll up to twenty-one. Two of the dead were brothers,

Eugene Thomas Reilly and Desmond William Reilly. The others were all named in the newspapers over the next few weeks. They were Trevor George Thrupp, John Rowlands, Stanley James Bodman, Maureen Ann Roberts, Paul Anthony Davies, Michael William Beasley, Jane Davies, Lynn Bennett, Charles Harper Gray, Marylyn Paula Nash, Anne Hayes, Pamela Joan Palmer, John Clifford Jones, Stephen Whalley, Maxine Hamilton, Thomas Chaytor, Neil Robert Marsh and James Caddick. The final victim, James Craig, died in hospital as late as December 9th. More than 200 people were injured, many of them very seriously indeed.

An instant appeal was made for any witnesses who might have seen anyone behaving suspiciously around the two pubs, or who might have information useful to the investigation. A number of witnesses came forward.

Roy Findon and his brother, Michael, had been walking up New Street just a few minutes before the first of the explosions. They had just passed the Rotunda when they saw two men outside Lloyds Bank. They were both in their twenties and one of them was carrying a parcel. As the Findons carried on walking they noticed two policemen on duty who were trying the doors of business premises to ensure that they were locked. The two men in the doorway had also seen the policemen and hid from them, finally running off towards New Street station when they had the chance.

Another suspicious character was seen by George Pugh and his wife, Edna, who were in the Odeon cinema watching 'Planet of the Apes'. At some time before 8.00 p.m., a man came in and sat on Edna's right. What attracted George's attention to him was that although this was a non-smoking part of the cinema, the man chain-smoked and constantly glanced at his watch. At the sound of the first explosion, which could be heard clearly inside the cinema, the man stood up and walked out.

By far the most valuable witness, though, was Clifford Godwin, a ticket clerk who worked in the booking office at the railway station in New Street. He recalled a group of Irishmen who had all purchased return tickets to Belfast via the port of Heysham, and the train left at 7.55 p.m., less than twenty minutes before the first bomb went off. The police at Heysham were notified to check all passengers leaving that train.

The Heysham train reached Crewe at 8.50 p.m., and five Irishmen alighted and went into the buffet together. They would have to wait for the connection that would take them on to Heysham. It was due in at 9.15 p.m.

In the meantime, back in Birmingham, a third bomb had been found. It was placed in a doorway at the General Accident Insurance Company and was made the subject of a controlled explosion. A later examination would show that it contained over thirteen pounds of a commercial explosive called Eversoft Frangex and its construction was similar to other bombs which had been placed around the Midlands, indicating that all had been planted by the same terrorist team.

The Heysham train was on time and the five Irishmen boarded in good spirits. Once on the train, one of the men produced a pack of cards and the men began playing. Meanwhile, in Heysham, a group of officers were gathering to meet the train. Amongst them were Sergeant Alan Dickie, Constable Gerald Baines, a dog handler and a Special Branch officer, Constable David Watson. The ticket collector, Arnold Taylor, was told to point out any tickets issued at Birmingham, especially if they belonged to a group of men.

The train arrived at 10.45 p.m., and amongst the 300 or so passengers were a group of four men all walking together. When Mr Taylor checked their tickets he saw that not only were they issued at New Street station, but they were also numbered consecutively. He nodded to the police and Constable Watson asked them if they would step into a small office nearby.

Inside that office was Detective Constable Fred Willoughby and he had just finished questioning another man, who gave his name as Paddy Hill and said he was going over to Ireland to see his grandmother. His suitcase was checked and was found to contain only clothes. Hill was allowed to go, so he walked to the ferry and found himself a place in the bar, where he ordered himself a drink.

Meanwhile, the group of four Irishmen were now in the office with Constable Willoughby. They readily identified themselves as Johnny Walker, Richard McIlkenny, Gerry Hunter and Billy Power. They gave various reasons for travelling to Ireland, after which all were asked to wait outside, near the ticket barrier. The identification documents the four men had shown were checked against police records. All were accurate, gave the correct addresses and none of the four was known to Special Branch as a possible IRA member. The ferry was due to sail at 11.45 p.m., and the police were all set to let the group go when the telephone rang.

The caller was Joe Mounsey of the Lancashire Criminal Investigation Department (CID) and he asked if there had been any developments at Heysham. Mounsey was informed that a group of four Irishmen had been held but that everything seemed to check out. Mounsey, though, was taking no chances. He ordered that the four be taken to Morecambe police station where they could be tested for explosives by Doctor Frank Skuse, a scientist at the Forensic Science Laboratory at Chorley.

Just ten minutes before the ferry was due to sail, the four were told that a couple of bombs had gone off in Birmingham and there were many dead and injured. It was explained to them that they were being taken to Morecambe for testing, so that they could be eliminated from the inquiry. The police apologized for the inconvenience but stressed that once it was all over, the men could catch another ferry, the following day. It was at that point that one of the four asked, "What about our mate?" Paddy Hill was then described and, moments later, Constable Willoughby was on the ferry asking Hill if he would come with him to join his friends.

What happened next was to be the subject of much debate over the years to come. The publicized version at the time was that the five were placed into separate rooms. Hunter, Walker and McIlkenny were placed in cells, Power in the female jailer's room and Hill in the charge room. Detective Superintendent George Reade and a team of men from the West Midlands Serious Crimes Squad travelled up to Morecambe from

Birmingham and began interviewing the men. They were also subject to forensic examination by Dr Skuse. The following day, the five were taken back to Birmingham for further interviews. During these, a positive reaction for the presence of nitro-glycerine was found on one of Power's hands, Hill also tested positive and there was a slight positive reaction from Walker. In addition to this, Power confessed to his part in the bombings and named a sixth man, Hughie Callaghan, as being involved.

Callaghan was arrested at his home on the night of November 22nd. The next day, November 23rd, Walker, McIlkenny and Callaghan also signed confessions and on Sunday, November 24th, all six men were charged with murder. Later, three more men were arrested on charges of conspiracy to cause explosions, being either workmates of some of the Six, or people named by them. They were James Kelly, Mick Sheehan and Mick Murray. The latter was a self-confessed member of the IRA and had been a workmate of both Walker and McIlkenny, adding to the suspicion against them.

The trial of the Birmingham Six, and their three fellow defendants, opened at Lancaster on June 9th, 1975, it being felt that they would have little chance of receiving a fair trial in Birmingham. The presiding judge was Mister Justice Bridge and the Crown's case was led by Mr Harry Skinner. Mr John Field Evans represented Callaghan, Hill and Power whilst the other three were defended by Mr Michael Underhill. The proceedings lasted until August 15th.

Much of the evidence against the Birmingham Six rested on two pillars – the forensic tests and the confessions signed by four of them. Before this, however, there were a number of other witnesses who gave evidence or whose statements were read out in court.

Hilda Wickett was the next door neighbour of Johnny Walker and she reported an incident which she said took place some time in August. One night, in the small hours of the morning, she was woken by the sound of a car pulling up outside. Looking though her window she saw Walker climb out of a car, go to his front room window and tap on the glass. He then returned to the car and two other men got out, opened the boot and dragged out two large sacks such as might contain cement or plaster. These were taken inside by Walker who then returned to the car and collected a cardboard box that was about a foot square in size.

Thomas Watt was a workmate of Walker and McIlkenny and he said that on a number of occasions, Walker had warned him not to go into the city centre. On each of these occasions, a bomb had exploded later, the last warning coming on the night of the pub blasts. In addition, Walker had once asked him where he might get some cheap clocks.

Julia Vines had been the barmaid in the Taurus Bar, which was situated on New Street railway station. She recalled a group of Irishmen in the bar at 7.45 p.m. on the night of the explosion. They were all carrying suitcases. However, the defence managed a rare victory by pointing out that in an earlier statement, Julia Vines had said that this was at around 7.30 p.m., thus reducing the time the group would have had to plant the bombs.

Next came the turn of the scientific experts. Donald Lidstone worked at RARDE, the Royal Armament Research and Development Establishment at Woolwich. He had sifted the rubble of the Tavern in the Town and had determined that there may have been two bombs placed close together, since the remains of two briefcases had been found. He estimated that up to thirty pounds of explosive had been used.

Douglas Geoffrey Higgs also worked at RARDE and he had examined the wreckage of the Mulberry Bush. He too thought that there were two bombs in briefcases or attaché cases, containing some twenty-five to thirty pounds of explosive. However, there was a problem for the prosecution here. The bomb had been placed inside the bar by the rear entrance. One of the confessions described the bomb as being outside the bar and another had it placed near the jukebox, both of which were incorrect. In addition, all four confessions said that the bombs had been in plastic carrier bags. Both experts had said that they were in some sort of case, like a briefcase.

No doubt the most important scientific evidence came from Dr Frank Skuse. He had first conducted a Greiss test on all five men held at Morecambe. According to Dr Skuse, this involved swabbing the hands of the suspect with ether. This was then squeezed out of the cotton wool into the first of three bowls. Next, more ether was added to this bowl and the contents were then divided into three roughly equal parts, which were now in three bowls.

Caustic Soda would be added to the first bowl, followed by a special chemical known as the Greiss reagent. If any organic sample was present, the liquid would turn pink. If such a positive result was obtained, then only Greiss reagent would be added to the second bowl. If nitro-glycerine was present, this liquid would remain clear. If it did, the third sample was then taken for further analysis in the laboratory.

Power and Hill had shown positive readings and Walker a faint positive reading. Dr Skuse had not left matters there, though. Back in the laboratory he had then subjected the samples from those three defendants to further tests. He had performed a TLC or Thin Layer Chromatography test, and a GCMS or Gas Chromatography/Mass Spectrometry test. The TLC was at least as sensitive as the Greiss and the GCMS up to a hundred times more sensitive.

One would have expected that if the Greiss tests had proved positive, or partly positive, for three of the prisoners, then the other tests should have confirmed Dr Skuse's Morecambe findings. Surprisingly, they did not. All the tests were negative except for the GCMS test on Hill's left hand. Asked to produce documentary evidence of this single success, Dr Skuse was unable to do so. He did say, however, that in his opinion, the Greiss test alone was ninety-nine per cent accurate and on that basis he was prepared to swear that the three defendants who tested positive had recently handled nitro-glycerine.

This was important evidence and the defence had to try to refute it. They called Doctor Hugh Black, who had been an inspector of explosives at the Home Office. He testified that in his opinion the Greiss test was not sufficient to determine contact with nitro-glycerine. A large number of other substances that were nitro-cellulose based, such as lacquers, varnishes and paints, might give the same positive reaction. However, the validity of Dr Black's opinion was greatly reduced when he admitted that he had performed no such tests himself and had never in fact set foot inside a forensic laboratory.

There remained the confessions signed by four of the Six. They held that these had been beaten from them by police officers and the prosecution now called a total of thirty-six officers who had played some part in the interviews or been present when they were made. None reported knowing of any violence used against any of the prisoners. The only dissent was the testimony of Sergeant Ronald Buckley, who had been in charge of the cells at Morecambe. He said that the five who were picked up at Heysham were interrogated by the Midlands police from 7.00 a.m. onwards on November 22nd. The Midlands police had always claimed that they did not take over the interrogation until 9.30 a.m., after the forensic tests had been completed. The prosecution hastily got Sergeant Buckley to confirm that he could not swear with any degree of accuracy what time the Midlands police took over.

All six defendants stepped into the witness box to explain their treatment at the hands of the police. Power was the first. He explained that at Morecambe he had been taken into a room by Detective Sergeant Alan Watson and Detective Constable Michael French. French had punched him on the back of the head then both men set about him, finally pushing him down into a chair. An officer sat on each side and Power was then jabbed in the ribs, punched and kicked. At one stage French told Power to put his hands flat on the table in front of him. French then took a pair of handcuffs and put them on like knuckledusters before using them to hit Power whenever he denied any involvement in the blasts.

After some time, Watson left the room leaving Power alone with French. French then said that they would kill Power on his way back down to Birmingham. They would push him from the car on the motorway and say he had tried to escape. Later a third officer entered and when French told him that he could take over he pulled Power into another room by his hair. There, six or more officers were waiting and they kicked and punched him from all directions. After being taken back to the other room he was asked to name the sixth man and when Power asked them what they meant one of the officers punched him and said "The man who stayed behind". He then named Callaghan as the man who had seen them off at the station. After this treatment Power was prepared to say anything the police wanted and signed a statement admitting his part in the bombings.

Callaghan was the next witness and he was followed into the witness box by Paddy Hill. Both described beatings at the hands of the police, Hill naming Detective Sergeant Ray Bennett and Detective Constable John Brand. One of them told him that he was going to make a statement admitting that he had planted the bombs and when he replied that he was not going to, they said they would kick it out of him.

Hunter said he was seen by Detective Inspector John Moore and Superintendent Reade himself. Both officers punched and slapped him and Reade grabbed hold of

Hunter's hair and slammed his head against the wall. He fell to the floor and Moore then kicked him in the stomach.

McIlkenny also named Moore as one of his attackers but added the name of Detective Sergeant James Kelly. At Morecambe, McIlkenny escaped relatively lightly. Moore threw a blanket over his head and then held it down so tightly that McIlkenny could not breathe. He blacked out and afterwards they left him alone.

The last one to give evidence was Walker, who said he was seen by Sergeant Kelly and Detective Constable Thomas Sutcliffe. As he entered the interview room another officer, who Walker later identified as Constable George Cole, kicked him in the base of the spine. As he fell his shirt came open, revealing an old operation scar on his stomach. The police now concentrated their punches and kicks on that area. Cole took out a gun and suggested shooting Walker. He then placed a blanket over Walker's head and Walker felt the muzzle of the gun jammed up against his temple. Someone in the room clapped loudly to mimic a shot being fired. After this they started hitting him again until Kelly saw a blister on Walker's right foot, which he then forced a lit cigarette into. Eventually, Walker too blacked out and woke up on a cell floor. These treatments were repeated back in Birmingham and even at Winson Green prison after the men had been formally charged.

The five men who had been picked up at Heysham also explained why they were going to Ireland. On November 14th, 1974, a known IRA terrorist named James McDade had been blown up whilst planting a bomb outside the Coventry telephone exchange. McDade was known to most of the six defendants, and had been to school with some of them. He had at one stage even lodged with Billy Power and his family. After McDade's death, the IRA announced that he would be given a military funeral in Ireland and five of the prisoners had decided that they would like to attend, not because of any IRA sympathies, but merely out of respect for a man who had been their friend. This knowledge, however, must have suggested to the jury that there might well have been closer links between the six and McDade than mere friendship.

The verdict came on August 14th. The Birmingham Six were each found guilty of twenty-one murders and sentenced to life imprisonment. On the other charges, Kelly was sentenced to one year but had already served that time in jail, so it was ordered that he be released in eight days once arrangements had been made for him to have a new identity, since the IRA might well wish to harm him. Sheehan was given nine years and Murray was sentenced to nine years. He, however, was already serving a twelve-year sentence for conspiracy to cause explosions.

An appeal was entered and heard on March 30th, 1976, before Lord Justice Widgery, Lord Justice Lawton and Mister Justice Thompson. They held that there was no evidence that the Six had been beaten apart from a black eye sustained by Walker, and this had been explained as occurring when he was moved from Morecambe. He had accidentally hit his head on getting into the car that was to take him to Birmingham.

It was not until May 1985 that the first real cracks began to appear in the prosecution's scenario. Two forensic scientists, Doctor Brian Caddy and David Baldock, both conducted Greiss tests on a large number of substances. Baldock found that many nitro-cellulose products gave a positive reaction. He also confirmed that in the 1970s, scientists would use nitro-glycerine to clean the equipment they used for the more sensitive GCMS tests.

Doctor Caddy's tests were more widespread and he found that the Greiss test gave positive reactions for, amongst other things, a cigarette packet, a picture postcard, varnish and two packs of old playing cards. All the items had been coated with some form of nitro-cellulose. Dr Caddy even had a television producer, Ian McBride, shuffle a pack of playing cards and then tested his hands. Mr McBride tested positive for having recently handled nitro-glycerine. The Home Office had their own team of scientists test out the findings of Caddy and Baldock. The report, received by the Home Office in February 1986, confirmed the results.

In October of that same year, former Constable Tom Clarke came forward to say that he had witnessed some brutality inflicted by his colleagues. The prisoners had been kept awake all night and he had seen Detective Constable Frederick Jennings and Constable Coffey pointing guns into two of the cells.

By this stage, the forensic evidence had been cast into doubt and there were the first admissions that brutality had been used to extract the confessions. As a result, on January 20th, 1987, Douglas Hurd referred the case back to the Court of Appeal. That appeal was heard at the Old Bailey on November 2nd, before the Lord Chief Justice, Lord Lane, Lord Justice O'Connor and Lord Justice Brown. It lasted for thirty-two days and a number of new witnesses were called.

Bill Bailey had been the head cleaner at Morecambe police station at the time of the men's arrests. He testified that officers told him that the cell block and detective offices were out of bounds to him. There was perhaps nothing sinister in that but the day after the men had been moved, Bailey was allowed back into those areas and found streaks of blood on three walls. He had also watched as all of the five prisoners were moved by car. None of them had banged their heads as they climbed in.

Joyce Lynas was a former police officer and had been on duty at Birmingham when the five were brought down from Morecambe. She heard many loud bangs and saw one of the prisoners actually being assaulted.

Peter Bourne had been one of the prison officers at Winson Green and he testified that he saw that they were all bruised as they came in, especially Walker. Finally, there was a strange document that was termed the Reade Schedule. This had been written out by Superintendent George Reade and appeared to be a timetable of the interviews. One of the entries on the list was an interview with Hill which the official version said had never taken place, though Hill always maintained that it had. The entry was crossed through and the word "Out" written next to it. This suggested that the published list of interviews was in fact a fabrication.

The judgement was given on January 28th, 1988. Each new witness was dismissed in turn. Lynas was not worthy of belief, Tom Clarke was unconvincing, Bourne was merely trying to play down the part played by other prison officers in the beating up of the appellants, Bailey was mistaken, and Reade was simply not capable of organizing the complicated conspiracy that would have been necessary if the version of events given by the Six were accurate. The appeals were dismissed.

On August 14th, 1989, the West Midlands Serious Crimes Squad was disbanded. They had been shown to have fabricated confessions from prisoners and in the preceding twelve months some twenty suspects had had charges dropped or convictions quashed. Two months later, the Guildford Four were released, though Douglas Hurd immediately maintained that the convictions of the Birmingham Six were safe. However, such was the level of public disquiet that in March of the following year, an inquiry into the police handling of the case was ordered. It was to be carried out by the Devon and Cornwall force.

Later that same year, on July 23rd, a television programme was broadcast in which a disguised man admitted to being one of those who had planted the bombs in the Birmingham pubs. He described the interiors of the two bars accurately and pinpointed almost precisely where the bombs had been planted. In short, he gave accurate information that had never been made public.

On August 29th, the case was referred back to the Court of Appeal. By now, part of the report from the Devon and Cornwall police had been submitted and this showed that many documents had been altered or tampered with. For instance, notes of an interview with McIlkenny had pages inserted that were not original. Dates had been altered in notebooks and what purported to be different signatures had been written by one officer.

The appeal opened on March 4th, 1991. No fewer than five Home Office experts stated that the Greiss test was insufficient to prove the presence of nitro-glycerine. Only now was it revealed that Dr Herbert Bamford, a colleague of Dr Skuse, had at the time of the initial investigation been sent to Liverpool to test the hands of passengers bound for Ireland. He had found two males who, according to the Greiss tests, showed a positive reaction for nitro-glycerine. Both men were released without charge when they showed that they had handled adhesive tape. So, at a time when Dr Skuse was swearing that no other substance but explosives could produce a positive test, it was well known that other cellulose products could. Furthermore, Dr Bamford had made a written statement to that effect on October 5th, 1987, a full month before the previous appeal had opened. That statement had not been disclosed to the defence.

Doctor David Baxendale reported a series of tests he had done on the original police notes and confessions. He had found many instances of documents not being correct. Indeed, some of the so-called contemporaneous notes had to have been made as late as 1975.

Acquitted members of the Birmingham Six, sent to prison in 1975 for the bombing of two pubs, gather with their Member of Parliament, Chris Mullin (with scarf), after their release on March 14th, 1991 (Chris Helgren/Reuters/Popperfoto)

The entire case had collapsed. The forensic evidence was worthless and the confessions and notes of interviews were totally unreliable. Added to this, the West Midlands Serious Crimes Squad had been disbanded in disgrace and many instances of brutality had been proved. The appeal was successful and on March 14th, 1991, six innocent men who had served more than fifteen years each were finally freed.

Suggestion for further reading:

Chris Mullin, *Error of Judgement: the truth about the Birmingham bombings* (Dublin: Poolbeg Press, 1997).

48

Stefan Ivan Kiszko

Jailed for life for the murder of
Lesley Susan Molseed, at Ripponden, Yorkshire

I T was a simple enough errand. The Molseed family needed a loaf of bread and the youngest daughter, eleven-year-old Lesley, said she would go. April Molseed, her mother, handed the slightly-built girl a pound note and watched her skip off down the street. It was 1.00 p.m. on Sunday, October 5th, 1975.

When Lesley still had not returned half an hour later, April Molseed asked her other daughter, fourteen-year-old Laura, to go and look for her. Perhaps she had been distracted, or got talking to one of her friends. Laura left the family house at 11 Delamere Road, Rochdale, and walked what would have been Lesley's most direct route to the shops on Ansdell Road. There was no sign of her sister. Laura returned home and enlisted help from her brother, Freddie, and when they still could not find Lesley, Freddie was sent to fetch his stepfather, Danny Molseed, from the pub. It was now 2.30 p.m.

After Danny too had searched for Lesley without success, the police were called in. Officers began a search of the estate and initiated door-to-door enquiries, again without success. The following day, the search was extended, but still there was no sign of the frail child who had a heart complaint. Appeals to the public for help were made and some people, mostly children, came forward to say that they had seen something of Lesley on that Sunday.

Dianne Reeves had seen Lesley turn from Delamere Road into Stiups Lane. She had also been seen on Stiups lane by Mark Conroy, who went to the same school as Lesley. Anita Owen, who had just been to the shop for her own mother, saw Lesley turn into Ansdell Road from a small entry that led to Stiups Lane. Two other witnesses, Bernadette Hegarty and John Cooper, also saw Lesley on Ansdell Road, walking towards the Spar shop. However, when the proprietors were spoken to, both Robert and Marion Ellidge reported that they had seen nothing of Lesley that day.

There was, in fact, one other early account of a sighting of Lesley, but it did not fill the police with hope. Jacqueline Reilly had been working in her kitchen, which overlooked Stiups Lane. She saw Lesley skip past, carrying her shopping bag and heading off towards Ansdell Road. There was a van, though, travelling slowly behind Lesley, as if it were following her. All that Mrs Reilly could say was that the van was yellow, but that was enough. There had already been reports of a yellow van seen parked near where children were playing on the estate. It was not encouraging news.

David Arthur Greenwell was working away from home. His budget did not stretch to expensive hotels, or even basic ones, but it was too far to drive home each night. He had the perfect solution. After the day's work was complete he would park in a lay-by on the A672, close to Ripponden on Rishworth Moor, and settle down for the night. After all, his van had everything he needed – a bed, a primus stove on which to cook breakfast, even a bowl in which he could wash. The only thing it did not have was a toilet. Still, that did not matter too much. Up here on the moors he could simply walk up off the road, find a secluded spot, and do whatever was necessary. Such was the case at 6.45 a.m., on Wednesday, October 8th, 1975.

From the lay-by, a bank of grass, gorse and heather led up the hill. It was a moderately steep climb but David scrambled up the bank and found a place hidden from the road. A flash of colour caught his eye. As David completed his task and turned to go back down to his van, he saw the flash of colour once again. It looked like someone had dumped a pile of clothes up there. David went closer and saw to his horror that it was the body of a little girl, lying face down on the hillside. Lesley Molseed had been found.

The murder investigation fell under the jurisdiction of Detective Chief Superintendent Jack Dibb, and he appointed Detective Chief Inspector Richard Holland to investigate the case. Very soon afterwards, Holland was himself promoted to Superintendent.

Lesley had been stabbed twelve times, around the chest, back and neck, with a small bladed knife, possibly a penknife. Though she had not been raped, her murder was clearly sexually motivated, for the murderer had masturbated onto her underwear. Immediately, Holland decided that whilst the details of the case would be released to the press, two facts would be withheld; that Lesley's underwear had not been removed, and that the killer had ejaculated onto her. In this way, when they finally caught the man responsible, these two details would enable them to be sure of their man. There was one other factor that would also greatly assist the police in confirming that they had the right man. Peter Guise, a forensic scientist, examined the semen stains on Lesley's clothes and determined that the perpetrator had a very low sperm count.

A further appeal for witnesses revealed a number of people who had driven past the lay-by in the days that Lesley had been missing. The post-mortem showed that Lesley had been killed where she was found and almost certainly on the day she had been abducted. This led Superintendent Holland and his team to concentrate their efforts on sightings made on the Sunday. A timetable of vehicles seen in the lay-by at various times was drawn up, but perhaps one of the most valuable sightings was that by Christopher Coverdale.

Mr Coverdale had been visiting friends in Rochdale and drove past the lay-by at 1.45 p.m. on the Sunday. Though he did not see a car parked there, he did see a man and a little girl climbing up the embankment. The man had his face towards the road and was pulling the girl up towards him. Mr Coverdale described the man as being white, aged thirty to thirty-five, with light brown or fair hair which was cut short and may have been receding. He was also quite plump and somewhere between five feet six and five feet eight inches tall. When Christopher Coverdale was taken to the lay-by to show where he had seen the couple, he pointed out a spot very close to where Lesley's body had eventually been found.

Meanwhile, back in Rochdale, and close to where Lesley had lived, there had been a number of incidents that involved a man exposing himself to children. The first of these incidents had taken place two days before Lesley vanished.

On Friday, October 3rd, two ten-year-old girls, Ann Marie Storto and Sheila Woodhead, had been walking home from the youth club and as they approached the corner of Stiups Lane and Kingsway, they saw a man standing in the clinic porchway, leaning against the wall with one hand in his pocket. Rather frightened of the way he looked, the two girls turned around and headed back towards the club, only for the man to follow them.

The children involved gave somewhat conflicting reports, but the summary of what happened next is that the two girls arrived back at the youth club and were then walked home by thirteen-year-old Debbie Brown and two of her friends, Maxine Buckley and Debra Mills. Later, that same man had dropped his trousers and exposed his penis to Debbie, Maxine and Debra.

There were other reports of a man behaving indecently in the area around the youth club that evening. At 9.50 p.m., three older girls, Catherine Burke, Gillian Cleave and Pamela Hind, were approaching the club when they too saw a man in the clinic doorway. He stepped out in front of them, opened his coat and allowed his trousers to fall, thus exposing himself. Once again, all three girls gave conflicting reports of what they had actually seen.

The following day, October 4th, two of the girls involved in the Friday night incidents, Maxine Buckley and Debra Mills, were walking along Vavasour Street when they saw a man on the corner of Jackson Street. He crossed the road so that he stood in front of the girls and exposed his erect penis to them. He then ran off towards Crawford Street. The girls ran off home and Maxine reported the matter to her mother. Furthermore, Maxine said she thought she knew where the man lived.

The police were called and Constable Peter Sergeant visited Maxine Buckley at her home. He took down the details of the incident and then drove both girls to Crawford Street, where Maxine said the man lived. She pointed out number thirty-one but when the constable knocked on the door, there appeared to be no one at home. Reports were made of all these incidents and, once Lesley Molseed's body had been found, these were passed on to the investigating team as a matter of routine. They had many other details to sift through, though, and for the time being, the reports of the flasher were buried under a growing mound of paperwork.

So far, Maxine Buckley had been involved in two incidents where a man had exposed himself to her. On November 5th, she attended a bonfire night party with a friend of hers, Michael Rigby. After the fireworks were over, Maxine and Michael were walking home together and passed down Vavasour Street at around 8.30 p.m. As they strolled, Maxine saw a man in front, walking towards them, and recognized him as the man who had exposed himself to her on October 4th. As he passed them, the man gritted his teeth and smiled awkwardly at them, frightening both children. Once again, Maxine ran home and told her mother and again the police were called.

Two uniformed officers attended and drove both children down to Crawford Street, where Maxine said the man lived. Once again number thirty-one was pointed out and even as the children identified the house, an elderly woman and a young man appeared at the doorway. "That's him, that's the man", called out Maxine, and Michael agreed that she was right. The man they had identified was twenty-three-year-old Stefan Kiszko.

It was 10.20 p.m. when Woman Police Constable (WPC) Shaw and Constable Oliver arrived at 31 Crawford Street. They explained that they were investigating a report of an indecent exposure on October 4th, but Kiszko explained that he had only just come out of hospital after being in there for six weeks. Asked about his movements on the 4th, Kiszko said that the family were in the process of moving to a new house in Kings Road. On October 4th he had been at home with his mother until after lunch, after which he had gone to Kings Road to move some things. He had then been here, at home in Crawford Street, for the rest of the day. Asked if he owned a vehicle he pointed out a bronze Hillman Avenger, registration VDK 157 K, parked outside. The police officers made their report and again passed it on to the Molseed team.

As part of the routine house-to-house enquiries being carried out by the officers working on the murder of Lesley Molseed, Detective Sergeant Mawson and Detective Constable Russell visited 31 Crawford Street on November 7th. As soon as they walked in the door, Stefan Kiszko began complaining about another visit from the police. Mawson and Russell knew nothing of a previous visit and asked Kiszko to tell them what it was about. He muttered something about a young girl in Vavasour Street on October 4th.

The two officers then asked Kiszko to outline his movements on the 4th and he replied that he had been thinking about this since the other two officers called and now thought that he had been in hospital on that day. He had had an operation on his foot and added that he had a discharge letter from the hospital that would prove he was correct. Only now was he told that they were investigating the murder of Lesley Molseed, and that they also wanted to know where Kiszko was on the following day, October 5th. Kiszko then went to look for his hospital letter but could not find it. He was asked to make a written statement confirming what he had said, and readily did so. According to that statement, as far as he could recall, he was in the Manchester Royal Infirmary on October 5th.

When the police contacted the hospital they received confirmation that Stefan Kiszko had been discharged not at the beginning of October as he had claimed in his statement, but on September 15th. Why had he lied if not to give himself an alibi? On November 10th, the police paid another visit to the Kiszko household, this time at their new address, 25 Kings Road.

Asked to explain the discrepancy in the hospital discharge dates, Kiszko said that he had not lied deliberately. He could not remember what date he had been discharged but had thought it was some time at the beginning of October. Whatever the real date was, he had spent October 5th helping his mother, Charlotte, pack items for the forthcoming move to the new house. Even so, he had difficulty walking at the time and the first time he had driven his car after his discharge from hospital had been on October 12th when he drove his mother to the cemetery so they could visit his father's grave.

It was not until December 16th that the report which WPC Shaw had filed on the indecent exposure came to the top of the pile in the murder investigation room. This was then linked with the report that Mawson and Russell had made and it was decided to organize a search of Kiszko's old house in Crawford Street. That search was made on December 20th, by Detective Sergeant Godfrey.

The following day, December 21st, Detective Sergeant John Michael Akeroyd, Detective Constable Robert McFadzean and Detective Constable Anthony Melvyn Whittle were back at Kings Road. They told Kiszko that they were investigating the indecent exposure report and asked him to come down to the police station to answer some questions. A somewhat irritated Kiszko agreed to go with them and once he had left the house, his bedroom was searched. At this stage, all that was taken away was a pile of girlie magazines and a soiled tissue.

Over the next few days, Kiszko was interviewed a number of times. At first he repeated that he had not been out on October 4th or 5th, his first trip after the hospital being to the cemetery on October 12th. Asked more specifically about October 5th, the day when Lesley was abducted, Kiszko repeated that he had not gone out due to being weak from the blood transfusions and injections.

Over the course of the interviews, though, Kiszko changed his story. First he admitted that he might have gone out that weekend after all, to take some things up to the new house in Kings Road. Then he admitted that he might have gone to a bonfire on November 5th, but had not left his car. It was then that Kiszko gave some information that the detectives found most interesting.

Told that the police were satisfied that he was the man who had exposed himself to Maxine Buckley and Debra Mills, Kiszko replied "I couldn't do anything like that, that's why I'm having these injections". Kiszko had mentioned injections before but it had not been picked up on then. Now he was asked to say what the injections were for and Kiszko said that he had been given them because he did not fancy girls. He was then asked to explain and said "Well, when I was in hospital I discussed my problem with a doctor and he gave me some injections to bring me on".

Was it possible that Kiszko had been receiving treatment for some sexual dysfunction and the injections had awoken feelings within him that had caused him to kill? A search of his car was organized and eleven more girlie magazines were found in the boot. Asked about them, Kiszko again blamed the injections and admitted that he had started to develop sexual urges since being treated in hospital. Questioned again about the indecent exposure on November 5th, Kiszko now admitted that he might just have rubbed his trousers up and down. This was then expanded to an acknowledgement that he had seen some little girls and had masturbated.

The search of Kiszko's car revealed another interesting piece of information. Two scraps of paper were found in the glove compartment and these were seen to be lists of car numbers. Kiszko explained that occasionally he had been cut up by bad drivers and had decided to take down numbers so that he could pass the information on to the police. He could not, however, explain one particular entry.

Only one number, ADK 539 L, was written in red ink. When the police checked, they found that this vehicle belonged to Derek and Doreen Hollos from Blackley. Mr and Mrs Hollos had not driven the car anywhere near places where Kiszko had admitted to being, so how then could Kiszko have taken down their number? However, when they were interviewed, they did confirm that they had driven past the lay-by where Lesley's body was found at 2.15 p.m., and again at 7.15 p.m., on Sunday, October 5th. From this, the police inferred that Kiszko must have been lying about his movements, and the reason for this was that he must have seen the car near the spot where Lesley's body was found.

The interviews continued on December 22nd, by which time Kiszko was admitting that he might have exposed himself on October 4th but that it must have been an accident. He recalled moving a carpet that caught his trouser zip and knocked it down. Then, at 11.30 a.m., Kiszko was left alone with Akeroyd and admitted that he was responsible for Lesley Molseed's death. He was asked to repeat this in front of Superintendent Holland and Chief Inspector Thomas Steele. Kiszko then made a written statement admitting responsibility in which he also confirmed that he had not taken the child's underwear off, that he had masturbated on to her, and that he had then wiped his knife on either her dress or her leg.

Later that same day Kiszko withdrew his confession saying that he had told lies in the hope that he would then be allowed to go home to his mother. Questioned again by Holland, Kiszko then once more agreed that he was the killer. He was charged with murder on December 23rd.

The trial of Stefan Ivan Kiszko opened at Leeds on July 7th, 1976, before Mister Justice Park. The proceedings lasted until July 21st, during which time Mr Peter Taylor led for the Crown, assisted by Mr Matthew Caswell. Kiszko was defended by Mr David Waddington and Mr Philip Clegg.

The prosecution case covered a number of points. To begin with, in addition to Kiszko's confession, which contained details that only the killer could know, there was the forensic evidence. In addition to the semen staining found on Lesley's body, a number of fibres taken from a carpet in Kiszko's car matched fibres found on Lesley's body, suggesting that she had been in the vehicle at some point. However, this was made less significant when both Kiszko and his mother stated that the carpet had not even been in the car at the time of the abduction.

Four knives had been found in Kiszko's home and when asked which one he had used to kill the child, Kiszko pointed out the only one that bore bloodstains. Finally, there was the car registration that Kiszko admitted writing down, and which was of a vehicle that had passed the murder scene on October 5th.

Ronald Outteridge was the forensic scientist who had examined much of the physical evidence. He reported light semen staining on Lesley's clothing, which showed that the killer had a low sperm count. There were, however, insufficient samples to determine the blood group of the killer. He had also recovered four fibres from Lesley's clothing – two pale yellow wool, one bright yellow wool and one orange rayon fibre. These matched samples taken from a carpet in Kiszko's car. As for the knife, though it did test positive for blood, it could not be typed. It could not even be firmly identified as being human.

After the various police officers involved in the case had given their evidence and details of the indecent exposures that Kiszko had admitted to were read out in court, the time came for the defence team to put their case. It was here that what turned out to be a fatal error was made.

The defence were in fact putting forward two suggestions. The first was that Kiszko was not the killer and was not in the vicinity where Lesley was abducted on October 5th. However, there was also a secondary defence that if Kiszko were the killer, then this was a case of diminished responsibility due to the injections he had received at the time. In short, the defence were saying that their client had not committed the crime, but if he had, he would not have been responsible for his actions.

Doctor David Anderson stated that Kiszko had been treated with a drug called Primoteston, a form of Testosterone. There could be side effects with this drug and these included aggressive or deviant sexual behaviour. However, such behaviour could only come about where there were already existing tendencies. The side effects could not result in the arousal of urges uncharacteristic for the individual concerned.

Another medical opinion was given by Doctor Michael Tarsh, a psychiatrist, who stated that whilst Kiszko had no history of mental illness, there were aspects of his behaviour, for instance the writing down of car numbers, which were symptomatic of paranoia.

The jury decided, by a majority of ten to two, that Stefan Kiszko was guilty of murder and he was sentenced to life imprisonment. A subsequent appeal, heard on May 25th, 1978, before Lord Justice Bridge, Mister Justice Wien and Mister Justice Eastham was rejected. The conviction was sound.

In due course, a new defence team began to review the evidence against Kiszko and found that there had been some problems with the original police investigation. For instance, one statement that had only been handed over to the defence on the morning that the trial opened was from Maurice Helm, a milkman.

Mr Helm had gone to the police voluntarily and made a statement in which he admitted that on October 4th, he had been forced to urinate in a doorway and upon emerging, three young girls had seen his exposed penis and run off. He was rapidly eliminated from the murder enquiry and no action was ever taken against him for the accidental exposure incident. This immediately eliminated one of the incidents that had been laid at Kiszko's door.

A petition was sent to the Home Office detailing this and other evidence that had never been properly investigated at the time. As a result, the Home Office asked Detective Superintendent Trevor Wilkinson to look at the original files on the case.

Amongst the statements Superintendent Wilkinson read was one from Mrs Emma Tong, who reported that she had seen Lesley in a white car, well after the time that Kiszko was supposed to have abducted her. Kiszko, of course, drove a bronze-coloured car and one fitting Mrs Tong's description had been seen by witnesses parked in the lay-by on October 5th. It had never been traced.

Then there were statements from Anne Marie Griffin and her mother, Maria Baran, testifying that Kiszko had been in their shop at 1.00 p.m. on October 5th. There was also a report from Doctor D'Vaz, who had treated Kiszko for his ankle injury. The doctor did not believe that there was any way that Kiszko could have climbed the embankment to the spot where Lesley's body was found.

Wilkinson realized that he would need help to tie up all these loose ends and eventually he took on board three other officers, Detective Sergeant John Mackerill, Detective Inspector Desmond O'Boyle and Detective Constable Alison Rose.

On December 3rd, 1990, the team contacted the laboratory at Wetherby where the samples in the case had been tested. There they interviewed Robin Falconer, who said he recalled the case. Kiszko's semen sample had been sterile with no sperm heads, but the original file stated quite clearly that the semen found on the child's clothing did contain sperm heads, albeit with a very low count. Wilkinson determined that he would seek expert advice on whether Kiszko could have been sterile at one stage but have produced spermatozoa with heads at another.

The children who had reported the various incidents of indecent exposure were all young adults now, but Wilkinson set about tracing them all and interviewing them again. Catherine Burke, who was interviewed on February 14th, 1991, readily admitted that she had lied back in 1975. She had only gone along with what Pamela Hind had said but had actually seen nothing untoward.

Pamela Hind, who was now Pamela Clarke, said she had not seen the man's penis after all, and when Debbie Brown, now Debbie Holt, was interviewed, she too said that she had just been going along with what her friends, Maxine and Debra, had said. Sheila Woodhead and Ann Marie Storto still claimed that they had seen a man exposing himself but this was now explained by the statement of Maurice Helm, who had admitted that it was him.

Maxine Buckley was the next witness to be traced and she too admitted that Kiszko had not been the man she saw on October 3rd. She had known Kiszko and was certain that it was not him.

All this testimony did not just mean that Kiszko was never guilty of any offence of indecent exposure, it also had more far-reaching consequences. If Kiszko had admitted to these offences, then he might well have admitted to other things that he had not done, such as the murder of Lesley Molseed. Furthermore, the details of the indecent exposure offences must therefore have been fed to him by the investigating police officers, and if they had fed him details of those incidents, then they might also have fed him details of the murder case, namely that the killer had ejaculated on to Lesley, that her underwear had not been removed and that the knife had been wiped on her body.

Dr Paul Belchetz was consulted and was given a sample of Kiszko's sperm. Dr Belchetz was an expert on hypogonadism, which Kiszko suffered from, and he made a statement saying that Kiszko was incapable of producing sperm with heads and always

Stefan Kiszko with his mother three days after his release from prison in February 1992. Kiszko died less than two years later (PA/News)

had been. This meant that Kiszko could not have produced the semen found on Lesley's body, as this contained sperm heads. This in turn meant that Kiszko could not be the killer.

Ronald Outteridge, who had done the original testing and who had now retired, met the investigating team. He swore that it had not been him who had requested a semen sample from Kiszko. It had simply been given to him by the police, who had never asked him to search for sperm heads. As for the fibre evidence, the fibres from the carpet in Kiszko's car were quite common, and no fibres from Lesley had been found in the car, as one might have expected had she been in the vehicle.

The establishment now knew that Stefan Kiszko could not be the killer of Lesley Molseed. The case was sent back to the Appeal Court, where it was heard on the 17th and 18th of February, 1992. It was chaired by the Lord Chief Justice, Lord Lane, who after hearing the new evidence summed up the entire case in two sentences. Giving his judgement, Lord Lane said, "It has been shown that this man cannot produce sperm. This man, therefore, cannot have been the person responsible for ejaculating over the little girl's knickers and skirt, and consequently cannot have been the murderer."

The police had known, since early 1976, that Kiszko could not produce sperm heads and so could not be the killer, but he had still spent sixteen years in prison, where he was subjected to at least two serious assaults by other prisoners who obviously believed him to be a sex offender.

Stefan Kiszko returned home a broken man to his beloved mother. The years in prison had taken their toll on both his mental and physical health and on December 21st, 1993, he collapsed and died at Kings Road. It was eighteen years to the day since he had been arrested.

Suggestion for further reading:

Jonathan Rose with Steve Panter and Trevor Wilkinson, *Innocents. How justice failed Stefan Kiszko and Lesley Molseed* (London: Fourth Estate, 1997).

The Bridgewater Four

49

Vincent Hickey, Michael Hickey,
James Robinson, and Patrick Molloy
Jailed for the murder of Carl Bridgewater at Wordsley, Staffordshire

D OCTOR Angus Macdonald was a chest physician, based at Wordsley Hospital in Staffordshire, who had recently treated an old lady named Mary Poole. Mary lived with her cousin, Fred Jones, at Yew Tree Farm, and from time to time, Dr Macdonald would call into the farm to see how Mary was recuperating. The doctor decided to pay one such visit late on the afternoon of Tuesday, September 19th, 1978.

Dr Macdonald was about to knock on the front door of the house when he noticed two things. Firstly, the paint around the lock was chipped and damaged, as if someone had tried to force an entry. Secondly, the door was slightly open. Pushing the door, Dr Macdonald tentatively walked into the hallway, calling out for Fred Jones and Mary Poole. There was no reply.

As soon as he stepped into the living room, Dr Macdonald could see that something was wrong. The room was in disarray with papers scattered about, drawers open and other general signs that there had been an intruder, or possibly a gang of burglars. It was then that Dr Macdonald's eyes fell upon the settee, and the figure of a small boy who was half lying there. The poor child had been shot in the head, by means of a shotgun, and was clearly beyond aid. Sensibly, Dr Macdonald decided to touch nothing but went home to telephone the police.

The call was answered, at 5.30 p.m., by Constable Michael Fallon, who immediately set out for Yew Tree Farm. He arrived there at 5.37 p.m., and soon afterwards, Dr Macdonald returned to see what assistance he might provide. Whilst Constable Fallon waited for other officers to arrive, he made a quick check of the premises. The killer or killers had certainly not gained entrance through the front door, for the lock itself was undamaged. More likely he or they had escaped this way. The point of entry had been around the back of the house, for Constable Fallon found a window open there, and a pane of glass broken.

At 7.30 p.m., Fred Jones and Mary Poole returned home to find their house filled with policemen and scene of crime officers. The two old people had enjoyed a day out in the country, having been taken for a drive by a friend, Mrs Kit Parrot. They were devastated to discover that their home had been broken into and a child murdered in their living room.

The officer in charge of the inquiry was Detective Chief Superintendent Robert Stewart and he and his men soon came to the conclusion that the most likely scenario was that the child had interrupted a robbery and been shot. This in turn strongly suggested that the killer might well have known the victim. After all, a chance thief would have easily been able to subdue a young boy. The victim had been delivering newspapers and still had his satchel with him when he died. This enabled a speedy identification to be made. The child was thirteen-year-old Carl Bridgewater.

What looked like a chance robbery soon developed into something more curious and the developments seemed to reinforce the suggestion that the killer had known Carl and was, in all probability, a local man. When Fred Jones was interviewed he stated that he had been receiving strange telephone calls. They would come at all times of the day and night but when he answered them, the line would go dead. Was someone checking to see if he and Mary were at home? Furthermore, Fred added that he had been paid £70 in cash for stabling some horses, and had put the money in a drawer in his bedroom. On August 19th, he had gone for that money and found it missing. Up to that point, Fred had been in the habit of leaving a key under a slate outside the house, so that a neighbour could get in and exercise the dog for him, but from then on, Fred had changed the front door lock and kept the key secure. Was this why the killer had first tried to gain access through the front door and then damaged it in the process?

There was one final puzzle to decipher. When Fred and Mary went out that morning, they had left the dog locked in the kitchen. The police, though, had found it in the scullery. The dog had not been heard barking, although surely it would have barked if a stranger had entered the house. All these factors indicated that the killer was someone local who knew the farm and its routine very well.

A careful search of the farm yielded further information. Some antiques that had been removed from the house were scattered about the back of the house, showing that the killer had left in a hurry after shooting Carl. Some items had been taken, though, and Fred Jones drew up a list of the missing items for the police. Also, Carl's bicycle, which he usually left at the front door when making his delivery, was found thrown over a wall, into a pigsty. It had presumably been put there by the killer.

One of the first lines of inquiry was to ask if anyone in the area had seen anything. A Mrs Jones, who was no relation to Fred, lived in a cottage that overlooked part of Yew Tree Farm, and from her house, the back door of the farmhouse could be seen. She told the police that at around 4.00 p.m., she had seen a light blue Ford Cortina estate car parked in the gateway, with its boot lifted as if someone were loading things into it. Mrs Jones did not see anyone but at 4.30 p.m., the car had gone.

Other people too reported seeing a vehicle, which was either a Cortina or a Viva, parked at the farm, or leaving through the gateway onto the main road, at various times throughout the day. Brian Clarke, for instance, was passing the farm at 4.55 p.m. when he saw a blue-coloured vehicle. There was a man standing by it, with his back to the road, but Brian saw that he was of heavy build, with light shoulder-length hair.

Terence Phelps was a most valuable witness for he had not only seen the car, but had seen Carl Bridgewater too. Terence had been chatting to a friend of his, Mrs Osborne, who lived in Lawnswood Drive, when she invited him in for a cup of tea, just as Carl passed on his bicycle. This was at 4.05 p.m., and when Terence left Mrs Osborne's at 4.55 p.m., he saw a blue car with perhaps two or three men in it, on the track leading to the farm.

Another witness, Roger Edwards, said that he had seen the driver, a man aged around fifty-five, who was wearing some kind of dark blue uniform with a single pip on each shoulder. The man had dark hair, which was greying a little, and which seemed to be wavy.

It was this statement, mentioning a man in uniform, that caused the police to investigate all workers who wore any kind of uniform and who drove a pale blue car. One of the names that came out of the police computer when these details were input was Hubert Vincent Spencer, an ambulance driver at the Corbett Hospital, Stourbridge. Spencer drove a light blue Viva, and was a known collector of antiques, but when Detective Constable Alan Mynott and Detective Constable Brian Withnall spoke to him, Spencer was able to provide them with an alibi for the time of the murder. He had been at the hospital, on duty, from 8.30 a.m. until 5.10 p.m., and this was confirmed by Mrs Barbara Riebold, who was the secretary at the hospital and responsible for giving the drivers their duties.

Diligently carrying out their duties, Constables Mynott and Withnall made further inquiries about Mr Spencer. Not only was he a keen antiques collector but he had also once owned an antiques shop. Furthermore, he also had links with Yew Tree Farm, where Carl was killed, having worked there sometimes for the owner, Hubert Wilkes. The Wilkes family had purchased the land some years before, Fred Jones and his cousin merely keeping the house.

There were other links too that deserved closer inspection. The hospital where Spencer worked was close to the farm, but the strongest link of all was that Hubert Spencer was known by Carl Bridgewater. The two families had once lived just two doors apart, in Ascot Gardens, though the Spencers had since moved to Kingswinford.

Matters proceeded slowly and carefully. On November 16th, Roger Edwards was interviewed again in the hope that he might provide more information on the man in uniform. That same night, Detective Chief Inspector Watson and Detective Sergeant Anthony Holdway went to Corbett Hospital and spoke to Spencer again. He confirmed to them that he had been at Yew Tree Farm hundreds of times over the past few years.

Two days later, on November 18th, Chief Inspector Watson and Sergeant Holdway interviewed Spencer's ex-partner in the antique shop. Kenneth Farndon confirmed that the business had folded but was also able to say that he knew that Spencer had once owned a twelve-bore shotgun, though he had not seen him with it for the past six months.

There could be little doubt that at this time, Hubert Spencer was high on the list of suspects for the murder of Carl Bridgewater. A month earlier a curious note had been found in a country lane. That note blamed a named person for the murder of Carl Bridgewater but when it was checked out, the gentleman named was exonerated. That note, surprisingly enough, was discovered on a stroll by Hubert Spencer.

Then, just as it seemed that police efforts would be concentrated on this one man, an incident took place, on November 30th, which altered the entire course of the investigation. It was on that date that news of another armed robbery reached the ears of the murder team.

Two men, one of them carrying a sawn-off shotgun, had burst into Chapel Farm at Romsley, near Halesowen. The occupants of the house, elderly people, had been threatened with violence and some cash had been taken. There had been at least one other man involved in the robbery, the getaway driver, adding to the similarities with the Yew Tree Farm robbery. In both cases a farmhouse where the occupants were elderly had been raided, a shotgun had been used, and a group of at least three men had been seen.

Once again there were witnesses who had seen the car believed to have been used by the team of robbers, but this time an observant cleaner had taken a note of the number. The car, a green Austin, was traced to Linda Galvin at an address in Birmingham. On December 1st, Linda was interviewed and she confirmed that on the day of the Chapel Farm robbery, the car had been driven by the man she lived with, Vincent Hickey.

In fact, Hickey had already been interviewed in connection with the Bridgewater inquiry. He too was one of the names printed out by the police computer as the owner of a pale blue Ford Cortina. All other lines were now dropped and the police concentrated on finding Vincent Hickey, especially since, as officers had arrived at Linda Galvin's house, Hickey had been seen darting out of the back and was now on the run.

Vincent Hickey had only recently suffered yet another brush with the law. On November 24th, he had appeared at St Albans, charged with deception, and had been awarded a two-year suspended sentence. Now he was wanted in connection with the Chapel Farm robbery, and had become a suspect in the Carl Bridgewater inquiry.

Three days after he had gone into hiding, Hickey contacted a solicitor, told him about the trouble he was in with regard to Chapel Farm and suggested that he believed he might be able to avoid a custodial sentence by informing on the other men involved in that robbery. After advising Hickey, the solicitor telephoned the police and then had his clerk, Joseph Roberts, escort Hickey to the police station at Bromsgrove. There he was interviewed by Superintendent Deryk Knight and Sergeant Herbert Dickenson, questioned about Chapel Farm and arrested on suspicion. At this stage, no mention had been made of the murder of Carl Bridgewater.

After some time languishing in his cell, Vincent Hickey decided that the time had come to offer information in the hope that he might make a deal for himself. At 10.55

p.m. that same night, he was interviewed again, admitted his part in the Chapel Farm robbery and named his cousin, Michael Hickey, as being involved too. He also said that there were two other men there, but he did not know their names. The police had by now told Vincent that they were also questioning him about the Carl Bridgewater case and he said that his cousin had mentioned that the older of the two strangers had committed the crime.

On December 5th, Vincent Hickey was interviewed again, after which he was formally charged with the Chapel Farm raid. Later that same day he identified one of the other men involved in that robbery as Jimmy Robinson. The next day, at 4.00 p.m., Vincent was seen by officers working on the Bridgewater case and named the fourth man as Pat Molloy. Warrants were now issued for the arrest of Michael Hickey, James Robinson and Patrick Molloy. Robinson became the first to be arrested, being apprehended on the day that the warrants were issued.

On December 7th, Jimmy Robinson admitted that he had taken part in the Chapel Farm robbery, naming another man, John Burkett. The next day, December 8th, Burkett and Molloy were both arrested. There followed a large number of interviews with all four of the men in custody. No notes or tape recordings of those interviews were made and each man was seen a large number of times. During this extensive questioning, Vincent Hickey admitted that he was the driver on the Yew Tree Farm robbery but then changed his mind and said that he was not there after all, and knew nothing about it. By now it was all academic, though, because on December 10th, Pat Molloy made a written statement admitting that he was involved in the Yew Tree Farm robbery, and naming both Hickeys and Robinson as the other men there.

According to Molloy's statement, he had been upstairs in the house, searching for valuables, when one of the other men called out that there was someone coming. He hid, but after a couple of minutes, heard the sound of a shot. Going downstairs he saw Carl on the settee and heard Jimmy Robinson say that the gun had gone off by accident. Over the next few days, Molloy made various verbal statements, changing parts of the narrative and at one stage even changing the name of the man who shot Carl. Meanwhile, Molloy's signed statement was shown to both Vincent Hickey and Jimmy Robinson, both of whom described it succinctly as "... a load of bollocks".

Meanwhile, Michael Hickey was still on the run. By this time he had admitted to his father that he had been involved in the Chapel Farm robbery and another armed robbery at a supermarket. He was finally arrested on December 20th, immediately confessed to the two armed robberies but, like his cousin and Jimmy Robinson, denied any involvement in the Yew Tree Farm robbery and the murder of Carl Bridgewater.

There was also no forensic evidence linking any of the four men to the Yew Tree Farm murder. Indeed, the only forensic evidence to be found at all was a set of fingerprints found on Carl's bicycle. These were positioned on the frame as if the bike had been grabbed by someone and thrown over the fence. However, the prints have never been identified, and did not belong to any of the four prisoners.

Nevertheless, the confession was enough to charge all four men. On December 28th, 1978, Molloy was charged with Carl's murder. The following month, once the police felt that they had enough evidence, Vincent Hickey was also charged with murder, on January 12th, 1979. Almost a month after that, on February 5th, both Michael Hickey and Jimmy Robinson were also charged with the same offence. John Burkett, on the other hand, was charged only with armed robbery, for his part in the Chapel Farm raid. He pleaded guilty and was later sentenced to twelve years in prison.

The trial of the Bridgewater Four opened at Stafford on October 8th, 1979, before Mister Justice Drake. The proceedings lasted until November 9th, during which the Crown's case was led by Mr Philip Cox, assisted by Mr Igor Judge and Mr W. Coker. For Molloy, Mr John Gorman was assisted by Mr Malcolm Lee. Mr Desmond Hollis, assisted by Mr Neil Jolly, acted for Vincent Hickey, whilst Michael was defended by Mr Richard Tucker and Mr Richard Wakerley. Finally, Mr Douglas Draycott and Mr James Pyke acted for Jimmy Robinson.

From the very beginning of the trial, the prosecution were highly selective in the witnesses they called. It had been established beyond doubt that the four were in various public houses, separately, in Birmingham until around 3.00 p.m. For that reason, any witness who had mentioned seeing a pale blue car at the farmhouse before around 3.20 p.m. was not called to give evidence. In all, eight witnesses who had seen some sort of car between 3.25 p.m. and 5.05 p.m. were called, but the court did not hear from, for instance, Robert and Janet Light, who said that they had seen a car reversing from the farm track at 12.25 p.m., or Roger Edwards, who had seen the uniformed driver at 2.50 p.m.

Even more selective was the line-up evidence. Vincent Hickey had never been placed on an identification parade. An attempt was made to place Michael on one but when his solicitor noticed that he was the only man there with a beard, he quite rightly advised him not to take part. Pat Molloy was placed on parade and eight witnesses failed to pick him out. The same, initially, applied to Jimmy Robinson, but after the parade had finished, three witnesses changed their minds and said that they had recognized him after all, despite the fact that witnesses were supposed to make any identification there and then.

Wendy Stagg said, after the parade, that she thought Robinson looked like a man she had seen standing on the pavement outside the farm. Mario Sabetta had seen two men, one of whom was carrying what he thought was a shotgun. No less than eight months after the parade he came forward to say that he now thought one of the men was Robinson. Finally, there was Terence Madeley, who had reported a green car, not a blue car, coming out of the farm driveway. He too picked out Robinson after the parade was over. All these three witnesses recalled Robinson's hair, describing it as various lengths but all agreeing that it was fair in colour. However, all three eye witnesses must have been mistaken for, on the day of the murder, Jimmy Robinson was almost bald, having had his head shaved on August 25th.

The shotgun evidence was also weak. Jimmy Robinson admitted to owning a twelve-bore and to having used it on two armed robberies, but the cartridges found in his possession were filled with size three shot. The weapon used to kill Carl had fired size five shot.

Next, the prosecution tried to show that one or more of the men had intimate knowledge of the area around Yew Tree Farm. Reginald Hickey, a relative of two of the defendants, gave evidence that he, Vincent and Michael had worked as labourers in the area. Both men denied this vehemently and the defence were able to show that Reginald did have a score to settle, having been brought to court from Gloucester prison, where he was serving a four-year sentence after Vincent Hickey had informed on him.

Helen Johnson was a barmaid at the Dog and Partridge public house where some of the prisoners were regular drinkers. She told the court that she had overheard Pat Molloy talking to Jimmy Robinson, soon after the murder had taken place. Molloy said, "If we are ever caught and seen by the police, you must say that the gun went off accidentally". According to Helen, this took place some three weeks after the murder, but this was impossible because from September 21st to October 23rd, Jimmy Robinson was in prison. The prosecution tried to explain this discrepancy away by suggesting that Helen had simply got the date wrong and the conversation must have taken place very soon after the murder.

Amongst the final prosecution witnesses were a number of prisoners and prison officers. Melvyn Ritter had been in Birmingham prison, where the Hickeys and Robinson were, and swore that on April 5th, Robinson had admitted that he had shot Carl, but claimed that it was an accident.

Brian Sinton, another prisoner, said that he had been in the showers with Michael Hickey when Hickey admitted that it was he, not Robinson, who shot Carl, because he was crying. Next came Peter Bryant, who had been on exercise with all three men and said that they had made various incriminating statements when talking about the antiques that they had taken from the farm.

No doubt the strongest single piece of evidence was Molloy's confession, even though he was now claiming that it had been extracted from him through threats and trickery. He also claimed that the only reason he had made it in the first place was because two police officers had shown him another confession, signed by Vincent Hickey. By making his own statement, incriminating the other three, he hoped to avoid a murder charge. In fact, the entire confession was untrue and neither he nor any of the others had been anywhere near the farm when Carl died. The court, though, did not even hear this retraction. Molloy's legal team advised him not to retract it as he would receive a stiffer sentence if found guilty of murder and, since no confession had ever been made by Vincent Hickey, this part of his claim would not stand up to scrutiny.

The jury retired at 3.00 p.m. on November 9th and returned to announce a unanimous verdict of guilty of murder against three of the defendants, and one of manslaughter against Molloy. Sentencing was held over until Monday, November 12th.

Both Robinson and Vincent Hickey were given life, with the recommendation that they both serve at least twenty-five years. Michael Hickey was to be detained at Her Majesty's pleasure and Molloy was given twelve years.

Almost exactly one month after the sentencing, on December 13th, 1979, the case was thrust back into the headlines by another killing. Four people were enjoying a pleasant night at Holloway House, the farm next door to Yew Tree Farm. At the gathering were Hubert Wilkes, who owned both farms, his daughter Jean, and his part-time secretary, Janet Spencer. Janet was accompanied by her husband, Hubert Spencer, who had once been a suspect in the Bridgewater case.

The group began talking about the Bridgewater case until Hubert Spencer said that he was going to the toilet and left the room. It was just after midnight when he returned with a shotgun, which he placed close to Wilkes' temple before firing. When he was arrested, early that morning, the investigating officers began looking again at the Bridgewater murder.

When he had been interviewed on that matter, Spencer had given an alibi, saying that he had been at work all day. That alibi had been confirmed by Barbara Riebold. Now though, when officers went to the hospital to collect the work sheets for the date of Carl's murder, they found that some were missing, including all those for the relevant day. As a matter of course, Mrs Riebold was interviewed again but she still maintained that Spencer had been at the hospital all that day.

Hubert Spencer faced his own trial for murder, at Stafford, on June 23rd, 1980, before Mister Justice Cox. The case lasted until June 26th, after which Spencer was adjudged to be guilty and sentenced to life imprisonment. This news, though, renewed the Bridgewater Four's claims that they were innocent of Carl's murder.

In October 1980, Pat Molloy claimed publicly that he had seen a confession signed by Vincent Hickey. This document had been shown to him by Detective Constable John Perkins. That same officer had also used physical violence against Molloy in an attempt to get him to confess. Still, no confession by Hickey had been found so again the pleas were ignored.

The following year, on June 12th, 1981, Pat Molloy was playing football in the exercise yard of the prison when he collapsed. He was rushed to Leicester Royal Infirmary where he died. That same year, in December, a leave to appeal by the other three was rejected by the Lord Chief Justice, Lord Lane, who ruled that there were no links between the Bridgewater case and the shooting of Hubert Wilkes.

Other attempts were made to keep the case in the public gaze. On February 26th, 1983, Michael and Vincent Hickey climbed onto the roof of Long Lartin prison with a sign stating that Spencer had killed Carl. They stayed up there until March 17th. Five days later, the Home Office announced an enquiry into the case. Despite the fact that a prisoner had come forward saying that he had heard Spencer admit the crime, the conclusion, announced on November 3rd, was that there was no reason to reopen the investigation.

Three weeks later, Michael Hickey mounted another roof top protest, this time at Gartree. He stayed on that roof until February 21st, 1984. Later that same year, in July, another Home Office enquiry was announced but in November, this too decided on no further action.

One by one, important witnesses for the prosecution at the original trial came forward to admit that they had lied, or that their evidence was had been flawed. On February 5th, 1985, Reginald Hickey admitted that he had lied about working in the area around Yew Tree Farm. The following year, 1986, Brian Sinton, the ex-prisoner who had said that Michael Hickey had confessed to him, admitted that he too had lied. Two prison officers had told him what to say. Yet another Home Office enquiry was launched, even though Sinton later withdrew his retraction and claimed that he had been telling the truth after all.

In October 1987, the Home Secretary referred the case to the Court of Appeal. Bundles of documents were now released to the defence for the first time, causing the proceedings to be repeatedly postponed whilst they were carefully read and examined. The new appeal finally opened on November 23rd, 1988, before Justices Russell, Leonard and Potts. It concluded on January 26th, 1989, but the dismissal was only made public on March 17th.

In 1990, Pat Molloy's original confession was examined by language experts who declared that the phraseology was different to Molloy's normal language. In short, he did not write it or dictate it. This, together with knowledge that other cases involving Detective Constable Perkins had involved violence and intimidation, led to yet another inquiry in October 1991. This dragged on until 1993 when, on February 3rd, it was announced yet again that there was no reason to re-open the case. In the meantime, in October 1992, Detective Constable Perkins had died.

The publicity continued though. On May 20th, 1993, Mr Timothy O'Malley, who had been the foreman of the jury that convicted the four men, stated that he was now completely convinced that they were innocent. On June 7th, Michael Chamberlain, a personal friend of Detective Constable Perkins, admitted that Perkins had told him that the confession had been beaten out of Molloy.

The year 1996 came, and Hubert Spencer was released from prison. More documents were released to the defence and plans for a new appeal were made. Then, in early 1997, the bombshell was dropped.

On February 6th, Pat Molloy's confession was subjected to an ESDA test, which can reveal the imprint of any document that might have been above the one tested. This showed that the page above had contained a statement that began, "I Vincent Hickey wish to make a statement..." The same tests showed a forged signature at the foot of the sheet. The 'confession' that Molloy had always maintained had been shown to him was proved to have existed, and been forged, almost certainly by D.C. Perkins. Days later, the Home Office's own expert confirmed that the document had existed. Furthermore, Molloy's own confession was examined by Dr Eric Shepherd, a psychologist, who stated that it could not have been written or dictated by Molloy in the time shown. That is to say, the period of time which was alleged to have elapsed between the start of the confession and its reported end was insufficient for all the words to have been written down.

The appeal was due to start in April but now that the case had totally collapsed, all three men were released on unconditional bail, on February 21st, 1997. The appeal itself opened on April 16th and grudgingly declared that the convictions were unsafe.

Even now there are those who believe that the three surviving prisoners were freed on a technicality. The truth is that all three men had alibis that were not believed, with witnesses not being called at the original trial. Jimmy Robinson, for instance, had been seen at his girlfriend's house, carrying a bunch of flowers, at around 3.30 p.m. on the day of the murder. Added to this, all four were subjected to physical and mental torture by the police, evidence was manufactured against them and witnesses who did not fit the prosecution's case were excluded from the trial.

In this manner, four innocent men were sent to prison where one died and the others served more than seventeen years.

Suggestion for further reading:

Paul Foot, *Murder at the farm: who killed Carl Bridgewater?* (London: Review, 1998).

The Cardiff Three

50

Steve Miller, Yusef Abdullahi and Tony Paris
Jailed for life for the murder of Lynette White in Cardiff

L EARNNE Vilday had not seen her friend, Lynette White, for five days now and over those days, had become increasingly concerned. Taking a cab to Lynette's flat at 7 James Street in the Butetown area of Cardiff, Learnne looked though the letterbox and saw that the kitchen door was closed. Normally it was held open by a piece of string. It was not a major change but allied to the fact that Lynette had not been seen for so long, it persuaded Learnne that it was time to take her concerns to the police.

It was 9.17 p.m. on Sunday, February 14th, 1988 when Sergeant William Bisgood and a colleague broke down the front door of Lynette's flat. In the small bedroom they found her body lying between the foot of the bed and a window. She had been stabbed more than fifty times and the room was awash with blood. An unused but unwrapped condom lay on the bed suggesting that Lynette, a prostitute, had been murdered by one of her clients.

The crime scene was examined by Professor Bernard Knight, who put the time of death at some time between midnight and 4.00 a.m. on February 14th. That estimate seemed to be confirmed when it was noted that Lynette's wristwatch had stopped at quarter to two. On the chimney breast, Professor Knight found a partial hand print with blood on it, suggesting that it had been put there either by the killer or by Lynette herself during the attack. A trainer or shoe print was found in the blood on the floor and swabs taken from Lynette showed the presence of semen in her body. Those samples were sent for DNA testing, as were a number of blood samples. These tests would show, amongst other things, that the semen had been deposited within six hours of Lynette's death, indicating that it might not have belonged to her attacker after all.

The officer in charge of the investigation was Detective Chief Superintendent John Williams and he was soon able to determine that although Lynette had not been seen much in her usual haunts over the previous five days, she had been spotted around Cardiff, the last reported sighting being just before midnight on February 13th, in the Montmerence Club. Witnesses were appealed for and it transpired that a number of people had seen a white man in his mid- to late thirties near the flat at about the time Lynette met her death. The man was said to be five feet eight inches in height, or perhaps a couple of inches taller, with dark greasy hair that had a white streak at the front. He was dishevelled, crying and, more importantly, his clothes had blood on them.

The first arrest was made on February 25th when a man named Malcolm Morris was detained. Fortunately for Mr Morris he was able to provide an alibi and forensic tests did not link him with the murder site, so he was released the next day. Less than two months later, on April 14th, Doctor Peter Gill announced that he had examined some of the blood samples taken from the scene and had discovered the male chromosome on five spots. This showed only that the killer had to be male.

One of the first people to be picked up for questioning had been Lynette White's boyfriend, a black man named Steve Miller. He gave details of his movements on the night of February 13th/14th, saying that he was with two friends, Eugene Savage and David Orton. The latter of these two men confirmed that Miller had been with him, at various clubs and pubs, from 9.00 p.m., or perhaps 9.30 p.m., on February 13th until around 3.00 a.m. on February 14th. Despite this, Miller's clothes were taken for scientific analysis, and a sample of his blood tested. There were no bloodstains on his clothing and his blood was not of the same rare type, AB, as that discovered at Lynette's flat, bearing the male chromosome. As a result, Miller was eliminated from the inquiry.

Over the next few months, various suspects were picked up, questioned, had blood samples taken and were then released. Then, on November 10th, Violet Perriam came forward to make a statement. She had already intimated to the police that she had seen a group of black men outside Lynette's flat and had said that she could name two of them but was too frightened to do so. Now she was prepared to name names and said that the two she had recognized were John Actie and Rashid Omar.

One week after this, on November 17th, Angela Psaila, who had been living with Learnne Vilday at the time she reported Lynette missing, was interviewed by the police. She too now said that she had seen a group of black men outside Lynette's flat on the night that she met her death. She was able to name John Actie, Steve Miller, Ronnie Actie, John's brother, and two others, Yusef Abdullahi and Tony Paris. Furthermore, Angela said that she had heard screams coming from the flat and went to investigate, seeing John Actie, Miller and Paris standing outside the open flat door.

A couple of weeks later, Angela made another statement claiming that when she went to investigate the screams, Learnne Vilday had gone with her. As a result of that statement, Learnne was interviewed again and now named Steve Miller, his brother Tony, Abdullahi, Ronnie Actie, and another man, Martin Tucker, as being in the room when Lynette died. The next day, the Miller brothers, Abdullahi, Ronnie Actie, Rashid Omar and Martin Tucker were all arrested.

Over the next four days, Steve Miller endured nineteen separate police interviews. By the eighth of those interviews he was admitting that on the night in question he might well have been high on cocaine and brandy and so might not have a clear memory of what took place. By the final interview, he had admitted being in the room when Lynette died, and had confessed to stabbing her at least once. It did not matter that his confession contradicted almost all of the facts of the case – for example, he claimed that the first wounds inflicted were to Lynette's belly, whereas this was not the case – he had now admitted his part and named others.

Two days after Miller's arrest, on December 9th, Tony Paris and John Actie were arrested, bringing the number of suspects being interviewed up to eight. In one of Fate's strange coincidences, Angela Psaila was subjected to a rape attack at about the same time and as a matter of routine, her blood was tested. It was found to be the same rare AB type as that found at Lynette White's flat. Interviewed about this, Angela now made another statement admitting that she was an eye-witness to the attack upon Lynette and had been forced to take part herself in order to secure her silence. She named the men involved in the murder as Tony Paris, the Miller brothers, the two Acties and Yusef Abdullahi. The police now maintained that the bloodstains and pools must have been cross-contaminated. The AB blood showed that Angela must have been there and that therefore her testimony could be relied upon, while the male chromosome showed that the killer, or at least one of the killers, had to be male. This hypothesis also meant, of course, that both Angela and a male killer must have bled at the scene themselves.

Despite the testimony of witnesses who had reported a white man, with bloodstained clothes, outside Lynette's flat, despite the fact that none of the prisoners had the rare AB blood group and despite the fact that Angela Psaila had amended her story with each new statement, five of the eight were charged with murder. Even now, the anomalies in the case are astounding. The same statements that had been used against the five men who were charged had named one or more of the other three men, but these men were not charged with murder. Instead, they were charged with lesser offences but in due course, these minor charges were also dropped, again without explanation from the police. On December 11th, 1988, Tucker, Omar and Tony Miller were released. The other five, Steve Miller, Yusef Abdullahi, John Actie, Ronnie Actie and Tony Paris, were all sent for trial.

There were many delays before the trial began and the proceedings only opened, before Mister Justice McNeill, in October 1989. Early discussions took place about whether or not Miller's confession was admissible, as it was argued that the interviews he had endured were oppressive and that he had a very low IQ, and was therefore highly suggestible. The argument was dismissed and the trial proper started.

On February 26th, 1990, five months into the proceedings, Mister Justice McNeill suffered a fatal heart attack and a new trial was ordered to take place. This opened on May 2nd, 1990, at Swansea, before Mister Justice Leonard.

Learnne Vilday repeated her story that the five men in the dock were the ones responsible for Lynette's death and also stated that they had forced her to take part in the crime. Angela Psaila testified that she too had been forced to watch and then take part. She had been made to cut Lynette's wrists whilst her friend and flatmate, Vilday, had been forced to cut Lynette's throat. She also stated that whilst the murder was taking place, another man, Mark Grommek, had come into the room. Mark Grommek, though, denied that he had set foot inside the room where Lynette was murdered. He had been at home that night in his flat above the murder scene, and had had a friend with him at the time, Paul Atkins. Furthermore, Grommek also testified that on the night of the murder, he had seen the prisoners congregating outside the flats.

Tessa Sidoric was a friend of Steve Miller's and had visited him in prison whilst he was on remand. According to Tessa, during their conversation Steve had denied having any involvement in Lynette's death but had admitted to walking in on the killers. Another witness was Jackie Harris, Abdullahi's girlfriend, who said that Yusef had confessed to her that he had committed the crime when he was high on drugs. Later, though, Jackie withdrew this story and said that she was worried about being arrested for perjury. The story was, however, confirmed by Debbie Taylor and Nicki Gordon, who had also visited Miller at the same time. Miller had also apparently added that he witnessed Tony Paris stabbing Lynette.

Ian Massey, a fellow prisoner at Cardiff, said that he had become friendly with Paris and that Paris had confessed to him that he and the others were guilty. There were, however, some unanswered questions that the prosecution could not explain away.

Detective Sergeant Stephen Steele had found 150 fingerprints at Lynette's flat. None of those prints belonged to any of the five defendants. Neither were any of Angela Psaila's prints found, despite her own statement that she had been present in the room when Lynette met her death.

Doctor Whiteside had examined the murder scene and testified that anyone standing near Lynette when she died, let alone taking part in her murder, would have had extensive bloodstaining on his or her clothes. No bloodstaining had been found on any of the defendants' clothing, or on that of Angela Psaila or Learnne Vilday.

The only evidence against the five prisoners can be summed up very briefly. Against Miller was his own confession and the testimony of Debbie Taylor and Tessa Sidoric, who claimed to have heard him confess to being involved in the murder when he walked in on it accidentally. Against Paris was the discredited testimony of fellow prisoner Ian Massey, the alleged comment from Steve Miller overheard by Debbie Taylor and Nicki Gordon, and the testimony of Angela Psaila and Learnne Vilday. For Ronnie Actie, there were only the statements of Vilday and Psaila that put him at the scene. Against Abdullahi was his supposed confession to Jackie Harris and the evidence of Psaila and Vilday, while against John Actie were the statements of Psaila and Vilday, and the statement of Violet Perriam, who had named him and one of the men who was never charged, Rashid Omar. It should be remembered, however, that even the prosecution put no great store on the testimony of Angela Psaila and Learnne Vilday, as they were unable to agree between them which men were at the scene.

On November 19th, the jury retired to consider their verdicts. The next day they returned to court to announce that they had found Miller and Paris guilty. On November 21st, Ronnie Actie was found not guilty and discharged. The next day, November 22nd, his brother John Actie was also found not guilty but Yusef Abdullahi was found guilty as charged. The judge then sentenced Miller, Paris and Abdullahi to life imprisonment.

By March 1991, the defence lawyers acting for the Cardiff Three had received statements from twenty-two witnesses who had not been called at either of the two trials. Neither had their testimony been declared to the defence. Between them, these twenty-two witnesses gave a complete alibi for all three men, though some were contradictory and others were of doubtful quality and so were not strong enough to have the case reopened. However, in September 1992, Jackie Harris made a full retraction of the evidence she had given, claiming that she had been put under pressure by police officers who in effect dictated what she was to say in court.

As a result of that retraction, the case was sent back to the Court of Appeal and a hearing set for December 7th, before the Lord Chief Justice, Lord Taylor and Justices Laws and Popplewell. The result was damning for what had always been a weak case against all of the three men.

The blood found in five locations at the scene did not belong to any of the defendants and must have come from a man as it bore the Y-chromosome. As far as Miller was concerned, it was shown that the story told by both Vilday and Psaila was in direct contradiction to the forensic testimony given by Professor Knight and other experts – for example, Vilday and Psaila stated that the throat wound had been inflicted at the end of the attack, but the forensic evidence showed that this was in fact the first offensive wound. The crime could not possibly have taken place, therefore, in the way they described. Once Jackie Harris had withdrawn her testimony about Abdullahi, the case against him also collapsed, and various witness statements gave Tony Paris an almost complete alibi for the night of the murder.

The appeal result was announced on December 16th. The convictions were not safe or satisfactory and as a result all three men were freed. They had each spent just over four years in jail whilst the real killer remained at large.

Suggestion for further reading:

Satish Sekar, *Fitted In: the Cardiff Three and the Lynette White Enquiry* (London: The Fitted In Project, 1997).

Recommended Further Reading

Brian Bailey, *Hangmen of England: a History of Execution from Jack Ketch to Albert Pierrepoint* (London: W. H. Allen, 1989).

William Beadle, *Wrongly Hanged* (Dagenham: Wat Tyler, c. 1995).

Christopher Berry-Dee and Robin Odell, *The Long Drop: Two Were Hanged – One Was Innocent* (London: True Crime Library, c. 1993).

Syd Dernley with David Newman, *The Hangman's Tale: Memoirs of a Public Executioner* (London: Pan Books, 1989).

John Eddowes, *The Two Killers of Rillington Place* (London: Warner Books, 1995).

John Ellis, *Diary of a Hangman* (London: True Crime Library, 1996).

Martin Fido, *Murder Guide to London* (London: Orion, 1994).

Paul Foot, *Murder at the Farm: Who Killed Carl Bridgewater?* (London: Review, 1998).

J. H. H. Gaute and Robin Odell, *The New Murderer's Who's Who* (London: Headline, 1989).

Jonathan Goodman, *The Daily Telegraph Murder File* (London: Mandarin, 1993).

Gordon Honeycombe, *The Murders of the Black Museum 1870-1970* (London: Hutchinson, 1982).

Ludovic Kennedy, *10 Rillington Place* (London: Victor Gollancz Ltd, 1961).

Brian Lane, *The Encyclopedia of Forensic Science* (London: Headline, 1992).

Brian Lane, *The Murder Guide to Great Britain: 100 Extraordinary, Bizarre and Gruesome Murders* (London: Robinson, 1993).

Sara Lee, *Strange Tales from Strangeways: and Other Extraordinary Prison Cases* (London: True Crime Library, 1995).

T. J. Leech, *A Date with the Hangman* (London: True Crime Library, 1992).

Grant McKee and Ros Franey, *Time Bomb – The Guildford Four* (London: Bloomsbury, 1988).

Chris Mullin, *Error of Judgement: the Truth about the Birmingham Bombings* (Dublin: Poolbeg Press, 1997).

Albert Pierrepoint, *Executioner: Pierrepoint* (London: Coronet Books, 1998).

Andrew Rose, *Stinie: Murder on the Common* (Harmondsworth: Penguin, 1989).

Jonathan Rose with Steve Panter and Trevor Wilkinson, *Innocents. How Justice Failed Stefan Kiszko and Lesley Molseed* (London: Fourth Estate, 1997).

E. F. L. Russell, *Deadman's Hill. Was Hanratty Guilty?* (London: Secker & Warburg, 1965).

Satish Sekar, *Fitted In: the Cardiff Three and the Lynette White Enquiry* (London: The Fitted In Project, 1997).

Professor Keith Simpson, *Forty Years of Murder* (London: Grafton Books, 1988).

Rocky Stockman, *The Hangman's Diary: a Calender of Judicial Hangings* (London: Headline, c. 1993).

Rupert Taylor, *Sussex: Murder Casebook* (Newbury: Countryside Books, 1994).

M. J. Trow, *'Let Him Have It Chris': the Murder of Derek Bentley* (London: Grafton, 1992).

Various, *In Suspicious Circumstances* (London: Boxtree, c. 1993).

Adrian Vincent, *A Gallery of Poisoners* (London: Warner Books, 1993).

416

Assizes Documents and Newspapers

Assizes Documents

Masset CRIM 1 58/5
Masset HO 144 1540
Bennett CRIM 1 65/2
Harrison ASSI 52 57
Devereux CRIM 1 97/7
Dickman HO 144 4202
Loake ASSI 6 46/9
Seddon CRIM 1 129/2
Kelly ASSI 52 203
Clinton ASSI 52 266
Hodgson ASSI 65 22
Beckett (Perry) CRIM 1 178/3
Thompson CRIM 1 206/5
Thorne ASSI 36 38
Kirby ASSI 13 57
Seymour ASSI 6 66/5
Burtoft ASSI 52 424
Blake ASSI 45 94/14
Hoolhouse HO 144 21121
Hoolhouse HO 144 21122
Myatt ASSI 13 70
Jennings ASSI 26 53/2
Grossley ASSI 84 35
Coffey ASSI 52 581
Rowland ASSI 52 589
Evans CRIM 1 2035
Evans CRIM 1 2116
Turnage ASSI 45 117
Moore ASSI 36 125
Mattan ASSI 84 135
Bentley CRIM 1 2282
Hooper ASSI 6 90

Newspapers

Birmingham Evening Mail
Bolton Evening News
Bristol Evening Post
Cambridge Evening News
Chronicle and Echo (Northampton)
Daily Post (Liverpool)
Dorset Evening Echo
East Anglian Daily Times
Eastern Daily Press
Evening Courier (Halifax)
Evening Echo (Bournemouth)
Evening Gazette (Middlesborough)
Evening News (Norwich)
Evening Press (York)
Evening Standard (London)
Express and Echo (Exeter)
Express and Star (Wolverhampton)
The Gazette (Blackpool)
Glasgow Evening Times
Gloucestershire Echo
Grimsby Evening Telegraph
Hartlepool Mail
Lancashire Evening Telegraph
Leicester Mercury
Northern Echo
North West Evening Mail
Nottingham Evening Post
Oldham Evening Chronicle
Southern Daily Echo
The Star (Sheffield)
Sunday Sun (Newcastle-upon-Tyne)
Sunderland Echo
Telegraph and Argus (Bradford)
The Times
Western Daily Press
Western Morning News
Yorkshire Evening Post
Yorkshire Post

Index

441